Merrill's Expanded Guide to Computer Performance Evaluation Using the SAS System

H.W. "Barry" Merrill, Ph.D.

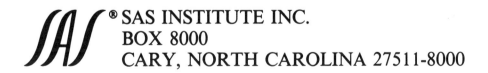® SAS INSTITUTE INC.
BOX 8000
CARY, NORTH CAROLINA 27511-8000

Merrill's Expanded Guide to Computer Performance Evaluation Using the SAS System

Copyright © 1984 by SAS Institute Inc., Cary, NC, USA.
ISBN 0-917382-54-4

84 85 4 3 2 1

SAS,® the basis of the SAS System, provides data retrieval and management, programming, statistical, and reporting capabilities. Other software products in the SAS System include SAS/FSP,® SAS/GRAPH,® SAS/IMS-DL/I,® SAS/ETS,™ SAS/OR,™ and SAS/REPLAY-CICS.™ These products are available from SAS Institute Inc., a private company devoted to the support and further development of Institute Products and related services. *SAS Communications*® and *SAS Views*® are publications of SAS Institute Inc.

To 99,
    who caught my eye in election line
    with an EXCP that felt like a never-ending channel program,
    who won my mind and heart with her fast CPUs,
    who showed me who I was
        and who I am
           and who I must be,
    who is my muse,
        and became my wife,
           and without whom this book would not be.

Contents

Preface

Many people helped make *Merrill's Expanded Guide to CPE* happen. The freedom to research CPE at State Farm resulted from my introduction to Dr. Norm Vincent by Dr. L. Rogers Taylor and my interview with Dave Vitek and Nick Fortney. After attending the 1972 BBUG meeting, Dave convinced Norm of the need for measurement, just as I arrived at State Farm. Four years later, I was ready to move from MVT to MVS and State Farm wasn't, so a chance call from Linda Wright led to an afternoon with Sun Company's Jack Schrodel, who, in turn, provided me with seven years of truly challenging and perceptive management issues to answer with measurement, which created what is, in my opinion, the best MVS shop in the world. Bill Fore and, especially, Dave Patterson provided excellent support for my research (and soothed many a justifiably ruffled feather for me). Both State Farm and Sun Company shared the belief that research should be shared; thus, they permitted me great latitude in presenting my papers before a wide range of audiences at many conferences.

The MVS/XA announcement stimulated this rewrite of the 1980 edition of *Merrill's Guide*. In April 1983, Mike Eubanks at Texas Instruments provided me with access to XA SMF data; so in June, I found a second home as a consultant to Computer Language Research, better known for its FASTAX product. With the support of Vice President Jim Charles and, especially, with Chuck Hopf's (the wizard) daily discovery of one more error or omission, I was able to solidify the code by October 1983.

Writing the *Expanded Guide* began with Charlan Ledbetter typing and transmitting the appendices of the earlier book (at 300 baud!), and Cheryl Byrd typed many of the written papers and some dictation for her husband Mark to transmit from his Cromenco (at least now it was at 1200 baud)! The acquisition of an IBM PC/XT and its Professional Editor provided sub-second response while all of the prior book and papers were being revised and all of the new material was being written.

The text was transmitted (still at 1200 baud) locally, copied to tape on the MVS system, and sent to SAS Institute Inc. for editing and typesetting. Kathryn A. Council edited *Merrill's Guide*, which was no small job. She chopped my paragraph-long sentences into byte-size pieces and still allowed most of my idiosyncrasies to show through. Kathy not only edited the guide, but she also organized all phases the guide went through at SAS Institute, and she served as the liaison between the Institute and me.

At the Institute, Kathy was assisted by the Technical Writing and Graphic Arts departments.

From Technical Writing: Judith K. Whatley, David D. Baggett, Gail C. Freeman, Gigi Hassan, James K. Hart, and Frances A. Kienzle.

From Graphic Arts: Arlene B. Drezek, Craig R. Sampson, Carol M. Thompson, Melissa H. Shipman, June L. Woodward, and Elisabeth C. Smith.

But the real credit belongs to my family: Judy, Rachel, and Nathaniel. They suffered through 90-hour weeks for a full year to see *Merrill's Expanded Guide to CPE* to fruition.

Barry Merrill
Dallas, Texas

chapter one

Introduction

This book introduces you to the vast array of information available from accounting records written by the IBM computer operating systems, MVS , VM, and DOS/VSE , and performance records written by subsystems such as CICS , IMS, TSO , CMS, and POWER that execute under these operating systems. These records frequently contain resource and response information important for managing, measuring, and planning for the delivery of shared computer resources to all multiple users. But to be understood by humans, these raw records require decoding and decomposition. The MXG software* described in this book performs the translation from raw data to information. The book describes how to use the information to manage and measure the performance of your computer system.

The sources of raw data are different for each operating system. For MVS/370 and MVS/XA operating systems, the majority of raw data records are written to the System Management Facilities (SMF) file. Additional records can be written by subsystems to their own files (such as CICS Monitor Facility data, which can be written to a CICS Journal File). For VM/370, accounting data and VMAP internal performance data are written to the spool as card images. For DOS/VSE, POWER accounting records are written to their own file, and CICS Monitor Facility or Performance Analyzer II data can be created. Most new data base management subsystems now provide some accounting or performance data, and the long-range goal of the MXG product is to provide SAS programs to process all important performance or accounting data.

The MXG software uses the SAS System to decode, interpret, and analyze this raw computer performance data. The SAS System is the de facto industry standard for the analysis and presentation of CPE information because it has proven to be both cost-effective and easily learned. The SAS System saves time and money. However, it is not necessary to know the SAS System to understand the information described in this book. The real value of the book is in describing the information found in each record of each data source, explaining what it means, and showing how it can be used to measure the computer installation's performance (response time, turnaround, capacity, and so forth).

You should be able to understand this book with a minimum knowledge of SAS syntax. If you are not a SAS user, chapter thirty-nine provides a summary of the SAS language to help you follow the examples.

The data sources described above are written by software monitors built into (or added onto) the operating system or subsystem. In almost every case, these software monitors simply write out control blocks and resource counts when a recordable event occurs. Since these control blocks are required for the operating

---

*The MXG software can be purchased separately through the SAS Institute Publications Division.

system, the only additional overhead associated with this software-captured data is the writing of the record. Thus, a strong motivation for using software-captured performance data is that they are free.

By choosing software-based measurement, we are building solid bridges into the future. Present and future dynamic operating systems provide general purpose features that are tailored to specific requirements by setting parameters to control the dynamic range permitted. The role of the system tuning function of performance evaluation is to optimize these user-chosen parameter values. The most effective way to optimize the performance of these systems is to use the measurements on which the dynamic algorithm is based. We are dependent on instrumentation built into the software component to provide measures for analysis. The only accurate representation of why the dynamic algorithm operates as it does comes from the data on which the algorithm operates.

The SMF-like data provided by the vendor may not be the total answer for all measurement of all subsystems. There are other software products that monitor TSO, IMS, CICS, and the operating system, and these tools can be useful. Tactical problems (firefights) often need data that are not available in the vendor-provided records. Furthermore, many of these measurement products also write records to SMF-like files. Commonly-used data records are supported by the MXG software, and the long-range goal of MXG is to provide SAS programs to support all performance related records written by any operating system or subsystem.

HOW TO USE THIS BOOK

This book begins with a discussion of the pragmatic approach to Computer Performance Evaluation in chapter two. Chapters three through six describe the structure and general contents of the data files that contain the CPE data MXG uses. Chapter seven takes an MVS job as a case study and follows it through the data events it creates in these records. Chapter eight discusses the critical tasks necessary to establish service objectives, and chapter nine suggests ways to obtain agreement from users concerning the legitimacy of the service objectives you define. Chapters ten through eighteen discuss how the MVS resources (CPU, I/O, memory, and so forth) can be measured. Chapters nineteen through twenty-three describe how MVS workloads (batch, TSO, CICS, and so forth) are measured and managed. Chapter twenty-four describes the differences between MVS/370 and MVS/XA data. MVS availability measurement is described in chapter twenty-five, and chapter twenty-six describes how to measure and distribute the MVS overhead to measure the capacity of a computer system. Chapter twenty-seven identifies ways of using the performance data to aid the productivity of the applications development area and discusses some specific COBOL performance problems. The organization of the CPE effort is described in chapter twenty-eight, and CPE organizations themselves are described in chapter twenty-nine. Chapter thirty discusses how benchmarks can be used in CPE for both performance measurement and setting CPU factors for common work measures. Chapter thirty-one is a tutorial on how the resources reported in CPE data can be used for chargeback and cost recovery.

A description of the MXG software begins in chapter thirty-two, with the installation procedures. Chapter thirty-three suggests ways for the beginner to get started, and chapter thirty-four describes the internal logic used to build the Performance Data Base (PDB). The JCL-oriented considerations of regularly building a PDB are discussed in chapter thirty-five, and examples of typical reports from a PDB are provided in chapter thirty-six. Chapter thirty-seven contains some features of the SAS System that are useful for analyzing CPE data. Chapter thirty-eight is a brief bibliography of CPE work, and chapter thirty-nine is a primer on the SAS System. Chapter forty describes each SAS data set built from the raw performance records by the MXG software. These descriptions are the detailed reference material on the variables and data sets that you will create and use. Chapter forty-one describes SAS utilities provided with the MXG software and members of the MXG Source Library (SOURCLIB) not covered in the preceding chapter.

This book is intended to be both a teaching tool and a reference manual. For management interested in what CPE can do for them, chapters two, seven, eight, nine, twenty-three, twenty-six, twenty-seven and twenty-eight are most relevant. For technicians who are charged to install and use the MXG software, start with chapters thirty-one through thirty-five to unload the SAS programs and read each of the data set descriptions in chapter forty to understand the data at your fingertips. Then skim each of the remaining chapters once and refer to them as necessary.

chapter two

The Pragmatic Approach to Computer Performance Evaluation

Computer manufacturers market a combination of hardware and software that provides general-purpose data processing. Their goal is to maximize profit while providing sufficient hardware and software to meet the purchaser's needs. The purchaser, however, wants to minimize the cost of the hardware and software while meeting his users' requirements.

This generality of hardware and software, which must provide flexibility for all potential users, can be tuned to provide maximum utility for a specific installation. Thus, the primary purpose of Computer Performance Evaluation (CPE) is to optimize a general-purpose computing system to meet the specific installation's objective of providing computing service to its users.

The Overall Approach

Two concepts are crucial to this approach: objectives and optimization. Without objectives for the computing system, there can be no optimization. When objectives have been established, change can be measured, and optimization (sometimes one small step at a time) can begin.

The key elements of this approach are:

- an automated system using the computer operating system's accounting file to build a Performance Data Base (PDB). The PDB provides measures of response time and resource consumption and is the basic measurement tool of data for reporting and tracking.
- measurable and meaningful performance objectives that are understood and relevant to both the user and the supplier.
- a charging scheme related directly to the performance objectives. The work requesting and receiving better service is charged more than the same work requesting and receiving less service.
- resource consumption measures and associated capacities so that resource shortages and excesses can be identified. Then the acquisition or release of equipment can minimize charges and maximize service.
- performance data base as an ongoing source of information to deduce correlations in the data. Exceptions to efficient consumption and degradation in service can be detected so that ongoing optimization through changing equipment and workloads can provide the most cost-effective, user-satisfying computing possible.

The implementation of this approach requires:

- a source of raw data that adequately describes the system to be measured
- a software system (a tool) that can build the PDB and effectively analyze the data
- analysis of the data with the tool to establish which measurables are appropriate to use as objectives.

Details of the implementation will be described later. The choice of the system accounting data is discussed in the next section.

Choosing the System Accounting Data

In the early days, when only uniprogramming existed, performance measurement was simple. Since only one job could be in the processor at a time, performance was measured simply by timing the program's execution with a watch (or in some cases, with a calendar). As the processor neared twenty-four-hour-a-day operation, the next larger processor was ordered. With the advent of multiprogramming, however, the measurement process became more complex. OS/360 allowed several jobs to share some of the resources by overlapping their execution. No longer could simple elapsed time measures be the performance metric. Contention for the shared resources could degrade performance of some jobs, and the need for metrics other than elapsed time became evident.

Out of this need for data, hardware monitors and software monitors were created in the late 1960s and early 1970s. Hardware monitors are digital counters that probe the electrical state of certain points inside the processor and log out data to a self-contained tape. Software monitors are specially written programs, either time-driven or event-driven, that periodically interrupt the processor and sample internal states, queue sizes, and so forth, and log out to a data storage device. Dudley Warner's System Utilization Monitor (SUM) box hardware monitor and Ken Kolence's Computer Usage Engine (CUE) program software monitor were the first successful monitors of each type, and their creators are generally recognized as the fathers of hardware and software monitors. Both tools came from outside the CPU vendor, who was not interested in providing tools that would reduce sales of their hardware.

One of the challenges of the CPE analyst in the early 1970s was that of deciding between hardware monitors and software monitors. By 1972 there were seven hardware-monitor vendors and five major software monitors available for OS/360. Whereas some were better than others, all were equally important in demonstrating to management that tools did exist, allowing technical decisions to be based on real measurements rather than on intuition.

Hardware monitors were a strong part of the early CPE effort. Because the technology was still transistor-based, any point in the electrical circuit could be probed, and the logic manuals described what signals were on what buses at what time well enough for you to probe the signal and run experimental batch jobs to create expected signals for the monitor to recognize. Hardware monitors were especially attractive to the installation that was out of capacity but incapable of convincing management of that fact. Since the hardware monitor impressed no overhead on the system being measured, it was a favored tool when CPU cycles were hard to come by. Furthermore, the sampling rates believed to be required for accurate software monitoring were measured in micro-seconds, and software monitors had a deservedly bad reputation as expensive to execute.

But times have changed, technology has changed packaging, and the hardware monitor has become much less important because of the great improvements in the software monitor, which is an intrinsic part of dynamic operating systems such as MVS and VM. Although hardware monitors have no overhead on the host processor, they are severely limited because they can only gather data at specific electrical interfaces. Critical data for measurement are often the condition of one or more gates deep inside a single LSI circuit, and it is not possible to connect the probe to the inside of an integrated circuit. The signals that need to be probed are often less than 10 nanoseconds long, requiring very expensive probes and fast counters that escalate the cost of the monitor. The limited number of counters does not permit comprehensive measurement of multiple processors. In the early years, processing of the data tape created on the hardware monitor was done on the mainframe during a slack hour, but now mini- and microcomputers are built into the hardware monitors to avoid consumption of host resources. Their high cost ($100,000+) shows the true cost of data reduction, which was offloaded from the host to the mini/micro.

Thus, hardware monitors have lost their place in performance measurement, at least as far as measurement of the central processor and its peripherals is concerned. Hardware monitors are sometimes still useful for measuring communications systems, but ultimately, intelligent software and firmware in the communications controllers will measure these systems. There is almost no information about the processor complex that cannot be directly measured or substantially inferred from the accounting software within the operating system.

Early software monitors, while providing useful data, often carried significant overhead and caused considerable bias since they tended to measure themselves. They usually produced predetermined reports instead of data and, thus, were not suited for continual measurement. More significantly, since they were not created by the vendor of the operating system, their vendors had to be reactive to hardware and software changes and usually lagged behind each new release by 6 to 9 months.

As operating systems became more dynamic and as vendors of processors and operating systems have become less protective of performance data, the accounting file has become a more complete source of data for billing and for performance analysis. In fact, the hardware monitor caused the vendor to enhance the accounting data with resource monitoring data so that the vendor's employees in the field could use software monitor data to answer customer complaints from a hardware monitor. The main argument for using the accounting file is that it is free. It is primarily an event-driven software monitor that copies various control blocks when certain events occur. Since these control blocks are required for the operating system, the only overhead associated with the file is in writing the accounting records. In addition, resource monitoring is an inherent design component of the dynamic operating system, which makes scheduling decisions and manages resource distribution from these monitored data. Again, there is almost no overhead, except for the physical writing of the data from the operating system's software monitor.

Cost distribution of the shareable computing resources (for example, the CPU) by the installation to its users is standard practice so that the data are collected anyway. Because of its availability, low cost, accuracy, and comprehensiveness, the system accounting file is the de facto standard source of CPE data.

Selecting the Software System

Having chosen the accounting data as the primary data source, the next step is to choose a software system to decode this collection of records into a usable performance data base. The data in the accounting file are complete but disjointed, with information spread across a number of different records (often with dissimilar formats) in many sequences. Thus, the key to the breakthrough in this approach was the discovery of the SAS System. In theory, nothing in this approach required the use of the SAS language; however, the practical implementation is almost cost prohibitive in languages such as PL/I, FORTRAN, or COBOL. The data-handling capabilities of the SAS System make the performance data base possible in the real world of large systems, and the statistical techniques of the SAS System are the analytical tools used against the data base. The SAS System is simply the worldwide standard for CPE. Throughout the remainder of this book, the term SAS refers to the base SAS product in the SAS System.

Measurement and Establishment of Objectives

The final implementation requirement is to measure and establish objectives. The marriage of measurement technique and performance objectives is the original contribution and the key to this approach. Objectives are statements of what values certain variables should assume. If measured values are significantly different from the objective, then there should be some associated measure of discontent; either users are not happy with service, or the comptroller is not happy with the cost of running the computing center.

The most basic objective is to recognize the need for objectives. Objectives already exist in each installation, even if they are not documented. At some level of service measurable by users, the computing center is not providing expected service, and at some value of investment measurable by the comptroller, the computer service is too expensive. The major role of the computer measurement effort is to select appropriate criteria to be defined as objectives, propose their acceptance, and measure them against the objectives.

Computer systems' service transactions, such as a job, interactive response, page printed, message switched, or other quanta that can be identified as belonging to a user and requiring resources, are introduced into the system at some time, receive service (that is, consume resources), and leave at some other time. Thus, the basic objectives can be described in terms of two variables:

- response time received
- resources consumed.

The methods of definition and acceptable values for response and resources may change for different systems, but the key element of this approach is the establishment of performance objectives defined in terms of response time and resource consumption.

No common set of objectives exists because each installation (in fact, each computer within an installation) can, and often should, have different objectives. The response requirement of an on-line system may be so rigid that the resource consumption is insignificant as a limiting criterion, whereas a batch system might have only low response criterion, and resource consumption may be a more important objective. The subjectivity of the owner of the computer resource is often needed to define the truly relevant objectives in management terms. The measurement analyst must translate these management goals (for example, "This is an insurance company. We must pay our claims within 24 hours") into measurable objectives ("All claims jobs will run at priority 15, and 95% must be turned around in 5 minutes").

The Performance Data Base

Since its inception in 1973, the PDB has been a dynamic collection of SAS data libraries containing performance data. The MXG software produces almost the same data as described below, although this example installation has created local SMF records not included in MXG. This example is included to give a general overview of the size and cost of a very comprehensive PDB. The PDB built by MXG is discussed in later chapters. In the example installation, the PDB comprises the complete source of resource consumption and response data for each of four major subsystems run there: batch, TSO, CICS, and IMS. The input accounting data used for these systems are tabulated below:

Subsystem	Resources measured by	Response time measured by
Batch	RMF/SMF	SMF
TSO	RMF/SMF	TSO/MON
CICS 1.4	RMF	Performance Analyzer II (PAII)
CICS 1.5+	RMF	CICS Monitor Facility (CMF)
IMS	RMF	CONTROL/IMS

The following paragraphs describe the subsystems that build the PDB and provide an idea of the magnitude of data processed and the required resources for this system.

For the CICS 1.4 systems, each evening when CICS is taken down, the SAS System reads the CICS Performance Analyzer II Data (PAII) and creates the backup as well as the daily CICS PDB from 110,000 (typical) daily transactions in 3:05 (maximum) 3033-CPU minutes.

For the CICS 1.5 systems, CICS Monitor Facility (CMF)* records are written to the SMF file and processed with the other SMF records.

Formerly, when IMS was taken down each night, the IMS log tapes (6 to 8 per day) were processed by the CONTROL/IMS-supplied program to build the IRUF file. This program, the only non-SAS step that processes data, reads 1,040,000 (typical) log records in 6:15 (maximum) 3033-CPU minutes. The SAS System then reads the output IRUF, producing the Daily IMS PDB in 5:23 (maximum) 3033-CPU minutes. Because of problems with this very large volume input file, CONTROL/IMS was modified so that the C/IMS records were written directly to the SMF file and processed with the normal SMF dump. The PRSEDIT program that created the IRUF file was reverse engineered in the SAS System, and CPU time that was being lost due to truncation in PRSEDIT was recovered.

At approximately 1:00 a.m., SMF or RMF data are dumped from all systems and combined into one daily SMF data set. The combined SMF or RMF data are then processed by the BUILDPDB job, which massages the data and builds the daily SMF or RMF PDB. This job processes all the SMF data to build a composite observation for each step and for each job and drives a number of other subsystems that are dependent upon SMF-type data. Furthermore, this job builds the input to the billing system and produces daily performance reports for three levels of management.

---

*The acronym CMF has also been used by a Boole and Babbage product that creates RMF-like data from MVS. In this book, CMF refers only to the IBM CICS Monitor Facility records written either to SMF or to a CICS journal file.

Table 2.1
Performance Data Base Weekly Resource Consumption

Description of component	Input record count	Transactions represented	3033 CPU minutes
CICS Daily Read PAII Data, Back it up, Produce CICS PDB	600,000	507,674	14.75
IMS Daily Read IMS Log, Produce "IRUF,"	6,000,000		22.01
Read "IRUF," Produce IMS PDB	500,000	311,811	18.27
SMF/RMF Daily Dump VSAM SMF Combine all systems	2,650,000		40.08
Read SMF, Produce daily PDB Produce billing input and so forth			
TSO transactions		636,327	
TSO sessions		12,370	
Batch jobs		28,995	
	2,650,000		103.27
Combined daily reports			22.18
Combined weekly reports			1.88
Build weekly PDBs			6.01
FDR and FDRDSF backups			3.93
Total Weekly 3303-CPU			222.30

Table 2.2
Contents of Weekly Performance Data Base

Name	Description	Number of variables	Number of observations
AUDIT	count of records passed to billing	21	7
CHANGES	priority changes and job releases*	18	23989
CICS	CICS transactions	24	507674
CONNECT	RJE sessions	18	2389
DSETS	use of critical data sets	9	184
IPLS	IPLs	4	35
JES	JES start/stops	9	71
JOBS	job, TSO session, and WYLBUR session resources	147	42733
PRINT	printing by job/remote/form/event	14	45589
PROPRIET	proprietary program executions	64	15759
RMF70	RMF CPU activity	17	980
RMF71	RMF paging/swapping	95	818
RMF72	RMF performance group statistics	30	9419
RMF73	RMF channel queuing/activity	36	18246
RMF74	RMF device queuing/activity	32	65811
RMF75	RMF page/swap data sets	22	7517
STEPS	steps and TSO call/resources	104	120586
TAPETRAN	tape transmission resources	8	371

Name	Description	Number of variables	Number of observations
TMSAUDIT	TMS change audit trail*	12	675
TSOMON	TSO response measure - 15 min per user	57	41122
TYPE10	allocation recovery	8	513
TYPE21	tape error statistics	13	35535
TYPE229	tape/disk mount time, tape swaps*	18	36140
WYLBUR	WYLBUR session detail	24	687

*These data sets are based on locally-created SMF records.

It should be clear that the PDB is a comprehensive system. Many subsystems use the PDB (automatically) as input for further management information. Among the significant systems based on the PDB are the following:

- tape mounting: time to mount tapes by teams, using TYPE229 data, part of the operator's bonus.
- tape cleaning: TMS identifies new scratch tapes, based on expiration date. This list is intercepted and merged with TYPE21 data to determine if the TMS-identified new scratch tape had temporary or permanent errors. Cleaning or certifications, rather than scratch, is defined by the error status if temporary or permanent errors were encountered.
- remote utilization: printer or form usage at remotes, especially print queue time, is reported by merging JOBS and PRINT.
- audit trails: since the billing system is fed by the PDB, audit of the data sent (AUDIT), the data sets used (DSETS), and TMS changes (TMSAUDIT) are traced for the auditors.
- trend reporting: weekly summary data of resources and responses are added automatically to the trend reporting system.

While the operators start the SMF dumps, the SMF merge job automatically submits the job to build the PDB, and no other intervention is required. SAS date functions are used to determine day-of-week and day-of-month, and appropriate jobs are automatically submitted to the internal reader from within this job, as described in chapter thirty-five. The completion code of one job is verified by data control to ensure successful completion. The entire system is maintained by one junior SAS analyst; design changes are made by a senior consultant. Only when the MVS system fails during execution does the junior analyst become involved in maintenance.

Many other ad hoc studies are performed using the PDB. Perhaps the most significant use is for capacity measurement, described in chapter twenty-six. There is no limit to the usefulness of the PDB. Since it contains data on resource consumption and response delivered during the same time frame, problem determination from a single source has been feasible and fruitful. By establishing valid performance measures and objectives for those measures and by reporting and tracking those objectives regularly, much of the need for firefighting is eliminated. Only when a performance measure goes out of its expected range (outside control limits) is firefighting involved, but even then it is rarely necessary to do more than selectively analyze those time periods (using PDB data) to identify the cause of the deviations and to take corrective action. In most instances, looking at the second or third level of detail on the daily reports provides the explanation.

chapter three

The Structure of MVS SMF Files

System Management Facilities (SMF) is an integral part of the IBM OS/360, OS/VS1, OS/VS2, MVS/370, and MVS/XA operating systems. Originally called System Measurement Facility, SMF was created as a result of the need for computer system accounting caused by OS/360. A committee of SHARE attendees and IBM employees specified the requirements, which were then implemented by IBM and were generally available with Release 18 of OS/360. The SHARE Computer Management and Evaluation Project is the direct descendant of this original 1969 SHARE committee.

Prior to OS/360, performance measurement was simple. A job was read in, and the run time was measured with a clock or, in many cases, a calendar. With the advent of OS/360, however, no longer did each job totally own the processor. The multiprogrammed operating systems were introduced to improve hardware utilization by overlapping one task's work with another. The sharing of resources (CPU, memory, and so forth) required an internal software measurement to permit accounting, and SMF provided this measurement capability. However, unlike its competitors, IBM went far beyond simple accounting data. The SHARE committee recognized that writing out control blocks when certain major events occurred would provide high quality information at a low overhead. That attitude has provided the capability to perform CPE from accounting data. The strides made with SMF have not been repeated by other vendors or even for other IBM operating systems. For example, compare the quality and range of performance data in SMF (even OS/360 SMF) with the present 80-byte accounting record begrudgingly written by VM/370.

SMF can mean different things from different perspectives. The most general reference to SMF is to the SMF files that are managed by the operating system and into which all SMF records are written. SMF also refers to the component of the operating system, the SMF writer, that moves the software records from memory to the disk SMF file. SMF also refers to the IBM-supplied utility that dumps the disk SMF file to tape. In addition, the SMF component provides EXITS—standard, supported interfaces between an operating system event (such as reading in a JOB card) and optional user written routines (such as account number validation at read-in time). SMF is usually a reference to the architecture that captures data and writes that data to the common SMF files for later processing.

Within the SMF architecture, the SMF files contain record numbers, record IDs, or record types, where each record type describes a class of events (for example, file close and step termination create separate record types in the SMF file). Many

SMF records are written by the SMF component, but many other components have properly exploited the fine architecture provided by SMF and write their data records into the SMF file. The best example is the Resource Measurement Facility (RMF), a sampling software monitor introduced with MVS that records its data in the SMF file. Many other IBM components use the SMF files as their archive, and almost all other MVS performance products that create data records write them to the SMF files.

The SMF records are variable-length, and each contains a standard SMF header with the record type, a time stamp indicating when the record was moved to the SMF buffer, and the software system identification on which this record was written. When the current buffer is filled, it is given to the SMF writer to process while new records are being added to other buffers.

SMF records are written to VSAM data sets. The installation can choose from two to thirty-six data sets named SYS1.MANx, where x is any number or letter. At IPL time, one of the defined data sets is selected as the active SMF data set into which new records are written. If the active SMF data set fills, SMF automatically notifies the operator that MANx is full, and SMF switches or begins writing subsequent records to the next-defined SMF data set that is not full. The operator then starts the dump program, which copies the contents of SYS1.MANx to tape and makes the disk data set available for reuse by the SMF writer. When all defined SMF data sets are full, SMF recording is suspended, and no records can be written until the data sets are dumped. (A nondeletable console message is the primary protection against this data loss. You should consider terminating the employment of any operator who permits this to happen.)

The installation specifies the parameters for SMF through the SYS1.PARMLIB member SMFPRMxx. The only critical parameter, BUF, should be set to the maximum value permitted, which is 8192, giving SMF two 4096-byte buffers. Any lower value also causes a significant increase in the cost of the SMF writer when creating the records. A lower value also causes the IFASMFDP dump utility to consume unnecessary CPU time when reading the VSAM files. Usually the SMF records are processed after they have been dumped from the VSAM disk data set to a BSAM tape or disk data set, but they can also be read from the VSAM data set. In fact, MXG Software is attractive because it processes SMF records from either a BSAM or VSAM file, with complete user transparency.

The required DCB attributes of the SMF records that must be specified for correct processing are DCB=(RECFM=VBS,LRECL=32756). The blocksize will be acquired from the data set. Although the Variable, Blocked, Spanned (VBS) record format is required, SMF does not create a normal VBS file. A normal VBS file contains variable length records, but each block is always filled (a logical record spans two or more blocks when necessary). SMF does write spanned records except when the logical record length is larger than the size of the SMF buffer. Thus, the overhead of partitioning a logical record into 2 blocks only occurs when it is absolutely necessary. Spanned records are appropriate because of IBM's poor choice of a maximum buffersize of 4096 for this sequential processing and because SMF has mostly small (for example, 260 to 400 byte) records and occasionally very large (18000 to 32756 byte) records. However, VBS files can cause problems with SMF analysis programs. Every time the system is started with an IPL, the logical records that were in the buffer are not written to the active SMF data set. Thus, if the system crashes after a block containing a spanned record is written, the active SMF data set contains only the first part of the spanned record. The other SMF records in the unwritten buffer are lost. The incomplete spanned record can cause the SMF processing program to fail with a SYSTEM 002 ABEND, as happened frequently when the SMF data sets were BSAM prior to MVS/SE2. The SAS System recognizes this broken segment problem without abending. It reports that an invalid segment was read, so the user knows that data were lost.

There is a lot of confusion surrounding the volume of activity to the SMF data set. A 3081K with a great deal of activity can generate 350,000 SMF records in a 24-hour period or, typically, about 175,000 records during the peak 8 hours; however, the VBS logical records are blocked about 16.6 records per physical 4096 block. That causes only 2636 physical I/Os per hour to SMF (an I/O rate of less than 1 record every second). Compared to the total I/O capacity of over 500 I/Os per second for a 3081K, this SMF activity is not a significant I/O workload. Even at the volume level, 1 I/O per second is far less than many other critical system volumes and should not be considered a problem. Prior to the VSAM SMF architecture, the SMF writer was the major bottleneck in heavily utilized systems. This is no longer true. IBM benchmarks on 3033s showed that the SMF writer could handle well over 4000 logical records per second without any problem.

The earlier BSAM architecture also required attention for performance that is no longer required for SMF but is described here to give you an understanding of BSAM in its entirety. Originally, BSAM used the WRITE VERIFY option for SMF records, and it was necessary to alter (zap) the SMF writer to disable this archaic I/O option, which doubles the time to read or write. Improved DASD devices and VSAM have eliminated this need. Because the BSAM architecture used a TCLOSE after every block to guarantee that a block once written could be read, it was very important to locate the SMF data sets adjacent to the Volume Table of Contents (VTOC) data set to reduce disk arm movement on the pack containing SMF data sets because each TCLOSE updates the last-block-written pointer in the VTOC. With MVS/XA, the SMF dump program preformats the SMF VSAM data set with a logical end-of-file (the string SMF EOF MA), providing the same integrity as the old TCLOSE for BSAM.

Formerly, it was impossible to guarantee that records in SMF were written in exact time sequence even though they were time stamped as they were moved to the buffer. This lack of sequence was caused by the various enqueue chains and the different dispatching priorities of tasks in the system. Additionally, the time stamp had different meanings. Since MVS, however, the IBM-created records written to SMF appear to be written in time stamp order, except for two records:

1. The type 2 and 3 (SMF DUMP HEADER and TRAILER records) time stamps are the time of the event and not the time the record was placed in the buffer.
2. A step termination record (type 4 or type 30, subtype 4) can be written out of sequence if the installation uses the SMF exit to tell the user why a job was canceled by the operator. Because of the logical location of that exit, the termination has occurred, and the time stamp has been filled in; however, the record is not placed in SMF until the operator responds, and, thus, the record is out of sequence.

For non-IBM-created records written to SMF, the time stamp may still be out of sequence. When a programmer calls on the SMF writer, he can either fill in the SMF time stamp and inform the SMF writer to pass the record through to the SMF file unchanged or pass the data to the SMF writer and have the SMF writer apply the time stamp, which causes the record to be written in sequence.

Many records written to SMF are job related; that is, they correspond to specific events for specific tasks. All records relating to an execution of a particular task, whether a job or a TSO session, can be tied together by the job log, which consists of the job name, the job reader date, and the job reader time. In the MXG code, job log is defined by two variables: JOB and READTIME, where READTIME is the datetime stamp of the job read-in event. Thus, even though the records relating to the job are written at different times, there is only one read time for each job or task, and all records relating to a single execution can be clustered by job name and read time. Since restarted jobs are not reprocessed by the reader, their records contain the same readtime stamp.

chapter four

SAS Data Sets Built from MVS Data

The preceding chapter described the structure of data records in SMF files. This chapter describes the kinds of data recorded in SMF and whether the data are created free as a part of MVS or by products (such as IBM's RMF, NPA, or CMF products). This chapter begins with a discussion of SMF record numbers or record IDs.

Most SMF and RMF literature refers to the records by their record number rather than by name, so you should learn the contents of SMF records by their ID number. SMF record IDs are 1-byte numerics ranging from 0 to 255. Records 0 through 127 are reserved for IBM's records, and records 128 through 255 can be assigned by the installation. For example, if you install a product like TSO/MON*, you must choose an unused SMF record ID from 128 to 255 for the product to use. Sometimes a second field, a subtype identifier, is also required to recognize the event that caused the record or to recognize the subsystem that created the record. IBM's records 22, 30, and 47 are examples of records with a subtype field. IBM currently writes the 69 SMF record types tabulated in Table 4.1:

Table 4.1
SMF Records

0, 2, 3, 4, 5, 6, 7, 8, 9, 10
11, 14, 15, 16, 17, 18, 19, 20, 21, 22
23, 25, 26, 30, 31, 32, 34, 35, 38, 40
43, 44, 45, 47, 48, 49, 50, 52, 53, 54
55, 56, 57, 58, 60, 61, 62, 63, 64, 65
66, 67, 68, 69, 70, 71, 72, 73, 74, 75
76, 77, 78, 79, 80, 81, 82, 90, 110

Job-related:	contain job name, TSO user ID, or STC name and are written when a certain event occurred in a job (records 4, 5, 6, 10, 14, 15, 16, 17, 18, 20, 25, 26, 30, 32, 34, 35, 40, 60, 61, 62, 63, 64, 65, 66, 67, 68, 69)

---

*a product that measures TSO response and writes two SMF records.

RMF-produced: written at regular intervals when RMF is active (records 70, 71, 72, 73, 74, 75, 76, 77, 78, 79)

SMF-information: relate to SMF activity (records 2, 3, 7, 23)

NPA activity: Network Performance Analyzer product statistic (record 38)

VSAM activity: VSAM data activity (records 60, 62, 63, 64, 67, 68, 69)

CATALOG activity: for Integrated Catalog Facility (ICF) activity (records 61, 65, 66)

JES activity: start and stop of JES, RJEs, and NJEs (records 43, 45, 47, 48, 49, 52, 53, 54, 55, 56, 57, 58)

VSPC activity: VSPC session activity (records 43, 44, 45, 47, 48, 49)

Configuration: IPLs, VARYs and other operator actions (records 0, 8, 9, 11, 19, 22, 31, 90)

VTAM activity: buffer usage by VTAM (record 50)

CICS activity: CICS Monitor Facility (record 110)

Tape activity: volume errors when dismounted (record 21)

RACF activity: security activity with RACF (records 80, 81)

CRYPTO activity: IBM's CRYPTOGRAPHIC system usage (record 82).

Most SMF records contain unique information; however, sometimes 2 or 3 records contain data in almost exactly the same format. For efficiency, when these groups of SMF records are logically related, MXG software processes the records together and builds 1 or more SAS data sets as appropriate. For example, the type 4 and type 34 records, both step determination records, are processed by 1 program and written to 1 SAS data set. The type 4 record is written when a batch step is terminated, and the type 34 record is written at the end of a TSO step. The type 14 and type 15 records for data set activity are also processed by 1 member. The type 14 record is written by SMF when a file is opened for input, and the type 15 is written for files opened for output.

The 78 SAS data sets built from the 69 IBM SMF records with the MXG software are shown in Table 4.2. Note that the MXG SOURCLIB member and the SAS data set built by that member have similar names and are consistent with the SMF record types being processed. In most instances, a single SAS data set will be built with the data set name TYPE*nnnn*. There are several cases where multiple SAS data sets are built from a single source member, either for performance considerations or because two records are logically related.

Table 4.2
SMF Records Written to SAS Data Sets by MXG

Source library member name	Record types processed	Records written by	MXG's SAS data set name	Record description
TYPE0	0	SMF	TYPE0	IPL
TYPE0203	2,3	SMF	TYPE0203	SMF dump/trailer
TYPE434	4,34	SMF	TYPE434	step termination
TYPE535	5,35	SMF	TYPE535	job termination
TYPE6	6	JES	TYPE6	print/punch (JES WRITER)
TYPE7	7	SMF	TYPE7	SMF data lost condition
TYPE8911	8,9,11	SMF	TYPE8911	I/O configuration
TYPE10	10	SMF	TYPE10	allocation recovery
TYPE1415	14,15	SMF	TYPE1415	data set closed
TYPE16	16	ICEMAN	TYPE16	ICEMAN sort invoked
TYPE1718	17,18	SMF	TYPE1718	data set SCRATCH/RENAME
TYPE19	19	SMF	TYPE19	ONLINE DASD volume
TYPE20	20	SMF	TYPE20	job initiated
TYPE21	21	SMF	TYPE21	tape volume dismounted
TYPE22	22-1	SMF	TYPE22_1	CPU configuration
TYPE22	22-2	SMF	TYPE22_2	VARY ONLINE command
TYPE22	22-3	SMF	TYPE22_3	STORAGE configuration

Source library member name	Record types processed	Records written by	MXG's SAS data set name	Record description
TYPE22	22-4	SMF	TYPE22_4	MSS configuration
TYPE22	22-5	SMF	TYPE22_5	VARY ONLINE, S
TYPE22	22-6	SMF	TYPE22_6	VARY OFFLINE, S
TYPE22	22-7	SMF	TYPE22_7	channel path configuration
TYPE22	22-8	SMF	TYPE22_8	reconfiguration channel path
TYPE23	23	SMF	TYPE23	SMF buffer statistics
TYPE25	25	JES3	TYPE25	JES3 SETUP/FETCH
TYPE26J2	26	JES2	TYPE26J2	JES2 PURGE
TYPE26J3	26	JES3	TYPE26J3	JES3 PURGE
TYPE30	30-1	SMF	TYPE30_1	TYPE30 job initiated
TYPE30	30-2,3	SMF	TYPE30_V	TYPE30 interval
TYPE30	30-4	SMF	TYPE30_4	TYPE30 step terminated
TYPE30	30-4	SMF	TYPE30_D	TYPE30 DD activity
TYPE30	30-5	SMF	TYPE30_5	TYPE30 job terminated
TYPE30	30-6	SMF	TYPE30_6	TYPE30 create data ASID
TYPE31	31	SMF	TYPE31	START TSO
TYPE32	32	SMF	TYPE32	TSO command
TYPE38	38	NPA	TYPE38EX	NPA exception
TYPE38	38	NPA	TYPE38IN	NPA interval
TYPE38	38	NPA	TYPE38NC	NPA/NCP statistics
TYPE40	40	SMF	TYPE40	dynamic allocation
TYPE43PC	43,44,45	VSPC	TYPE43PC	VSPC
TYPE4345	43,45	JES	TYPE4345	JES START/STOP
TYPE47PC	47	VSPC	TYPE47PC	VSPC
TYPE4789	47,48,49	JES	TYPE4789	JES BISYNC RJE SIGNON

Source library member name	Record types processed	Records written by	MXG's SAS data set name	Record description
TYPE48PC	48	VSPC	TYPE48PC	VSPC
TYPE49PC	49	VSPC	TYPE49PC	VSPC
TYPE50	50	VTAM	TYPE50	VTAM buffers
TYPE5234	52,53,54	JES	TYPE5234	JES SDLC RJE SIGNON
TYPE5568	55,56,58	JES	TYPE5568	JES NJE START/STOP
TYPE57	57	JES2	TYPE57J2	JES2 NJE SYSOUT
TYPE57	57	JES3	TYPE57J3	JES3 NJP SYSOUT
TYPE60	60	SMF	TYPE60	VSAM VVDS updated
TYPE6156	61	SMF	TYPE61	ICF activity
TYPE62	62	SMF	TYPE62	VSAM opened
TYPE6367	63,67	SMF	TYPE6367	VSAM DEFINE/DELETE
TYPE64	64	SMF	TYPE64	VSAM EXCP statistics
TYPE68	68	SMF	TYPE68	VSAM RENAME
TYPE69	69	SMF	TYPE69	VSAM data space
TYPE7072	70	RMF	TYPE70	RMF CPU
TYPE7072	72	RMF	TYPE72	performance group
TYPE71	71	RMF	TYPE71	paging and memory
TYPE73	73	RMF	TYPE73	MVS/XA channels
TYPE73	73	RMF	TYPE73L	MVS/370 logical channel
TYPE73	73	RMF	TYPE73P	MVS/370 physical channel
TYPE74	74	RMF	TYPE74	device activity
TYPE75	75	RMF	TYPE75	paging data sets
TYPE76	76	RMF	TYPE76	RMF trace
TYPE77	77	RMF	TYPE77	ENQUEUE conflict
TYPE78	78	RMF	TYPE78	MVS/XA device queuing
TYPE78	78	RMF	TYPE78CF	MVS/XA device configuration

Source library member name	Record types processed	Records written by	MXG's SAS data set name	Record description
TYPE78	78	RMF	TYPE78PA	MVS/XA virtual storage-private area
TYPE78	78	RMF	TYPE78SP	MVS/XA virtual storage-subpools
TYPE78	78	RMF	TYPE78VS	MVS/XA virtual storage
TYPE79	79	RMF	TYPE79	MONITOR II session
TYPE80	80	RACF	TYPE80	RACF processing
TYPE81	81	RACF	TYPE81	RACF initialization
TYPE82	82	CRYPTO	TYPE82	CRYPTO security
TYPE90	90	SMF	TYPE90	operator changes
TYPE110	110	CICS	CICSACCT	CICS 'accounting'
TYPE110	110	CICS	CICSEXCE	CICS exceptions
TYPE110	110	CICS	CICSTRAN	CICS transactions
TYPE110	110	CICS	CICSYSTM	CICS system resources

A complete description of these SMF records is contained in chapter forty. There is a section in chapter forty that describes each SAS data set listed above. The events creating each record and each SAS variable contained in the data set are documented. Chapter forty is your reference source when you need a specific analysis. If you are a new CPE analyst, you should take the time to read all of chapter forty. Although most of the data you analyze come from only a few important SMF records, you should read the contents of all the SMF records to be aware of what SMF does and does not record.

chapter five

The Structure of DOS/VSE Performance Data

MXG code executes only under the MVS version of SAS software. To analyze data created by DOS/VSE, you must copy the DOS/VSE POWER and CMF data to a data set on the MVS system where you execute MXG.

DOS/VSE is a simpler, more efficient operating system than MVS, but it has physical limits that can be easily exceeded as the number of terminals and devices increases. Usually the migration from DOS/VSE to MVS results from the success of the enterprise; that is, the business requires more services than DOS can provide. As a result, the quantity and quality of DOS performance measurement data is less than that of MVS SMF and RMF data. Nevertheless, the data available from DOS/VSE are very adequate for responsible analysis of capacity with a SAS performance data base, as the case study presented in this chapter illustrates.

DOS/VSE operating systems sometimes do not need to be measured. These operating systems occur frequently in 4331-class machines used to drive laser printers at an RJE site. For this purpose, the smallest 4331 is only about 22% CPU busy. But as soon as people get one of these single purpose DOS systems, they try to use it for something else as well. With your demonstrated skills as an MVS performance expert, it will be natural for your management to expect you to be able to solve "Wayne's" performance problem on his DOS/VSE RJE system.

DOS installations using CICS as their on-line system are well provided with CICS response and resource data in the records written by the CICS Monitor Facility (CMF). This free component of CICS became available with Release 1.5 and writes a record on every transaction and typically a 15-minute summary of resources record to a CICS journal data set. The accounting records written by DOS/VSE POWER provide data similar to the step termination record written by the earliest version of SMF. MXG software processing of the CICS CMF records is discussed in chapter twenty-one since the CMF records written to the journal file are the same format under DOS/VSE as under MVS. MXG software that processes the DOS/VSE POWER accounting records is described in the following sections of chapter forty:

section and data set	contents
DOSJOBS	step resources
DOSLIST	printing event resources
DOSPUNCH	punch event resources
DOSREAD	input card reader resources
DOSRJE	Remote Job Entry (non-SNA lines)
DOSSNA	Remote Job Entry (SNA lines)

The DOS/VSE logical equivalent to RMF data, the DOS/PT, (IBM FDP XYZ-1234) is also important in the analysis of DOS/VSE installations, but it is not currently processed by MXG code.

A historical note on the /PTs is appropriate: around 1972 software monitors began to be sold for OS/360 systems, and IBM made available a marketing aid called Operating System Performance Tool (OS/PT). Users were not allowed to execute it themselves, and they could look at, but not keep, the output of the runs. In fact, it could only be used by the IBM marketing team if users were trying to decide which IBM processor (either a 145 or a 155) to install. It was a very good sampling software monitor, and SHARE petitioned IBM to make the product available for a fee. Only after MVS became viable and RMF's predecessor, MF/1, began to be accepted as the software monitor of choice did IBM finally make OS/PT, VS1/PT, and DOS/PT available for a fee.

DOS/PT executes in a DOS partition, sampling utilizations on hardware and partition, and writes data to a log, usually tape. Like all monitors, its overhead is determined by the sampling rate; but in the author's opinion, the slowest sampling rate has been adequate. The report software provides some selection. If the data are written every 10 minutes, adequate detail is available for subsequent investigation. If reports are summarized every hour, you can manually extract the most important utilizations, the total CPU active and the CPU active for each partition for each hour as percentages, and enter them into a SAS data set to merge with CMF and POWER data. Since DOS/PT provides overall CPU activity and CPU activity by partition, you can determine true CPU cost-per-transaction in a CICS system, as shown below. Much of this book is specific to the data available with MVS. Although DOS data may be less complete, the philosophy of computer performance evaluation is based on analyzing available data.

The following analysis of DOS/VSE serves two purposes: first, DOS/VSE sites can see how solid analyses can be from available data, and, second, non-DOS/VSE installations get a sample of the analysis that the rest of the book offers.

DOS/VSE 4331-2 COMPUTER CAPACITY ANALYSIS

The following analysis was presented to the president and staff of a widget company in Widgetville, WD. The analysis used POWER account data to determine the split between CICS and other work on this 4331-2 processor. That the site was out of capacity was demonstrated by CICS internal response time from CMF data. The CPU cost of a CICS transaction was determined by regression of the CMF transaction counts with the partition busy measured by DOS/VSE PT. Twelve data values for each hour were manually extracted from the DOS/VSE PT reports.

Analysis of the computer performance data from the 4331 in Widgetville shows the present system is operating at capacity, and the CPU itself is the limiting component. The conclusions and supporting data follow.

Replacement of the 4331 is required and, based on the projected computer requirements, a 4361 processor should provide sufficient capability to meet the company's needs until late 1986 or early 1987.

The Widget Company system is well designed, using state-of-the-art software designs that do not exist in many MVS systems. The DOS/VSE operating system will meet the needs of Widget Company for some time, and until a physical limitation in the software that requires migration is encountered, no conversion to the more powerful, flexible, and expensive MVS operating system is needed.

The capacity of the Widget Company computer system was measured in the number of CICS transactions because that number most clearly relates to the business activity of the enterprise. Tracking the CICS transaction count per day provides an excellent management indicator of capacity utilization. It is also wise to confirm periodically that the transaction count continues to track processor utilization. A major change in the application design could alter the present strong relationship between daily business transactions and processor utilization.

Hourly CICS Transaction Capacity Is 2250

Analysis of the Widget Company processor shows that each CICS transaction requires 1 CPU second of processing time on the present 4331 CPU (Figure 5.1). Since there are only 3600 seconds in each hour, the maximum transactions needed if the 4331 were to process only CICS work is 3600 transactions per hour.

However, business needs at the Widget Company require that other computer work be accomplished during prime time as well. During the month analyzed, 38.33% of the total prime-time work was this other work, and CICS made up the remaining 61.77% (Figure 5.2).

With only 62% of the prime-time capacity available for CICS, the 4331 CPU can actually process only 2224 transactions per hour. The analysis of response time of CICS (Figure 5.3) showed that the response time of CICS begins to degrade

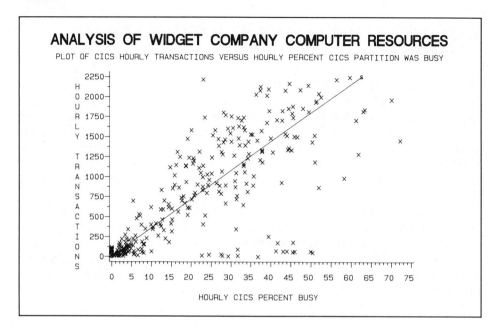

Figure 5.1

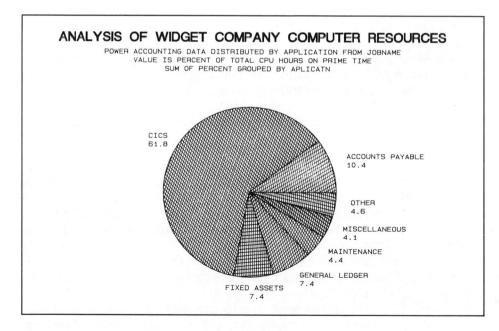

Figure 5.2

at transaction rates above about 1800 per hour, but the elongation of response at a rate of 2224 transactions per hour is still acceptable.

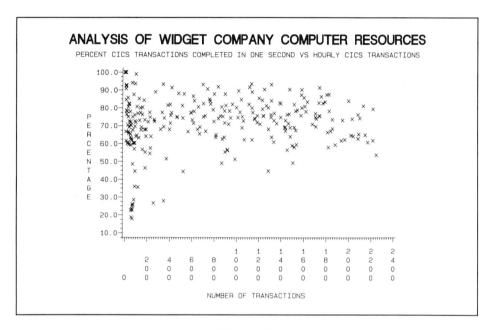

Figure 5.3

Thus, the maximum hourly CICS transaction rate that the present 4331 CPU can achieve, without degraded response and allowing for the non-CICS work, is 2224 transactions per hour.

Daily CICS Prime Shift CICS Transaction Capacity Is 16000

There are 9 hours in the prime-time shift at the Widget Company, but the daily CICS capacity is not 9 x 2224 = 20016. Although this is the rate that the hardware could support, the widget business does not generate constant demand all day. The profile of average transactions that the Widget Company requires for each hour of the day shows the classic double-peak (Figure 5.4). The shape of this profile changes only if working hours change since this shape is the result of Widget Company's business requirements. The hourly capacity at which response time degrades is 2224 transactions. If you keep the same shape but raise the curve until the peak hour is at hourly capacity, the area under the raised profile is the daily capacity. Thus, the true daily capacity is 16928 transactions per day (Figure 5.5). This technique is completely described in chapter twenty-six.

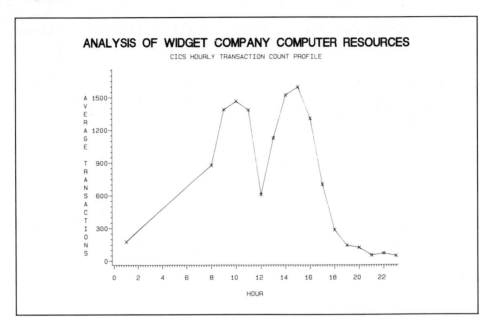

Figure 5.4

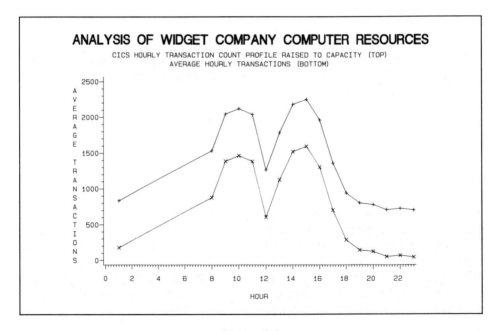

Figure 5.5

Table 5.6
November 1983, Daily CICS Activity

Date	Day	Transactions	Date	Day	Transactions
31 OCT	M	16452	14 NOV	M	15458
01 NOV	T	11565	15 NOV	T	13307
02 NOV	W	12434	16 NOV	W	8624
03 NOV	T	13177	17 NOV	T	15161
04 NOV	F	12718	18 NOV	F	10697
05 NOV	S	5760	19 NOV	S	2753
06 NOV	S	1746	20 NOV	S	3804
07 NOV	M	16142	21 NOV	M	12722
08 NOV	T	17374	22 NOV	T	14622
09 NOV	W	12704	23 NOV	W	11412
10 NOV	T	9089	27 NOV	S	10082
11 NOV	F	8888	28 NOV	M	7194
12 NOV	S	4927	29 NOV	T	19584
13 NOV	S	2218	30 NOV	W	11152

Number of days	Transaction count was above
2	17000
4	16000
6	15000
7	14000
9	13000
13	12000
16	11000

Widget Company Is at Capacity

Data processing managers find that user complaints rise rapidly when response time is poor for more than two days in any week, for two consecutive weeks with two or more days of poor service, or when four or more days in a month are poor. During the month investigated (November 1983), daily CICS capacity was exceeded on two days and approached on two more days (Table 5.6). Although transaction count can increase above the daily capacity value, the result is an elongation of response time and a reduction in productivity of the computer user. Thus, the present 4331 configuration is operating at capacity to provide unelongated response. The limiting resource is the speed of the processor (the CPU). The capacity of the other computer resources used by CICS transactions (real memory, I/O paths or channels, and disk devices) is adequate. (Although proof is not demonstrated here, it was determined by comparing CMF response to DOS/PT measures of these resources.)

Projected Life of a 4361 Is through the End of 1986

The published estimate that the 4361 CPU is 3.3 times faster than the present 4331 capacity of 16928 daily transactions was used to estimate daily CICS transaction capacity for the 4361 processor of 55862 transactions. (This estimate also assumes that the distribution of work between CICS and batch remains constant.)

Widget Company has provided two scenarios (Table 5.7) of growth, termed historical and aggressive, that are based in part on expected widget tonnage but grow faster than widget growth because of planned new computer applications (Figure 5.8).

Table 5.7
Projected Growth of Widget Company

End of year	Tons of widgets (millions)	Composite growth factor		Required daily CICS transaction capacity	
		Historical	Aggressive	Historical	Aggressive
1983	4.4	1.00	1.00	17000	17000
1984	5.6	1.44	1.49	24480	25330
1985	8.3	2.40	2.68	40800	45560
1986	9.5	3.02	3.69	51340	62730
1987	10.2	3.55	4.69	60350	79730
1988	10.6	4.02	5.64	68340	95880

A 4361 should provide adequate CPU capacity through second quarter 1987 if the historical trend is followed or would be exceeded by the third quarter of 1986 if aggressive growth is achieved (Figure 5.9).

Note: although the CPU capacity of a 4361 is projected to be adequate until 1986-87, by that time it will be necessary to expand real memory and probably disk volumes, control units, and channels if the 4361 is to operate at its true capacity. Since the present capacity of these ancillary resources is adequate, tactical acquisition of these resources should pose no strategic problem for the data processing department of Widget Company.

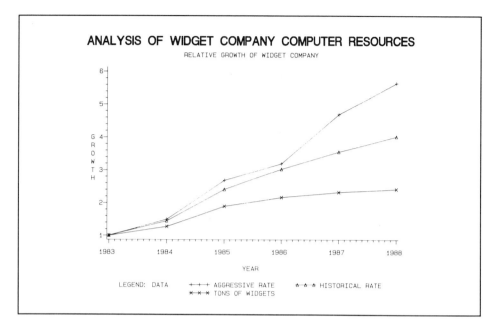

Figure 5.8

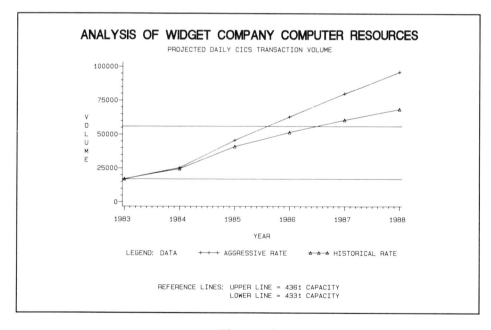

Figure 5.9

The preceding case study shows that the use of POWER accounting data and CICS CMF data with MXG software, merged with manually extracted CICS partition busy data from DOS/PT, can be easily used for DOS/VSE capacity analysis. Expressing computer capacity in transactions and tons of widgets rather than in CPU seconds is important for management's understanding and acceptance of technical analysis.

chapter six
The Structure of VM/370 Measurement Data

The VM/370 virtual machine operating system is an outgrowth of the TSS and CP-67 operating system, so it has two primary uses in today's corporate data centers. First, its interactive system, conversational monitor system (CMS), is used heavily as a basis for decision support systems, office communications and calendaring with IBM's professional office system (PROFS), and program development. Second, its ability to permit one processor to execute multiple operating systems finds VM filling a role in migration and conversion as well as supporting production systems like DOS/VSE concurrent with MVS testing.

The utility of VM has been well demonstrated to its small group of believers for many years, but only in the past few years has IBM begun to support the VM product as a production system. Although many improvements in the software have been noted, IBM has still not provided accounting and performance data of value; SMF under OS/360 at release 18.6 was far better instrumented than VM is at release SP3. In the author's opinion, VM succeeded in spite of its relatively poor support because its source was distributed with the product. By making the source available to users, facilities that did not exist could be easily coded as modifications, at source level, by the VM system programmer. The purported "user friendly" attribute of CMS does not come from an intrinsic human engineering design, but rather from the more powerful EXEC language that enables programmers to wrap complex tasks with an apparent single command image to their users. CMS is less expensive to use than TSO for many functions, although the recent announcements of extensions for TSO show that MVS designers are responding to those differences.

There are only two sources of VM data: the 80-byte VM account records (that until recently had to be physically punched unless the installation modified VM) and the VM monitor data that can be processed by the IBM VMAP software. MXG software is currently available only for VM account data. A future enhancement to MXG software will allow processing of VM monitor data, the only source of response time measurement to CMS users.

The measurement and management of VM resources is possible with only VM account records, although no response data are available. Several events create account records, but the session record is the basis of most VM analysis. At logoff time, resources used by each CMS user or each virtual machine are written to the VM account file on spool. Periodically, a VM utility is executed to collect these VM account records and present them to the reader on a VM machine. The VM machine collects and sends these records to an MVS data set where the MXG software processes the records and creates the following SAS data sets:

VMSESSN   one observation for each virtual machine session containing resources (CPU and I/O) consumed (see below).

VMUSRDA   one observation for each user data record created.

VMDEVICE   one observation for each device attached to a virtual machine.

VMLOGON   one observation for each failed logon attempt.

VMDISK   one observation for each failed disk attempt.

VMLINK   one observation for each failed link attempt.

VMVCNA   one observation for each SNA session on behalf of a virtual machine. VTAM communications network application, VCNA, executes in a VS1 or DOS/VSE machine under VM and manages the SNA resources connecting SNA devices with their virtual machine. At SNA session completion, data are passed from the VCNA machine to VM and written to the VM account file. The data describe the VTAM resources (input bytes, output bytes, and so forth) used by the virtual machine.

In addition to these data, which could be used to describe adequately the resources consumed by VM sessions, VM provides another facility that aids the CPE task. Any virtual machine can issue VM commands at specified times during the day. If a special virtual machine were to issue the ACCOUNT ALL command every hour, a VM account record on each virtual machine is created at the end of each hour rather than just at logoff. These records contain resources consumed by that machine during that hour and are created simultaneously for all logged on machines. By summing all these interval records during the hour, the total resources captured by the VM account record can be determined, and individual user records can be gathered (by USERID or ACCOUNT) into business elements to report hourly usage of the VM system's resources by using group or business elements. An example of this technique is provided in the MXG software member ANALVM.

The only resources provided in the session record are two CPU times; SIO counts to disk, page-in, and page-out; and SIO counts for spool cards read, lines to print, and cards to punch. The two CPU times recorded are V-time, or CPU seconds consumed in the virtual machine, and T-time, or total of V-time and the

CPU consumed by CP, (as the VM operating system is referred to) on behalf of this virtual machine. In data set VMSESSN, these two CPU times are expanded into three variables, CPUVIRTM, CPUVMTM, and CPUCPTM. When ACCOUNT ALL is used to create (for example) hourly data, these three values provide the total CPU consumed in all virtual machines, on the hardware, and in VM operating system on behalf of its virtual machines. Data set VMSESSN contains one observation for each ACCOUNT ALL interval that each virtual machine was logged on, and the resources in that observation are the resources consumed during that interval. Furthermore, these interval records are written simultaneously for all users.

Although VM provides only account records, machines executing under VM produce other performance records. For example, a DOS/VSE machine executing under VM creates VM account records that describe CPU time used by the entire machine. In addition, DOS/POWER account records that describe the CPU consumed by each job executed under DOS are written by DOS to its account file. If the DOS/VSE machine also executes CICS and if CICS monitor facility is enabled, the CMF records are written to a DOS CICS journal file and the transaction response time and resources can be analyzed even though CICS is executing under DOS/VSE, which is executing under VM. An MVS machine executing under VM creates SMF and RMF records as well. In the example ANALVM, RMF data and VM account records are created hourly, and both are combined to report the portion of the VM system used by MVS and the distribution of MVS CPU captured by RMF versus MVS CPU not captured (MVS Overhead). Although VM itself is weak on performance data, non-VM systems executing under VM handle reporting nicely.

chapter seven

Events in the Lifetime of an MVS Task

To perform CPE analysis, the analyst must understand the computer system under investigation and know what functions the operating system performs for a task. Although operating systems are different, they all manage the shared resources in response to requests by tasks for those resources. Since the operating system is the manager of the many queues for these requests, a large part of CPE data analysis is to determine who is in what queue, for how long, and why.

All operating systems provide some accounting data for each task (job, session, and so forth) that contain time stamps when certain events occur for that task. By comparing these time stamps to the logical structure of the services provided by the operating system, the analyst can understand how an operating system interaction is mapped to the CPE data. By subtracting successive time stamps, the duration in certain states (allocation, CPU execution, I/O execution, and so forth) can be determined at the task level. Documentation of CPE data from the vendor often does not tell enough about the meaning of these events. Sometimes you can read the microfiche (when the vendor makes the source available) and perhaps decipher the conditions under which a time stamp is valid, but even then, the experimental confirmation of suspicion is required. By executing tasks that you understand (that is, your own computer workload) and by examining detail data in the detail records written on your tasks, you can gain the necessary knowledge.

The SAS System provides features for manipulating numeric values that represent durations and time stamps. SAS date, time, and datetime variables are stored as numeric values, and SAS date, time, and datetime formats can express the values as day, month, year, hour, and so forth. MXG code defines all durations and time stamps with these SAS date, time, and datetime formats.

In this book and in the MXG software variables whose names end in TIME (for example, READTIME) are time stamps—the date and time that an event occurred. The default format is DATETIME19.2, so they are printed in the form 18DEC83:11:10:56.99. (The internal value of a datetime variable is the number of seconds since January 1, 1960.) Variable names ending in DATE (for example, BILLDATE) are SAS date values with format DATE7, printed as 18DEC83. (The internal value of a date variable is the number of days since January 1, 1960.) If a variable's name ends in TM (for example, CPUTCBTM), the variable contains a SAS time value. Its format is TIME12.2, printed as 27:16:58.87. Time values usually represent durations, although they are occasionally used for the time of day when the date is not directly available. Since time values and datetime values are internally stored in units of seconds, they can be added or subtracted. For example, to find the duration between two datetime values, subtract them. Similarly, the end time of an event can be found by adding the datetime value at the start of the event and its duration.

A technical note on time stamp variables: datetime values must be stored in SAS variables with a length of 8 bytes, whereas date or time values require only 4 bytes of storage. The SAS default of 8 bytes for storing numeric values is altered by MXG to save storage space. (DEFAULT=4 is specified in a LENGTH statement, and 8 bytes are allocated explicitly for each datetime stamp variable.) To save further storage, only the start (a datetime value) and duration of an event are kept (12 rather than 16 bytes) since the end time can be reconstructed by addition.

Figure 7.1 maps the time stamps that exist in the SAS MVS data sets from most of the job-related SMF records. The main function of BUILDPDB , the MXG module that builds the MVS Performance Data Base (PDB), is to collect these time stamps from their many event records and place them into a single SAS observation per job. The number in parentheses under each variable name identifies the SMF record type used to create this variable. More information on these events and their variables can be found in chapter forty. The following paragraphs describe the event represented by each variable and identify the source clock used for this event. In multiple CPU installations, various events on behalf of a job can occur on different processors, and the time stamp of that event uses the clock on that processor. JES data identifies the system on which these events occurred (SYSREAD, SYSCVRT, SYSEXEC, SYSOUTP, SYSPUR), and the following descriptions use the same names to identify the source clock.

Reading in the task   The physical card images (JCL) for the job, TSO session, or started task are read by JES from a reader (real or internal) and stored in the JES SPOOL data set. If syntax errors in the JCL are detected in the reader, the task is terminated with a JCL error at the end of read-in.

READTIME	date and time the read-in began (actually, when the task's JOB card was recognized in the host). READTIME is the common time stamp in all records created on behalf of this task because a task can be read in only once. READTIME uses the clock on read-in CPU (SYSREAD).
RDRTM	duration required to read in the task. Although normally quite short for jobs processed by internal readers, it represents transmission time for jobs read in from physical readers.

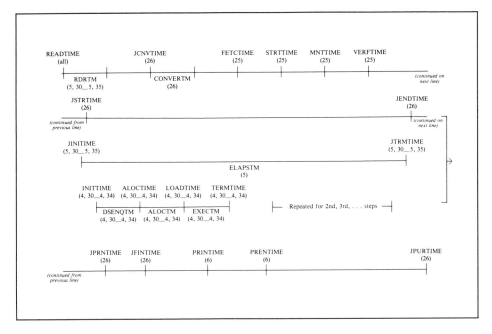

Figure 7.1
Job-Related Time Stamps

JES conversion   Now the JCL card images on the JES SPOOL must be processed by the JES converter into internal text and control blocks, which are then rewritten to the SPOOL data set. JES determines the functions (SCAN, EXECUTE, PRINT, PUNCH) that are required for this task in the converter. When JCL syntax errors are detected here, the converter flushes the job at JCNVTIME + CONVERTM.

> JCNVTIME   time the converter began processing this task. This normally occurs immediately following the completion of read-in, and, thus, the duration from reader-end (READTIME + RDRTM) to JCNVTIME is not created as a variable. JCNVTIME uses the clock on conversion processor (SYSCVRT).

> CONVERTM   duration required to convert job control statements.

JES3 main device scheduling (MDS)   For JES3, mountable devices can be allocated first. Then only after all required devices are available is the task eligible for execution scheduling. When the installation chooses this option, events in device scheduling are reported only in the JES3 type 25 record.

FETCTIME   time stamp when it was requested that mountable volumes be fetched from the library.

STRTTIME   time stamp when operators issued the start set-up that the needed volumes had been fetched.

MNTTIME   time stamp when first mount was issued by JES3.

VERFTIME   time stamp when first mountable volume was verified (that is, the mount was completed and the correct volume serial was verified).

JES execution processor   After the JES conversion (and JES3 MDS, if any), the task is considered for execution (unless the task was read into the HOLD queue). The job waits in the execution queue until it is the highest priority job in a job class for which there is an idle initiator. Execution begins when JES issues a JOB STARTED message and passes the job's control blocks from the SPOOL to the idle MVS initiator. MVS then initiates the job, allocates devices needed by the job, and executes the steps of the job. When the last step is complete, when a step abends and terminates the job, or when the job is canceled by an MVS cancel command, MVS terminates the job and returns the job to JES with a JOB ENDED message. All time stamps use the clock on the execution CPU (SYSEXEC).

JSTRTIME   job start time stamp, when JES passed the job to the MVS initiator.

JINITIME   job initiation time on the MVS execution processor. JSTRTIME and JINITIME should be the same.

JTRMTIME   job termination time on the MVS execution processor.

JENDTIME   job end time stamp, when JES received the job back from MVS. JTRMTIME and JENDTIME should be essentially the same.

ELAPSTM   duration from initiation to termination. Called elapsed time for jobs, session duration for TSO, and up time for started tasks.

MVS initiation process   A job consists of one or more steps. Job initiation begins at INITTIME of the first step when the initiator issues the data set enqueue (ENQ) request for each data set name that will be used by the job. JES3 has already guaranteed availability by issuing the enqueue request earlier, but in JES2, the request is made for the first time here.

If the data set name is not available for this request (because this request is for OLD, NEW, or MOD and the data set is being shared, or vice versa), the job has a "data set ENQUEUE conflict" and this message is issued to the operator:

"FOLLOWING DATA SETS RESERVED OR UNAVAILABLE."

If the operator cancels* the job, MVS initiation is terminated with a SYSTEM 222 ABEND, and the job is returned to the JES2 execution queue in HOLD status to be released by the operator at a later time. Later, this will be a restarted job. Otherwise, the job waits, holding its initiator until the needed data set becomes available. The delay between INITTIME and ALOCTIME (called DSENQTM) measures this delay.

Once the data set names are acquired by ENQ, step allocation commences at ALOCTIME. During allocation, all devices required by this step are acquired one at a time, in the order of the DD statements for the step. If a tape drive or a mountable disk drive is needed but all of those on-line are in use, the job enters allocation recovery, and the operator can either give an off-line drive to the job (by replying with the address of the off-line drive), cancel the job (causing a SYSTEM 222 ABEND and the termination of the job), or leave the job waiting, holding its initiator until a drive becomes available.**The delay between ALOCTIME and LOADTIME (called ALOCTM) measures this delay. Allocation is complete when all needed devices have been given to the job and all mountable disk devices have been mounted. Mounts for the first tape volume on each tape drive are issued at the end of allocation, but allocation does not wait for tape mount completion as it does for disk mount completion.

Once allocation completes at LOADTIME, the program to be executed by this step can be loaded into memory by the FETCH program and begin to execute instructions. Note that although the job has been in initiation since JSTRTIME, it is not until now that the user's program is given any processor (that is, CPU) time. When this program terminates at TERMTIME, this step terminates. Subsequent steps are initiated, allocated, and executed until the last step terminates, and control is given back to MVS job termination at JTRMTIME.

INITTIME	MVS step initiation time stamp .
ALOCTIME	beginning of MVS device allocation time .
LOADTIME	completion of allocation and beginning of problem program execution for this step.
TERMTIME	MVS step termination time stamp .
DSENQTM	duration from INITTIME to ALOCTIME. Represents any delay for data set enqueue in the first step, usually very small for subsequent steps.
ALOCTM	duration from ALOCTIME to LOADTIME. Represents length of time job step waited for allocation.

---

* Actually, the operator must issue three JES commands; $HJ to hold the job, then $CJ to cancel the job, and ultimately $AJ to release the job from hold.
** This HOLD option prompts for another operator response to allow the job to keep devices allocated thus far or to free resources and start anew later.

EXECTM   duration from LOADTIME to TERMTIME. This is the maximum elapsed time during which the step could have executed its program's instructions. This duration and its components are expanded in Figure 7.2, below.

JES output processor   After the execution processor has completed its control for JES, the task may require output processing if the task created any SYSOUT (printing or punching). The JES output processor does not print or punch anything but is a brief phase from JPRNTIME to JFINTIME, during which the JES output control blocks for printing (called JOEs, for job output elements) are collected and organized into proper order for printing or punching. Beginning at JFINTIME, however, each printing event is a separate element in the JES print queue. (Loosely defined, a printing event is a printing or punching on the same form and same printer.) A separate SMF record is created for each printing event containing the start of printing, PRINTIME, and the end of printing, PRENTIME.

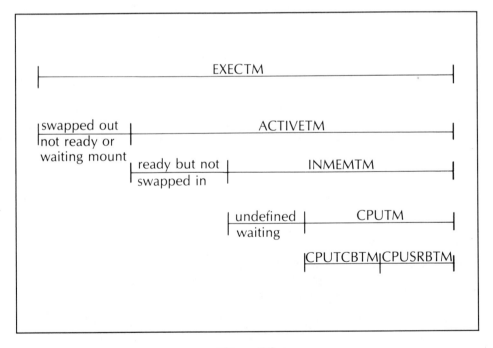

Figure 7.2
Events within EXECTM

JPRNTIME   start time of the output processor. Uses the clock
            on the CPU that executed the JES output processor
            (SYSOUTP).

JFINTIME   finish time of the output processor. Uses the same
            clock as JPRNTIME.

PRINTIME   signifies start of printing. Uses the clock on the
            CPU where printer is connected, which is the same
            as the CPU where the JES line serving this printer
            is connected (SYSTEM in the type 6 record or in
            the PRINT data set).

PRENTIME   signifies end of printing for each file. Uses same
            clock as PRINTIME.

JES purge processor   When JES has completed all printing or punching for this
task or if the task is purged with the $PURGE command, all traces of this job
are removed from the SPOOL and the JES job number is available for assignment
to a new job. JES purge processor uses the clock on the CPU that purges the job.

JPURTIME   purge event time stamp.

Figure 7.2 expands the events within MVS step program execution duration
EXECTM, shown above. Whereas the preceding durations were calculated from
time stamps stored in SMF records, these components of EXECTM are durations
accumulated by MVS and stored in the step (type 4, 30, and 34) SMF records.

EXECTM   duration of program execution from LOADTIME to
            TERMTIME. See above.

ACTIVETM   duration, measured by the System Resource
            Manager (SRM) component of MVS, that the SRM
            had selected this task to be active. The difference
            between EXECTM and ACTIVETM is the time the
            step was either swapped out by the SRM, waiting a
            mount, or not ready (usually only due to physical
            I/O device problems).

INMEMTM   duration, measured by the SRM, that the task was
            in real memory. The difference between
            ACTIVETM and INMEMTM is the total duration
            spent swapping in and out this task. This difference
            is usually insignificant unless there is significant
            contention for the physical paths to the swapped
            data sets.

CPUTM   sum of CPUTCBTM and CPUSRBTM, total
            processor time consumed by this task. The

difference between INMEMTM and CPUTM is the duration that this task was in real memory but not executing instructions. It includes waiting for dispatch (this task is not the highest priority task in this CPU) and waiting for I/O.

The preceding nineteen variables provide an awesome opportunity for analysis. Understanding the sequence of events and the points in that sequence that are available in the operating system's task accounting records significantly eases the CPE analyst's task. However, it is necessary to understand the limitations and potential errors that can occur in the time stamps and durations. There are numerous exposures in these software-captured values from the CPU clock(s).

The multiple system environment probably causes the most confusion. A multiple operating system environment is often referred to as loosely coupled to indicate that processors are coupled by the JES SPOOL rather than tightly coupled or multiple engine processors that are coupled by sharing one operating system and one real memory. In such an environment, it is possible for a job to be read in on one system, executed on another, printed on a third, and so forth. No vendor has found a way to synchronize clocks in these multiple system environments. Each system's clock is set by human operators comparing wristwatches and pressing the SET CLOCK switch (or its equivalent) on the hardware. If clocks for the two systems are not synchronized, it is possible to have jobs start before they were read in, execute in negative time, and so forth. Since there are no real hardware or software solutions to synchronization, the operators must understand the importance of accuracy when setting the system clock. Although there are no solutions, below are suggestions that have been implemented by some installations:

- modify JES to compare clocks when a new processor is brought into the complex. Do not allow a processor to enter the complex if its clock is not operating within some predetermined value, usually 15 to 30 seconds.
- require operators to record the differences among clocks as a part of the shift turnover procedures, and create competition between crews to see how closely they can set the clock.
- negate the crew that fails to synchronize the clocks adequately if the operator bonus program based on performance exists.

Restarted jobs in a JES2 environment also cause confusion. For example, if a job enters data set enqueue conflict, frequently the job that went into data set enqueue is restarted and placed on hold until the job owning the data set finishes. At this time, the second job is manually released by the operator and enters execution. This is all one job to JES2. The detail SMF records written for the job may appear to refer to more than one job since there are step and job termination records written for the canceled execution, and there are additional step and job termination records written when the job is reexecuted. All contain the same READTIME. There is only one execution purge record, and the JES execution processor time stamps JSTRTIME and JENDTIME contain the start and end time of the last execution.

Although BUILDPDB resolves this possibility in its JOBS data set by counting the number of job termination records (RESTARTS) and keeping the minimum value of INITTIME, many other accounting and performance systems falsely report the count of job termination records as the number of jobs processed.

A final warning about these time stamps concerns how the operating system builds them. The images for some SMF records, especially type 26, are initialized with hexadecimal zeros, and time stamps are filled in as events occur. If an event never occurs, then the time stamp remains hexadecimal zeros in the written record. By design, the SMFSTAMP8. format sets the time stamp value to a missing value. When a missing value is subtracted from a nonmissing value, the result is a missing value. Test the variables to make sure they are nonmissing before you subtract.

- READTIME is the only variable guaranteed to be nonmissing.
- JCNVTIME can be missing for a job placed on hold that is canceled before conversion.
- the JES3 time stamps, FETCTIME, STRTTIME, MNTTIME, and VERFTIME, are only nonmissing for jobs that go through JES3 main device scheduling.
- JSTRTIME is missing for all JCL errors detected at converter time or for any job canceled (CANCELED = 'Y') before execution.
- JENDTIME is missing for any job with a missing JSTRTIME and, more importantly, for any job active when the operating system crashes. Furthermore, JENDTIME can be nonmissing and less than JSTRTIME if a job executed was restarted and the system crashed during the restart.
- JPRNTIME and JFINTIME can be missing for JCL errors.
- PRINTIME and PRENTIME are missing for any job that does not produce printed output.

chapter eight

Establishing Service Objectives

Service objectives already exist at every installation. When response time or turn-around is below an acceptable level, users complain. When service is better, there are no complaints. The first task of the CPE analyst in developing service objectives is to standardize a measure of service so that both the user and the supplier are using the same metric for service. The second task is to correlate values of that service metric with user requirements and satisfaction levels to set a goal or objective value for the service metric. Then you can begin to optimize service delivered and resources consumed while minimizing costs.

The choice of the service metric itself is crucial to the success of establishing service objectives. The following five criteria for a service metric are necessary and sufficient conditions:

1. be measurable
2. be repeatable
3. be understandable by a typical user
4. correlate strongly with the user's perception of service
5. be directly controllable by the amount of resources made available at the computer installation.

Be measurable   The measurement must be automatic and continuous so that a complaint made yesterday or last week can be investigated. It should be measurable at the individual interaction so that those interactions with poor service due to poor design (rather than due to insufficient resources) can be identified. Furthermore, at the individual interaction level, both the interaction name (program, command, and so forth) and the individual user's name (job, user, operator, and so forth) are known. This permits measurement of functionality and productivity from the same data used for measurement of service delivered.

Be repeatable   The measurement must be repeatable; the measurement tool must exclude itself from the metric. The choice of expression of the metric (mean, percentiles, and so forth) can influence the repeatability of the metric.

Be understandable by a typical user   You should not need to be a CPE analyst to understand what is being measured and how. Even if the metric uses highly internal phenomena (for example, DL/I calls, EXCPs) the description to the user must be in his terms. The purpose of the service objective is to communicate to the user, not to show off your technical knowledge. Keep in mind that users are not programmers and jargon should be minimized. The closer the description of the measurement is to the business purpose of the enterprise, the better understood it will be.

Correlate with perceived service   The measurements that are currently available may not capture all the response time of an interaction. For example, interactive work measured in the host does not include the communications response time. But if the measurement includes the actual number of bytes in the communications messages, the estimated communications delay can be added to the measured internal response, and the total must be correlated with the user's actual response at the terminal. It is necessary to perform measurements at the terminal and compare them to the planned measurement tool to confirm this correlation. If less than half of the terminal response time is recorded in the total response measurement, there may be significant disparity between the user's perception and the supplier's claims.

Be directly controllable   The purpose of the service objective is to manage properly the computer resources necessary to service the users. If the service measure cannot be improved by additional resources, the metric is not useful as a service objective. This usually occurs because of a poor definition of the service measurement. For example, batch turnaround time is usually a poor metric because the time a job spent in HOLD (before execution or for TSO output processing of its SYSOUT) is not available in SMF. If batch service is based on turnaround time and does not exclude the time spent in HOLD, there is little the supplier can do to change the measured batch turnaround time for those jobs.

The driving force for your service objectives is the type of workload and the type of data available for your important workloads. Because of the structural difference between batch and interactive and because of the different data sources available, different service objectives are needed for batch and interactive.

BATCH SERVICE OBJECTIVES

For batch service measurement to be repeatable, the batch workload should be classified into groupings with similar service measures. To achieve the service levels required by users, the user must indicate the job's requirements before it executes, using either a job class parameter or a job priority parameter. Then the response a job receives is classified by the user-supplied parameters that are determined by the design of batch scheduling algorithms. Establishing service objectives for batch must be tied to (and may be a part of) the batch scheduling algorithm .

Historically, there have been two approaches to establishing batch scheduling. One approach is to provide batch service based on the urgency of the job. These user-oriented scheduling systems recognize that the purpose of the computer installation is to provide service, and they design batch scheduling to meet the user's needs. The second approach is to schedule jobs based on resource requirements in order to make the computer manager's life easier. These computer-oriented scheduling systems require the user to determine the resource requirements (number of tape drives, expected CPU seconds, and so forth) and to label his job in a language the computer understands. (Many operations managers in these computer-oriented systems believe that users exist only to provide a test load.)

The author favors user-oriented scheduling . Although the resource consumption of jobs is of concern to the installation, it should not prohibit the execution of a job when that job is needed immediately. Rather, a comprehensive user-oriented system calls on the CPE analyst to identify jobs whose resource consumption creates a problem for the installation. The analyst must justify (through resource costs) either acquisition of the needed resources or modification of the application design to reduce that resource requirement. This is especially appropriate for the tape drive resource. Rather than placing restrictions (for example, jobs needing more than six tape drives are run only on weekends), examine the jobs that exceed this arbitrary value and assist the user in redesigning his job to serialize this resource where possible. (In MVS, most jobs that use a large number of tape drives usually do so because the JCL did not specify UNIT=AFFINITY, and the user often does not even realize how many tape drives his job requires.) Applications that cannot be altered provide a clear financial case: if the application is important, let it buy and pay for the additional resources.

The most common method of batch categorization is to use priority to distinguish urgency. The most common failing of this approach is when there are too many categories. A good approach, which has been confirmed by measurement, is to recognize that humans need only 3 time-sensitive categories and 1 or 2 deferred categories for batch work. Consider your own batch submissions. The categories NOW, IN-A-LITTLE-WHILE, LATER, TOMORROW, and NEXT-WEEK will meet all your needs. NOW is the job you need before you can go to the meeting. IN-A-LITTLE-WHILE are the jobs you want to pick up after the meeting. LATER are the jobs you want to see before you go home. TOMORROW is the resource hog you want to run at low rates this evening, and NEXT-WEEK is the annual growth analysis you want to work on next week. Mapping NOW to 15 minutes, IN-A-LITTLE-WHILE to 1 hour, and LATER to 4 hours has been very successful.

Although you can add granularity to the categories, the experience at one installation was that they were not used, even when significant price differences existed among the added categories. The installation had 5 time-sensitive batch categories called the Initiation Wait Time (IWT), which described how long the user was willing to wait for initiation. Users can specify an IWT request of 15 minutes, 30 minutes, 1 hour, 2 hours, or 4 hours. Even though the cost of the job varied from $2.25 per unit for 15 minutes down to $0.80 per unit for 4 hours, the users requested only 15-minute, 1-hour, or 4-hour work categories. Less than 5% of all time-sensitive jobs were submitted in the 30-minute or 2-hour categories.

The categorization of batch can have a positive political value as well. The most common (and probably the most effective) batch scheduling systems categorize based on some sense of urgency. If the categories are expressed in terms of business purpose, the computer facility becomes more a part of the enterprise and less a separate facility. Insurance companies have differentiated batch work between PREMIUM and CLAIMS since the premiums have to be in the bank before the claim checks can be written. Airlines have differentiated between today's and tomorrow's flights. Although the underlying computer technology may still be a simple priority system, the presentation in terms of business will be much more palatable to the "I don't trust the computer department" users. CPE analysts, who bridge the chasm between computer technology and business purpose, must abandon computerese in favor of company jargon to be most effective.

Although separate categories for different types of batch work must be created, the service measurement must be the same for each category. Turnaround time should not be used for one class and initiation wait time for another because the service measure is not repeatable if the user switches classes for the same job; a common service measure for all categories should be used. The goal for each category is different, reflecting the expected response time of that category. Thus the initiation wait time metric is used for all categories of batch, and only the expected value of each category changes from 15 minutes to 4 hours.

Should the scheduling category affect execution time? Some installations use the user's requested scheduling priority to set execution priority. To do so causes the same job to finish sooner when placed in a high priority category. Alternatively, all batch work can be executed at the same execution priority, independent of the requested scheduling priority. In that case, the job should have the same execution duration, no matter which category was used to schedule the job. The choice depends on whether you believe response or consistency is more important to your users and on what portion of the job's lifetime (from read-in to purge) is spent in execution versus waiting for execution. If the job is wait-intensive, as most IBM data processing jobs are, its execution time is typically small when compared to its lifetime, and consistency of execution is more important to the user. However, in execution-intensive jobs, typical of high resource, scientific analyses, it is often more important to complete the work now than to provide consistency of execution time. The choice must be made by each installation.

Batch service objectives are usually determined by looking at the time that jobs spend in various queues. The operating system and job entry subsystem can be regarded as a pair of queue managers operating in tandem. Since SMF data provide a nearly complete time stamping of the events in the life of a job, the time in most queues for any job can be easily calculated by subtracting time stamps.

There are two basic measures of batch service: turnaround time and time-in-queue .

Turnaround time was the only measure available before SMF, but it can be defined in at least two ways:

1. Execution wait plus execution time duration from read-in until the job is ready to print. This definition usually excludes the time to read in the job and is often expressed as last-card-read to ready-to-print.
2. Total turnaround time is the duration from read-in until the job is purged. This definition is essentially the same as execution wait plus execution time with print queue and printing time added.

With either definition, however, the computer installation may be at the mercy of the user. Without other constraints, a user can control his turnaround (independent of your scheduling of his job) by the amount of data his job processes. Your measurement might show that same job took 10 seconds one day and 10 hours the next as the user changed the input from 10 to 36,000 records. In addition, the time in HOLD must be addressed when turnaround is used. Furthermore, if print queue and printing time are included in the turnaround measurement, turnaround may be controlled by the owner of the printing resource, which may be a remote site out of your control. Turnaround time, if used at all as your service metric, must be used carefully and should be influenced by the resources required by each job, as the case study below shows.

Time-in-queue batch service measurement must deal with the three phases in the life of a job, which can be measured separately. The advantage of this approach is that it separates the three dissimilar phases of a job so that installation resources can be applied separately as necessary.

Phase One: Input queue time—calculated from the end of read-in (or the end of converter) until the job first enters execution. This metric is directly under your control and should be used to report batch service. You have designed the batch scheduling scheme, allocated resources to batch, and should be able to control the time in the input queue. This metric is directly observable by the user with the STATUS command under TSO.

Phase Two: Execution time duration—elapsed initiation time of the job is not included as a service metric but must be acknowledged to users since it is a part of the total response time they see. If the service objective is based on input queue, the installation should guarantee that elapsed time be consistent so that the user can plan his schedule accordingly. With any well-tuned batch system, and especially with MVS, providing stable batch execution time is achievable. Furthermore, the day-to-day variability of the user's data volumes tends to mask much of the variability that the data center can cause.

Phase Three: Print queue and printing time—although part of total turnaround, scheduling printing bears no relationship to a job's urgency. The printing may deserve its own service objective and be reported to the user and owner of the printers, but it should not be combined with batch job scheduling. Furthermore, if printing is centralized with manual delivery to each floor, the time spent waiting for printing may be insignificant compared to the delivery system service time.

Choosing the statistic to report the batch service measurement is just as important as choosing turnaround or input queue time. Each batch job has a measure of its response time. Statistically, three measurements have been used: the mean (or average) value, the value of the 90th percentile, and the percent meeting a stated goal.

Average values do not represent reality   The average (or mean) value is the sum of the observations divided by the number of observations. It is mathematically appealing, but has very little applicability in measuring service objectives. To a typical user, average means most of the time, something by which he can choose alternatives. In many interactive systems, the average value of response time is received by 65% to 70% of the interactions because the data have a small number of very large values that make the average quite far from the median (or 50% value). (See chapter twenty-one for an example.)

Percentile value   If jobs in a category are sorted in ascending magnitude and then counted to a given percentile value (say 90%), then the value of that observation can be reported as the value met by 90% of that category. Although at first, this seems a good choice for measuring batch service, it is not a repeatable measure; whereas service (by all subjective criteria) was consistent, this value would vary from 30 to 50 minutes for the 1-hour category. It does not correlate well, but it comes closer to users' needs than average values.

Percentage meeting a stated value is by far the best technique for expressing service objectives   It is easy to understand, easy to calculate, and mathematically robust. You simply set a goal value for the metric (for example, 1-hour batch has a goal of initiation within 1 hour), count how many tasks met the goal, and report "last week 96.2% of all 1-hour jobs met their goals."

Batch Turnaround Case Study

Although turnaround is less desirable as a measure for batch service, it may be necessary to use it. Perhaps your installation does not like this philosophy. Perhaps you have always used turnaround time as your measure and do not want to change. Or perhaps you have a scientific environment that requires batch service to take into account the execution time because scientists are waiting for the job to end. In any of these cases, the following implementation may provide useful suggestions.

In one system, a slow scientific processor was needed by engineers who submitted several small test jobs and then executed a job that might run for 5 to 15 hours, while they went home to wait for the job to complete. At the same time, other users ran much shorter jobs. To serve both sets of users, the service objective was designed as the sum of input queue time requested plus an after-execution-calculation (based on consumed resources) of how much time the job should have required. If measured job turnaround time was greater than the sum of expected queue time (EQT) and expected execution time (EET), the job failed to meet its objective.

The difficulty in this approach is calculating the correct EET. EQT is defined based on the priority of the job when it is submitted:

Priority	EQT
Super Express	30 minutes
Express	60 minutes
Standard	120 minutes

The equation for EET was developed using linear regression to predict elapsed time as a function of the CPU and I/O time of a job. The CYBER Dayfile (equivalent of SMF) gave the CPU and I/O times explicitly (as MVS/XA does). If the operating system provides only I/O counts (MVS pre-XA), I/O time can be fabricated from I/O counts by measuring the average I/O time per I/O for each device type. The resources of the job were expressed as the variable JOBTM:

```
JOBTM = CPUTM + IOTM;
```

and the relationship to job elapsed time (ELAPSTM) was calculated by analyzing the performance data base built from the Dayfile:

```
PROC SYSREG DATA=CYBERPDB;
    MODEL ELAPSTM = JOBTM;
```

The regression equation showed that for every second of JOBTM, elapsed time was 2.1 seconds. With these facts, expected turnaround time of a job could be calculated from Dayfile data:

```
expected turnaround = EQT + EET
                    = EQT + 2.1 * JOBTM + MOUNTTM
```

Mount time was added because the data center staff thought it was important. Only very short jobs with many mounts have MOUNTTM values large enough to affect the measure. (Remember, EQT ranges from 30 minutes to 120 minutes.) The proposal of new batch scheduling and new service objectives generally causes negative feedback because change is an alien creature to data centers. By understanding the staff's concerns for your plans, you can include resource measures in the EET equation that please the requestor but have little effect on the results.

The calculated value of expected turnaround was compared to turnaround measured from read-in to ready-to-print. If turnaround was less than expected, the job met its service objective and was priced at the requested priority rate. If turnaround was greater than expected, the job missed its objective and the user was not charged the rate of the requested EQT. Failure of the data center to provide expected turnaround means a discount to the user; the failed job is charged at the next lower EQT rate.

This approach treats jobs with small resource consumption as if their objective is the EQT specified by their priority, and the objective of jobs that consume significant resources increases with resources.

Batch Input Queue Case Study

The discussion of batch service objectives cannot be independent of the batch scheduling scheme, which must be concerned with more than just service times. In proposing new service objectives, the CPE analyst must also suggest how to redefine groups, change initiator structure, modify operational procedures, and so forth. Thus, the following case study is appropriate to the typical data processing (as opposed to scientific processing) center. In the typical IBM DP shop, the average job elapsed time is approximately 15 minutes, and you want to give users a cheaper rate when they give you more time to schedule their jobs. (The longer time available means you can spread peak arrivals across more time, requiring less peak hour capacity and reducing real cost.) The following scheme, which met batch processing needs at one installation, required JES modifications to create SMF records not offered by IBM.

Batch service categories are defined based on users' requests for initiation wait time (IWT). The IWT request is specified on a JES control card and is one of the following:

```
15MIN  30MIN  1HR  2HR  4HR  OVERNITE  WEEKEND
```

The IWT clock starts when the job is read in unless the job was read into the HOLD queue. A local SMF record is written by JES when a job is released from

HOLD, and the IWT clock is restarted when the job is released. If the IWT request is changed by the user after the job was read in, the IWT clock is restarted also. The IWT clock ends when the job is initiated, and the IWT received is the difference between IWT start and job initiation. The IWT received is the time the job waited for execution, excluding time in HOLD.

The scheduling scheme that supports this design uses JES2 aging to ensure that the lower IWT categories are not preempted by higher categories. By initially setting the job's priority as:

```
IWT:        15MIN   30MIN   1HR   2HR   4HR   OVERNITE   WEEKEND
Priority:    12       11     10     8     4       1          0
```

and then aging priority at the rate of 1 unit every 30 minutes, a 4-hour IWT job read in 3 hours ago will be at the same priority as a newly arrived 1-hour IWT job. Aging stops at the 30-minute IWT for 2 reasons: first, the 15-minute category was to be a hot batch category that always met its goals, and, second, in a JES2 multi-access spool, aging proceeds even if the batch machine is not available; each processor can independently age tasks. When a batch outage occurred, if aging continued into the 15-minute IWT, all jobs would soon be at the same priority and the truly hot recovery job could not be serviced. This scheme guarantees a higher probability for success in the 15-minute category, but the remaining categories have equal probability of success.

Jobs should not be executed until they have waited half of their IWT, which is the same as causing them to wait until they are in the next IWT category. This ensures that a user's request is legitimate. If a 4-hour job gets 15-minute service, the consistency of response is lost and users exploit the system. Delaying jobs can lead to idle resources during certain periods but ensures that the profile of job IWTs reflects the true requirements of the business.

If the job fails to meet its requested IWT, the price is determined by the IWT category it received. Thus, the supplier reports service delivered and is financially motivated to ensure that service is good. Even if finances are only internal budget transfers, the supplier appears more honest if failure to meet service has a budgetary impact, and it greatly simplifies the CPE analyst's task in measuring the cost of missed service.

Since the cost of a job is based on IWT, operators do not alter the priority of jobs. The user is given RJE and TSO commands to alter his job's IWT after submission, placing responsibility in the user's hands and freeing console operators.

Operators do not alter the initiator structure since there is only one class for all batch initiators. The only criterion for scheduling is the requested IWT, which maps directly to priority, so there is no need for multiple batch classes.

The IWT scheme meets 95% of the jobs' needs. Other jobs are treated as exceptions to standard IWT batch work. Jobs that require special processing because they must execute on a particular processor (data base jobs such as IMS BMP's and ADABAS batch) are submitted at special classes. Initiators of these special classes exist only on the correct processor. Additionally, production jobs are scheduled by IWT but are priced less than normal. The users identify critical jobs in their production job stream by name, and these jobs can be submitted at the 15-minute IWT at a discount.

The preceding case studies describe two approaches to establishing batch service objectives. Although development of batch service objectives is clearly a non-trivial task, a first pass approximation to the measurement of batch service is easily accomplished with the SMF data in the following examples.

Batch Examples Using PDB Data

SAS data set TYPE26 (or PDB.JOBS) contains the scheduling time stamps for all batch jobs. The data set TURNARND is created by selecting batch jobs (not TSO sessions or started tasks) and deleting jobs with a missing value of JSTRTIME. A missing value of JSTRTIME indicates a JCL error and including these jobs in average turnaround statistics would unfairly bias the average to a lower-than-actual value. The turnaround time in minutes, TURNMINS, is calculated by subtracting READTIME from JPURTIME, and dividing by sixty. The SHIFT variable is contained in PDB.JOBS, being defined in the IMACSHFT installation macro by the start time of the job. The data are sorted by shift and job class, and the count and average turnaround are calculated by PROC MEANS and placed in the TURNSTAT data set. Finally, PROC PRINT creates the example report (using the SPLIT= option to print labels instead of variable names):

```
DATA TURNARND;
   SET PDB.JOBS;
   IF TYPETASK NE 'JOB' THEN DELETE;
   IF JSTRTIME EQ . THEN DELETE;
   TURNMINS=(JPURTIME-READTIME)/60;
   KEEP SHIFT JOBCLASS TURNMINS;
PROC SORT;
   BY SHIFT JOBCLASS;
PROC MEANS NOPRINT MAXDEC=2;
   BY SHIFT JOBCLASS;
   VAR TURNMINS;
   OUTPUT OUT=TURNSTAT
            N=NRJOBS
          MEAN=AVGTURN;
   LABEL
```

(continued on next page)

(continued from previous page)

```
            SHIFT   ='EXECUTE'SHIFT'
            JOBCLASS='JOB'CLASS'
            NRJOBS  ='NUMBER'OF'JOBS'
            AVGTURN ='AVERAGE'TURNAROUND'MINUTES'
          ;
      PROC PRINT SPLIT='';
        ID SHIFT;
        VAR JOBCLASS NRJOBS AVGTURN;
      TITLE 'BATCH SERVICE DELIVERED';
      TITLE2 'AVERAGE TURNAROUND (MINUTES)';
```

```
                   BATCH  SERVICE  DELIVERED
                   AVERAGE  TURNAROUND  (MINUTES)


            EXECUTE      JOB        NUMBER       AVERAGE
            SHIFT       CLASS         OF       TURNAROUND
                                     JOBS        MINUTES

             EVE          A          210          2.58
             EVE          B          109          5.13
             EVE          C           13         10.31
             EVE          D          109         22.40
             NIGHT        A           19          3.02
             NIGHT        B          209          7.11
             NIGHT        C          109         14.22
             NIGHT        D           13         31.88
             PRIME        A          583          2.00
             PRIME        B          333          5.33
             PRIME        C           99         18.22
             PRIME        D           84         24.29
```

Example 8.1 Calculating Average Turnaround Minutes

At this installation, jobs are submitted at priorities 3, 4, and 5. Priority 3 jobs have an objective of 12-hour queue time, priority 4 jobs have a 4-hour queue time goal, and a priority 5 job's goal is a 1-hour queue time. All the information comes from the JES2 type 26 records. First, exclude nonbatch jobs and JCL errors by testing for JSTRTIME not equal to missing. The queue time (INQUETM), converted to units of hours (INQUEHRS), is defined as the time from read-time to start of execution. Set NRJOBS=1 for each record and then set NRMET=1 if the job meets its objective. PROC MEANS creates an output data set named INQUECNT that contains the number of jobs and the number of jobs that met their objectives for the shift and input priority. The percentage of jobs meeting the goal is calculated and stored in data set INQUEPCT and then printed:

```
             DATA INQUETM;
               SET PDB.JOBS;
               IF TYPETASK NE 'JOB' THEN DELETE;
               IF JSTRTIME EQ . THEN DELETE;
               INQUEHRS=(JSTRTIME-READTIME)/3600;
               NRJOBS=1;
               IF      INPRTY=3 AND INQUEHRS LT 12 THEN NRMET=1;
               ELSE IF INPRTY=4 AND INQUEHRS LT  4 THEN NRMET=1;
               ELSE IF INPRTY=5 AND INQUEHRS LT  1 THEN NRMET=1;
               KEEP INPRTY INQUEHRS SHIFT NRJOBS NRMET;
             PROC SORT;
               BY SHIFT INPRTY;
             PROC MEANS NOPRINT;
               BY SHIFT INPRTY;
               VAR NRJOBS NRMET;
               OUTPUT OUT=INQUECNT
                      SUM=NRJOBS NRMET;
             DATA INQUEPCT;
               SET INQUECNT;
               PCTMET=100*NRMET/NRJOBS;
               FORMAT PCTMET 5.1;
             LABEL
               SHIFT ='EXECUTE*SHIFT'
               INPRTY=' INPUT*PRIORITY'
               NRJOBS='NUMBER*OF*JOBS'
               NRMET =' NUMBER*MEETING*GOAL'
               PCTMET=' PERCENT*WHICH MET*GOAL'
               ;
             PROC PRINT SPLIT=*;
               ID SHIFT;
               VAR INPRTY NRJOBS NRMET PCTMET;
               TITLE 'INSTALLATION PERFORMANCE OBJECTIVES';
               TITLE2 'BATCH JOBS MEETING GOAL';
```

```
               INSTALLATION PERFORMANCE OBJECTIVES
                      BATCH JOBS MEETING GOAL
```

EXECUTE SHIFT	INPUT PRIORITY	NUMBER OF JOBS	NUMBER MEETING GOAL	PERCENT MEETING GOAL
OFF PRIME	3	155	149	96.1
OFF PRIME	4	99	99	100.0
OFF PRIME	5	83	83	100.0
PRIME	3	198	197	99.5
PRIME	4	281	281	100.0
PRIME	5	496	446	89.9

Example 8.2 Calculating Percentage of Jobs Meeting Input Queue Goal

Management understands the statistics in Example 8.2, and the user understands what the supplier means when he advertises that 90% of the work submitted at priority 3 will be executed in less than 12 hours.

Once the batch categories SHIFT and INPRTY are defined and performance reporting has begun (for example, average turnaround, percent meeting goal), the CPE analyst can learn who is submitting work and tell what priority is being used. Any batch system can be abused by users who do not play by the rules, and the CPE analyst can identify user groups that need management attention. If service delivered is poorer than anticipated, the supplier can often find which group within his installation is abusing the job scheduling scheme and preventing others from receiving good service. Although accounting information can be used to classify work if the first letter of the job name can identify the submitter, it is a simple matter to identify who submits work at each priority by crosstabulating a portion of the job name with input priority. Economic sanctions (charging more for higher priority) or management control can be applied to people who abuse the system so the service provided for all users is equalized.

```
TITLE 'CROSSTABULATION OF FIRST LETTER OF JOB NAME WITH INPUT PRIORITY';
PROC FREQ DATA=TYPE26J2;
   TABLES JOB*INPRTY;
   FORMAT JOB $1.;

   CROSSTABULATION OF FIRST LETTER OF JOB NAME WITH INPUT PRIORITY
                       TABLE OF JOB BY INPRTY

      JOB                      INPRTY

      FREQUENCY |
        PERCENT |
        ROW PCT |
        COL PCT |     3  |     4  |     5  |  TOTAL
      - - - - - - - - - - - - - - - - - - - - - - - - - -
      A          |    38  |    92  |    87  |    217
                 |  2.41  |  5.83  |  5.51  |  13.74
                 | 17.51  | 42.40  | 40.09  |
                 |  6.55  | 22.66  | 14.67  |
      - - - - - - - - - - - - - - - - - - - - - - - - - -
      B          |    40  |    27  |    63  |    130
                 |  2.53  |  1.71  |  3.99  |   8.23
                 | 30.77  | 20.77  | 48.46  |
                 |  6.90  |  6.65  | 10.62  |
      - - - - - - - - - - - - - - - - - - - - - - - - - -
```

(continued on next page)

(continued from previous page)

C	18	26	201	245
	1.14	1.65	12.73	15.52
	7.35	10.61	82.04	
	3.10	6.40	33.90	
D	10	12	5	27
	0.63	0.76	0.32	1.71
	37.04	44.44	18.52	
	1.72	2.96	0.84	
T	180	31	0	211
	11.40	1.96	0.00	13.36
	85.31	14.69	0.00	
	31.03	7.64	0.00	
V	79	17	14	110
	5.00	1.08	0.89	6.97
	71.82	15.45	12.73	
	13.62	4.19	2.36	
X	33	58	92	183
	2.09	3.67	5.83	11.59
	18.03	31.69	50.27	
	5.69	14.29	15.51	
Y	10	42	13	65
	0.63	2.66	0.82	4.12
	15.38	64.62	20.00	
	1.72	10.34	2.19	
Z	172	101	118	391
	10.89	6.40	7.47	24.76
	43.99	25.83	30.18	
	29.66	24.88	19.90	
TOTAL	580	406	593	1579
	36.73	25.71	37.56	100.00

Example 8.3 Distribution of Jobs by Input Priority

This example provides a simple crosstabulation of the first letter of job name by input priority. If the first letter of the job name indicates the submitting department, then the report provides a profile showing which departments submit the most work at higher priority (note Department C with 12% of the priority 5 work), a breakdown by priority of the percentage of work within each department (82% of Department C's work is at priority 5), and a breakdown of overall priority assignment (37% of all jobs were at priority 5). This profile can be used to persuade out-of-line departments to stop abusing the service.

If your batch service objectives relate to your users' perceptions of computing and if the batch service objectives are met consistently, you have satisfied the users. If you meet the batch service objectives and your users are dissatisfied, either they are unreasonable or, more likely, the batch service objectives are not relevant to their concerns. If you consistently meet batch service objectives and users are satisfied, it is possible that you have excess resources. They should be identified in order to reduce operation costs. If, however, realistic service objectives are not being met, resource consumption in the system should be examined to determine why batch service objectives are missed.

INTERACTIVE RESPONSE SERVICE OBJECTIVES

The difference between batch and interactive service objectives has more to do with measurement availability than philosophy. If you have detailed response measurement for each interaction in an interactive system, you can treat it as the transaction turnaround time and continue as described earlier. Even with an estimate of average response time for a time interval, you want to make the best use of the response data you have in order to measure and manage the quality of interactive service.

Just as you categorized batch work into similar groups, you need to classify interactions. Otherwise, there will be such variability in the metric that no statistical measurement correlates with the user's perception of response. Similar to the three time-sensitive categories appropriate for batch, most interactive systems can be adequately described using three groupings of FAST, MEDIUM, and LONG, or similar labels of expected response. Classification of each interaction into its group can be accomplished by using either a table of command names or an after-the-fact measurement of resources consumed by the command.

Classification by command name works well when the commands themselves are stable; however, the same named command may have widely varying response (TSO LISTD command response is greatly affected by the number of members in the library listed). When you choose classification by command name, you are also committed to the constant maintenance of the table of names. Every new command must be added to the table. Nevertheless, classification by command name is a frequently-used technique. TSO/MON used this technique for years (although additional options now exist). Even when the alternative classification technique is used, command name classification must often be used for certain command names when response is inconsistent with resource consumption.

Classification by projecting expected response time based on resources consumed is very much like the CYBER batch example discussed earlier. You perform measurements of response time versus measured resources captured in the interactive record and develop an equation for expected response. You then process today's interactions, dynamically calculate (from the equation) their expected response, and compare that calculation to the actual response each inter-action received, tabulating the percentage meeting its expected value. Obviously, the accuracy of this technique is determined by the accuracy of the response projection equation, but the technique is commonly used because it works. Some specific examples are:

CICS I/O Count   Chapter twenty-one is a case study on CICS measurement , where the response of a CICS transaction was predicted solely on the number of calls the transaction made on the access method (although a few anomalies were classified by name because they used their own access method).

IMS CPU, I/O, and DL/I   Data from CONTROL/IMS, which contained several CPU and I/O measures and DL/I calls, are used in a linear equation to calculate expected response time of a credit card system.

TSO RMF-measured response   TSO/MON is the only good source-of-detail TSO transaction response; however, the average response of TSO transactions that finish in the first period can be calculated from the type 72 RMF data (or from RMVINTRV in the PDB). First period is defined by some number of service units; if a transaction uses more than that amount, the transaction is switched into second period. Thus, the common RMF-based TSO-trivial average response is nothing more than the average response of all TSO transactions that used less than some number of service units, which is just a linear equation of CPU, I/O, and, possibly, memory page seconds.

The development of the classification equation requires some research and vali-dation of clusters (PROC FASTCLUS is good for this purpose). Once you have determined the equation, the classification algorithm is simple. The only major caution is the effect that system changes have on the classification. The equation must be revalidated or even changed when the hardware, software, or application is altered. For example, changing a processor alters the meaning of TSO service units, and changing from ISAM to VSAM for CICS data bases alters the resources measured in CICS CMF or PAII. Often, however, the equation does not need to be changed; the goal value of the objective can be changed instead. If your objec-tive is to have 92% of CICS transactions meeting their (dynamic) goals, installing a faster processor may require the objective to be raised to 95% instead of changing the equation.

Unlike batch, interactive service objectives must at least address the issue of internal versus external response. The user sees a response at his terminal; only part of the response can be measured by our source of measurement. Further com-plicating the issue (even within internal response time) is the fact that the mea-surement tool may intercept a point in time different from what the user perceives.

For example, the TSO LISTDSname command is a nontrivial command in terms of resources used. It issues many I/O commands to read the directory of a partitioned data set. In terms of response measured by TSO/MON, it is a trivial command because of that product's definition of TSO command response. (This is true of any monitor based on GTF SYSEVENTs.) SYSEVENT-based monitors can only see response time from command entry to the first TPUT (that is, when the data are sent to the screen). The LISTDSname command reads the name of the requested data set and immediately sends the DSNAME back to the terminal before it begins to process the request. The measured response is rarely more than 0.5 seconds, but the user may wait 30 seconds more before he sees anything else sent to his terminal.

What should you do? Understand the architecture of the software system you are trying to measure. Discuss with its systems programmer the exact steps for serving a transaction and where your measurement tool gets its time stamps. Read the vendor's manual - it cautions you about the system's limitations. Then, carefully describe the response time you are measuring. There is no consistent naming convention among interactive systems, as the following list shows: SIGNON, SIGNIN, LOGON, LOGIN, BEGIN MENU, START, and so forth.

Validate the Vendor's Data Before You Believe It

Before you automatically accept the response time measurement from any source, confirm it by experimenting. Conduct a simple session with the interactive system you want to measure Log on and execute typical transactions for 15 minutes. Set a tape recorder by your terminal and record when events occur, noting the time occasionally, using the system's TIME command. The recorder picks up the sound when you press ENTER, and if you say what you see on the screen, you can go back later and extract the exact time between events. The now-standard CPE accessory digital stopwatch with a built-in calculator wristwatch can resolve to under 100 milliseconds. Extract the durations of commands as you expect the response monitor to have captured them and compare your terminal response, command by command, to the recorded data. If there are differences, explain them. If there is a measure of the number of characters in the messages to and from the screen, you can calculate an estimate of the minimum transmission time by dividing number of characters sent and received by the line speed in characters per second, taking into account data compression. This estimated transmission time for each transaction should be added to internal response time to provide a better estimate of perceived response. If you encounter a situation such as the LISTD command, make sure it is classified correctly for the response time and realize that classification in the short response time category does not necessarily come just from small resource transactions.

While conducting the experimental validation, execute from a script so that you can repeat the experiment. Execute your script under an unloaded line (that is, no other terminals active on your line) under the peak load condition. This allows you to estimate queuing on the line. If your peak line load condition occurs at the same time of day as the peak internal response load and you execute your script then as well as unloaded, the variation in both the internal processor response and the external transmission response can be measured. See chapter twenty-one for an example using CICS.

For TSO systems, MXG SOURCLIB contains a very simple measurement tool. Member CLTIMER executes a TSO CLIST that calls a SAS program that instructs the user to press enter as fast and as often as possible; then the program reports on the true total elapsed time of each of these trivial interactions. This tool is extremely powerful since an end-user can conduct his own experiment.

One common situation can be aided with CLTIMER. A large number (20 to 40) of TSO terminals share a 9600 BPS line with several JES VTAM printers. Although this may be cost-effective, it rarely provides good response to interactive users because the printers often cripple the line. In one instance, executing CLTIMER with the printers enabled showed an average response time of 4.2 seconds, whereas disabling the printers dropped the response to 0.7 seconds. Although the user had been advised previously of the cause (and cure) of his specific problem, it took this demonstration on his own terminal to convince him of the need to add additional line capacity to improve response.

Subsecond Response Time

Walt Doherty, of the IBM T.J. Watson Research Laboratory, long involved in performance evaluation, was the first and most effective proponent of subsecond response time objectives. He has repeatedly confirmed and enhanced his early 1970 conclusions, which have been further substantiated by the work of Arvin Thadani. Their more formal demonstrations are listed in the bibliography.

Their research shows that, for human-intensive interactive work, productivity increases as response decreases, but the rate of productivity increase is significantly greater when response time is less than 1 second, with increasing productivity down to the limits of human perception of perhaps 150 milliseconds. Several of their studies cite improvements in productivity (typically measured in user-transactions per-session-hour for a specific interactive system) in the range of 4 to 6 times productivity at response improvements of only 2 or 3 times, when the base response measure was on the order of 1 second.

Also impressive is recent work done by G. N. Lambert, who examined the quality of the end product, on code developed by programmers as a function of response time. Two development projects believed to be highly similar were compared. The earlier group had received 2.3 seconds average response, and the second group was attached locally and averaged only 0.84 seconds. Not only did the second group accomplish its task in 22% less time at 63% of the cost, but the quality of their finished product increased from 14.5 function points-per-error to 33.6!*

The case for increased line speed is easily made by calculating the time required to send a typical full screen (1920 bytes) of data at available line speeds:

Line speed "BPS"	Characters (or bytes) per second	Seconds for transmission of 1920 bytes
300	37.5	51.2
1200	150	12.8
2400	300	6.4
4800	600	3.2
9600	1200	1.6
56000	7000	.275

It is impossible to provide subsecond response on a 9600 BPS line, even with a single user. Although few questioned the response or productivity impact of subsecond response for human-intensive interactions, until very recently the fastest line speeds supported for terminal controllers was 9600 BPS. This meant that to achieve better than 1.6 seconds response for a screen required a local processor, and that solution was cost-effective only with a relatively large number of users at one location. In 1983, IBM announced that its 3274 family of terminal controllers support direct communications at 56000 BPS; so for the first time, it is possible to provide users with subsecond response without the cost of (and management problems associated with) distributed processing. Some early measurements have shown that productivity of users on 56000 BPS lines is indistinguishable from that of locally attached users on the same processor, and human interactions per session hour increased from 100 for users on 9600 BPS to more than 500 for both the locally attached and the remote 56000 BPS users. Additional measurements suggest that a single 56000 BPS line with two 3274 controllers supporting 20 terminals each can provide 40 TSO development programmers with subsecond response. The cost-effectiveness is easily shown at late 1983 line costs:

---

*To the author this is highly plausible. When he develops code and does not have to wait for the response, he is able to keep a much larger sphere of reference and can keep more mental tasks active. As soon as he has to wait for the response, however, he seems to purge the active stack, loses all his pointers, and has to restart his mind.

Line speed (BPS)	Cross-town line cost (monthly)	Cross-town cost per user	Dallas to East Coast (monthly)	Dallas to East Coast user
9600	$150	$ 3.75	$1000	$ 25
56000	$800	$20.00	$8000	$200

For a cross-town user, an investment of $16.25 per user per month could produce a 5-fold increase in productivity, whereas for the cross-country user it requires $175 per month more per user to provide subsecond response time for the same productivity increase. In both cases, improvement can be made without software changes with only the telecommunications function involved and no capital expenditure. An experimental verification can be conducted by upgrading a single 3274 to install the required V35 interface (with a one-time cost of between $200 and $1500, depending on the model) to use a 56000 BPS Digital Data Service with a minimum cost and with no risk.

chapter nine

Obtaining Agreement on Service Objectives

Once you have determined the measurement of service objectives, you still have to get your user community and management to accept the legitimacy of the measurements. It is relatively easy to convince them that CICS response measurement should be based on the internal response of transactions classified as fast, and that a percentage of these transactions completes in some number of seconds. It is more difficult to reach an agreement on the percentage and the time involved. A second challenge exists after you establish goal values: how do you control users so they do not abuse the system and subvert your planned service? This chapter suggests methods for meeting both challenges.

A major part of the problem is psychological. You are proposing a change in how computer services are measured. The end user may feel threatened by your proposal and fear that you are going to set the numbers to look good and still give him what he perceives as poor service. He wants service goals that keep the operations staff's feet to the fire. The operations manager may not trust your numbers either because he is afraid that you **are** going to hold his feet to the fire! The best way to counteract these human fears is to communicate your intentions, explain how measures are made, and provide concrete evidence that the numeric values you choose as goals correlate with the threshold of user complaints. The goal values most easily accepted are those that are most honest. The goal value of a service objective should be set at the value below which users complain and above which users do not complain.

There are three ways to set the goal value of a service objective: a measure of the user's subjective perception, management dictate, and guidance from others' experiences.

Of course, the best method for setting the service objective goal value requires the most effort. Record the user's subjective perception of response and then correlate perception with internal response measures.

The following case study demonstrates how this method was used to set the goal for a CICS system with twenty-four operators at one location.

CICS OPERATOR HOURLY RESPONSE

Operator _____ Date _____ Terminal _____

Hour starting at	You felt the service during that hour was:				
	Excellent	Good	Fair	Poor	Rotten
7a.m.	———	———	———	———	———
8a.m.	———	———	———	———	———
9a.m.	———	———	———	———	———
10a.m.	———	———	———	———	———
11a.m.	———	———	———	———	———
12a.m.	———	———	———	———	———
1p.m.	———	———	———	———	———
2p.m.	———	———	———	———	———
3p.m.	———	———	———	———	———
4p.m.	———	———	———	———	———
5p.m.	———	———	———	———	———
6p.m.	———	———	———	———	———

Figure 9.1
CICS Operator Hourly Response Form

The form shown in Figure 9.1 was given to each operator every morning for 2 weeks. At the end of each hour, the supervisor rang a bell to remind each operator to pause 10 seconds and place a check mark in the appropriate column for that hour. No quantitative value was ever associated with the 5 response descriptors. The operators were told only to answer how they honestly felt about response during each hour, and their responses were then analyzed.

The first analysis is the honesty check of the operators' responses. The columns were given numeric values 1 (Excellent) through 5 (Rotten) and then tabulated by the operator. Although most operators showed a range of responses, 1 person (obviously bucking for a promotion) reported Excellent for every hour, including 2 hours when CICS was down. A second person (obviously displeased with his job) graded the response Rotten, even when his peers rated the response Excellent. These two responses were removed from the analysis.

Once these outliers were removed, the operators' response data were merged with the response measurement from CICS Performance Analyzer. If CICS Monitor Facility data had been available, it would have been used. The subjective response from the operators was plotted against the proposed service measures (average, percent in 1 second, percent in 2 seconds, and so forth). All proposed measures correlated highly with users' perceptions, but the percent in 4 seconds was the clearest pattern. Whenever over 93% of CICS transactions in this system completed in under 4 seconds, all operators rated the service as Excellent or Good. Whenever the percentage dropped below 89%, the operators rated service Poor or Rotten. Management and the end users had no problem accepting the following service objective goal value of:

90% of fast CICS transactions must complete in 4 seconds.

They could see that this goal did relate directly to their users' perception of response. The subjective study validated the measured response.

Many installations have not only conducted individual studies of interactive systems, gathering user perceptions and correlating with the measured response, but they have also captured subjective response as an ongoing part of CPE. TSO and CMS LOGOFF EXITS are used to ask the user what he thought of response during his session, and his response is written to SMF in an installation record, which is then plotted along with other service measures. CICS and IMS transactions have been written that allow the user to notify the CPE analyst that response was very poor at some particular time and to allow investigation of the problem with minimum human interruptions. By allowing users to participate in establishing and evaluating service objective goals, their fears are allayed, and you can gain validation of your proposal.

It may not be possible to measure the subjective response of your users. In many cases, the service objective is established by a management directive: "hot batch jobs have 15-minute turnaround 95% of the time." This method works when the director has good technical knowledge of what can be achieved within the configuration, which you can provide by measuring the service you now deliver, and by understanding the needs of the end user, which you can provide in terms of jobs per user per day or transactions per user per session hour.

In this case study, batch service had fallen into disrepair. Job scheduling was aimed at optimization of computer resources (users specified Class A, B, or C if their jobs were I/O bound, mixed, or CPU bound) rather than service, and users never knew when to expect their jobs back. The director was willing to specify service objectives, but he suggested that users be polled as to their needs. The supervisors (about 50) were asked to define what portion of their work was required in 1 hour, 4 hours, or overnight. Their responses were very consistent, with only 10% of the work needed in 1 hour, 30% needed in 4 hours, and 60% overnight. Therefore, the director decided that service goals would be 1-hour, 4-hour, or overnight. He also decided that users must submit only 10% of their jobs in the 1-hour category, 30% in the 4-hour category, and the remainder could be designated for overnight. The scheduling system was then redesigned with these objectives in mind, and the strong backing of the director assured compliance by both users and suppliers.

The third way to establish goal values is to take advantage of literature. Although each installation is different, there are some rules of thumb that are easy to defend when you show management that someone else (preferably in the same industry grouping as your enterprise) has done it first.

For example, data entry clerks usually require less than 1 second response when they press enter. If these staff members have to wait at the end of each line to continue typing, their productivity is degraded. Even worse, their frustration causes them to become dissatisfied with their job, and the installation may lose highly skilled employees to other companies that provide needed response.

It is also well documented in the TSO and CMS literature that response between 2 and 3 seconds is required for trivial interactions to satisfy most users. If their work is human-intensive, they need even better response in the subsecond range to maximize their productivity. Thus, if a 10-second service objective were proposed, it would probably fail. Users know that they become asynchronous themselves when trivial response exceeds 10 seconds and would reject such a goal.

Installations have attempted to persuade TSO users to do more batch work and less in TSO since TSO is more expensive to deliver. They offer a fast or hot batch category as the inducement and have found that if turnaround time for this category is greater than 15 minutes, users will not move work to batch but will continue to execute under TSO. This fact can be used in establishing the service objective goal value by placing an upper limit on acceptable values.

Examples like these in the literature can be used in your proposal for service objectives, but they are never a substitute for direct measurement of your own users. Establishing the service objective and obtaining agreement on that goal may appear to be the easiest part of the task since the installation must then manage its resources to ensure the service objectives are being met; however, any service objective can be destroyed by an unconcerned user who abuses the system. Although the user is the reason you have the computer in the first place, you must gently control the user to keep him from misusing the shared resources. The most effective technique for ensuring that each department, group, or individual user does not abuse the system is to report to management since management supports the concept of managing by service objectives. Management is also responsible for controlling usage. Therefore, provide the manager with data so he can see who is violating the precepts on which the objectives are based. Then let managers manage. You can influence and increase the effectiveness of management feedback by what data you choose to report and how you report them.

Pricing computer services is still the most effective control mechanism, provided pricing is based on real cost that results from a well-tuned environment. You charge more for faster service than for slower service because faster service costs more to deliver. As chapter twenty-six shows, the cost of your installation is set by the peak hour of day since that hour determines the hardware capacity required. If you can defer some of the peak hour work to nonpeak hours, you require less capacity, and the cost to the user is ultimately less. Since your true cost for work in these nonpeak hours is much less than the work that determines the configuration, you should pass this cost-reduction back to the end users by offering discounts or pricing differentials when they execute in nonpeak hours. You should discount the price even more if the user submits work in a lower-urgency category. The overnight batch should be much cheaper than 1-hour batch, and a transaction in a test CICS (without memory fencing or fast response objective) should be cheaper than the same transaction in the production CICS system.

If you have given the user the capability to choose the service category (that is, shift, batch class, Test versus Production system, and so forth), you must charge more for faster service and more in prime time because the user's choice affects how well you can supply service. Although many installations have implemented such schemes, the quality of control is very much affected by the range of prices. Installations with effective control have price ranges so that the highest-priority, prime-time work costs six to eight times more than the lowest-priority, weekend-shift work. A price discount measured in tens of percents is simply not large enough to cause a user (who must shuffle his work) to take advantage of the discount.

With a reasonable pricing scheme for computer work, the control of the service objectives is made easy. Since the same piece of work can have a widely varying price that is dependent on service requested and shift differential, you can report to management the cost-per-work unit by an individual or a group and compare those who disregard the possible discounts to those who take the effort to request service appropriate to their needs. Psychology helps in the manner data are presented. Assume a structure where several users report to a supervisor, several supervisors report to a manager, several of whom report to the director. You should report the average cost-per-work unit as follows:

Table 9.2
Average Cost-Per-Work Unit

report to	contains one line for each	frequency
Supervisor	Individual	daily or weekly
Manager	Supervisor	weekly
Manager	Manager	weekly and monthly
Director	Manager	weekly and monthly

This scheme communicates without alienating, especially if you send reports to the supervisors first. Then wait a few weeks before the managers see supervisor's data. Your purpose is to aid the supervisors, not to place them on report.

Allow lower-level people time to absorb and understand the data and to react to it correctively before you begin reporting to management. Provide average cost-per-work unit, subtotaled by the supervisor, to the manager each week. Provide average cost-per-work unit by manager to the director each month. Even in the absence of real pricing, the same reporting strategy should be used to report the percentage of work that is in higher-priority-work categories. You must show management who is using and who is abusing performance categories until no one abuses the system.

Even though the timing and hierarchy of the reports are important for effective control, the format of the report can generate change. On the report, use the actual name of the individual, supervisor, or manager rather than his title. Although this requires more maintenance on your part, it is worth the effort since no one likes to see his name placed in a bad light. Peer pressure to conform to the published service objectives and work categories provides effective control. Table 9.3 gives an example relating to the case study above for 1-hour, 4-hour, and overnight batch categories.

Table 9.3
Weekly Peer Listing of Batch Work

supervisor	1-hour category		4-hour category		overnight category	
	% of jobs that met goal	% of their jobs run here	% of jobs that met goal	% of their jobs run here	% of jobs that met goal	% of their jobs run here
Fortney	91.4	7.2	93.5	25.5	99.2	67.3
Johnson	90.3	8.6	95.3	28.4	99.4	63.0
Fuerst	94.5	9.3	96.2	33.3	99.6	57.4
Crockett	93.4	8.4	95.9	29.6	99.3	62.0
Wright	92.0	6.2	96.7	31.4	99.5	62.4
Fore	95.0	22.3	95.3	46.8	99.2	30.9
Patterson	93.6	7.9	94.2	25.9	98.9	66.2
Spencer	90.9	9.9	99.9	19.9	99.9	70.2

Note that whereas the directive demanded less than 10% of batch work be submitted in the 1-hour category, supervisor Fore's group exceeded this objective.

When this scheduling system was implemented, the first week's report showed the above pattern; all groups had complied with the objectives except Fore's group. Each Monday morning the supervisors met to match coins and see who would pay for the coffee. Since Fore's group had abused the new scheduling system by submitting too much 1-hour work, none of his peers would allow him to participate in the game. Peer pressure is the simplest and most effective management tool to ensure work is submitted so that service objectives can be met.

chapter ten

Resource Measurement - Processor Utilization

The central processor is the most expensive single component in any installation. Although the percentage of the DP budget allocated to the CPU declines as channels, control units, tapes, and disks increase, the CPU is the reason these peripherals are acquired, and measuring it is the most important task. The disks and tapes may total more than the CPU, but they are at least initially of much less concern because they can be expanded in small increments. Furthermore, since the growth of disks and tapes results directly from application growth and since each data set on disk is owned by someone, the cost recovery or justification of peripherals may not require direct measurement. Justification of processor upgrades and replacements, as well as tuning of the present configuration, makes measurement of the CPU resource your most important job; since the CPU is shared, that job is made more complex.

There are two sources of CPU utilization in MVS. The SMF step records provide utilization at task level for the portion of processor usage recorded in the step records. The RMF records capture total processor utilization and utilization in each performance group. Before proceeding with CPU measurement, first examine the impact of two RMF parameters on resource measurement.

RMF interval   The RMF interval is set by the INTERVAL parameter (in member IEAIPS00 of SYS1.PARMLIB), which determines how frequently RMF data are written to the SMF file. The duration of each RMF interval is recorded in variable DURATM and can be greater than the specified interval if RMF is not able to regain control of the CPU at the exact end of the present interval. For example, it may have to wait for its own pages to be brought back in real memory. If RMF is ever stopped, the duration is less than the interval value.

Once you have gained control of performance at an installation (that is, after service objectives have been defined, measured, and used to tune the system and the workload), there is little need for the interval to be less than 60 minutes long. During tactical firefights, however, you may find it desirable to write RMF records with an interval as short as 10 to 15 minutes, and in benchmarks an interval of only 1 minute can be advantageous. The accuracy of the CPU measurement is not affected by the interval. Writing records with higher frequency provides more granularity for specific measurement but also increases the amount of data written. Unfortunately, RMF does not permit a different interval for each RMF record, and to obtain higher granularity for CPU or paging data, you must accept more very long type 74 records. In addition, a 60-minute recording interval for RMF is consistent from day to day. Since MVS/SP1, RMF records are automatically synchronized so that hourly data are written on the hour. This allows direct comparison between today and yesterday at 9 a.m.

Sampling rate   Some RMF data are acquired by sampling. The rate at which samples are taken is set by the CYCLE parameter (also in member IEAIPS00 of SYS1.PARMLIB). CYCLE is the number of milliseconds between samples and is normally set at 1000 milliseconds (or 1 second).* However, the value of CYCLE can have a significant affect on CPU utilization since sampling at a high rate (small value of CYCLE) can consume appreciable resources. A CYCLE parameter of 1000 milliseconds (or 1 second) is usually adequate.

A historical note: a few years ago, a weekly computer newspaper published a front page article attacking the accuracy of RMF data. The unreviewed article compared measurements from RMF to a hardware monitor and claimed that there was as much as 60% error in RMF. Subsequent discussion with the person providing the data (not the article's author) showed that the error was in the analysis, not in the data. The RMF and hardware monitor data were tabulated by time stamp, but the start of the RMF data was aligned with the end of the hardware monitor data. When the interval data were properly aligned, there were no significant differences.

In 1979, a COMTEN/COMRESS 7900 hardware monitor was taken out of storage and connected to a 370/168 processor. Block time had been purchased on the 168 by another computer manufacturer, who had always used hardware monitor measurements to establish the relative power of its machines as compared to IBM's. After the manufacturer was introduced to RMF, the RMF CPU measurement was validated by synchronizing the hardware monitor and RMF to the same 10-minute intervals. Since the resolution of the hardware monitor time stamp was 1 second, you could be off as much as 2 seconds CPU active in each 10-minute interval or a CPU busy percentage of 0.3%. The comparison of data from both monitors showed no 10-minute interval in which the difference in CPU busy was greater than 0.3%. The other computer manufacturer was impressed and began using RMF data in its analysis in lieu of hardware monitor data. It was also noted that when no work other than RMF was in execution, the CPU busy recorded by the hardware monitor was never greater than 0.6%, confirming the very low overhead of RMF data capture. These measurements were made with a CYCLE value of 1000 milliseconds.

---

* The CPU measurement in RMF and SMF is not the result of sampling, but is acquired by subtraction of successive values of the CPU clock. Thus, accuracy of the CPU is limited initially by the CPU clock resolution of the hardware in microseconds. Since RMF and SMF software resolve CPU hardware measures to .01 of a second (or 10 milliseconds), the RMF software monitor sets the CPU measurement accuracy.

Sources of CPU Utilization

The primary sources for measuring CPU utilization come from the RMF type 70 and 72 records, described in sections TYPE70 and TYPE72 of chapter forty, and from the SMF type 30 step record, described in section TYPE30_4 of the same chapter. Please read these sections and familiarize yourself with the variables that contain CPU measurements.

The RMF type 70 provides the number of seconds in the interval that the processor was not executing instructions, called the wait state. By subtracting wait time from duration of the RMF interval, seconds of CPU active are calculated directly. This measure of CPU busy is as accurate as a hardware monitor measures. Expressing the ratio of CPU active to interval duration as a percentage provides the common measure of percent CPU busy, PCTCPUBY. For a single processor (a uniprocessor or UP), there is one CPU busy. There are processors with more than one CPU, such as multiprocessors (MPs), attached-processors (APs), and two- and four-way dyadic processors. What is their CPU busy? How do we describe these processors?

These processors are part of a hardware environment that is called tightly coupled. In a tightly coupled processor , a single copy of the operating system is in control of two or more central processing units that share a common (real, rom, core) main memory area. Each CPU in a tightly coupled machine can usually execute instructions on behalf of any task, and all CPUs can be concurrently executing different tasks. More recently, the term multiengine has been applied, as the number of tightly-coupled processors has gone from two to four, with expectations for continued monotonic increase.

To understand CPU measurement, you should understand how instructions are executed. When your program is loaded into main memory at program load time (see chapter seven), the first part of the first page of your instructions is moved into the high speed buffer, or cache memory, where all instructions are decoded (by the I unit). The I unit then controls the actions of the E, or execute unit. If your program executes instructions sequentially, you can continue executing in cache until you run out of instructions. Cache memory is divided into lines of 32 to 128 bytes, depending on the vendor and the model of the processor. When you run out of instructions in the cache or when you branch to an instruction not currently in the cache, the processor requests that instructions be moved by the hardware from their main memory location into an available line in the cache. This event is called a buffer miss, and the internal performance of the processor is very much affected by the buffer hit ratio or the percent of time that an instruction was executed in the cache. When a task encounters a buffer miss, it continues to record CPU busy while the instructions are being fetched from main memory and placed into the cache.

Two UPs can be combined into an MP by adding hardware that allows the main memory to be shared. Each of the UPs still has its own cache memory, and all instructions are executed in the cache of the engine where the task is executing. A task can execute in CPU zero, issue an I/O instruction, and wait for the data to come back. When the block of data is ready for the task and if CPU zero is busy with another task, your task can resume its execution in CPU one, which requires the lines in cache zero owned by this task to be moved to the cache in CPU one. So, the size of the cache memory permits processor speedup within one IBM family of CPUs. (See chapter eleven for examples.) There is a problem encountered in multiengine systems: since there can be only one main memory controller shared by all CPUs, there is contention for that memory path. As a result, the same task accumulates more CPU time in a multiengine system than in a uniprocessor as the system waits to access main memory after each cache miss. On 370/168-MPs, the increase in measured task CPU time was over 15%, whereas the 3033-MPs showed about half that increase.

Although this chapter deals only with the processor, a primary source of CPU measurement is the decoding of service units. A description of MVS service units follows.

One of the SRM's responsibilities is to make sure that work is delivered equally to equally important tasks. Thus, a measure of work is needed. The SRM's measure of work is the service unit, a weighted function of the CPU, I/O, and storage units consumed by a task. The installation chooses the relative importance of these resources by specifying service definition coefficients, and the SRM calculates service units (using variable names in TYPE72) as:

Service units = CPUUNITS + SRBUNITS + IOUNITS + MSOUNITS

where

CPUUNITS = CPUCOEFF * raw CPU TCB service units

SRBUNITS = SRBCOEFF * raw CPU SRB service units

IOUNITS = IOCCOEFF * raw I/O service units

MSOUNITS = MSOCOEFF * raw storage service units.

Each of these raw service units is defined on other basic measures captured by SMF and RMF:

1 raw CPU TCB service unit = CPU TCB seconds * SU_SEC

1 raw CPU SRB service unit = CPU SRB seconds * SU_SEC

1 raw I/O service unit = EXCP count or = 8.33 milliseconds of I/O connect time

1 raw storage service unit = 50 pages owned for 1 raw
CPU TCB service unit

where SU_SEC is the hardware dependent constant (for example, 368.4 for a 3081K) discussed in the TYPE70 section of chapter forty and where the choice between EXCPs or connect time is discussed in chapter thirteen.

Figure 10.1 profiles the various measures of CPU time that are available in SMF and RMF records. If you IPL a processor, execute work until all tasks have completed, and wait until the final RMF interval record is written, you can compare these records. (Note that the figure is not drawn to scale because the labels are too long.)

From the total CPU active captured by RMF type 70, line two of Figure 10.1, the sum of the control performance group CPU times (TCB plus SRB) captured by RMF type 72 is subtracted to measure unassigned CPU time in line three.

The difference between TCB and SRB CPU time is discussed in the next chapter; the sum of TCB plus SRB is the real CPU usage by a task and is the important metric. The portion of a task's CPU time recorded under TCB versus SRB was determined by the operating system architect; some logical functions are performed under a task's TCB, whereas other functions (for performance or reliability) are performed under an SRB. SRB time is usually on the order of 10% of the total CPU time for most tasks unless the task is specifically designed to process under an SRB.

This unassigned CPU time is the CPU active not directly attributed to any performance group. It is sometimes called the MVS (overhead) CPU time and is discussed further in chapters eleven and twenty-six. The portion of CPU active that is unassigned is directly related to the subsystems that are executed. If many MVS services are required (for example, TSO, IMS, and, to a lesser degree, CICS), the unassigned CPU time can approach 50% of total, whereas a pure batch machine may see only 20% of the total CPU time unassigned.

All CPU active measurements from RMF and SMF fall into the three states of TCB, SRB, or MVS of line three. Although this RMF perspective on CPU utilization is accurate and useful, RMF data can only be resolved to the performance group. Since many tasks can accumulate resources in the same performance group, RMF cannot map CPU usage to a job, TSO session, or group of account numbers. You must use the CPU time reported in the SMF step (TYPE30_4) or job termination records (TYPE30_5) for that perspective, as shown below.

The fourth and fifth lines of Figure 10.1 show the CPU time captured by the SMF step and job termination records, respectively, as compared to the RMF captured CPU times in line three. Not all the RMF performance group CPU time is captured in the SMF step and job records, and some of the unassigned MVS CPU time is captured in these SMF records. The magnitude of these differences

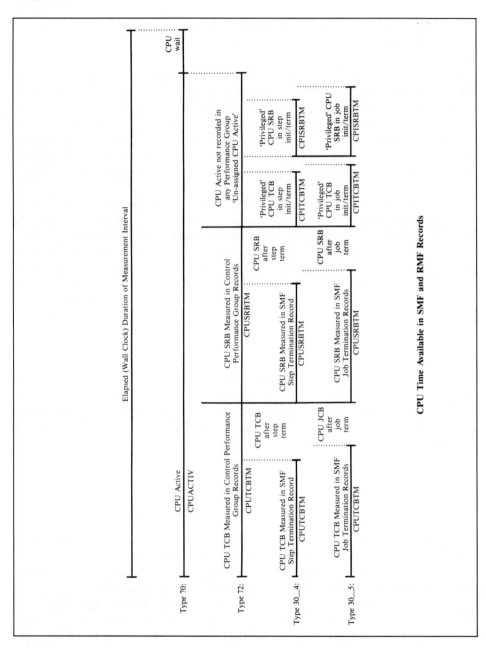

CPU Time Available in SMF and RMF Records

Figure 10.1

is so small that they are almost always ignored, but the differences do exist. There is a small amount of CPU time (usually small fractions of a second) captured in RMF performance group data that is not captured in SMF step and job records. This measures the CPU time consumed in the termination of the step or job after the SMF record has been built and includes the time to write the step or job record to SMF. It could be appreciable if the installation uses the IEFU83 or IEFU84 exit to create a banner page with step or job CPU and I/O statistics since the CPU time used by the banner page code is not included in the step resources in SMF but is captured in the task's performance group.

Unassigned MVS CPU time captured in the SMF step and job records that is not captured in the RMF performance group data is the privileged state or initiator times. These measures are also separated into TCB and SRB portions and represent CPU time consumed in the privileged state as the initiator starts and supports the new task being initiated. As soon as the task exists as an address space, this privileged state ends, and the CPU time is recorded under the RMF performance group and the SMF task. This is the only portion of the unassigned MVS CPU that can be attributed to a task, but it is usually insignificant and not worth the effort.

Million instructions per second (MIPS) was a fashionable metric in past years and is useful for loosely comparing processors. Within a family of processors, like the 370/1x8s or the 370/303xs, which were architecturally similar and differed mostly in the size of their cache memory, MIPS could be used as a relative-speed measure between them. However, comparing 2 processors of different families using MIPS can be misleading. Each hardware design tries to optimize instruction speed while minimizing costs. In so doing, the same logical function may take 5 instructions and 500 nanoseconds on one machine and 2 instructions and 1000 nanoseconds on another machine. Thus, whereas the first machine might be rated at 17 MIPS and the second at 14 MIPS, the second can actually perform 7 functions in 7 microseconds for every 3.4 functions performed in 8.5 microseconds on the first machine. Since all instructions are not equal, the total number is of little use, especially if the two processors to be compared are implemented differently.

MIPS can cause conceptual problems if they are used to measure capacity or speed. The classic example was the announcement of the 3081-D processor, a dyadic (that is, two-engine) machine. Each of the two CPUs in a 3081-D is essentially a 3033 in speed, at about 5 MIPS rate. The capacity of a 3081-D is about 10 MIPS because of the twin processors or about twice the capacity of a 3033 UP. Many translated 10 MIPS of capacity into 10 MIPS of speed and thought they could expect transactions to complete in half the time. In fact, the 3081-D was not faster than a 3033-U; it was simply wider. It would not halve the transaction response time anymore than would making an MP out of a UP. If transactions are processed in multiple address spaces (as are TSO and IMS message regions), the extra processor increases the transaction rate by parallelism, not by reducing transaction service time. Only an increase in the speed of the processor always reduces transaction service time.

The TYPE70 data set contains a separate variable for percent CPU busy for each CPU in a multiengine processor, PCTCPBY0 through PCTCPBY4. (Additional variables may exist in the future when more than 4-engined machines are available.) TYPE70 also contains PCTCPUBY, the percentage of time all processors were in use concurrently. Note that 50% PCTCPUBY on a 3084-Q (with 4 3081-K engines) is the same number of CPU seconds as 100% PCTCPUBY on a 3081-K with 2 engines. If you utilize individual engines of a tightly-coupled processor complex, be sure to compare results to see if there is any significant imbalance that occurs if any tasks specify CPU affinity in the program properties table or if differing levels of microcode are installed in the different engines.

Although the TYPE70 and TYPE72 data sets provide CPU measures directly from RMF, data set RMFINTRV has already combined these two RMF data sets (plus others) into a single observation per interval. RMFINTRV is part of the MXG performance data base or can be built directly from RMF records, and it provides the source of all CPU analysis from the RMF perspective. The variable names shown in Figure 10.1 (lines one through three) are contained in RMFIN-TRV. Note that RMFINTRV also uses the IMACWORK installation macro to collect and combine RMF performance group data into your WORKTYPE definitions.

The reports provided with RMFINTRV, described in chapter forty-one, provide hour-by-hour plots of processor utilization . The following general comments suggest ways to analyze CPU utilization.

For the first analysis, plot PCTCPUBY versus time of day. Any interval during your busiest times of day with less than 90% CPU active warrants further investigation since this represents a significant waste of the most expensive resource. One of the main virtues of MVS is its ability to maintain both high CPU utilization (high throughput and cost-effectiveness) while providing fast response for important work.

The installation's work priorities are defined to MVS in the system resource manager's installation performance specification (SRM's IPS), especially through the dispatching priority of each period of each performance group and the assignment of work groups into competing domains. MVS responds to those assignments and ensures that good service is provided to the more important tasks as long as resources are undercommitted.

A resource managed by the SRM is overcommitted if its measured value exceeds an upper limit for that resource, and undercommitted when the measured value of the resource is less than a lower limit. These two limits are referred to as the happy values for that resource and are set in member IEAICS of SYS1.PARMLIB for each resource that the installation selects.

When the SRM detects ANY overcommitted resource, it begins to manage the workload by swapping out unimportant address spaces based on the IPS definition of important. Only when all resource utilization measures are below their lower happy values does the SRM declare the system undercommitted and begin to swap tasks back in.

The happy values for CPU utilization are typically 98% and 100.9%. Since CPU utilization is calculated by software, the sampled value of CPU utilization is set to 101 whenever the true value was 100 and the SRM detected that it still had an undispatched ready task in memory. If 9 out of 10 samples are set to 101, the average short-term CPU utilization would be 100.9%. (Under an RMF Monitor II or interactive RMF session, you can see the actual 101 value.)

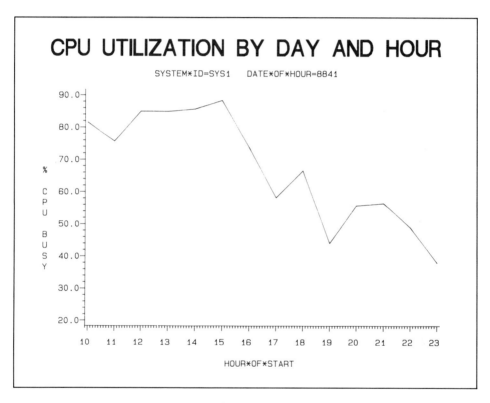

Figure 10.2

With this dynamic management of CPU resource by MVS, any interval with low CPU utilization when you have significant work to do suggests a problem. Either insufficient work was presented, the system was under initiated, or external effects to the operating system (such as high paging wait or I/O reserves), prevented utilization of the processor. A daily plot of PCTCPUBY versus STARTIME is a good indicator of problems.

Tracking down CPU utilization problems is part of tactical CPE and usually requires detail at the hourly level for the previous day. The examples in ANALDALY (see chapter forty-one) provide perspective in CPU utilization analysis. Figure 10.2 shows the daily profile of CPU active, and Figure 10.3 shows how the proper definition of performance groups into work types can be used to track who is using the processor and when it is being used. Execute ANALDALY against your own data to begin to understand how your processor resource is consumed.

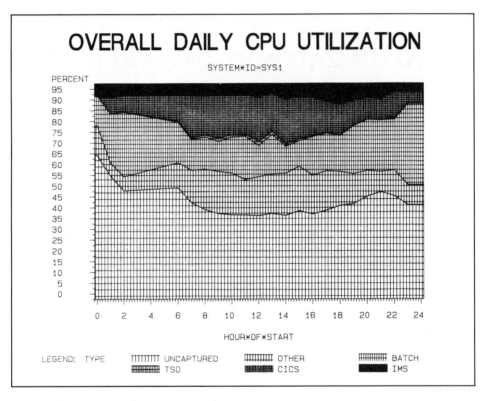

Figure 10.3

chapter eleven

Variability of CPU Measurement

Repeatability is the measure of CPU timing consistency between executions in the same hardware or software configuration. Variability is the measure of consistency between executions in different configurations. Both result from a trade-off between performance and accountability in the design of hardware and software. In addition, application options and design can have profound effects on CPU timing consistency.

This chapter documents many sources of CPU timing consistency: program design effects, processor architecture, microcode implementation, and system software effects due to higher multiprogramming levels and low utilization throughput improvements. The use of TCB alone versus TCB plus SRB measures is also discussed.

REPEATABILITY VERSUS VARIABILITY

When discussing the consistency of CPU timing measurements, *repeatability* is used to describe the change in measured CPU time when the same job is executed on the same hardware, software, and firmware. *Variability* is used to describe the impact of executing the same job on different processors, different system control programs (SCPs), and different releases of firmware. From an accounting perspective the repeatability of CPU timing is increasing. Workload throughput delivered, however, is improving, regardless of the status of repeatability and variability. IBM has always placed accounting issues behind performance issues (which is probably appropriate from their perspective and does improve cost-effectiveness), and the concerned user must recognize and identify potential accounting inconsistency.

CPU TIME

CPU time, as reported by the System Management Facility (SMF) and the Resource Measurement Facility (RMF), is a measure of the time a task was in control of the central processing unit (CPU). Only one task can be in control of the CPU at any time. At the beginning of a task's acquisition of the CPU (that is, when a task is dispatched), the operating system stores the current value of the clock. When the task relinquishes the processor, by voluntarily entering the

WAIT state or by being preempted by the operating system, the previously stored clock value is subtracted from the present clock value to provide the duration that the task used the CPU.

If the task in control was executing under a task control block (TCB), the duration used is called TCB time and is added to the TCB CPU time field of the task's step accounting record (SMF record type 4 and type 30, subtype 4). This TCB time is converted to TCB service units and added to the TCB service units field of the period of the control performance group in which the task was dispatched (in the type 72 RMF workload record). If the task is also in a REPORT performance group, that segment of the type 72 record is also updated.

If the task in control was executing under a service request block (SRB), the duration used is called SRB CPU time and is added to the SRB CPU time field of the task's step accounting record, and the SRB service units are added to the RMF workload record.

Technical note: TCB service units are calculated by multiplying an installation-chosen software constant (CPUCOEFF) by an IBM-defined hardware-dependent constant (service units per CPU second) times the CPU time.

Similarly, SRB service units are calculated by multiplying another installation-chosen software constant (SRBCOEFF) by the same IBM-defined hardware-dependent constant (service units per CPU second) times the SRB CPU time.

If the task in control was neither under a TCB nor under an SRB, then the time is not stored in step accounting records nor in workload records but rather in the operating system record. Thus, the duration of every second of every task's CPU utilization is recorded in one and only one of the three software buckets: the task's TCB bucket, the task's SRB bucket, or the operating system's bucket.

There is actually no discrete operating system bucket. Instead, there is another software bucket into which all WAIT time is recorded by RMF (type 70 record). RMF records are written at an installation-defined interval, typically one every hour. By taking the actual interval duration and subtracting the accumulated WAIT time, the total hardware CPU active time is measured. This is the same measure you would get by measuring CPU busy with a hardware monitor. By summing the TCB and SRB Service Units from all control performance groups in the type 72 RMF workload record for the same interval, the operating system CPU time can be calculated.

First, TCB service units and SRB service units in the RMF workload record are converted back into TCB time and SRB time for each control performance group and then summed for all control performance groups. This sum represents total identifiable CPU time during the interval (that is, the total CPU time that can be identified to a performance group).

Second, the difference between hardware CPU active time (from the WAIT records) and this total identifiable CPU time measures the operating system CPU time (that is, the CPU time consumed during the interval that was not attributable to any control performance group). The operating system CPU time can be as high as 35-45% of total hardware CPU active time in a processor executing an application (such as TSO or IMS) that requests many OS services or can be as little as 15-20% in a pure batch machine, which requires much less operating system services.

The portion of total hardware CPU time that is contained in the total identifiable CPU time is often called the capture ratio (that is, the portion captured by RMF in the performance group records). Capture ratio is discussed in chapter twenty-six.

If a processor was IPLed and quiesced after all work was completed, the total TCB time in the SMF step accounting records would equal the total TCB time in the RMF workload records, and the total SRB time in the SMF step accounting record would equal the total SRB time in the RMF workload records.

Technical note: the TCB and SRB CPU times reported in the SMF type 30 records are the same TCB and SRB times reported in the SMF type 4 step accounting record. With MVS/SE2 and subsequent operating systems, two additional CPU times are reported in the SMF type 30 record: the initiator TCB and initiator SRB CPU times. These represent the TCB and SRB times spent in the operating system in privileged state to initiate the task. Although RMF does not include this time in any control or report performance group record, it is included in the total hardware CPU active time and, thus, would also be included in the operating system CPU time calculated above.

PROGRAM DESIGN EFFECTS

The CPU time to process a task is directly affected by the program and the data used by the program. Many reports of variability and repeatability in CPU timings were attributed to the operating system but were actually related to application implementation attributes such as these:

1. **Data dependencies.** Users can see executions of the same program vary greatly because of changes in the quantity or quality of the data processed:
   a. Volume of data: the same program uses significantly more CPU time processing 10,000 records than 500 records.
   b. Order of data: sort execution of unsorted data uses significantly more CPU time than a second sort of the same data already sorted.
   c. Block size of data: increasing the blocksize of sequentially processed data reduces the CPU time necessary to process the I/O. Since the input output supervisor's (IOS) CPU time is charged to the task causing the I/O and since IOS is invoked for each block of data (EXCP) transferred, reducing the number of EXCPs by increasing the

blocksize always reduces the total (TCB + SRB) CPU time for the program. In one IEBGENER copy, CPU time was reduced from 60 seconds to 1 second when a file of 80-byte logical records was reblocked from a blocksize of 80 to a blocksize of 19040.

    d. Number of I/O buffers specified: increasing the number of buffers for sequentially processed data reduces the CPU cost of I/O by reducing the number of start I/O (SIO) commands needed to perform the I/O.

2. **Compiler versions.** The identical source language program can have great differences in CPU time, depending on the version of the compiler used to create the load module.

    a. Programs compiled by the PL/I optimizing compiler have typically shown a 30% reduction in CPU time compared to programs compiled by the PL/I F compiler.

    b. Reductions on the order of 50% have been observed between executions of the same source program compiled by the FORTRAN H and FORTRAN G compilers and between the CAPEX optimizing COBOL compiler and the IBM COBOL compiler.

3. **Compiler options.** Even within the same compiler, language options can dramatically alter the resultant load module, causing the same source program to use very different amounts of CPU time.

    a. COBOL STATE option: this debugging option causes the last 50 instructions (the state of the program) to be recorded and printed when an abend occurs. Storing of these data consumes a small amount of CPU time, typically on the order of 5-15%.

    b. COBOL FLOW option: this debugging option keeps track of the number of times each instruction is executed. The additional code required to add these counters typically doubles the CPU time of the program.

    c. COBOL TRUNC option: this option causes rounding and truncation of numeric fields after certain mathematical operations. In one highly numerical COBOL program, TRUNC also caused doubling of the measured CPU time.

    d. COBOL compiler BUF and SIZE options: these options do not affect the execution of the resultant load module but do affect the cost of the compile itself. The blocksize of the compiler's utility files is determined by these parameters. If set large enough, full track I/O is performed; if set too small, the compile CPU time can be doubled because of the extra I/O operations required.

4. **Dynamic programs.** The CPU time of some programs varies because the program itself is not static.

    a. Simulation and iteration techniques: all are used to solve mathematical problems and involve generation of a random starting point, followed by successive iteration toward a solution. If the starting point is accidentally close to the final solution in one run, its CPU time can be many times less than a run in which the random starting point was many steps further away from the solution. Additionally, changing the step size of the iteration (that is, how far the model moves between steps) can change the CPU time by tens or hundreds of times. Scaling and transformations, such as Polar versus Rectangular perspective, can also radically alter the CPU time of two runs. None of these effects leaves any visible trace in the SMF and RMF data, and they are often difficult to recognize, even with the complete SYSOUT listings for the two runs since they are often specified by only an application control card.

b. I/O chaining: many high efficiency utility programs (such as fast dump restore) use smart I/O programs that chain blocks of data together. The number of blocks successfully chained together in one operation is a function of the system loading on that logical I/O path. If I/O path loading is low, many blocks are chained together, with only one pass through the IOS logic, leading to significant CPU time reduction.

c. Sorts are dynamic programs: the volume of data and the memory allocated (virtual and real memory as well as auxiliary tape/disk working space memory) alter the CPU time of sorts. For instance, if enough address space exists for the task, a sort can be accomplished in memory without any calls for the processing of SORTWORK, leading to reduced CPU time. The same unsorted data in a smaller address space take more CPU time because of the spilling of data onto SORTWORK files.

5. **Monitor effects.** Software and hardware monitors exist in the software and in the processors that can be enabled (typically from the master console) without any knowledge of the executing tasks, yet the enabling of the monitor can increase the measured CPU time of the task.

a. Generalized Trace Facility (GTF): the GTF software monitor executes some of its code under the TCB or SRB of the task it is monitoring, and GTF's code processing time causes the monitored task's CPU time (TCB or SRB) to increase by up to 50% when ALL is specified.

b. Program Event Recording (PER): PER is a hardware monitor that, when enabled, increases measured CPU time for the monitored tasks. PER has also been reported to approach a doubling of the measured CPU times.

c. Data base monitors: these monitors can be enabled by users to trace their logical and physical I/Os. Resources used by the trace are charged to the address space in which the application monitor executes. For example, ADABAS logging of data base calls causes a significant increase in the CPU time of the ADABAS nucleus and can be invoked by a single ADABAS user or by the data base administrator.

6. **TSO command list (CLIST) effects.** Using TSO CLIST language around a simple program can make the execution easier, but the TSO CLIST language is a program and consumes resources that are charged to the TSO user. Using a TSO CLIST that is simply a list of TSO commands for a program, such as all the ALLOCs and a CALL, can be significantly cheaper than a very interactive CLIST that provides user friendliness, interrogates the user, and then allocates only the specific files to be used in this execution.

PROCESSOR ARCHITECTURE EFFECTS

Increased Power of the CPU

Processor power can be increased in two ways. Either the processor executes instructions faster or multiple processors are added in parallel. In the latter case (for example APing or MPing a 3033), processor power is essentially doubled, but execution time of a task is not changed. This is why the 3081D has double the power (capacity) of a 3033UP but will not reduce response time of a CICS or TSO transaction. It is little more than a 3033MP in one box.

Unfortunately, even when power is increased by increasing the speed of instruction execution, not all instruction executions are treated equally. New hardware not only has a faster clock cycle time, but some instructions change and require a fewer number of cycles to complete. In a pipeline design, the time to execute a series of instructions is a function of how little interference occurs (that is, how seldom the pipe breaks), which varies for different instruction sequences. Not all instructions are made faster by the same factor. The end result, regarding CPU timing, is that there is significant variability between two runs of one task and two runs of a different task on different CPUs, depending on the machine instructions that make up the two tasks and their sequence of execution.

For example, the TCB time variability measured between the 168 and 3033 was found to be:

Task	168 seconds	3033 seconds
Best Improvement	6.49	1.00
Worst Improvement	1.48	1.00
"Average" Improvement	2.11	1.00

In another analysis by instruction, similar variability was noted between a 3033N and a 3081D:

Instruction	3033N TCB (sec.)	3081 TCB (sec.)	Speedup ratio
Short-packed decimal	75.19	42.73	1.76
Long-packed decimal	220.73	69.06	3.20
Integer storage to register	12.39	18.80	0.66
Integer register to register	11.50	13.82	0.83
Single-precision floating point	24.70	23.71	1.04
Double-precision floating point	26.99	25.81	1.05
Double-precision register to register	26.91	21.63	1.25

Additionally, when work comparison between a 3033N and 3081D was classified by work type, the TCB reduction was found to be:

CICS	17%
TSO trivial	18%
COBOL batch	20%
SAS System	25%
CPU intensive FORTRAN	25%

Note that the service unit per CPU second constant for a 3033N is 216.4, and for a 3081D, it is 276.3, which predicts a speedup ratio of 1.276 or a reduction of 21.7%.

In a 3081D to 3033MP comparison, the BXLE instruction has been reported to require 40% more CPU time in the 3081D. The divide packed with more than 9 digits has been reported to take more time on 3081D than on a 168. Yet overall, the 3081D seems to be the same or slightly faster (6-8%) than the 3033MP. The problem is apparent when the average value of 7% faster does not apply to your BXLE-heavy workload and you measure a 40% increase rather than the expected 7% decrease.

Cache Design Effects - All Processors

In IBM 370 processors, instructions are executed from the high speed buffer, commonly called the cache memory. When the instruction to be executed is not in the cache, hardware storage management causes the transfer of the instruction and several subsequent instructions into the cache from real memory. Although the processor cycle time may be only 26 nanoseconds (ns), the storage transfer time is currently 12 times as long, requiring 312 ns to bring in the next 8 bytes of instructions. Thus, when a program's instruction is not in the cache, the task has to wait for some 300 ns to fetch the next instruction(s). During this wait, no productive execution of work occurs, but the CPU active clock continues to run for the processor and for the CPU time (TCB or SRB) of the task that had the cache miss or buffer miss event. The CPU clock keeps running during the hardware servicing of the cache miss, and the CPU time is charged to the task. Several factors influence the impact of cache design on CPU timings:

- **Size of cache**. The size of the cache directly affects CPU time. More cache means fewer misses, which means less measured CPU time for the same work. The only significant performance change between the Model I and Model III 370/158 and 370/168 was an increase in the size of the cache. Note that in the 3033 family, all have the same processor cycle time of 37 ns, but the cache sizes describe the performance and, hence, probable CPU measures:

CPU	Size of cache
3033-S	512
3033-N	16394
3033-U, A, M	65536
3081-D	32768
3081-K	65536

- **Data pass through**. Another impact of processor change in the 3081 is the way all data are transferred via the cache buffer, whereas in the 3033, it was not necessary to transfer through the cache. Thus, CPU time recorded for a task that transfers data (for example, IEBGENER) can be radically different in a 3033 than in a 3081. Moreover, tasks can encounter high repeatability error even in the 3081, depending on the storage conflict between real memory and the cache.

Cache Design Effects - Tightly-Coupled Processors

The design of a tightly-coupled multiengine interacts with both main and cache memory.

Serialization   Because there is a serial path to access main memory in a tightly coupled machine, there is the potential that one processor will be required to wait longer for a buffer miss than in a UP. When the access is to transfer data to or from the high speed buffer in the execution unit of the processor, this wait due to storage conflict is recorded and charged as CPU time. The end result is that the CPU time for the same task is larger on a tightly-coupled machine than on a uniprocessor. The effect has been as large as a 15% increase in the past, although present dyadics seem to measure about 7% more CPU time than their uniprocessor equivalents. The higher CPU time recorded on the multiengine processor can be compensated for in accounting by maintaining different CPU charging rates between uniprocessors and tightly-coupled processors.

Redispatch   Cache buffer design in tightly-coupled machines also causes variability between processors. In multiengine systems, a task can move from processor to processor. For example, a task in CPU 0 might issue an I/O. When the I/O operation completes, if CPU 0 is now busy but CPU 2 is free, the task is redispatched in CPU 2 to get its I/O. Since each CPU has its own cache memory, the lines of cache for this task that are now in CPU 0 must be moved to CPU 2 so that the task can be redispatched. In the 3081 Model D, the task's lines in CPU 0's cache are moved from the cache to real storage and then from real storage to the cache in CPU 2. In the Model K, however, the movement is directly from CPU 0's cache to CPU 2's cache, typically taking one half the time. Again, this provides throughput improvement at the expense of variable CPU charges to the task when comparing 3081D runs to 3081K.

3033 AP Channel Microcode   Another tightly-coupled impact occurs in the 3033AP. Microcode used by the channels resides in read-only storage (ROS). Each CPU in an AP or MP has its own ROS area. Since the AP side does not have any channels, the existing ROS store on the AP, which would have held channel microcode, was used to optimize CPU instructions. Thus, when a task executed on the AP side, it consumed less CPU than when it executed on the UP side. IBM's own measures showed up to 15% reduction, yet neither the user nor the installation has the ability to decide on which processor of an AP a task will execute.

Tightly-Coupled (Software) Effects

By sharing memory and operating system code, tightly-coupled machines create additional problems of repeatability and variability because of synchronization, contention, and serialization. Software designs to improve throughput often result in variability and repeatability effects. In handling interrupts in a UP, only higher priority tasks are serviced, permitting a simple determination with very low overhead. In a tightly-coupled machine, however, the interrupt is examined and a software check of the other processor is made to see if the new task is higher in priority than the task executing on the other processor. This increases overhead and potential CPU charges but provides better service and throughput.

Tightly-coupled machines use locks to serialize resources. As contention for a lock increases, the delay to the other processor (called spinning) increases:

Processor A Assumed hold time (%)	Processor B Theoretical spin time (%)
10	1
20	4 ---Design Point
30	9
40	16

This spin time is frequently chargeable to tasks (as above, when the spin is for memory access in the execution unit). By reducing the path length through ENQ and XSWAP, the SP1.3 system has reduced this variance, and in MVS/XA, multiple locks are used where possible to reduce the spin time.

MICROCODE DEPENDENCIES

The CPU measure is directly affected by the level of microcode. IBM does not provide a record of the level of the microcode in effect. If the level were in either the IPL record type 0 or the RMF CPU type 70 record, billing and accounting compensation factors could be adjusted for microcode, as it is for the CPU type and operating system release.

An example of the impact of replacing software functions with faster microcode implementation is the first time page fault handling, implemented by microcode, which was installed in 3081s shipped in 1982 and available for 3033s as extension feature 6850. When a program issues a getmain to allocate virtual storage, a new virtual storage page is acquired unless space still exists in the previously acquired virtual pages. No real storage page is allocated by the getmain. When the virtual page is referenced for the first time, a page fault results. The operating system must process this page fault by executing the following sequence:

1. Acquire a real storage frame from the available frame queue.
2. Clear the new page to zeros (for security).
3. Set the new page's storage protect key to that of the task.
4. Update the task's page table entry in the page vector table.
5. Redispatch the task so that the interrupted instruction can resume.

In an SP1.1 system or in SP1.3 without the extension feature or if no frame is on the available frame queue, a page translation exception is generated, and the MVS software performs the above sequence of stealing an unchanged real storage page. In MVS SP1.3, however, these five functions are processed without causing an actual page fault interruption. The first time reference is recognized as such, and the five functions are now executed in microcode. The first time, page fault handling via microcode improves throughput. However, the processing time of the microcode is now charged to the task's TCB time, whereas when the MVS software handled the page translation exception, that CPU time was charged to MVS rather than to the task. IBM believes that this single effect accounts for the increase (up to 14%) in CPU TCB time recorded on 3081D when compared to 3033 MP without the extension feature, both executing SP1.3.

SYSTEM SOFTWARE DESIGN

Higher Multiprogramming Level (MPL) Effects

With larger processor power, more tasks can be executed concurrently. With this higher MPL comes more system overhead, some of which is chargeable to TCB or SRB CPU time tasks. The magnitude of this effect is the same for a multi-processor (MP) or a uniprocessor (UP); however, since migration usually proceeds from a UP to an MP of essentially twice the power, the effect is often noticed when a UP is replaced by the larger power MP.

Example: if a queue search of length N searched S times per second and requires X instructions, it takes $N * S * X$ instructions per second. In a machine twice as fast, the queue is searched $2S$ times per second, and the increased power might support an MPL twice as high so that the queue is twice as long. Hence, it requires $2N * 2S * X$ or $4NSX$ instructions per second. Thus, the queue search can require 4 times as many instructions or twice the overhead because of the higher MPL.

Solution: whenever possible eliminate the queue or at least reduce its length. The following are known problem areas:

1. **ENQ/DEQ.** ENQ/DEQ was moved to its own address space in SP1.3 to reduce the queue length of getmains in SQA. Prior to this change, 60% repeatability error due to the best-fit SQA algorithm was discovered in 1979. Furthermore, in SP1.3 a hashing search is used, rather than the former serial search to reduce the search time from N to log N, which is a substantial reduction. If N increases from 10 to 1000, log N increases from 1 to 3.

2. **Nonspecific allocation.** Formerly, each candidate device would be selected and all on-line devices serially scanned for the selected device, causing $N * M$ searches. In SP1.3, the candidate is immediately checked in the UCB table, requiring only N searches.

3. **System queue area (SQA).** Finding a free queue element in the SQA (that is, a free area of a specific number of bytes) still uses the best-fit algorithm to reduce fragmentation. This algorithm requires full scan of all free elements unless an exact match is found.

4. **The XSWAP installed user program.** The original SP1.1 IUP was designed into SP1.3 to correct a design error that reduced the number of SQA getmains substantially by requesting the correct size on the first try.

Low Utilization Effects

Low utilization effects are designed into SP1.3 to improve throughput. The philosophy is to delay the entry into the WAIT state by allowing the operating system to find something to do if it is not 100% CPU busy.

Wake-up of other processors   During periods of low utilization for the tightly-coupled machines, an active CPU wakes up the other CPU periodically (via SIGP) to see if there is any work that can be given to the idle CPU. This wake-up communication is charged to an SRB that runs in the idle machine and can induce a 30% to 50% increase in the measured SRB time on the idle machine, compared to SP1.1 where no wake-up was issued.

Recursive scan   Another low utilization effect is the recursive scan of the dispatch queue. The normal first scan runs disabled (will not be interrupted). When utilization is low, the operating system, on finding no dispatchable work, rescans in its enabled mode to see if any interrupts occurred during the first scan. This results in additional CPU processing in the operating system, but the time is not charged to any task. This effect primarily alters the measures of operating system overhead and increases with larger queue size, more logical scans, higher counts of address spaces, and lower utilization (because there is more wait state). It is also dependent on the system control program level (SP1.1 versus SP1.3 versus XA). An example of the change in OS overhead was estimated by sponging the wait state in a low utilized benchmark with a low priority BR15 task that does nothing but branch to itself:

	No Sponge (%)	Sponge (%)
Wait State	52.5	0
Sponge State	0	63.0
Real Work	28.7	23.2
System Overhead	18.8	13.8

Note the significant increase in system overhead when the wait state was high. This effect is pronounced when comparing a highly used 3033UP to a lowly used 3081.

TCB VERSUS SRB

The MVS operating system accumulates CPU time by storing the clock before and after each task dispatch. Clock times are subtracted, and the difference is the CPU time. It will be recorded in one of three possible states:

TCB   the CPU was executing for a specific task under a task control block; the logical equivalent to what OS/MVT recorded as billing CPU time.

SRB   the CPU was executing for a specific task under a service request block. This measure was not separated from operating system overhead in MVT. In MVS, the SRB architecture allowed for better identification of this formerly unreported CPU time. A separate field was established in SMF/RMF records to record this CPU time.

OS   the CPU was executing, but the software architects either could not identify which task caused the execution or they decided that the time could not be properly charged to a task. For example, the time spent searching the dispatching queue or servicing an interrupt may not be properly assigned to the task that is dispatched, nor can it necessarily be assigned to the task that was interrupted.

All CPU activity is recorded by SMF/RMF into one of these three states. The system designer chooses the method of recording. Furthermore, IBM has moved functions from under the operating system to under a task's TCB and between TCB and SRB with different operating systems. Compilers have been rewritten so that generated code uses an SRB rather than a TCB. Variability and repeatability problems occur. Usually these changes occur with an operating system release, but even routine maintenance can alter the state under which CPU time is recorded. This problem is most pronounced for installations that use only TCB time for billing. As functions moved from TCB to SRB to operating system and back to TCB, the billing system had to be more reactive to equalize billing, whereas the sum of TCB and SRB remained more consistent across these software changes. IBM stated that it "tries to make TCB time, as reported by SMF, repeatable within a given range on a given processor configuration. Repeatability is not an objective across processor types (168 to 3033) or even from uniprocessor to MP/AP (3033 to 3033 AP/MP). IBM does not strive to ensure SRB time, as reported by SMF, is repeatable, nor do we even measure the effects of any changes." *

However, no quantification of the "within a given range" was stated. More important is the formal acknowledgment that even its best attempts are confined to a range of TCB time within the same CPU and system; that is, IBM addresses only repeatability and makes no claim for variability.

---

* IBM MVS Conversion Guide (GC28-0689-6).

It is the author's belief that SRB time is a legitimate measure of processor time when it is applied correctly to the task that caused the service request block; thus, it should be summed with the TCB time to distribute the processor utilization. Analysis of the repeatability of TCB alone versus the repeatability of the sum of TCB and SRB has shown no significant difference in repeatability, and in several experiments, the repeatability of the sum was better than the repeatability of the TCB alone. The variability of the sum of TCB and SRB has seldom been worse than the variability of TCB alone. Between MVS and MVS/SE1 for example, TCB alone ranged from a plus 19% to a minus 41% change, yet the sum of TCB and SRB saw a net minus 3% change.

SUPERVISOR STATE AND PROBLEM STATE MEASURES

In the early 1970s, the CPU time reported by SMF was inconsistent, and the lack of software tools (such as the SAS System) to analyze SMF caused many to use an external measurement device called a hardware monitor. The hardware monitor attached a probe to certain hardware test points and periodically sampled the voltage at that test point, counting true and false values of the test point. The program status word bits were directly measurable at a test point and thus became the prime source of CPU measurement. Bit 14, the wait state bit, was false when the CPU was active; and Bit 15, the problem state bit, was true when the problem state bit was on. A false Bit 15 meant that the processor was in supervisor state. Problem state and supervisor state were available and extremely useful measures of MVT because the time in supervisor state measured in this way actually measured the MVT nucleus CPU time.

In MVS, although the PSW measures can still be made with hardware monitors, the supervisor state active measurement no longer measures the nucleus, nor does it measure MVS operating system overhead. In MVS, the supervisor state measure from a hardware or software monitor measures how long that bit is in that state.

Supervisor state means that the system can execute a privileged instruction. When MVS was redesigned, the PSW bit was no longer an accurate measure of operating system busy time. In many cases, operating system architects turned on the PSW bit for supervisor state simply because a privileged instruction might be executed at some later time. There is no reason not to turn the supervisor bit on earlier; it creates no overhead but is simply a flag to the hardware to permit the execution of certain hardware instructions. The sum of problem state and supervisor state matches CPU active (from the hardware monitor or from RMF type 70 WAIT records), but the distribution of processor busy between problem and supervisor states has no relationship to TCB, SRB, OS overhead, or other measures.

BENCHMARK CONSIDERATIONS

All well known problems of benchmarking (that is, representativeness, accuracy, repeatability of the task code, and so forth) are made more difficult by the preceding problem. You must be careful only to compare systems that have:
- equal and high system utilizations. This tends to reduce the low utilization effects cited above.
- similar resource constraints. For example, MVS/XA SP2.1 requires over 1 megabyte more real storage than MVS/370 SP1.3. Thus, a storage constrained SP1.3 benchmark might not be correctly executed on the same hardware with SP2.1 installed.
- similar I/O configuration. Changing from UP to tightly coupled in an I/O constrained environment could produce deceptive results because of SIGP activity due to channel availability.
- service level responsiveness. Changes in service delivered can easily alter the conclusions of the benchmark.
- user modification impact. Functions within the SCP can degrade user modifications that should have been changed or eliminated.
- proper analysis of second level effects. For example, a memory constrained UP3033 was compared to a 3081D with the same size memory, yet the 3081D was not memory constrained. Due to the increased processor capacity of the 3081D, the average memory-resident time of transactions was significantly reduced in the 3081D, freeing up memory faster and eliminating memory bottlenecks.

Table 11.1 shows the wide range of CPU TCB times from a benchmark executed across a range of hardware, software, and microcode. It demonstrates the range of error that has been observed across these operating systems, processors, and microcode levels. Note especially the impact of the fourth column, when the SP1.2 microcode was used with the SP1.3 operating system. (It was not planned this way, but only after the benchmark was seen to consume inordinately high CPU times was it discovered that the IBM CE had installed the wrong level of microcode.)

Table 11.1
CPU TCB Timings for Various Combinations

Hardware:	3033UP	3033UP	3033MP	3033MP	3033MP	3081D	3081D
Software:	SE1	SP1.1	SP1.1	SP1.3	SP1.3	SP1.3	SP1.3
Microcode:				1.2	1.3	1.3	1.3
level:				Extn	Extn	Extn	Extn
Program							
ASSEMBLY	3.45	3.43	3.68	4.40	3.56	3.03	3.11
IEBCOPY	0.82	0.76	1.11	2.48	1.47	1.62	1.51
EASYTREV	7.15	6.63	7.72	8.65	7.75	7.76	7.46
FORTRAN Compile	0.93	0.92	1.04	-	0.93	-	0.93
IEBGENER	3.40	2.99	3.25	-	3.34	-	3.37
SAS System	54.39	53.85	58.59	54.63	53.37	53.95	54.11
OS COBOL Compile	10.01	9.80	10.50	11.00	10.49	8.96	9.01
VS COBOL Compile	8.95	8.85	9.42	9.88	9.43	7.78	7.89

chapter twelve

Resource Measurement - Memory, Paging, and Swapping

Real memory is needed to process data; the CPU can only execute instructions and operate on data that are in real memory. Without enough real memory, the operating system writes old pages to disk and reads new pages from disk so that needed data and instructions are in memory. The I/O necessary to read and write to and from the paging disks is called paging. Thus, paging is not a resource, but it is the operating system's reaction to insufficient real memory. Swapping is not a resource; it is the operating system's reaction to an overall insufficiency of some or all of the resources under the control of the operating system. Swapping occurs when too many tasks are perceived to be competing for limited resources. It is the physical movement of an entire task. For example, all the real memory pages of an address space can be moved in one fell swoop. Memory is the resource; swapping and paging are manifestations of insufficiency of the real memory resource.

DIFFERENCE BETWEEN REAL MEMORY AND VIRTUAL MEMORY

The total size of a program (the user's code, buffer space, operating system code required by the program, and so forth) is called the address space size or virtual storage size. The virtual storage size of a task is set when the task is initiated and is determined by the REGION parameter. (Under MVS/XA, the minimum region size is 1 megabyte.) The only true resource associated with a task's virtual storage requirement is that each page (that is, frame or 4096 bytes of address space) referenced must be backed or assigned to a physical page on auxiliary storage (a paging disk). Although each such page must exist on an auxiliary storage device, only pages that are currently being used need to be in the (expensive) real memory. (For a far more complete discussion of virtual memory, Peter Denning's 1970 paper is unsurpassed.)

Note: virtual storage size became a severe limitation in MVS/370 for a small number of very large installations, and Virtual Storage Constraint Relief (VSCR) was a buzz word prior to MVS/XA. The VSCR problem of MVS/370 primarily affected large IMS systems because of their usage of Common Storage Area (CSA) for each terminal; the number of physical terminals was limited by the size available for the CSA. The problem was compounded by a lack of data describing the allocation and fragmentation of virtual storage areas. MVS/XA has expanded the size of the critical areas and moved much of MVS out of these areas so that VSCR is much less of a problem. However, now there are complete data that describe usage of the shared virtual storage areas (CSA, SQA, FLPA, MLPA, PLPA) by subpool and protect key in TYPE78VS. Individual address space usage of the private area can be monitored (selectively) in TYPE78PA and TYPE78SP data sets, which is new with RMF Version 3.2. These data sets are described in chapter forty.

The resource of true concern is real storage. Real memory is the single most critical resource to any operating system, especially for IBM's virtual storage systems MVS, VM/370, and DOS/VSE. Although the following discussion is specific to MVS, the principles of memory management are similar for VM and DOS/VSE.

Real memory in MVS exists in a three-level hierarchy from the extremely fast to the fairly slow.

High speed buffer   The high speed buffer , or cache memory, is the fastest and most expensive real memory. All instructions are executed from cache, as described in chapter ten. Cache memory is measured in kilobytes (where 1 kilobyte is 1024 bytes), and sizes varying from 16K to 128K are common. The size of the cache is usually fixed for a particular model and type CPU, and an increase in cache is only available as a processor upgrade. In fact, the only appreciable difference between the 3 models (S, N, and U) of the 3033 line is the size of their cache (see chapter eleven).

Main storage   Main storage is slower than cache and, therefore, less expensive. Whereas cache memory access is measured in nanoseconds, main memory access is measured in microseconds. Main storage is measured in megabytes (1 megabyte is 1024 K-bytes or 1,048,576 bytes), and sizes ranging from 1MB to 96MB are currently offered. Incremental additions of main memory, typically in 4MB increments, provide an increase in the effective capacity of a processor by eliminating the CPU cost of some paging and swapping. Additional memory also improves the responsiveness of the processor.

Auxiliary storage   Auxiliary storage is the slowest memory managed by the operating system and is, therefore, the largest and least expensive. Because auxiliary storage exists on disks and drums, its access time is measured in milliseconds. There must be sufficient auxiliary storage to contain the peak number of virtual storage pages referenced. Usually, however, the performance of a system is limited not by the number of cylinders of auxiliary storage but by the number of actuators that can access auxiliary storage. High performance requires parallelism of the paging operations, which in turn may require that you increase the number of paging devices even though the total paging space need not be increased.

As MVS evolved, the real memory—Real Storage Manager (RSM)—and auxiliary memory control systems—Auxiliary Storage Manager (ASM)—have undergone continued improvement. The original design of MVS memory management has changed little structurally, but the controlling algorithms, especially the internal measurements and happy values used by those algorithms for decisions, have changed with each release of MVS. The Performance Notebook and the Initialization and Tuning Guide (cited in chapter thirty-eight) should be used for detail values for the specific version and level of the operating system in use. The following sections describe the overall attack on measurement and management of the memory resources.

PAGING: THE MANAGEMENT OF PAGES FOR TASKS IN MEMORY

Paging is the movement of individual pages between main storage and auxiliary storage (or between real memory and the page data sets) because there is not sufficient real memory to hold all the pages needed. A page fault occurs when an in-memory task tries to execute the next instruction, and the next instruction is not in real memory but is out in a paging data set. As a result of the page fault, the operating system makes the in-memory task wait. The paging supervisor then directs the RSM to get an available real memory frame from the Available Frame Queue (AFQ) and assign it to this task, and then it directs the ASM to locate the page in its page data set and issue the I/O to bring the needed page into real memory. When a page fault is resolved by transferring the needed page into memory, it is called (and counted as) a page-in.

Where did the available real memory page come from? At least once every second the SRM checks to see that there are enough real pages on the AFQ. Typical values for enough have been 20-30 frames. When the number of frames falls below the 'enough' constant AVQLOW, page steal is invoked, and RSM steals pages in memory that have not been recently used.

Page steal   Every page in real memory has an associated counter called the unreferenced interval count (UIC). When a page is referenced (read from or written into), its UIC is set to zero, and every second that passes without the page being referenced increments the UIC by one. Thus, a page with a UIC of eight has not been referenced for eight seconds. The maximum value of UIC for all pageable pages in memory is called the system high UIC and is taken as the initial criterion for the page steal algorithm. Page steal scans all address spaces looking for pages whose UIC is equal to the system high UIC and takes no more than two old pages from one address space and places them in the available frame queue. (If there are not enough pages of this age, the algorithm decrements the steal criterion and repeats until the required number of pages has been acquired.) Thus, page steal ensures that there are always some real memory frames available for immediate reassignment.

Page-out   Every page in real memory also has a change bit that is turned on if the page has been altered since it was last read into memory. If the data in a page being stolen have not been changed, there is no need to write the page-out to the page data set. Only when the change bit is on does the page steal algorithm direct the ASM to perform physical I/O to move the data to the page data set. When a page steal results in a physical transfer of the data from memory to the page data set, it is counted as a page-out.

Page reclaim   Before the paging supervisor directs the ASM to read in the page, he checks to see if the needed page was stolen earlier but not reassigned to another task. If the page is still unassigned on the available frame queue, the page fault is resolved without a physical I/O, and this event is counted as a page reclaim. Although a page fault resolved by an actual page-in will take milliseconds, a page fault resolved by page reclaim will be measured in microseconds. Note, however, that today's page reclaim, under a slightly higher memory utilization, is tomorrow's page-in.

A page fault results when a page is needed by a task that already has its other pages in real memory. The task must wait for the page to be physically transferred (wait for page-in) from disk to memory. **A page-in always delays a task**.

SWAPPING: TASK MANAGEMENT

The SRM's primary management task in MVS is to respond to overcommitment of resources, as measured through the happy values discussed in chapter ten. When these measures are exceeded, the SRM concludes that the system is overcommitted and attempts to swap-out or move all pages of a task from real storage to auxiliary storage. This type of swap is called a unilateral swap, and the count of unilateral swaps is a primary indicator of how overcommitted the system is. The intent is to free real memory but also, by swapping out a task, to reduce the system multiprogramming level, which reduces consumption of all resources.

Although some of the resource controls available to the SRM (for example, dispatching priority) manage resources even when the system is undercommitted, swapping only controls in an overcommitted system. The installation defines the relative importance of groups of tasks (called domains), and when swapping is required to manage resources, the less important tasks suffer.

The purpose and processes of swapping and paging are quite different. Paging moves single pages for waiting tasks, and swapping moves a group of pages at a time. Thus, the I/O paths for paging are more critical for good performance. Swapping acts like a long burst of sequential I/O; typical swap sizes and number of pages to be moved in or out at one time for one task are measured in tens and twenties of pages. Configuration of the auxiliary storage system can be comprised of one or more swap data sets, with separate paging data sets for the link pack area and common storage area and one or more local area page data sets. When zero swap data sets are defined, all swapping goes to the local page data sets. If swap data sets are defined, a minimum of three is recommended by IBM so that parallel I/O can occur.

Choice of the auxiliary storage configuration is beyond the scope of this book but is addressed in detail in the IBM references of Tom Beretvas and Siebo Friesenborg. This chapter helps you determine whether memory and paging are a problem and, if so, suggests some solutions. Because all tasks must wait for a page fault to be resolved by page-in, it is important to avoid creation of contention on the I/O path to the page data sets. The best performance is always obtained with page isolation or pristine paging—paging on a channel, control unit, and device used only for paging. Intermixing swapping devices and paging devices on the same physical paths is not recommended because of the dissimilarity in duration of paging and swapping I/O. If sufficient real memory is available to the workload, however, paging and swapping can be minimized and the auxiliary storage configuration can also be minimal. Insufficient real memory always requires a more complex auxiliary storage subsystem to maintain service objectives.

MEMORY

The most important measurement concerning the real memory resource, the CPU busy, is discussed in chapter eleven. The first and best clue that there is insufficient memory in an IBM virtual system is that the CPU utilization is too **low**. This clue seems contradictory since high paging results from insufficient memory and drives up CPU utilization. Also, high paging is thought to thrash the operating system by causing the CPU to spend all its time moving pages in and out, with CPU utilization of 100% and no productive work accomplished. Thrashing does not occur in IBM's implementation of virtual storage systems because the main memory is shared between users' programs and the operating system. As paging increases because of insufficient real memory, the operating system is as likely as a user's program to have a page fault and, like a user's program, causes a program to wait. When the page fault is in the operating system and the function being performed is one of the critical functions that must be completed before any other task is dispatched (for example, if the operating system is executing with interrupts inhibited or masked), then the entire system must wait until that page fault is resolved. If it takes 33.3 milliseconds to queue and transfer that operating system's page into real memory, the entire system must wait that long. It only takes 3 of these critical page faults per second to limit CPU utilization to a maximum of

90% because 3 x 33.3ms = 100ms = .100 seconds of wait time in every second. **High paging causes low CPU utilization.**

Real memory size can be measured in the number of pages in use at a point in time, or memory usage can be measured in page-seconds, which is the number of pages times the number of processor seconds that number of pages was in use. Alternatively, the paging rate can be measured to quantify the flow of pages due to an insufficiency of real memory. Pages and frames are used interchangeably in measuring memory. Both RMF and SMF provide similar measures but from different perspectives on memory and paging. Swapping, controlled by the SRM, is also measured both in RMF and SMF. As always, RMF provides a global perspective while SMF offers a measure for each task. Chapter forty (particularly TYPE30_4, TYPE71, TYPE72, TYPE75, and TYPE78) contains SMF and RMF measures of these resources, as well as a tutorial.

The primary source of memory resource measurement is TYPE71, which provides the RMF global perspective on memory utilization. There are statistics on the number of frames in use in the major virtual memory areas of the Link Pack Area (LPA), Common Storage Area (CSA), System Queue Area (SQA), Local System Queue Area (LSQA), and local or private area. For each of these areas, TYPE71 counts the number of fixed frames and the number of pageable frames. For each of these counts, three statistics are provided for each RMF interval: the minimum, maximum, and the average values during the interval. Table 12.1 presents the thirty SAS variables that describe those statistics. Note that there are no statistics on pageable frames in the SQA and LSQA because pages in those two areas are fixed rather than pageable.

Table 12.1
Memory Frame Statistic Variables in TYPE71

storage area	pageable frame count variables (min, max, and avg)	fixed frame count variables (min, max, and avg)
LPA	LPAPGMN, MX, AV	LPAFXMN, MX, AV
CSA	CSAPGMN, MX, AV	CSAFXMN, MX, AV
CSA and LPA	(none)	CSLPFXMN, MX, AV
local	PRVPGMN, MX, AV	PRVFXMN, MX, AV
SQA	(none)	SQAFXMN, MX, AV
LSQA	(none)	LSQFXMN, MX, AV
Total	PAGBLMN, MX, AV	FIXEDMN, MX, AV
Below 16BM	(none)	FIXLOMN, MX, AV

One frequent cause of memory problems is an unexpected step increase in fixed memory usage, often resulting from a new release of a product (like IMS, CICS, and so forth). Changing the number of buffers allocated to IMS could cause a jump in the average number of fixed pages in the CSA, and a page that has been fixed cannot be paged-out for reuse by another task. Thus, an increase in fixed pages reduces the shareable memory available, and that reduction could cause a dramatic increase in the page fault rate that could also drive down the CPU utilization, even during hours when there is plenty of work. Although the data in TYPE71 do not identify tasks using real memory frames, using the weekly TYPE71 data to plot the average number of fixed frames versus the start time of the interval might show when a step increase occurred.

```
PROC PLOT DATA=WEEK.TYPE71;
   PLOT FIXEDAV * STARTIME;
```

If the plot shows an increase, examine which area caused the increase:

```
PROC PLOT DATA=WEEK.TYPE71;
   PLOT (LPAFXAV CSAFXAV LSQFXAV SQAFXAV PRVFXAV) * STARTIME;
```

Although this still does not tell you which task caused the problem, it narrows the scope. Discussion with senior systems programmers can tell you which memory areas are used by each software system at your installation. Then, with a step increase in fixed memory at a particular time of day, you can examine the SMF step records (TYPE30_4 or PDB.STEPS) to see if a candidate step initiated during the same interval as the increase. If the problem recurs, further investigation with a tactical tool like RMF Monitor II or tracing memory fields with the RMF Trace Facility (which creates TYPE76 observations) may be required. Look at the TYPE78VS data as well. Even though it describes virtual size, it can help identify tasks that may use large real storage.

The same plot can identify the other frequent cause of memory shortage, a gradual growth over time rather than a step increase. Some installations have experienced a slow erosion of memory. One case occurred when the LOGREQ component issued a GETMAIN for 1F6 bytes, but when finished, the FREEMAIN was for 1F0 bytes. This left 6 unfreed bytes for every LOGREQ record written. TYPE71 data confirmed the slow growth over time, but it took additional research in the form of a dump and an examination of ownership of CSA to find the problem, which was ultimately corrected by IBM. Another problem is the failure of a task to clean up its CSA space when it fails. Data base management systems are a particularly prevalent example because they use a great deal of CSA and are vulnerable to user-caused ABENDs. When the DBMS nucleus fails, its CSA allocation may not be properly de-allocated, causing every restart to eat up another chunk of CSA. TYPE71 does not identify the cause, but it shows that there is a problem and can limit possible causes.

Analysis of the number of fixed frames in the virtual memory areas can often identify memory shortages, but it takes intuition to identify the causing task from frame counts. A measurement of memory usage that maps to owning tasks is needed. The performance group resources in TYPE72 and the step and interval statistics in TYPE30_4 and TYPE30_V provide memory service units consumed. Memory service units and other service unit components were defined in chapter ten. A raw storage service unit is the ownership of 50 real pages (200 kilobytes) for 1 raw CPU TCB service unit. Recall that on a 3081K processor, 1 CPU TCB second generates 373 of these raw CPU TCB service units, and, thus, a 3081K raw storage service unit is the ownership of 50 real pages for about 0.0027 CPU seconds or about 0.1345 page-seconds. Although the mapping of memory service units to page-seconds is processor dependent in magnitude, the 2 measures are related by a constant and can be used interchangeably for qualitative measures of memory usage.

Note: if the address space uses a cross memory function (a cross memory call or a secondary address space), pages in the secondary address space are not counted in the memory service units of the calling address space but in the memory service units of the secondary address space.

This raw storage service unit value is then multiplied by the installation's chosen service definition coefficient for memory service (MSOCOEFF, in TYPE72) to produce the actual memory service units (MSOUNITS in TYPE72 and TYPE30_4). In the TYPE30_4 step data, the number of page-seconds itself is also provided.

In theory, memory should be managed by tracking MSOUNITS, but in practice that has not been the case. The number of pages in use by a task is only partially under control of the task. Since real storage management is based on a least recently used replacement algorithm, the number of pages you require depends on your program's requirements and on memory utilization of other tasks executing at the same instant. MSOUNITS are not repeatable for the same task because of this environmental dependence. Tracking memory usage is made more difficult because the metric itself is not a stable measure, and the repeatability error of memory service (or page-seconds) can be on the order of 40%. Thus, it is not possible to recover accurately the cost of real memory through direct charge back (see chapter thirty-one).

The lack of repeatability of memory service units does not prevent its use in performance evaluation. Although not repeatable, it represents memory usage, especially if the task being measured used on the order of tens of CPU seconds. Much of the repeatability error is associated with the sampling of memory size, and there is some indication that repeatability error decreases with sample size. If two tasks, executing in the same processor at about the same time show a five-to-one ratio of memory service, you can conclude that one requires five times the memory of the other. Whereas data on memory usage are captured in page-seconds, the average working set size can be estimated by dividing page-seconds by CPU TCB seconds. You must be careful when comparing average working set size because it reflects the average amount of memory in use but not how long it was used. Nevertheless, it is often the preferred metric to report to management because it is easier to understand.

Page-seconds are reported for each task in the TYPE30_4 and TYPE30_V step and interval records. The TYPE30_4 data apply to the entire step, and the TYPE30_V interval data apply to each SMF elapsed interval. So if you choose, MXG software can create TYPE30_V only for on-line and long running tasks and, thus, capture average working set and memory service units for each interval of selected tasks (as well as paging, swapping, and other resources at the interval level). In addition, RMF captures memory service units delivered to each performance group, and the percentage of total memory service units consumed by each performance group during an RMF interval can be calculated. Although the percentage distribution will be reasonable, the absolute value may be appreciably in error. In one specific example, the sum of the average working sets on a 16MB machine totaled 27 MB, but the percentage distribution agreed with intuition. The average working set of a performance group period, calculated in TYPE72, must be multiplied by the average multiprogramming level of that performance group period to reflect properly total memory usage by the performance group since only one task in the performance group period is usually accumulating CPU service at one time.

Insufficient real memory causes paging, and the TYPE71 data on overall paging is again the starting point. No paging by address space is provided, but paging by area is readily available, as described in the eleven variables in Table 12.2. (There are no LPA page-outs because the link pack area must be re-entrant, and re-entrant code cannot be altered; that is, the change bit can never be turned on for an LPA page, and MVS does not write out an unchanged page.) These and other paging rate variables are described in section TYPE71 of chapter forty and are reported in example paging reports in section DAILYRPT of chapter forty-one.

Table 12.2
Paging Rates by Area Variables in TYPE71

Storage area	Page-in rate variables	Page-out rate variables	Page-reclaim rate variables
LPA	LPAGINS	(none)	LPARECLM
CSA	PVTCAIN	PVTCAOUT	PVTCAREC
VIO	PVTVAMI	PVTVAMO	PVTVAMR

non-VIO   PVTNPIN   PVTNPOUT   PVTNPREC

$$PAGING = PVTNPIN + PVTNPOUT$$
$$PFRATE = PVTNPIN + PVTNPREC$$

PAGING   Physical I/O was necessary to move a page in or out of real memory but does not necessarily cause any task to be delayed.

PAGE FAULT   An in-memory task needed a page that was not available. The task had to wait until the page was brought in (or located via reclaim).

In addition to the memory service units for each SMF interval available in TYPE30_V, paging at the address space is also available. The RMF TYPE71 data can provide a picture of the area where paging occurs during each RMF interval, but only the SMF interval data identify tasks involved in paging. Unfortunately, you get only the total page-ins, page-outs, and page reclaims, with no mapping to memory area, but the TYPE30_V data do provide excellent resource data on paging.

Translating paging rate into delays   If you know the time to process a page fault, you can use the TYPE30_4 for each step (or the TYPE30_V interval data for long running steps) to estimate the impact of paging on a task. For example, if you examine a CICS address space type 30 record and find that there were 3000 page-ins in a 10-minute SMF interval (a page-in rate of 5 pages per second), you can estimate the delay to that CICS address space. Assume you know that the average time needed to resolve a page fault (that is, queuing in ASM plus I/O queuing and service time) is 50 milliseconds or .05 seconds. Then, since CICS is a single task in its address space, page wait time for this CICS is calculated:

page wait time per second $= .05 \times 5 = .250$ seconds

This means that for every second of elapsed time, when page-in rate is five pages per second, this CICS task is waiting one-quarter of the time. By this calculation, you can show the impact paging has on a single address space, and the calculation can be extended to groups of tasks. For example, if you took all batch jobs during prime time and totaled their page-in count (from TYPE30_4), multiplied by the average time per page-in, and divided by the duration that these jobs were swapped-in (INMEMTM), you could inform management of the percentage of time that batch jobs were waiting due solely to insufficient real memory:

percent wasted time $= 0.05 \times (PAGEINS / INMEMTM) \times 100$

How do you know that it takes 50 milliseconds to resolve a page fault? You may have already examined your I/O system and seen that the TYPE74 data show average I/O time to your paging system is 50 milliseconds. An alternative approach is to take the step records for your work and estimate the increase in elapsed time for a page fault. If you take step records for prime batch, for example, you can first plot elapsed execution time (EXECTM, described in chapter seven, excludes delays due to allocation and data set enqueue) versus the page-in count for each step:

```
PROC PLOT DATA=PDB.STEPS;
   PLOT EXECTM*PAGEINS;
```

Then use linear regression to give an equation describing the relationship between execution time and page-in count:

```
PROC SYSREG DATA=PDB.STEPS;
   MODEL EXECTM = PAGEINS;
```

If you have removed outliers, such as jobs with very large CPU times or I/O counts whose EXECTM is not directly driven by PAGEINS, the coefficient of PAGEINS from the regression is the average time in seconds that execution time is elongated for every page. Thus, you can estimate the time to resolve a page fault with that coefficient.

The stress in this analysis is on page-in or page fault rate, not total paging. Although MVS systems can have overall paging rates measured in hundreds per second, those total paging rates are combining pages moved for paging and pages moved for swapping. Swapping is the result of overcommitment and is discussed further in the workload measurement chapters. Although swap pages must be moved between real and auxiliary memory, the page faults reflect insufficient real memory and are the preferred metric.

TYPE75 records describe page data sets and swap data sets in use. TYPE75 is valuable because the type of page or swap data set and its physical address (UNITADR) are listed along with the percentage that the data set is busy (DSBUSY). This is a significant indicator and should be compared to device busy from type 74. The DSBUSY in type 75 is the auxiliary storage manager's view of the page data set's percent-busy, whereas the type 74 is the IOS's view of the device's percent-busy. A significant discrepancy between the type 74 and 75 records suggests either multisystem usage of the volume on which the page data set is used or incorrectly set parameters in the SRM, which cause the ASM to schedule I/O inefficiently. Both SIO counts and the number of pages transferred for each interval are in type 75 records. Both counts appear to be good indicators of page activity and permit calculations of the average number of pages per start I/O.

chapter thirteen

Resource Measurement - I/O and Data Set Activity

Information on I/O activity in MVS is reported in several SMF and RMF records. The RMF TYPE73P data report physical channel utilizations. TYPE73L provides MVS/370 logical channel utilizations and logical channel queuing. Under MVS/XA, the logical channel no longer exists, but equivalent queuing is reported in TYPE78 along with enhanced control unit reporting. TYPE74 provides measurement of utilization and queuing at the device level with limited control unit information. These data sets provide resource measurement data for global I/O analysis from the perspective of the device to the path but provide no information on the impact of I/O on workloads. TYPE72 provides the I/O service units delivered to each performance group during each RMF interval; if performance groups map to logical workloads, TYPE72 is an excellent source of workload I/O data. For further detail at task rather than just performance group, SMF step records provide I/O counts (and, under MVS/XA, the duration of I/O connect time) for each DD for each task. The detail DD level statistics are available in TYPE30_D (if enabled for specific tasks in IMAC30DD), and these I/O counts are summarized by device type for each step in TYPE30_4. Further detail is available in TYPE1415 (non-VSAM) and TYPE64 (VSAM), which describe each task's I/O usage at the data set level. Additional data specific to tapes are reported in TYPE21 for each tape volume dismounted, with no information on the tape's user. TYPE75 reports I/O operations specific to paging and swapping workload, by page or swap data sets. In MVS/XA, even TYPE70 contains I/O information in the count of I/O interrupts processed (and the percentage delayed) by each processor.

You must first understand the different perspectives of these I/O measures. Read the following sections in chapter forty before proceeding: TYPE73L, TYPE73P, TYPE73, TYPE78, TYPE74, TYPE72, TYPE30_4, TYPE30_D, TYPE1415, TYPE64, TYPE21, and TYPE75. TYPE73L, which describes events in the processing of an I/O request as it can be measured, is especially enlightening.

Measuring I/O Activity

Three metrics are used to measure I/O activity.

1. EXCP - number of blocks of data transferred.

> Originally the execute channel program, EXCP is the OS/360 macro that caused the execution of all channel programs (the set of

instructions from the CPU to the I/O components). Since most EXCPs in OS/360 caused a block of data to be read and written and because EXCP counts were maintained by SMF, it has historically been the primary metric for I/O activity, especially for billing I/O. Although it has been defined and redefined in different operating systems and releases, MVS now defines an EXCP count as a block of data transferred. One major weakness still remains: both a 16-byte block and a 32756-byte block count as one EXCP. Furthermore, the MVS definition applies only if the I/O access method or I/O driver counts blocks transferred and passes that count to the SMF count routine, IEASMFEX. The BSAM, QSAM, and VSAM access methods do conform, and, thus, their EXCP counts reflect the transfer of 1 block of data. ISAM EXCP counts are specifically undefined as not being a count of blocks transferred, and an INFO/SYS entry describes ISAM EXCP counts as the value returned by the access method. If the access method is EXCP, the value in the EXCP count fields is dependent on what the I/O programmer chose to do, and only by examining actual code can the value be understood. Frequently, EXCP access method programmers branch to IEASMFEX after each block, providing the correct value of blocks transferred in the EXCP count. Just as frequently, however, the I/O programmer counts the number of start I/O macros and at close time passes that value instead of the correct count of blocks transferred to the EXCP count routine.

Note: sort programs use the EXCP access method. Sorts in general and SYNCSORT in particular provide a count of SIOs rather than EXCPs to the SORTWORK DDs. SYNCSORT, through a SCZ zap, allows the installation to count EXCPs instead of SIOs for the SORTIN and SORTOUT segments, which should be done for consistency with other access methods.

2. SIO - count of physical I/O operations necessary to transfer I/O.

The start I/O macro is a privileged instruction issued by the input/output supervisor (IOS) component of MVS, as a result of a program issuing an EXCP. The access method can take several blocks (EXCPs) from a program, allocate several buffers (through the BUFNO parameter), and transfer the BUFNO blocks with one SIO. Under the sequential access method, extended (SAM/E), the BUFNO defaults to five. (SAM/E was the optional selectable unit nine until it became free with MVS370 Release 3.8.) Thus, for QSAM, five EXCPs are counted for every SIO. For BSAM I/O, buffering is done by the programmer rather than by the access method. BSAM usually counts one EXCP per

SIO, although IEBGENER uses BSAM with two EXCP per SIO. For ISAM and VSAM, however, it is possible to have many SIOs issued for a single block of data (consider an ISAM data block in an overflow area that must be located via search). Although both EXCP and SIO count I/O operations, they do not map directly to one another.

3. IOTM - I/O connect time duration.

This metric, also called device connect time, became available with MVS/XA and is the standard measure of I/O utilization. Accumulated by hardware monitors built in the channels, it represents the duration that a task was actually transferring data or commands to or from a device. The IOTM is captured at the device level in RMF TYPE74. Additionally, SMF captures IOTM just like EXCP counts in the step type 30 records, with total IOTM captured separately from the individual connect time for each DD. In the future, capacity analysis will be able to apply the techniques of CPU capacity analysis (see chapter twenty-six), based on CPU connect time, to the analysis of I/O capacity based on this I/O connect time.

Note: analysis of early MVS/XA data uncovered an error in the IOTM in the DD segments of type 30 records; the error was accepted as a problem by IBM as APAR OZ77081. Make sure that you have installed the anticipated PTF to this APAR before using the IOTMTODD and IOTMNODD variables in TYPE30 data sets. The DEVCONTM in RMF TYPE74 and the IOTMTOTL TYPE30_4 are valid; only the IOTM to the DD segments of the type 30 records (IOTMTODD and IOTMNODD) is invalid.

Analysis of the I/O subsystem begins with an understanding of the I/O configuration at your installation. The configuration of the I/O path from the software I/O request to the physical device can prevent or create contention for shareable I/O devices.

Since tape drives are never shared by tasks or processors, tape I/O contention can only occur at the control unit or physical channel; so, it is much easier to manage. The tape subsystem is treated separately in chapter fourteen.

The physical configuration is the responsibility of installation management; users do not choose the channel, control unit, or device number of their data. Thus, delays caused by the physical path must be resolved by installation management. Users can cause I/O delay when they create contention by executing applications in parallel (for example, a TSO session and batch job) that concurrently access the same physical I/O device or by allowing their applications to exceed the physical capacity of the isolated physical path to a device. The first charter of the I/O performance analyst is to identify whether I/O delays are the installation's fault or the user's.

Data in TYPE73L (or TYPE78) identify this level of causality for I/O queuing delays. During peak hours, data can be printed to identify whether I/O deferrals are for the path or control unit (the fault of the configuration) or for the device or logical device (usually blamed on the user). I/O contention can occur even in a single processor when two tasks try to access the same device simultaneously, but MVS resolves the conflict by treating it as a logical channel/device queued request with less overhead, and this conflict is more readily addressed than shared DASD conflicts.

The most expensive form of I/O contention results from shared DASD. Shared DASD refers to the ability of two processors to access the same DASD volume. A two-channel switch is installed in the control unit, one channel to each processor, and the connection switches between the other processors as I/O requests occur.

The only purpose of shared DASD is to enhance availability at the expense of performance. In a multi-system installation, DASD must be shareable so that in an outage, work can be moved from its normal system to another system, and the business can continue (although in a degraded mode while the failed system is under repair). In a normal configuration there should be no sharing of the DASD because it lengthens the time to process an I/O. In other words, every installation should aim for pristine I/O when planning its I/O configuration.

Pristine I/O occurs when all devices behind each head-of-string controller talk to only one application within one processor, and there is no other I/O occurring on the physical path (channel and control unit) except from this application for the period of peak work when responsiveness is paramount.

Pristine I/O is ideal for all day, but the cost of extra I/O paths can be greater than the gain. Therefore, we compromise performance for cost-effectiveness and design I/O configuration so that I/O elongation occurs only during the processing times when throughput is more important than response time. In most installations, this means that peak prime hours define I/O configuration, which is pristine and response oriented for productivity.

In a pristine I/O configuration, there is a specific purpose for each head-of-string and the numerous devices that exist behind the controller. Their existence is determined by the space and access arms required for ensuring pristine I/O configuration. Each MVS system has separate strings for temporary work space, paging, and swapping, and none of these strings is used by another processor. There is application data for each production of IMS, CICS, ADABAS, MODEL204, and so forth, on its own string(s). The control unit and channels to which the strings are attached are normally used only between the string and the CPU in which its owning application executes. By managing the I/O configuration at this level (a string of DASD talks over an isolated path to the CPU in which its owning application normally executes), I/O elongation due to path delay is eliminated.

Pristine I/O is quite feasible. The most difficult task is not in planning the configuration but in getting from where you are to where you want to be. Although you may not be able to isolate I/O fully (catalogs and other master data sets must be shared), all strings owned by the installation (that is, paging and temporary work space) should be pristine. Paging must be isolated from other I/O if responsiveness is to be maintained. Temporary work space should never be shared among processors since the linkage editor always issues a reserve macro that prevents any other system from issuing any I/O to the entire volume for the elapsed time of the linkedit step. There are other benefits with isolated I/O. When CICS data bases are pristine, a heavy CICS workload may degrade itself, but the extra I/O load does not affect other workloads. Capacity planning for I/O is much easier with pristine I/O since measurements of channel, control unit, and device busy are clearly the result of the real workload; management can easily see why you need more paging actuators when your measurements are unclouded by other I/O on the string.

Once on your way toward a pristine I/O configuration and having eliminated the installation's path delays, you can begin to attack I/O delays due to the user. The largest cause of inefficiency in I/O that is due to the user is the use of small blocksize for sequential I/O. **Increasing sequential blocksize provides better response with less cost.** The second paper in chapter forty-two provides a complete analysis of the real costs (CPU, memory, I/O, and so forth) for QSAM I/O and discusses the steps needed to minimize I/O resource costs. That discussion proves that the present architecture of MVS and 3380 minimizes jointly the CPU (TCB plus SRB), real memory page-seconds, I/O operations, blocks of data, physical tracks of storage, and elapsed time of tasks when the bytes transferred in each physical I/O operation equals the byte capacity of the track or when full-track I/O is performed. Full-track I/O on a 3380 can mean 2 buffers at 23440 or 7 buffers at 6640, and the CPU cost of the 6K blocksize typically is 45% more than, or 1.5 times the CPU cost of full-track blocksize with minimum BUFNO, the optimum for sequential I/O. In simpler terms, to minimize CPU, I/O, real memory costs, and the number of tracks required to store data, sequential I/O should be blocked to full-track blocksize on devices with track sizes less than 32760. For devices with a track size that exceeds the software blocksize limitation (currently 32760), 32670 byte blocks minimize CPU, I/O, and real memory but not tracks used; thus, the compromise of half-track blocksize on 3380s is recommended for sequential I/O.

These conclusions apply only as long as the I/O subsystem operates in the same manner. If the logical structure of the software processes of issuing an I/O or if the physical devices change in structure, there might be a different set of criteria for minimizing I/O costs. A new design could totally eliminate the problem. If I/O were dynamically managed by the system (system-managed storage), attributes such as blocksize and buffers could be dynamically set to be optimum for the device and operating system characteristics, with no user involvement. Users could request storage in megabytes and describe planned usage (20 times per hour,

1 time per week, and so forth) as well as the response requirements (for example, 30 milliseconds per I/O) and its application owner, and let the system do the rest. It is within the scope of operating system design to manage the storage in a manner that dynamically optimizes the processor, memory, and response of an I/O.

Meanwhile, however, you must find the users who process sequential I/O with poor blocksize and buffers, causing you to buy a larger processor than needed. With the data available in SMF, QSAM and BSAM files can be accurately analyzed and frequently used files identified. The purpose of the analysis routine ANALDSET (see chapter forty-one) is to analyze I/O usage by data set and user.

SMF provides comprehensive information on data set placement, usage, and audit trails. The SAS data set TYPE1415 contains most of the needed information; however, TYPE1415 must be processed first in order to calculate I/O activity because EXCPs accumulate across multiple opens, and the number of EXCPs in an individual 14 or 15 record has no meaning unless it is known that no multiple open occurred. Furthermore, to analyze the usage of data sets properly, data set information should be combined with program information so that file usage by program can be examined and the program that creates files, especially files with poor I/O attributes, can be identified. This requires an interleave of TYPE1415 and TYPE30_4 data sets to build the DATABASE data set and is done with the program ANALDSET.

The process is complex for three reasons:

1. Multiple type 14 or 15 records can be written for the same data set in the same step because a 14 or 15 record is written each time a file is closed.
2. There is no step number in type 14 or 15 records. Thus, use of the same file and data set names in 2 different steps cannot be differentiated (in TYPE1415) from the same file in 1 step.
3. The EXCP count in each type 14 or 15 record has no meaning because the EXCP count to a file accumulates across multiple opens.

These problems are resolved in ANALDSET, which uses either the MXG PDB.STEPS data set for step information or the same SMF file from which TYPE1415 was built. Because of the volume of 14 and 15 records, ANALDSET uses tapes for large data sets and minimizes the use of tape drives by using unit affinity (UNIT=AFF) in its JCL. ANALDSET extracts and builds 2 data sets, SORTSTEP and SORT1415, and then interleaves them by time into data set ADDPROG, which adds step number, program name, step ABEND and condition code, and step name to the TYPE1415 information. If MXG PDB.STEPS is used, the first 2 job accounting fields are also added to the observation.

Data set ADDPROG is then resorted within the job by STEP, DDname (DDN), unit address (UNITADR), and SMF time. The logic then unaccumulates the accumulated EXCPs to produce entries in data set SUBEXCP with correct EXCPs for each OPEN of each file. After SUBEXCP has been sorted, the data set

DATABASE is built from the individual opens, accumulating the EXCP count
to produce 1 observation with the total EXCPs for each type of OPEN for each
file and the data set and volume serial used in each job. DATABASE can be the
source of many analyses. In fact, because of the relatively high cost of ANALDSET
(approximately 10-15 3081K CPU minutes to process 1 week's data from a
3081K) and because data set attributes change so slowly, it is sufficient to build
DATABASE from 1 week's data once every quarter.

DATABASE is useful for identifying exceptionally light and heavy users of I/O
resources. The output, resulting from the MEANS procedure is shown in Example
13.1. By scanning the minimum and maximum values of important variables, you
get a profile of I/O usage at your installation.

For example, the maximum value of NROPENs, the number of times a file was
opened in the same step is 572. Although multiple OPENs are sometimes necessary, 572 OPENs in the same step can indicate poor programming. By selecting
records with NROPENs greater than from DATABASE, programs with many
OPENS can be identified.

```
                   OVERALL STATISTICS ON DATABASE ANALYSIS

 VARIABLE      N        MEAN       MINIMUM        MAXIMUM         SUM
                                   VALUE          VALUE

 RECIND    11299     37.19055    0.00000000      112.00       420216.0
 NUCB      11299      1.21860    1.00000000       11.00        13769.0
 TIOESTTA  11299      1.68103    1.00000000       17.00        18994.0
 TIOEWTCT  11299      1.00690    1.00000000        3.00        11377.0
 TIOELINK  11299     30.64342    0.00000000      128.00       346240.0
 TIOESTTC  11299      0.00000    0.00000000        0.00            0.0
 BUFNO     11299      0.00000    0.00000000        0.00            0.0
 MSSCVOLI  11299      0.00000    0.00000000        0.00            0.0
 VOLSEQ    11299      0.00292    0.00000000        4.00           33.0
 JFCBUFNO  11299      0.49553    0.00000000       32.00         5599.0
 BUFTEK    11299      9.23480    0.00000000       98.00       104344.0
 BUFFLEN   11299    361.43402    0.00000000    12960.00      4083843.0
 JFCBOPCD  11299     13.81069    0.00000000      219.00       156047.0
 BLKSIZE   11299   5265.12497    0.00000000    32760.00     59490647.0
 LRECL     11299    841.05301    0.00000000    32768.00      9503058.0
 NRVOLS    11299      1.01097    1.00000000        5.00        11423.0
 JFCFLGSI  11299    126.53297    0.00000000      160.00      1429696.0
 AVGBLK    11299    495.51748    0.00000000    19069.00      5598852.0
 DCBOFLGS  11299     55.03151   19.00000000      159.00       621801.0
 DCBOPTCD  11299      3.47482    0.00000000      219.00        39262.0
 DEBOFLGS  11299    131.34038    0.00000000      255.00      1484015.0
```

(continued on next page)

(continued from previous page)

DEBOPATB	11299	10.65953	0.00000000	255.00	120442.0
DEBVLSEQ	11299	1282.17639	0.00000000	65416.00	14487311.0
FILESEQ	802	1.38653	1.00000000	10.00	1112.0
TRTCH	802	0.00000	0.00000000	0.00	0.0
DEN	802	5993.51621	200.00000000	6250.00	4806800.0
KEYLEN	10497	0.66114	0.00000000	58.00	6940.0
PRIALOC	10497	61.16519	0.00000000	6000.00	642051.0
JFCBCTRI	10497	130.37744	0.00000000	201.00	1368572.0
SECALOC	10497	1192.83748	0.00000000	25688.00	12521215.0
TTRN	10497	2788074.85567	0.00000000	3777429504.00	29266421760.0
TRKREL	10497	2.01943	0.00000000	1470.00	21198.0
EXTREL	10497	0.00171	0.00000000	15.00	18.0
CRDATE	11299	74837.06178	0.00000000	78203.00	845583961.0
EXPDT	11299	3344.67298	0.00000000	99366.00	37791460.0
LIMCT	983	100.49339	0.00000000	19254.00	98785.0
UCBSTAB	11299	13.40933	8.00000000	80.00	151512.0
NEXTENT	11299	1.92619	0.00000000	16.00	21764.0
UNITADR	11299	744.49075	512.00000000	1663.00	8412001.0
DSSEQCNT	802	1.38529	0.00000000	10.00	1111.0
DSSEQNR	802	1.38529	0.00000000	10.00	1111.0
TRKSALOC	10497	364.81433	0.00000000	16650.00	3829456.0
NRLEVELS	598	0.90301	0.00000000	1.00	540.0
EXCPOFLO	598	12.09030	0.00000000	447.00	7230.0
RECPRIME	598	62519.76087	2.00000000	2784179.00	37386817.0
TRKSLEFT	598	33.59197	0.00000000	298.00	20088.0
RECOFLOW	598	88.85452	0.00000000	2093.00	53135.0
CYLOFULL	598	0.08027	0.00000000	2.00	48.0
EXTINDEX	598	0.35284	0.00000000	1.00	211.0
EXTPRIME	598	1.33445	1.00000000	2.00	798.0
EXTOFLO	598	0.19732	0.00000000	1.00	118.0
CYLINDEX	598	0.42809	0.00000000	10.00	256.0
CYLPRIME	598	20.09365	1.00000000	420.00	12016.0
CYLOFLO	598	0.61538	0.00000000	10.00	368.0
STEP	9910	4.73986	1.00000000	60.00	46972.0
CONDCODE	9910	57.32886	0.00000000	8264.00	568129.0
NROPENS	11299	1.96557	1.00000000	572.00	22209.0
EXCPS	11299	399.43075	0.00000000	155330.00	4513168.0
BLKCNTS	11299	102.85485	0.00000000	44253.00	1162157.0

Example 13.1 Overall Statistics on DATABASE Analysis

Example 13.2 shows how to trace unblocked I/O through a simple crosstabulation of record format (RECFM) and data set organization (DSORG) weighted by the number of EXCPs. The output shows the breakdown of unblocked files and the kind of data sets and record formats in use at this installation.

Weighting in the FREQ procedure is helpful in initial data surveys. Column percentages show that 61.6% of this installation's I/O is physical sequential. Over 20% of all EXCPs (921,648) are counted by fixed record format against physical sequential data sets (which should be fixed-blocked). One crosstabulation has identified 20% of the EXCPs needing improvement.

```
PROC FREQ;
  TABLES RECFM*DSORG;
  WEIGHT EXCPS;

                        TABLE OF RECFM BY DSORG
    RECFM           DSORG

    FREQUENCY  |
      PERCENT  |
      ROW PCT  |
      COL PCT  | DA          | IS          | PO          | PS          | TOTAL
```

	DA	IS	PO	PS	TOTAL
F	158214	111610	13467	921648	1204939
	3.51	2.47	0.30	20.42	26.70
	13.13	9.26	1.12	76.49	
	38.17	11.98	3.51	33.11	
FB	32	819758	32267	1025870	1877927
	0.00	18.16	0.71	22.73	41.61
	0.00	43.65	1.72	54.63	
	0.01	88.02	8.42	36.85	
U	99048	0	336540	480850	916438
	2.19	0.00	7.46	10.65	20.31
	10.81	0.00	36.72	52.47	
	23.89	0.00	87.81	17.27	
V	0	0	0	10816	10816
	0.00	0.00	0.00	0.24	0.24
	0.00	0.00	0.00	100.00	
	0.00	0.00	0.00	0.39	
VB	157235	0	996	157004	315235
	3.48	0.00	0.02	3.48	6.98
	49.88	0.00	0.32	49.81	
	37.93	0.00	0.26	5.64	

(continued on next page)

(continued from previous page)

VBS	0	0	0	176097	176097
	0.00	0.00	0.00	3.90	3.90
	0.00	0.00	0.00	100.00	
	0.00	0.00	0.00	6.33	
VS	0	0	0	11716	11716
	0.00	0.00	0.00	0.26	0.26
	0.00	0.00	0.00	100.00	
	0.00	0.00	0.00	0.42	
TOTAL	414529	931368	383270	2784001	4513168
	9.18	20.64	8.49	61.69	100.00

Example 13.2 Table of RECFM by DSORG

Why is so much I/O done with RECFM=F at physical sequential? Although other record types could be used, Example 13.3 follows the fixed physical sequential data usage to find the answer. Here, DATABASE is subsetted for only those observations that are physical sequential files with RECFM=F. Perhaps a program specifying fixed-record format is poorly written, so a frequency tabulation of program names that could be causing the problem is produced. (The 5405 EXCPs with no program names are from TYPE1415 observations that did not match with TYPE30_4 because the step was still active when SMF was dumped.) The program EASYTREV stands out because it produced over 33% of the total I/O.

```
DATA;
  SET DATABASE;
  IF DSORG='PS' AND RECFM='F';
PROC FREQ;
  TABLES PROGRAM;
  WEIGHT EXCPS;

   PROGRAM      FREQUENCY        CUM FREQ    PERCENT   CUM PERCENT

                  5405               .           .            .
   CLEARS2K        366              366        0.040        0.040
   CPXUPTSM         68              434        0.007        0.047
   CSCBDB01          7              441        0.001        0.048
   DFSRRC00        212              653        0.023        0.071
   DGFP2C02          2              655        0.000        0.071
```

(continued on next page)

(continued from previous page)

DGIS2C03	10	665	0.001	0.073
DGIS2C07	9600	10265	1.048	1.120
DGIS2C17	9000	19265	0.982	2.103
EARCSC75	1368	20633	0.149	2.252
EASYTREV	308342	328975	33.653	35.905
FSPSCOMP	893	329868	0.097	36.002
FSPSREPL	8	329876	0.001	36.003
FSSM3100	16	329892	0.002	36.005
HEWL	5735	335627	0.626	36.631
HMPGA112	754	336381	0.082	36.713
HSPGA112	259	336640	0.028	36.741
HWFA0C10	12900	465640	14.079	50.821
IBISCON	3	465643	0.000	50.821
IEBGENER	6114	471757	0.667	51.488
IEHLIST	22364	494121	2.441	53.929
IEV90	158	494279	0.017	53.946
IEWL	3325	497604	0.363	54.309
IKFCBL00	9608	507212	1.049	55.358
IKJEFT01	46647	553859	5.091	60.449
INIT3350	34501	588360	3.765	64.214
MFEDIT1	430	588790	0.047	64.261
NITAWL	500	589290	0.055	64.316
OPSSMF	5	589295	0.001	64.316
PCOMPMP	304	589599	0.033	64.350
PRCOMC	15208	604807	1.660	66.009
RAIL1390	1507	606314	0.164	66.174
SIMIFSS	40417	646731	4.411	70.585
SYS2K	31	646762	0.003	70.588
S2000	183	646945	0.020	70.608
TCRCREAT	372	647317	0.041	70.649
TMSDATA	150505	797822	16.426	87.075
TP2000	2884	800706	0.315	87.390
UPDTWR	13	800719	0.001	87.392
VMSEDIT	115524	916243	12.608	100.000

Example 13.3

Example 13.4 shows 3 different tabulations, weighted by EXCPs, of DATABASE observations that executed EASYTREV. The file name (DDname) tabulation shows that all are user-specified file names rather than those files created internally by EASYTREV. Examination of data set names shows that most unblocked I/O by EASYTREV went to temporary data sets.

From a look at the jobs using EASYTREV, the problem becomes clear. One job, DRUGNOL, accounts for 71% of the fixed EXCPs. These data, combined with the preceding information, show that 1 user of EASYTREV is creating user-specified temporary files that are physical, sequential, and RECFM=F.

```
DATA;
  SET DATABASE;
  IF PROGRAM='EASYTREV';
PROC FREQ;
  TABLES DDN DSNAME JOB;
  WEIGHT EXCPS;
```

DDN	FREQUENCY	CUM FREQ	PERCENT	CUM PERCENT
FILEA	95226	95226	30.833	30.883
FILEB	213083	308309	69.106	99.989
FILE2	33	308342	0.011	100.000

DSNAME	FREQUENCY	CUM FREQ	PERCENT	CUM PERCENT
CPM.A3E500.SUNMA	88508	88508	28.704	28.704
SYS78203.T063055	177015	265523	57.409	86.113
SYS78203.T084554	19755	285278	6.407	92.520
SYS78203.T093251	19329	304607	6.269	98.789
SYS78203.T100637	3150	307757	1.022	99.810
SYS78203.T122239	206	307963	0.067	99.877
MVTVY03.T124809	206	308169	0.067	99.944
SYS78203.T131639	2	308171	0.001	99.945
CPM.SORT.UPDATE	42	308213	0.014	99.958
CPM.SORTED.ADDS	129	308342	0.042	100.000

JOB	FREQUENCY	CUM FREQ	PERCENT	CUM PERCENT
VECXA71	171	171	0.055	0.055
DRUGNOL	221269	221440	71.761	71.816
C35CA20	86488	307928	28.049	99.866
WKD601F	414	308342	0.134	100.000

Example 13.4

Except for several SMF anomalies described in section TYPE1415 of chapter forty, the preceding discussion and analysis of DATABASE is complete. Not all type 14 and 15 records reflect the number of EXCPs issued: EXCP accounting does not occur for cases when the access method is EXCP. As described earlier, EXCPs done by program FETCH from STEPLIBs are partially counted in MVS/370 and are counted slightly differently in MVS/XA, as described in chapter twenty-four. Concatenated partitioned data sets accessed by BPAM* reflect only the name of the first data set in the concatenation list and create only one type 14 or 15 record per open, even though many different data sets can be involved.

---

* A PDS name without a member name appears in the JCL, as it does for STEPLIB, SYSLIB, SORTLIB, and so forth. When the member name is specified in the JCL, the access method is BSAM, not BPAM.

In some cases, it may be necessary to find all tasks that use a specific unit address, for example, in a conversion from 3350 to 3380 disks. DATABASE can provide tasks that open a data set on the device. What may be needed instead is to identify tasks that still have DD cards pointing to the device to be removed. If you can identify all users of the departing device, you can advise them to change their JCL in advance of the change in hardware, preventing a JCL error in their production job stream and allowing you to gain their goodwill. Type 30 records contain a segment for every device allocated, whether opened or not, and macro IMAC30DD, described in chapter thirty-two, can create data set TYPE30_D for those devices whose usage is to be monitored.

It may be unnecessary to look at DATABASE to analyze I/O since PDB.STEPS contains total EXCPs to each device class. In many cases, identifying which job and which class of device the I/O comes from is sufficient.

A final example of the value of DATABASE is given in Example 13.5, a series of frequency distributions on significant variables that thoroughly describe the use of the I/O resource in an installation.

```
 TITLE 'OVERALL STATISTICS ON DATABASE ANALYSIS';
PROC FREQ DATA=DATABASE;
  TABLES ALOC;
PROC FREQ DATA=DATABASE;
  TABLES ACCESS DSORG RECFM TEMP OPEN;
  WEIGHT EXCPS;
PROC FREQ DATA=DATABASE;
  TABLES DISP*TEMP TEMP*OPEN;
  WEIGHT EXCPS;
```

                  OVERALL STATISTICS ON DATABASE ANALYSIS

ALOC	FREQUENCY	CUM FREQ	PERCENT	CUM PERCENT
	3269	.	.	.
ABSTR	819	819	10.199	10.199
BLOCK	2634	3453	32.802	43.001
CYL	4577	8030	56.999	100.000

(continued on next page)

(continued from previous page)

OVERALL STATISTICS ON DATABASE ANALYSIS

ACCESS	FREQUENCY	CUM FREQ	PERCENT	CUM PERCENT
BDAM	143240	143240	3.174	3.174
BDSAM	14634	157874	0.324	3.498
BISAM	181765	339639	4.027	7.526
BPSAM	89850	429489	1.991	9.516
BSAM	666994	1096483	14.779	24.295
EXCP	1009853	2106336	22.376	46.671
QISAM	749603	2855939	16.609	63.280
QSAM	1657229	4513168	36.720	100.000

OVERALL STATISTICS ON DATABASE ANALYSIS

DSORG	FREQUENCY	CUM FREQ	PERCENT	CUM PERCENT
DA	414529	414529	9.185	9.185
IS	931368	1345897	20.637	29.822
PO	383270	1729167	8.492	38.314
PS	2784001	4513168	61.686	100.000

OVERALL STATISTICS ON DATABASE ANALYSIS

RECFM	FREQUENCY	CUM FREQ	PERCENT	CUM PERCENT
F	1204939	1204939	26.698	26.698
FB	1877927	3082866	41.610	68.308
U	916438	3999304	20.306	88.614
V	10816	4010120	0.240	88.854
VB	315235	4325355	6.985	95.839
VBS	176097	4501452	3.902	99.740
VS	11716	4513168	0.260	100.000

TEMP	FREQUENCY	CUM FREQ	PERCENT	CUM PERCENT
PERM	3392791	3392791	75.175	75.175
TEMP	1120377	4513168	24.825	100.000

(continued on next page)

(continued from previous page)

OPEN	FREQUENCY	CUM FREQ	PERCENT	CUM PERCENT
INOUT	159148	159148	3.526	3.526
INPUT	2643042	2802190	58.563	62.089
OTHER	152790	2954980	3.385	65.475
OUTIN	107990	3062970	2.393	67.867
OUTPUT	1259718	4322688	27.912	95.779
UPDATE	190480	4513168	4.221	100.000

OVERALL STATISTICS ON DATABASE ANALYSIS

TABLE OF DISP BY TEMP

DISP FREQUENCY PERCENT ROW PCT COL PCT	TEMP PERM	TEMP	TOTAL
MOD	750681 16.63 45.39 22.13	903300 20.01 54.61 80.62	1653981 36.65
OLD	1092240 24.20 83.74 32.19	212122 4.70 16.26 18.93	1304362 28.90
SHR	1549870 34.34 99.68 45.68	4955 0.11 0.32 0.44	1554825 34.45
TOTAL	3392791 75.18	1120377 24.82	4513168 100.00

(continued on next page)

(continued from previous page)

OVERALL STATISTICS ON DATABASE ANALYSIS

TABLE OF TEMP BY OPEN

TEMP   OPEN

FREQUENCY PERCENT ROW PCT COL PCT	INOUT	INPUT	OTHER	OUTIN	OUTPUT	UPDATE	TOTAL
PERM	144083	2289135	152665	35420	661247	110241	3392791
	3.19	50.72	3.38	0.78	14.65	2.44	75.18
	4.25	67.47	4.50	1.04	19.49	3.25	
	90.53	86.61	99.92	32.80	52.49	57.88	
TEMP	15065	353907	125	72570	598471	80239	1120377
	0.33	7.84	0.00	1.61	13.26	1.78	24.82
	1.34	31.59	0.01	6.48	53.42	7.16	
	9.47	13.39	0.08	67.20	47.51	42.12	
TOTAL	159148	2643042	152790	107990	1259718	190480	4513168
	3.53	58.56	3.39	2.39	27.91	4.22	100.00

Example 13.5

It is difficult to provide any stable guidelines for the analysis of I/O because of the diverse applications, goals, and purposes of installations. However, the complete information in RMF 73 and 74 records permits a good analysis of which device is causing significant I/O delays. At that point, data set usage can be identified through SAS data set TYPE1415 and the ANALDSET routine, or, less optimally, GTF analysis can be used to determine data set placement on the volumes causing delays. The key to success in management of the I/O subsystem, however, begins with minimization of contention first and application changes second.

chapter fourteen

Resource Measurement - Tapes and Tape Drives

The number of tape drives required by an installation depends not only on the tape usage but also on the job entry subsystem allocation algorithm. Although JES3 is described, the analysis techniques of tape usage apply only to the JES2 algorithm. The SMF step records determine if we are delaying jobs because of insufficient tape drives and identify tape drive usage by job. SMF does not provide measures of time to mount volumes, but the step information does count mounts by job. Finally, the TYPE21 (tape error statistics) data set is used for both JES2 and JES3 to address management of tape media.

There are major differences in JES2 and JES3 algorithms for allocating tape drives. JES3 main device scheduling offers several options that permit FETCH, which tells the tape librarian to get a tape volume and bring it to the tape drive area, and SETUP, which causes drive allocation and mount, in advance of job execution. The time stamps of these scheduling events are provided in the TYPE25 data set, and their interpretation depends on the choices made by the JES3 installation. JES3, following the design of its predecessor ASP, allows tape resources to be pre-allocated before the job is selected for initiation. This means that the job is ready to execute when initiated, but this approach usually requires more tape drives since drives are allocated but not usable until the job is initiated. Furthermore, a JES3 job that requires a tape drive in a later step will have owned its tape drives for the elapsed time of all preceding steps. Although not the only option JES3 offers, it is a common implementation, dependent on local installation requirements.

In JES2, allocation occurs after step initiation. JES2 does not pre-allocate tape drives, so it uses fewer tape drives. One tape drive is allocated for every DD statement that points to a tape data set unless UNIT=AFF is specified to serialize tape volumes on the same unit(s). The tape drive at allocation causes an allocation recovery event, and the job step may have to wait (owning an initiator) until a tape drive becomes available.

Note: allocation recovery offers the operator three choices: the operator can reply CANCEL to cancel the job (this action wastes all work accomplished by the job so far and requires at least that the job be rerun); WAIT to allow the job to wait until a tape drive is freed by another job; or enter a device number to vary that off-line tape drive on-line and allocate it to the job in allocation recovery. This command is seldom used since the drive should have been on-line in the first place. If the operator replies WAIT, he must decide whether resources allocated to this job so far are to be held or released. For example, perhaps the job has allocated two tape drives and is in allocation recovery for the third and final drive it needs. Do you want to keep the two drives and wait for one more (YES to HOLD)? Or should the two drives be released for other jobs to use while you still wait for this task (NO to HOLD)?

Tape Drive Utilization in a JES2 Environment

How many tape drives are needed? What impact do tape drives have on work scheduling? The following discussion deals with tape drive utilization in a JES2 environment. (In JES3 with pre-execution volume fetch, the analysis is slightly more difficult, but data in the type 25 records may be adequate to permit a similar approach.) Since tape drives are allocated at the step basis in JES2, step records provide most of the information concerning tape drive utilization.

Type 10 SMF record (allocation recovery)   A type 10 SMF record is only written when the operator replies with a device number to the allocation recovery event to vary that device on-line for that job. Tape drives should not normally be off-line; thus, the typical strategy is to reply WAIT with NOHOLD. In that case, the job step waits until sufficient devices become available as a result of other step terminations, but no type 10 allocation recovery record is written. Even when written, type 10 records contain no measure of how long the task was delayed.

Allocation recovery   All is not lost, however, because job steps that enter allocation recovery do so at the time stamp ALOCTIME, as discussed in chapter seven. All allocations for that step are completed by LOADTIME. By analyzing ALOCTM in data set TYPE30_4 or PDB.STEPS, particularly the difference between LOADTIME and ALOCTIME, those job steps with an allocation recovery can be detected.

It is sometimes possible for ALOCTM to be significant and yet not be the result of an allocation recovery. If the processor is placed in STOP while the step is in allocation or if a RESERVE conflict prevents the operating system from responding to the allocation, the ALOCTM duration could imply that an allocation recovery occurred when actually one did not. These occurrences are rare but should be considered when using ALOCTM to infer that a delay did occur.

The time to allocate a DD depends on the device type and the disposition of the data set being allocated. Allocating a pre-existing disk data set or any tape data set is simple when compared to allocation of a new disk data set. (For a new disk data set, the volume table of contents must be scanned to find space.) Unfortunately, SMF provides only the total number of DDs allocated in each step, so you must estimate the time required to allocate an average DD. By taking a normal day's SMF data, one without allocation recoveries, STOP, and so forth, you can calculate the typical time to allocate each DD by dividing the step ALOCTM by NUMDD. This analysis usually shows an average time per DD of about 0.5 of a second, with a standard deviation of about 1 second. Thus, if you take 5 seconds per DD as the worst possible time to allocate a DD, you can multiply 5 by the number of DDs in each step and compare that expected allocation time to actual ALOCTM. If the step required an average of more than 5 seconds per DD, assume it was a step delayed by allocation recovery.

Tape drive allocation   Example 14.1 shows how delays caused by tape drive allocation can be observed. By selecting TYPE30_4 records for jobs that allocated tape drives and by calculating DELAYTM for steps that were delayed, the PROC MEANS output shows that for all steps that used tape drives, total step elapsed time was 3,219,724 seconds; total delay time for the 262 delayed steps (ALOCTM greater than 5 seconds per DD) was only 85,432 seconds. Thus, less than 3% of the total initiated time of all steps using tape drives was spent waiting for tape drive allocation.

```
DATA DELAYS;
  SET TYPE30_4;
  IF TAPEDRVS > 0;
  IF ALOCTM > 5*NUMDD THEN DELAYTM=ALOCTM;
  KEEP NUMDD EXECTM SELAPTM TAPEDRVS ALOCTIME ALOCTM DELAYTM;
PROC MEANS;
  TITLE 'STATISTICS ON ALLOCATION DELAYS';
```

```
                STATISTICS ON ALLOCATION DELAYS
```

VARIABLE	N	MEAN	MINIMUM VALUE	MAXIMUM VALUE	SUM
NUMDD	8231	12.537	0.00	179.00	1.031940E+ 05
EXECTM	8231	374.177	0.05	58577.02	3.079852E+ 06
SELAPTM	8231	391.170	0.09	58657.60	3.219724E+ 06
TAPEDRVS	8231	0.459	0.00	9.00	3.778000E+ 03
ALOCTIME*	8231	586087818.733	584983231.58	586147534.23	4.824089E+ 12
ALOCTM	8231	15.932	0.01	3823.55	1.311327E+ 05
DELAYTM	262	326.078	0.01	3823.55	8.543236E+ 04

Example 14.1*

The plot in Example 14.2 of the delay time versus time-of-day shows that around midday on July 28, an event occurred that caused a series of job steps to be delayed much longer than at any other time during the day. Investigating SYSLOG showed that an operator had varied a bank of ten tape drives off-line and that it was not discovered for nearly an hour.

---

*Units are seconds since Jan. 1, 1960. SAS DATETIME19.2 format would print value of about noon on July 28, 1978.

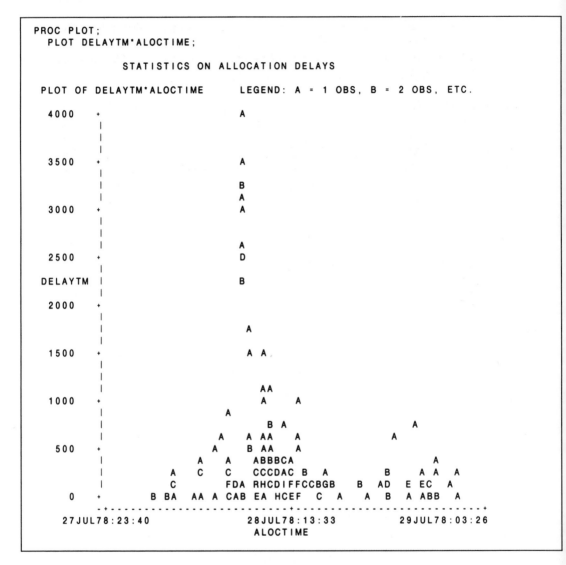

```
PROC PLOT;
  PLOT DELAYTM*ALOCTIME;

               STATISTICS ON ALLOCATION DELAYS

  PLOT OF DELAYTM*ALOCTIME        LEGEND: A = 1 OBS, B = 2 OBS, ETC.

   4000   +                       A
          |
          |
          |
   3500   +                       A
          |
          |                       B
          |                       A
   3000   +                       A
          |
          |
          |                       A
   2500   +                       D
          |
 DELAYTM  |                       B
          |
   2000   +
          |
          |                      A
          |
   1500   +                      A  A
          |
          |
          |                       AA
   1000   +                       A      A
          |                     A
          |                        B  A                   A
          |            A     A AA    A              A
    500   +            A     B AA     A
          |        A    A    ABBBCA                    A
          |     A    C    C    CCCDAC B  A          B     A  A   A
          |     C         FDA  RHCDIFFCCBGB    B   AD  E  EC   A
      0   +  B  BA   AA  A CAB EA HCEF   C   A     A   B   A ABB   A
          -+-------------------------+-------------------------------+
       27JUL78:23:40          28JUL78:13:33           29JUL78:03:26
                                 ALOCTIME
```

Example 14.2

The percentage of initiator time acceptable as delayed time depends on the nature of the installation's service objectives and the nature of the workload. For example, had this long delay occurred during nonprime hours, it would have been of less concern, provided that the delayed jobs met their service objectives. But a significant number of delays lasting over an hour during prime shift could indicate that the installation needs more tape drives.

On the other hand, the total number of tape drives might be adequate; it may be work scheduling that caused peak drive usage. In those cases, the TYPE30_4 data set can still be used to identify job steps that were delayed, job steps that were active during the time of day when jobs were delayed, and the number of tape drives in use by each task. A listing of active jobs and delayed jobs might suggest that certain jobs could be moved to a different time of day to reduce conflicts for tape drives.

The tape drive resource is an uncommonly visible one to operations management because many people are involved in mounting tape volumes. Thus, it is easy to lose perspective and create a major issue concerning the correct number of tape drives. Instead, the preceding approaches provide data that allow rational decisions to be made.

JCL considerations   Frequently, lack of JCL knowledge in programming and data control groups causes jobs to overallocate tape drives. Example 14.3 shows typical JCL that requires four tape drives, even though only one could be used at a time, and it shows how UNIT=AFF should be specified so that this sequential input can be processed with one tape drive.

```
      JCL THAT ALLOCATES FOUR DRIVES


//SMF  DD  DSN=SMF.DAILY(0),DISP=OLD,UNIT=TAPE
//       DD  DSN=SMF.DAILY(-1),DISP=OLD,UNIT=TAPE
//       DD  DSN=SMF.DAILY(-2),DISP=OLD,UNIT=TAPE
//       DD  DSN=SMF.DAILY(-3),DISP=OLD,UNIT=TAPE


      JCL THAT ALLOCATES ONE DRIVE WITH UNIT AFFINITY


//SMF  DD  DSN=SMF.DAILY(0),DISP=OLD,UNIT=TAPE
//       DD  DSN=SMF.DAILY(-1),DISP=OLD,UNIT=AFF=SMF
//       DD  DSN=SMF.DAILY(-2),DISP=OLD,UNIT=AFF=SMF
//       DD  DSN=SMF.DAILY(-3),DISP=OLD,UNIT=AFF=SMF
```

Example 14.3
Unit Affinity to Reduce Allocated Tape Drives

It is tedious to identify directly from SMF that a job should have specified UNIT=AFF by comparing OPENTIME and SMFTIME for each DD using the ANALDSET program discussed in chapter thirteen. A better way is to tabulate jobs that used more than four tape drives. The need for three concurrently open tape files is not unreasonable for many applications, and four concurrently open tape files may be needed occasionally. There are few applications, however, that truly need more than four tape files opened concurrently. Identification of all jobs steps that allocated more than four tape drives usually identifies two or three valid ones, and the remainder are jobs where the user caused more tape drives to be allocated than were required. If the list of such jobs is circulated to the job's owner, along with a brief description of how to specify unit affinity, concerned users can take steps to reduce unintentional overallocation. To motivate users to change their JCL, explain how their carelessness costs them in longer elapsed time since it takes longer to allocate more drives.

The final user effect on tapes is the multiple mounting of the same volume by the same job because RETAIN was not specified in the JCL. Even though there is no guarantee that MVS allocation keeps the same device across steps in a job, the absence of RETAIN almost always guarantees that the tape mounted in step one will be unmounted and remounted in step two, increasing the workload on the tape hangers and the elapsed time of the job. Examination of PDB.JOBS variables TAPEDRVS, TAPSMNTS, and TAPMNTS identifies jobs with many mounts per drive. TAPEDRVS counts the maximum number of tape drives allocated in any step in the JOBS data set; TAPSMNTS counts specific tape mounts with volume serial specified; and TAPNMNTS counts scratch tapes mounted. Those jobs should then be discussed with their owner for possible JCL enhancement to RETAIN the tape volume from step to step.

If there are appreciable I/O errors in accessing tapes, you see much more tape usage since jobs are rerun because of errors, yet you would not normally know if the jobs were original or rerun. For this reason, the data provided in the type 21 SMF record, called the error statistics by volume or ESV record, which contains error counts during that mount, are important. Read section TYPE21 of chapter forty.

Each time a tape is dismounted, a type 21 record is written. This record describes the volume serial number and the unit address on which the tape was mounted and provides statistics for different kinds of errors. The count of errors does not differentiate between media errors and path-caused (device, control unit, and channel) errors and is not conclusive; but it is valuable. Example 14.4 performs a tabulation of the TYPE21 records, using the MXG routine ANALESV. For each unit address, you can see the statistics for all tapes dismounted. This tabulation (especially PCTMNT, the percentage of mounts with errors) shows which tape drives may need cleaning, although a high error count on a particular drive could result from a defective tape volume. The second report also provides a detailed listing of each drive and gives the volumes with errors. The third report tabulates those volume serial numbers with permanent I/O errors.

Again, the fact that a volume mounted had a permanent error does not mean that the volume is defective; the permanent error could have been hardware-related. Nevertheless, volumes with high error frequencies or permanent errors should be candidates for physical cleaning or, perhaps, certification.

By monitoring error-statistics-by-volume on a daily basis, the problem of tape errors can be brought under control. Often, most of the volumes involved in tape errors are in a particular series, perhaps a series that is five or six years old, and it may be appropriate to replace those volumes. On the other hand, installations with poor tape head cleaning practices have a significant number of errors on all tape drives. Showing management the ESV report, by shift, usually leads to cleaner tape drives and fewer problems.

```
DATA FOR THIS RUN WERE COLLECTED BETWEEN FOLLOWING DATE/TIMES

        SYSTEM          MINTIME                 MAXTIME
        C168       29JUL78:03:43:05.42      29JUL78:08:31:55.22

  TAPE READ/WRITE ERRORS BY CHANNEL, CONTROLLER, AND DRIVE ADDRESS

- - - - - - - - - - - - - - - - - - - - - - SYSTEM=C168 - - - - - - - - - - - - - - - - - - - -
```

UNIT ADDR	NR USER	NUSER	PCTMNT	SIOCOUNT	ERRORS	PCTER	TEMPPREAD	TEMPPWRERIT	PERMRWRIAD	PERMRWRIT	NOISE	ERASE	CLEAN	SIO_CHAR
470	5	1	20.0	7108	1	0.0	0	1	0	0	0	1	0	
471	8	2	25.0	10329	8	0.1	1	7	0	0	0	7	0	
472	3	0	0.0	5766	0	0.0	0	0	0	0	0	0	0	
473	7	1	14.3	11776	1	0.0	0	1	0	0	0	1	0	
474	8	3	37.5	26850	11	0.0	0	11	0	0	0	11	0	
475	4	0	0.0	3342	0	0.0	0	0	0	0	0	0	0	
476	5	0	0.0	9084	0	0.0	0	0	0	0	0	0	0	
478	4	3	75.0	7466	5	0.1	2	3	0	0	0	3	0	
479	6	0	0.0	2211	0	0.0	0	0	0	0	0	0	0	
47B	2	0	0.0	230	0	0.0	0	0	0	0	0	0	0	
47C	2	0	0.0	622	0	0.0	0	0	0	0	0	0	0	
47D	1	0	0.0	284	0	0.0	0	0	0	0	0	0	0	
47E	1	0	0.0	214	0	0.0	0	0	0	0	0	0	0	
47F	1	0	0.0	30	0	0.0	0	0	0	0	0	0	0	
490	1	0	0.0	2	0	0.0	0	0	0	0	0	0	0	
491	22	2	9.1	38627	3	0.0	0	2	0	0	0	2	1	
492	5	1	20.0	21471	452	2.1	0	255	0	0	0	452	0	
493	5	0	0.0	5884	0	0.0	0	0	0	0	0	0	0	
494	15	1	6.7	83788	1	0.0	0	1	0	0	0	1	0	

(continued on next page)

(continued from previous page)

```
495   11   2   18.2   15448    4   0.0   0    4   0   0   0    4    0
496   12   3   25.0   43516   51   0.1   0    4   0   0   0    4   47
497   16   3   18.8   19626   11   0.1   0    7   0   0   0   11    0
498    5   0    0.0    6551    0   0.0   0    0   0   0   0    0    0
49B    5   0    0.0   21332    0   0.0   0    0   0   0   0    0    0
49C    5   0    0.0   21165    0   0.0   0    0   0   0   0    0    0
49D    4   1   25.0     319    1   0.3   0    1   0   0   0    1    0
49E    1   0    0.0       2    0   0.0   0    0   0   0   0    0    0
49F    3   0    0.0   16649    0   0.0   0    0   0   0   0    0    0
670    2   0    0.0     533    0   0.0   0    0   0   0   0    0    0
671   13   3   23.1    9390   14   0.1   3    1   0   0   0    1   11
672    4   0    0.0    1320    0   0.0   0    0   0   0   0    0    0
673    3   0    0.0    2823    0   0.0   0    0   0   0   0    0    0
674    7   3   42.9   47928    5   0.0   0    5   0   0   0    5    0
675    5   2   40.0   14610    8   0.1   6    2   0   0   0    2    0
676    6   0    0.0    5746    0   0.0   0    0   0   0   0    0    0
678    1   0    0.0      21    0   0.0   0    0   0   0   0    0    0
679    1   0    0.0    5368    0   0.0   0    0   0   0   0    0    0
67A    2   1   50.0     342    1   0.3   0    1   0   0   0    1    0
67C    4   1   25.0    2071    2   0.1   0    2   0   0   0    2    0
```

UNIT ADDRESS STATISTICS WITH ALL ERROR VOLUMES LISTED BY VOLSER

- SYSTEM=C168   UNITADR=492 -

```
              N                 S                      T  T      T  P  P                    S
              R                 I                      E  E      E  E  E                    I
   V          U      P          O         E       P    M  M      M  R  R                    O
   O    N     S      C          C         R       C    P  P      P  M  M   N       E   C    _
   L    R     E      T          O         R       T    R  R      W  R  W   O       R   L    H
   S    U     E      M          O         O       E    E  E      R  E  R   I       A   E    A
   E    S     R      N          U         R       E    A  A      I  A  I   S       S   A    R
   R    E     R      T          N         R       R    D  D      T  D  T   E       E   N    D

234928   1   1   100.0    359     2   0.3   0   0     2   0   0   0     2   0
238578   1   1   100.0   3306   452   0.0   0   0   255   0   0   0   452   0
```

(continued on next page)

(continued from previous page)

UNIT ADDRESS STATISTICS WITH ALL ERROR VOLUMES LISTED BY VOLSER

- SYSTEM=C168   UNITADR=494 -

V O L S E R	N R U S E R	N S E E R S E R	P C T M N T	S I O C O U N T	E R R O R S	P C T E R R R S	T E M P R R E A D D	T E M P R R E A A D D	T E M P R W R I T E	P E R R M R E A D D	P E R R M W R O I S E	N O R I S E	E C R L A E S E	S I O _ C H A R D
238598	1	1	100.0	1727	1	0.1	0	0	1	0	0	0	1	0

UNIT ADDRESS STATISTICS WITH ALL ERROR VOLUMES LISTED BY VOLSER

- SYSTEM=C168   UNITADR=495 -

V O L S E R	N R U S E R	N S E E R S E R	P C T M N T	S I O C O U N T	E R R O R S	P C T E R R R S	T E M P R R E A D D	T E M P R R E A A D D	T E M P R W R I T E	P E R R M R E A D D	P E R R M W R O I S E	N O R I S E	E C R L A E S E	S I O _ C H A R D
197553	1	1	100.0	5368	1	0.0	0	0	1	0	0	0	1	0
214091	1	1	100.0	1541	3	0.1	0	0	3	0	0	0	3	0
218586	1	1	100.0	2529	1	0.0	1	1	0	0	0	0	0	0
240824	1	1	100.0	168	1	0.6	0	0	1	0	0	0	1	0

(continued on next page)

(continued from previous page)

VOLSERS WITH HIGH NUMBER OF USES WITH ERRORS OR HIGH ERRORS

- SYSTEM=C168 -

VOLSER	NRUSES	NRUSER	PCT	SIOCOUNT	ERRORS	PCTERR	TEMPREAD	TEMPWRIT	PERMREAD	PERMWRIT	NOISE	ERROR	CLEAN	SIO_HARD
208211	3	3	100.0	3692	65	1.8	1	7	0	0	0	7	58	
238578	1	1	100.0	3306	452	13.7	0	255	0	0	0	452	0	
239176	2	1	50.0	525	8	1.5	0	4	0	0	0	8	0	

Example 14.4

The SAS source code for these examples of tape resource analysis is found in member ANALTAPE of SOURCLIB.

chapter fifteen

Resource Measurement - Printing

Just as operations management often sees tape drives as a limiting resource, printer utilization is of concern because printed output is the final feedback to the user. It is not uncommon to find a $6 million computer not meeting objectives because of insufficient $10 thousand printers.

Printers are owned by JES. When a job or session is executing, if it opens a sysout data set, JES intercepts the program I/O and writes the data to be printed (perhaps in compressed form) on the spool data set owned by JES. When the job ends on MVS (or if FREE=CLOSE is specified in the DD), the output can be processed by a JES writer, which actually prints the sysout data from the spool. For each sysout data set printed on a printer, a separate type 6 SMF record is written by JES, containing information that includes lines actually printed, form number, destination (remote number and printer number), and so forth. When the final print file is processed, the job is purged and the type 26 job purge record is written. This record contains the count of records written to spool. Read sections TYPE6 and TYPE26J2 of chapter forty.

In addition to statistics on the actual printing, duration of printing and duration in the print queue can be calculated from SMF records. TYPE26J2 and TYPE26J3 data sets contain time stamps for the time that the output processor finished making all output for the job available for printing (JFINTIME) and for the time all printing was completed (JPURTIME). Unfortunately, between JFINTIME and JPURTIME many things occur, including printing. The duration should represent the time in the print queue plus the time to print. Sometimes, however, output is held (especially output to be viewed by TSO users) at the user's request, and this causes a long duration. Thus, you should not take the duration from JFINTIME to JPURTIME as the print queue plus printer elapsed time.

The best approximation for analyzing printer delays requires merging the TYPE6 and TYPE26 data sets as shown in the code preceding Example 15.1. This merge is an implicit part of BUILDPDB in building data sets PDB.PRINT and PDB.JOBS data sets. PRINTIME is the time in TYPE6 when each file begins to print. The selection must eliminate TSO sessions for two reasons.

1. Much of the TSO SYSOUT printing is done while the session is still in execution (prior to JFINTIME) because FREE=CLOSE is specified for TSO SYSOUT to cause printing before LOGOFF.
2. The print queue time is not measurable (at least not without significant labor and gross assumptions) because it would require matching the time of the TYPE40 record, which freed the file, with the TYPE6 record,

which indicates that the file was printed. There is (not yet) a time stamp
SMF 6 when the file was actually made ready (FREE) to print.

```
     PROC SORT DATA=TYPE6;
       BY READTIME JOB;
     PROC SORT DATA=TYPE26J2;
       BY READTIME JOB;
     PROC MEANS DATA=TYPE6 NOPRINT;
       BY READTIME JOB;
       OUTPUT OUT=PRINTGOT SUM=NRLINES MIN=PRINTIME;
       VAR NRLINES PRINTIME;
     DATA PRINTER;
       MERGE TYPE26J2(IN=INJES) TYPE6(IN=INWTR);
       BY READTIME JOB;
       IF INJES AND INWTR;
       IF JOB TSO='J';
       PRQUETM=(PRINTIME-JFINTIME)/60;
       PRINTTM=(JPURTIME-PRINTIME)/60;
       KEEP NRLINES PRINTTM PRQUETM;
     PROC CHART;
       HBAR NRLINES PRQUETM PRINTTM;
       TITLE 'DISTRIBUTION OF CALCULATED PRINT QUEUE AND PRINT
          EXECUTION TIMES';
```

```
        DISTRIBUTION OF CALCULATED PRINT QUEUE AND PRINT EXECUTION TIMES
                          FREQUENCY BAR CHART
 MIDPOINT
 NRLINES                                 FREQ  CUM.    PERCENT    CUM.
                                               FREQ               PERCENT

          |
   15000  |**************************  277   277    96.85     96.85
          |
   45000  |                             1    278    0.35      97.20
          |
   75000  |                             2    280    0.70      97.90
          |
  105000  |                             3    283    1.05      98.95
          |
  135000  |                             2    285    0.70      99.65
          |
  225000  |                             1    286    0.35     100.00
          |
          ----+----+----+----+----+---
              50   100  150  200  250
                FREQUENCY
```

(continued on next page)

(continued from previous page)

DISTRIBUTION OF CALCULATED PRINT QUEUE AND PRINT EXECUTION TIMES
FREQUENCY BAR CHART

MIDPOINT
PRQUETM

	FREQ	CUM. FREQ	PERCENT	CUM. PERCENT
60	216	216	75.52	75.52
100	18	234	6.29	81.82
300	7	241	2.45	84.27
420	13	254	4.55	88.81
540	21	275	7.34	96.15
660	3	278	1.05	97.20
780	2	280	0.70	97.90
1020	6	286	2.10	100.00

```
          |
       60 |* * * * * * * * * * * * * * * * * * * * * * * * * * *    216   216   75.52   75.52
          |
      100 |* *                                                       18   234    6.29   81.82
          |
      300 |*                                                          7   241    2.45   84.27
          |
      420 |* *                                                       13   254    4.55   88.81
          |
      540 |* * *                                                     21   275    7.34   96.15
          |
      660 |                                                           3   278    1.05   97.20
          |
      780 |                                                           2   280    0.70   97.90
          |
     1020 |*                                                          6   286    2.10  100.00
          |
          - - - -+- - -+- - -+- - -+- - -+- - -+- - -+-
             30   60   90  120  150  180  210
                          FREQUENCY
```

DISTRIBUTION OF CALCULATED PRINT QUEUE AND PRINT EXECUTION TIMES
FREQUENCY BAR CHART

MIDPOINT
PRINTTM

	FREQ	CUM. FREQ	PERCENT	CUM. PERCENT
40	278	278	97.20	97.20
120	4	282	1.40	98.60
200	3	285	1.05	99.65
600	1	286	0.35	100.00

```
          |
       40 |* * * * * * * * * * * * * * * * * * * * * * * * * *      278   278   97.20   97.20
          |
      120 |                                                          4   282    1.40   98.60
          |
      200 |                                                          3   285    1.05   99.65
          |
      600 |                                                          1   286    0.35  100.00
          |
          - - - -+- - - -+- - - -+- - - -+- - - -+- - -
             50   100   150   200   250
                          FREQUENCY
```

Example 15.1

The estimated time in the printer queue (PRQUETM) and the estimated time to print (PRINTTM) are easily calculated, and the CHART procedure is then used to produce the 3 frequency distributions, as shown in Example 15.1. Even though there are still potential errors in both the queue time and the printing time, these 3 charts show that the vast majority (75%) of printing is started within 2 hours (midpoint=60 minutes implies interval lengths of 120 minutes) and that 97% of printing took less than 80 minutes. The third chart shows that 96% of all jobs printed less than 30 thousand lines, although at least 1 job printed over 225 thousand lines. The durations here are affected by mounting forms, stopping the printer to replace paper, and so forth. It is possible to do a more detailed analysis of the type 6 record, but accuracy seldom requires it.

```
        PROC CHART DATA=PDB.PRINT;
        HBAR PRQUETM;
        TITLE 'DISTRIBUTION OF PRINT QUEUE TIME FOR JOBS WAITING
           LESS THAN 120 MIN';

DISTRIBUTION OF PRINT QUEUE TIME FOR JOBS WAITING LESS THAN 120 MIN
                      FREQUENCY BAR CHART
 MIDPOINT
 PRQUETM                              FREQ  CUM.     PERCENT     CUM.
                                            FREQ                 PERCENT
          |
       8  |* * * * * * * * * * * * * * * * * * *  167   167    77.31     77.31
          |
      24  |* *                          15   182     6.94     84.26
          |
      40  |*                            10   192     4.63     88.89
          |
      56  |*                             7   199     3.24     92.13
          |
      72  |*                             6   205     2.78     94.91
          |
      88  |*                             5   210     2.31     97.22
          |
     104  |                              3   213     1.39     98.61
          |
     120  |                              3   216     1.39    100.00
          - - - + - - - + - - - + - - - + - - - + - -
            30   60   90   120  150
                 FREQUENCY
```

Example 15.2

By taking the preceding data for PRQUETM and excluding those jobs that exceeded 2 hours, a more meaningful distribution of queue time is pictured. Of this sample, 77% of the jobs waited less than 16 minutes in the print queue. This type of analysis, which selects and individually excludes exceptions while presenting the other more typical data, provides management with a realistic evaluation of the delays for printing devices (Example 15.2).

The time to mount forms can also be estimated from the PDB.PRINT data set. The assumption is made in this example that the time between end of print on one form until start of print on a new form is the time required by the operator to mount the form. This is not always true; if form A finishes at 2 a.m. and no new printing is scheduled until 6 a.m. for a different form, then the algorithm reports a form mount of 4 hours. By restricting the analysis to those times of day when you expect to have constant demand for the printer, however, the estimated forms mount time FORMMNTM may approximate reality.

```
PROC SORT DATA=PDB.PRINT OUT=FORMS;
 BY RMOTID OUTDEVCE PRINTIME FORM;
DATA FORMOUNT;
 SET FORMS;
 BY RMOTID OUTDEVCE PRINTIME FORM;
 IF FIRST.FORM THE DO;
   FORMNTTM=PRINTIME-FORMEND;
   OUTPUT;
   FORMEND=PRENTIME;
   RETAIN FORMEND;
   DELETE;
 END;
 ELSE FORMEND=PRENTIME;
PROC SORT DATA=FORMOUNT;
 BY FORM;
PROC CHART DATA=FORMOUNT;
 BY FORM;
 HBAR FORMMNTM;
TITLE 'DISTRIBUTION OF ESTIMATED FORMS MOUNT
     TIMES BY FORM NUMBER';
```

Printing at remote stations (RJE printing) may require examination of more than just the printing information in TYPE6. Before an RJE station can print, it must have signed on to the network. Many times, end users complain of poor printing; that is, they did not get their printed output back in the morning. They blame the data center when in fact the RJE operator did not sign on early enough in the morning to complete printing the previous night's output. The TYPE4789 or TYPE5234 data sets, discussed in chapter seventeen, identify when the remote signed on for the remote in question and provide proof of the situation.

Another event can occur on RJE lines that dramatically elongates printing, but it is not at all visible through the TYPE6 data. Both lines to be printed at the RJE station and cards being read in from the RJE station must be transmitted across the RJE line. If there is an appreciable volume of cards being read in while there is outbound printing, JES must slice the line between input and output, and lines printed per minute may fall when input is being read. Analysis of TYPE26J2 (or PDB.JOBS) provides the only clue that this event is occurring, for JES2 provides the input cards processed for each job (SPOOLCRD), the remote read from (INROUTE), the start time of input (READTIME), and the duration of input (RDRTM). JES3 installations do not fare so well.

The source for these analyses of printer usage is found in the ANALPRNT member of MXG.SOURCLIB.

chapter sixteen

Resource Measurement - Initiators

JES2 initiators are defined by the job entry subsystem system generation and can be started either automatically at JES startup or individually by operator commands. Each initiator is defined by the job classes it can initiate. When a job ends, its initiator is idled. JES looks to see if there are any more jobs on the input queue that can be started by this initiator; that is, it looks to see if there are jobs in this initiator's class structure. Several job classes can be assigned to an initiator; the input queue is scanned for work in the first class before work in the second class is considered. Within any class, the job with highest priority that is eligible for execution at this instant is scheduled first.

The total number of initiators started determines the total number of batch jobs that can be executed concurrently, and the classing definitions determine how the incoming batch workload is scheduled. Chapter nineteen discusses alternative ways to manage batch scheduling, including initiator classing, but this chapter is concerned with measuring initiator utilization and the techniques for establishing how many initiators should be concurrently started.

There are two sources of performance data on initiators. SMF job records (type 30, subtype 5) provide the job class of each job and the duration of execution. These data are gathered in the PDB.JOBS data set, and they can be analyzed (as shown below) to determine multiprogramming level by class and overall. The main difficulty in using JOBS data for the analysis of multiprogramming level (MPL) is that the job must be purged before its data are available in PDB.JOBS, so yesterday's initiator utilizations may not be known for several days. The second source of information on multiprogramming level is the statistics provided in RMF TYPE70 data set. For each RMF interval, statistics are maintained on the percentage of time that 0, 1-2, 3-4, and so forth (up to 36 and over) initiators were active and the average number of batch initiators (BATCHAVG) during the interval. These statistics give no information concerning the class of the initiators, but for the analysis of total initiators, the data are more valuable than data from SMF. If the RMFINTRV data set is used, the number of active initiators can be known; the correlation between number of initiators and paging, swapping, and so forth can be easily shown; and the optimal number of initiators can be determined.

Frequently, the major impediment to throughput is a combination of allowing the operation staff to start and stop initiators and an archaic class scheduling scheme. Well-designed scheduling algorithms that match class and number of initiators often fail to meet objectives because of manual, untrackable manipulation by operators. SMF does not log initiators' starts and stops in any explicit fashion;

therefore, changes in the class structure of initiators dramatically affect job scheduling.

Example 16.1 shows an approximation of the average multiprogramming ratio from PDB.JOBS. First, batch jobs are selected from data set JOBS. Then, the MEANS procedure is used to calculate some simple statistics. JELAPSTM is the number of total initiator seconds. The difference between the minimum and maximum values of the variable JTRMTIME is the duration of the interval for which the sum of elapsed time is accumulated.

The sum of the elapsed time of all jobs run, when divided by the duration of the overall interval, is a measure of the average multiprogramming level (that is, the average number of active initiators, such as 14.9 on system SYS1 in this example). If operations expects twenty active initiators from the processor and the workload has been normal, investigate why only three-fourths of the expected initiators were used.

Remember that the result is an approximation. The interval is defined by the minimum and the maximum termination times, whereas the elapsed time is defined by the total elapsed time of all batch jobs terminated in that interval. If a long job initiates before the interval begins and terminates during the interval, a significant portion of the job's elapsed time may occur outside the interval. Therefore, the average multiprogramming level calculated by this ratio is only an approximation of the actual average MPL. Furthermore, long jobs that initiate in the interval but do not terminate contribute to the true MPL and are not reflected in this average. If the interval spans a typical working day and these effects are balanced, the following calculation can be used:

```
DATA JOBS;
   SET PDB.JOBS;
   IF TYPETASK='JOB';
   KEEP SYSTEM JELAPSTM JTRMTIME;
PROC SORT DATA=JOBS;
   BY SYSTEM;
PROC MEANS N MEAN MIN MAX SUM;
   BY SYSTEM;
   VAR JELAPSTM JTRMTIME;
   OUTPUT OUT=AVGMPL(DROP=X) SUM=JELAPSTM
      MIN=X MINTIME     MAX= X MAXTIME;
   TITLE 'EXAMPLE 16.1 FIRST PART';
   TITLE2 'INITIATION SUMMARY STATISTICS';
DATA AVGMPL;
   SET AVGMPL;
   AVGMPL=JELAPSTM/(MAXTIME-MINTIME);
   FILE PRINT;
   PUT //' THE ESTIMATED AVERAGE MULTI-PROGRAMMING LEVEL IS '
      AVGMPL 5.1 ' INITIATORS ' /
      +5 ' FOR THE PERIOD FROM ' MINTIME DATETIME16.
      ' TO ' MAXTIME DATETIME16. / +5 ' ON SYSTEM ' SYSTEM;
   TITLE 'EXAMPLE 16.1 SECOND PART';
   TITLE2 'ESTIMATION RESULTS';
```

```
                         EXAMPLE 16.1 FIRST PART                        1
                     INITIATION SUMMARY STATISTICS

VARIABLE    LABEL                     N        MEAN       MINIMUM        MAXIMUM
                                                          VALUE          VALUE


- - - - - - - - - - - - - - - - - - - - SYSTEM·ID=SYS1 - - - - - - - - - - - - - - - - - - - - - - - - - - - -

JELAPSTM    JOB·ELAPSED·DURATION    2670         460             1          34920
JTRMTIME    JOB·TERMINATION·EVENT   2670   766158780     766112743      766195010

VARIABLE         SUM

- - - - - - - - - - - - - - - - - - - - SYSTEM·ID=SYS1 - - - - - - - - - - - - - - - - - - - - - - - - - - - -

JELAPSTM       1228850
JTRMTIME   2045643943095

- - - - - - - - - - - - - - - - - - - - SYSTEM·ID=SYS3 - - - - - - - - - - - - - - - - - - - - - - - - - - - -


VARIABLE    LABEL                     N        MEAN       MINIMUM        MAXIMUM
                                                          VALUE          VALUE

- - - - - - - - - - - - - - - - - - - - SYSTEM·ID=SYS3 - - - - - - - - - - - - - - - - - - - - - - - - - - - -

JELAPSTM    JOB·ELAPSED·DURATION      80         791             1          11608
JTRMTIME    JOB·TERMINATION·EVENT     80   766155199     766120409      766194702

VARIABLE         SUM

- - - - - - - - - - - - - - - - - - - - SYSTEM·ID=SYS3 - - - - - - - - - - - - - - - - - - - - - - - - - - - -

JELAPSTM       63258.2
JTRMTIME   61292415950.4

                         EXAMPLE 16.1 SECOND PART                       2
                          ESTIMATION RESULTS

   THE ESTIMATED AVERAGE MULTI-PROGRAMMING LEVEL IS  14.9 INITIATORS
       FOR THE PERIOD FROM 11APR84:01:05:43 TO 11APR84:23:56:50
       ON SYSTEM SYS1

   THE ESTIMATED AVERAGE MULTI-PROGRAMMING LEVEL IS   0.9 INITIATORS
       FOR THE PERIOD FROM 11APR84:03:13:29 TO 11APR84:23:51:42
       ON SYSTEM SYS3
```

Example 16.1

Whether 15 is the correct number of initiators depends on the size of the processor and the nature of the batch and nonbatch workload. If the processor is a 3081Q with ADABAS, TSO, and CICS systems in addition to batch, then 14.9 may be an appropriate average multiprogramming level for batch work. However, if it

is a 3081Q processing only batch jobs, you would expect far more than 15 active
initiators.

Plotting the multiprogramming level versus time-of-day is a more informative
approach. By plotting only the average number of initiators, the operations manager can see a profile of the batch multiprogramming level. If operator manipulation of initiator classes is preventing jobs from being scheduled, this plot shows
the periods of idleness. Although you cannot tell which classes are not being executed from the TYPE70 data, you can always tell if problems exist:

```
PROC PLOT DATA=PDB.TYPE70 ;
  BY SYSTEM;
  PLOT BATCHAVG*STARTIME;
  FORMAT STARTIME DATETIME13.;
  TITLE1 'EXAMPLE 16.2';
  TITLE2 'AVERAGE BATCH INITIATORS FROM RMF TYPE 70 DATA';
```

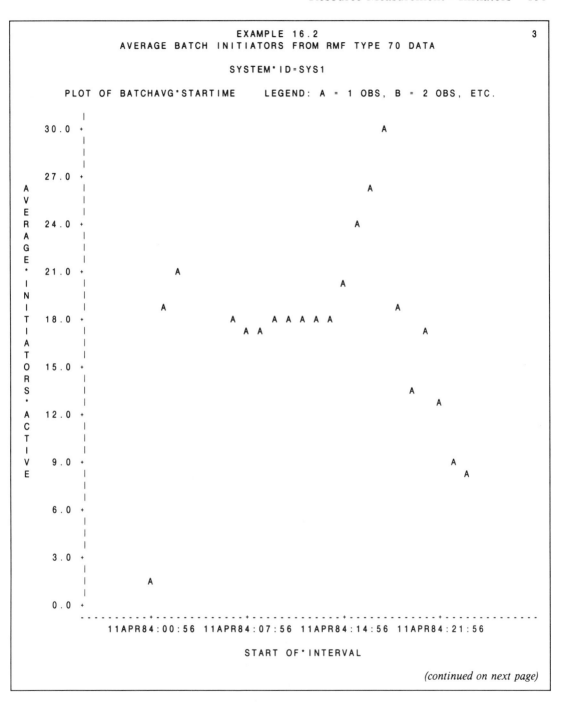

EXAMPLE 16.2   3
AVERAGE BATCH INITIATORS FROM RMF TYPE 70 DATA

SYSTEM·ID=SYS1

PLOT OF BATCHAVG·STARTIME   LEGEND: A = 1 OBS, B = 2 OBS, ETC.

(continued on next page)

(continued from previous page)

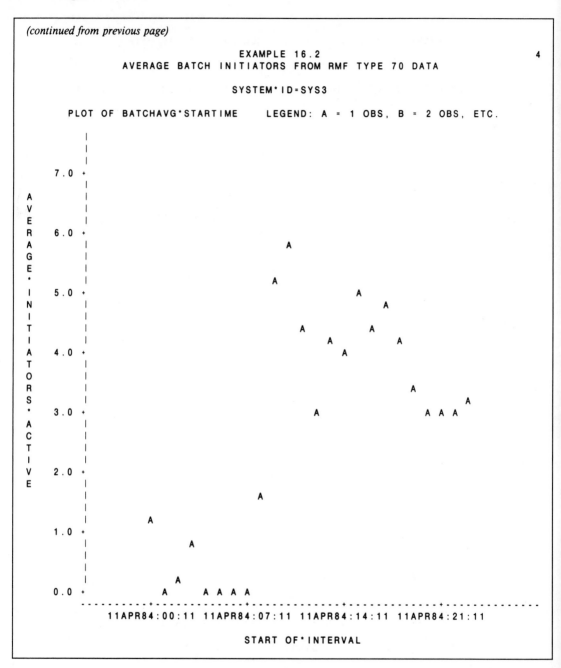

Example 16.2

Another approach to tracking initiator usage is provided in Example 16.3, which takes data set PDB.JOBS and builds a subset called MULTPROG with only batch jobs. Each batch job is subdivided into one observation for each 10-second interval that the job was active. A job with elapsed time less than 10 seconds is discarded. These observations are then sorted by time and counted into data set INTRVAL, which contains the number of active initiators for each 10-second interval.

A 10-second data plot would look very busy, so the FORMAT statement is associated with the BY variable TIME so that output observations are summarized by each minute of the day and contain the average number of initiators for that minute. The interval in data set MULTPROG could have been set to 60 seconds initially, but jobs under 60 seconds would have been lost. Sampling at 10-second intervals and then averaging adjacent samples gives a more accurate representation than taking the average of active initiators. It also significantly reduces the data to be plotted.

```
DATA MULTPROG;
  SET PDB.JOBS;
  IF TYPETASK='JOB';
  IF JINITIME=. OR JTRMTIME=. THEN DELETE;
  /* SPECIFY INTERVAL IN SECONDS */
  INTERVAL=10;
  IF (JTRMTIME-JINITIME) LT INTERVAL THEN DELETE;
  TIME=JINITIME-MOD(JINITIME,INTERVAL);
  DO UNTIL (TIME GE JTRMTIME);
    OUTPUT;
    TIME=TIME+INTERVAL;
   END;
  FORMAT TIME DATETIME19.2;
  KEEP TIME SYSTEM;
PROC SORT DATA=MULTPROG;
  BY SYSTEM TIME;
PROC MEANS DATA=MULTPROG NOPRINT;
  BY SYSTEM TIME;
  OUTPUT OUT=INTERVAL
  N=NRACTIVE;
  VAR TIME;
PROC MEANS NOPRINT DATA=INTERVAL;
  BY SYSTEM TIME;
  FORMAT TIME DATETIME13.;
  OUTPUT OUT=MINUTE
  MEAN=AVGINIT;
  VAR NRACTIVE;
PROC PLOT DATA=MINUTE;
  BY SYSTEM;
  FORMAT TIME DATETIME13.;
  PLOT TIME*AVGINIT/VREVERSE VPOS=144;
  TITLE 'EXAMPLE 16.3';
  TITLE2 'MULTI-PROGRAMMING LEVEL (AVERAGE INITIATORS ACTIVE)';
```

```
                          EXAMPLE 16.3                                    5
            MULTI-PROGRAMMING LEVEL (AVERAGE INITIATORS ACTIVE)

                          SYSTEM*ID=SYS1

      PLOT OF TIME*AVGINIT    LEGEND: A = 1 OBS, B = 2 OBS, ETC.

          TIME |
11APR84:00:20 +
              |
              |     CAAAA
              |       J
11APR84:01:01 +      A |
              |   IA A
              |   E
              |
11APR84:01:43 +
              |           A       BA A  B
              |                   A AB A    A   A ABA
              |                           AAG A
11APR84:02:25 +                           BED
              |                           F  BB
              |                           E C A A A
              |                            CBBAB
11APR84:03:06 +                           AAAAAD A
              |                            CBAD A
              |                            BA C ABA
              |                            CBAAABA
11APR84:03:48 +                           AAB BD
              |                     AA   ABCAA
              |                     AADCB
              |                     AADA  C
11APR84:04:30 +                    C F A A
              |                    B  CD A
              |                    I AA
              |                    J
11APR84:05:11 +                    J
              |                    K
              |                    J
              |                    K
11APR84:05:53 +                    J
              |                    J
              |                    K
              |                    J
11APR84:06:35 +                    K
              |                    J
              |                    K
              |                    J
11APR84:07:16 +                    FABA
              |                      AABA    ABC
              |                            BBABC
              |                         A A A CA ABA
11APR84:07:58 +                         AA A BABB
```

(continued on next page)

(continued from previous page)

```
                                                  CA B CA
                                                  AA A ACAB  A
                                                       CFA
11APR84:08:40 +        A    A A    A    DB            A
              |             AAAB AB    B
              |                       DEB
              |                       BCCB
11APR84:09:21 +                       ADDA
              |                       ABH
              |                       DCAB
              |                       CEBA
11APR84:10:03 +                        BBDB
              |                       EDA
              |                       AIA
              |                       GBA
11APR84:10:45 +                       AFAA AA
              |                        C  CD
              |                        DEB
              |                        EDA
11APR84:11:26 +                        CFA
              |                        CG A
              |                        CDC
              |                       BCABBA
11APR84:12:08 +                       AH A
              |                        FBB
              |                       ABEBA
              |                       AABBAAAA
11APR84:12:50 +                          CAEB
              |                        AA BBCA
              |                        BEBB
              |                        HB
11APR84:13:31 +                        FD
              |                        DG
              |                        CFA
              |                       DDAAA
11APR84:14:13 +                       AAACAA B
              |                           BFAA
              |                           BAFB
              |                          BACD
11APR84:14:55 +                           BEABA
              |                        GC
              |                        AACF
              |                           GBA
11APR84:15:36 +                         DE A
              |                            BFC
              |                           AAEBA
              |                            A EDA
11APR84:16:18 +                           BCBBA
              |                                 DD  B
              |                                  ABABACA
              |                          ABA ACB
```

(continued on next page)

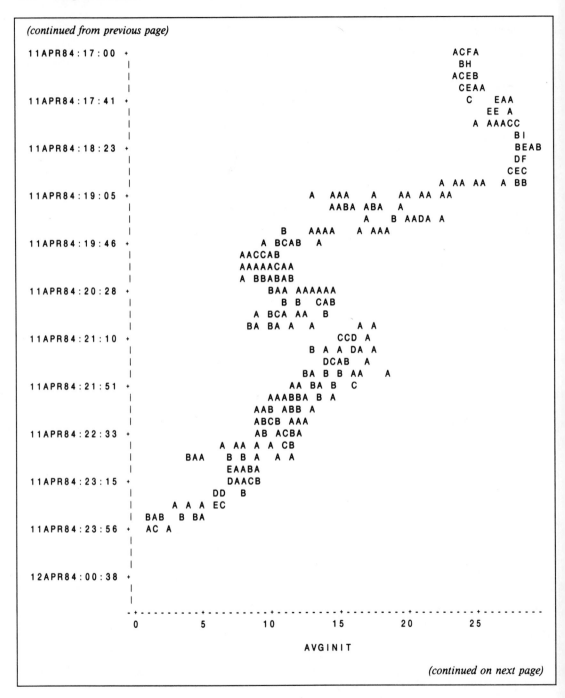

(continued on next page)

(continued from previous page)

```
                              EXAMPLE  16.3                              6
                MULTI-PROGRAMMING  LEVEL  (AVERAGE  INITIATORS  ACTIVE)

                           SYSTEM*ID=SYS3

           PLOT  OF  TIME*AVGINIT     LEGEND:  A = 1 OBS,  B = 2 OBS,  ETC.

           TIME |
11APR84:03:06 +   B            A      F
              |   I         A         A
              |   J
              |   K
11APR84:03:48 +   J
              |
              |
              |
11APR84:04:30 +
              |   C
              |   B
              |
11APR84:05:11 +
              |
              |
              |
11APR84:05:53 +
              |
              |
              |
11APR84:06:35 +
              |
              |
              |
11APR84:07:16 +
              |
              |
              |
11APR84:07:58 +
              |
              |   D         B        D
              |   J
11APR84:08:40 +   K
              |     A     A  A      E      A      A
              |   G     A           B
              |   B
11APR84:09:21 +   D         A                      F
              |                                     K
              |                 D        A  A       D
              |                                     J    A
11APR84:10:03 +                                     J
              |                                     J
              |                 C           A           A    A       E
```

(continued on next page)

(continued from previous page)

```
                   |                         J
11APR84:10:45  +                             D            A              B         A              C
                   |                             E              A    D
                   |                             A    A             I
                   |                             F              A    C
11APR84:11:26  +                             E              A    A  C
                   |   D         A             F
                   |   D                           A                   A
                   |   G
11APR84:12:08  +   A
                   |
                   |   A              A
                   |   A
11APR84:12:50  +   A
                   |
                   |
                   |   B
11APR84:13:31  +   A
                   |   H              A       A       A
                   |                             D       A  A  A       C
                   |                             B  A  A       A  F
11APR84:14:13  +            A                        A       G  A
                   |   C         A             F
                   |   G                       B              A
                   |   E              A
11APR84:14:55  +
                   |
                   |   A
                   |   G         A       A
11APR84:15:36  +   A         A       A  A              F
                   |                                 K
                   |                                 J
                   |                             E  A  A  A       A  B
11APR84:16:18  +   I         A             B              A
                   |   G                       B              A
                   |   A                       J
                   |   J
11APR84:17:00  +   I  A       A
                   |                             J
                   |                             I       B
                   |                             J
11APR84:17:41  +                             J
                   |   B         A             H
                   |   G  A             A       A
                   |   K
11APR84:18:23  +   J
                   |   B         A       A  F
                   |   K
                   |   J
11APR84:19:05  +   K
                   |   F
```

(continued on next page)

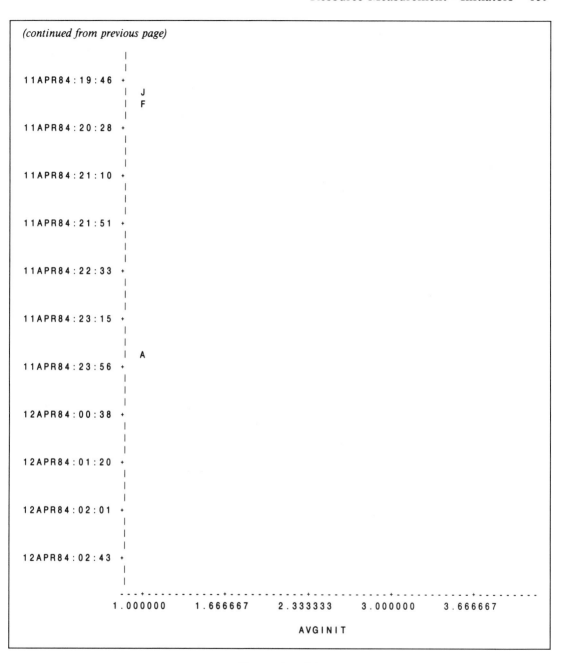

Example 16.3

In this installation, the SYS1 system is fairly inactive until a brief peak of work from 2 a.m. until 4:30 a.m. Then the system sleeps again until around 7:15 a.m. Work builds up until the peak at about 6:30 p.m.

With the PLOT's VPOS = 141, two and one half pages are required, and each value on the Y axis represents a duration of about 10 minutes. Thus, the range of values represented by a line is the profile of the number of initiators used during each 10-minute period, providing a form of visual integration over time.

```
PROC MEANS DATA=INTERVAL;
   BY SYSTEM;
   VAR NRACTIVE;
   TITLE 'EXAMPLE 16.4 FIRST PART';
   TITLE2 'AVERAGE, MINIMUM, AND MAXIMUM INITIATORS';
PROC FREQ DATA=INTERVAL;
   BY SYSTEM;
   TABLES NRACTIVE;
   TITLE 'EXAMPLE 16.4 SECOND PART';
   TITLE2 'PERCENTAGE OF SAMPLES WITH NRACTIVE INITIATORS';
```

```
                        EXAMPLE 16.4 FIRST PART                    7
                 AVERAGE, MINIMUM, AND MAXIMUM INITIATORS
```

VARIABLE	N	MEAN	STANDARD DEVIATION	MINIMUM VALUE	MAXIMUM VALUE	STD ERROR OF MEAN
------------------------------------- SYSTEM*ID=SYS1 -------------------------------						
NRACTIVE	8197	15.2880322	5.70013823	1.00000000	31.0000000	0.06295901
------------------------------------- SYSTEM*ID=SYS3 -------------------------------						
NRACTIVE	3470	1.84005764	0.86909594	1.00000000	4.00000000	0.01475377

```
                        EXAMPLE 16.4 SECOND PART                   8
                 PERCENTAGE OF SAMPLES WITH NRACTIVE INITIATORS

                              SYSTEM*ID=SYS1
```

NRACTIVE	FREQUENCY	CUM FREQ	PERCENT	CUM PERCENT
1	114	114	1.391	1.391
2	52	166	0.634	2.025
3	40	206	0.488	2.513

(continued on next page)

(continued from previous page)

4	152	358	1.854	4.367
5	23	381	0.281	4.648
6	86	467	1.049	5.697
7	112	579	1.366	7.064
8	121	700	1.476	8.540
9	170	870	2.074	10.614
10	1159	2029	14.139	24.753
11	272	2301	3.318	28.071
12	251	2552	3.062	31.133
13	199	2751	2.428	33.561
14	434	3185	5.295	38.856
15	679	3864	8.284	47.139
16	1069	4933	13.041	60.181
17	870	5803	10.614	70.794
18	603	6406	7.356	78.151
19	341	6747	4.160	82.311
20	299	7046	3.648	85.958
21	155	7201	1.891	87.849
22	101	7302	1.232	89.081
23	49	7351	0.598	89.679
24	226	7577	2.757	92.436
25	123	7700	1.501	93.937
26	121	7821	1.476	95.413
27	80	7901	0.976	96.389
28	201	8102	2.452	98.841
29	82	8184	1.000	99.841
30	10	8194	0.122	99.963
31	3	8197	0.037	100.000

EXAMPLE 16.4 SECOND PART   9
PERCENTAGE OF SAMPLES WITH NRACTIVE INITIATORS

SYSTEM'ID=SYS3

NRACTIVE	FREQUENCY	CUM FREQ	PERCENT	CUM PERCENT
1	1545	1545	44.524	44.524
2	1022	2567	29.452	73.977
3	816	3383	23.516	97.493
4	87	3470	2.507	100.000

Example 16.4

Example 16.4 extends the analysis to provide statistics on the distribution of the actual number of initiators active during each 10-second interval. Although 3 intervals had as many as 31 initiators active, 60% of the intervals had 16 or fewer initiators active. In this case, the average MPL calculated from the elapsed time ratio (14.9) is very close to the true multiprogramming ratio. If the range of initia-

tors is less than the 36 maximum of TYPE70, examine BATCH0 through
BATCH12 for a similar but less detailed profile.

In the example, all batch initiators were grouped together. In more typical analyses, data may be sorted by class to produce separate plots of the active initiator
count by class. This type of information, especially the graph, is very useful in
management communications, particularly to operations management since the
operations manager has the most direct control over the multiprogramming level.
Shops that permit operators to modify initiators' classes or to start and stop initiators at their discretion are rarely able to maintain as high an MPL as installations
that do not permit operator intervention. The manipulation of initiator structure
by operators should be avoided for several reasons. First, operators can forget that
they changed Initiator 7 to class X. Even though the class X job was important,
by dynamically restructuring the initiators, the operator may have destroyed a
well-designed batch scheduling system. Second, the operating system can respond
much faster than an operator. Frequently the operator's response to a resource
problem is to reduce the number of initiators, but by the time the operator enters
the command, which takes seconds, the SRM has responded with its command,
taking only microseconds, and the operator's alteration of initiator structure may
be inappropriate. Third, the clues available to the operator at the console are rarely
good indicators of the actual state of the system. Even with tools such as
OMEGAMON, RESOLVE, LOOK, and RMF MONITOR II and III, the operator
must have the education of a systems programmer and the skills of a performance
analyst to integrate those screens to conclude the resource commitment of the system. The number of jobs in the queue can indicate backlog, but it does not suffice
for ad hoc redesign of batch scheduling. It is far better to define the initiator structure based on the job scheduling schema (see chapter nineteen) and to prohibit
operators from altering the scheme on their own.

Although operators should not be allowed to alter initiator structure, it is reasonable for the performance analyst to define several initiator structures for specific periods of the day (for example, prime time for hot batch, midnight structure
for backup, and so forth) and to expect the operations staff to effect these defined
changes at specified times of day. It is the unsolicited alteration that must be
avoided if batch service objectives are to be met. Plotting actual multiprogramming level versus time-of-day is most effective in convincing operations management to keep the operators' hands off the initiators.

In the early years of MVS, when it was still known as VS2, IBM systems engineers cautioned against over-initiation. Before VS2 was fully understood, several
installations migrated from OS/360 MVT to VS/370 VS2 on the same processor
and found the number of initiators VS2 could support to be somewhat less than
their (well-tuned) MVT system had supported. When VS2 executed with the same
number of initiators as MVT had used, batch work elongated dramatically. It was
only later that the real culprit, insufficient real memory for the expanded size of

VS2, was understood, but the concern for over-initiation is still a common initial response by IBM to batch performance problems.

How can the correct number of initiators be determined? As with all performance questions, begin with the performance effect of an incorrect value and then measure the effect on your system. In the case of batch initiators, if there are too many, the result is recognized first by the SRM. When the resources required by all these batch jobs exceed the resources available, the SRM reduces the system workload by swapping out jobs with unilateral swaps. Data set RMFINTRV contains the unilateral swap rate (SWAPUS) from TYPE71 and also contains the average number of batch initiators (BATCHAVG) from TYPE70. If a week's data are examined graphically and if too many active initiators caused excessive unilateral swapping, a simple plot shows the number of initiators used when swapping becomes excessive:

```
PROC PLOT DATA=PDB.RMFINTRV;
  BY SYSTEM;
  PLOT SWAPUS*BATCHAVG;
  TITLE 'EXAMPLE 16.5';
  TITLE2 'UNILATERAL SWAP RATE VERSUS AVERAGE INITIATORS ACTIVE';
```

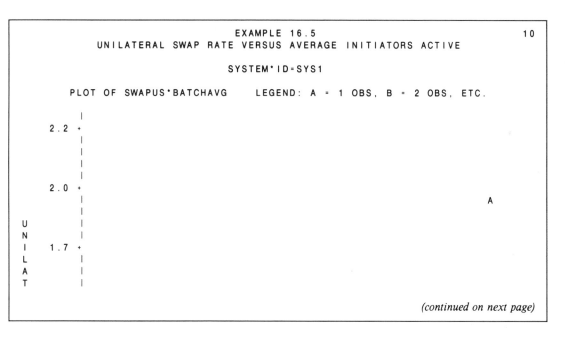

(continued on next page)

(continued from previous page)

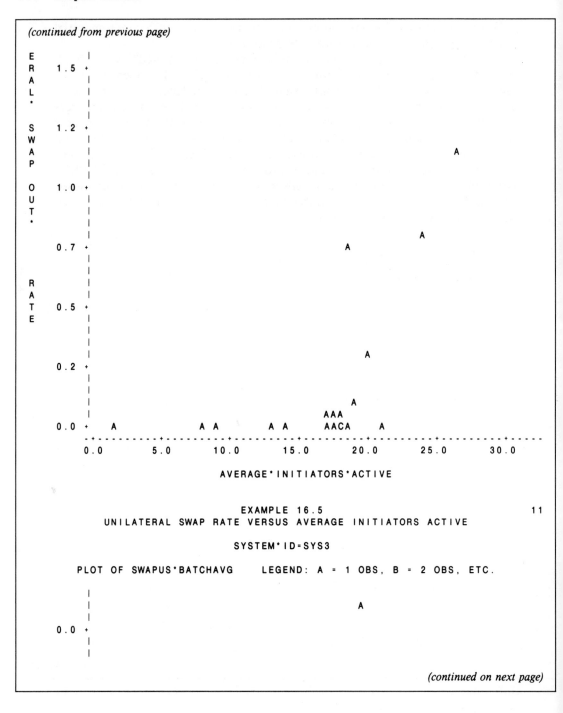

EXAMPLE 16.5   11
UNILATERAL SWAP RATE VERSUS AVERAGE INITIATORS ACTIVE

SYSTEM·ID=SYS3

PLOT OF SWAPUS·BATCHAVG   LEGEND: A = 1 OBS, B = 2 OBS, ETC.

(continued on next page)

(continued from previous page)

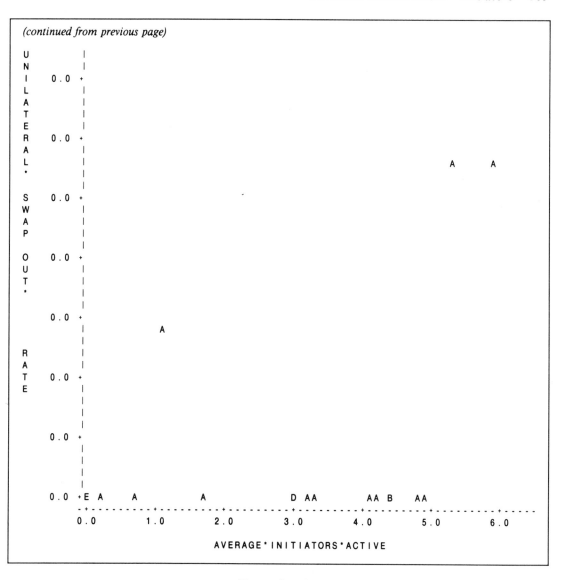

Example 16.5

How much unilateral batch swapping is too much? Since swapping rates are expressed as the number of tasks being swapped per second, a SWAPUS rate of 0.05 means that there are 5 tasks swapped every 100 seconds or that a batch task is swapped out, on average, every 20 seconds. Since elapsed time to swap out a task is on the order of 250 milliseconds assuming 3 parallel paths to the swap data sets, a batch job with 15 pages to swap out, and an average of 50 ms per page, this swap rate of 0.05 suggests that the system is in good shape, only occasionally bumping into an overcommitted state. If the swap rate were increased to 0.5, a batch task would be swapped every 2 seconds, and the portion of time spent moving tasks in and out begins to be appreciable. Batch swapping rates much higher than 0.5 usually indicate that either too many initiators are active or that the other work in the system is consuming more than its share of resources. The key is to use a unilateral swapping rate to set the correct number of initiators based on the amount of resources you are willing to give to batch and to measure the effect of too many rather than assuming that some number of initiators is too many.

Unilateral swapping rate can only be used when the SRM coefficients (the happy values discussed in chapter seven) have been tuned. If the happy values themselves are set incorrectly, the operating system may vote overcommitted when resources are idle. This was the case in a series of benchmarks reported by IBM at SHARE 55 in 1980. The IPO team used a dedicated 3032 from midnight to 8 a.m. for several months, iterating the number of initiators and measuring the elapsed run time of a commercial job mix (see chapter thirty for more information on benchmarking). When its results were plotted and presented, they showed that a minimum elapsed run time occurred with between 5 and 6 initiators and concluded that their benchmark demonstrated the correct initiator level for that processor. Fortunately for the audience, it was pointed out that at 8 a.m. each morning, the 3032 was given back to the IBM systems center and ran production batch and TSO all day long, with 24 batch initiators! How could the benchmark conclude 5 on a machine that can clearly support 5 times that number? The benchmark team used the MVS/SE1 default SRM coefficients, and the systems center listened to its own gurus and made the then standard changes to the default values. Do not trust anyone else's rules of thumb for the number of initiators, but do measure the impact on overinitiation. Operate for a few days with some number, observing the unilateral swap rate, page fault rate, CPU active, and so forth, and then increase batch initiators by 1 for a few more days until the level of swapping becomes excessive. Set your own values by measuring your own system.

chapter seventeen

Resource Measurement - RJE and NJE

This chapter discusses RJE and NJE measurement for JES2. Remote job entry (RJE) and network job entry (NJE) are IBM facilities that transmit batch jobs to be executed and their output to be printed from one location to another. An RJE site is a slave to a single JES shared spool at a single installation. There may be several CPUs that can access this spool to select and execute batch jobs. An RJE station sends jobs as a JCL data set to that spool for execution or reads the printed lines, SYSOUT data sets, from that spool for that station's jobs. The RJE console can communicate with its JES by issuing JES commands to control input and output processing at the RJE station. NJE interconnects two or more JES spools so that an RJE site in Kentucky, connected to its JES in Tennessee, can send a job to be executed at the company's Los Angeles computer center where the data base needed by the job is located. NJE picks up the job from the Tennessee spool and sends it to the LA spool for execution. When the job completes in LA, NJE sends its sysout back to Tennessee where it resides on spool until the Kentucky RJE operator allows it to print. Note that the Kentucky RJE could have dialed directly into the LA computer; NJE is used primarily to reduce line costs by allowing many RJEs to share the line.

The increase in on-line and interactive systems seems to imply that batch is decreasing, yet batch computer work is growing faster than all other work. It should not be surprising that batch is still the primary consumer of total work units in many installations measured since batch is inherently less expensive than any other delivery vehicle. Chapter twenty-six shows that to deliver a work unit to batch requires 1.36 hardware work units, whereas delivering 1 unit to CICS and IMS costs about 2 units; MVS/SE1 TSO consumes 3.5 work units for every 1 unit consumed by the TSO user. **Batch will always be cheaper.**

RJE delivers batch service to users who are not located adjacent to the computer room. Even with all users in the same building, RJE workstations on each floor are common since they reduce the time required to deliver printed output to the user. The explosion in RJE from personal computers is just around the corner. A HASP workstation package for the IBM PC has been developed. The elegant implementation includes a communications line monitor, and it can handle line speeds of at least 19.2KB. The top line of the PC screen prints a ticker tape of each block transmitted, the ACKs, NAKs, errors, and so forth. One user drives 2 Xerox 10-page per minute laser printers on a 19.2 KB line! The BARR/HASP software or hardware card and a PC provide full RJE workstation capability that dramatically outperforms 8100s or 3277s for a total purchase price of well under $5000!

The more typical PC owner will likely use 2400 BPS because it is the slowest common speed for HASP protocol at which the cost of the modem for a single user is cost-effective. Although PCs currently struggle with asynchronous communications to TSO and CMS, when volumes of data begin to be transmitted between hosts and PCs, synchronous communications are mandatory to reduce error rates and communications costs. HASP protocol is not only synchronous, but it also offers data compression that further reduces communications costs. Because it is also supported by every mainframe vendor, users with real data transmission requirements will demand HASP capability. It is not unreasonable to expect that every TSO/CMS user will also have an RJE remote number (and node) by 1990, allowing interaction with VTAM for interactive applications and using a hot-key to switch states and interact with JES to process printing, with the PC's hard disk as the local spool. Thus, this chapter is not about a dinosaur on the decline, but will be a mainstream to analysis of the future.

What do we need to measure about RJE stations? The TYPE4789 (for bisynchronous protocol) and TYPE5234 (for SDLC protocol) data sets are the primary sources for analysis of the RJE station itself. There is an observation for each sign-on and each sign-off, and there is a security record if an invalid password is attempted. The sign-on and sign-off observations from the same remote can be matched to create an observation for each RJE session.

Note: the MXG member ANALRJE, described in chapter forty-one, provides this capability when building the RJESESSN data set. Note that TYPE4345, the JES2 start/stop event records must be interleaved with the RJE records because when JES2 is stopped, or abends, no sign-off record is written. Additionally, JES2 stops writing SMF records if there are no free SMF buffers in the JES2 workspace, which has occasionally resulted in an incomplete RJE session.

RJESESSN data can be analyzed from several perspectives. Since each session contains the JES line number used, examination of the line being used by each remote can identify unexpected use of dial-in lines. For example, one remote user attempted to sign on using the newly installed dedicated line. When sign-on failed, he was advised by the data center to try the dial backup line today and try the dedicated line tomorrow. Seven months later, it was noted that the dedicated line had never been used; the dial backup had worked and had been used thereafter.

Error statistics for each session are provided in RJESESSN; the activity on the line is more comprehensive for SDLC than for BISYNC, but either source can adequately distinguish those lines that have high error rates from those that do not. Absolute error rates are not as important as comparing rates by type of line. Although it requires an external table for you to map JES lines to telephone companies, you can compare how well you are served by using error counts. Note that high error rates can be the result of the workstation rather than the line.

Sharing the information in RJESESSN with telecommunications personnel can aid their problem analysis and also begin to open a dialog with the data processing group. Telecommunications personnel generally have no knowledge of how much the performance analyst really knows about the line usage, and each group can learn from the other.

RJE service is often the culprit for complaints of poor batch service. For example, one data center frequently received complaints of poor batch service for a particular remote. Although selection of all jobs executed for that remote showed job scheduling was accurate 100% of the time, complaints continued monthly. When RJESESSN records for that remote were examined, the source of the complaint was recognized. The remote was not being signed on until after 8:00 a.m. when it would begin printing output from the night before, which was finally distributed to end users around 11:00. The end users saw poor batch response because of poor RJE printing practices. Provide the RJE managers with monthly reports of the availability of their remote from RJESESSN.

Frequently, one group of programmers may move to a new location, and an estimate of their RJE utilization is required. Although the real resource of concern is the printing load they generate at the new site (or remove from the old), management also wants to know how many jobs they submit. The PDB.JOBS data set in MXG (or its source for this information, TYPE26J2) can be used to count jobs submitted from a remote. The INROUTE and INNODE identify the remote (and node, in NJE) from which the job was read if it was read in by a physical reader at that remote. Frequently, however, users submit their batch work from an interactive session (WYLBUR, ROSCOE, TSO, and so forth) in which case INROUTE is zero (it is always zero for jobs processed by an internal reader, and it is zero for jobs read in on a local reader at the data center). For those jobs, an approximation to the real owning remote is to use the PRROUTE remote number instead of INROUTE since PRROUTE is the remote where the job's SYSMSG was printed. Note that whereas PDB.JOBS contains the total lines printed by each job, it does not tell the remote users those lines were printed. The PDB.PRINT data set must be used to count the number of lines printed at a particular remote. Finally, do not be confused by the SPOOLINE variable in PDB.JOBS. It counts the number of lines of print that a job placed on the spool, but it does not count how many print lines resulted from the spooled data. A job could place 1000 print lines on the spool and print none if the job were canceled by the user before being printed, or it could print 1 million lines if 1000 copies were printed. PDB.PRINT is the only source of actual lines printed at a remote.

NJE is in common usage as enterprises have more computer systems in different cities that process other cities' jobs. Analysis of these NJE systems has not been required because there are probably more pressing problems, and the volume of traffic across the NJE lines tends to be small. So far, NJE provides a capability that a small number of users actually use. As a result, the author has not had extensive experience in analysis of NJE performance. The following notes were gathered empirically in 1981 while attempting to understand the contents of JES2 data in the SMF records written in an NJE environment. They have not been reverified.

In JES2/NJE, a purge record is written at each node when a job leaves that node. In the example at the beginning of this chapter, the job created a type 26 SMF purge record at the Tennessee node as it was sent to LA, one at the LA node when the SYSOUT was sent back to Tennessee, and a third record at the Tennessee node when the remote in Kentucky finished printing.

When SYSOUT is transmitted between nodes, a type 57 SMF record is written by JES2, describing the transmission volume and duration. Unfortunately, it contains accounting information, and its READTIME is not the true READTIME of the job, so TYPE57 data is not of much use for accounting.

JES services jobs with a series of processes that includes read-in, converter, execution, output, and purge processes. In JES/NJE, each process can occur at a different node.

MXG's BUILDPDB requires only the purge record that was written on the execution processor because that record contains the important time stamps that describe job scheduling at that node. This is the only purge record that BUILDPDB processes and is identifiable by the SYSEXEC variable, which is blank in all other purge records for a job.

Although it is possible to tell if the job has completed execution from a single purge record, it is not possible with the data in a purge record to know if all purge records for the job were written. Several new variables created in MXG TYPE26J2 and used as input to BUILDPDB elaborate on why a particular purge record exists. These variables are SOURCE, INREASON, EXECSTAT, SYSOUTPR, and NJETRANS, described in section TYPE26J2 of chapter forty.

NJE has other effects on values of performance variables, and a lot of the information on NJE comes from variables in TYPE26J2 observations:

1. The existence of NJE can be detected from the INDEVICE name, which previously contained only local names READER1, PRINTER3, PUNCH6, or the standard RJE format of

$$Rnnn.XXm$$

where

nnn is the remote number

RD for a reader

XX is PR for a printer

PU for a punch

m is the device number.

R196.PR2 is the second printer at remote 196. When the input device is not an RJE station on this JES spool but is an NJE JES at some other spool, INDEVICE format is

$$Lnnn.YYm$$

where

nnn is the JES2 NJE line number,

YY is

JR   for a job received for execution or further transmission

SR   for sysout received at this node to be printed

m is a number.

2. When the job has executed, all its subsequent purge records written at any node contain a nonmissing value for JSTRTIME and JENDTIME, the JES job start and end times.

3. The purge record from the execution processor is the record containing a nonblank value for SYSEXEC, the execution processor system ID.

4. The purge record from a job that was transmitted from this node can be identified in one of several ways:
   a. SYSTRANS is nonblank
   b. TRANBEGN and TRANEND are nonmissing
   c. INDEVICE form is Lnnn.JRm (that is, not SR)
   d. NEXTNODE is nonblank.

5. EXECNODE contains the name of the node at which the execution takes place.

6. ORIGNODE is blank in the purge record on the read-in system, but all subsequent purge records on this job contain the read-in node name.

7. LASTNODE is blank in the purge record on the read-in system, but in all subsequent records on this job, it contains the node name from which the job was received.

8. NEXTNODE is nonblank only in job transmission purge records.

9. Make sure that the PTF issued in 1980 for APAR OZ43707 that affects time stamps is installed. It preserves the READTIME in NJE record types 4, 5, 6, 14, 15, 20, and 26 (but not type 57) written at other nodes. READTIME in TYPE57 contains the start time of the specific read-in associated with that sysout transmission, which means that type 57 records cannot be matched with the job whose sysout is being transmitted. In all NJE purge records, JRDRTIME is the actual end-of-reader time on the node (on the receiving system if the job was transmitted).

With the expected large number of RJE users, NJE appears to offer flexibility in managing the remote user; therefore, analysis of NJE data will also increase.

chapter eighteen

Resource Measurement - Communications Lines

Response time at terminals directly affects productivity. The discussion on subsecond response time later in this chapter demonstrates the need for rapid response. Often you hear of the office at home and of the possibility of computer networking. What data do SMF and RMF provide for this area? Actually, they provide nothing.

If you install the Network Performance Analyzer, you gain the TYPE38 data on utilization, described in that section of chapter forty, and an example of reporting is provided in section ANALNPA in chapter forty-one. There may be a gold mine of information here, but little is known about how much money can be saved by measuring communications lines. Our knowledge about the measurability of communications lines is at the same point as it was for the measurement of CPUs in 1972. At that time, the hardware monitor proved its worth as the only source of data.*

A hardware monitor is not the tool for studying CPUs or their peripherals executing MVS, VM, or DOS/VSE. Those software operating systems provide excellent qualitative and quantitative measurements. Although these measurements are still imperfect, they do allow us to measure performance costs effectively. In the author's opinion (which he respects very much), the expense of a hardware monitor to measure those systems cannot be justified.

But the hardware monitor is the only tool that can measure hardware. At CMG XIII in 1982, the use of a hardware monitor to measure the performance of a Z80-based microprocessor system, a four-user word-processing office system was described. Until IBM decides to provide network measurements as a design criterion for their terminals and chooses to design measurement software in the communication controller (the 3725s and so forth), it may take a hardware monitor to measure response time. The announcement letter suggests that the data available to the CPU in the new 3274 control units may provide quantitative response measures of interactions on the line and some limited resource statistics.

But it is not clear that you need such sophisticated tools to manage teleprocessing line resources. Since line capacity is always measurable in total bytes per second, many telecommunications performance problems either diminish as insignificant or loom like the Navassa Island lighthouse in the night when you apply a little paper and pencil to the problem.

---

* Charles Dudley Warner was awarded the A. A. Michelson Award in recognition of his development of the first hardware monitor tool—the System Utilization Machine (SUM).

TRANSMISSION BETWEEN HOST AND PERSONAL COMPUTERS

The following discussion of interfacing personal computers and mainframes required only simple measures. Frequently the role of the performance analyst is to teach users how their choices affect performance.

Transferring data from a mainframe to a personal computer is called downloading, whereas sending data back to the mainframe is called uploading. If you are concerned with the time required to transfer data, there are four phases to be considered:

1. **LOGON phase.** This phase includes the time to power up the PC and the start-up time of the PC transfer program that communicates with the host. This time is constant for a given PC and software. For example, starting up an IBM PC, executing the IBM Asynchronous Communications Support Program (ASYNC) on the PC, then dialing up the host and logging on to TSO requires about 5 minutes of elapsed time.

2. **Extract and formatting host data phase.** This phase is generally required only for downloading. A mainframe program must read the mainframe data, select the records or fields desired, and build a file in the format required by the communications program (typically 80-byte records are expected). This program can be executed by a CLIST; so to the user, it is a single command. The execution duration of this phase depends on the size of the mainframe data base and the efficiency of the mainframe program. If the downloading is a regular event, this phase could be executed automatically as a batch program in the production system that updates the mainframe data base prior to logon. The extracted data must contain not only the data elements, but labeling information also needs to be imbedded in the file to be transmitted. For example, if the data are for a spreadsheet on the PC, then the row and column assignment must be provided for each data value. This labeling requirement increases the volume of data to be transmitted. At SUGI '84, several examples of using the SAS System for this phase were presented.

3. **Transmission phase.** The amount of data, line speed, and communications software all affect the duration of transmission. The line speed for data transmission is described in bits per second, sometimes erroneously called the baud rate after Baudot, who developed the Baudot code used for teletype. A baud is the inverse of the minimum time to transmit a pulse. If there are 2 states for the pulse, on and off, the baud rate and the bit per second rate are the same. There are sophisticated encoding schemes that permit multiple states for every pulse; for example, a pulse of -5, 0, or +5 volts allows 3 states in one pulse width,

and that system's bit rate would be 1.5 times its baud rate. Because baud rate no longer maps directly to bit rate, communications speeds should always be expressed as bits per second, which can be translated to more understandable terms like characters per second or even screens (that is, 1920 characters, the size of a 3270 terminal screen). Commonly available line speeds are:

Table 18.1
Transmission Rates at 100% Line Utilization

Bits per second	Characters per second	Seconds per 3270 screen	3270 screens per minute
300	37.5	51.2	1.2
1200	150	12.8	4.7
2400	300	6.4	9.4
4800	600	3.2	18.75
9600	1200	1.6	37.5
14400	1800	1.2	57.25
19200	2400	0.8	75.0
56000	7000	0.275	218.75

A modem modulator-demodulator connects to the PC and translates digital characters into serially transmitted audio tones that can be transmitted over telephone lines in speeds of up to 14400 BPS. Speeds of 4800 BPS and below can be used for switched, dial-up modems, whereas higher speeds require nonswitched or dedicated conditioned telephone lines. Speeds above 14400 BPS do not use modems, generically described as analog devices; instead a dedicated dataphone digital service (DDS) is leased, and the telephone company provides a data services unit (DSU) that replaces the modem. At 9600 BPS and above, either analog or digital technology can be used, but analog is usually used because it is about half the cost of digital transmission. Digital transmission does offer much reduced error rates, which can justify the additional cost at 9600 BPS. Although all speeds are used currently, the 300/1200 BPS rates are most commonly used for dial-in services because of the low cost of modems. Speeds of 2400 and 4800 are used for HASP and SDLC dial-in workstations, and 9600 and above are common for dedicated 3274 control units serving VTAM terminals, JES 3277 and 8100 remotes, and so forth. Heretofore, 19.2 KB and 56 KB lines have primarily been used with multiplexors between concentrations of computers and users to reduce line costs or for heavy RJE printing. Two 600 line-per-minute printers, even with 50% data compression by JES with 100 bytes printed per line requires 1000 CPS, or 83% of a 9600 BPS line.

Unfortunately, the above transmission speeds are based on the assumption that the communications software can drive the line to its rated speed. Although production protocols between real terminals (HASP workstations, 3274s, and so forth) lose little capacity, the software currently available for PCs performs poorly. Not only is there appreciable time wasted in the PC software itself, but also most present packages are aimed at transmitting to TSO, which causes further delay. Measurements of several PC transmission packages are detailed below in Table 18.2:

Table 18.2
Measurements of PC Transmission Packages

Rated line speed (CPS)	Software communications package	Host program	Actual line speed (CPS)	Minutes to transfer 10 screens
37.5	IBM ASYNC	TSO EDIT	21	15.24
150	IBM ASYNC	TSO EDIT	52	6.15
150	CROSSTALK	CMS EDIT	119	2.69
1200	IRMA	TSO EDIT	30	10.66
1200	PCOX	TSO PCOX	342	0.94

Note that the time to transfer the same volume of data ranges from less than 1 to more than 15 minutes. Recognize that vendors make no claim regarding transmission speed, and the ability to transfer, no matter how slowly, was more important in their original design than was speed of transmission. As more performance analysts begin to measure the performance of the software (see below), vendors will design performance as well as functionality into communications software.

4. **Processing the data received**. To process the file, time is still required on the PC once the data have been downloaded. If the data are for a spreadsheet application, for example, the data base on the PC must be updated by using a utility from the spreadsheet to read the transmitted data. Of course, this phase can be done after the communications path is disconnected, but its elapsed time must be considered in the total time required to download data, and it must be measured experimentally.

Therefore, the overall transfer of data is made up of three phases whose durations are relatively constant and one phase, transmission, whose duration grows linearly with the data. Based on the frequency of transmission (hourly, daily, and so forth), the appropriate line speed and communications package can be selected.

SUBSECOND RESPONSE TIME

For ten years, Walt Doherty, IBM T.J. Watson Research Center, has been proposing subsecond response time. Until recently, however, only through distributed computing networks, typically with local 4341 class machines, could response time in the 200-300 millisecond range be delivered. With the recent announcement of an inexpensive modification to the 3274 51C control unit family, which allows the 3274 to operate into a DDS 56000 BPS line, the need for the extra CPU has been eliminated. Note that Table 18.1 shows the time to transmit a 3270 screen of 1920 bytes, an SPF scroll, is over 1.6 seconds at 9600 BPS but only 275 milliseconds at 56000 BPS. Therefore, a group of TSO users across town could have subsecond line response by replacing their present 9600 BPS line with a 56000 BPS line. The monthly cost in January 1984 of a crosstown 56KB line was only $800, whereas the cost of a Dallas to Philadelphia line is only $8000 per month. Unpublished measurements by 2 TSO installations experimenting with 56KB lines have suggested that subsecond response can be provided to 40 development programming TSO users sharing 1 56KB line with 2 3274 control units and no more than 20 terminals per control unit. This is a crosstown cost of only $20 per terminal per month for the increased line cost to provide subsecond response time.

MEASURING ACTUAL LINE SPEED

Line speed, in real characters per second, can be measured with a stop watch. You can get a good estimate of the real character transfer rate by timing the duration to scroll through a file.

Scrolling or even transmitting a file, measuring the duration of transmission, measuring the size of the file in characters, and then dividing to calculate line speed in characters per second can provide an accurate engineering estimate. Consider the following:

- The software in the host, especially TSO, can be swapped out (or JES can take a page fault) during the transmission. This increases the duration, slowing the measured line transfer speed from its theoretical value.
- The software in the terminal, especially an IBM PC with the IBM Asynchronous Communications Support software, may not be able to handle the line speed, slowing the measured line transfer speed.
- The protocol of the line (Asynchronous, Bisynchronous, or SLDC) affects measured line transfer speed.

- Because of differing software protocols, transmitting to the host is usually faster than receiving from the host.
- Measuring the file size can be nontrivial. If measured on the PC, are data stored in a compressed mode? Does the file size reported by the operating system include blank lines? If measured on the host in tracks, remember that 19069 bytes are how many might be there, not how many are there. The last block might even be a short block.
- The file size to be transferred should require at least 10 seconds and preferably 100 seconds of elapsed time. Humans can respond to a stop watch in under a quarter of a second. Ten seconds duration would have a potential error of 2.5%, or 175 characters per second error on a 56000 BPS, 7000 CPS line.
- The number of characters sent can be less than the number in the file. The software might use data compression. Although it would seem intuitively obvious to the casual observer (or certainly casually obvious to the intuitive observer) that trailing blanks would be removed before transmission, not all transmission packages do. HASP protocol not only removes blanks at the end of the line, each installation can optionally compress replicated characters. Even though you want compression when you transmit real data, you may find measurement easier if you build your file with nonreplicated characters. The following SAS program builds a nonreplicated character file of 64000 bytes:

```
DATA _NULL_;
   FILE NOREPLIC RECFM=FB LRECL=80 BLKSIZE=23440;
   A='0123456789ABCDEFGHIJKLMNOPQRSTUVWXYZYXVW';
   DO _I_= 1 TO 800;
     PUT A $CHAR40. A $CHAR40.;
     END;
```

Error retry by the communications path elongates the transmission time. This frequently occurs when a telephone extension on the transmission line is taken off the hook accidentally. In one case, human error caused termination of the partial transmission.

These concerns are surmountable, and you can measure the capacity of the line to transmit data. Taking the measurement at various times of the day would identify any queuing on the communications path. The elapsed time to transmit the same file is a starting point to begin measuring. If the transfer rate never changes during the day, then the communications path has sufficient capacity unless some factor external to the path is constraining the arrival rate to a constant value. Although variation in the transfer rate across the day confirms contention on the communications path, it cannot isolate the cause (line, software, 3725, and so forth).

Note: the 327x normal sized, 80 character by 24 lines, contains 1920 possible bytes, or characters, per screen. Scrolling through 10 full screens of nonreplicated data on a 9600 BPS dedicated line requires a minimum of 16 seconds for the 19,200 bytes. Time it, record it, and check it next week to see if it has changed.

The final communications tool, this one for TSO only, is provided with the MXG software in member CLSTIMER, described in that section of chapter forty-one. This module prompts you to press enter as often as you possibly can, and then it reports in tabular and graphical form the total response time between two successive trivial interactions. Total response time on a 9600 BPS line has been measured as low as 690 milliseconds, with many interactions in the 700-1000 ms range; an abrupt jump to 2-3 seconds occurs when the TSO user is swapped out. Simply running the program at a user's terminal shows exactly how good or bad the end user's response time for trivial interactions is. CLSTIMER is especially useful for demonstrating degradation caused when JES printers share a line with TSO users.

Forty-two 3270 terminals and a JES 328X RJE printer on a single 9600 BPS line were used in one comparison, and the response time dropped dramatically when the printer was moved to another line. The summary of CLSTIMER measures is shown in Table 18.3.

Table 18.3
Trivial Response Measured with CLSTIMER

Measurements with printer

Midpoint response value (seconds)	Cumulative percent of total responses
0.6	18
1.2	33
1.8	55
2.4	87
3.9	95
3.6	100

Measurements without printer

Midpoint response value (seconds)	Cumulative percent of total responses
0.4	29
0.8	67
1.2	84

1.6	90
2.0	96
2.4	100

Ninety percent of these trivial interactions were serviced in under 1.6 seconds when no printer was sharing the line, whereas with the single 3286 printer on the same line, the 90th percentile response was 1 second longer at nearly 3 seconds. This analysis only required the execution of CLSTIMER with and without the printer. Combining JES printing and TSO users on a single line might seem cost-effective, but when JES protocol dominates the line, the TSO user loses.

The CLSTIMER program was very effective for visually communicating the impact that printers were having on response time on a very saturated line. All users perform a measurement experiment on your system when they log on. Why not give them access to a simple CLIST tool that allows them to see the response time with the line speeds they have chosen.

chapter nineteen

Workload Analysis - Batch

In most installations, the batch workload is the largest consumer of resources. Although on-line systems continue to make inroads by offering interactive answers, batch is significantly less expensive because of its inherent lower overhead; thus, you can always expect to have significant batch work. Intelligent terminals, like the IBM PC, only increase batch workload; data centers of the twenty-first century will be capable of managing large data libraries that execute batch jobs for users to manage data movement between the host and a desktop computer that will probably be a 2 MIP 4 MB processor. Batch will still be used to update, backup, and report from these large data libraries of the future corporate data center.

This chapter discusses the measurement of the batch workload, but most of the analytic tools have been previously discussed. Resources consumed by batch work are usually no different from other workloads, and, thus, individual resources can be tracked, as discussed in the resource measurement chapters. Of particular importance to batch users are chapter seven, which describes the events in the life of a job; chapters eight and nine, which discuss service objectives for batch; chapter sixteen, which discusses measurement and determination of initiators; and chapter seventeen, which deals with remote job entry (RJE).

This chapter addresses the following topics:

1. Scheduling batch work
2. Analyzing execution events that delay batch work
3. Identifying ownership of batch work.

SCHEDULING BATCH WORK

Scheduling batch work is implicit in the definition of the installation's batch service objectives. If classing is used to differentiate batch categories, then the number of initiators and their classing structure determine the scheduling of batch work. Because the needs of installations vary widely, there are few general guidelines. The following sections identify several methods for resolving users' complaints about batch service or batch pricing.

Managing Scheduled Job Streams with Urgency Job Scheduling

The use of an urgency job scheduling system, such as the initiation wait time example in chapter eight, can only be controlled with a pricing differential that costs the user more if higher urgency is required by a job. This philosophy uses economic pressure to motivate users to delay execution of less critical work, thereby saving their budgets. Most batch work is amenable to this urgency scheduling, but there is a class of work usually called scheduled job streams that must be handled separately. The user claims a need to execute in the highest urgency category because once this scheduled job stream is started, it must execute with minimum interjob delay in order to complete. But the user argues for a lower rate because the job stream must execute regularly.

It is usually most effective to agree with the user, offer his job stream execution at the highest urgency, and reduce the price for those jobs in the job stream. This can be managed by accounting; jobs in this special pricing category can be identified by a unique account number assigned by data processing and could be validated against a table of authorized job names in the job initiation security validation routine to prevent abuse or misuse. Since these production job streams should be a relatively small percentage of the workload, they should be treated as exceptions to the normal urgency-scheduled job only in their pricing, and special initiators should not have to be established.

Investigating User Complaints with Batch Service

Measuring the installation's batch service and reporting the quality of service rendered to end users greatly reduces questions and complaints. Not only should the overall batch work be measured, but the batch work from different groups should be tabulated and compared so that the users themselves know the level of service being provided, especially to their own groups. If a variance between groups does exist, it can be analyzed. Often, however, a user may complain of poor batch service when the real problem is not connected with the job scheduling itself. Two specific examples follow.

JCL errors occur at end of job read-in   One user not only complained bitterly that batch service was poor, but also that even JCL errors took 15 minutes. Since the JCL error should occur immediately, we were concerned also. By examining several of his jobs with JCL errors (in MXG data set PDB.JOBS the variable ABEND will have value JCL), we discovered that the value of variable SPOOLCRD, the number of JCL and SYSIN statements put on the spool by JES, was 2010. A subsequent execution of the same job name showed that when the job executed it had a SYSINCNT value of 2000. This proved that the user's job contained a SYSIN data set of 2000 80-byte cards (160 KB of data, or about one half the data that fit on a PC's 360 KB floppy disk). The INROUTE variable gave the remote number, and the JES system programmer confirmed that this was a 2400 BPS dial-in RJE site. On a 2400 BPS line with no contention, 160,000 bytes would require a minimum of 9 minutes for transmission. Thus, the problem of poor batch service for JCL errors had nothing to do with batch scheduling, but rather was the time required to read in the job. The JCL error occurs immediately **after** the last card (JCL or SYSIN) has been read.

Further investigation with the end user showed that the SYSIN data being transmitted had never changed; the user did not know how to copy the case of cards to a data set. We gave him the JCL to copy a SYSIN data set to TSO disk space, gave him a second job with a total of eleven card images to submit to use the data, and we made a friend for life!

Impact of RJE operation on batch service   A separate occurrence of batch complaints from one group of users served by a single RJE station caused investigation of the hours of service for that RJE. The RJE connect records (TYPE4789 for this Bisync RJE, but also TYPE5234 for SDLC remotes) showed the RJE site did not sign on until 7:45 a.m. to begin printing the prior evening's output. When informed, the management at the RJE site chose to pay an RJE operator to arrive 2 hours earlier, solving the poor batch service complaint.

ANALYZING EXECUTION EVENTS THAT DELAY BATCH WORK

If the batch jobs are elongated during execution, the user complains of poor batch service. If the elongation is due to insufficient resources (memory, I/O, CPU, and so forth), the previously discussed techniques for resource analysis identify the cause. However, poor design of the batch job or job stream can be the culprit. Thus, an examination of the following possibilities can prove helpful.

Job Stream Design Effects

Many streams of production jobs should not exist as a job stream, but rather the individual jobs should be combined into a single, multi-step job. Although this should be the responsibility of the applications programmers and the data control function, both of those groups usually suffer from a lack of JCL expertise. There is a great fear of changing anything that works, a reticence to redesign JCL streams because the redesign must be documented, and there is a great deal of foot-dragging in this area. The performance analyst can do the organization a great service by measuring just how much elapsed time is wasted between jobs in these streams. The analysis can be elementary if the stream is truly a serial sequence of jobs; the time wasted between the selected jobs can be determined by using the following analysis of the job stream durations.

In this example, all jobs in the job stream start with the letters PROD. The first job in the stream is named PRODFRST, and the last job in the stream is named PRODLAST:

```
DATA JOBS;
 SET PDB.JOBS;
 IF JOB=:'PROD';
PROC SORT;
 BY JSTRTIME;
DATA JOBSTREM;
 KEEP JOB ELAPSTM STREAMTM BETWENTM JSTRTIME JENDTIME;
 SET PRODJOBS;
 BY JSTRTIME;
 IF JOB EQ 'PRODFRST' THEN FIRSTIME=JSTRTIME;
 RETAIN FIRSTIME PREVTIME;
 IF JOB EQ 'PRODLAST' THEN DO;
   LASTTIME=JENDTIME;
   STREAMTM=LASTTIME-FIRSTIME;
 END;
 BETWENTM=JSTRTIME-PREVTIME;
 IF . LT BETWENTM LT 0 THEN BETWENTM=.;
 PREVTIME=MAX(JENDTIME,PREVTIME);
PROC PRINT SPLIT='*';
 VAR JOB JSTRTIME JENDTIME ELAPSTM BETWENTM STREAMTM;
 SUMVAR ELAPSTM BETWENTM STREAMTM;
 LABEL
   BETWENTM='TIME WASTED*BEFORE THIS*JOB EXECUTED'
   STREAMTM='JOBSTREAM*BEGIN-TO-END*DURATION';


 TITLE 'JOB STREAM ANALYSIS';
 TITLE2 'TIME SPENT IN JOB EXECUTION AND TIME WASTED
   BETWEEN JOBS IN THIS JOB STREAM';
```

This analysis shows beginning and ending times of each execution of this stream, the elapsed time of each job, and the time wasted between each job in the stream. By quantifying the delay, the effort to modify the stream can be justified. A frequent response to this analysis can be that the output of each job must be checked before submitting the next. This attitude results from the data control area because the application programmer was lazy. If a human can be directed to perform checks on a printed page, algorithms can be written to perform those same checks in a separate step. If the checks are invalid, that step can then issue an abend to terminate the job. Otherwise, the next job becomes the next step of this single multi-step job that replaces the many single-step jobs. Call for human evaluation only when it cannot be programmed and thereby avoid the delay in human notification, in printing, or in retrieving the output for review. Most of all, avoid the scheduling delay for the next job in the stream by making it a step.

Examine Internal Delays within the Elapsed Time of Each Job

Frequently production jobs are delayed after they are initiated. As discussed in chapter seven, the delay due to data set conflicts can be detected by examining the variable DSENQTM in JES2 installations. If there are production jobs with any DSENQTM delay, the SYSMSG output must be examined to determine which data sets are causing the delay. Armed with the data set name, the TYPE1415 data set can be examined to identify other jobs causing the delay, and the owners of both jobs can agree on the correct shared usage of the needed data set in order to minimize contention.

Another delay can occur when there are insufficient tape drives available for allocation. Production jobs wait in an initiator for tape drives to become available. Of course, as discussed in chapter fourteen, the tape drive resource must be analyzed. This analysis can identify the jobs being delayed and how long their ALOCTM values are delaying them, and it also can identify other noncritical jobs submitted at the same time of day that are creating contention for tape drives. Do not forget that the use of UNIT=AFFINITY to reduce the number of tape drives required by a job not only reduces the time to allocate and, hence, the run time of that job, but it also makes wasted tape drives available to other jobs.

Rerun and Abend Analysis

It is not uncommon for a recurring failure in the application to cause poor batch service. Users perceive poor batch service when the real cause is reruns, especially with applications that undergo frequent design changes. The frequency of rerun can be identified by counting the occurrence of the same production job name if the reruns are executed with the same job name. Production jobs should be tabulated by the ABEND and associated CONDCODE variables in PDB.JOBS to determine if a particular type of ABEND is recurring. This is true especially if the tabulation can group jobs coming from the different application areas. Many production failures actually result from JCL problems. For example, system x13 abends occur at open time, usually resulting from a misspecified data set and member names in the JCL. By identifying the abends that are most common from each application, the performance analyst can offer educational seminars on the causes of abends. For example, a discussion of DASD space allocation JCL rules can reduce the occurrence of B37, D37, and E37 abends.

Program Analysis - ANALPROG

The MXG analysis routine, ANALPROG, described in chapter forty-one, can tabulate the resource consumption of production jobs by program. Programs that should be examined because of high resource usage or because of high frequency of execution are identified. Once identified, the program can be monitored with a program monitor, such as the ANALYZER program that comes with the CA/CAPEX COBOL OPTIMIZER product, and that analyzes any program written in any language. Chapter twenty-seven also offers suggestions about COBOL options that elongate execution duration.

IDENTIFYING OWNERSHIP OF BATCH WORK

A major task in analyzing the batch workload is the identification and categorization of batch jobs to their owning business function. If the installation has dealt with this problem in the past, there should exist a standard classification algorithm for the performance analyst. The billing or accounting classification should be exploited first since senior management may already be accustomed to that classification. Alternatively, the CPE analyst can take the lead and establish a batch work classification scheme by which the resources and service can be mapped to business groups. The following items are associated with each job and can be used in this classification:

Accounting Fields — should be used as the primary source of work classification. Since accountants must keep track of expenses, any existing categorization should be used. Often this can be as simple as the first letter(s) of the account number. If the installation has a jumble of account numbers with no algorithmic capability, consider creating a SAS format to map each account or group of accounts to its owning department. The format value could also contain information, such as physical location of the customer, and would reduce the stored size of the job level data. This use of PROC FORMAT is discussed in chapter thirty-seven.

RACFUSER Name — contains the RACF user name and identifies the user submitting the job in installations with a security system that is RACF or that uses the RACF interfaces. Since this entity is usually associated with an individual, it can provide a simpler scheme for identifying the owner of batch work.

Programmer Name Field (PGMRNAME) — contains the actual application description of up to twenty characters in the JOB statement. If it cannot be used directly because of a lack of enforced standard format, it can be used to verify that other classification schemes are accurate.

USERINFO field — is an 8-byte field available to the SMF JOB-related exits, and it is frequently filled in by installation code with information about the job, such as department, business element, and so forth.

Job Name   provides the best categorization of batch work. The power of the SAS System's character manipulation functions, like SUBSTR, permits easy identification based on different characters in different positions of job name.

In the final analysis, you may have to test all five of the items described in this section in order to identify the owner of batch work. After a classification algorithm has been written, its validation must include a tabulation of the job names that were classified to different groupings. By giving the list of unique job names identified to a particular application to the manager of that application, anomalies to your algorithm can be identified before any formal analysis is accomplished on the classification.

chapter twenty

Workload Measurement - TSO

A TSO logon creates a session's JCL, which is submitted through a reader that is almost like a job. The job name is the TSO session's userid, and the accounting fields are filled by prompting the user or by the User Attribute Data Set (SYS1.UADS). The job executes a program usually named IKJEFT01 from SYS1.LINKLIB, with a step name that is the TSO procedure name supplied either by the user or by default in the UADS. In execution, the TSO session exists in its own address space like a batch job; the only major difference is the connection between the address space and the terminal. Thus, resource measurement and workload measurement of TSO are very similar to batch measurement discussed in chapter nineteen.

This chapter describes the following aspects of TSO workloads:

- response time techniques
- terminal usage in VTAM networks
- measures of user productivity
- benchmarking TSO by stimulation.

RESPONSE TIME TECHNIQUES

Establishing response time objectives for TSO was discussed in chapter eight. Two sources of measurement data that can be automatically gathered and included in the performance data base are the records written by RMF and the records written by Morino Associates' product TSO/MON. Another source of response measurement is the CLTIMER TSO command list that accompanies MXG software. It is also possible to measure TSO user response by accessing an ADABAS data base.

RMF Measurement of Response Time

RMF sums the elapsed time of all transactions that end in each period of each performance group, and it counts the number of transactions summed. If total elapsed time is divided by the number of transactions, then the average response time of transactions ending in that period is known. The average elapsed time of ended transactions exists for every period of every performance group; it is not just a TSO metric. As described in section TYPE72 of chapter forty, the statistic is used primarily for measuring TSO, but it is occasionally used for batch.

This measurement is free with RMF, but it is somewhat limited in use. It cannot be used as a service time objective since only one value, or average response, is measured. The idea that average response time values relate to what actually happens with interactive systems is a fallacy, and this is demonstrated with the numeric example in chapter twenty-one. RMF response measure also suffers because performance groups are not commonly defined in a manner that allows data to be captured on individual users.

If every TSO userid had its own performance group, you would know the RMF measured average internal response time for each user. What would be the resource cost of added performance groups? Intuition and the fact that there was no observed effect when 20 performance groups were increased to 120 suggest that the only impact on increasing the number of performance groups is that the size of the type 72 record is increased by 56 bytes for every period in the definition of that performance group. Even with 4 periods defined, the additional resource cost would be that of adding 224 bytes of SMF data per hourly RMF interval for every user. Since MVS permits up to 999 performance groups, it is possible to record these data for every user. Many installations define performance groups to gather response statistics, but usually several TSO users who perform similar business functions are placed in the same performance group. This allows you to track both the average response and, more importantly, the hourly resources consumed by these business functions.

As an overall system measure, the response time measurement available from RMF is very useful when clearly understood. Within one operating system and hardware configuration, the average elapsed time for transactions that ended in the first period is an excellent indicator of internal response time trends and correlates well with perceived response, as long as neither the CPU nor the software is changed. Categories such as this, which are based on any resource measure, do not normally survive a processor or operating system change, and, thus, neither does the average value of such a category of transactions. The redefinition of service unit, perhaps because of a different CPU, can cause a group of transactions that formerly ended in second period to end now in first period. Since the population being measured has changed, there is no guarantee that the measured value will be stable.

Within a stable configuration, the RMF response time measure can be used when no better measure is available. Named TSORESP, it is calculated in TYPE72 and is in the RMFINTRV built by BUILDPDB. Examples of its use are included in DAILYRPT, described in chapter forty-one.

TSO/MON for Response Time

From the preceding section, it should be clear that TSO/MON offers much of what is missing in the RMF response time measure. The architecture and value of TSO/MON are best described by Morino Associates, but a brief description of the data capture algorithm is worthwhile because it is an excellent model of how to monitor systems other than TSO.

- Transactions are categorized. TSO/MON traps every command and categorizes it as trivial or nontrivial, based on an installation choice: either the names of commands are looked up to categorize the transaction or service units consumed determine the classification.
- The response time measurement is distributed into 8 response intervals, with magnitudes set by the installation. Typically these intervals are 1, 2, 3, 4, 8, 15, 30, and over 30 seconds.
- Data are captured for each TSO user individually. A separate logical segment is maintained for each user, with response distributions data enhanced by resource consumption statistics and the SMF READTIME by which other records for this TSO session can be directly related for cross-analysis.
- Accumulated data are written to SMF periodically at an installation-chosen interval, usually in the range of one to four intervals per hour. The same interval applies to all users in the same CPU; thus, data can be compared directly to RMF.
- The volume of data to be analyzed grows only with additional concurrent users and not with their transaction rates. This design typically creates only 16 SMF records for a user during a 4-hour TSO session. These 5 items describe the data created in the TSOMSYST data set built by MXG software and are described in that section of chapter forty.
- In addition to the response and resource statistics captured in each user's interval record, an unrelated SMF record can be created by TSO/MON for each program or command that the installation chooses to monitor individually. This record describes the user and resources for the duration of the call and contains within it the eight response intervals for trivial and nontrivial interactions rather than transactions that the user performed while in this called program. For example, since the SAS System can be executed as a called program, a single TSOMCALL observation is created, containing all interactions during that execution of the SAS System.

The documentation provided with the TSO/MON product can answer any further questions on its use.

CLSTIMER for Actual Response Measurement

The TSO CLIST utility distributed with MXG software, CLSTIMER, is described in that section of chapter forty-one. It provides a simple SAS routine that can be installed in the master CLIST library so that it seems to be a command named TIMER. The command performs a response measurement experiment for a TSO user and provides a graphical and tabular analysis of the user's total (internal plus communications path) response at the terminal. It demonstrates the true impact of changing line speed or comparing the effect of a printer on the line, and it allows the end user to gather his own response measures to compare the alternatives himself.

TERMINAL USAGE IN VTAM NETWORKS

The VTAM terminal name in the type 30 step and job records exists in the PDB.JOBS data set whenever RACF exits are enabled. All current security packages for MVS use the RACF exits and, thus, should cause this field to be nonblank. It can be extremely valuable since it permits analysis of what terminals are being used by what users. To see if it is valid for your sessions, execute these statements:

```
DATA TSO;
  SET PDB.JOBS;
  IF TYPETASK='TSU';
PROC FREQ DATA=TSO;
  TABLES VTAMTERM;
  TABLES JOB*VTAMTERM/NOROW NOCOL NOPERCENT NOCUM;
  TITLE 'VTAM TERMINAL NAMES USED BY TSO USERS';
```

MEASURES OF USER PRODUCTIVITY

Productivity can be measured in many ways, and no one has determined which is best. Several measures used in the literature can be readily evaluated from your own data.

TGETS as Counts of Interactions

The count of TGET macros, a GET from the terminal, should signify that the user has pressed enter once for each TGET. Thus, the number of human interactions can be counted whenever TGETS are counted. Both the type 30 step record and the type 30 interval data contain TGETS; the interval data can be used to track the number of interactions per user. IBM studies have found that interactive programmers require 300 to 400 interactions per hour when provided subsecond response for human intensive computing. By comparing the TGETS per hour for your users, you can estimate how well you are providing for your TSO users' productivity.

CPU Seconds Per User Hour

The CPU (TCB + SRB) seconds consumed in each session hour have been a good way to measure the intensity of this resource required by different types of users. For example, on 3033 processors, response for users whose primary use of TSO was EDIT and SUBMIT (relatively nonintensive) were found to cluster around 5 to 10 seconds per hour, but interactive debugging users response clustered around 12 to 16 seconds, and very intensive SAS users processing large amounts of data (that is, the author) typically used 20 to 30 CPU seconds for every hour logged on. When a new TSO facility is benchmarked, its intensity is compared to the current average for all TSO users, and if the new facility is 3 times the average CPU intensity per logged on hour, the new facility is described as being the equivalent of 3 logged on users. As always, care must be taken with these univariate comparisons.

CPU Per Transaction

This alternate measure of TSO workload utilization was also used to demonstrate the change in usage of TSO over time. Calculated from RMFINTRV (or TYPE72) as

```
CPU_TRAN=CPUTM/NRTRANS;
```

CPU_TRAN was plotted for several years, normalizing CPUTM for the different processors. It was stable for 2 years, began to grow in early 1982, and 9 months later it had doubled its initial value. It has remained at the second plateau ever since. Prior to 1982, the nonprogrammer population had little training in TSO. Starting in 1981 and culminating in 1982, a concerted effort to introduce the power and capability of TSO to end users, especially through packaged decision support systems like SAS, RAMIS, EMPIRE, and so forth, was undertaken through classes and seminars on these tools. The growth of CPU per transaction intensity correlated with this increase in education, raising the intensity as the user population raised from trivial to serious TSO users.

BENCHMARKING TSO BY STIMULATION

Because a TSO session executes almost like a batch job, you can conduct a benchmark of TSO usage without either TPNS or without having 200 users log on over the weekend. The following program executes as a batch job and creates the load equivalent to several TSO users:

```
//      EXEC    PGM=IKJEFT01,DYNAMNBR=40
//SYSPROC  DD  DSN=nameofsystem CLISTlibrary
//SYSTSPRT DD  SYSOUT=A
//SYSTSIN  DD  *
  LISTDS 'SYS1.LINKLIB' M
```

This batch step executes the commands that follow the SYSTSIN DD statement. A CLIST could be prepared that exercises several functions, but executing the single TSO command to list all members of a large PDS has correlated well with more sophisticated benchmarks. It is not surprising; the majority of the work (hence, the majority of instructions executed and paths tested) and any interactive system seem to be independent of the actual command executed. For TSO, handling of the input, swap-in of the address space, loading of the command to be executed, paging the results, parsing associated with the command, output processing, and termination are the same for every command. The measured CPU consumption of the LISTDS command from benchmarks has correlated exactly with CPU comparisons taken from the real TSO workload executed on the same before and after configurations. It is not without concern; it once showed dramatic changes that were not anticipated in CPU across an operating system maintenance release. Investigation showed that the actual size of the SYS1.LINKLIB data set had changed with the maintenance release. Although comparing I/O counts and CPU usage make this point obvious, it further demonstrates that the benchmark technique is vulnerable to error, as chapter thirty mentions.

Before stimulating a TSO workload, you should be aware of two possible problems. First, only TSO commands that internally use GETLINE/PUTLINE instead of TGET/TPUT macros can be executed under TSO in batch. You can tell by trying it, and if it works, then the command used GETLINE/PUTLINE. A command using TGET/TPUT causes the job to act like it was not executed or to terminate at that point without executing further commands in the input stream. Second, realize that this batch job stimulates just like a logged on user in memory, but this user has no think time. Therefore, one stimulated user (that is, batch job) represents an in and ready user, not just a logged on user. By comparing the in and ready user count to the average TSO users logged on (both are in RMFINTRV), you can estimate the ratio of logged on to active for your normal TSO. This ratio can then be used to extrapolate the number of batch jobs stimulating to the number of logged on users being simulated. It is common to find 5 to 10 logged on users for every in and ready user. Thus, stimulating 200 logged on users could require only that you execute stimulate with 20 copies of the above job in 20 initiators. Conduct this benchmark as suggested in chapter thirty by iterating initiators from 1 until total saturation occurs, perhaps starting a new initiator every 3 minutes. This stimulates the system over the range of logged on TSO users. Considering the minimal expense involved in this experiment, it is worth trying any time a serious question of TSO capacity is raised. Finally, note that neither TSO/MON nor RMF supports response measurement of TSO transactions issued from batch jobs, so this technique is useful only for resource measures of TSO workloads.

chapter twenty-one

Workload Measurement-CICS

There are very few software products that run on IBM systems with users as enthusiastic as CICS bigots (except SAS users, of course). One of the most successful of IBM's interactive transaction processing systems, Customer Information Control System (CICS) was the result of a joint project called a Major Application Program Evaluation, or MAPE, in 1975-ish IBM-ese. CICS grew out of the need to meet the business application of a power utility to process utility customer's calls about their electric bills.

This chapter discusses the entire CICS subsystem as it can be measured for response time (service objectives) and for resources (cost distribution of the shared computer resources). The primary data source discussed is the data created by the IBM component of CICS releases 1.5 and later, the CICS Monitor Facility or CMF data. CMF records can be written by CICS to a journal file under both MVS and DOS/VSE, or under MVS, they can and should be written to the SMF file as the type 110 record.

The development of CICS measurement tools by IBM is a fascinating history because it demonstrates how long it took to realize the necessity of having recorded performance data in the development of interactive systems. Since there was no measurement built into the CICS product, IBM's field force designed and supported the first good CICS measurement tool, the CICS Performance Analyzer II, which was distributed as a Field Developed Program. The wide acceptance of this FDP resulted in the development of CMF, which provides everything that was in PAII and much more.

This chapter covers a range of topics appropriate for CICS and any other interactive system. Topics include:

- *RESPONSE TIME CLASSIFICATION CASE STUDY*
- *AVERAGE VALUE OF RESPONSE TIME*
- *CICS INTERNAL RESPONSE MEASUREMENT*
- *CICS CMF DATA STRUCTURE*
- *DEBUGGING FEATURES BUILT IN MXG CMF PROCESSING*

RESPONSE TIME CLASSIFICATION CASE STUDY

The following paper, entitled "Performance Evaluation of CICS Using the SAS System and the CICS Performance Analyzer Data," was originally presented at CMG X in Dallas. The study used PAII data, the only data available when this research was conducted. Now the same analysis would use CMF data with the same results, as the internal response measured by both tools is measured at essentially the same points.

Performance Evaluation of CICS Using the SAS System and the CICS Performance Analyzer Data

Abstract Response time and resource usage measures are gathered on the CICS system by the IBM Product CICS Performance Analyzer II (PAII). The product was validated to determine that the percentage of total response time measurable by the PAII was 85% under isolated line decreasing to 72%, with 12 terminals on a shared line. Analysis showed that only I/O count was needed to provide accurate classification of transactions into groupings based on response time. Finally, human factors of satisfaction were compared to response measures, and response objectives were established based on user satisfaction.

User satisfaction in any interactive on-line system is based on perceived adequate response. For such a system, you want to obtain actual measures of response, establish objectives for these measures, and provide reports to both the user and the supplier of service that describe how well objectives are met.

Although PAII produces information on CICS resource consumption as well as response measures, the primary interest in this study was to answer the following questions:

1. How much of the user perceived response time was recovered by CICS PAII?
2. Can a simple classification scheme for transactions be developed?
3. Can user satisfaction be correlated with response measures?
4. Is regular reporting economical?

Figure 21.1, modified from the PAII manual, identifies the events in the life of a CICS transaction. The four components that provide service are the application code, task control program (KCP), terminal control program (TCP), and supervisor control program (SCP, or operating system). Although the user sees response as the elapsed time from terminal entry until response display, some elapsed time occurs between entry and task create (the start of transaction time stamp in PAII) and between the time the application ends (the end of transaction time stamp in PAII) and the display at the terminal. If a significant portion of user perceived response time is measured by PAII, then realistic objectives can be based on such measures. However, if only a small portion of response is measurable, then the difference between measurement and perception can invalidate the usefulness of the tool.

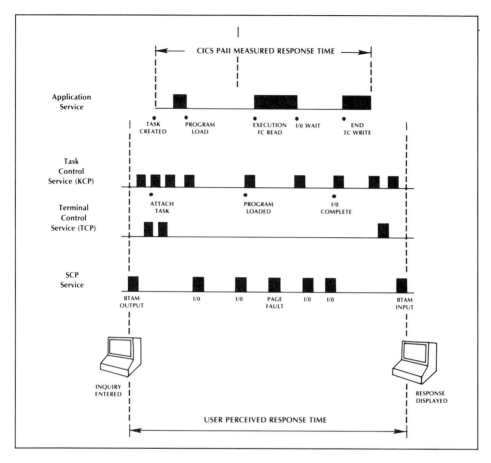

Figure 21.1

To determine the response recovery of this tool, 30 transactions representative of the workload and selected by the user were measured internally with PAII and externally at the terminal with a Questronics, Inc., Terminal Response Time Monitor by measuring the time the inhibit light on the 3270 Terminal was on. The series of transactions was executed in 2 different environments: with CICS on a dedicated 168-MP with no other terminals active on the 4800 baud line and at peak load on the 168-MP, with 16 CICS terminals and 1 controller on the same 4800 baud line. After the experiment, hardware response was matched with the PAII response, and a difference was calculated for each transaction. These differences were averaged for the 2 environments, and Table 21.2 shows the remarkable recovery of response time by PAII. Clearly, the major portion of user perceived response time was measured by PAII.

Table 21.2
Response Time Recovered

	Average hardware response time	Average difference in response time	Percent recovered
Isolated line and CPU	2.5	.4	84%
Fully-loaded line and CPU	2.8	.7	75%

The next step was to investigate the resource measures contained in PAII. Table 21.3 lists these fields. There are two CPU fields in the transaction record: TRCCPUR and TRCCPU. TRCCPUR is the true CPU time used by the transaction. The TRCCPU field contains the duration that CICS thought the transaction was dispatched and, thus, includes any wait time outside CICS's control, such as preemption by higher dispatching priority tasks, paging, and so forth.

Table 21.3
Resource Measures in Transaction Record

Field Name	Description
TRCCPU	CPU time as perceived by CICS
TRCCPUR	Actual "Real" CPU time of transaction
TRCWAIT	Wait time as perceived by CICS
TRCSIO	Count of Start I/Os issued by transaction
TRCPGIN	Count of page-ins
TRCPGOUT	Count of page-outs
TRCMSGIN	Number of input messages
TRCMSGOT	Number of output messages
TRCMILTH	Total length of input messages
TRCMOLTH	Total length of output messages
TRCHISTG	Highwater mark of terminal + user address space
TRCPCPH	Highwater mark of program address space

RESPONSE = TRCCPU + TRCWAIT

In addition to the resource fields, there is a flag field that indicates when the transaction was delayed by CICS. If insufficient address space was available or if the maximum number of concurrent tasks was exceeded, the transaction was forced to wait, and its response time is not related to resources. Thus, these trans-actions are classified separately as delayed and excluded from further analysis.

The problem of classifying CICS transactions was addressed next. Intuitively, some transactions are fast and some slow, and there are only two valid classification techniques. Either the transactions are classified by a name lookup table, or the transactions are classified by some resource measures. Classification by name should be used only as a last resort. Name classification requires manual mainte-nance whenever new transactions are added, and it usually assumes that the name describes the transaction completely, which is not generally true. The same transaction name can have widely differing responses, based on different arguments. For example, an alpha search for a customer will have a radically dif-ferent response for all SMITHs than for all SYZYGYs!

The most likely predictors of response are CPUR and SIO. The daily PAII data of 45,452 nondelayed transactions were initially profiled and are given in Table 21.4.

Table 21.4

CPU Distribution

TRCCPUR (seconds)	Number	Cumulative percent
.00	4290	9.4
.01	9564	30.5
.02	10580	53.8
.03	11967	80.1
.04	6302	93.9
.05	1580	97.4
.06	631	98.8
.07	265	99.4
.08	94	99.6
.09	36	99.7
.10	18	99.7
>.10	125	----

Response Distribution

Response (seconds)	Number	Cumulative percent
0	10462	23.0
1	16262	58.8
2	12156	85.5
3	2875	91.9
4	733	93.5
5	248	94.0
6	155	94.4
7	161	94.7
8	184	95.1
9	229	95.6
10	175	96.0
11-19	1383	99.3
>20	208	----

I/O Distribution

TRCSIO (count)	Number	Cumulative percent
0	4985	11.0
1	372	11.8
2	5709	24.3
4	6211	43.0
5	3058	49.8
6	5990	63.0
7	4453	72.7
8	2118	77.4
9	1859	81.5
10	1592	85.0
11	1837	89.0
12	2010	93.5

13	648	94.9
14	160	95.2
15	167	95.6
16	100	95.8
17	176	96.2
18	82	96.4
19	96	96.6
20-29	822	98.4
30-39	500	99.5
40-49	113	99.7
>50	117	----

Initially, an attempt was made to select classifications using linear regression to fit a linear equation to the data. Three regressions were executed; 1 against all 45,610 transactions, 1 against the 45,452 nondelayed transactions, and 1 against the 45,231 transactions after outliers (CPUR over .10 seconds or SIO count over 40) were removed. Table 21.5 describes the regression results and highlights the variability created by removing a very small number of transactions. Significance for the first 4 variables and the fact that response was so unrelated to SIO were unexpected results.

Stepwise Linear Regression Results

	All Transactions $N = 45610$		Non Delayed $N = 45452$		Cleaned $N = 45231$	
R^2 value:	.8837		.69763		.69580	
	Coefficient	F	Coefficient	F	Coefficient	F
Intercept:	.0746	-	.1448	-	.1003	-
TRCMSGOT (number output messages):	1.5035	11861	1.5087	69511	1.5024	69732
TRCMOLTH (length output messages):	.0080	4145	.0078	23308	.0078	23231
TRCHISTG (terminal storage):	-0.0002	1002	-0.0002	2714	-0.0017	2444
TRCMILTH (length input messages):	-0.0107	367	-0.0087	1420	-0.0092	1497
TRCCPUR (CPU):	57.31	4122	31.7023	1270	47.1416	713
TRCPCPH (program storage):	-0.00001	144	-0.00002	879	-0.00002	947
TRCPGIN (page-ins):	.1263	21	.1833	241	.1538	168
TRCPGOUT (page-outs):	.2456	16	.2629	105	.2259	78
TRCSIO (SIO):	-0.0504	224	-0.0088	23	-0.0292	66
TRCMSGIN (number input messages):	.3407	8	-0.2030	16	-0.0862	3

Table 21.5
Stepwise Linear Regression Results

Further investigation of the most significant variables is given in Table 21.6, and the deception produced by linear regression can be seen. The number of output messages, TRCMSGOT, is unusable as a classification variable since 91% of the transactions have only 1 message. Similarly, whereas output message length, TRCMDLTH, and terminal and user storage, TRCHISTG, showed high influence on the response equation, they appear to impact response due to a bimodal distribution with a high frequency at large values. Thus, linear regression did not produce good classification variables.

Table 21.6

Number Output Messages

TRCMSGOT	Number	Cumulative percent
0	3957	8.7
1	40387	97.2
2	301	97.9
3	5	97.9
4	7	97.9
5	32	97.9
6	63	98.0
7-11	28	98.2
12	62	98.3
13	765	99.9
>13	3	----

Output Message Length

TRCMDLTH	Number	Cumulative percent
0	5594	12.3
100	6936	27.6
200	7738	44.6
300	2245	49.5
400	11025	73.8
500	10399	96.7
600	433	97.6
700	271	98.2
800	92	98.4
900	70	98.6
1000	27	98.6
1100	59	98.8
1200	561	99.9
>1200	2	----

Terminal + User Storage

TRCHISTG	Number	Cumulative percent
2000	3901	7.1
4000	782	8.7
6000	962	10.9
8000	367	11.7
10000	316	12.38
12000	16783	58.0
14000	5835	62.1
16000	2795	68.3
18000	7934	85.8
20000	6380	99.7
>20000	97	----

Intuitively, either SIO count or CPU time should provide reasonable classification. Statistics were computed for all transactions with the same SIO count. Figure 21.7 plots average response time by SIO count, and a strong linear relationship is found to exist for transactions with less than about 15 SIOs, and response seems relatively constant beyond 15 SIOs. Figure 21.8 plots mean CPU time versus SIOs and shows an even stronger relationship to suggest that either CPUR or SIO could classify transactions. This is further endorsed by Figure 21.9, where mean response is plotted by mean CPU for each SIO count. The final plot shown in Figure 21.10 shows the distribution of transactions and suggests that roughly equal groupings of SIO count could be made.

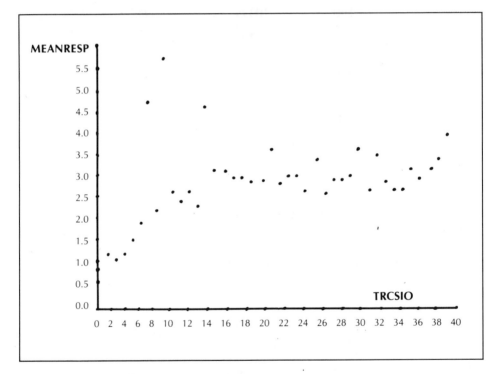

Figure 21.7

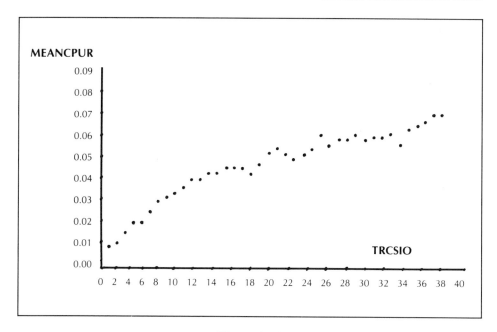

Figure 21.8

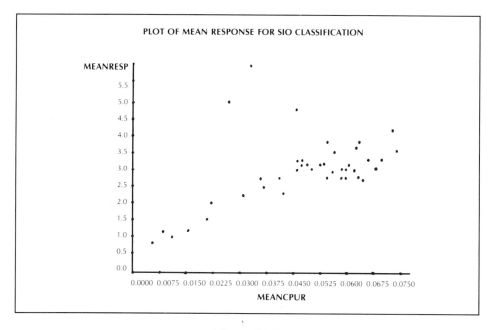

Figure 21.9

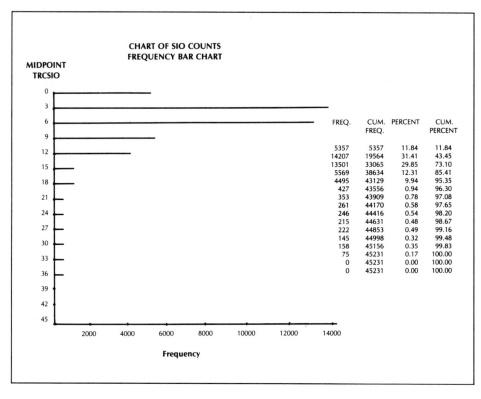

Figure 21.10

Having seen the response almost essentially constant for over 15 SIOs, the following classifications were defined:

Fast   - 0 to 4 SIOs

Medium   - 5 to 14 SIOs

Long   - over 14 SIOs

Delayed   - Transactions marked as delayed.

With these classifications, the percentage of each group's response was tabulated and is given in Table 21.11, which is now the CICS Performance Report.

CICS Performance Reports for Tuesday, June 19, 1979
Cumulative Response Percentage Report by Transaction Category

Group	Transaction count	0 to 1 secs	1 to 2 secs	2 to 3 secs	3 to 4 secs	4 to 5 secs	5 to 10 secs	10 to 15 secs	15 to 20 secs	Over 20 secs
FAST	19564	50.72	86.72	95.66	97.42	97.88	99.04	99.84	99.90	0.10
MED	23725	2.24	39.58	79.41	88.13	90.17	92.73	95.07	98.86	1.14
LONG	2163	0.42	17.11	59.32	82.76	89.92	96.53	97.78	99.17	0.83
DELAY	158	5.70	27.85	55.06	64.56	75.95	84.18	85.44	87.97	12.03

Hourly Profile of Average CICS Response Time for Tuesday, June 19, 1979

Hour	Fast transactions Number	Response	Medium transactions Number	Response	Long transactions Number	Response	Delayed transactions Number	Response
8	1888	1.1	2330	3.2	240	3.1		
9	2892	1.1	3250	3.7	286	2.8		
10	2156	1.3	2680	3.2	186	2.9	1	6.7
11	1654	1.1	1965	3.3	262	3.0		
12	1633	1.1	2157	3.3	217	3.1		
13	1621	1.7	2774	3.9	223	4.8	26	107.2
14	1796	1.9	2185	3.4	275	4.8		
15	1592	1.6	1793	3.0	155	4.4		
16	950	0.7	984	3.1	72	3.3		
17	1139	1.0	1304	2.8	61	4.0		
18	740	0.8	1121	3.1	68	3.7		

Tabulation of Transactions Delayed for Known Causes Tuesday, June 19, 1979

Event	Occurred
Maximum task delay	152
Analyzer timer err	4
Analyzer chain err	2

Table 21.11
CICS Performance Reports for Tuesday, June 19, 1979

Natural response clusterings are obvious, especially the fast and medium groupings in the 0-1 and 1-2 second responses. In addition, hourly average responses are not only stable across the day but show clear grouping. In a final test of grouping, the nearest neighbor classification distance was calculated by the SAS procedure NEIGHBOR and was used to determine misclassification. Because of the high CPU costs of nearest neighbor calculations, only the first 1000 transactions were evaluated, but only 7 were misclassified according to that procedure.

To establish goals for these measures that related to customer satisfaction, the supervisor of the 16 terminal operators recorded his subjective impression of CICS's response for each 2-hour period of each day for 2 weeks. The scale had the ranges ROTTEN, POOR, FAIR, GOOD, EXCELLENT, mapped to numerical values 1 through 5. Because of hardware failures on other CPUs during the 2 weeks of the test, there were some overloaded conditions, and, thus, all values occurred. The distribution was about 15% POOR and FAIR, 40% GOOD, and 30% EXCELLENT. The percentage of CICS transactions (nondelayed) that were under 3, 4, and 5 seconds was also calculated for each of the 2-hour periods. The scatter plots all showed a strong linear relationship; the 5-second group correlation coefficient was .89.

Several hourly measures were considered for the service objective. The average response and the percentage of transactions completed in 1, 2, 3, 4, and 5 seconds were considered for the service objective; the average value did not group responses very well. However, all of the percentage metrics did demonstrate good categorization. The PERCENTAGE OF FAST TRANSACTIONS IN 4 SECONDS was chosen as the service objective because it most clearly related to user's perceived response. Whenever the percentage of FAST CICS transactions that completed in less than 4 seconds was less than 89%, the users graded response as POOR or ROTTEN, and when the percentage was above 93%, the grade was always EXCELLENT or GOOD. The service objective value of 90% of FAST transactions in 4 seconds was easily accepted because it had been shown to both supplier and user to map to human perception.

AVERAGE VALUE OF RESPONSE TIME

Average values do not relate to human perceptions or to the reality of interactive systems. In addition to being discussed in chapter nine, an example here that uses actual CMF-measured internal response measurements from all executions of a specific transaction during one day shows how poorly average internal response time describes the response received by a user.

Measured values:

Average internal response = 0.57 seconds
Standard Deviation = 0.85 seconds
Maximum internal response = 5.57 seconds
Response value at AVG plus one STD

Calculated values:

Response value at average plus 1 std dev = 1.42 seconds
Response value at average plus 2 std dev = 2.37 seconds

Measured values for comparison:

Percentage of transactions with:

Response less than the average (0.57 sec) = 66%
Response less than average plus 1 std (1.42 sec) = 92%
Response less than average plus 2 std (2.37 sec) = 98%

The average value of 0.57 seconds does not describe the user's response because more than two-thirds of the transactions took less than the average value. These data do not have a normal or bell-shaped distribution, where approximately 67% of the observations fall between plus and minus 1 standard deviation from the mean. In these data, where negative values are not possible, 92% of the observations fall between mean and 1 standard deviation, or 92% of the transactions were completed in less than 1.42 seconds.

The distributions of response time tend to have average values much higher than that seen by the majority of transactions because a small number of transactions with long response time can have a large numeric effect on the average value. Thus, the percentage of transactions meeting a goal is a much stronger metric than the average value because it measures what the user really sees.

CICS INTERNAL RESPONSE MEASUREMENT

There are two measures of transaction response time: elapsed time, ELAPSTM, includes user think time, TCWAITTM; and the internal response time, IRESPTM, excludes user's think and typing time. IRESPTM must be used for analysis of CICS internal response time.

An even better estimate of the user response time can be made by the installation if it takes advantage of the data CMF provides on characters sent or received by each transaction. If the line speed (in characters per second) is known, the estimated minimum transmission time could be added to IRESPTM. The terminal identification (TERMINAL) could be used to determine the line speed, as discussed in chapter eighteen. For example, if terminal names starting with TWX operate at 300 bps and all other terminals operate at 1200 cps (9600 bps line), the estimated user response time, USRESPTM, could be calculated by the following algorithm:

```
IF TERMINAL=: 'TWX'    THEN    LINECPS=37.5;
ELSE LINECPS=1200;
ESTRANTM=TRMCHRCN/LINECPS;
USRESPTM= IRESPTM + ESTRANTM;
```

This measure is not coded in MXG since it can be used only for installations that have embedded line speed intelligence in their choice of terminal names. If calculated, it represents the best case user response time that would occur if there were no contention on the user's line. If line delays were measured, as in the first example in this chapter, those results could be used to refine the estimate of transmission time, ESTRANTM. That analysis showed that the line delay of 400 milliseconds per transaction when only 1 terminal was active increased to 700 milliseconds when all terminals were in use. It would not be unreasonable to multiply the calculated minimum transmission time, above, by 7/4 for this installation to reflect the probable peaktime transmission time for each transaction. Before expending a great deal of effort, however, determine if the transmission time is even a significant part of user response by calculating it and comparing it to IRESPTM.

CICS CMF DATA STRUCTURE

Creating CMF Records

Creating CMF records requires that the CICS system programmer enable the CICS Monitor Facility by specifying parameters in several of the CICS "gen" tables. Enabling CMF and specifying the choice of destination for the CMF records either to a Journal File (MVS and VSE) or to the SMF File (MVS only) is accomplished with the following parameters:

In the CICS table	Specify Parameters
Journal Control File	JFILEID=number
SIT	CMP=YES MONITOR=(ACC, PER, EXC)
JCT	JTYPE=SMF FORMAT=SMF
MCT	TYPE=RECORD CLASS=(PERFORM, ACCOUNT, EXCEPTION), FREQ=900, this is the CMF interval DATASET=number in JFILEID CPU=*xxxx*, where *xxxx* is the appropriate value for your operating system. See the *IBM CICS* *System Programming Reference Manual*, under the section "CICS Monitor Facility."

If the CMF records are to be written to a CICS Journal File, the only change in the above parameters is the JCT entry, which must be changed to either JTYPE=DISK or JTYPE=TAPE to correspond to the journal file whose journal number was specified in the JFILEID= and DATASET= keyword. Of course, an appropriate DD statement for that journal file may be required. In the above example for SMF, the DATASET= operands are ignored because of the presence of the JTYPE=SMF operand. Maintenance on both the operating system and CICS must be current, and MVS/370 must be at PUT level 8307. For MVS/XA there are additional PTFs that are required.

CICS Data Sets Created by MXG

The data available in these CMF records are described in detail in chapter forty in the sections that describe the four data sets built by MXG software:

CICSACCT   a count of each CICS transaction issued from a terminal by an operator. It has little useful information. The CICSACCT data set contains one observation for each CMF accounting class record. Accounting data are accumulated for each separate combination of transaction name (TRANNAME), terminal identification (TERMINAL), and operator identification (OPERATOR). The accumulated accounting data include only the transaction counts, message counts, and the number of abending transactions. Since they contain no other resource data, the data set is of questionable use for resource accounting. Furthermore, it contains only the ending time of the interval being reported; start time is not provided.

CICSTRAN   a detail transaction record containing response time, CPU and I/O resources, and wait time durations for several types of CICS delays. This is a superset of the information formerly available in CICS PAII. The CICSTRAN data set contains 1 observation for each CMF performance class record. Each observation is the result of the completion of a CICS transaction, and it contains the response time given that transaction, the CPU and I/O resources consumed by that transaction, as well as terminal, operator, system, application id, and so forth. This data set is the backbone of CICS transaction reporting and analysis since it permits crosstabulation and investigation of response, resources, and sources of CICS transactions. Because it contains 1 observation per CICS transaction, it can be relatively large. For example, 50,000 transactions require 20 cyl of 3350 space for the CICSTRAN data set.

CICSYSTM   an interval record that describes the global CPU and I/O resources consumed by all CICS transactions during the interval. This data set provides a superset of the ACR and TCP/KCP data that were available in PAII. The CICSYSTM data set contains 1 observation for each CMF performance class record. This is the global system data produced at (typically) 15-minute intervals on the entire CICS system.

CICSEXCE   an exception record that identifies transactions delayed due to VSAM file waits, ISAM overflow file delays, and delays in acquiring main and temporary CICS storage. The CICSEXCE data set contains one observation for each CMF exception class record and provides data on exceptional conditions raised by a transaction, including VSAM queuing, ISAM overflow file waits, and temporary storage waits. The transaction that caused the exception record can be selected from the CICSTRAN data set by the common value of TASKNR. There can be more than one exception record produced for a single

transaction, and all will have the same value of
TASKNR in both CICSEXCE and CICSTRAN data
sets.

CICS Reports

A starter set of reports is provided with the MXG software to demonstrate the
analysis of transactions response time and resources in member RPTCICS,
described in chapter forty-one.

Dictionary Record

In addition to the four CMF records that create the above data sets, CMF also
creates a dictionary record when it is started. The dictionary record describes the
length and type (numeric or character) of each data element. If the CMF dictionary
records could be used, the SAS code could be impervious to change since a change
in a data element would be reflected in the dictionary. This would ease the maintenance burden of the MXG software, but the execution cost of using the dictionary
was found to be prohibitive. A system using the dictionary records was developed
and tested, but it required almost four times the CPU processing time to look up
each data element in the dictionary, when compared to the direct coding technique
employed in member VMAC110 of SOURCLIB. Furthermore, since a dictionary
record is written only when CMF is started, there may not be a dictionary record
included in a day's CMF data. This would necessitate a SPIN file architecture to
hold the CMF dictionary record received last (one for every CICS system since
they can be at different maintenance levels and, hence, have different dictionaries).
Although the idea of a data dictionary is attractive, in the large volume environment of CICS transactions, it is not cost-effective.

The price you pay for this pragmatism is possible coding changes when IBM
adds additional information or modifies data elements as seen when IBM
expanded the file control browse count from 2 to 4 bytes, with a PTF to CICS
1.5. IBM is not likely to alter the data radically since IBM's own product,
CICSPARS, which uses the CMF records, is also hardcoded and does not use the
dictionary record. Note that the debugging feature described below does provide
a simple way to print the dictionary entries for those interested in its structure.

JCL Considerations for Processing CMF Data

The JCL for processing the CMF records depends on whether the data to be processed were written to a journal file or to the SMF file. The JCL for the journal
file is different if the file was created on DOS/VSE, even though the file must be
on a tape that will be read from an MVS system. MVS CMF records should be
written to the SMF file to eliminate the human costs of designing, testing, and
monitoring the job stream to dump and manage the journal file's data. Installa-

tions that use BUILDPDB to build their PDB will process CMF records as part of that job. Thus, there are a number of JCL options that should be considered.

Destination of the CICSTRAN data set determined by IMACCICS macro   The default destination DD of all four CICS data sets is the WORK DD. However, because of the potential large size of the CICSTRAN transaction data set, the default DD destination of that data library can be set by the IMACCICS installation macro. This setting allows transaction data to be written to a tape SAS data library, independent of the other, smaller CICS data sets. For consistency, the destination specified in IMACCICS is also used as the source of CICSTRAN data in the example reports that use the CICS transaction data set. If the IMACCICS member of SOURCLIB contained

```
          MACRO _CICTRAN CICSTRAN %
```

and the execution JCL contained

```
//CICSTRAN DD DSN=PDB.CICSTRAN,DISP=(,CATLG),UNIT=TAPE
```

the CICS transaction data set CICSTRAN would be written to tape.

Journal formatted CMF data are input through the JOURNAL DD   For DOS/VSE journal files that have been written to tape to be read on the MVS system, the JOURNAL DD will be reading a tape that is foreign to the tape management system. More important, many DOS/VSE tapes require the specification of LTM for the tape label processing. The MXG member TYPE110J is used to process the journal file instead of member TYPE110, which processes an SMF file. In the following example, DOS/VSE input is expected (hence, the LTM parameter on the JOURNAL DD), a tape data library is used for CICSTRAN, and the other three CICS data sets are initially written to the WORK DD in the SAS procedure, but the SAS COPY procedure puts them on the end of the SAS data library pointed to by the CICSTRAN DD. The following example processes MVS journal data if the LTM is changed to SL, and the EXPDT=98000 is removed. (This assumes the MVS journal data is on a standard label tape data set; the EXPDT parameters in both jobs assume that UCC-1, TMS, is used.)

```
//DOSVSE   EXEC SAS,OPTIONS='GEN=0 ERRORABEND NOSOURCE'
//SOURCLIB   DD DSN=MXG.SOURCLIB,DISP=SHR
//SASLIB     DD DSN=MXG.SASLIB,DISP=SHR
//CICSTRAN   DD DSN=MXG.CICSTRAN,DISP=(,CATLG),UNIT=TAPE,
//              LABEL=EXPDT=99000
//JOURNAL    DD DSN=VSE Journal tape data dsname,DISP=SHR,
//              LABEL=(1,LTM,EXPDT=98000)
```

```
//SYSIN    DD   *
   %INCLUDE SOURCLIB(TYPE110J);
   PROC COPY IN=WORK OUT=CICSTRAN;
   %INCLUDE SOURCLIB(RPTCICS);
                      ANALCICS
```

Standalone processing of SMF CMF data   The input data are expected via the SMF DD when the CMF data are in SMF format. The preceding example requires only minor modifications to accomplish the same task:

```
//MVSSMF    EXEC SAS,OPTIONS='GEN=0 ERRORABEND NOSOURCE'
//SOURCLIB  DD DSN=MXG.SOURCLIB,DISP=SHR
//SASLIB    DD DSN=MXG.SASLIB,DISP=SHR
//CICSTRAN  DD DSN=MXG.CICSTRAN,DISP=(,CATLG),UNIT=TAPE,
//             LABEL=EXPDT=99000
//SMF       DD DSN=SMF data set dsname,DISP=SHR
//SYSIN     DD *
   %INCLUDE SOURCLIB(TYPE110);
   PROC COPY IN=WORK OUT=CICSTRAN;
   %INCLUDE SOURCLIB(RPTCICS);
                      ANALCICS
```

Inclusion of CICS CMF data in the BUILDPDB is automatic Four data sets are built by BUILDPDB. However, the IMACCICS macro may need to be changed, as above, to create the detail transaction data on tape, and the appropriate tape DD statement must be added to the JCL.

DEBUGGING FEATURES BUILT IN MXG CMF PROCESSING

This section describes the debugging features built into the CMF code. Although it is unlikely that you will need to debug a problem, code is included in MXG. Also, the capability to print the CMF dictionary records is included as one debug option.

The three most useful options are enabled by adding a specific string as a SYSPARM on the EXEC statement in batch or on the SAS/SASGO statement under TSO. This provides three levels of debugging: high, medium, and a third with lots of detailed printout. The second and third options can use a great deal of CPU time and can print thousands of lines, if indiscriminately invoked. The first option should not produce any significant output. The fourth debug option modifies the data sets built and requires a change to the SAS source code and, thus, is least likely to be needed.

Documenting CMF Problems

If you are requested to provide the author with the output of a CMF run with a debug option enabled, execute the requested debug run as described below and then execute the same job a second time, with the debug EXEC statement replaced by the following EXEC:

```
// EXEC SAS,OPTIONS='OBS=1 SOURCE MACROGEN'
```

This produces a complete listing of the source and expansion of macro statements in effect.

Debug Option One: SYSPARM=TYPE110-1

This option provides a printout of the dictionary records encountered in the SMF input. These records might be needed if new data are added to the type 110 record by IBM or if you use any of the optional clock, counter, or character fields available. It can be invoked with the following EXEC statement in place of the normal EXEC statement:

```
// EXEC SAS,
// OPTIONS='ERRORABEND SYSPARM='''TYPE110-1'''''
```

Note the MVS requirement for four apostrophies before and five after the actual parameter value.

Debug Option Two: SYSPARM=TYPE110-2

This option invokes option one and also prints the string of identifiers encountered in each data section segment and provides some of the internal variables that might be needed to understand what is in a type 110 record. Because there are many data sections in each CICS block, it is suggested that you use the SAS parameters FIRSTOBS and OBS to restrict the amount of printing produced. If you encounter a problem (for example, a STOPOVER abend condition), then the SAS log indicates the VBS record being processed by the value of the SAS internal variable _N_ (printed when a STOPOVER abend or a PUT _ALL_; is invoked). Use this value of _N_ as the value of the FIRSTOBS= and OBS= options. In the following example, JCL for invocation of debug option two, the third VBS record is to be examined (remember that there are many data segments in each of the (typically) 32,760 byte type 110 records).

```
// EXEC SAS
// OPTIONS='ERRORABEND FIRSTOBS=3 OBS=3,
//           SYSPARM='''TYPE110-2'''''
```

Debug Option Three: SYSPARM=TYPE110-3

This option invokes options one and two, and then it prints lots of detail on each record encountered. This option should also be used with restrictive values of FIRSTOBS and OBS to prevent excessive CPU and printing.

```
// EXEC SAS
// OPTIONS='ERRORABEND FIRSTOBS=75 OBS=75,
//         SYSPARM='''''TYPE110-3'''''
```

Debug Option Four: Enable _DBUG110 macro

The preceding three debug options use the SAS SYSPARM facility. A macro named _DBUG110 is defined in VMAC110, but immediately after its definition, the definition is nullified by the statement

```
MACRO _DBUG110 %;
```

Should it be necessary to enable the _DBUB110 macro, comment out the above statement to activate the macro. When the _DBUG110 macro is activated, it causes a number of internal variables to be added to the four SAS CICS data sets. Note that these additional SAS variables significantly increase the amount of disk space required. Table 21.12 describes the contents of those debugging variables that will be kept when the _DBUG110 macro is activated.

Table 21.12
Alphabetic Description of CICS CMF Debugging Variables

Variable	Type	Length	Description
MCTSSDCA	NUM	4	offset to the start of data descriptors.
MCTSSDCL	NUM	4	length of each data descriptor (should be 1).
MCTSSDCN	NUM	4	number of columns in data descriptor segment. This is the number of identifiers that must be skipped when reading the data record. More important, this is the number of variables (fields) that exist in this record. Compare this value to the number of variables in the INPUT statement if there is a problem. As long as the INPUT statement is reading fewer variables, the code should work, but additional variables beyond the INPUT statement will not be input.

MCTSSDID	NUM	4	type of record: 0 = dictionary record for this class given by MNSEGCL. The dictionary records are not output to a SAS data set, but they can be printed on the log by invoking debug option one. 1 = normal value for MNSEGCL=2, account, output in the CICSACCT MXG data set. 1 = normal value for MNSEGCL=4, exception, output in the CICSEXCE MXG data set. 1 = normal value for MNSEGCL=3, transaction, output in the CICSTRAN MXG data set. 2 = used for MNSEGCL=3, global performance, output in the CICSYSTM MXG data set.
MCTSSDL	NUM	4	total length of section.
MCTSSDRA	NUM	4	offset to start of first data record.
MCTSSDRL	NUM	4	length of real data in each data record of this class and type.
MCTSSDRN	NUM	4	number of data records of this class and type in this data segment.
MNSEGCL	NUM	4	class of these data: 2 = accounting class (output in CICSACCT data set) 3 = perform class (output in CICSTRAN or CICSYSTM depending on MCTSSDID) 4 = exception class (output in CICSEXCE).
MNSEGID	CHAR	4	machine on which data produced—always CICS.
MNSEGREG	NUM	4	reserved, or region.
SECTLLBB	NUM	4	section header length including the length field, the section header, the section descriptor, the field identifiers, and all of the data records in this section.
SEGLEN	NUM	4	length of the section header including this 2-byte field—always 18 decimal.

SMFAPS	NUM	4	offset to start of product section, currently 32 decimal.
SMFLPS	NUM	4	length of product section, currently 17 decimal.
SMFNPS	NUM	4	number of product sections, currently 1.
SMFPSJID	NUM	4	journal log identification—user journal ID for monitoring.
SMFPSPRN	CHAR	8	recording product name—application known to VTAM. This field is redundant with the variable named APPLID taken from MNSEGSYS in the CICS SAS data sets.
SMFPSRSN	NUM	4	block sequence number of this block in this log.
SMFPSRVR	NUM	4	record version, CICS 1.5 is 1, CICS 1.6 is 2.
SMFPSSTY	NUM	4	product subtype, currently 1.
SMFSSS	CHAR	4	subsystem identification, currently CICS.

chapter twenty-two

Workload Measurement - IMS

This chapter discusses the sources of measurement data on IBM's information management system, IMS. IBM recently produced the second version of Walter Scholz's "Annotated IMS/VS Performance Reports," GG24-1559-1, which provides an excellent discussion of performance factors in IMS systems, discusses the IBM tools IMS DC Monitor and IMSPARS, and mentions RMF and SMF. That document is the best overall description of IMS CPE.

An IMS system is composed of an IMS control region and one or more message regions. The control region usually executes as a started task and manages scheduling of transactions in the message regions, loading of programs to process those transactions, and servicing of DL/I calls for data from the DL/I data bases or from the IMS queues. Each message region executes as a batch job in its own address space. Thus, both control and message regions can produce type 30 SMF records with resource data.

As suggested earlier, all on-line systems should be placed in their own control performance group and, thereby, take advantage of RMF interval reporting. For IMS, this means assigning a separate performance group to each control region and each message region. Each of these performance groups can map to the same set of performance characteristics (priority, objective, and so forth) so as not to discriminate between the message regions for service.

Although SMF and RMF provide no information on response time or transaction counts, these separate performance groups can be trended over time to determine not only the growth of the entire IMS system, but also the growth of individual regions. Since IMS transactions are scheduled in the various message regions based on the transaction class, this usually permits direct mapping of message region resources to the business element that produces that class of transaction.

RMF provides accurate measures of CPU and memory in the TYPE72 (and hence in RMFINTRV) data sets for each region; however, there are inconsistencies in I/O counts reported for IMS. First, data base I/O operations do not occur under the address space of their message region but under the control region's address space. Second, it has been reported to IBM for several years that a large part of the I/O counts is not reported to RMF from IMS until IMS is taken down, causing the interval RMF records to reflect very little I/O activity until the last interval during which IMS was active.

There is no source of IMS response from IBM. Although there are records written to the IMS log when events occur in IMS, these records do not calculate response time. Papers describing the use of the IMS log records for performance reporting have been presented, but, in general, calculation of response time is not possible from the IMS log.

Even more than the lack of data on the IMS log itself, there is concern about the appropriateness of the IMS log as a source of performance data. The purpose of the log is to record all data base alterations so that the data bases can be recovered after a failure. As a result, there are more records written to the log than there are transactions, and these records require long processing times. Since copies of data base records before and after change are contained in the IMS log, the issue of security must also be raised.

The only source of IMS response time known to the author is the product of Boole and Babbage (originally written by Mario Morino) called CONTROL/IMS. Boole and Babbage has recently renamed its product IMF (for IMS measurement facility). It is still referred to as CONTROL/IMS or CIMS in this book and in the MXG software. The CIMS data recorder component writes a transaction record and a program record to the IMS log tape. The PRSLEDIT program in the CIMS product uses these records to create files from which CONTROL/IMS reports can be run. A transaction record is created for every transaction and provides resources, response, and accounting for each transaction. The program record is created when a program is terminated and reports on resources consumed by transactions scheduled during this load of the program. The vendor's documentation for the CONTROL/IMS product should be examined for specific details on the product and its records.

The MXG software supports these CONTROL/IMS records. Member TYPECIMS of the SOURCLIB processes these records from the log tape and builds these SAS data sets (whose contents are described in chapter forty):

CIMSTRAN   one observation for each transaction, with resource and response measures and total DL/I call activity for the transaction.

CIMSDBDS   one observation for each DBD referenced in processing each transaction, describing the name and DL/I activity (both counts of calls by type and resultant physical I/Os).

CIMSPROG   one observation for each terminated program.

The CIMSTRAN data set is the primary source of IMS transaction analysis, and it was used as the basis of response classification in establishing service objectives for IMS. Since there are two phases in the flow of an IMS transaction, two separate measures of an IMS transaction's response are needed: the input queue time (INPQUETM) and the execution service time (SERVICTM). Their sum is the transaction's total response (RESPONSTM).

Input queue time is controlled by the class (INPUTCLS) of the transaction and the number of message regions that can execute that class transaction. By tracking the number of transactions of each class that arrives at each time of day, scheduling IMS transactions can be matched to business needs, and service objectives for input queue time can be set in a way similar to the establishment of batch service objectives for initiation time of batch jobs of various classes. The service time objective must be based on the resources consumed by the transaction, as suggested for batch jobs with long execution times. In the CIMSTRAN observation, there are seven measures of CPU time consumed by the transaction and four measures of physical I/O, as well as counts of DL/I calls by type.

Table 22.1

Daily Computer Center IMS Performance Measurement Report
Wednesday, August 15, 1983

Service Time

Category	Volume(%)	Goal	Half Goal	The Goal	Twice Goal
Credit Card	19826 (47.4%)	1.0	83.9%	95.9%	99.1%
00-04.9 IWU	5825 (13.9%)	1.0	93.4%	99.0%	99.8%
05-09.9 IWU	10639 (25.4%)	1.5	90.6%	98.9%	99.8%
10-19.9 IWU	2651 (6.3%)	4.0	88.4%	98.1%	99.6%
20-39.9 IWU	1774 (4.2%)	6.5	85.9%	96.7%	99.4%
40-59.9 IWU	336 (0.8%)	12.0	84.5%	96.7%	98.2%
60 plus IWU	768 (1.8%)				
Total	41819 (100.0%)		87.4%	97.3%	99.4%

Input Queue Time

Class	Volume (%)	Goal	Half Goal	The Goal	Twice Goal
001	2240 (5.4%)	0.5	95.8%	98.2%	99.6%
002	9773 (23.4%)	1.0	98.7%	99.7%	99.9%
003	6845 (16.4%)	4.0	87.2%	91.9%	96.0%
004	314 (0.8%)				
005	2822 (6.7%)	4.0	82.2%	88.1%	94.2%
006	19825 (47.4%)	1.0	95.4%	98.0%	99.3%
Total	41819 (100.0%)		93.9%	96.7%	98.5%

In an unpublished analysis of IMS response time by the author and several co-workers at Sun Information Services, the elapsed execution time of IMS transactions was found by linear regression to depend only on the CPU, I/O, and DL/I call counts, and an equation to predict expected response based on those resources was developed. When a transaction completes, its expected response time is calculated from that equation, which is then compared to the actual measured response.

If the transaction completed earlier than expected, it is considered to have met its service objective. The service objective metric for IMS was then established as the percentage of IMS transactions that met service objectives. A separate input queue objective as the percentage of transactions meeting their queue time objective is also reported. To reduce the amount of data presented to management, the reporting (Table 22.1) shows the percentage of transactions that met the goal as well as the percentage meeting half and twice the goal, for input and service times separately.

For each observation in CIMSTRAN, the variable NRDBD tells how many DBD segments were referenced by that transaction. There are NRDBD observations in CIMSDBDS for that transaction, describing the DBD (name, type, and so forth) and activity by that transaction. Observations in CIMSDBDS are matched with their parent observation in CIMSTRAN, using the variables LTERM (logical terminal), TRANSACT (transaction name), and STRTTIME (start time of transaction execution).

The CIMSPROG data set is less frequently referenced. Its most significant value has been the additional CPU times recorded there and nowhere else describing CPU time to schedule the program. When comparing the CPU time reported in SMF/RMF and CONTROL/IMS, you must include the CPU time in CIMSPROG.

In summary, IMS resource usage can be easily tracked by the RMF performance group data (TYPE72) or by type 30 interval records, TYPE30_V from SMF. The addition of a tool such as CONTROL/IMS to provide transaction resources and responses allows IMS to be managed and measured with much higher precision. The absence of transaction reporting greatly increases the difficulty of managing IMS. Unlike the CICS product, which offers the excellent CICS Monitor Facility, the IMS user must rely on non-IBM software for measurement of IMS response objectives.

chapter twenty-three

Workload Measurement - Other On-line Systems

This chapter discusses ways to investigate new on-line systems, and it describes experiences with non-IBM on-line systems.

When an applications area sees a promising new on-line system, a project to evaluate that system should be formed with a CPE analyst participating. The primary focus of the project should initially be on the system's suitability for business. However, the CPE analyst must also identify how response can be measured so that service objectives can be established, and he must determine how to accomplish accounting at the individual user so that using departments can pay their fair shares of the resource cost.

The most effective data for response measurement are detail records of each interaction's response and resources, but getting these data requires the designer to build a monitor and recording component into the on-line system. For some interactive systems, a detail interaction record may include too much detail, depending on how the system defines an interaction. Even though tracking every interaction every day can be too expensive, the data are indispensable in the initial evaluation of a new on-line system.

If no detail transaction records are provided by the product, there are other alternatives that can provide response measurement. In all cases, a transaction can be created that time stamps itself, calculates the time difference between successive interactions, and reports this measurement to the interactive terminal. An example of this technique for TSO is provided in member CLSTIMER of the MXG SOURCLIB. In addition to reporting the response to the user's screen, the transaction can write out the resultant responses to a data set, and the transaction can be scheduled automatically several times per day so that responses at different times and on different days can be analyzed from the recorded data. This simple technique provides samples of response time that are usually adequate for managing most on-line systems. As with any sampling monitor, its major defect is that it does not provide continuous data.

RMF SYSEVENT can also be used by the on-line system to provide RMF with counts of interactions and the elapsed time of each interaction. This approach allows calculation of average response for each RMF interval. As discussed earlier, this is a poor metric, but it is far superior to no metric at all. This approach does require fairly serious modifications to the on-line system.

Initially, resource measurement of the proposed on-line system can be far more important than response measurement. Although vendors provide glowing descriptions of their products' functionality, they rarely provide real cost of execution. Whether or not your installation actually uses cost accounting to charge back resource costs, you must act like the installation when evaluating a new system. Since your management has to acquire the hardware on which the new system will execute, you should know just how much hardware the new system requires.

Of course the 2 best sources of resource data are the SMF type 30 record, especially the SMF interval data (TYPE30_V), and the RMF performance group data, TYPE72. A new on-line system being evaluated must be placed in its own performance group, and if multiple address spaces are used by the new system, each address space must be placed in separate performance groups. Initial measurements should be aimed at determining resource costs of the business functions to be performed. A simple method of determining these costs is to conduct a benchmark of functions with RMF recording at a 1-minute interval and to perform 1 business function during each minute. A tape recorder at the terminal can be used to describe the function being performed, and it provides a transcript of events without interrupting the operator. At the conclusion of the benchmark, the RMF TYPE72 records can be printed and matched to the business function performed to estimate the minimum cost of the function. You should remember to take into account the design of the on-line system. Measurement of resources for 1 user may not be directly extendable to many users because there may be additional resources consumed by the on-line system to manage other concurrent users. In addition, the startup and shutdown resource costs can be captured from the RMF interval records; those costs should be distributed to all users. The RMF data are suggested first because they provide the CPU, I/O, and memory resource at synchronized intervals. The SMF step interval data could also be used, but their intervals are keyed to initiation time rather than to the wall clock, requiring a little more complexity in synchronization. The additional data in TYPE30_V (notably, the I/O counts by DDNAME and the paging statistics) often make the extra complexity worthwhile.

If the on-line system produces accounting or response data records, evaluation of the system must validate the accuracy of those records. The preceding benchmark example also provides data for validating the vendor's data. The CPU and I/O measurements of the RMF or SMF interval can be compared to the sum of vendor data records for the same interval to validate transaction level accounting. In some systems, however, the vendor's records can only be created at the end of a user's session, with no detail transaction or interaction data. Even then, the benchmark data can be used by summing RMF intervals after startup and before shutdown and comparing them to the sum of resources in user session records. Most on-line systems that measure their CPU time do a good job, but they usually only capture the TCB CPU time. Their I/O counting is frequently excellent, although data base management systems often count calls for data and do not provide counts of the physical I/O operations that result. Detailed examination of the vendor's data records, as compared to SMF and RMF, is an essential part of the evaluation process.

A detailed discussion of other on-line systems is beyond the scope of this chapter. However, the ADABAS system was evaluated as described above, and it is useful here as a case study.

ADABAS, as proprietary software product of Software AG, manages its data bases through a single address space, called the nucleus. ADABAS users, under TSO, CICS, or in batch, use either the natural language or subroutine calls to request data from the ADABAS. Implementation of these requests uses a supervisor call (SVC), which is issued from the user's address space, to communicate with the nucleus. The SVC moves the user's request into the common storage area (CSA), an area dedicated to ADABAS. The nucleus periodically scans the CSA, moves the new request into its address space, and then parses the request and schedules it in a thread, much like a batch job is scheduled into an initiator. The thread executes the call, acquiring the requested data, returns the data to CSA, and posts the user, who then receives the response to his request.

Therefore, resources associated with ADABAS are consumed both in the address space of the user and in the nucleus address space. The user's TSO session or batch job can be accounted through the SMF step records, and the CICS ADABAS user's resources are available in the CMF transaction record. Total nucleus resources are available in the SMF step records and in the RMF performance group record (if the nucleus is in its own performance group).

The only source of data on the nucleus at the individual interaction level is the ADALOG facility, which can record resources consumed by each SVC call. The ADALOG data can be voluminous because a single interaction can generate many SVCs, and many interactions can be required to perform a single business transaction. In addition, there is no explicit measurement of CPU time; only the ADABAS command type (one of approximately 32 commands), its elapsed time, and the count of I/O operations to the 4 ADABAS files are recorded.

The elapsed time of the SVC provides the duration that call was being serviced by ADABAS. Calls can be put-back on the CSA queue for a later recall without the elapsed time being reset. The duration is a good trend indicator, but it is of questionable use in response measurement because it does not include the duration between issuance of the SVC by the user and start of the command in the nucleus, nor does it include the time to get the data back to the user. Both of these durations tend to be much longer than the duration the SVC was actually in the nucleus.

The physical I/O counts recorded in the ADALOG matched very well with the SMF I/O counts. The structure of processing an ADABAS call compared so favorably with initiation that it was postulated that the CPU cost of ADABAS could be predicted by the number of calls issued and the number of physical I/Os that resulted. The ADALOG data were captured for several days, and linear regression of the interval RMF data on CPU TCB seconds as a function of the number of calls and the number of I/Os confirmed the relationship. During the interval, 85% of the CPU TCB seconds were accounted for by the number of ADABAS calls issued, and the remaining 15% were attributable to the number of physical I/O operations. This is certainly consistent with the structure; the majority of CPU time consumed in the nucleus is the movement of the command from CSA into the nucleus, decoding that command, and scheduling the call in a thread. These functions are independent of what the call does when executed. If the call causes significant I/O, then the CPU time to process these I/Os was reflected in the regression coefficient for IOCOUNT. The result of this validation was an equation for the CPU time used by each call and the CPU time used by each physical I/O.

Because of the large volume of calls, the detailed ADALOG data could not be used effectively. An alternative capture mechanism was designed by the author and implemented by Ron Root of Sun Company. The general design followed the philosophy of TSO/MON in that data were captured in the ADALOG exit at completion of each call, and statistics were added to a storage area in CSA for that user. At 15-minute intervals, the data in these individual storage areas were written to SMF with a segment for each ADABAS user. The summarized interval data contained the count of each of the 32 ADABAS command types and the count of I/Os to each of the 4 ADABAS files, the sum of the elapsed time for all calls during the interval, and statistics on the maximum elapsed time of any call during the interval. The elapsed time divided by the number of calls provides an estimate of average response per call during the interval, and the number of calls and I/O counts are used in the CPU equation to calculate the nucleus CPU seconds that resulted from each user's activity during the interval. These data are used both for performance objective measurement and for cost recovery of the nucleus.

The modifications to ADABAS to create the installation SMF record required several weeks of development, validation, and testing. It was appropriate for Sun Company because of the large commitment to ADABAS made by several applications. Although not required at all sites, this is typical of the effort required if on-line systems are to be managed effectively.

chapter twenty-four
Measurement Differences between MVS/370 and MVS/XA

For MVS/XA, IBM has made major changes in SMF and RMF records and their contents. These changes include:

- RMF records are completely reformatted. They are now in the same relocatable format as the SMF records introduced in MVS/SE-2 (for example, types 30 and 32).
- Type 30 (Common Address Space Work) records are expanded with new data.
- Several new SMF records exist.
- All SMF and RMF records generated on an MVS/XA system are identified by bit 5 in the first byte (after the RDW) that is on.

Aside from these specific changes, there remains the perennial SMF accounting question: what will happen to CPU times and I/O counts (and therefore users' satisfaction with the consistency of the bills they get for computer usage) when I migrate to the new release?

EFFECT OF MVS/XA ON CPU TIMES RECORDED IN SMF RECORDS

The good news is that the TCB and SRB CPU timings recorded in the step records (type 4 step termination record and type 30, subtype 4) appear to have only minor increases from MVS/370 to MVS/XA, and their variability has decreased somewhat. Preliminary benchmarks with 26 unique steps executing repeatedly as initiators were increased from 5 to 60 with an increment of 5 initiators every 5 minutes, showed the results displayed in Table 24.1.

In addition, the repeatability of these measures within MVS/370 and MVS/XA was measured and compared. How much the CPU time measured for identical jobs varies according to what else is going on in the system. The results are shown in Table 24.2.

Table 24.1
Ratio between MVS/XA and MVS/370 CPU Timings
for Benchmark Jobstream

Metric	Average ratio	Minimum ratio	Maximum ratio
Minimum TCB + SRB	1.03	.88	1.24
Minimum TCB alone	.99	.86	1.18
Average TCB + SRB	1.02	.85	1.24
Average TCB alone	.98	.83	1.17

Table 24.2
Repeatability of CPU and I/O Measurements for Multiple Runs
of Benchmark Jobstream

Metric	Repeatability as percent of mean for MVS/370			Repeatability as percent of mean for MVS/XA		
	Min	Avg	Max	Min	Avg	Max
TCB Time	0	4.5	15	0	3.5	11
TCB + SRB Time	0	5.3	23	0	3.8	12
I/O Count Total	0	.5	10	0	0.2	2
Connect Time Total	.	.	.	0	7.4	34

CHANGES IN MVS/XA THAT AFFECT I/O COUNTS

The bad news is not really that bad, but I/O counts are increased in MVS/XA. The primary cause for the increase is the rewrite of the program FETCH. To understand the increase, you must know something about the implementation of this MVS component.

FETCH loads programs from load libraries into virtual storage. On the disk, a program consists (among other things) of a series of text records, each of which is followed by a number of Relocation Dictionary (RLD) records. Text records contain the actual instructions and data of the program. Their lengths vary, but they are large (thousands of bytes). RLD records, on the other hand, are always just 256 bytes long and contain information that FETCH uses to find relocatable addresses within the preceding text record so that it can add the starting address of the load module to them as part of its processing.

Under MVS/370, the channel programs with which FETCH reads a module are not all initiated via the STARTIO interface to IOS. Once FETCH issues the I/O request for the first text record and any RLD record following it, FETCH will, if possible, issue requests for subsequent records (both RLD and text), by extending the original channel program in its Program Controlled Interrupt (PCI) Disabled Interrupt Exit (DIE). Text blocks that are read in as a result of processing in this exit are not counted in MVS/370.

In MVS/XA, FETCH has been completely rewritten and no longer uses PCI. In MVS/XA, the segment for STEPLIB in the step termination records now contains the true number of I/O requests issued by program FETCH to load the program from disk. This count usually is equal to the number of text records loaded, but if a text record has a very large number of RLD records following it, FETCH may have to issue a second I/O request. For all intents, however, the STEPLIB DD now contains the true I/O count to load the module. MVS/XA frequently records ten I/Os where MVS/370 could count only one STEPLIB I/O.

There is a flag bit in each Channel Command Word (CCW) called the PCI flag. When this bit is on, a special I/O interruption is generated when the CCW takes control of the channel. The channel program's execution continues unaffected, but the interrupt allows the issuer of the I/O request to take certain actions, such as chaining more CCWs to the end of the running program.

PERFORMANCE OF PROGRAM FETCH IN MVS/XA

There is a more significant potential impact on your installation in the rewrite of program FETCH for MVS/XA than the change in STEPLIB I/O counts. MVS/370 FETCH can load programs in MVS/XA format with no performance degradation. However, for MVS/XA FETCH to perform well, there are a number of steps you must take.

Need for RLD Count Fields to be Filled In

MVS/XA FETCH can perform well only if it can build channel programs to read in a text block and all of its associated RLD records. To build the necessary CCW string, FETCH must know how many RLD records are present. The necessary counts are available only in load modules produced by the DFDS or DFP levels of the linkage editor or reprocessed by the XA level of IEBCOPY. (The RLD count for the first text block is in the PDS directory entry for the load module; the RLD count for subsequent text blocks is in the last RLD record for the previous text block.) Lacking these counts, FETCH cannot optimize the I/O requests with which it reads in the RLD records, and its performance suffers.

Impact of Having Incorrect RLD Counts

Besides the possibility of performance problems because the RLD record count fields used by XA FETCH are left zero by the MVS/370 linkage editor, there is a possibility that you may have load modules whose RLD counts are filled in but are incorrect. An early version of release 1.4 of the DFDS linkage editor created wrong count values. There were later versions of release 1.4 that did not have this problem, and it did not exist in release 1.5 and later releases. When XA FETCH encounters a nonzero count value and then finds that the actual count of RLD records is not the same, a console message (CSV300I) is created. (More typically, thousands of console messages are created.) The message simply advises that an incorrect count of RLDs was encountered. Instead of ignoring the error, IBM is helping us by letting us know of a possible performance improvement by the console message, but we only need the message once to identify the member and library in error.

A load module with incorrect RLD count fields can be corrected by IEBCOPY with either the ALTERMOD or COPYMOD option. If you do not wish to allocate the extra space to do a copy, you can use the ALTERMOD option to correct the counts, but a 75-cylinder library on a 3380 with 1449 members required 31 minutes elapsed time, 12 seconds TCB, and 7 seconds SRB on a 3081K.

Despite this effort, the CVS300I message still can occur. There are some members that IEBCOPY cannot correct. The IEBCOPY listing identifies the members that were not corrected because they were either marked nonlinkeditable (for example, if the ESD records have been stripped by the SAS procedure PDSCOPY for performance) or were in OVERLAY or SCATTER load module format.

However, if you decide to do it, by all means correct your RLD counts because, aside from the messages generated, asking MVS/XA FETCH to load programs with incorrect RLD counts can double both device busy time and I/O rates to the program libraries. This is because when FETCH discovers the incorrect count, it abandons the work it has done so far and redoes the entire program load.

Importance of Blocking Load Libraries

Even with correct RLD record counts, MVS/XA FETCH can still be a poor performer unless the load library is blocked up. Load libraries can be blocked with IEBCOPY's COPYMOD facility, but it cannot be executed in place; you must copy to tape and back or from one disk to another. On the same 75-cylinder load library, running a COPYMOD used 37 minutes elapsed time with 31 seconds TCB and 13 seconds SRB on the 3081K. The load library could also be relinkedited with the XA linkage editor (if you still have any necessary linkage editor control cards for the individual modules) to reblock the library.

Especially for IMS, TSO, certain non-IBM transaction processing systems, and all other cases where dynamic LINKs and LOADs are frequent, it is prudent to fill in or correct the RLD record counts in all of your load libraries (IEBCOPY can do this; you may also relinkedit them) and also to reblock your libraries (IEBCOPY can do this). Without these steps, FETCH performance in MVS/XA will be inferior to its performance in MVS/370. With RLD counts filled in and correct and with the load library blocked, it appears that the MVS/XA program FETCH gets back to the same level of CPU consumption and general performance that MVS/370 FETCH has.

CHANGES TO SMF AND RMF RECORDS

There is potential for confusion concerning the use of the terms SMF and RMF when referring to those records that are the subject of this chapter. In a sense, all the records discussed in this chapter are SMF records because they are written to the SYS1.MAN*x* data sets via the SMF record writing mechanism. They all have a standard record header that, among other things, contains their SMF record numbers. Nevertheless, in this chapter, when a record is referred to as being an SMF record, it means that the record is one of those whose content is collected by the System Management Facilities data gathering portion. (An example of such a record is the type 30 common address space work record.) On the other hand, when reference is made to RMF records, those records indicate that their contents are gathered by the IBM Resource Measurement Facility program product. These records all have an SMF record number ranging from seventy to seventy-nine.

The major changes that have been made to SMF and RMF records for MVS/XA that will be of interest to performance analysts and capacity planners are identified below. Some entirely new records have appeared, some fields in existing records are no longer filled in or have been removed entirely, and some fields in existing records have a different meaning.

New SMF Records

Six new records are documented in the XA SMF manual:

- The type 16 record is written by IBM's ICEMAN sort program product
- A new record (type 60, VSAM volume data set) exists in support of the Integrated Catalog Facility (ICF), and three new record types (61, 65, and 66) describe ICF/VSAM activity
- RMF now creates a type 78 I/O queuing activity record.

Record Fields That No Longer Exist

There are two ways IBM can drop support of a record field. Either the field can be made reserved, which means the bytes it occupied are still in the record but their values are no longer defined, or the field can actually be removed. The latter method can affect programs that process the record even if they do not use the deleted field because the offset of each field in the record that follows the deleted field is changed. In MVS/XA, IBM has used both techniques:

> Type 6   JES Output Writer - SMF6IOE (JES3 Control Buffer and Data Buffer Errors) is now reserved.
>
> Type 6   JES Output Writer - SMF6DFE (JES2 bad record length truncated) is now reserved.
>
> Type 71   Paging Activity - PVTSPREC (LPA swap pages reclaimed) was deleted.
>
> Type 71   Paging Activity - SMF71LVL (Record Level - Total or Pageable, documented in TNL-GN28-4962) went away.

Record Fields That Have Changed in Some Way

- The device number replaces the unit address in record types 4, 8, 9, 10, 11, 14, 15, 19, 21, 30, 34, 40, 64, 69, 74, and 75.
- VIO is now identified by a device number of X '7FFF' (because the old value of X '0FFF' is now a valid device number).
- MSS virtual devices are now identified by one in the first bit of the first nybble of device number (formerly, one in the second nybble of unit address identified these devices).

Miscellaneous SMF and RMF Issues

- There are many typographical errors in the original (-0) XA SMF manual. About half of these are corrected in -1, but it will require a -2 to clean up the rest.
- No device connect time is recorded in the type 14/15/64 (data set activity) records. Although the DD segment in the type 4 or type 30, subtype 4 corresponding to a step's use of a data set will contain this time, its absence from the data set record itself will effectively prevent analysis of device connect time by data set.
- RMF reports still truncate fractional values rather than rounding them.

Changes to Specific SMF Record Types

The following sections discuss changes made to various SMF record types in MVS/XA:

Type 0 (IPL) SMF Record   This record is written as MVS initializes. The data in it include virtual and real storage sizes and the SMF options that are in effect. The following has changed in MVS/XA:

- SMF0BUF contains X '4000' to indicate a 4096 byte SMF buffer size where you would have expected X '1000'.
- SMF0VST contains X 'FFE00000' for the virtual storage size of MVS/XA.

Type 22 (Configuration) SMF Record   This record describes the system hardware configuration (main storage, devices, and so forth). One is written at IPL and whenever a VARY command is executed. Note the following for MVS/XA:

- The MSS device segments are documented as extending through device 0EF, but the length of the data indicates a maximum MSS address of 0DF.
- Real storage pages for MVS/XA appear to be zero.

Type 26 (Job Purge) SMF Record (JES2 Only)   This record is written by the job entry subsystem when it has totally finished processing a job or a started task. The following change has been made for MVS/XA:

- The XA level of JES2, which will also run on 370, has added a new print section that contains (or will soon contain) the number of bytes printed or punched. (This segment also exists in MVS/370 records.)

Type 30 (Common Address Space Work) SMF Record   This record type was introduced in MVS/SE2 to provide a better source of information about address space activity than was available from the types 4, 5, 20, 34, 35, and 40 records. The five subtypes of this record provide not only resource usage information for an address space but also identification information (job name, JES job number, accounting fields, and so forth). Note the following for MVS/XA:

- The major change in the type 30 record is the addition of device connect time. Each DD segment in a type 30 is expanded to contain the I/O connect time for that DD. In addition, the total I/O connect time for the address space for the time covered by the record (step, job, or interval) is recorded in a separate field. There are corresponding I/O counts and connect times in each DD segment and total I/O counts and connect times for the address space.
- When doing capacity planning, you should look at all I/O activity, not just the activity that can be tied back to a DD card. By summing total I/O activity * (both I/O counts and connect time) recorded in the DD segments and subtracting the totals from the overall address space totals stored in the record,** you can compute the I/O counts and connect time not recorded at the DD level.*** This unrecorded I/O is primarily the SPOOL I/O activity in JES2, although I/O to the LINKLIST data sets,

---

* variables IOTMTODD and EXCPTODD in MXG step data sets
** variables IOTMTOTL and EXCPTOTL
*** variables IOTMNODD and EXCPNODD

certain catalog management I/O, and I/O done during data set
OPEN/CLOSE (other than priming or purging QSAM buffers) is also
included. Thus, even though the JES3 shop is still in the cold, the
non-DD related I/O allows the JES2 shop to estimate SPOOL activity at
the step level.

- Although SPOOL I/O in JES2 is not recorded in a DD segment, it is
  recorded at the address space level because the actual I/O requests are
  done out of the requesting address space. The implementation of SPOOL
  I/O in JES3 uses global buffer pools, with the I/O to and from SPOOL
  being done by JES3 on behalf of call users. For this reason, JES3 SPOOL
  I/O counts cannot be made available in SMF data for individual address
  spaces. JES2 counts and times should be used in accounting and capacity
  planning analysis to recover the cost of SPOOL I/O activity. Appendix
  8-2 of the SMF manual discusses what is and is not captured in the DD
  segment statistics and also what is captured in the address space totals.
  Whereas that discussion only mentions I/O counts, it applies equally to
  device connect time.

- Under MVS/370, when a DD segment referred to a device with multiple
  physical paths, that DD segment might be identified with any of the
  possible hardware addresses that MVS could use to access that device (it
  depends on the path used just before allocation picked up the address
  from a field in the UCB). For this reason, tying I/O back to the base (or
  primary) device address was a problem. In MVS/XA, since units are
  referred to with a single device number, regardless of the number of
  physical paths to it, this uncertainty is eliminated. Another change caused
  by the substitution of device number for unit address is that there are
  cases when the same set of DD cards results in fewer DD segments in the
  type 30 record. An example is a concatenated DD with multiple
  UNIT=AFF tape references. Under MVS/370, there could be multiple
  DD segments, all referencing the same tape but with different hardware
  unit addresses as explained above. In MVS/XA there is only one DD
  segment for such a concatenation.

- SMF30JNM (incorrectly documented in the -0 SMF manual) should
  contain the JES job identifier (JOBnnnn, STCnnnn, and so forth), but for
  some STCs (started tasks), it contains the jobname of the STC.

- A new field, ABEND reason code, is available.

- A flag is set (SMF30SFL) if IEFUSI was used to change the region size of
  the extended private area of the task.

- Six new fields describe storage and paging:

    SMF30RGB   region size below 16MB

    SMF30ERG   region size above 16MB

SMF30ARB   maximum LSQA + SWA subpools below 16MB

SMF30EAR   maximum LSQA + SWA subpools above 16MB

SMF30URB   maximum user subpools below 16MB

SMF30EUR   maximum user subpools above 16MB.

Changes to Specific RMF Record Types

The following sections discuss changes made to various RMF record types in MVS/XA. These changes are in addition to the reformatting of all the RMF records into the now standard SMF relocatable format.

Type 70 (CPU Activity) RMF Record   This record identifies each CPU in the complex. It provides the amount of wait time accumulated by the dispatcher for those CPUs during the RMF interval. The following changes were made for XA:

- This version of the CPU has been added. This field identifies which model of 3081 or 3083 is being used. This value is needed to determine which (model-dependent) CPU speed constant was used by SRM in converting CPU seconds to service units. This constant reflects the speed of a single processor in the complex rather than the capacity of the complex as a whole. It is necessary to know this value in order to reverse SRM's calculation and derive CPU times from the CPU service numbers that come out in the RMF type 72 (workload activity) records.
  In MVS/370 only, the CPUTYPE (3081 or 3083) was provided. The model-dependent constants currently in use are shown in Table 24.3.

Table 24.3
SRM Speed Coefficients for 3083 and 3081 Models

CPU version from RMF type 70	Service units per second of a single CPU	Processor	Speed relative to 3081D	Capacity relative to 3081D
X '03'	276.30	3081-D	1.00	1.00
X '13'	291.65	3081-G	1.05	1.05
X '23'	368.40	3081-K	1.33	1.33
X '01'	204.80	3083-E	0.74	0.37
X '11'	306.50	3083-B	1.11	0.55
X '21'	388.80	3083-J	1.41	0.71

Use these values with caution since the numbers are often changed by PTF or even by user modifications. The safest way to determine the proper CPU speed coefficient to use for a given system is to calculate it from the value of RMCTADJC, a field in the main SRM control block for that system. The following method of determining the proper CPU speed coefficient with the TSO TEST command was adapted from Volume 4, Number 8 (April 15, 1982) of the Candle Computer Report:

```
TEST  'SYS1.LINKLIB(IEFBR14)'
L     10.%+25C?+40  F    for MVS/XA
L     10.%+25C%+40  F    for MVS/370
```

Note: the % operator indicates 24-bit indirect addressing, which will not work for a control block above 16MB. Thus, ? (31-bit indirect addressing) must be used in place of the last % only for MVS/XA.

The LIST (L) command will display:

HHHHHHHH   NNNNN

where *HHHHHHHH* is the hex address of the (decimal) constant *NNNNN*.

Then:

SU_SEC = (16,000,000) / *NNNNN*

- As discussed in Candle Report Volume 5, Number 9, MVS/XA can handle I/O interrupts in batches rather than always having to absorb the cost of an interrupt to handle each I/O completion. (This is done by issuing a TEST PENDING INTERRUPTION (TPI) instruction in IOS.) For each CPU, the type 70 record now contains the count of I/O completions handled by an I/O interrupt; the SMF manual refers to such I/Os as having been handled by the Second Level Interrupt Handler (SLIH). The type 70 record also contains the count of the number of I/O completions that were handled by TPI (and thus were batched). These numbers are of interest since, in multiprocessor configurations, MVS/XA disables processors for I/O interrupts if the percentage of I/O interrupts that are handled by TPI is sufficiently low. This process is called selective disablement. Selective disablement saves CPU time because an interrupt is much more expensive than a TPI. On the other hand, any I/O completion that is handled by TPI on one CPU because another is selectively disabled has been delayed by some amount of time.
- SMF70FLA is documented as a field in the SMF manual, but in fact, it never contains any field other than zero. The SMF manual was apparently created from the RMF report program DSECT, which does document this internally-used field.

Type 71 (Paging Activity) RMF Record   This record reports on the demands made on the system paging facilities and the utilization of real and auxiliary storage during the reporting interval. Only a very minor change has been made for MVS/XA:

- In MVS/370, if the processor had more than 16MB of real memory, the type 71 record used 3 fields to report the number of pages moved above and below this line as MVS/370 tried to optimize the real page location constraints. In MVS/XA, the constraints are eased, and MVS/XA no longer attempts these optimizations. Thus, the 3 fields that individually identified page movement are replaced by a single count of pages moved. However, the designers took advantage of the 12 bytes already defined in the record, and now they contain the average, minimum, and maximum numbers of frames below 16MB real that are fixed.

Type 72 (Workload Activity) RMF Record   This record reports on activity for all address spaces that fall into each performance group defined in the IPS. For each performance group period in the group, metrics (such as the number and elapsed time of terminated transactions), CPU, I/O, and main storage service absorbed by all transactions are provided. Note the following differences between MVS/XA and MVS/370:

- Certain data must reside in frames whose real addresses are below 16MB. For example, format 0 CCWs must be below the line because only 24-bit addresses are available to point to them.
- In MVS/XA, I/O service units can be calculated either from I/O counts (the only possibility in MVS/370 and the default in MVS/XA) or from the new Device Connect Time (DCTI). The choice is made by setting the IOSRVC parameter in IEAIPS*xx*. Unfortunately, there is no bit set in any SMF/RMF record that indicates whether I/O service units were based on I/O counts or on connect time. This creates measurement problems until a flag is added to the record.
- If device connect time is used for I/O service units, the I/O service unit is defined as 65 connect time units. One connect time unit is 128 microseconds. Thus an I/O service unit based on connect time represents 8.32 milliseconds of connect time, which is just about one-half of a revolution of a 3600 RPM disk drive. Thus, if all your I/O were at half-track blocking, I/O service units based on I/O counts or connect times should be equivalent.
- Note that to SRM and, therefore, to RMF, transaction is not just a TSO interaction. The term can also refer to a batch job, a batch job step, or a CICS transaction.
- The bit map that formerly described the Selectable Units (SUs) installed no longer exists. It never was reliable, as bits could be on or off (that is,

independent of the SU they represented). Several fine software vendors attempted to use this bit map to choose optimum I/O if SU9 (SAM-E) was installed, and they received program abends for their efforts.

- A small point, but the last 2 bytes of the ICSNAME field contain a value of X '6060' for the default ICSNAME.
- SMF72FLA and SMF72FLG are also RMF fields like SMF70FLA, described above.

Type 73 (Channel Activity) RMF Record   This record provides information about on-line channels. Due to the major restructuring of the I/O subsystem that was done for XA, this record has undergone a major change:

- Since MVS/XA no longer has logical channels, the logical channel queuing data has disappeared from the type 73. In fact, the type 73 now contains only physical channel busy percentages. There is no longer a count of SIOs by physical channel since I/Os in MVS/XA does not control (or even know) what channel the channel subsystem will use for a START SUBCHANNEL (SSCH) instruction.

  Technical Note: it is interesting to note that in MVS/XA, RMF attempts to cut down on its measurement overhead. In MVS/370, RMF acquired physical channel data by issuing TEST CHANNEL instructions. In MVS/XA, RMF steals the results of the STORE CHANNEL PATH STATUS (STCPS) instruction that is issued by the SRM to collect the information it needs about channel busy to perform its I/O load balancing. The SRM attempts to schedule STCPS every 200 milliseconds, but it can be preempted from sampling. Thus, the type 73 record also contains the count of STCPS instructions that were stolen and used in the RMF calculation of physical channel busy. This is the first case wherein the sampling rate of RMF data is not set by RMF.

Type 74 (Device Activity) RMF Record   This record type provides information about all on-line devices for which RMF was instructed to gather statistics. A number of changes (and problems) has resulted from the introduction of the channel subsystem for XA. The following should be noted:

- Ensure that UZ58785 is installed, along with its pre- and co-recs and their associated microcode levels. Without these fixes, the device segment in each type 74 record is 8 bytes short, and RMF reports show negative connect times. This cluster of fixes is referred to as the Channel Measurement Overflow PTF.
- The four connect time measurements (connected, active, disconnected, and pending) are separately measured for each device. No longer is the RMF device busy measurement made by sampling UCB bits at the RMF sampling interval. Rather, the percentage of connect and disconnect time is added to the percentage of time the device was

blocked by another system to measure the device utilization. This definition of utilization is good because it reflects when the device was unavailable to another user.

Type 78 (I/O Queuing Activity) RMF Record   This record is new in MVS/XA. Besides queuing statistics, certain I/O configuration information is available. Note the following when writing programs to use this new record:

- In all other SMF and RMF records that use the relocatable format, offsets are based on the beginning of the logical record. In this record, however, R781CPDS is an offset from the start of the I/O Queuing Control Section. Additionally, R781CPDN (the count of configuration data sections) contains four, even when there are only two sections with data (four sections exist, the last two are all hex zero).
- The logical queuing statistics, which were maintained in the logical channel segments of the type 73 record in MVS/370, are now recorded at the device level in the type 78 record. New fields report the percentage of I/Os that were delayed because all paths were busy because the control unit was busy or because the device was busy, and the percentage of successful I/Os to the device can also be calculated from the data.

Type 78 (Virtual Storage) RMF   A subtype of the type 78 (new with RMF Version 3.2) provides good measures of virtual storage. Sizes of areas (LPA, CSA, SQA, LSQA, and so forth) are provided in total by protect key and by sub-pool for CSA and SQA areas in the MXG TYPE78VS data set. Optionally, recording can be enabled for selected address spaces, individual private areas (TYPE78PA), and for subpools within these private areas in TYPE78SP.

All in all, the performance analyst and capacity planner will be very pleased with the improvements made in SMF and RMF data with MVS/XA. As with any major architectural change, there will be minor errors to be corrected and new measures to be understood, but the data added by MVS/XA can only serve to provide better measures of resources and service.

Those responsible for computer usage billing systems will be especially happy that CPU time measures in MVS/XA are very close to those that would be found in MVS/370 and, if anything, are even more repeatable. The I/O count increase associated with STEPLIBs, although potentially significant, should be easy to deal with.

chapter twenty-five

Availability Measurement

Information on availability in SMF was limited to IPLs and JES outages until the SMF enhancements added in MVS/370 System Extensions Release 2 started task accounting and interval accounting with the new type 30 workload record. Now that an interval record can be created for each active address space, it is possible to identify when on-line systems are executing. MXG provides installation macro IMACINTV (chapter thirty-two) to select jobs by criteria such as JOBNAME, PERFGRP, JOBCLASS, and so forth. The type 30 interval records for these jobs are stored in SAS data set TYPE30_V, which is built by both TYPE30 and BUILDPDB.

The availability of this new information allows measurement of the up time of each CICS, WYLBUR, ADABAS, IMS control region and IMS message region, at least to within the granularity of the chosen type 30 interval duration. However, nothing in SMF provides us with internal availability of those subsystems. For example, although the type 30 SMF analysis would show that CICS was up for a 30-minute interval, if the 3705 communications controller was being reloaded with a new NCP program, which can take 2 to 20 minutes, no transactions would have been serviced during that time. Similarly, if the IMS master terminal operator STOPs an IMS data base, TYPE30_V records up time, and users of transactions that use the stopped data base (correctly) claim IMS was not available to them. Exploit the data in TYPE30_V to show data center management when their systems are up, but be careful when attempting to use these figures as measures of true end user availability.

End user availability measurement can only come from data records written by the application control program (that is, IMS or CICS) when major events within the application occur or are written from an external software monitor that interfaces with the application control program. These data records are unique to each subsystem because they must describe the events in that subsystem that inhibit processing of user interactions and record results of periodic tests of the communications path from the application to the terminal and back. No such measurement system currently exists.

SMF provides no information on the status of initiators, so batch availability cannot be determined very well. SMF provides no information about which initiators were started or drained, the time being drained, which initiators were active, and so forth, and no description of the classes that could be initiated was provided. There is not even a record written when the operator makes a change, much less what the change might have been. Data set PDB.JOBS and the JOBCLASS variable can be used to show what classes were initiated (see chapter sixteen), but we cannot tell what classes might have been initiated.

Only two other subsystems create SMF data useful for availability analysis. RJE availability, measurable by remote from JES SIGNON/SIGNOFF records, is discussed in chapter seventeen. JES's own up time can be determined from its START/STOP records in the TYPE4345 data set, which is described in chapter forty. However, two records in SMF are useful for tracing incidents that affect availability, although they may not provide precise numeric values of the availability.

The first and most obvious record for tracking availability is the type 0 record, the IPL record. By printing the TYPE0 data set each day, you can learn several things. First, the existence of a type 0 indicates that the operating system was IPLed. An IPL may or may not be desirable. Some installations schedule IPLs daily; thus, the existence of an IPL is expected. Unexpected IPLs should be confirmable on the shift supervisor's log of system incidents. Further examination of the list of IPLs may show that at a given time of day several IPLs occurred in very short order. This could result from the operator pressing the LOAD key several times in close succession. (This is no longer possible literally since the LOAD key has been replaced by less accident prone devices on all but the most ancient systems.) This is usually indicative of repeated attempts by an operator to recover when the IPL begins and then fails. Multiple IPLs occurring at very close intervals can suggest a need for operator education in proper recovery.

How long was the system down? There is no accurate method to determine how long the operating system was down prior to an IPL; however, you can deduce the probable periods of down time by determining the time between the previously written SMF record and the IPL record time stamp. This is accomplished in MXG by processing type 0 records into data set TYPE0 as the variable DOWNTM. As SMF records are processed, the time stamp of the prior record is retained in the VMACSMF module. When an IPL record is encountered, the down time is calculated as the difference between the IPL time stamp and the time stamp of the SMF record that is physically preceding from the same system.

A warning about this technique is necessary. First, some locally written SMF records can have time stamps that do not relate to the time they were written to the SMF buffer; thus, it may be necessary to exclude certain (or all) record types higher than 127 if 1 of these local records could precede a type 0 record. Second, the fact that no SMF records were written does not necessarily mean the system is down for the duration calculated. The system could have had no work to do, so it sat idle for hours until a scheduled test IPL occurred. For this reason, analysis of this estimate of DOWNTM should never be provided to anyone above the data center manager. SMF cannot easily record why an IPL was needed, although you can have the operator reply to the IPL message, and the reply is carried into a type 90 SMF record in TYPE90. The operations shift-to-shift log should record the when and why of all major changes or incidents. Provide the TYPE0 analysis to the data center manager to help ensure that the manual logs are complete.

The second record directly relating to availability is the type 7 SMF record, which indicates that all defined SMF VSAM data sets have been filled with SMF data and that SMF is no longer recording. A type 7 record should never occur. Its impact can be disastrous on a billing system as well as on a performance system based on SMF. It usually means that the operators have missed several messages and have not properly submitted the SMF dump job on that system, although it can occur when a runaway job is creating SMF records at an extremely high rate. For example, if a file is opened and closed repeatedly in a tight loop, it is possible to fill up VSAM SMF files with type 14 SMF records and, thus, cause the lost data event.

chapter twenty-six

Capacity Analysis and Measurement

GOAL LEVEL CAPACITY MEASUREMENT

Introduction

Goal level capacity is defined as the capacity of a computer system to do work and concurrently meet specified response objectives (that is, meet the performance goals for the system). Therefore, we are not only concerned with the ability to produce work, although that may be important to some, nor are we concerned with predictive models derived or developed from internal estimates of performance and extended upward and outward. We are concerned with engineering measures of the ability of our computing system to deliver required service economically. We will use the performance data on the system to measure its present capacity to meet service objectives. We will evaluate how the measured capacity compares with what we think the hardware or software configuration should deliver, but we are primarily concerned with how much we can do with what we have. Furthermore, work is measured in the same units that we recover and account for computer usage. The capacity measurement then relates directly to dollars and is, therefore, easily understood by nontechnical management.

This technique of measuring capacity requires that a stable configuration exists for an adequate measurement period. To measure the relationship between work and service, the configuration must have been saturated (at least to the point of degraded service) during some periods in the measurement interval. If the configuration contains multiple systems, it is usually easy to find a period of time during peak workload when one or more CPUs are unavailable, sufficiently saturating the remaining CPUs. Even a well-designed single system can be driven into saturation (especially following an outage), and so the approach is equally valid in large and small environments. We measure goal level capacity by analyzing measured response versus the measured workload. The actual measures of response and resources consumed or delivered are taken from the PDB and summarized for identical 1-hour time periods.

There are three steps to the process:

1. Determine the hourly goal level capacity of each of the major subsystems (for example batch, TSO, IMS, and CICS). This presumes that you have specified performance groups so that work delivered to each subsystem can be identified by performance group and that you have established measurable service objectives for each subsystem.

2. Use the preceding hourly capacity results to estimate weekly hardware capacity by extending hourly capacity by the shape of the daily workload profile. Assume that work will increase but that its arrival pattern does not change.

3. Determine excess capacity by comparing calculated capacity (above) to the actual resource delivered.

Definition of Work and Hardware Capacity

Begin by defining the unit of work by which capacity will be measured. The resource measure or work unit used can affect the accuracy of this approach, but experience has shown that this is a sound approach. The best measure of capacity is the installation's billing work unit since the billing unit bridges the gap between technical measures and management comprehension. If there is no billing unit by which computer usage costs are distributed, still tailor the work unit to management. If CPU seconds are the perceived measure, use them, and if service units are understood as work units, use them. Since billing units and service units are functions of CPU seconds, it is not surprising that all three measures work well. Any measure of work that correlates closely with CPU busy is adequate, and the closer the unit is to the cost-recovery or billing system unit, the easier it will be understood by management.

Hardware capacity, defined in terms of this work unit, is the number of these units that can be measured in one hour. For example, take the IBM service unit as the measure of work. Service units consumed by a task are calculated from an equation containing four terms:

Service Units = CPUCOEFF * CPU TCB seconds * hardware constant

+ SRBCOEFF * CPU SRB seconds * hardware constant

+ IOCCOEFF * I/O Units

+ MSOCOEFF * Memory (page seconds) units

The hardware constant* is set by the operating system at IPL time based on the CPU model, and it represents the number of raw CPU service units generated in 1 second of CPU time on this processor. Its purpose is to ensure that this work unit is consistent for different processors. The same job should record the same number of work units; the work units equation you choose must be independent of the processor on which the work executed.

The four COEFF values are chosen by the installation (in member IEAIPS*xx* of SYS1.PARMLIB) to set the relative weight of the four components of service unit. The COEFF values in effect are reported in the type 72 RMF record.

---

* Usually called the "Machine Dependant Constant" by IBM, it is the variable SU_SEC in the MXG TYPE70 data set.

The hardware capacity of a computer system is the number of work units that system would generate if the CPU, I/O, and memory were operating at 100% capacity. The maximum value recorded in RMF during the last week is 100% capacity. For example, if we examine last week's hourly RMF data and find the following values:

CPUCOEFF=10 SRBCOEFF=10 IOCCOEFF=5 MSOCOEFF=0.1

Processor: 3081K (hardware constant = 368)

Type 70 CPU active (maximum)   = 3600 seconds

Type 72 I/O units (maximum)   = 1,440,000 EXCPs

Type 72 memory units (maximum)   = 3,000,000 raw units

we can now calculate hardware capacity in service units for this system:

Service Units = 10 * 3600 * 368
              + 5 * 1,440,000
              + .1 * 3,000,000
              = 13,248,000 + 7,200,000 + 300,000
              = 20,748,000 total service units per hour

In other words, this 3081 K system has a hardware capacity of 20 million service units per hour, based on the present service unit equation and the work consumed last week. Not all of this hardware capacity can be delivered to a user's program, but it is the present capacity of this measured system. By measuring actual hardware capacity, you know how much you have. By measuring service units delivered to each workload, you know how much of this hardware capacity is delivered to a workload (such as TSO, IMS, and so forth).

Does a capacity of 20 million units per hour really describe what the hardware can do? If the numbers show that last week you always generated less than 20 million units, then 20 million units is, in fact, the real hardware capacity. It may be possible to generate more units by adding memory, changing operating systems, and so forth, but until those things are done, you still have only 20 million units as the capacity of the present hardware and software configuration. Your first concern is to measure how much work you currently generate, determine how much of that hardware work is delivered to major subsystems, and then determine the operating system overhead consumed but not recorded on behalf of these major subsystems. Later you will be concerned with how close to a theoretic capacity you are. Hardware capacity is constant only as long as the configuration (hardware, software, and microcode) is unchanged.

The preceding example shows how simply hardware capacity can be determined. Examine the work unit equation your installation currently uses (or the one you propose) and evaluate the equation using each resource at the maximum observed value.

What if not all the resources in the billing unit equation exist in the RMF data? You can use RMF data to track total resources in each hourly interval, but can you compensate for nonexistent resource data in RMF? In the following example, the billing unit was originally called the computer work unit (CWU), a linear composite of four resource measures: CPU TCB seconds, I/O counts, tape volume mounts, and tape drive hours. The latter two resources are not recorded in RMF data. Additionally, the CWU equation used TCB time alone,* yet the SRB time is equally important and was to be treated just like TCB time for capacity analysis. To carry out the capacity analysis, the computer resource unit (CRU) metric was defined to be that portion of the CWU that could be captured from RMF data. The CRU from RMF was compared directly to the CWU from SMF for the same workloads, and a conversion factor (a constant of proportionality) that mapped CRU to CWU for each subsystem was determined for each subsystem. For example, since TSO does not use mountable devices, the ratio between CRU and CWU is different from batch subsystems.

This chapter uses CRU units as the work unit. Although the coefficients of the CRU equation are different from the service unit equation described above, the CRU equation is in principle a service unit equation. The only real difference is magnitude. If you use the same resource measures (in the proprietary CRU equation) that you used to calculate the 20 million service units, then the result is hardware capacity measured in CRU rather than in service units. The purpose of this discussion is to demonstrate the technique with a case study. Therefore, whereas the CRU equation itself is proprietary, it is actually nothing more than service units based on CPU TCB, CPU SRB, and I/O; the coefficient for memory service in the CRU equation is zero. Hardware capacity measured in CRU for the case study configuration was:

Processor	CRU equation value at 100% capacity
3033 "A"	236800
3033 "B"	236800
168-MP	226800
Total of the three CPUs	700400

The Hour As the Appropriate Time Interval

The hour is chosen as the time interval for each observation in this approach because it works and because it is representative of the way work flows through the system. Several things make the hour an appropriate choice:

---

* This was not desirable, but the use of TCB + SRB had not yet been implemented.

1. Using the hour, you can gather sufficient data in a reasonably short time. If you concentrate on peak hours of the day, you typically find 6 peak hours each day (3 in the morning and 3 in the afternoon), giving a total of 30 peak hours per week. In 3 weeks, you would have nearly 100 data points and 1 bad hour would have a small effect on the results.
2. A long interval tends to smooth out the data too much. Every installation seems to be alike in that demand peaks during mornings and afternoons and falls off during lunch time. An interval of more than an hour would hide the valley.
3. Although an argument can be made for a 30-minute interval, intervals of 15 minutes or less suffer wide variability because of human interactions (notably by the console operators). Most problems require 15 to 30 minutes to resolve, and these short-term effects can bias the analysis since they can slip through the outlier detection phase.
4. Most batch jobs execute in less than 15 minutes. When measuring batch service, you should be sure that the length of the interval is relative to service time to ensure that events counted in the interval actually occur during that interval.
5. Management accepts the hour as the basic interval because it is easy to work with mentally. An 11-hour prime shift maps easily to 11 RMF intervals but not as easily to 22 half-hour intervals or to 44 quarter-hour intervals. The use of hourly or half-hourly data provide good results, but intervals longer or shorter can provide less stable analysis.

Service Objective Measurement

The importance of service objectives is discussed in chapter eight. For capacity measurement, you can measure how increased work affects the ability to meet service objectives:

Table 26.1

Subsystem	Measure	Goal
Batch	Percentage of jobs meeting requested initiation wait time (IWT). Users submit jobs and specify the IWT they require (15 min, 30 min, 1 hour, 2 hours, 4 hours, or overnight). Time to initiate is measured by SMF.	94%
TSO	Trivial transactions meeting 4-second response. TSO/MON name table defines trivial. Internal response is measured by TSO/MON.	92%

IMS	IMS queue met expected response.	98%
	Service time met expected response.	95%
	CONTROL/IMS measures input queue	
	time and service time separately.	
	Expected queue time is table lookup	
	based on transaction class/priority.	
	Expected service time is calculated	
	based on resources measured by	
	CONTROL/IMS.	
CICS	Fast transactions met 4-second response.	92%
	Internal response measured by PAII.	
	Transactions classified as fast if	
	AMCT (I/O count) is less than 5 and	
	transaction name is not in a table	
	of anomalous transactions.	

Defining the RMF and SMF Data Used

Measurement of capacity begins with gathering data from RMF and SMF. The analysis requires several preconditions:

1. RMF data must describe workloads. That is, control performance groups must be defined so that each major subsystem can be identified by performance group(s). To maximize the use of RMF data for capacity measurement and planning, a separate control performance group should be defined for each started task and every unique address space that services multiple users. This means that each CICS, IMS control region, IMS message region, and so forth is in its own performance group, and the growth of these applications can be measured and tracked by using the RMF performance group data (TYPE72). There is no execution performance degradation apparent with 100-150 performance groups other than the small increase in the size of the type 72 record. This level of detail is needed primarily for the capacity planning and tracking that follows capacity measurement. During the present capacity measurement, you want to sum individual control performance groups from each type of subsystem to reduce the complexity of the analysis. The RMFINTRV program in SOURCLIB, which uses the installation macro IMACWORK to define the subsystem (variable WORK), produces the RMFINTRV data set containing the needed summarization by subsystem and hour. The RMFINTRV data set is also built by the BUILDPDB program.
   Note: RMF has control performance groups and report performance groups. In the analysis of capacity, you should use only the control performance groups. If report performance groups are defined, work

delivered to a report performance group will be counted twice in both the control and report performance group buckets. The double accounting invalidates calculation of system overhead and, hence, the analysis. Variable PERFRPGN in TYPE72 flags observations from a report performance group that must be deleted before summarizing the RMF data (RMFINTRV deletes those observations).

2. RMF data for each time interval must be combined across CPUs at a node to calculate the capture ratio of the workload. The capture ratio reflects the amount of MVS overhead attributed to each workload and is a characteristic of the workload, not of the CPU. In a JES2 multi-access spool system, JES must execute in each processor, but the primary expenditures of JES resources occur in the processor to which the JES remote lines are attached. The primary JES work is often expended on a CPU different from the one where the batch is executed. (Moving the high speed [56 KB] JES lines is an effective way of distributing work.) You cannot calculate capture ratios by CPU because the overhead in CPU A is directly affected by the workload in CPU B. Experience and knowledge of the structure of MVS shows that the most stable method of determining the distribution of MVS overhead (that is, calculating the capture ratio) requires the summation of work units by workload across all processors that share the same spool volumes (or node).

3. Success in meeting performance objectives for each subsystem must be summarized into hourly statistics. The success of this approach has been best where the service measurement was of the form "x percent met its goal this hour" and is less stable when the service metric was an average value. Be sure that the hour of the service intervals matches the starting hour of RMF data. Batch service should be assigned to the interval in which it initiated rather than when it terminated.

4. Better success is achieved if JES work is combined with batch work into a single workload called JESBATCH. Because JES resources are so closely related to batch work, this combined workload reduces the complexity of the analysis without losing utility.

5. Work delivered from RMF is combined with service delivered from SMF, CMF, TSO/MON, and CONTROL/IMS, in this case study, and placed into a single SAS observation per hour. This data is first cleaned of outliers and then used in subsequent analysis. The resulting SAS data set contains the following variables:

Table 26.2

Variable	Contains	Source
TIME	Date and hour interval started	constructed
BATCHCRU	CRU - Batch performance groups	TYPE72
JESCRU	CRU - JES performance groups	TYPE72
JESBATCH	CRU - Sum of BATCHCRU and JESCRU	TYPE72
TSOCRU	CRU - TSO performance group	TYPE72
IMSCRU	CRU - IMS (control + message)	TYPE72
CICSCRU	CRU - CICS performance	TYPE72
TOTALCRU	CRU - MVS overhead CRU plus the sum of CRU delivered to all control performance groups	TYPE70 + TYPE72
BATCHMET	Percentage of batch jobs meeting IWT	SMF
TSOMET	Percentage of TSO meeting 4 sec	TSO/MON
IMSMETSR	Percentage of IMS meeting service goal	CIMS
IMSMETQU	Percentage of IMS meeting input queue goal	CIMS
CICSMET	Percent CICS meeting fast goal	PAII

TOTALCRU is the total work delivered, including MVS overhead. The MVS overhead is the difference between CPU active seconds (in TYPE70) and the seconds of CPU (TCB + SRB) delivered to all control performance groups (in TYPE72). These MVS overhead CPU seconds are then converted to work units (or service units), and this MVS overhead work is added to total work units delivered to all control performance groups. Although the work is called MVS overhead, it is actually MVS work not attributed to a performance group. Our goal in measuring capture ratios is redistributing MVS overhead back to the workload that caused it.

Removing Outliers

After you have gathered hourly data for a period of 3 to 6 weeks of stable workload and configuration, you can begin analysis of the data. First, looking at plots of the data, determine if there are outliers that should be removed. Outliers are those data observations that lie outside of the normal data. You are interested in measures taken when the system is at or near its peak workload because that is when you can measure the relationship between work and service delivered. Hours with no significant demand and hours when TCAM went into a loop are not typical peak workload hours. Therefore, you can visually inspect plots of work consumed and service delivered and use common sense to identify hours that must be excluded from analysis. If you know peak hours of the day, you can further refine the analysis by choosing only those hours that you expect significant workloads. In this study, data for known peak workload hours (8 a.m. to 11 a.m. and 1 p.m. to 3 p.m., Monday through Friday) were selected. Each workload and response were then plotted individually:

```
PROC PLOT;
     PLOT(BATCHCRU JESCRU TSOCRU IMSCRU CICSCRU TOTCRU)*TIME;
     PLOT(BATCHMET TSOMET IMSMETQU IMSMETSR CICSMET)*TIME;
```

Any hour causing outliers was examined in detail. Operation's logs were examined to determine if there was a known anomaly during that hour. Data for hours with TOTALCRU less than one-half the maximum were deleted because such data represented lightly loaded intervals and were redundant with the peak hour selection. The result of this outlier analysis was a set of hourly observations from each system that was cleaned of operation interventions and software and hardware failures. These data were used for the subsequent analysis.

Overview of Linear Regression to Distribute MVS Overhead

Consider the following work profile for a batch processor:

BATCH CRU	JES CRU	SYSTEM TASK CRU	MVS CRU	PERFORMANCE BUFFER	IDLE

0   work==>   100%

Clearly, not all of the hardware capacity to do work can be used productively (that is, be billed directly). To measure the portion of hardware work required to produce some measure of billable work, you must understand the measures used in the model above.

A portion of hardware capacity can be unused because of **idle time**, which usually results when there is insufficient work. But even at peak load, there are times when all tasks are waiting for I/O and the processor is idle. To meet performance goals, it may be necessary to operate at less than 100% of hardware capacity. Therefore, a **performance buffer** that may require a portion of hardware capacity is defined. **MVS overhead** is used in dispatching tasks and in memory management, functions that are not directly related to individual tasks. This unidentifiable resource consumption can be measured, but it is not attributed to individual tasks by RMF. **Systems tasks** (such as security, tape mount accounting, RMF, RESOLVE, and multiple system support) require a portion of hardware capacity. Their resources are not charged to individual tasks. JES performs job scheduling and printing facilities for batch work, but a portion of its resource consumption is not attributed to the batch work. **JES resource consumption** requires a portion of hardware capacity.

In the above profile, RMF data provide the work delivered to batch, JES, and systems tasks from the performance group (type 72) data. The CPU portion of the MVS CRU can be measured by subtracting the sum of the performance group CPU times (TCB + SRB) in the type 72 data from total CPU active in the type 70 data. Although the I/O work done by MVS is not available in RMF, the estimate of total work using the sum of performance group data and the MVS CPU work is the best measure available.

Total work in any batch system is clearly related to batch workload. As discussed before, JES work units and batch work units are combined into the JESBATCH workload. The functional relationship of TOTALCRU to JESBATCH can be determined by using linear regression. Linear regression calculates coefficients in a linear equation between one independent variable (TOTALCRU) and one or more dependent variables (JESBATCH), and it provides other statistics on how the regression line fits the data. From algebra, the equation of a line is

$$Y = B_1 * X + B_0$$

where B_1 is the slope of the line and B_0 is the intercept. In our present analysis, Y is TOTALCRU, and X is JESBATCH CRU. The SAS procedure SYSREG calculates B_1 and B_0:

```
PROC SYSREG;
   MODEL TOTALCRU=JESBATCH;
```

The B_0, or INTERCEPT value, is an estimate of static work that is independent of the JESBATCH workload, and B_1 provides an estimate of the slope of the line relating total work to JESBATCH work. The inverse of the slope, $1/B_1$, is the capture ratio of this workload. Expressed as a percentage, the capture ratio describes the portion of TOTALCRU that is captured by the JESBATCH CRU measure. Using the equation relating TOTALCRU and JESBATCH, you can show where hardware capacity is consumed in this simple batch example.

Multivariate Linear Regression for Capture Ratio Measurement

The simple batch model described above can help you understand regression, but, typically, there is more than just batch in the configuration. Taking the case study with its four major workloads, the total work can be graphically displayed as:

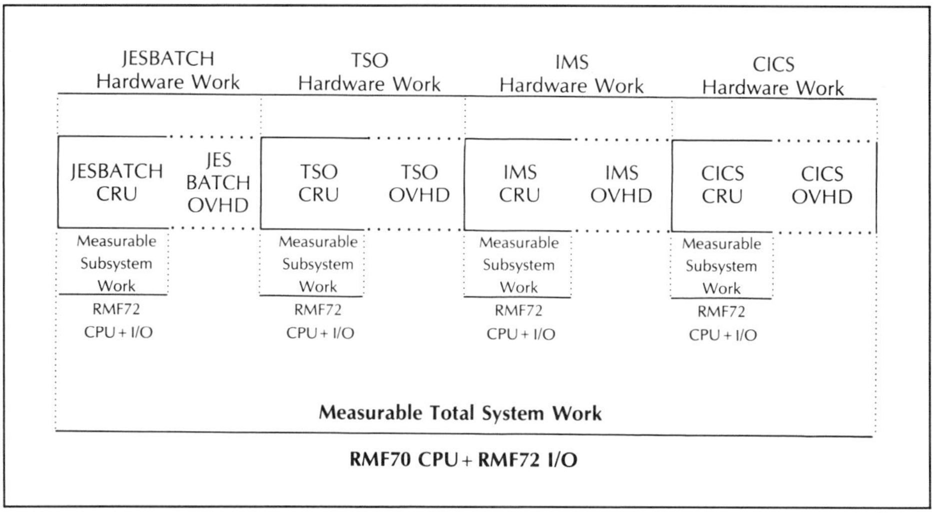

Figure 26.3

Assume that the portion of total overhead to be attributed to each subsystem is a function of the actual work measured in that subsystem and use the linear model:

$$WORK = B_0 + B_1 * Workload_1 + B_2 * Workload_2 + ...$$

The SAS procedure SYSREG calculates the linear regression coefficients and R^2 value:

```
PROC SYSREG;
    MODEL TOTALCRU=JESBATCH TSOCRU IMSCRU CICSCRU;
```

From the resulting output, the R^2 and coefficient values are extracted:

Table 26.4
SYSREG Output

R-SQUARE .9974

Variable	Parameter Estimate
INTERCEPT	24800
JESBATCH	1.239
TSOCRU	1.738
IMSCRU	1.311
CICSCRU	1.503

Therefore, the equation describing how much overhead is attributable to each subsystem is given by:

TOTAL WORK = 24800 + 1.239*JESBATCH + 1.738*TSOCRU
+ 1.311*IMSCRU + 1.503*CICSCRU

This equation shows that for every unit of work delivered to the JESBATCH performance group 1.239 units of hardware work were expended. For every unit delivered to a TSO user, 1.738 units of hardware work were consumed. In both cases, the additional work (.239 and .738 units per unit delivered) was the work actually consumed by the MVS overhead measure, which was then distributed to the tasks (JESBATCH and TSO) that caused the MVS overhead.

Statistics provide the illusion of certainty. Linear regression always finds an equation through any scatter of data. The task of the CPE analyst is to ensure that the mathematical equation provided by linear regression is a valid expression of the true world. You can validate the regression by comparing the results with common sense:

- The INTERCEPT value (representing static work that is always present) must be small compared to the maximum value of TOTALCRU. In this example, it is less than 3% of peak TOTALCRU.
- Each coefficient must be greater than one. Since the coefficient represents TOTALCRU as a function of subsystem CRU, a coefficient less than one is not physically possible. However, if there are outliers, missing data, or if the data are bimodal (for example, analyzing data before and after a major software or hardware change), the coefficients can be less than one or even negative, a clear indication of an invalid equation.
- R^2 (the square of the correlation coefficient) should be 95 or more. When expressed as a percentage, it describes how much of the variance of the data is accounted for by the linear equation.

The regression is rerun across several subsets of the original data (such as BY WEEK), and the magnitude of the coefficients are compared for stability. If the regression equation truly describes a physical phenomena, subsets of the original data should produce similar coefficients. If very different coefficients result, the data are suspect.

The inverse of the regression coefficients is the capture ratios of the subsystem:

Table 26.5

Subsystem	Regression Coefficient	Capture Ratio (%)
JESBATCH	1.239	80.71
TSO	1.738	57.54
IMS	1.311	76.28
CICS	1.503	66.53

Remember that these coefficients describe how much overhead is attributed to a subsystem. If changes were made (for example, adding memory or an MVS maintenance release), these coefficients can change. When memory is added, these coefficients change because overhead should be reduced with reduced paging. The capture ratio is not a constant, but it describes how much of the MVS overhead was caused by that workload for a specific workload and configuration. If you reduce MVS overhead, these coefficients decrease, and the capture ratio increases with the increased capacity.

These capture ratios can be larger than you see in the literature because this analysis includes the SRB CPU time recorded by RMF, whereas most other analyses have not taken advantage of measured SRB time consumed by a workload.

You have now distributed unmeasured MVS overhead to workloads. The capture ratio allows you to compare the maximum amount of usable work that a subsystem could produce. For example, the 100% hardware capacity of a 3033 was 236800 CRU. The 80.71% capture ratio shows that you could deliver 191121 CRU per hour (.8071 * 236800) to the JES and batch performance group. The 57.54% TSO capture ratio shows that this 3033 could deliver only 136254 CRU per hour to TSO.

However, you do not know if service goals can be met when the processor is operating at 100%. Because the PDB provides resource data and response data, you can determine the amount of hardware capacity to set aside for the performance buffers.

The Scientific Guess (the SWAG)

The case study was performed against data from the MVS/SE1 Operating System. An artifact of that operating system (fixed in MVS/SE2 and later systems) was its inability to drive a pure TSO machine to 100% utilization. Although the particular causes of the TSO inefficiency were eliminated in SE2, the analysis needed to describe a workload that could not effect 100% utilization. An approach that worked is presented below.

As a part of the analysis for outliers, each subsystem's response versus resource plots was produced. A pure TSO CPU never achieved 100% utilization, and processors supporting the other subsystems were driven to 100%. The data were analyzed by processor, and periods when only TSO was in execution were selected. Analysis showed that the hardware CRU consumed on the TSO processor never exceeded 165,900 CRU per hour or never exceeded 70% capacity. There are several possible reasons why this occurred: TSO resources cannot be consumed until the command can be brought into memory I/O conflicts, memory constraints, or the larger number of active address spaces may have prevented 100% utilization of the hardware. In any event, the 70% limitation was a measured fact, and it was necessary to set aside this unusable hardware capacity. For this purpose, the TSO inefficiency factor was defined as a function of the subsystem CRU. During the peak hour, when 165,900 total CRU were consumed on the TSO processor, the TSO CRU itself was 890,000 CRU, and, therefore,

$$\text{TSO inefficiency factor} = (2368000 - 165900) / 890000 = .797 .$$

This meant that for every CRU delivered to the TSO subsystem at peak load, an additional .797 CRU must be set aside for unusable hardware due to the inherent inefficiency of TSO under MVS/SE1.

For batch systems, there were no such inefficiencies. The IMS and CICS subsystems never approached filling a processor in the measured period, so similar phenomena for IMS and CICS were not measured.

The Performance Buffer - Mapping Failed Service to Capacity

The performance buffer is the portion of hardware capacity that must be set aside to guarantee that performance goals are met. As resource consumption increases above some threshold, the responsiveness within that subsystem decreases, so response versus resource was plotted for each subsystem to determine the resource level at which response was below goal level. Even though only the peak hours within prime shift were investigated, goals were based on the entire shift. Thus, rather than using the percent of goal, the plotted data were tabulated to count the percentage of peak hours when subsystem goals were met, as shown below:

Table 26.6
Performance Buffer Analysis

Subsystem	CRU in subsystem	Hours of data	Hours meeting goal	Hours meeting goal (%)
Batch	0-189000	164	163	99.9
TSO	0-40000	36	26	72
	40000-50000	66	46	59
	50000-60000	93	61	65
	60000-70000	39	19	49
	70000-85000	14	4	18
CICS	0-15000	81	74	91
	15000-18000	61	56	85
	18000-21000	46	34	74
	21000-24000	16	12	75
	over 24000	6	4	66
IMS*	0-21000	31	28/31	90/100
	21000-24000	19	13/18	68/95
	24000-27000	33	25/28	75/84
	27000-30000	24	19/19	79/79
	over 30000	11	7/7	82/64

With the exception of batch, response of each subsystem decreases as the subsystem work increases. The consistent performance of batch is the result of several choices. In the case study, batch scheduling, based on user-provided definitions of urgency (15 min, 30 min, 1 hour, 2 hours, or 4 hours) coupled with billing rates, which escalate with urgency, has caused users to request service properly. Therefore, batch work can be configured and scheduled to meet its goals almost always, although to do so can cause poor service to other workloads.

---

*The pairs of entries in the last two columns for IMS are the service time and queue time statistics, respectively. The count and class of IMS message regions determine the queue time for transactions, and the memory and priority of IMS determine service time. Both were tracked separately primarily because the data center manager was the former IMS system programmer, and to gain his approval of this analysis, it was necessary to include both IMS measures to assuage his concerns. As you can see, the trend is strongest for the IMS service time, which is more directly affected by resources than is the IMS queuing time.

For the other subsystems, however, you want to measure the impact of degraded responses. Because these data start with peak hours and then include only hours with very high workloads, you cannot afford to establish 90% goals for the entire day. A reasonable criterion was to set an acceptable subsystem workload as the workload at which the subsystem met its response goals for at least 60% of the time. In other words, when you encounter excessive, rather than expected, workload in a subsystem, you can tolerate a few hours of missing the performance goal, assuming that you will make up the performance goal outside of these overload hours.

If you define the acceptable workload as that workload meeting 60% of the peak hours and compare that value with the peak workload delivered to the subsystem, you find that whereas 84000 CRU were delivered to TSO, the acceptable value of 60000 CRU at 60% peak hours means you must set aside 24000/60000 = .40 subsystem CRU for the TSO performance buffer. The capture ratio showed that for every one unit in the performance group, 1.738 units were spent in the hardware. Therefore, the performance buffer of 0.40 units in the performance group must be inflated by the capture ratio:

$$0.40 * 1.738 = 0.695 \text{ hardware CRU}$$

Thus, 0.695 hardware CRU must be set aside for every CRU delivered to the TSO subsystems. Similar calculations were made for the other subsystems and are tabulated in Table 26.7.

For every one CRU delivered in the TSO subsystem, an additional .695 CRU of hardware CRU capacity was set aside so that TSO goals would be met.

Table 26.7

Subsystem	Maximum subsystem CRU delivered	Subsystem CRU for 60% peak hour goal	Difference between maximum and 60% hours	Hardware CRU performance buffer factor
Batch	198000	198000	0	0.0
TSO	84000	60000	24000	0.695
IMS	34000	30000	4000	0.174
CICS	28000	24000	4000	0.249

TSO factor − (24000) / (60000) x 1.738 − .695

The 1.738 factor, the inverse of the TSO capture ratio, converts from subsystem CRU to hardware CRU.

Combining MVS Overhead, TSO Inefficiency, and Performance Buffer

The preceding results are summarized in Table 26.8, showing the amount of hardware CRU necessary to produce one billable unit for each subsystem.

This table shows the development and the bottom line of this analysis. For each unit of billable work in each subsystem, the actual hardware work necessary to produce that billable work is given. These four capacity coefficients become the basis for all further capacity analyses.

Table 26.8
Development of Hardware CRU Required to Generate 1 CWU

	Batch JES		TSO	
	Factor	Result	Factor	Result
1. Start: 1 CWU		1.000		1.000
2. Convert to subsystem CRU	1.111	1.111	1.087	1.087
3. Calculate additive overhead CRU (factor times subsystem CRU)	.239	.265	.738	.802
4. Calculate additive inefficiency CRU (factor times subsystem CRU)	0	0	.797	.866
5. Calculate additive performance buffer CRU (factor times subsystem CRU)	0	0	.695	.755
6. Add 2 through 5 to obtain goal level hardware CRU for one CWU		1.376		3.510

	CICS		IMS	
	Factor	Result	Factor	Result
1. Start: 1 CWU		1.000		1.000
2. Convert to subsystem CRU	1.154	1.154	1.009	1.009
3. Calculate additive overhead CRU (factor times subsystem CRU)	.503	.580	.311	.314
4. Calculate additive inefficiency CRU (factor times subsystem CRU)	0	0	0	0
5. Calculate additive performance buffer CRU (factor times subsystem CRU)	.249	.287	.174	.176
6. Add 2 through 5 to obtain goal level hardware CRU for one CWU		2.021		1.499

The end result of our analysis of the hourly goal level capacity shows the number of hardware work units that must be expended when 1 billable CWU is delivered to the 4 subsystems and meets service objectives of each subsystem at the same time. Thus, whereas batch requires 1.376 units of capacity for 1 billable CWU, TSO requires 3.510 units of capacity, or over 2½ times the capacity, to produce the same billable work as batch. It is no wonder that service bureaus love batch!

However, this warning is appropriate: these capacity coefficients are not constant. A major change in MVS could make a major change in any of the factors forming the capacity coefficients. For example, adding memory reduces paging, which is a portion of the MVS overhead; the capture ratio (regression coefficient) would change to reflect the increased capacity of the added memory. Change could also occur in the TSO inefficiency factor. You should not accept these capacity coefficients as a permanent measure; they describe the state of a hardware or software complex at a point in time. If major changes are made to the complex, the analysis must be repeated against the data from the new configuration to calculate new capacity coefficients. By comparing the new to the old, the change in capacity by subsystem can be determined.

The final warning on these numbers is that they should not be taken as invariant. Not only are they affected by the tightness of the service objective, but the TSO inefficiency factor disappears with changes in the operating system. The numbers were included in this case study to quantify typical orders of magnitude, but they are no longer representative of actual operating systems. Measure and determine your own configuration's capture ratios for your major workloads. The analysis of MVS overhead using regression is solid, but the TSO inefficiency factor and the performance buffer calculation are engineering approximations at best.

Using the Results of the Hourly Goal Level Analysis

To summarize the hourly goal level capacity, the capacity coefficients can be used to compare and combine work from the different subsystems. Since capacity coefficients map delivered work to hardware work necessary to deliver that work, you can determine:

- how much work a 3033 can do.
- the hardware capacity of a 3033. Earlier the hardware capacity was shown to be 236,800 CRM/hour. Using the capacity coefficients and assuming a 3033 is dedicated to a subsystem, you can calculate 3033 capacities:

Table 26.9

Subsystem	Capacity coefficient	Maximum billable work
Batch	1.376	172,093
TSO	3.510	67,464
CICS	2.021	117,169
IMS	1.499	157,971

- how much more work can be added to a 3033. Assume that you measured the 3033 and found that CICS is delivering 30,000 CWU per hour, and IMS is delivering 24,000 CWU per hour.

Used Capacity = 30000 * 2.021 + 24000 * 1.499 = 96600 CRU

Excess Capacity = 236,800 − 96,600 = 140,200

Available for batch = 140,200 / 1.376 = 101,900 CWU

  or

Available for TSO = 140,200 / 3.51 = 39,900 CWU

Determination of Weekly Capacity from Hourly Capacity

The preceding analysis gives the technique for measuring hourly capacity. Although you could multiply the results by 168 hours (the number of hours in a week) to get weekly capacity, the result does not represent the realities of computer usage. Our goal is to measure capacity in a manner that is accurate and relevant to management, especially to financial managers making major acquisition decisions. Capacity measures should relate directly to the real needs of the business.

The week is the best unit of time for reporting capacity to management. A week allows short-term trends to be spotted and eliminates the inconsistency of monthly reporting due to the variable number of working days in each month.

You can further partition the work into prime and nonprime shifts, but the real analysis should be concerned only with the shift during which the configuration limits the ability to meet service. For most installations and for this case study, the configuration is limited by prime shift usage.

Suppose you want to take hourly capacity and correct the number of hours in prime shift so that the unusable capacity due to unavailable workload is not considered. Assume that the workload growth over time will be in magnitude, but not in the arrival pattern: peaks will remain where they are, with only the amount of work done in each hour changing. With this assumption, you need to determine the shape of the daily prime workload.

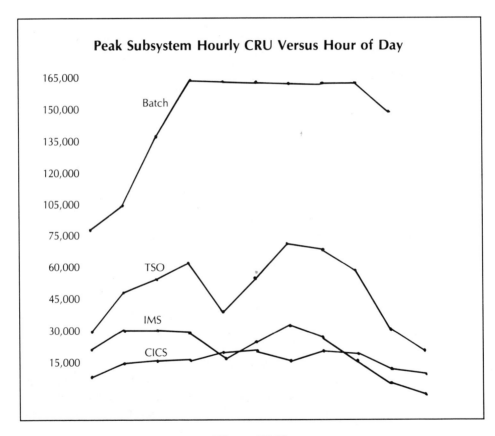

Figure 26.10

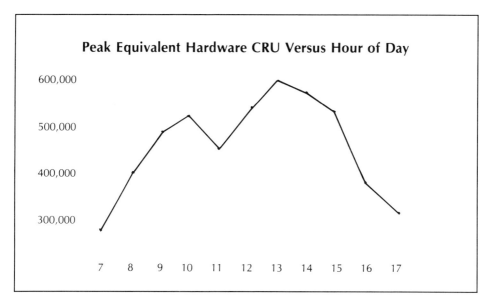

Figure 26.11

Subsystem CRU per hour versus hour of day for each subsystem was plotted. The typical peak hourly value was the fifth highest value of each hour for each subsystem CRU. Since there were 30 days data for each hour, that represented the 83rd percentile. Figure 26.10 shows the resulting profile for the peak hourly subsystem CRU for the 4 subsystems. Using the capacity coefficients to convert these profiles to hardware CRU and summing across the subsystems for each hour gave the equivalent hourly hardware CRU for the complex, shown in Figure 26.11.

The assumption that the workload shape is constant means that you will run out of capacity (that is, service objectives will not be met with increased workload) when the peak hour of the daily profile exceeds the 700,400 CRU hourly hardware capacity. Therefore, you want to raise the present workload profile until its present peak hourly value is equal to 700,400 and then calculate the area under that profile. The profile, with peak value of 700,400, is the amount of work that can be accomplished in this configuration in one day. The tabulation of this analysis is given in Table 26.12. The first 4 columns are peak hourly CRU. The fifth column is the sum of the first 4 columns after each was converted to hardware capacity by the capacity coefficients. This sum represents total peak hardware CRU consumed. The peak hour of the day was 1:00 p.m.; column 6 uses the peak daily value to normalize the other hours of the day.

Table 26.12
Construction of Weekly Peak Hardware CRU

Peak Subsystem Hourly Hardware CRU

Hour	JESBATCH	TSO	CICS	IMS
7	95000	30000	6000	21000
8	105000	52000	14000	29000
9	140000	56000	17000	29000
10	165000	60000	18000	28000
11	165000	42000	22000	20000
12	165000	58000	24000	27000
13	165000	72000	22000	32000
14	165000	68000	23000	28000
15	165000	60000	22000	19000
16	155000	36000	17000	6000
17	150000	22000	16500	4500
Daily Total	1635000	556000	201500	143500

Hour	Equivalent hardware CRU hourly sum	Ratio to peak hour	CRU extended to hardware capacity
7	280700	.490	343,100
8	39700	.698	488,600
9	467700	.817	571,700
10	516500	.901	631,400
11	448500	.783	548,200
12	519600	.907	635,000
13	572700	1.000	700,000
14	554300	.968	677,500
15	510100	.891	623,500
16	382000	.667	466,900
17	322600	.563	394,300
Daily Total	4974500	8.686	6,080,200

The basic assumption is that the shape of the hour-by-hour profile does not change; instead, only the magnitude of the profile changes. Since the shape, normalized to its peak value, is calculated in the Ratio to peak hour column, you can extend each hour's shape by multiplying the ratio times the 700,400 hardware CRU capacity. If the peak hour consumed the maximum possible value of 700,400 hardware CRU, the shape of the workload would cause a daily total of 6,080,200 CRU to have been consumed. This value, which is the integral of (or area under) the daily profile when extended so that the peak hour equals hardware capacity, is daily hardware CRU capacity. Note that the sum of the ratios, 8.686, indicates that the shape of the curve gives an area equivalent to 8.686 hours per prime shift. Since there are 11 hours in the prime shift, usable capacity is not 11 hours times the hourly capacity, but only 78.9% of absolute capacity. In other words, 21% of prime shift capacity can never be used because there is no workload presented to the system. This is a measure of noontime dip and early morning and late afternoon demands.

Weekly prime shift hardware capacity is then taken as 5 times the daily value of 6,080,200 or 30,401,000 prime shift hardware CRU per week. Notice that if you multiplied the 700,400 hourly hardware CRU by 5 days times 11 hours, you would have calculated 38,522,000 CRU, 26.6% greater than the actual usable capacity. Failure to discard unusable capacity causes the reported utilization never to reach 100%, even after the system is saturated and tends to discredit the capacity analysis.

Tracking Capacity Utilization

Once you have a legitimate measure for capacity, you want to determine and track ongoing utilization. You especially want to plot the data to predict when new hardware is required. The PDB contains the subsystem CRU delivered during prime shift each week. However, the hardware capacity set aside for the performance buffer and the TSO inefficiency is not actually consumed and must be added to the raw RMF data to get the goal level workload consumed last week. For the TSO, CICS, and IMS subsystems, the consumed CRU (as measured in RMF) must be inflated by the total:

Table 26.13

Subsystem	Inefficiency	Performance	Total
Batch	0	0	0
TSO	.797	.695	1.492
CICS	0	.249	.249
IMS	0	.174	.174

Each subsystem's CRU is multiplied by the total coefficient, and the resulting CRUs are added to total CRU delivered (that is, the total CRU of all performance groups and the MVS overhead CRU) to produce the hardware CRU delivered. This number is then plotted by week against a hardware capacity of 30,401,000. The weekly data can be tracked over time, and as the systems are reconfigured, the hardware capacity line is raised or lowered. Management is provided with weekly graphs, which are created by the SAS/GRAPH product and are shown in chapter forty-two.

chapter twenty-seven

Application Improvement

Performance measurement has traditionally been limited to the evaluation of the overall computing system and has only become a factor with applications when a high resource-consuming application became visible or when the response of an application system failed to meet objectives.

However, included in the data gathered for system performance measurement is a large volume of useful information for the application development process. This chapter presents several techniques useful for improving the application development process.

In a discussion of improved performance, there are two areas of performance to address. First, the development of the application can be measured and analyzed, and assistance can be provided to improve productivity of the development programming group. Second, the end product, the application, can be analyzed and performance improvements suggested to improve execution performance of the application.

PERFORMANCE OF THE APPLICATION DEVELOPMENT WORKLOAD

The applications development group is limited by two factors in any development: calendar time to complete the task and people and computer resources consumed. A reduction in either completion time or resources used is a performance improvement, and the techniques for improved performance address both goals.

The most important technique for accomplishing both goals is to establish and report response objectives so that the applications group knows what response it can expect to receive.

If the primary tool for development is batch, then a scheduling system (that is, priority, class, and so forth) with clearly stated objectives must exist, and feedback confirming that objectives are being met is crucial. The applications development group can then appropriately classify its jobs, knowing that response requirements will be met and permitting better estimates of time-to-complete. Table 27.1 shows an example of the type of objectives and reporting that the applications development group needs each week. Feedback is provided on batch response received by the applications group, as well as on resource consumption by each group and on each group's fairness to other groups in terms of abusing a priority scheduling system. At one installation, the only mechanism for controlling priority abuse is a listing such as Table 27.1. Peer pressure from the different groups is enhanced by listing the name of each applications group supervisor on the weekly report. Management interest and peer pressure can prevent abuse of the high-priority classes.

Table 27.1
Weekly Batch Performance Report for Application Groups

	15 Minutes		1 Hour		4 Hours		Overnight	
	Jobs met this goal (%)	Jobs at this PRTY (%)	Jobs met this goal (%)	Jobs at this PRTY (%)	Jobs met this goal (%)	Jobs at this PRTY (%)	Jobs met this goal (%)	Jobs at this PRTY (%)
All Groups	96	7	94	31	93	42	99	20
Group A	92	11	91	26	91	40	100	23
Group B	99	4	95	35	90	43	99	18
Group C	100	6	94	32	96	41	99	21

Objectives:

- 90% of jobs must meet service time objective
- 10% or less of a group's jobs can be in the 15-minute category.

If the primary tool is TSO, a similar reporting tool is needed, as shown in Table 27.2. Response measures are provided, and usage of TSO by the two groups is seen in the percentage of trivial transactions - 33% by the A (APL) Group and 57% by the B (COBOL) group.

Table 27.2
Application Development Group TSO Response Performance

	% in 2 sec	% in 4 sec	% in 8 sec	% in 30 sec	Count of trans	Avg resp sec	% of trans
All Groups	69	80	88	97	206,364	9.6	
Trivial	82	88	92	97	105,624	6.2	51
Nontrivial	55	72	85	96	100,740	13.2	49
Group A	66	80	91	98	52,670	6.7	
Trivial	86	93	97	99	17,403	5.7	33
Nontrivial	51	71	87	98	35,267	7.1	67

Group B	70	80	87	97	153,694	
Trivial	81	87	91	97	88,221	57
Nontrivial	57	73	84	96	65,473	43

Number of Sessions 3384

Average Users Logged On 63

Maximum Users Logged On 101

Average Session Duration 54 minutes

The two reports provide overall performance statistics concerning service to the applications group, but they do not address resource consumption of the application development. For this purpose, a daily report of resource consumption by development batch jobs (Table 27.3) and TSO sessions (Table 27.4) should be provided to first-line supervisors. Knowing who should be working on what and how programmers code job names, the supervisor can detect high resource usage by scanning the reports. For that reason, it is best to sort the list by submitter so that work is grouped by individuals.

Table 27.3
Daily JOB Listing

Development Group A

Job	JES#	Read-in Time	REQ	REC	Execute	Print
VECBWMDY	398	02FEB79:05:40	4:00	2:48	0:04	0:18
VECBWMDY	2990	02FEB79:11:33	4:00	3:07	0:12	0:14
VECBWMNW	2699	02FEB79:14:08	4:00	2:15	0:52	0:13
VEXJSMFF	9969	02FEB79:09:14	0:15	0:06	0:06	0:25
VEXJSMLN	7777	02FEB79:08:08	0:15	0:08	1:09	1:15
VEXJSMLN	7924	02FEB79:12:45	0:15	0:07	1:06	1:19

Cost	CPU	EXCP	Pages	ABEND	COND	TAPEDRVS
16.42	0:14	11140	16	USER	999	0
9.11	0:09	9061	42			0
180.04	2:12	36904	149	SYST	613	3
7.32	0:10	837	20	SYST	813	3
6.69	0:08	1100	16	SYST	213	5
7.46	0:09	1306	21	SYST	213	5

The batch detail is valuable not only for resource tracking (note the relatively high cost of the third job), but, if properly designed, it can often help detect education problems. For example, this sample has repeated occurrences of X13 abends relating to OPEN, but they usually result from JCL errors such as incorrect PDS member names. Perhaps this group would benefit from a seminar on JCL conducted by the CPE analyst. By providing these data daily or weekly to the first-line supervisor, you are emphasizing the need for education, which should be recognized.

Table 27.4
Daily TSO Listing

Development Group A

User ID	JES#	Logon time	Logoff	Session Duration	Cost	Trans Count	Terminal
VECBWM	3712	04NOV80:08:20	16:14	7.53	36.38	496	TD703I1a
VEXJSM	3604	04NOV80:07:17	07:32	0:14	.56	4	TD703I1b
VECJSM	3641	04NOV80:07:40	07:44	0:03	1.42	16	TD703I1b
VEXJSM	3702	04NOV80:08:18	08:30	0:12	12.95	47	TD703I1c
VEXJSM	3778	04NOV80:08:51	10:16	1:24	7.06	38	TD703I1b
VEXJSM	3792	04NOV80:11:13	12:47	1:33	.93	8	TD555I2d
VEXJSM	4163	04NOV80:13:13	15:10	1:56	4.01	52	TD703I2b

Similarly, the TSO report shows resource consumption. Moreover, it provides interesting information about work habits of the group. Since these data come from the JOBS data set in the PDB, which contains the VTAM terminal name of each session, this report shows who is using each terminal. This may also be useful to defend the number of terminals allocated to the group, or it can show that more terminals are needed by the group.

Both of these reports provide ongoing data to the applications development group. Their usefulness, however, is largely a function of the supervisor.

In addition to ongoing reporting, the applications development group can benefit from several periodic analyses. A major failing of daily reporting is that overall impact may be lost when such a short period is observed. Frequently, monthly reports will show trends and frequencies that are missed in daily reporting. Thus, several periodic analyses of the work submitted by the applications development group can complement the daily reports.

Table 27.5
Abend Analysis

	Group A	Group B	Group C	Group D	Total
JCL Errors:	357	109	446	204	1116
Return Codes:	888	206	1090	501	2685
04	371	85	428	136	1020
08	290	22	118	127	557
12	119	25	266	207	617
16	83	11	203	26	323
Other	25	63	75	5	168
System Abend Codes:					
x01	18	6	30	6	60
x06	9	3	17	4	33
x0A	1	—	2	6	9
x13	65	11	106	29	211
x37	20	4	49	13	86
x3B	9	—	6	—	15
x3D	3	—	—	—	3
OC1	12	2	9	2	25
OC2	5	1	4	—	10
OC3	15	—	—	—	15
OC4	8	2	21	1	32
OC6	44	—	13	—	57
OC7	2	4	30	6	42
XF1	—	3	8	—	11
User Abend Codes:	28	15	39	50	132
Total Jobs:	4491	2147	7225	3179	17042

ANALYSIS OF ABEND AND CONDITION CODES

A simple frequency count of batch terminations by group and by individuals within a group is very informative. Since most abnormal terminations result from users' errors, reducing abend frequency should improve productivity. The first step is to identify what type of terminations are occurring. Table 27.5 shows the type of data readily available. The interpretation of these data depends on the installation, but there are some obvious observations. Group A seems to need education in JCL; compare its JCL error count with the other groups' JCL errors and totals. Groups B and C could use education in tape management system (TMS) JCL parameters since ABENDs xFx are issued for TMS error conditions. The occurrence of x3B abends (ISAM) in Group C was unexpected because that group supposedly had converted to VSAM. An ongoing ISAM development was discovered despite a corporate decision to terminate new ISAM applications. These examples show only a small part of information to be obtained from abend analysis.

IDENTIFYING DEVELOPMENT JOBS THAT ARE DELAYED FOR TAPE DRIVES

Jobs submitted by applications development programmers frequently request more tape drives than they need. This increases turnaround time for the job since it takes time to allocate tape drives. Usually the applications development programmer has no idea of the number of tape drives actually used by a job since it is not normally printed on the listing. Frequently the same JCL deck is used over and over again, resulting in tape drives being allocated and never used. (Once the programmer gets the JCL to work, why not avoid the chance of a JCL error by never touching the JCL again!) Most programmers have never been shown how to minimize the number of tape drives allocated to a job.

Using the JCL parameter UNIT=AFF= (on the DD statement) the same tape drive can be reused by a different data set in the same step. MVS operating systems allocate one tape drive for every DD statement that points to a tape data set. Even if DDs are concatenated and read sequentially, one tape drive is allocated for each DD. Typical JCL to read in the last four daily tapes might look like:

```
//IN      DD    DSN=DATA.DAY(0),DISP=OLD,UNIT=TAPE
//        DD    DSN=DATA.DAY(-1),DISP=OLD,UNIT=TAPE
//        DD    DSN=DATA.DAY(-2),DISP=OLD,UNIT=TAPE
//        DD    DSN=DATA.DAY(-3),DISP=OLD,UNIT=TAPE
```

The preceding JCL causes four tape drives to be allocated. The following JCL uses the UNIT=AFF= parameter to allocate the second through fourth tape data sets to the same physical drive on which the first tape was allocated:

```
//IN    DD    DSN=DATA.DAY(0),DISP=OLD,UNIT=TAPE
//      DD    DSN=DATA.DAY(-1),DISP=OLD,UNIT=AFF=IN
//      DD    DSN=DATA.DAY(-2),DISP=OLD,UNIT=AFF=IN
//      DD    DSN=DATA.DAY(-3),DISP=OLD,UNIT=AFF=IN
```

By periodically analyzing tape drive usage, you will discover whether the need to educate users in UNIT=AFF exists. By helping the programmer use fewer tapes, you will improve his turnaround, and you will reduce unnecessary demand on tape drives. Select from the JOBS data set of the PDB those jobs that use more than four tape drives (variable TAPEDRVS) and ask their owners if the number requested is appropriate. Recall that in MVS/370, the installation macro IMACCHAN affects the count of tape drives. Make sure the count is correct before presenting these results:

Table 27.6
Tape Drive Usage
Jobs Using 5 or More Tape Drives

Tape Drives = 5			Tape Drives = 6		
Jobname	Number of times executed	Tape EXCPs	Jobname	Number of times executed	Tape EXCPs
KG4CS	3	16	WILLIAMS	16	0
VR6TC	2	325	KA5PQD	16	24061
W5GN	3	12000			

In Table 27.6, note the very small number of EXCPs on jobs KG4CS and VR6TC with five tape drives, and job WILLIAMS with no tape EXCPs and six drives. Investigation of WILLIAMS shows that a junior programmer has taken over maintenance of a daily, weekly, monthly, and quarterly system. His predecessor gave him a JCL that would always work because it had a DD statement for every data set that the production system could ever use. When the JCL was subdivided into the 4 jobs the programmer actually needed, no job ever required more than 3 tape drives, and the programmer's productivity quadrupled as his compile job no longer waited for 6 tape drives.

IDENTIFYING OTHER HIGH RESOURCE-CONSUMING JOBS

Tape drives are not the only concern. Execution duration and resource consumption of both applications development programs and production programs can have a significant effect on schedules. Jobs that use high resources require longer to run and receive fewer turnarounds per day for the programmer. Analysis of the execution resources by program execution (from the PDB STEPS data set) identifies candidate programs for further analysis. Resources typically considered are CPU, I/O, paging, and so forth, and there are many excellent ways to categorize these high resource programs. Table 27.7 is a partial example of the output of the HIUSEAGE program in SOURCLIB, which identifies programs that rank in the top fifty on any of several resources.

Table 27.7
PDB Analysis - HIUSEAGE Report - High Resource Program Usage
All Programs Ranked in Highest 50 on Any Resource

Program	TCB rank	SRB rank	EXCP rank	Page rank	Elapsed rank	Number of times
EASYTREV	1	1	1	1	1	4931
SORT	5	2	6	2	2	1023
IEWL	14	11	14	3	10	1011
XREF	11	5	5	4	8	352
ADRLIBR	12	9	9	5	5	1603
CPLAGON	3	6	15	6	7	219
IEBGENER	13	7	10	7	3	1155
IKFCBLOO	4	12	7	8	9	522
PGM=*.DD	7	4	8	9	4	256
DBULTRG	8	23	25	10	16	21
IERRCOOO	17	19	22	11	14	486
DGMALTGG	21	18	19	12	18	31
EAMATOLU	20	21	11	13	20	44
DPROOFU	2	15	17	14	12	38
ETBILDUG	10	17	13	15	15	22

DTAB49	9	8	12	16	6	44
WYLISTR	25	25	21	17	24	346
DSDUMP	16	10	3	18	13	227
IEHLIST	18	13	16	19	17	196
PCSTRUN	15	14	4	20	19	21
GGAL3164	6	3	2	21	11	23
DGPROBM	19	16	18	22	21	34
DATTESTR	24	24	20	23	25	333
EIDISTDST	23	20	23	24	22	33
IEHPROGM	22	22	24	25	23	174
IEFBR14	26	26	26	26	26	230

This tabulation of program usage often reveals significant, unexpected information. Does Table 27.7 look like a development group or a reporting group? The program DPROOFU certainly is CPU intensive; it ranks second in CPU TCB time consumed, yet it was executed only thirty-eight times. It is a strong candidate to be examined in further detail.

Analysis of program usage by development group can also reveal structural differences in program usage. For example, the compiler program name (or perhaps the compiler step name) identifies which version of the compiler is being used by which development groups, and it may uncover use of archaic or nonsupported language compilers.

The preceding examples show how the performance measurement group can routinely assist the productivity of the development process itself. The same techniques can be applied to the production execution of the application itself. Identifying trends in abend analysis of major applications can provide improved maintenance. Tracking high resource consumption production programs can reveal unexpected production programs and identify candidates for extended analysis with program performance monitors (such as the ANALYZER program, a free part of the CA/CAPEX COBOL Optimizing Compiler product and analyzes any program, not just those compiled by CAPEX).

The best assistance the performance measurement group can provide the applications development group is information on how applications and the application development groups use resources. The information needed should be in the Performance Data Base since the JOBS and STEPS data are normally needed by the CPE analyst. Thus, the analyses described above can be accomplished by little more than PROC PRINTs, FREQs, and MEANSs against the PDB, at very little cost.

Providing this information to the applications development group also carries with it a possible political benefit. In many installations, the junior applications programmers are self-conscious about asking for help from their application peers; they do not want their officemates (who may be competing for the same promotions) to know what they do not know. The CPE analyst, from outside the applications group, poses no threat to the programmer and frequently becomes the support center for applications programmers. In so doing, the CPE analyst becomes more aware of activity in the applications group and frequently can influence the quality and performance of future development.

chapter twenty-eight

Organization of the CPE Function

The success of the CPE function can be affected more by the position CPE occupies in the organizational chart of the enterprise than by the technical skills of the CPE personnel.

There are two major functional areas of Computer Performance Evaluation:

- Strategic CPE: the long-range, concerned with tomorrow rather than today, analytic, and pro-active.
- Tactical CPE: the here and now, firefighting today's battles, ad hoc, and re-active.

The organizational chart in Figure 28.1 is typical of medium to large MVS installations. The line functions that supply computer services, operations, and systems programming, report to the same director as the staff function that plans, advises, audits, and analyzes the line function.

When the DP organization is as large as in Figure 28.1, strategic and tactical CPE functions should be separated in their formal management reporting chains. Installations that have had successful strategic and tactical CPE reporting up the same management chain are the exception rather than the rule. The functions should be split, even when the organization needs less than a full-time person in either function.

Why separate the two functions physically as well as logically? Inevitably, conflict will occur between the two functions. Strategic wants a new performance group structure, and tactical does not see that to be of sufficient importance to do it in the time frame strategic requires. The strategic function requests changes to the operating system, suggesting that operations personnel change their habits, and, in general, creating work for the tactical function. Since management above the tactical CPE function is the data center manager and since the data center manager hates change because almost every single failure is the result of change, strategic's change requests frequently fall on deaf ears. The CPE function must report up a different chain to a manager at the same level as the manager who can say no.

The main virtue of the location of the strategic CPE function shown in Figure 28.1 is that changes can be initially proposed directly to the tactical CPE function for agreement. Only when there is a conflict do the managers above each function become involved. If the data center and technical staff managers still disagree, the director makes the choice between supplier and the observer or user's representative.

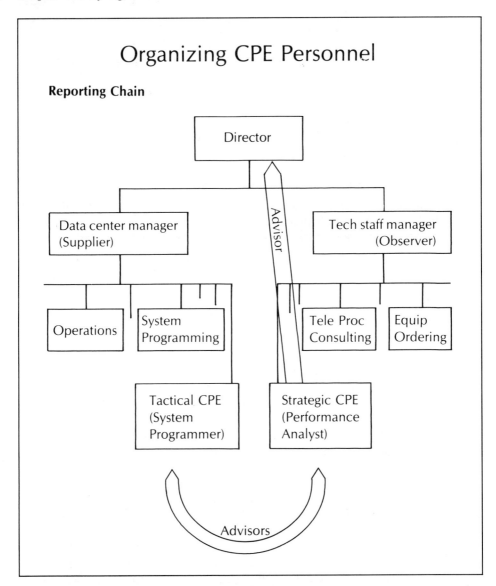

Figure 28.1
Organizing CPE Personnel

What about installations that do not require a full-time person for both functions? Even if the work is done by one person, it should be reported under two functional headings. As the enterprise grows, the staffing also grows, and by tracking where time is spent, it will be easier to recommend staffing increases.

Whether or not the two functions are separated, the two functions do exist. Management must recognize that there are two largely independent functions of CPE and that the talents required for each function are quite different. The strategic function depends on the performance analyst skills of analysis, measurement, projection, and the ability to understand what the operating system does. The tactical function depends on the system programmer skills of programming in the system language (Assembler) and the ability to understand how the operating system works. Obviously, there is an overlap in the skills, and there should be frequent consultation between the two functions.

The following sections describe a typical separation of responsibility for the two functions. Although the choice of functions performed by strategic versus tactical depends on personnel skills, as well as on the history of the organization, all the functions are needed and must be assigned to one or the other.

RESPONSIBILITIES OF THE STRATEGIC CPE FUNCTION

The strategic CPE function:

- requires performance analyst skills.
- reports to a staff manager rather than a line manager.
- establishes performance objectives in concert with management direction, customer requests, and tactical concurrence that the objectives are achievable.
- develops the measurement system, designs the reports, and is responsible for building the performance data base. In addition to being hierarchical, reporting should be daily, weekly, and monthly:

Table 28.2

Report	Quantifies	Destination
high-level	objectives met and work delivered	management
mid-level	resources consumed to deliver work	strategic
detail	hours and tasks that consume resources	tactical

- performs trend analysis. The performance data base data are summarized weekly, after verification that the data themselves are clean (that is, no duplicates and so forth). The data are then added to the trending data base, which extends back at least eighteen months. Trends are plotted weekly and examined to detect any changes, which may then invoke discussion with tactical for further analysis and discovery.

- performs capacity measurement, analysis, and planning. The results are first communicated to the tactical function for concurrence, then jointly to both managers, then to the director. After resources are approved, the strategic function monitors delivery dates with the equipment ordering function on the technical staff.
- evaluates new products that offer improved performance and proposed applications. Analysis includes the impact the proposal may have on resources as well as the wisdom of acquiring the product. (For example, is it the most effective solution to the business problem? Is this a wise expenditure or does a solution to this problem already exist under a different name?)
- evaluates new hardware and new operating systems. Whereas the tactical function performs the IPL and tests, the responsibilities of the strategic functions are constructing the benchmark, evaluating the performance of the new system, and, especially, determining the correct billing factors (for example, for a CPU upgrade).
- audits billed resources versus delivered resources. When the performance data base is under the control of the strategic function, resources consumed (as measured in the PDB) can be audited against the cost-transfer or billing data to ensure the work of the data center is properly accounted. This is always required if the PDB is the source of billing data, and it is always valuable.
- investigates users' problems, especially recurring problems or problems referred to strategic from tactical. Although the tactical function can and does use the PDB for analysis, the intelligent division of labor lets the strategic function act as the analyst for the tactical function, leaving the tactical function free to attack critical problems.
- advises senior management of trends in the enterprise's use of computer services. The strategic function knows which work is growing, which is declining, and the advisory relationship with the director provides an opportunity to expound the CPEers view of the future.
- communicates suggestions directly to the tactical function. If a performance degradation is noted by the strategic function, it is discussed with the tactical function directly. When resolved, the staff and line managers are notified, but there is no need to communicate up and over first.
- answers marketing management's request when the enterprise is a service bureau. In that environment, the marketing function frequently calls on the strategic function for analysis of the profitability of competing products.
- performs "blue sky research." Once the CPE function is functioning properly, the role of the strategic analyst is to look for trouble and investigate ways to improve service or reduce resources.

RESPONSIBILITIES OF THE TACTICAL CPE FUNCTION

The tactical CPE function:

- requires senior systems programmer skills. This function must understand the operating system and be well versed in the subsystems that the installation executes (for example, IMS, CICS, and so forth). Often this is the only place concerned with interfacing these subsystems with each other and with the operating system.
- reports to a line manager rather than a staff manager. The primary responsibilities of the tactical CPE function are to ensure that today's users are able to perform their business functions with adequate response, which is a line function.
- understands and accepts the performance objectives. Without this common agreement between tactical and strategic, the two functions march in different directions. Although it is the responsibility of strategic to establish the objectives, tactical must see that they are met, and, thus, it must be involved in their establishment.
- uses daily reports primarily to confirm that planned changes were installed correctly or to detect that performance degraded after maintenance was applied to the installation. When a problem is recognized, the strategic function is often invoked to aid in the analysis phase, but correction is usually within the tactical function.
- suggests design changes to strategic function. The flow of information between tactical and strategic is in both directions. The tactical function is closer to the problems and can see better ways for reporting and managing problems.
- applies performance modifications. The tactical function must perform the system programming function to ensure that change control is in effect. Although strategic can recommend installation of a modification (for example, memory fencing, DASD relocation, and so forth), installation and testing are tactical function's task.
- manages DASD location. Although tactical and strategic have agreed on the philosophy of which strings contain which application's data (see chapter thirteen), the day-to-day placement of data sets and volumes is tactical's responsibility.
- is called upon by operators or the hotline when problems occur. The strategic function can be invoked by tactical, but orderly problem tracking centralizes performance problems through the tactical function and prevents both CPE functions from being tasked independently to solve the same problem.
- uses tactical tools. The tactical function is skilled in the problem

resolution tools like RMF Monitor II and III sessions, has access to the consoles for MVS and JES console commands, and can invoke the tactical monitors like RESOLVE, LOOK, or OMEGAMON, or can gather detail data with GTF.

- signs off on ALL changes. The tactical function does not approve or disapprove change, but must always be notified when changes occur. By requiring that the change notification form used by operations and the other systems programmers pass by the tactical function, the effectiveness of the tactical CPE personnel is greatly enhanced. Now when a failure is noted at 8 a.m., the tactical function knows what was changed earlier that morning and can immediately back out the changed component, without delay. This procedure has also paid other dividends by preventing the installation of conflicting changes that were recognized by the tactical CPEer.

STAFFING OF THE CPE FUNCTIONS

The number of personnel required in both the tactical and strategic functions is difficult to predict. Not only is the size of the enterprise relevant, but the management style and personnel attitudes also determine the effectiveness of the CPE effort. More people will be required initially when there are more fires to fight and procedures to establish, but as the CPE function matures, more can be done with less. Thus, the following description of one organization does not suggest what is optimal for all organizations.

The organization is structured as shown in Figure 28.1, and the director's annual budget is about $36 million in 1984. All personnel, hardware, software, and communications costs are included in this figure, although applications programmers or end users are excluded. The organization operates three 3081-K processors under MVS, and a VM 3033. The shift operations crew consists of a supervisor, an MVS console operator, a master terminal operator responsible for the on-line applications MTO functions (CICS, IMS, and so forth), a network operator for the telecommunications lines, and several tape hangers. This data center serves remote users, so there is little printing support. The systems programmers group consists of 25 people, ranked from most junior to most senior, and the technical staff consists of 10 people.

Within the line organization, two persons perform tactical CPE. One is a senior systems programmer who is also responsible for additional functions and spends approximately 50% of his time on CPE matters, and the second person is a junior systems programmer, fully dedicated to CPE.

Within the staff function, four people are involved with strategic CPE. A senior CPE person heads the function full-time, and an entry-level clerk-programmer manages the day-to-day PDB runs and reports in 66% of his time. The remaining

2 CPE analysts are also responsible for the billing and cost-recovery, using the PDB data, but they spend only 33% of their time on the strategic CPE functions described above.

In this organization, a total body count of 1½ tactical persons and 2⅓ strategic persons is required to perform the CPE effort. This ratio between tactical and strategic is appropriate for a mature CPE organization that has had effective service objectives in place for several years. An immature CPE organization requires more personnel in tactical initially, as it takes time to develop service objectives and gain their acceptance as objectives for managing resources. Furthermore, since there is a dearth of trained CPE professionals, most personnel in a newly emerging CPE function must be trained from within, which requires time and an education budget. With more tactical work to do initially and with lesser-skilled CPE personnel, a similar sized installation just recognizing the need for CPE could easily require double the personnel of the mature CPE organization described above.

chapter twenty-nine
CPE Organizations

There are several professional organizations that provide continuing education and publish literature on current research. This chapter identifies those groups and provides the author's opinion of their strengths and weaknesses.

COMPUTER MEASUREMENT GROUP (CMG)

PO Box 26063
Phoenix, Arizona 85068
602/995-0905

This group is the premiere professional organization for CPE users, with almost 1000 users attending the 1983 national conference. The group originated as the Boole and Babbage User's Group meeting in 1969 for installations using their products. In 1975 the meeting was opened to all CPE professionals. Under the leadership of Donald Deese, CMG incorporated in 1976 as an independent professional society with no ties to any vendor. Now CMG is open to anyone with an interest in the field. Its national conference is held in early December (usually in a warm climate). The national conference offers a large vendor area where almost every vendor of a CPE product shows its wares. The CMG national conference papers are reviewed and edited, and the proceedings are provided at registration. If you can attend only one conference a year, this is the one to attend.

CMG awards the A.A. Michelson Award for significant professional contributions to Computer Metrics. The National CMG also publishes its *Transactions* quarterly. As with any volunteer professional organization, obtaining and keeping a good editor is difficult, and the CMG *Transactions* has had its ups and downs. Currently, the quality of the *Transactions* is excellent.

The national CMG also supports autonomous regional CMG Groups that meet in local areas and set their own organizational patterns. Regional groups meet monthly, quarterly, or semi-annually, depending on the willingness of two or three people to make arrangements. These meetings last from one to two days and may be free, or a small fee may be charged. These meetings are always worthwhile opportunities for inexpensive education and provide a chance for users to meet others working on similar projects. Regional groups are currently active in Seattle, San Francisco, Los Angeles, Denver, Southwest (Texas, Oklahoma), St. Louis, Chicago, Northeast (New York City, Boston), South (Atlanta, North Carolina), Washington, D.C., and Pittsburgh.

The administrative headquarters in Phoenix can provide you with the name of the regional chairman nearest you and let you know when the next meeting is to be held.

SAS USERS GROUP INTERNATIONAL (SUGI)

c/o SAS Institute Inc.
Box 8000
Cary, North Carolina 27511-8000
919/467-8000

At the annual SUGI meeting, an entire section is devoted to CPE and includes both invited and reviewed papers. In addition, although other tracks are not specific to CPE, many SAS programming techniques useful to CPE users are presented. Analysts who use the SAS System for CPE should consider attending this valuable conference; it is second only to CMG. Meeting announcements are sent to all who are on the *SAS Communications* mailing list. If you do not receive this quarterly news magazine, you can contact SAS Institute Inc. to get on the mailing list.

SPECIAL INTEREST GROUP ON METRICS OF ACM (ACM SIGMETRICS)

c/o Association for Computing Machinery
1133 Avenue of the Americas
New York, New York 10036

SIGMETRICS originated at a conference in Palo Alto in 1973 and bloomed in the mid-1970s, but it has been on the wane ever since. Some excellent conferences were sponsored, including two sponsored in conjunction with CMG; however, conflicts over finances that erupted between ACM headquarters and ACM special interest groups drove many former ACM members to CMG. The *Performance Evaluation Review* has also been up and down, depending on the skills of the editor to extract articles from researchers.

SHARE

c/o SHARE Inc.
111 East Wacker Drive
Chicago, Illinois 60601

SHARE (not an acronym) is the oldest, and some think it is the best, IBM user's group. Membership in SHARE is offered to installations—not individuals—with large IBM systems (currently 4341 or larger). SHARE holds major meetings in March and August with attendance over 4000 in favored cities; the 1-week meeting offers 800 separate sessions, with over 50 sessions frequently held concurrently. SHARE deals with much more than just CPE, but several of its projects are quite specific to CPE. The SHARE headquarters can be contacted to determine the name and address of the current project manager for the projects described below.

The Computer Management Evaluation Project of SHARE(CME)

This project was formerly named the Computer Measurement and Evaluation Project, and its origin was the SHARE-IBM joint committee on accounting, started in 1968, that specified the SMF facility for OS/360. The CME project is a closed project; that is, the sessions are closed, and you must be a member to attend. The primary requirement for membership is a short written paper demonstrating that you are actively involved in CPE, in order to ensure that project members are contributors to the field.

The project publishes the *CME Newsletter* for members 4 to 6 times a year. Because it is a closed newsletter, some organizations have allowed their employees to publish timely papers here without the normal legal delays for corporate approval, making this newsletter quite valuable. About every 2 years, the newsletter editor publishes through SHARE the *CME Compendium* (Volume VII is expected in 1984), which is typically 800 pages of the best papers from the *Newsletter*. The *Compendium* is automatically sent to every SHARE installation and is available for a small fee from SHARE headquarters.

The Modeling and Analysis Project of SHARE (MOAN)

This project is oriented toward simulation and mathematical queuing models and is predominately concerned with models of computer performance. There are no individual membership requirements, but contribution is expected from attendees at project meetings.

MVS Performance Project of SHARE (MVSP)

This is the project to attend if you are a tactical CPE person. A part of the MVS group, this project publishes the *MVS Tuning Report* available to SHARE installations and is one source of the MVS project's "MODS" tape, a library of mods, routines, and code for MVS systems programmers. Since many active CPE professionals find attending both this project and CME of such value, both projects schedule to avoid conflict (frequently by jointly sponsoring a common topic).

GUIDE

c/o GUIDE Inc.
111 East Wacker Drive
Chicago, Illinois 60601

GUIDE is similar to SHARE in that it requires an installation to have an IBM processor to gain membership, but its composition is different from SHARE. IBM representatives relate that whereas SHARE attendees are the technicians who want to make the system work, GUIDE tends to attract the first-line manager who supervises the technicians. Historically, GUIDE has had a very active DOS project, whereas SHARE has had little to do with DOS until quite recently. As of 1984, GUIDE has eliminated interim meetings and schedules three major meetings a year. GUIDE has great strength in the operations area and tends to be stronger in the application side of subsystems like IMS and CICS. In the area of CPE, however, the SMME project (systems management, measurement, and evaluation), which was quite effective in the mid-1970s, has disbanded.

EUROPEAN COMPUTER MEASUREMENT ASSOCIATION (ECOMA)

Scott N. Yasler, CDP
ECOMA
Scheurhzerstrasse 5
CH-8006 Zurich, Switzerland

This organization is managed in an excellent fashion to permit Europeans to share CPE information. It is similar to CMG in that vendors' exhibits are offered, papers are reviewed, and the proceedings are provided at registration for the annual October meeting. A spring newsletter is rich in content, often containing papers prepared too late for the October conference. Attendance is expensive, with registration and hotel room alone exceeding $1100.

There are meetings on CPE sponsored by other organizations. CPE product vendors with appreciable numbers of users sponsor their own user's groups, which are always of value to the CPE personnel who use those products. The best single source of information on professional meetings, whether sponsored by organizations or vendors, is the *EDP Performance Review*, which provides timely meeting announcements of these and other CPE meetings worth attending.

chapter thirty

Benchmarking

An entire book could be written on benchmarking. When IBM presents the results of its performance evaluations, it frequently requires 50 to 70 pages to dissect, analyze, and conclude comparisons. In this brief chapter, the following topics are discussed:

- motivation for a benchmark
- development of a benchmark work stream
- considerations for executing and monitoring a benchmark work stream
- analytic approaches for comparison of two runs
- unique problems when comparing uniprocessors to multiprocessors
- an alternative—the consistency system approach.

MOTIVATION FOR A BENCHMARK

The primary motive for benchmarking in this chapter is the need for a consistent work unit metric. In principle, the service unit equation, the computer work unit, or even the simple number of CPU seconds consumed are valid expressions of computer work. Although there are proponents of software physics who proclaim that one work is the movement of one byte, many do not accept this theory proposed by Ken Kolence. Kolence was awarded the first A. A. Michelson Award for his development of the software monitor embodied in the computer utilization engine CUE product used to found Boole and Babbage in 1969.

Work should be measured at an installation in computer terms that relate to the data processing department's acquisition of hardware. The work measure should be extended to the end user's applications, and we must move to package the data processing costs in end user's terms. You want to charge per business function (for example, $0.99 for an airline reservation request) rather than per CPU second for better understandability, applicability, and to simplify the jargon of computer processing. However, you always need to measure the business function in terms of computer work because you buy hardware in computer terms, not business terms. Thus, the benchmark process is mandatory so that a job, TSO session, or transaction records the same work units in our SMF data today on our 3081 as it does the next day on the new 3084. Although elapsed time, response time, and so forth are important, the first and foremost measure of pragmatic importance is the CPU factor of the new box. The CPU factor, in general, sets the upper limit of performance between two processors. Other resources (memory, I/O, and so forth) can limit a real workload and keep it from achieving full utilization of the processor, but the relative speed places an upper bound on how much better the faster processor could be, and the CPU factor between them allows a good first approximation to the real capacity of the machine.

Whether service units or a homegrown equivalent is used to measure capacity, the accuracy of capacity trends is directly affected by the consistency of the work measure across hardware and software changes. To guarantee the consistency of the work equation, you must determine the CPU factor or the relative speed of the 2 processors and then use the inverse of the factor to normalize work to common units. Benchmarking on your own CPU with your own operating system and workload is the only accurate method of determining the correct CPU factor for your installation. The factor is not a constant, but it has been found to change with maintenance level of the operating system and with microcode changes of the processor, as described in chapter eleven. The benchmark stream does not require months of preparation nor hours of execution. The benchmark stream described below executes in 1 hour, and it requires at most a total of 2 hours of dedicated system time to set up, submit, execute, and terminate. In benchmarking, there is no better adage than K.I.S.S. (Keep It Simple, Stupid)!

DEVELOPMENT OF A BENCHMARK WORK STREAM

The available benchmark stream, used for processors since 1977, is a batch stream comprised of 28 steps. Nine of the steps are the execution of the same FORTRAN program, called a synthetic program.

The use of synthetic programs was first described in 1969 by Buckholtz, and similar programs are often described as Buckholtz job streams. The programs are called synthetic because through parameters read at execution time, they can theoretically synthesize the resource consumption of widely varying programs. The program itself is comprised of nested loops around CPU instructions and I/O instructions. A SYSIN control statement specifies which loops are to be executed, and, thus, it sets the ratio of CPU to I/O activity. The DD statement for input files determines the I/O attributes (including access method), offering a wide range of I/O possibilities. The only real failing of synthetic programs is the inability to prove to management that they are representative of your workload.

The benchmark includes nine additional steps of a functionally similar synthetic program, differing only in that it is written in COBOL but executed with a different set of SYSIN control statement parameters. There are actually eight unique parametric executions in either the FORTRAN or COBOL synthetic programs because one step is intentionally replicated as a validity check in both sets.

The benchmark stream above had pre-existed the author's involvement and gave data references back to several prior comparisons. To this pre-existing set of 18 programs, 8 additional programs were added to answer the real concern for representativeness. The IBM utilities IEBGENER and IEBCOPY were added, and 5 language processing compilers, Assembler, FORTRAN H, OS COBOL, VS COBOL and PL/I programs were added with an arbitrary typical (that is, non-error-free source) program as input, as well as the execution of the linkeditor utility. Finally, the two most heavily used non-IBM programs at this site, the base SAS product and EASYTREV, were added for a total of 26 unique steps. The composite benchmark is not advanced as the best design, but it is, simply, the engineer's approach to testing. If your goal is to measure the CPU factor between 2 configurations, you should see that difference if you examine the data from a controlled experiment with typical programs. The combination of real and synthetic programs has provided a range of data points in every analysis that has been confirmed in fact after the benchmarked hardware has been installed. The CPU factor chosen by the benchmark (often hastily executed 2 days before production) is not expected to be the final factor chosen, for that number is best determined after several days of full production workload. It is needed to provide the initial estimate for billing system and banner page adjustment during the first days of production, and it is reviewed after a week's production workload. In no case have the results of the above benchmark analysis been more than 5% from the final CPU factor chosen.

CONSIDERATIONS FOR EXECUTING AND MONITORING A BENCHMARK WORK STREAM

The purpose of the benchmark is to examine the impact on billing and capacity of the new configuration so that the CPU factor can be set (at least approximately) in advance of production work. Especially when the causes of CPU variability are understood, it becomes wise to repeat the benchmark steps under differing system loads. The procedure that provides this facet is the variation of the number of initiators during the hour of the benchmark. The system is IPLd (isolated) from other processors, with a separate spool and with no shared DASD to confuse the analysis. Because the aim is for the CPU measure, you are not hurt by shared DASD because its impact is almost exclusively on the elapsed time of the run, but if you selectively elongate jobs using shared DASD, you may have fewer repetitions of some steps than others. With all initiators drained, you read in twenty or so sets of the benchmark jobstream. Each copy contains jobs one through twenty-eight, all with the same job class and priority so that JES scheduling cycles through the jobs as read in. The job names for each job in each copy of the twenty-eight steps end with a unique job name suffix (to avoid duplicate job name delays), and they start with a prefix that encodes the program being executed. This eases analysis, and it makes anomalies during the benchmark run identifiable by job name.

When all jobs have been read in, the benchmark is started by starting initiators 1 through 5. Beginning 5 minutes later and continuing every 5 minutes thereafter for an hour, 5 more initiators are started. After 1 hour, all initiators are drained, and the jobs then in execution are allowed to complete, typically requiring 20 to 30 minutes. The analysis of this style benchmark is provided in MXG software member ANALBNCH, described in chapter forty-one, which uses the TYPE30_4 and RMF data sets created during the benchmark. At IPL of the isolated system to be benchmarked, RMF is modified from its normal 1-hour interval to an interval of 1 minute to provide 60 data points from the hour's execution.

Following are some additional comments on benchmarks:

- The benchmark described above provides extremely accurate CPU power ratios, but its use to determine throughput or the analysis of elapsed time for such a benchmark is fraught with peril. The above portable benchmark requires only a single disk volume, where all data and libraries used by the benchmark are unloaded. Although most of the real file I/O in the benchmark is public work volumes, the access to the single library volume can cause delays that would not occur in a true I/O configuration. These I/O delays can elongate elapsed time of individual jobs. Of course the ending time of the last job has no bearing on the power of either processor. This tail-end effect is determined by the longest running job that happened to initiate before the initiators are drained. The number of jobs that completed cannot be used as a measure of throughput because I/O delays in one configuration can affect only some of the jobs in the benchmark stream. This benchmark serves to define CPU power; once this is accomplished, the techniques of chapter twenty-six can be extended to determine the capacity of the benchmarked configuration.

- Jobs that use tape data sets are frequently excluded for fear of biasing the elapsed time; however, they should be included in the benchmark. The characteristics of tape-oriented processing can be appreciably different from disk-oriented jobs, and wrong conclusions can be reached. If the benchmark JCL specifies specific tape volume serial numbers and if there are fewer total tape volumes than there are tape drives, each tape data set can be premounted with the MVS MOUNT command before execution begins. When the tape step is initiated, MVS knows the volume is mounted, and it allocates the drive with almost no delay.

- Be extremely careful if you suppress printing of output. If suppression is achieved by using a SYSOUT class that is not printed, resources consumed by the JES writer, both CPU and especially memory, are excluded from analysis. If suppression is achieved by using DD DUMMY, the further impact of I/O to the SPOOL data sets is excluded.

- Iteration of initiators is required for performance comparisons of two configurations. Many have gone astray by comparing today's workload to today's initiator structure on today's processor against tomorrow's processor and today's initiator structure. There is no a priori reason to expect that a different configuration will be optimal with today's initiator structure; you should iterate initiators for the optimum under both configurations and conclude performance comparisons between the optimal structure from today and tomorrow.

ANALYTIC APPROACHES FOR COMPARING TWO RUNS

The primary measure to be compared is CPU time recorded in the step records for the benchmark steps. The secondary measure is the operating system overhead, that is, the unassigned CPU activity that is the difference between total CPU busy (TYPE70) and the sum of the control performance group CPU active (TYPE72), CPUMVSTM in the RMFINTRV data set. In spite of the potential variability of the CPU measures recorded by SMF, it is the only source of data you can use to transfer cost or bill for processor utilization. It is also the true utilization of the processor by each step, and it can be used safely if you are careful. The minimum step CPU time recorded for a repeated execution of the step in the varying initiator level benchmark, above, must represent the absolute amount of processor required for that business function. Any increase in recorded CPU time above the minimum comes not from the program itself, but rather from operating system effects due primarily to multiprogramming effects, described in chapter eleven. By comparing the minimum CPU time recorded for each step, the power of the two processors is best determined. However, the ratio of average CPU time of all executions of each step between the two benchmarks provides insight into how repeatable the step CPU time is in the two configurations.

The correct CPU measure to use is the sum of TCB plus SRB CPU time for each step. This is the true total recorded CPU time caused by that step. However, if the installation still uses only TCB CPU time in its chargeback equation, it is also necessary to report the effect on TCB alone. By calculating the ratios of TCB and TCB plus SRB for minimum and average values, the range of interpretable values and an estimate of accuracy of the analysis can be made. For each step in the benchmark, the minimum and average values of CPUTCBTM and CPUTM are calculated. These four values from each step are then divided by the four values for that step from the baseline run to provide four ratios. Then, the average value of these four ratios is calculated for all steps in the benchmark. This process treats each step in the benchmark equally, or, in other words, it assumes that the true workload is distributed among the benchmark steps equally. The individual step ratios are also tabulated in ascending order, listed with their causing program, to verify the accuracy of this assumption. Table 30.1 tabulates the summary of the step CPU ratios from three past benchmarks:

Table 30.1
Benchmark Step CPU Summary

Configuration	Step TCB CPU		Step TCB + SRB		MVS
Name	Average ratio of minimum	Average ratio of average	Average ratio of minimum	Average ratio of average	Overhead CPU active (%)
TEN-TEN	.767	.772	.747	.757	20
TEN-ELEVEN	.672	.673	.653	.659	35
TEN-ALPHA	.982	.990	1.010	1.030	17

This summary provides the ratio among the 3 configurations and a prior benchmark on the baseline configuration. The TEN-ELEVEN configuration showed that the average ratio of minimum TCB time of the steps was .672, or configuration TEN-ELEVEN recorded 67.2% of the CPU time recorded by the baseline configuration. In the second column, the average TCB time ratio of .673 shows very little change from the minimum, suggesting a small repeatability error. Similarly, the minimum TCB + SRB ratio of .653 and the average TCB + SRB ratio of .659 also show consistency. Moreover, the smaller ratio for TCB + SRB, when compared to TCB alone, demonstrates that the TEN-ELEVEN processor is faster in executing the machine instructions typical of SRB time than it is in executing the machine instructions that typify TCB Rtime. The final column provides average percentage of processor busy recorded by SMF/RMF as CPU active but not recorded in any performance group. This unassigned CPU active, or MVS overhead, shows that the TEN-ELEVEN configuration required significantly more processor resources for this function than did either of the other 2 configurations. This additional 15-17% of the processor used by TEN-ELEVEN must be accounted for in the final comparison; although TEN-ELEVEN records 67% less CPU time in the step records, it also records significantly more CPU in the MVS overhead state.

Care must be taken when expressing comparisons with ratios or percentages because the average of the ratios is not necessarily the ratio of the average. Table 30.2 tabulates the two comparison techniques:

Table 30.2
Percentage Versus Ratio Comparisons

Percentage	Ratio	Percentage	Ratio
If "A" CPU is faster by this percentage	"A" CPU time divided by "B" CPU time will be	If "A" CPU is faster by this percentage	"A" CPU time divided by "B" CPU time will be
0	1.000	60	0.625
10	0.909	66	0.600
20	0.833	70	0.588
25	0.800	75	0.571
30	0.769	80	0.555
33	0.750	90	0.526
40	0.714	100	0.500
50	0.666	200	0.250

UNIQUE PROBLEMS WHEN COMPARING UNIPROCESSORS TO MULTIPROCESSORS

For a uniprocessor to have the same capacity as a multiprocessor, the ratio of UP CPU to MP CPU with 2 engines must be .50; that is, the faster UP must record half of the CPU time recorded on an MP with 2 processors (for example, a 3081). This is not strictly true because if the uniprocessor were found to record less CPU active in the MVS overhead state than the MP, the saved MVS CPU time could be used to offset a CPU ratio greater than a half. This did not happen in the above benchmarks; the faster uniprocessors failed to halve the step CPU time, and their measured MVS overhead was higher than the baseline MP runs. The equation below expresses the relative capacity of processors benchmarked, taking into account the impact of the measured difference in overhead (taking care to note the sign of the difference):

$$\text{UP Capacity Relative to MP Capacity} = \frac{N}{M * \text{STEP CPU RATIO}} + \frac{\% \text{ MP Overhead} - \% \text{ UP Overhead}}{100}$$

where

N is the number of processors in the benchmark configuration

(1 for the UPs in this example, 2 for the TEN-ALPHA)

M is the number of processors in the baseline benchmark

(2 in this example of a multiprocessor baseline).

With this ability to compare differing numbers of processors of differing speeds, based on their step CPU ratios and the measured change in MVS overhead, Table 30.3 compares the capacity of the two uniprocessors (TEN-TEN and TEN-ELEVEN) and the two-processor multiprocessor (TEN-ALPHA), relative to the baseline two-processor system:

Table 30.3
Relative Capacity of Benchmarked Configurations

Configuration name	CPU metric	Metric step ratio	Overhead percentage change	Resultant relative power
TEN-TEN	Minimum TCB	0.647	−0.150	0.493
TEN-TEN	Minimum CPU	0.660	−0.150	0.510
TEN-ELEVEN	Minimum TCB	0.742	−0.050	0.692
TEN-ELEVEN	Minimum CPU	0.758	−0.050	0.708
TEN-ALPHA	Minimum TCB	1.010	+0.030	1.040
TEN-ALPHA	Minimum CPU	0.971	+0.030	1.001

Thus the TEN-TEN configuration is marginally estimated at half the capacity of the baseline configuration; the TEN-ELEVEN, although appreciably faster on a per-step basis than the TEN-TEN, did not establish the necessary doubling of speed, and it lost capacity due to increased MVS overhead. Thus, the TEN-ELEVEN is only 70% of the capacity of the baseline configuration. TEN-ALPHA, a multiprocessor itself, appears to have almost the same capacity as the baseline configuration. These results in no way favor or reject any of the 3 configurations; one must go beyond sheer capacity and evaluate the cost of the processor. For example, if the cost of TEN-ELEVEN is half of the baseline configuration, it would be a more cost-effective processor, even though it is only 70% of the capacity of a baseline machine.

AN ALTERNATIVE—THE CONSISTENCY SYSTEM APPROACH

Is there life after benchmarking? The ease with which the benchmark can be executed by operations personnel suggested that it be scheduled regularly after every major system change, and this was done for some time. However, a better choice has proven valuable for confirmation of the benchmark process and also as a part of change management, and it provides a clear, simple confirmation of the consistency of the capacity and performance measures. This system is called the consistency system.

The consistency system is the analysis of specific jobs that are automatically executed three times a day on each processor. The jobs are taken from the benchmark stream because of the historical measures on resources consumed by those jobs. By including those jobs most vulnerable to system change, the consistency system has allowed detection of maintenance application to the system that altered the resources of these programs. The 4 language compilers, the linkage editor, the IBM utilities, and the SAS and EASYTREV benchmark steps are automatically submitted at 10, 2, and 4 each day. As part of the building of each weekly performance data base, these unique job names are selected and stored in a SAS data library that contains all prior executions of these jobs. The resources consumed (CPU, EXCP, mount count, and so forth) are compared to the expected based on plus or minus 10% of the last 6 month's running average for that resource. An exception report is produced when an exception is noted.

Since there is no change in these jobs, any of their resources can be tracked over time to demonstrate the actual delivery of service. Plotting elapsed time of individual jobs over the past year showed that there had been no elongation. Plotting work units recorded for each job overlayed from all systems shows how well the desired goal of a constant work unit equation has been met. CPU times from the consistency system are shown in SAS/GRAPH output in chapter forty-two.

In practice, benchmarking of a new processor or operating system proceeds as follows: when the new configuration is available, operations executes the benchmark system twice and dumps the SMF/RMF data for the performance analyst who builds a PDB from the data. ANALBNCH is then executed to provide a summary analysis similar to Table 30.3. These results are presented to management, along with a qualitative description of individual step CPU ratios. A preliminary CPU factor is defined from this analysis for implementation in the banner page and billing algorithms, as well as in the measure of work used by capacity measurement. When the system is first placed in production, the frequency of execution of the consistency system is doubled, and on Wednesday of the first week, plots of the consistency system are reviewed and needed changes are made to the initial CPU factor. A final review, again using the consistency system plots, is completed at the end of the first month of the new system. Because the CPU factor is determined ultimately from the consistency system, repeated at many times of day, the stability of the work unit measure is easily demonstrated to management. The cost of implementation is trivial, and the total CPU resource of their execution is only 30 seconds per day per processor. Because the trend can be examined for 18 months into the past, management has found the system to be believable and accurate.

chapter thirty-one

Accounting, Cost Transfer, and Billing

Computer system accounting is implicitly tied to an organization's financial attitude. Chief executive officers want effective cost accounting for their data processing budgets. Many DP departments and DP application groups have dragged their feet because they did not want to be held accountable for poor designs. Whether or not you are capable of successfully installing computer system accounting is both a technical and a political issue. This chapter is a technical tutorial on possible resource capture mechanisms and suggested ways of distributing the cost of major hardware components.

CPU AND MEMORY

The CPU and memory are the largest shareable resources in any data processing system. Thus, charges must be based on utilization in order to distribute equitably the cost of the processor in memory. Although you might want to charge for memory, real memory usage is not repeatably measurable. Therefore, memory as an isolated resource cannot be recovered; however, since the primary purpose of memory is to permit the CPU to execute code, it is reasonable to take the total cost of CPU plus memory and divide by the number of billed CPU seconds to determine the cost of a CPU second.

CHANNELS AND CONTROL UNITS

Channels and control units are meant to allow programs in execution to read and write blocks of data. Channels and control units are shareable resources, and their charges should be distributed based on usage. If channels and control units serving tape devices are separate from channels and control units serving disk devices, it is reasonable to sum the cost of tape channels and control units and divide by the number of tape EXCPs in order to establish a price-per-tape EXCP. Similarly, sum the cost of disk channels and disk control units and divide by the number of disk EXCPs to establish a cost-per-disk EXCP. Under MVS/XA, using I/O connect time instead of EXCPs eliminates the inequity of charging the same for a 99 byte EXCP as for a 32760 byte EXCP. In either case, the cost of the channels and control units should be distributed to users who make use of the channels and control units in passing blocks of I/O.

DISK DRIVES

Disk drives are not a shared resource. If an entire volume is dedicated to an application, the monthly cost of that disk drive can be billed to the entire application. If a disk drive has shared users, each data set on the disk is owned by someone. The disk management system, or disk naming conventions, can be used to identify the owner of each data set who can then be charged for the number of tracks in use. It is not uncommon to take the actual cost of a disk drive, divide by the number of tracks on the volume, and inflate this price per track by dividing it by the percentage of volumes that usually contain data. Thus, if 100% of all tracks are allocated, the true cost is the volume cost per track. But, if only two-thirds of the tracks are allocated at your installation, you would inflate the per track cost by three halves to cost recover the disk space.

TAPE DRIVES

Tape drives are owned for the life of a step by a specific job, but then they are used sequentially by multiple users. Thus, it is the duration of usage by job steps that must be used to distribute the cost of installed tape drives. Since the step data contain the number of unique tape drives allocated by the step and the step elapsed time represents the duration of allocation of that tape drive, you could determine the cost of a tape drive hour by taking the total cost of all tape drives and dividing that by the product of tape drives by elapsed hours summed across all steps. This measure reflects actual elapsed time of a job step and is a good measure if your installation is reasonably well tuned, causing job elongation to be constrained.

If you have widely varying execution times, however, it may be unfair to charge tape drives based on true elapsed time. If the installation wants to eliminate the variability of tape drive hours incurred in using actual elapsed hours, it is possible to estimate the number of hours the job would have used the tape drive if it had been the only job in the system. This estimate is crude but sometimes politically necessary. You can run sample tape programs and determine the average millisecond of elapsed time-per-tape EXCP or, in MVS/XA, per-tape I/O connect-second, and then you can establish an equation that estimates the billable tape drive hours from each EXCP count or from each I/O connect second. These billable tape hours can be summed and divided into the cost of tape drives to establish a per unit rate for billable tape drive hours to redistribute your cost of tape drives.

TAPE VOLUMES

Storage of tape volumes requires floor space and racks. The total cost of storage can be divided by the number of tapes in the library to establish a monthly cost for a stored volume. The tape management system catalog can be used to determine ownership of each volume, and a daily or weekly program can determine the number of days each volume is owned by its creating user, who can then be charged at one-thirtieth of the monthly rate for each day of tape storage. The job costs of the tape management system runs can also be added to the storage costs if they are significant.

TAPE MOUNTS

Tape mounts require people time. Scratch tape mounts require a great deal less people time than permanent tape data sets do. Unfortunately, SMF does not record any durations for tape mount time but provides only the count of mounts for each step for billing. The TYPE30 step data in PDB.STEPS can be used to identify scratch requests from specific volume requests. A work study analysis must be used to identify the ratio of time to fetch and mount permanent volumes versus the time to fetch and mount scratch volumes, and, thus, the relative cost of a permanent mount to a scratch mount can be established. The total cost of tape mount personnel's salaries can then be distributed by time to mount a scratch or permanent tape at different rates, and the job steps causing mounts can be charged appropriately.

PRINTERS

The TYPE6 record data in the PDB.PRINT data set provide the number of lines, the form, and the account number of each job printed at each location. The cost of personnel and printed paper at each site can then be distributed by the number of lines printed and based on the number of forms mounted. A surcharge can be established for mounting unique, nonstandard forms. It is reasonable to make end users pay and store unique forms in the printing area and thereby eliminate the need for data processing personnel to tabulate when each form is used.

TERMINALS, CONTROL UNITS, AND PORTS

If a terminal is shared across applications (for example, a VTAM terminal used for CICS, TSO, and CMS), it is difficult to distribute the cost of that terminal since not all applications provide a connect time measure. If the terminal is exclusively or mostly used by a single application, say CICS, then the monthly cost of the terminal and its share of the control unit and 3705 can be distributed directly to that application by monthly billing.

For TSO terminal usage that is frequently shared by different departments, the duration of each TSO session is contained in PDB.JOBS. For VTAM terminals, the physical terminal ID is contained in the session record, allowing numerous opportunities for distributing the cost of terminals to individual departments and identifying which terminals are used by which departments.

For terminals used by IMS and CICS and other applications, there are no connect time records, and cost accounting is still a complex, political, and technical issue.

The ideas expressed in this chapter are opinions based largely on successful implementations of cost accounting. But, since the purpose of cost accounting can range from honest cost recovery to influencing the behavior of users, the major role of the performance analyst is to establish a base line approximate cost for each of these resources. In many instances, the individual costs of a resource are so small that they can be disregarded if they are very difficult to acquire and not a significant portion of the budget.

OTHER COSTS

Other costs are the everyday costs that are typically forgotten until just before the billing system is installed. These include the costs of personnel, software, consumables like power and water, floor space, and supplies for the computer room. Accounting for these costs is usually a major political football since no one really wants to include them as part of his bill. Two common methods used are:

1. Billing each user the same portion of these costs as spent on all other resources.
2. Amortizing these unassignable fixed costs of the data processing facility across the entire organization, letting corporate policy dictate the assignment.

The more serious challenge is outside the domain of the computer performance analyst and in the domain of the financial analyst. For example, if you take the cost of the CPU plus the cost of the memory and divide by CPU seconds, the denominator is easy to determine. But what is the true cost of CPU and memory when you have three on different term leases at different times of acquisition, with differing residuals and differing costs of money? This is a management problem since management determines the fiscal policies employed at your company, and for these matters, your business analyst becomes your ally.

chapter thirty-two

Installing the MXG Software

INTRODUCTION

Merrill's Expanded Guide to Computer Performance Evaluation (MXG) consists of a book, software, and a support subscription. You are reading the book now. The software consists of more than 200 SAS programs stored on tape. The support subscription provides maintenance, enhancements, and updates to the software.

This chapter describes how to install the software so that you can begin executing the MXG SAS code. The total installation takes less than a day and includes these three steps, which are listed below and then detailed.

1. Unload the software you received into a partitioned data set to be referred to as SOURCLIB .
2. Edit the Installation Macros (members of SOURCLIB that begin with the letters IMAC) to define your installation parameters.
3. Build the format library, referred to as SASLIB.

Step 1: Unloading the Tape

The heart of *Merrill's Expanded Guide to CPE* is SAS software. MXG is distributed in machine-readable form as a Partitioned Data Set (PDS) on magnetic tape. It contains over 200 members and was built using the SAS procedure SOURCE. You will use IBM's utility IEBUPDTE to build the PDS on your disk, using the output of PROC SOURCE as the input. The PDS requires the equivalent of 10 cylinders of 3350 space and 50 directory blocks and consists of members containing standard 80-byte numbered SAS data sets.

To unload the partitioned data set from tape to disk, use the installation JCL shown below. It is suggested that you use a DSN with SOURCLIB as the final qualifier to facilitate communications about the software. The JCL below is also contained in member JCLFIRST of SOURCLIB.

```
//JOBNAME JOB ACCOUNTING INFORMATION,REGION=2048K
//S1 EXEC PGM=IEBUPDTE,PARM=NEW
//SYSPRINT DD SYSOUT=A
//SYSIN    DD DSN=MXG.SOURCLIB,DISP=SHR,UNIT=TAPE,
//            VOL=SER=MXGnnn,LABEL=(,NL,EXPDT=98000),
//            dcb=(recfm=fb,lrecl=80,blksize=6160)
//SYSUT2   DD DSN=MXG.SOURCLIB,DISP=(,CATLG),VOL=SER=xxxxxx,
//            DCB=(RECFM=FB,LRECL=80,BLKSIZE=19040),UNIT=3350,
//            SPACE=(CYL,(10,1,50))
```

Note that the JCL above is only a pattern. You will need to change the following fields:

SYSIN DD   The VOLSER MXG*nnn* must be replaced by the actual VOLSER printed on the tape you received.

SYSUT2 DD   The VOLSER*xxxxxx* must be replaced by the DASD volume on which you plan to unload the SOURCLIB. You may also need to change SYSDA as the unit type, based on your installation standards.

When you execute this job to unload the tape, you get a complete printout of the library in alphabetical member list order. Since SOURCLIB contains over 22,000 lines of print, make sure that you have specified sufficient maximum SYSOUT lines (a parameter of your job accounting information). Otherwise a system abend 722 results.

The following are general comments about SOURCLIB:

- Although the code is very general, some portions of the code must be modified before you execute this package. You also need to determine whether all or part of the data in some of the SMF and RMF records creates unique SAS observations.
- The naming conventions for the members of SOURCLIB identify the general purpose of each member.
- Members with names that start with the letters TYPE read an input file, process closely-related record types, and create one or more SAS data sets from the input file. Even though the TYPE members could be concatenated in SYSIN to create multiple SAS data sets in one execution (since each TYPE member rereads the input file), it is generally unwise to execute in that fashion.
- There are members of SOURCLIB with names that start with the letters VMAC that contain SAS macros invoked by other programs to build multiple SAS data sets in one pass of an input SMF or RMF file. In fact, most of the TYPE members simply invoke the appropriate VMAC member.
- Members with names that begin with the letters IMAC are the Installation Macros needed to tailor MXG to your own installation. These macros are discussed later in this chapter.
- Members with names that begin with the letters VMAC are the MXG Master Macros, the macros commonly used in several modules of MXG. These macros should not need your attention unless you want to understand how the records are decoded.
- The other members of SOURCLIB perform various analyses discussed in later chapters. For each member in the SOURCLIB that processes

data records, chapter forty describes the contents, function, and use of that member. The utility and remaining miscellaneous SOURCLIB members are described in chapter forty-one.

Step 2: Editing the Intallation Macros

After the tape has been unloaded to a DASD PDS, examine the Installation Macros for possible editing for your installation. The sections below describe each of the IMAC options that you may need to modify.

IMACACCT: Setting the number and length of accounting variables

The accounting fields in the SMF records are variable in number and length. Installations usually use JOB level accounting, where accounting fields are specified in the JOB statement, but it is possible to specify accounting fields in the STEP statement. Although MVS supports up to 100+ bytes of accounting information, it is uncommon for an installation to have accounting standards that require that much information. As written, the MXG code decodes the MVS accounting fields in up to nine unique variables (ACCOUNT1 through ACCOUNT9). Member IMACACCT allows you to tailor these account variables to your installation's accounting standards. You should edit that member and change the length attributes in the LENGTH statement for each of the account fields that your installation uses. The LENGTH statement determines the size of each of the account variables kept in your data base. If you underspecify the length of an account variable, accounting information is truncated and lost. If you overspecify the length, you create character variables that are longer than necessary. Thus, tailoring member IMACACCT to the length of your account fields saves you storage in your SAS data libraries.

When you edit IMACACCT, you see that ACCOUNT1 through ACCOUNT9 are defined in a LENGTH statement and created in the DO group, where _ I _ ranges from one to ten. Suppose your installation uses only the first two accounting fields in JCL. In that case, you can use the following steps to create only the ACCOUNT1 and ACCOUNT2 variables:

1. Specify the desired maximum length of variables ACCOUNT1 and ACCOUNT2 in the LENGTH statement for your installation's standards.
2. Disable ACCOUNT3 through ACCOUNT9 in the LENGTH statement. You can disable a block of code (and not delete it) by preceding the block with a /* comment symbol and following the block with a */ comment symbol. (Avoid placing the /* in column one since it may be treated as JCL.)
3. Prevent the creation of variables ACCOUNT3 through ACCOUNT9 by disabling the code block that starts with

```
ELSE IF _I_ EQ 3 ...
```

and ends with the END statement immediately before the

```
ELSE IF _I_ GE 10
```

statement.

4. Change the number ten (10) in the two statements beginning

```
ELSE IF _I_ GE 10 ... and
```

```
IF _I_=10 THEN ...
```

to a number two (2).

Note: the variables ACCOUNT3 to ACCOUNT9 and their associated length variables LENACCT3 to LENACCT9 appear in the list of variables to be kept in DATA statements in other modules in MXG code. By removing references to those variables as described above, you prevent their creation without creating a SAS syntax error later. This method works because the KEEP= data set option in the DATA statement was used in MXG instead of a KEEP statement. (The SAS system validates system variables in a KEEP statement but not those listed in the KEEP= data set option.)

IMACCHAN: MVS/370 two-channel definitions

The member IMACCHAN maps alternate channel paths for MVS/370 data. This member is not used in MVS/XA because each device in MVS/XA is identified by a unique device number. However in MVS/370, each DD statement segment in a step record has the unit address. An MVS/370 unit address is comprised of one hex character of the physical channel address and two hex characters of the unit address. When MVS/370 does I/O to a DD, it keeps track of the physical path to which the I/O occurred, and the DD segment contains the last address used. These unit addresses are used to count the number of mountable devices into the variables TAPEDRVS for tapes and D3330DRV for mountable 3330 devices.

To make sure that a tape drive used by a step is counted only once, the MXG code that processes the MVS/370 DD segments needs to know the alternate channel paths for each device. Installation Member IMACCHAN defines these alternate paths to MXG. The IMACCHAN supplied code contains a simple example in which channel 7 is the alternate for channel 2, channel 5 is the alternate for channel 4, and channel 8 is the alternate for channel 3. Check with the systems programmer who does the I/O GENS at your installation to determine the primary and alternate channels and then code the algorithm so that the alternate channel is changed to the primary channel by this code.

If your installation has a more complex environment where alternate channels are a function of the range of unit addresses, the variable UADR in IMACCHAN can be used to define more complex relationships for primary and alternate paths. When IMACCHAN is executed, the variable SYSTEM (containing the SMF system identification) exists, and if you have different alternate paths on different processors, you can use the variable SYSTEM in your algorithm to convert alternate channel to primary channel.

IMACJBCK: Specific job selection

It is not necessary to make changes to member IMACJBCK during installation, but you should understand its existence during the installation of this code. IMACJBCK is %INCLUDEd in every module in MXG that processes SMF records containing the job name. The member is located logically after the system SMF time stamp, job name, read-in time, and user information fields have been read. Thus, if you want to select observations from only a specific job or from a specific execution of a specific job, you do not need to modify the mainline MXG code in SOURCLIB. Instead, edit this member to select the desired job(s).

For example, if you know the true read time and job name of the job you want, replace the IF statement in IMACJBCK with, for example:

```
IF JOB EQ 'BUILDBLD' AND
   READTIME='04NOV80:14:30:00.01'DT;
```

This code selects only SMF records from the BUILDBLD job that were read in at the time given. Note that JES number does not exist in most SMF records and, thus, cannot be used for selecting any records except records 6, 26, and 30.

IMACSHFT: Shift definitions

Member BUILDPDB builds the Performance Data Base (PDB) and is described in a separate chapter. The member IMACSHFT is included in BUILDPDB to define the three shifts: prime, nonprime, and weekend. The default code example defines the prime shift as 8 a.m. to 5 p.m., Monday through Friday. Nonprime is 5 p.m. until 8 a.m., and weekend begins at 8 a.m. on Saturday and ends at 8 a.m. Monday. Edit this member to define your installation shifts.

IMACWORK: Mapping performance group number to workload category

The primary use of Performance Groups is to gather data for capacity measurement and capacity analysis. Chapter twenty-six recommends that every unique on-line system be placed in its own performance group. Member IMACWORK allows you to group the individual performance group data into a smaller number of high-level workload categories that are of interest to your installation.

The code defines the mapping of performance groups into work categories. For example, you may have several categories of batch work, each in its own performance group, but you may want to cluster those performance groups at the high level into a work group known as BATCH. Performance groups not explicitly defined are combined in the workload grouping OTHER.

The grouping defined in IMACWORK is used in member BUILDPDB when member RMVINTRV is invoked to build the RMF composite interval data set. The values of service units delivered to workload categories will be incorrect in this data set unless you map your performance groups to your logical work categories as described in the member IMACWORK.

IMAC30DD: Selecting type 30 DD segments to be output in TYPE30_D

In the type 30 step and job termination subtype records, there is a detail data segment for each DD statement that contains the EXCP count and the device address, blocksize, DDname, and so forth. The MXG code TYPE30 that processes type 30 records, sums the EXCP counts (and for MVS/XA, the I/O connect time) by each device type, reducing the data to manageable proportions. However, if you need specific information on a DDname, on a unit address (Device Number), or about EXCP counts to each DD within a particular job output, you can specify your selection criteria in IMAC30DD and then the selected observations to data set TYPE30_D. Member IMAC30DD is %INCLUDEd in TYPE30 after each DD segment has been processed by MXG. The variables DDNAME, EXCPCNT, BLKSIZE, IOTM, DEVNR, DEVCLASS, DEVTYPE, and DEVICE exist when this code is executed. If you remove the comment symbols from around the IF statement in the example provided, one observation would be output to TYPE30_D for every DD segment in every step record with an allocated device address (hex) 38B. No change is required to this member unless you want to create observations in TYPE30_D for analysis.

IMAC3330: Counting mountable 3033 devices

It is not possible to identify from a DD segment that a 3330 device is mountable. The mountable attribute is specified by the installation but is not included in data available in the SMF record. Thus, if you offer 3330 mountable devices and you want to know how many of these drives are used by jobs and which jobs are using these devices, you must provide a list of device numbers in IMAC3330 so that MXG code recognizes the device as a 3330 mountable device. Note that the variable DEVNR is used for both MVS/XA and MVS/370 since the MVS/370 device number is the unit address of the primary channel path to the device. If IMAC3330 is inaccurate, variable D3330DRV will be invalid but no other problems result.

Other installation-dependent code   Member TYPE7072 , which builds both TYPE70 and TYPE72 data sets, must set the Hardware Dependent Constant or the Service Units per CPU second correctly in order for the CPU time measures in the TYPE72 data set to be correct. In MVS/370, only the CPU Model (3081, 3083) was available in RMF, whereas in MVS/XA, the CPU version (for example, 3081-K or 3081-G) is provided, making it easier to set the correct factor. A detailed discussion of the Hardware Dependent Constant and its value is given in the TYPE70 and TYPE72 sections of chapter forty. Make sure that the SU_SEC value is set correctly in member VMAC7072 so that the TYPE72 CPU measures and any MVS Overhead CPU measures (for example, TYPE70 CPU minus TYPE72 CPU) will be correct.

For 370 systems, it will be necessary to examine the code more closely than for XA systems. The logic that builds the constant for SU_SEC is a long list of CPU types and models. In some cases, where multiple entries are given for a single model of CPU (for example, 3081-K, 3081-G, 3081-D, and so forth), you should arrange the code so that your type of CPU is the first in the list. If you have two processors of the same model and different versions (for example, 3081-K, System SYS0, and a 3081-G, System SYS1), use the following test:

```
IF CPUTYPE='3081'X AND SYSTEM='SYS0' THEN SU_SEC=368.4;
ELSE IF CPUTYPE='3081'X AND SYSTEM='SYS1' THEN SU_SEC=291.65;
```

Step 3: Building the SASLIB Format Library

SAS formats are a powerful tool for the CPE analyst. The use of formats is described more completely in chapter thirty-seven, but to install the software, you must build the Format Library (hereafter called SASLIB), which contains the SAS formats used by the MXG code. This step is necessary because MXG uses formats in many places to reduce the size of SAS data sets, and the SAS System will abend if a needed format cannot be found.

SAS formats are defined using PROC FORMAT. When PROC FORMAT is executed, the procedure builds the format and creates a member of the SASLIB load module library. Formats created by PROC FORMAT can be used in subsequent SAS programs when a SASLIB DD statement points to the SASLIB Format Library you created.

It is easy for you to allocate and build your own SASLIB load library using member FORMATS of SOURCLIB as input. The TSO commands and SAS statements needed to allocate and build your format library are shown below.

```
ATTR LIB RECFM(U) BLKSIZE (19069) /* for 3350 */
ATTR LIB RECFM(U) BLKSIZE (23440) /* for 3380 */
ALLOC F(SASLIB) DA('MXG.SASLIB')
     USING(LIB) CYL SPACE(3,1) DIR(10)
          VOL(XXXXXX)
ALLOC F(SOURCLIB) DA('MXG.SOURCLIB') SHR
SAS
%INCLUDE SOURCLIB(FORMATS)
```

When these statements are executed, the SAS System reads member FORMATS of SOURCLIB and executes the PROC FORMAT contained in that member. The DDname SASLIB is used by PROC FORMAT to create the formats needed by MXG code. (It is a good idea for SASLIB to be part of the data set name of the SASLIB format library to avoid confusion later.)

Below is the code needed to build the formats in a batch job.

```
//BLDFMT EXEC SAS
//SASLIB   DD DSN=MXG.SASLIB,DISP=(,CATLG),
//              SPACE=(CYL,(3,1,10)),VOL=SER=xxxxxx,
//              DCB=(RECFM=U,BLKSIZE=19069)
//SOURCLIB DD DSN=MXG.SOURCLIB,DISP=SHR
%INCLUDE SOURCLIB(FORMATS)
```

The code that builds the formats (shown above) is included as the first step of the job in member JCLTEST. New SAS users may find it easier to use JCLTEXT to create SASLIB in batch rather than under TSO.

JCL Requirements for Executing MXG

Once the software is installed, you are ready to begin executing the code. However, you must add two additional DD statements to the JCL of your SAS job in order to execute MXG. Below is the typical JCL required to execute MXG code.

```
//     EXEC SAS,OPTIONS='GEN=0 ERRORABEND NOMACROGEN NOSOURCE2'
//SASLIB    DD DSN=MXG.SASLIB.DISP=SHR
//SOURCLIB DD DSN=MXG.SOURCLIB,DISP=SHR
```

The two additional DD statements bring in the formats (SASLIB) and the source (SOURCLIB). The options specified in the EXEC statement are not mandatory but will provide better performance when MXG is executed.

The following example illustrates the importance of the GEN option to good performance. When you build a SAS data set, if GEN=1 is specified, the source statements used to build the data set are stored in the SAS data library. If GEN=2 is specified, the source statements used to build the current data set and the statements used to build the preceding data set are both stored in the data library. As values given to the GEN= option become larger, a large amount of disk space is used, especially when MERGE statements are also used. For example, when the BUILDPDB code from the original *Merrill's Guide* (which MERGEs six SAS data sets to build twelve SAS data sets) was executed, the following elapsed and CPU times were noted on a 370/3033 Model N:

Table 32.1 compares a small run with GEN=0 and GEN=5 and a large run with the two GEN= values.

Table 32.1

Input volume	SASGEN option	Elapsed time	CPU time
Small	GEN=5	1 hr. 18 min.	1 min. 17 sec.
Small	GEN=0	0 hr. 07 min.	0 min. 22 sec.
Large	GEN=5	3 hr. 58 min.	32 min. 11 sec.
Large	GEN=0	1 hr. 42 min.	13 min. 04 sec.

The small input volume was 8 tracks of 3350 raw SMF data containing 486 logical records. The large input volume was 2 reels of tape containing 757,470 input records. For the small runs, 138 tracks of work space were used when GEN=5 and only 22 tracks were used when GEN=0. For the large runs, the GEN=5 run took over 30 minutes before the input tape was even moved. With GEN=0, the large run moved the tape in 30 seconds! The impact of GEN=0 as the default execution parameter cannot be overstated.

The ERRORABEND option should always be used on any SAS execution that builds or updates SAS data sets. An error condition that would normally result in a return code 12 is changed to a User 999 ABEND condition when ERRORABEND is specified. The ERRORABEND option is required when processing SMF files so that the STOPOVER condition on the INFILE statement will cause the expected ABEND when invalid data are processed with MXG code.

The NOMACROGEN option tells the SAS System not to print the expanded macros when they are referenced. This option simply reduces the pages printed. However, if you experience problems, it may be necessary to remove NOMACROGEN in order to determine the actual line number that caused the problem.

The NOSOURCE2 option tells the SAS System not to print source statements brought into the program with the INCLUDE statement. The option shortens the SAS log and makes it more readable.

In production systems, once you are experienced in using SAS software, you should add the SAS option NOSOURCE to suppress all SAS source statements. This option reduces the amount of printed output.

OTHER INSTALLATION CONCERNS

The MXG code has been written and tested using SAS release 82.3. If your installation uses an earlier release of SAS software, the MXG code will require major changes. Those using later releases of the SAS System can disregard the rest of this chapter.

If your installation has applied all SAS maintenance (using the SAS DIAL-A-ZAP facility), then you have applied SAS zap Z0706, which corrects an OC1 ABEND due to inputting a PIB8. field. If you encounter an OC1 ABEND, you can confirm that the zap was not applied by executing the following simple SAS program:

```
DATA;
  A=1.2;
  FORMAT A PIB8.2;
```

When this step is executed, if an OC1 abend occurs, the SAS installation representative should install the following zap:

```
NAME SASINPUT SASINPUT
VER 01B4 0000,0000
VER 0210 0000,0000
VER 0550 0000,0000,0000,0000,0000,0000
REP 01B4 4530,F550
REP 0210 4530,F550
REP 0550 6820 CDCB,6A20,CCD8,2A02,07F3
IDRDATA Z0706
NAME SASLPA SASINPUT
VER 01B4 0000,0000
VER 0210 0000,0000
VER 0550 0000,0000,0000,0000,0000,0000
REP 01B4 4530,F550
REP 0210 4530,F550
REP 0550 6820,CDC8,6A20,CCD8,2A02,07F3
IDRDATA Z0706
```

SHARING THE MXG SOFTWARE AND MAKING MODIFICATIONS

It is not advisable to alter MXG SOURCLIB. Changes must be made in some cases to the IMAC.... members as discussed above, and you may choose to alter the code, especially the report code; however, you will create a serious maintenance exposure if you alter the master source library. In addition, managing changes in a single master library would be quite difficult if more than one person is using the software.

The simplest mechanism for preventing problems is never to change the master library, except when you receive a maintenance update from Merrill Consultants. Maintenance will be supplied as a complete replacement for member(s) of the master library.

Fortunately, there is a very simple solution that allows you to change the members that must be changed, never altering the master library and allowing multiple users to have different versions of the software. In addition to creating the master source library, allocate a partitioned data set with the same attributes as the master sourclib for each user who will execute the software. Call it the user's source library. If the user's source library is allocated to the DDNAME of SOURCLIB ahead of the master source library, the %INCLUDE facility of the SAS System first looks in the user's source library for the member to be INCLUDEd, and then it retrieves the needed member from the master source library only when the member is not in the user's source library. The IMAC.... members that must be changed for your installation should be copied into each user's source library and changed there rather than in the master library. Should you desire to alter other members, simply copy them into your own source library and make the changes there. If you only copy the members to be altered, you will have only a small number of members in your user library, and when a new maintenance update to the MXG software is provided, you can copy the update directly into the master library without any affect on your local changes.

For example, if the user source library name is USERID.MXG.SOURCLIB, the execution JCL would then be:

```
//      EXEC SAS,OPTIONS='GEN=0 ERRORABEND NOMACROGEN NOSOURCE2'
//SASLIB    DD DSN=MXG.SASLIB,DISP=SHR
//SOURCLIB DD DSN=USERID.MXG.SOURCLIB,DISP=SHR
//          DD DSN=MXG.SOURCLIB,DISP=SHR
```

It would be wise to protect the master source library (MXG.SOURCLIB) against update by users and to promulgate the above JCL as the standard for shared usage of the MXG software.

chapter thirty-three

Learning to Use MXG
Software

A good place to begin learning to use the MXG SAS code is with the member JCLTEST, which reads your SMF file and extracts ten records for each record ID it encounters. JCLTEST also creates an output OS file containing SMF records in the SMFOUT DD and a SAS data library containing SAS data sets decoded from the selected SMF records in the TEST DD.

Step 1 of JCLTEST extracts up to 10 records from your input SMF file and stores them in the SMFOUT DD. Step 2 reads the output from step 1, stores it in the TEST DD, and then prints all the data sets built in step 2. Note that JCLTEST does not analyze the data. It simply creates each possible SAS data set that the MXG code can create from SMF records. If no records of a particular SMF record ID are encountered, the corresponding SAS data set is created with zero observations. Then JCLTEST prints all variables in all SAS data sets that have at least 1 observation.

The performance data base described in the next chapter contains data that can be used to manage your installation. However, there are times when you need specific information from SMF records not found in the performance data base. Understanding the structure of the MXG code will help you comprehend the function of the BUILDPDB algorithms, which are discussed in the next chapter.

UNDERSTANDING SMF RECORD ID NUMBERS

Since most literature about SMF and RMF records refers to the records by their record numbers, you should become familiar with the contents of SMF records by their ID numbers.

In general, each SMF record ID contains unique information; however, there are some occurrences of two different record IDs that contain data in almost exactly the same format. For efficiency, and because these pairs of SMF records are logically related, many MXG modules process more than 1 record ID and build a single SAS data set with observations from all record types. For example, type 4 and type 34 records are step termination records. Type 4 is for a batch step; type 34 is for a TSO step. Both records are processed by the module TYPE434. Type 14 and type 15 records report data set activity; both are processed by member TYPE1415. You should learn each SMF record ID and the SMF record type processed by each MXG member.

There are two ways to process the same SMF record type using the MXG library. Members that begin with the letters TYPE read an SMF file once and create a single SAS data set for the desired records. Other members of MXG (those beginning with the letters VMAC) can be used to construct SAS programs that read the SMF data set once and create several SAS data sets from different SMF record types.

For example, member TYPE6 contains the following SAS program to process the type 6 SMF record.

```
%INCLUDE SOURCLIB(VMACSMF,VMAC6);
DATA
_VAR6
_SMF
_CDE6
```

The %INCLUDE statement tells the SAS System to bring in the SAS code contained in members VMACSMF and VMAC6 of the PDS referenced by the SOURCLIB DD. Member VMACSMF is a SAS macro named _SMF. Note that in MXG an underscore is always used as the first character of a SAS macro name. VMAC6 contains two SAS macros named _VAR6 and _CDE6. Note that the %INCLUDE statement brings in these SAS macros; the macros are not executed until they are called later in the program.

The keyword DATA following the %INCLUDE statement tells the SAS System to begin building a SAS data set. The name of the SAS data set to be built is found in the macro _VAR6 along with the alphabetical list of variables included in this SAS data set. Similarly, the system replaces macro name SMF with its contents, which define the INFILE attributes, open the input file, determine whether you are reading BSAM or VSAM SMF data, and perform other functions for SMF processing. For example, _SMF decodes the standard SMF header common to all SMF records. The SMF header contains the record ID (ID), the date and time this SMF record was written (SMFTIME), and the system on which this record was written (SYSTEM). Macro _CDE6 contains the SAS INPUT statements and SAS code unique to the type 6 SMF record and then operates on type 6 records to create the variables and output the data to the TYPE6 data set.

Since the default storage for all SAS data sets is a temporary data set pointed to by the WORK DD card, the program above processes an SMF file and extracts and decodes type 6 records into a data set named TYPE6, but TYPE6 disappears at the end of the job. To make TYPE6 a permanent SAS data set, you can override the temporary WORK DD statement in the SAS JCL. A better way is to use the SAS system option USER= to specify a DDname that points to a SAS data library where you want your data sets permanently stored. Note that in member JCLTEST, the USER= option is given the value TEST in the EXEC SAS statement, so SAS software uses the TEST DD to store any SAS data sets created.

The following example shows how to process multiple SAS record types in one pass of the SMF file.

```
%INCLUDE SOURCLIB(VMACSMF,VMACSMF,VMAC0,VMAC6,
                  VMAC21,VMAC26J2,VMAC30,
                  VMAC7072,VMAC71,VMAC73,
                  VMAC74,VMAC75,VMAC78);
DATA
ID(KEEP=ID SYSTEM)
_VAR0   _VAR6   _VAR21 _VAR26J2 _VAR30  _VAR7072
_VAR71 _VAR72 _VAR73 _VAR74    _VAR75 _VAR78
_SMF
OUTPUT ID;
_CDE0   _CDE6   _CDE21 _CDE26J2 _CDE30  _CDE7072
_CDE71 _CDE72 _CDE73 _CDE74    _CDE75 _CDE78
```

These lines of SAS code read an SMF file once and create nineteen SAS data sets representing RMF job, step, printing, IPL, and tape mount data. This code is the first phase of member BUILDPDB, which is discussed in chapter thirty-four.

To build a SAS program from macros, make sure that the correct SOURCLIB members are included. Follow the %INCLUDE statement with the DATA statement, _VAR macros, _SMF, and the corresponding _CDE macros. The example above creates a SAS data set named ID and data sets named by the _VAR and _CDE macros.

Table 33.1 maps SMF record types to members of the library that build the corresponding SAS data sets. Note that the library member, the _VAR macro name, and the _CDE macro name end with the number of the SMF record type or types being processed. The contents and a complete description of each data set appear alphabetically in chapter forty as appendices.

Table 33.1

Member name	Processed record type	From	SAS data set name	Description
TYPE0	0	SMF	TYPE0	IPL
TYPE0203	2,3	SMF	TYPE0203	SMF dump/trailer
TYPE434	4,34	SMF	TYPE434	Step termination
TYPE535	5,35	SMF	TYPE535	Job termination
TYPE6	6	JES	TYPE6	Print/punch(JES WRITER)
TYPE7	7	SMF	TYPE7	SMF data lost condition
TYPE8911	8,9,11	SMF	TYPE8911	I/O configuration
TYPE10	10	SMF	TYPE10	Allocation recovery
TYPE1415	14,15	SMF	TYPE1415	Data set closed
TYPE16	16	ICEMAN	TYPE16	ICEMAN sort invoked
TYPE1718	17,18	SMF	TYPE1718	Data set SCRATCH/RENAME
TYPE19	19	SMF	TYPE19	ONLINE DASD volume
TYPE20	20	SMF	TYPE20	Job initiated
TYPE21	21	SMF	TYPE21	Tape volume dismounted
TYPE22	22-1	SMF	TYPE22_1	CPU configuration
TYPE22	22-2	SMF	TYPE22_2	VARY ONLINE command
TYPE22	22-3	SMF	TYPE22_3	STORAGE configuration
TYPE22	22-4	SMF	TYPE22_4	MSS configuration
TYPE22	22-5	SMF	TYPE22_5	VARY ONLINE, S
TYPE22	22-6	SMF	TYPE22_6	VARY OFFLINE, S
TYPE22	22-7	SMF	TYPE22_7	Channel path configuration
TYPE22	22-8	SMF	TYPE22_8	Reconfiguration channel path
TYPE23	23	NEWSMF	TYPE23	SMF buffer statistics
TYPE25	25	JES3	TYPE25	JES3 SETUP/FETCH
TYPE26J2	26	JES2	TYPE26J2	JES2 PURGE

Table 33.1 (continued)

Member name	Processed record type	From	SAS data set name	Description
TYPE26J3	26	JES3	TYPE26J3	JES3 PURGE
TYPE30	30-1	NEWSMF	TYPE30_1	TYPE30 job initiated
TYPE30	30-2,3	NEWSMF	TYPE30_V	TYPE30 interval
TYPE30	30-4	NEWSMF	TYPE30_4	TYPE30 step terminated
TYPE30	30-4	NEWSMF	TYPE30_D	TYPE30 DD activity
TYPE30	30-5	NEWSMF	TYPE30_5	TYPE30 job terminated
TYPE30	30-6	NEWSMF	TYPE30_6	TYPE30 create data ASID
TYPE31	31	SMF	TYPE31	START TSO
TYPE32	32	NEWSMF	TYPE32	TSO command
TYPE38	38	NPA	TYPE38EX	NPA exception
TYPE38	38	NPA	TYPE38IN	NPA interval
TYPE38	38	NPA	TYPE38NC	NPA/NCP statistics
TYPE40	40	SMF	TYPE40	Dynamic allocation
TYPE43PC	43,44,45	VSPC	TYPE43PC	VSPC
TYPE4345	43,45	JES	TYPE4345	JES START/STOP
TYPE47PC	47	VSPC	TYPE47PC	VSPC
TYPE4789	47,48,49	JES	TYPE4789	JES BISYNC RJE SIGNON
TYPE48PC	48	VSPC	TYPE48PC	VSPC
TYPE49PC	49	VSPC	TYPE49PC	VSPC
TYPE50	50	VTAM	TYPE50	VTAM buffers
TYPE5234	52,53,54	JES	TYPE5234	JES SDLC RJE SIGNON
TYPE5568	55,56,58	JES	TYPE5568	JES NJE START/STOP
TYPE57	57	JES2	TYPE57J2	JES2 NJE SYSOUT JES2 NJE SYSOUT
TYPE57	57	JES3	TYPE57J3	JES3 NJP SYSOUT
TYPE60	60	SMF	TYPE60	VSAM VVDS updated
TYPE61	61	SMF	TYPE61	ICF DEFINE

Table 33.1   (continued)

Member name	Processed record type	From	SAS data set name	Description
TYPE62	62	SMF	TYPE62	VSAM opened
TYPE6367	63,67	SMF	TYPE6367	VSAM DEFINE/DELETE
TYPE64	64	SMF	TYPE64	VSAM EXCP statistics
TYPE65	65	SMF	TYPE65	ICF DELETE
TYPE66	66	SMF	TYPE66	ICF ALTER
TYPE68	68	SMF	TYPE68	VSAM RENAME
TYPE69	69	SMF	TYPE69	VSAM data space
TYPE7072	70	RMF	TYPE70	RMF CPU
TYPE7072	72	RMF	TYPE72	Performance group
TYPE71	71	RMF	TYPE71	Paging and memory
TYPE73	73	RMF	TYPE73	MVS/XA channels
TYPE73	73	RMF	TYPE73L	MVS/370 logical channel
TYPE73	73	RMF	TYPE73P	MVS/370 physical channel
TYPE74	74	RMF	TYPE74	Device activity
TYPE75	75	RMF	TYPE75	Paging data sets
TYPE76	76	RMF	TYPE76	RMF trace
TYPE77	77	RMF	TYPE77	ENQUEUE conflict
TYPE78	78	RMF	TYPE78	MVS/XA device queuing
TYPE78	78	RMF	TYPE78CF	MVS/XA device configuration
TYPE79	79	RMF	TYPE79	MONITOR II session
TYPE80	80	RACF	TYPE80	RACF processing
TYPE81	81	RACF	TYPE81	RACF initialization
TYPE82	82	CRYPTO	TYPE82	CRYPTO security
TYPE90	90	NEWSMF	TYPE90	Operator changes
TYPE110	110	CICS	CICSACCT	CICS 'accounting'
TYPE110	110	CICS	CICSEXCE	CICS exceptions

Table 33.1   (continued)

Member name	Processed record type	From	SAS data set name	Description
TYPE110	110	CICS	CICSTRAN	CICS transactions CICS transactions
TYPE110	110	CICS	CICSYSTM	CICS system resources

328

chapter thirty-four

Building the Performance Data Base

BUILDPDB creates the Performance Data Base from an input SMF file and, optionally, creates the SPIN data base to hold data on partially completed jobs until the next execution of BUILDPDB. The input file can be a day's SMF data, a week's, or even a monthly SMF file and uses the file name SMF. The Performance Data Base is written to the file name PDB, but the CICS transactions can be optionally written to a different DD (with the _CICTRAN macro in MXG member IMACCICS), perhaps on tape, to reduce disk space resources required by BUILDPDB.

BUILDPDB creates the data sets listed below, which are documented in chapter forty.

PDB Data Set	Contents	Source
IPLS	Each IPL event	SMF type 0
TAPES	Each tape volume dismounted	SMF type 21
TYPE70	CPU activity	RMF type 70
TYPE71	Paging and swapping	RMF type 71
TYPE72	Performance group resources	RMF type 72
TYPE73	MVS/XA physical channel use	RMF type 73
TYPE73P	MVS/370 physical channel use	RMF type 73
TYPE73L	MVS/370 logical channel queuing	RMF type 73
TYPE74	Device activity	RMF type 74
TYPE75	Page and swap data set use	RMF type 75
TYPE78	MVS/XA device queuing	RMF type 78
TYPE78VS	Virtual storage usage	RMF type 78
TYPE78PA	Private area virtual storage monitoring	RMF type 78
TYPE78SP	Sub-pool virtual storage monitoring	RMF type 78
SMFINTRV	SMF interval resources by job	SMF type 30
DDSTATS	DD-level I/O statistics by job	SMF type 30
CICSYSTM	CICS system performance resources	CMF type 110

CICSEXCE	CICS exceptions	CMF type 110
CICSACCT	CICS accounting by transaction	CMF type 110
CICSTRAN	CICS transaction response and resources	CMF type 110
RMFINTRV	Combined RMF resource, workload, response, paging, and so forth	RMF types 70, 71, 72, 73, 74, 78
JOBS	Job/TSO/STC resource, response and billing (one per job)	SMF types 6, 26, 30
STEPS	Step level detail	SMF type 30
PRINT	Printing resources, queuing, and so forth	SMF types 6, 26

These data sets, produced either daily or weekly, can be the complete source of performance reporting, resource analysis, capacity planning, and computer performance evaluation. Their uses are demonstrated in the many examples in this book, especially in the reports produced by member ANALDALY in chapter forty-one. The remainder of this chapter describes the logic by which SMF and RMF observations are combined in the member BUILDPDB.

This chapter describes the SAS program in member BUILDPDP that builds the performance data base. It will be easier to understand the chapter if you look at the code as you read.

The %INCLUDE statement brings in macros needed to process SMF record types 0, 6, 21, 26, and 30; RMF record types 70, 71, 72, 73, 74, 75, and 78; and CMF record type 110. Following the %INCLUDE statement is the DELETE procedure to delete the data sets in the PDB data library. This step is necessary if you build your PDB in the same OS data set each day so that sufficient space is available for the day's data. Be sure to remove this PROC DELETE if you make a partial rerun.

Next, BUILDPDB processes the day's SMF input data. It builds the data sets from the SMF records listed above and a data set named ID that contains record ID and SYSTEM for all SMF records encountered, even those not processed by this program. Then the program prints a frequency tabulation of record ID versus SYSTEM so that you can see what SMF records were received on the input SMF file. Then the SAS System deletes data set ID.

Each SAS data set created in the work file that does not need to be merged with other data sets is sorted directly into the PDB. Thus, the following data sets in the WORK file are sorted into the PDB directly after the SMF file is processed.

```
IPLS (from TYPE0), TAPES (from TYPE21), RMF data sets
TYPE70, TYPE71, TYPE72, TYPE73, TYPE73P, TYPE73L, TYPE74,
TYPE75, TYPE78, TYPE78VS, TYPE78SP, TYPE78PA, SMFINTRV,
DDSTATS, CICSYSTM, CICSEXCE, and CICSACCT.
```

The CICS transaction data, CICSTRAN, was written directly to the CICSTRAN DD, which should be on tape for appreciably-sized CICS systems. The PROTECT= option prevents inadvertent writing into or scratching of the PDB by a subsequent program that does not use the PROTECT= string.

The next %INCLUDE statement brings in the module, RMFINTRV, which is described separately in chapter forty-one. RMFINTRV creates the RMFINTRV data set, which contains a summary of RMF records merged into one observation per interval with all important RMF variables and is the primary data set used for reporting RMF resources, such as CPU, paging, and work, that are delivered to various workload categories. Examine SOURCLIB members IMACWORK and IMACSHFT, which affect the data in RMFINTRV, before executing BUILDPDB. After the SAS System builds the RMFINTRV data set, the RMF data sets in the work file are deleted to make room for the steps and job data sets.

First, today's data sets, TYPE30_1, TYPE30_4, TYPE30_5, TYPE6, and TYPE26J2, that contain the day's job, step, and printing resources are sorted by READTIME, JOB, and JESNR to arrange records for the same job together. In addition, initiation records from TYPE30_1 are sorted by initiate time, step records by increasing step termination time, and job termination records by decreasing job termination time. Data set TYPE26J2 is then rebuilt from the original version with unwanted PURGE records (records with blank SYSEXEC values) deleted. In a network job entry (NJE) environment, PURGE records are written for each job as it passes through every node. BUILDPDB, however, requires only the PURGE record that represents execution rather than pass-through.

The NODSNFERR option handles the first execution of this program. Since the SPIN data sets do not exist initially, the SAS System would abend when it encountered the statement set SPIN.SPIN30_1, issuing a "data set not found" error message; however, when option NODSNFERR is specified, reference to the nonexistent data set is replaced by _NULL_. In this way, there is no initialization of the SPIN data set required by BUILDPDB. If this is not the first execution, the next five SAS DATA steps interleave the day's data with the corresponding data sets spun yesterday. These SPIN data sets hold records for jobs that were not complete when the SMF data were dumped. BUILDPDB expects to find a purge record and the associated step and job records for every job. If the purge record has not yet been processed or if one of the conditions described below indicates that all records have not yet been received for this job, those partial records are stored in the SPIN file to wait for the next execution of BUILDPDB. Thus, yesterday's spun records in the SPIN30__ data sets are interleaved with the day's TYPE30__ data sets in this execution so that they can be matched in the next segment of this program. After combining yesterday's spun data sets with today's data, the option DSNFERR is restored so that a data set not found generates an error.

The section of code that begins with DATA GOOD30__1 is the heart of the BUILDPDB logic. In this DATA step, the five data sets, TYPE26J2, TYPE6, TYPE30__5, TYPE30__4, and TYPE30__1, are merged, and the IN= variable associated with each input data set is tested to determine whether all records were received on this job. Each job is tested when first encountered, and if all records for the job were received, a variable OKFLAG (a RETAINed variable) is set to one, and individual observations in the input data sets are output to their corresponding GOOD data sets. If all records for this job were not received, these observations are placed in the corresponding SPUN data set for processing during the next execution of BUILDPDB.

The preceding description is implemented following the label INBITS, where the SPIN variables are initialized to prevent a compiler note that a variable has been uninitialized. Such a circumvention for nonexistent variables is only needed for the first pass of BUILDPDB, but it can be left in the code permanently. OKFLAG is initialized to zero, and INBITS is initialized to a character string containing five underscores. By testing the status of each IN= variable and substringing into INBITS, a character string is created that identifies whether an initiate, step, job, writer, or purge record was received for this job.

Each time a record is spun by BUILDPDB, the SPIN variable for that data set is incremented by one. Then SPINCNT is initialized to the maximum value of the SPIN variables or one so that SPINCNT is always at least one. If records come from both TYPE26 and TYPE30__5, then IN26 and IN30__5 are true, and you have a purge and a job termination record. This does not mean that you have received all records for this job. Since restarted jobs create multiple job termination records, you might not have received the final job termination record. You should compare the time in the job termination record to the time in the purge record. Since the job termination records are sorted by descending termination time, if a job was restarted several times, then the job termination record encountered is the last job termination received on the job. Thus, you test to see that JSTRTIME (JES job start time from the purge record) is less than or equal to JTRMTIME (MVS job termination time from the job record), which must be less than or equal to the JENDTIME (JES termination time from the purge record). Only if the job termination record time stamp matches the purge record time stamps do you know with assurance that you have received all records on the job.

To explain further, if a job is canceled and requeued by the operator (for example, by using a $EJ command because the job entered a data set enqueue conflict), a type 30__5 record is written when the job is canceled. When the job is released from hold by an operator command and later re-executed, the purge record contains the start time and end time of the subsequent execution. However, if SMF data sets are not dumped simultaneously, the data presented to BUILDPDB could be the purge record on the job and the first 30_5 job termination record, but the final job termination record may have been written on a different system from the purge record. The JTRMTIME in the received 30_5 record would be earlier than the JSTRTIME of the second execution, so you would not want to pass these records to the PDB today but would SPIN these received records until tomorrow when the second job termination record is received from the undumped SMF data.

If the first IF statement is not true, the ELSE clause assumes that you have received a TYPE26 record and that either the JSTRTIME job start time or JENDTIME job end time are missing or that the JENDTIME is less than JSTR-TIME. In all three cases, you want to set OKFLAG to one and output this job to the day's PDB since a missing JSTRTIME signifies a JCL error or a job canceled before execution, and a missing JENDTIME or a JENDTIME less than JSTRTIME signifies a job that was active when the MVS system crashed. In these cases, you will not find additional records, and you will want to pass the records you have received into the PDB.

If that IF condition is not met, the final test to determine job status checks for a SPINCNT greater than zero and then sets OKFLAG to one. This is the system default for BUILDPDB as shipped, but it is not the desired normal execution default. Since SPINCNT is always at least one, this default value of the test forces all records to be passed through the PDB, regardless of whether or not you have received all records on the job. This default ensures that the PDB contains whatever data was input. If you truly want accuracy more than timeliness, then you should take advantage of the SPIN architecture. The SPIN architecture maximizes the quality of the job and step data by building an entry in the steps and jobs data sets only when all records on each job have been received. The purpose of this test is to ensure that all jobs are passed eventually into the PDB, but not until they have been spun for enough days. Thus, the value against which SPINCNT is tested must be greater than one if this system is to try to spin in completed jobs. Decide how large to make the test for SPINCNT based on two factors: (1) the frequency with which BUILDPDB is run since SPINCNT is incremented by one each time BUILDPDB is executed, and (2) how long the job remains on the JES spool before it is purged. If you do not have a command or a job that automatically purges jobs from the spool after some number of days, you are giving free storage for spooled output and significantly subverting the design of BUILDPDB. Without an automatic purge, or at least a regularly scheduled forced-purge of unprinted jobs that have been on the spool for a long time, the purge record is never received. It is strongly suggested that you discuss with your JES systems programmer an architecture that automatically purges jobs from the spool after some period of time. Many installations modify JES to purge jobs that are held for TSO output class after they have remained on the spool for one work day and to purge all other jobs after remaining on the spool seven days.

Once you have determined how many days a job can remain on the spool and how frequently you will execute BUILDPDB, then the test for SPINCNT can be changed from zero to an appropriate number. For example, if you are running BUILDPDB daily and purging jobs at least every seventh day, then a SPINCNT test of

```
ELSE IF SPINCNT GT 10 THEN OKFLAG=1;
```

should replace the default test of

```
ELSE IF SPINCNT GT 0 THEN OKFLAG=1;
```

to allow for minor errors in purged jobs execution and still pass jobs to the PDB within ten days of their execution. If you execute BUILDPDB weekly, a SPINCNT of two or three would be appropriate.

This segment of code for the default SPINCNT test was executed only if FIRST.JESNR was true (that is, if the first set of records is being processed). The value of OKFLAG is set to one if the job is good and leaves OKFLAG at zero if this job is to be spun. If OKFLAG is not set to one (turned on), then the DO group, which spins individual input records from each data set to their corresponding SPIN data set and counts the times spun, is executed.

After the TYPE26 record is spun, IN= variables are reset to zero and if the current record is not the last from this job, then the RETURN is executed. The program is re-executed from the top, OKFLAG is still zero, and the IN= variables are set to one for those data sets in the MERGE statement with another observation. Thus, each of the input data sets are effectively popped off the stack by resetting the IN= variables to zero until all observations from this READTIME-JOB-JESNR have been exhausted.

Since the spun variables are retained across observations, after all observations are spun, the spun variables are set to missing, and INBITS and SPINBITS are set to blanks. If OKFLAG is on, this DO group is not executed, and execution skips to the series of small DO groups beginning with IF IN30_1 THEN DO that output records to the GOOD data sets in preparation for sorting and summing the good jobs into the STEPS, PRINT, and JOBS data sets. After each input record is processed, IN= variables are reset to zero. When LAST.JESNR is on, indicating that processing is complete for this job, the spun counts are reset to missing.

Resetting IN= variables to process the MERGE as if it were a parallel series of stacks allows you to recognize whether all records were received and output to either GOOD or SPIN data sets. Unneeded data sets are deleted from the

MERGE, and the first observation of GOOD30_1 is kept since subsequent initiation records provide no additional information, and you only need the time of first initiation for restarted jobs.

Types 30_4 and 30_5 (step and job) records are then sorted by SORTTIME. When processing the good records, SORTTIME is set equal to the step initiation or job initiation times, respectively. Then data set STEPS and GOOD30_5 are built by interleaving the good step and job records. Two new variables are created: RESTART contains the number of job termination records encountered, and STEP contains the number of step records encountered.

Next, three macros are defined: _SUMSTEP, _MAXSTEP, and _MINSTEP. All three identify the step variables that are summed, maximized, or minimized when the step records are combined into the jobs data set. Data set STEPS is sorted by descending step within each job so that the first observation contains the last step's data. The MEANS procedure sums the resources from these step records into a single observation per job. The ID variables are output to SUM30_4 and contain the values of the first observation for each job, which, because of the descending step sort, is the last STEPS observation. SUM30_4 is set aside, and we return to the job termination records. Only one job termination record is needed, and that is the last termination. However, the job records are processed, JINITIME and JTRMTIME extracted, and the first job restart and the final JOB initiate time stamps created as these records are processed. The 30_5 records are now set aside, and the TYPE6 (print) records are processed by storing the number of lines in variables PRINTLNE for printed output, PUNCHCRD for punched card output, or EXTWTRLN for lines created by an external writer. PROC MEANS creates the sum of the PRINT records; INBITS appears in the BY list so that it appears in the output data set SUM6.

The summed step records, the single job record (with first and last initiation times), the summed print records, the purge record, and the jobinit record are now merged. The jobinit record is needed only if no 30_5 record is encountered, which occurs in a job that was active when MVS crashed. In that case, job accounting information comes from this jobinit record. DATETIME is set to the maximum value of READTIME, first step INITTIME, first JOBINIT time, last JOBINIT time, or last JSTRTIME to use the last nonmissing value of the job's starting execution. Member IMACSHFT is %INCLUDEd and uses the just set value of DATETIME to set the SHIFT based on your installation's definitions of SHIFT in that member.

The final piece of logic exploits our knowledge of what records were received in processing this job, and the variable ABEND is set based on what happened to this job. ABEND is also set by the step and job abend conditions, such as SYST, USER, RTRN, and so forth. ABEND is expanded to be a global termination indicator as follows: if a PURGE record is received as indicated by INBITS, JSTRTIME is tested to set ABEND='JCL' if this is recognized as a JCL error. Jobs canceled prior to execution are also classified as JCL errors, and the variable

CANCELED differentiates true JCL errors from jobs canceled before execution. JENDTIME is compared to JSTRTIME to identify if the job was active when the system crashed (ABEND='CRSH'). Finally, if no PURGE record is received, ABEND is set to NOPU.

Two data sets are built concurrently by this phase—the PDB.JOBS with all variables; and ACCOUNT, which keeps the READTIME, JOB, JESNR, and (arbitrarily) the first three ACCOUNT numbers and JFINTIME. Should your installation use more than three account parameters, you need to change ACCOUNT3 to ACCOUNT*n* where *n* corresponds to the number of account fields.

Data PDB.PRINT is then built by merging ACCOUNT with the PRINT data set. Since the PRINT records have no ACCOUNT number, this merge serves to calculate print queue time (PRQUETM) for each file (PRINTIME minus JFINTIME) and also allows you to associate the ACCOUNT number of the job with each file printed by that job. Similarly, STEPS is merged with ACCOUNT to add ACCOUNT number to the STEPS data set in the performance data base.

The final piece of logic outputs the five SPIN data sets to the SPIN file for the next execution of BUILDPDB. Two executions of PROC CONTENTS give us the size of the PDB and work file, and BUILDPDB ends by printing the first fifty observations of JOBS, STEPS, and PRINT from the day's PDB. In a normal production environment, the PROC PRINTs would not be needed.

chapter thirty-five

PDB Execution Considerations and Automatic Submission

The BUILDPDB module of MXG software, described in chapter thirty-four, processes an SMF file and builds the Performance Data Base. To move the PDB to production, however, you need to consider the functions described in this chapter and add them as necessary to the production job stream you develop. This chapter also discusses how the SAS System can be used to submit daily, weekly, and monthly jobs automatically, based on logic you define. Your goal should be to automate the execution stream so that your time is spent in analysis, not in checking JCL.

PRODUCTION EXECUTION CONSIDERATIONS

- The SMF dump program cannot be used alone. The example provided by IBM in SYS1.SAMPLIB of an intelligent dumping sequence should be packaged for operations. Without an intelligent dump program, when SMF fills, the operator must first switch SMF recording to an empty SMF data set, submit an IFASMFDP program execution to dump the full data set, switch back, and submit a second IFASMFDP program to dump the data written while the first dump was executing. An intelligent dump program requires the operator to submit only one job, which determines what data sets need to be dumped, issues the switch as necessary, and manages this function without operator assistance and, hence, without operator error.
- SMF must be dumped regularly. The size of the primary SMF VSAM data set determines the frequency with which SMF must be dumped, and that size is set by your choice of instructions to operations. Smaller VSAM data sets require more frequent operator attention to submit the intelligent dump program, but they do save disk space. If you can afford the disk space, dumping late each night further minimizes human error.
- Consider the impact of a head crash on the VSAM SMF file. If you dump only once a day, how much revenue (chargeback) do you lose with a pack failure at 6 p.m.? Compare this to the cost of executing the IFASMFDP program periodically (dump without clear) to backup the SMF file.
- Copy the SMF VSAM file immediately prior to dumping the program or

create two copies of the dumped output with IFASMFDP. Once the VSAM file has been cleared, the only SMF data source is the tape built by the dump program. A second copy of that tape, kept only until today's processing or until the weekend backup of SMF data is built, is usually worth the cost of an additional tape.

- The dump job must permit multiple executions without loss of data. Since a runaway job can flood the SMF file with records until it fills, the design of the SMF dumping job must provide for multiple executions, preferably without requiring any operator changes to the job's JCL. The day's SMF data should be processed during nonprime shift, and the JCL for that job should not depend on how many times the SMF dump job ran yesterday. There are two possible output file structures for the SMF dumping program that provide this capability:

  1. Create a generation data group (GDG) for each operating system and write the SMF dumped output to GDG(+1) each time the dump program is executed. Then, in the job that processes the SMF dump output, which should combine all SMF data from all systems at a node into a single daily SMF file for backup and processing, the GDG name without relative generation number can be used on the DD statement

```
//SMF  DD  DSNAME=SMF.SYSTEM1.DAILYGDG,
//                  DISP=(OLD,UNCATLG,KEEP)
```

  to read in all currently cataloged members of the GDG. Upon successful completion, the DD disposition uncatalogs all members and resets the GDG for tomorrow's creation.

  2. Write the SMF output to its data set with disposition MOD so that additional data are added to the end of the preceding data. This file must also be uncataloged after daily processing so that new dumps go to tomorrow's data set.

  The best choice is the second structure, using MOD on the output of the SMF dump program and uncataloging by the program that reads and combines the SMF data from multiple systems. Use of MOD is more expensive when a second dump is required since the first dump's data must be reread. The GDG alternative saves this (small) expense, but it suffers from one drawback: when a GDG is brought in without relative reference, the members are brought in as generation 0, then -1, then -2, and so forth and not in the sequential order that the SMF data were created. To guarantee the accuracy of duplicate or missing SMF data checking algorithms, the incoming SMF data must be presented in the order it was written. By demanding that the data be in order, an out-of-order algorithm can verify the expected order and issue an abend when the order is not as expected. One algorithm of this type is provided in MXG software and discussed below.

- Combine all SMF data from all systems at a node into a single daily SMF file for BUILDPDB. This can be an IEBGENER (with SYSUT2 specifying RECFM=VBS,LRECL=32756,BLKSIZE=32760) that reads and reblocks individual output files from the dump jobs. This combining job can be automatically submitted when (and only when) its feeder jobs have completed with the design described in Figure 35.1.

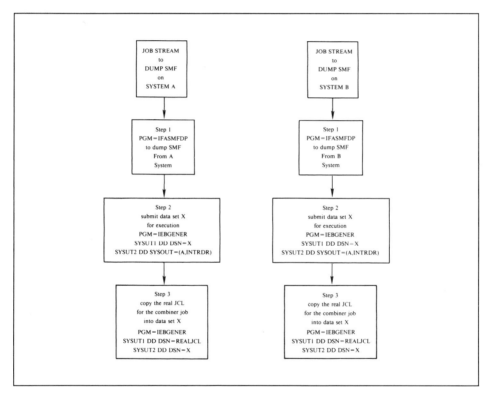

Figure 35.1
Submitting the SMF Combiner Job after Two Systems
Have Been Dumped

This pair of three step jobs first dumps the SMF data on their respective systems and, in the second step, submits a data set X into the internal reader; that is, it submits a job if its JCL is in data set X. Initially data set X is null so that the first of the pair to execute its second step accomplishes nothing in Step 2. However, the first job to execute, in Step 3, copies the real JCL for the combiner job into data set X from the job's permanent JCL library so that when the second job to execute executes Step 2, the combiner job is submitted only after both Step 1 dumps are complete. The first job primes data set X, and the second job submits data set X. The first task of the combiner job is to initialize data set X back to a null file in preparation for tomorrow's processing. The job then combines the SMF data from the multiple systems and submits the BUILDPDB job to process the daily SMF data.

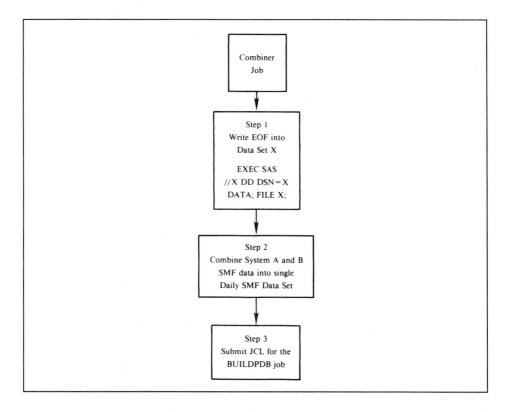

Figure 35.2

- The PDB system uses a SAS data library, called SPIN because of both its DD name and its purpose, to spin (or hold until tomorrow) data received from jobs that were partially complete when SMF was dumped. This data library is also used to store several SAS data sets that are used in the validation of BUILDPDB functionally. These functional enhancements to

the BUILDPDB should be considered for your own implementation if
BUILDPDB executes daily.

Upon completion of each day's run, data set SPIN.LASTRUN is
created containing the date of the last successful execution.

```
DATA SPIN.LASTRUN;
  LASTDATE=TODAY();
  OUTPUT;
  FORMAT LASTDATE MMDDYY8.
```

The first function of BUILDPDB is to compare today's date to the date
in SPIN.LASTRUN. Since this system runs seven days a week, the simple
test is:

```
DATA SPIN.ABEND;
  SET SPIN.LASTRUN;
  IF LASTDATE NE TODAY()-1 THEN DO;
    PUT ' BUILDPDB RUN TWICE OR MISSED A DAY ' /
        5X  TODAY= LASTDATE=  /
        ' RUN ABENDED WITH USER 001 ABEND ' ;
    ABEND=001;
    OUTPUT;
  END;
DATA _NULL_;
  SET SPIN.ABEND;
  IF ABEND THEN ABORT ABEND 001;
```

This serves two purposes. If a day was skipped or if BUILDPDB was
already executed today, this execution abends. Additionally, the
SPIN.ABEND data set has a nonmissing value for the variable abend,
signifying that a problem has been encountered. All subsequent jobs that
use the PDB as input, especially those that create other permanent data
sets and those that create reports, test SPIN.ABEND and terminate
themselves if abend has been previously set. Since no one in operations
knows how to turn off the SPIN.ABEND data set, no further work is
executed until the CPE analyst is called, the problem corrected, and
SPIN.ABEND reset.

When you want to abend the run and update a data set, note that the
data set must be updated in one SAS DATA step, and a second DATA
step must issue the ABORT ABEND. Otherwise, the ABORT overrides
the OUTPUT, and no observation is created in SPIN.ABEND.

BUILDPDB executes and builds today's PDB in a SAS data library
named DAY. DAY always contains the data created that day, which
represents the work accomplished between yesterday's and today's SMF
dump.

Yesterday's SMF data are validated for duplicate or missing data. The RMF data from yesterday in DAY.TYPE70 are summarized and added to the previous day's accumulated up time in the SPIN.ANALDUPE data set, summing the system up time for each CPU for each hour's data encountered. After SPIN.ANALDUPE is updated, each observation, representing in theory 1 hour's up time, is tested to see if more than 3600 seconds up time was recorded, indicating that duplicate data were received, or if less than 3600 seconds up time was recorded, then a system outage occurred. Duplicate data cause SPIN.ABEND to be updated with a nonzero abend variable, and then the run is aborted. After normal termination, however, SPIN.ANALDUPE is printed to provide a somewhat crude up time report. This algorithm is in MXG software member ANALDUPE.

- The daily data PDB for yesterday is always in DAY. The permanent PDB exists as 7 separate daily PDBs, named SUN, MON, TUE, and so forth, after the day whose data are contained therein. The PDB built on Monday at 3 a.m. is copied into SUN, and so forth. The duplicate data check ANALDUPE is applied to DAY, and if no duplicate data are encountered, the BUILDPDB job copies all SAS data sets from DAY to the correct day-of-week data set. Although this could be accomplished by manually editing the JCL for each day's run, job streams that require ANY human intervention should be avoided whenever possible. Let the humans do things that require thinking, and let algorithms perform tasks that have closed-form solutions. The following example accomplished the needed task of copying today's data into the correct day-of-week data set without any JCL or program changes by humans.

Note that what is described here is a dynamic, self-modifying program that writes the final program executed. Also, the modifications the program chooses to make upon itself depend on the time (day-of-week) when it runs and on the environment in which it finds itself.

BUILDPDB writes a single 80-byte record to an OS data set named INSTREAM. This record is the SAS code for defining a macro named _DAY. The contents of macro _DAY is yesterday's day of the week.

```
//BUILDMAC EXEC SAS,OPTIONS=ERRORABEND
//INSTREAM DD UNIT=SYSDA,SPACE=(TRK,(1,1)),DISP=(,PASS)
DATA_NULL_;
   FILE INSTREAM RECFM=F BLKSIZE=80;
   TODAY=TODAY()-1;
   DAY=PUT(TODAY, WEEKDATE28.);
   PUT 'MACRO_DAY' DAY $CHAR3. '%';
```

After this code is executed on a Monday morning, file INSTREAM contains the macro call

```
MACRO _DAY SUN %
```

File INSTREAM is then %INCLUDEd to interpret this SAS statement, thereby defining the value of _DAY for this execution, and PROC COPY copies from the DAY PDB to the correct day-of-week PDB:

```
//BUILDDAY EXEC SAS,OPTIONS=ERRORABEND
//DAY      DD DSN=DAY,DISP=OLD
//SUN      DD DSN=SUN,DISP=OLD
//MON      DD DSN=MON,DISP=OLD
//TUE      DD DSN=TUE,DISP=OLD
//WED      DD DSN=WED,DISP=OLD
//THU      DD DSN=THU,DISP=OLD
//FRI      DD DSN=FRI,DISP=OLD
//SAT      DD DSN=SAT,DISP=OLD
//INSTREAM DD DSN=INSTREAM,DISP=OLD
//SYSIN    DD *


%INCLUDE INSTREAM;


PROC COPY IN=DAY OUT=_DAY;
```

- BUILDPDB submits the weekly and monthly job streams. Since BUILDPDB can know the day of the week when it is executing, it is a simple matter to submit the weekly jobs and the monthly jobs. The following example is useful in explaining the power of the SAS System to application programmers. This program is designed to meet the following conditions:
  1. Weekly job is always submitted on Monday.

  2. Monthly job is submitted on the first day of the month unless the first day is a Monday. If the first day of the month is a Monday, the monthly job is submitted by a similar step attached to the weekly job so that the monthly job uses the weekly data set. For example:

```
// EXEC SAS,OPTIONS=ERRORABEND
//WEEKJCL   DD DSN=WEEKJCL
//MONTHJCL DD DSN=MONTHJCL
//INTRDR    DD SYSOUT=(A,INTRDR)


DATA_NULL_;
   IF NOT WEEKFLG THEN DO;
      WDAY=PUT(TODAY(),WEEKDATE3.);
      IF WDAY='MON' THEN WEEKFLG=1;
      ELSE STOP;
      RETAIN WEEKFLG;
   END;
   INFILE WEEKJCL;
   FILE INTRDR;
   INPUT;
   PUT_INFILE_;


   DATA_NULL_;
   IF NOT MONTHFLG THEN DO;
      WDAY=PUT(TODAY(),WEEKDATE3.);
      DAY=DAY(TODAY());
      IF DAY=1 AND WDAY NE 'MON' THEN MONTHFLG=1;
      ELSE STOP;
      RETAIN MONTHFLG;
   END;
   INFILE MONTHJCL;
   FILE INTRDR;
   INPUT;
   PUT_INFILE_;
```

• The weekly job creates the weekly PDB as a new member of a generation
data group that contains the data from the preceding seven days. Since
the SAS data sets in the daily PDB were sorted, the sorted order of the
data is preserved with the BY statement. A separate DATA step is
required for each data set in the weekly PDB. This JCL assumes that
there is a model DSCB for GDG's names SYS1.MODEL. The attributes
of the model DSCB are unimportant since the DCB attributes are set by
the SAS System, but the job fails with a JCL error if some model DSCB
is not specified as shown.

```
// EXEC SAS,OPTIONS=ERRORABEND
//WEEK DD DSN=CPM.WEEK(+1),DISP=(,CATLG),UNIT=TAPE,
    DCB=SYS1.MODEL,LABEL=EXPDT=99000
//SUN DD DSN=SUN
```

```
//MON DD DSN=MON
//TUE DD DSN=TUE
//WED DD DSN=WED
//THU DD DSN=THU
//FRI DD DSN=FRI
//SAT DD DSN=SAT
DATA WEEK.JOBS;
    SET MON.JOBS TUE.JOBS WED.JOBS THU.JOBS
        FRI.JOBS SAT.JOBS SUN.JOBS;
    BY READTIME JOB JESNR;
DATA WEEK.STEPS;
    SET MON.STEPS TUE.STEPS WED.STEPS THU.STEPS
        FRI.STEPS SAT.STEPS SUN.STEPS;
    BY READTIME JOB JESNR;
DATA WEEK.PRINT;
    SET MON.PRINT TUE.PRINT WED.PRINT THU.PRINT
        FRI.PRINT SAT.PRINT SUN.PRINT;
    BY READTIME JOB JESNR;
DATA WEEK.IPLS;
    SET MON.IPLS TUE.IPLS WED.IPLS THU.IPLS
        FRI.IPLS SAT.IPLS SUN.IPLS;
    BY SYSTEM IPLTIME;
DATA WEEK.TAPES;
    SET MON.TAPES TUE.TAPES WED.TAPES THU.TAPES
        FRI.TAPES SAT.TAPES SUN.TAPES;
    BY SYSTEM;
DATA WEEK.TYPE70;
    SET MON.TYPE70 TUE.TYPE70 WED.TYPE70 THU.TYPE70
        FRI.TYPE70 SAT.TYPE70 SUN.TYPE70;
    BY SYSTEM STARTIME;
DATA WEEK.TYPE71;
    SET MON.TYPE71 TUE.TYPE71 WED.TYPE71 THU.TYPE71
        FRI.TYPE71 SAT.TYPE71 SUN.TYPE71;
    BY SYSTEM STARTIME;
DATA WEEK.TYPE72;
    SET MON.TYPE72 TUE.TYPE72 WED.TYPE72 THU.TYPE72
        FRI.TYPE72 SAT.TYPE72 SUN.TYPE72;
    BY SYSTEM STARTIME;
DATA WEEK.TYPE73;
    SET MON.TYPE73 TUE.TYPE73 WED.TYPE73 THU.TYPE73
        FRI.TYPE73 SAT.TYPE73 SUN.TYPE73;
    BY SYSTEM STARTIME;
DATA WEEK.TYPE73P;
    SET MON.TYPE73P TUE.TYPE73P WED.TYPE73P THU.TYPE73P
        FRI.TYPE73P SAT.TYPE73P SUN.TYPE73P;
    BY SYSTEM STARTIME;
DATA WEEK.TYPE73L;
    SET MON.TYPE73L TUE.TYPE73L WED.TYPE73L THU.TYPE73L
        FRI.TYPE73L SAT.TYPE73L SUN.TYPE73L;
    BY SYSTEM STARTIME;
DATA WEEK.TYPE74;
```

```
    SET MON.TYPE74 TUE.TYPE74 WED.TYPE74 THU.TYPE74
        FRI.TYPE74 SAT.TYPE74 SUN.TYPE74;
    BY SYSTEM STARTIME;
DATA WEEK.TYPE75;
    SET MON.TYPE75 TUE.TYPE75 WED.TYPE75 THU.TYPE75
        FRI.TYPE75 SAT.TYPE75 SUN.TYPE75;
    BY SYSTEM STARTIME;
DATA WEEK.TYPE78;
    SET MON.TYPE78 TUE.TYPE78 WED.TYPE78 THU.TYPE78
        FRI.TYPE78 SAT.TYPE78 SUN.TYPE78;
    BY SYSTEM STARTIME;
DATA WEEK.SMFINTRV;
    SET MON.SMFINTRV TUE.SMFINTRV WED.SMFINTRV THU.SMFINTRV
        FRI.SMFINTRV SAT.SMFINTRV SUN.SMFINTRV;
    BY READTIME JOB JESNR INTETIME;
DATA WEEK.RMFINTRV;
    SET MON.RMFINTRV TUE.RMFINTRV WED.RMFINTRV THU.RMFINTRV
        FRI.RMFINTRV SAT.RMFINTRV SUN.RMFINTRV;
    BY SYSTEM STARTIME;
DATA WEEK.DDSTATS;
    SET MON.DDSTATS TUE.DDSTATS WED.DDSTATS THU.DDSTATS
        FRI.DDSTATS SAT.DDSTATS SUN.DDSTATS;
    BY READTIME JOB JESNR INITTIME;
```

- The monthly PDB is built by MONTHBLD, which is submitted on the first day of the month. Because no editing of the monthly job is acceptable, the JCL for MONTHBLD includes all possible PDBs that might be needed. All of the past five week's PDBs are in the JCL, as are all of the daily PDBs. The program determines what day of the week it is, fabricates macro definitions in INSTREAM, %INCLUDEs them, and, thus, dynamically sets which of the daily and weekly data sets are read. Since the fifth week typically spans both this month and last month, MONTHBLD also creates two macros in INSTREAM that define the beginning and ending dates of each month.

  A key part of this design is a consistent definition of month. The most appropriate definition is based on the ZDATE variable in each data set in the PDB, which contains the date each observation was added to the PDB ("ZDATE is zee date zee data were added to zee PDB"). Since ZDATE is the date of creation, records with a ZDATE of the second day of the month represent work that executed on the first day of the month (though there will be a small amount of data from today as well), and records with a ZDATE of the first day of the month represent work that executed on the last day of the preceding month. Therefore, last month is defined as all observations with a ZDATE value between the second day of the previous month and the first day of the current month.

  MONTHBLD first writes macros to select the dailies that will be needed to build monthly. Then simple SAS date functions make the

determination of the dates of the second of last month and the first of
this month to create the ZDATE selection macros _BEGIN and _END:

```
// EXEC SAS,OPTIONS=ERRORABEND
//INSTREAM DD UNIT=SYSDA,SPACE=(TRK,(1,1)),DISP=(,PASS)
//DUMMY    DD UNIT=SYSDA,SPACE=(TRK,(3,1)),DISP=(,PASS)
DATA _NULL_;
   TODAY=TODAY();                          /* EG 7652 */
   IF DAY(TODAY) NE 1 THEN DO;
      PUT '*** MONTHLY JOB NOT EXECUTED ON FIRST DAY OF MONTH '
      ABORT ABEND 1111;
   END;

   LASTDAY=TODAY-1;                        /*    7651 */
   DAYSIN=DAY(LASTDAY)                     /*      31 */
   FIRSTDAY=LASTDAY-DAYSIN+1;              /*    7621 */
   SECONDAY=FIRSTDAY+1;                    /*    7622 */
   FILE INSTREAM RECFM=FB LRECL=80 BLKSIZE=800;
   PUT 'MACRO _BEGIN' SECONDAY 5. '% MACRO _END' TODAY 5. '%';
   DAY=PUT(TODAY,WEEKDAY3.);
   IF      DAY='MON' THEN PUT
    'MACRO _D1 DUMMY % MACRO _D2 DUMMY % MACRO _D3 DUMMY %' /
    'MACRO _D4 DUMMY % MACRO _D5 DUMMY % MACRO _D6 DUMMY %' ;
   ELSE IF DAY='TUE' THEN PUT
    'MACRO _D1 MON   % MACRO _D2 DUMMY % MACRO _D3 DUMMY %' /
    'MACRO _D4 DUMMY % MACRO _D5 DUMMY % MACRO _D6 DUMMY %' ;
   ELSE IF DAY='WED' THEN PUT
    'MACRO _D1 MON   % MACRO _D2 TUE   % MACRO _D3 DUMMY %' /
    'MACRO _D4 DUMMY % MACRO _D5 DUMMY % MACRO _D6 DUMMY %' ;
   ELSE IF DAY='THU' THEN PUT
    'MACRO _D1 MON   % MACRO _D2 TUE   % MACRO _D3 WED   %' /
    'MACRO _D4 DUMMY % MACRO _D5 DUMMY % MACRO _D6 DUMMY %' ;
   ELSE IF DAY='FRI' THEN PUT
    'MACRO _D1 MON   % MACRO _D2 TUE   % MACRO _D3 WED   %' /
    'MACRO _D4 THU   % MACRO _D5 DUMMY % MACRO _D6 DUMMY %' ;
   ELSE IF DAY='SAT' THEN PUT
    'MACRO _D1 MON   % MACRO _D2 TUE   % MACRO _D3 WED   %' /
    'MACRO _D4 THU   % MACRO _D5 FRI   % MACRO _D6 DUMMY %' ;
   ELSE IF DAY='SUN' THEN PUT
    'MACRO _D1 MON   % MACRO _D2 TUE   % MACRO _D3 WED   %' /
    'MACRO _D4 THU   % MACRO _D5 FRI   % MACRO _D6 SAT   %' ;
   RUN;
   %INCLUDE INSTREAM;
```

If this code executed on a Wednesday morning, INSTREAM contains the
following macro definitions:

```
MACRO _BEGIN 7622 % MACRO_END 7652 %
MACRO _D1 MON    % MACRO _D2 TUE    % MACRO _D3 DUMMY %
MACRO _D4 DUMMY % MACRO _D5 DUMMY % MACRO _D6 DUMMY %
```

The MONTHBLD program continues now that the eight macros above
have been defined. Macro _MNTHBLD defines the structure of creating a
monthly data set symbolized here by _DSET, a macro name that is
redefined prior to the invocation of _MNTHBLD. First, a dummy data
set is built in the temporary DUMMY DD. Then, MONTH._DSET is
built from the six daily and five weekly PDBs. Note that the contents of
INSTREAM (see above) cause only two dailies, MON and TUE, to be
read in since _D3 through _D6 are DUMMY.

```
MACRO _MNTHBLD
OPTIONS OBS=0;
DATA DUMMY. _DSET  ;
SET  MON. _DSET  ;
RUN;
OPTIONS OBS=MAX;
DATA MONTH._DSET;
SET _D1._DSET _D2._DSET _D3._DSET _D4._DSET _D5.DSET _D6.DSET
WEEK1._DSET5 WEEK2._DSET WEEK3._DSET WEEK4._DSET WEEK5._DSET;
BY _BYLIST  ;
IF _BEGIN LE ZDATE LE _END;
RUN;
%
```

To complete the building of each SAS data set in the monthly PDB,
_DSET and _BYLIST must be defined and _MNTHBLD invoked for
each data set to be built:

```
MACRO _DSET JOBS     % MACRO _BYLIST READTIME JOB JESNR %
     _MNTHBLD
MACRO _DSET STEPS    % MACRO _BYLIST READTIME JOB JESNR %
     _MNTHBLD
MACRO _DSET PRINT    % MACRO _BYLIST READTIME JOB JESNR %
     _MNTHBLD
MACRO _DSET IPLS     % MACRO _BYLIST SYSTEM IPLTIME %
     _MNTHBLD
MACRO _DSET TAPES    % MACRO _BYLIST SYSTEM %
     _MNTHBLD
MACRO _DSET TYPE70   % MACRO _BYLIST SYSTEM STARTIME %
     _MNTHBLD
MACRO _DSET TYPE71   % MACRO _BYLIST SYSTEM STARTIME %
     _MNTHBLD
MACRO _DSET TYPE72   % MACRO _BYLIST SYSTEM STARTIME %
     _MNTHBLD
MACRO _DSET TYPE73   % MACRO _BYLIST SYSTEM STARTIME %
```

```
            _MNTHBLD
MACRO _DSET TYPE73L   % MACRO _BYLIST SYSTEM STARTIME %
      _MNTHBLD
MACRO _DSET TYPE73P   % MACRO _BYLIST SYSTEM STARTIME %
      _MNTHBLD
MACRO _DSET TYPE74    % MACRO _BYLIST SYSTEM STARTIME %
      _MNTHBLD
MACRO _DSET TYPE75    % MACRO _BYLIST SYSTEM STARTIME %
      _MNTHBLD
MACRO _DSET TYPE78    % MACRO _BYLIST SYSTEM STARTIME %
      _MNTHBLD
MACRO _DSET SMFINTRV  % MACRO _BYLIST READTIME JOB
      JESNR INTETIME %
      _MNTHBLD
MACRO _DSET RMFINTRV  % MACRO _BYLIST SYSTEM STARTIME %
      _MNTHBLD
MACRO _DSET DDSTATS   % MACRO _BYLIST READTIME JOB
      JESNR INITTIME %
      _MNTHBLD
```

A final step of the weekly and monthly jobs is an IEBGENER step that submits the reporting job(s) for both time periods. Thus, the entire system can be run unattended and automatically. BUILDPDB must be submitted daily, but all subsequent weekly and monthly jobs need only a verification of successful completion. By using the NOTIFY= operand on the JOB statement of these jobs, the data control clerk responsible for monitoring the weekly and monthly jobs is notified of any failure, and the data control clerk can then call the CPE analyst when a problem occurs. Some problems have been identified on the run sheet to be solved by resubmission without calling the CPE analyst. The ERRORABEND condition turns any error into an abend. This is communicated on the notify message sent to the data control clerk. Because no human intervention or editing is required for this production system, it is very stable, and it eliminates the need for human attention until an error occurs.

chapter thirty-six

Reporting Performance Data to Management

The presentation of reports to management is dependent on the organization, its management style, the business group within which the enterprise falls, and so forth. This chapter does not propose that the reports shown herein are all that are needed, but it is a collection of the reports that have been the primary source of management information for a number of years at one installation. Their purpose here is to demonstrate the contents of reports that were developed in direct response to management requests. These are not all the reports that can be generated from PDB data, nor are all these reports produced by the MXG software. Most reporting will be tailored to your installation, and reporting is easy with a SAS PDB.

CPE reports should be categorized by their intended audience.

Table 36.1

Audience	Report level	Contents
Management	High Level Summary	Objectives met and Work volumes
Strategic CPE	Medium Summary	Daily Resources Consumed
Tactical CPE	Detail	Hourly Events and Resources

Management needs to know how well computer services are meeting user's response and throughput requirements—the objectives and how much work users are delivering. Work should be measured in units that relate to cost so that management can look at a one page summary, see that service was good, and determine whether budgets will be met.

The strategic CPE function receives management level reports, reports necessary for the strategic function map workload, and objectives concerning necessary resources. Although management is concerned with the number of billable TSO units, the strategic CPE analyst must compare that to hardware resources needed to process the billable load.

The tactical CPE function needs both of these reports and also requires detailed reports that map resources consumed to time of day. If service was poor yesterday, the tactical CPE analyst must determine if it was due to insufficient resources or to a momentary increase in work requested. Providing resources by the hour gives immediate answers to most of these questions.

There is a trade-off between producing a report regularly from the PDB and writing a SAS job to produce reports on request. Time and experience confirm the best choice. These reports were designed to minimize time to solve problems without creating an inordinate amount of reporting. Placing the daily reports on-line, with a menu for report selection, reduces paper generation. If the menu offers all levels of reports, a technically oriented manager can select the data he wants to see. These reports do not replace ad hoc analysis nor are all questions answered by any set of reports; however, well-designed information content can improve the productivity of CPE personnel.

TOTAL WORK UNITS DELIVERED

This report summarizes work delivered by the shift on which the work was executed. Data are from the PDB.JOBS data set, and identification of type of work (batch, CICS, IMS BMP) requires decoding of job name, job class, performance group, and so forth. Under each work type, work units delivered are tabulated by the various business organizations decoded from the account (billing) number to which work is charged. Units are in computer work units, the common work unit for cost transfer.

Daily Network System Performance Analysis
3 am Wednesday, August 15, 1984 thru 3 am Thursday, August 16, 1984
Total Work Units Delivered

	7am-4pm	4pm-12am	12am-7am	Overnight	Weekend	Total
Total Workload						
All Work						51849
Batch						
All Jobs	17130	16104	6995	4822	6	45058
DCC	3186	1496	1677	12		6370
Dallas	2421	1244	48	771		4485
Tulsa	1134	1763	1359	208		4464
Philadelphia	8852	7466	3269	3235		22822
AFS	1289	3975	569	71		5905
CSC	247	160	73	526	6	1012
Miscellaneous	0	0				0
CICS						
Dallas						
AFS	161	4				165
IMS BMP						
All Jobs	1	15	310			326
Dallas		15				15
Tulsa			310			310
Philadelphia	1					1

PERCENTAGE OF JOBS MEETING INITIATION WAIT TIME REQUESTED

This is the primary report showing batch service delivered. See chapter eight for a description of initiation wait time (IWT) scheduling. Under each column representing an IWT category (for example, 15 minute category), the percentage of jobs meeting requested service and the percentage of work on that line submitted at that IWT category are provided, allowing management to see how good and how much on the same report. The performance of all batch work by shift and for all shifts is reported in the first section, and then each major business element's service (DCC and Dallas) is tabulated so that comparisons between groups can be made.

Daily Network System Performance Analysis
3 am Wednesday, August 15, 1984 thru 3 am Thursday, August 16, 1984
Percentage of Jobs Meeting IWT Requested

	15 min		30 min		1 hour		2 hours		4 hours		Overnight		Weekend		Total	
	%met	%jobs	%met	%jobs	%met	%jobs	%met	%jobs	%met	%jobs	%met	%jobs	%met	%jobs	%met	Jobs
All Jobs																
7am-4pm	98.9	51.9	100.0	1.8	100.0	25.2	100.0	3.9	100.0	17.1		0.0		0.0	99.4	
4pm-12pm	99.3	25.5	100.0	1.2	99.7	27.3	100.0	2.5	99.8	43.5					99.7	
12pm-7am	95.3	49.8	100.0	1.0	100.0	20.1	100.0	3.0	100.0	26.1					100.0	
Overnight											100.0	100.0			100.0	
All Shifts	98.6	39.1	100.0	1.4	99.9	23.5	100.0	3.1	99.9	25.0	100.0	7.9	100.0	0.1	99.4	
DCC																
7am-4pm	100.0	28.6	100.0	3.8	100.0	57.3	100.0	0.5	100.0	9.9		0.0		0.0	100.0	
4pm-12pm	100.0	7.0	100.0	2.3	100.0	58.1			100.0	32.6					100.0	
12pm-7am	96.4	47.5	100.0	3.4	100.0	32.2			100.0	16.9					98.3	
Overnight											100.0	100.0			100.0	
All Shifts	98.9	28.8	100.0	3.4	100.0	52.0	100.0	0.3	100.0	14.1	100.0	1.3		0.0	99.7	
Dallas																
7am-4pm	100.0	34.6	100.0	2.6	100.0	36.4	100.0	1.5	100.0	24.9					100.0	
4pm-12pm	100.0	11.8			100.0	36.5	100.0	1.8	100.0	49.8					100.0	
12pm-7am							100.0	10.0	100.0	90.0					100.0	
Overnight											100.0	100.0			100.0	
All Shifts	100.0	22.0	100.0	1.3	100.0	32.7	100.0	1.6	100.0	33.6	100.0	8.8			100.0	

PERCENTAGE OF CWU MEETING INITIATION WAIT TIME REQUESTED

This report is in the same format as the preceding report, but the values reported are percentages of CWU, the work units. Reporting batch service based on job counts identifies how many users were satisfied, but when the price of a work unit is dependent on whether or not IWT was met, the revenue lost due to missed service is important. By tabulating the number of CWU that met IWT and comparing it to the percentage of jobs that met, you can be sure that both the users and the supplier are happy. Note that from the previous report, 15-minute IWT jobs made up 51.9% of all prime-time jobs, but the same jobs represented only 37.3%

of prime-time work units. Users were submitting many small jobs in the more expensive IWT categories and were deferring larger resource jobs to the cheaper (and less time-sensitive) IWT categories.

Daily Network System Performance Analysis
3 am Wednesday, August 15, 1984 thru 3 am Thursday, August 16, 1984
Percentage of CWUs Meeting IWT Requested

	15 min		30 min		1 hour		2 hours		4 hours		Overnight		Weekend		Total	
	%met	%jobs	%met	%jobs	%met	%jobs	%met	%jobs	%met	%jobs	%met	%jobs	%met	%jobs	%met	Jobs
All Jobs																
7am-4pm	98.2	37.3	100.0	2.8	100.0	24.4	100.0	2.0	100.0	33.5		0.0		0.0	99.3	17130
4pm-12pm	96.6	34.9	100.0	0.3	96.6	12.4	100.0	0.3	99.4	52.1					98.1	16104
12pm-7am	88.5	44.6	100.0	0.1	100.0	20.9	100.0	2.2	100.0	32.3					94.9	6995
Overnight											100.0	100.0			100.0	4822
Weekend													100.0	100.0	100.0	6
All Shifts	95.6	33.5	100.0	1.2	99.1	17.0	100.0	1.2	99.7	36.4	100.0	10.7	100.0	0.0	98.3	45058
DCC																
7am-4pm	100.0	15.1	100.0	0.2	100.0	40.6	100.0	0.0	100.0	44.1		0.0		0.0	100.0	3186
4pm-12pm	100.0	0.3	100.0	0.1	100.0	10.2			100.0	89.3					100.0	1496
12pm-7am	98.0	41.3	100.0	0.0	100.0	21.9			100.0	36.7					99.2	1677
Overnight											100.0	100.0			100.0	12
All Shifts	98.8	18.5	100.0	0.1	100.0	28.5	100.0	0.0	100.0	52.7	100.0	0.2		0.0	99.8	6370
Dallas																
7am-4pm	100.0	22.5	100.0	0.4	100.0	23.5	100.0	0.3	100.0	53.2					100.0	2421
4pm-12pm	100.0	2.7			100.0	16.9	100.0	2.3	100.0	78.1					100.0	1244
12pm-7am							100.0	0.0	100.0	100.0					100.0	48
Overnight											100.0	100.0			100.0	771

BATCH JOB RESOURCE AVERAGES

Resources consumed by each batch IWT category are tabulated by shift. Average times in the IWT queue, in execution, and in the print queue are reported, as are their sum and the average CPU time, EXCP count, and CWU per job. This strategic report gives a broad picture of typical batch resources for each category on each shift. Because of the small number of jobs in the 30-minute and 2-hour categories, their statistics are not meaningful, but comparison of the average CWU for 15-minute jobs shows that they increase from 4.47 during prime time to 18.65 during evenings and to 20.93 CWU per job at night, showing the users take advantage of pricing discounts.

Daily Network System Performance Analysis
3 am Wednesday, August 15, 1984 thru 3 am Thursday, August 16, 1984
All Jobs
Batch Job Resource Averages

IWT Requested	Queue Time HH:MM	Execution Time HH:MM:SS	Print Queue Time HH:MM:SS	Queues + Execution HH:MM:SS	CPU Time HH:MM:SS.HH	EXCP Count	CWU	Total Jobs
All jobs 7am-4pm								
0:15	0:04	0:06:18	0:23:24	0:34:08	0:00:07.91	6747	4.47	987
0:30	0:00	0:05:34	0:02:14	0:08:04	0:00:21.04	6174	14.28	34
1:00	0:01	0:07:24	0:35:56	0:44:35	0:00:13.40	5850	8.70	480
2:00	0:03	0:09:09	0:06:09	0:16:43	0:00:08.48	3803	4.62	75
4:00	0:20	0:10:20	0:08:21	0:38:06	0:00:27.56	15326	17.61	326
All jobs 4pm-12pm								
0:15	0:00	0:15:00	3:08:45	3:23:46	0:00:22.35	17233	18.65	301
0:30	0:00	0:04:14	0:08:13	0:13:13	0:00:03.24	3459	3.07	14
1:00	0:01	0:09:01	3:56:53	4:06:28	0:00:06.97	7606	6.22	322
2:00	0:00	0:05:24	0:11:08	0:14:55	0:00:02.86	2928	1.73	29
4:00	0:05	0:09:28	1:02:50	1:17:22	0:00:22.06	12347	16.36	513
All jobs 12pm-7am								
0:15	0:11	0:08:58	1:10:53	1:31:00	0:00:44.37	16517	20.93	149
0:30	0:00	0:07:42	0:00:01	0:03:20	0:00:05.26	1578	1.55	3
1:00	0:03	0:13:23	0:21:59	0:38:30	0:00:34.45	22536	24.33	60

DETAIL JOB SUMMARY

This report is split into 2 pages but fits in 131 print positions. It is primarily used by the hot-line function of operations to answer "what happened to my job yesterday" questions. Important time stamps, durations, and the job's CWU are provided. IWT CHG status reflects events that affect or change the IWT, such as released from hold or delayed due to data set enqueue. The input (IN), print (PRN), and punch remotes (Remote PUN) reflect source and route card information, and the IWT requested and received answer complaints. Finally, termination type (SYST, USER, RTRN, and so forth) and the associated condition code are provided.

Daily Network System Performance Analysis
3 am Wednesday, August 15, 1984 thru 3 am Thursday, August 16, 1984
DETAIL JOB SUMMARY

Job	JES #	Submitter	Read Time of Day	IWT Start Time of Day	IWT End Time	Purge Time of Day
DACCSMFD	5906	VCCPRO	15AUG79:03:26	15AUG79:03:26	3:26	15AUG79:03:38
DACCSYSC	5852	VCCPRO	15AUG79:03:00	15AUG79:03:00	3:01	15AUG79:03:11
DACCSYSD	5853	VCCPRO	15AUG79:03:00	15AUG79:03:00	3:01	15AUG79:03:07
DACCSYSM	5851	VCCPRO	15AUG79:02:59	15AUG79:02:59	3:00	15AUG79:03:07
DAVAILDY	6476	VDCFMS	15AUG79:09:01	15AUG79:09:01	9:02	15AUG79:09:16
DAVAILDY	6480	VDCFMS	15AUG79:09:02	15AUG79:09:15	9:15	15AUG79:09:32
DAVAILDY	6719	VDCFMS	15AUG79:09:47	15AUG79:09:47	9:48	15AUG79:10:11
DCICSDAY	9571	VECBWM	16AUG79:02:33	16AUG79:02:33	2:33	16AUG79:02:41
DCPAFSDY	5934	VECBWM	15AUG79:04:12	15AUG79:04:12	4:12	15AUG79:04:30
DCPAFSDY	7032	VECBWM	15AUG79:10:57	15AUG79:10:57	11:00	15AUG79:11:11
DCPBKDAY	5941	VECBWM	15AUG79:04:12	15AUG79:04:12	4:15	15AUG79:04:19
DCPCSCDY	5933	VECBWM	15AUG79:04:12	15AUG79:04:12	4:12	15AUG79:06:08
DCPCSCDY	7031	VECBWM	15AUG79:10:57	15AUG79:10:57	10:59	15AUG79:11:05
DCPDALDY	5935	VECBWM	15AUG79:04:12	15AUG79:04:12	4:13	15AUG79:04:29
DCPDALDY	7034	VECBWM	15AUG79:10:57	15AUG79:10:57	11:01	15AUG79:11:11
DCPDCCDY	5931	VECBWM	15AUG79:04:12	15AUG79:04:12	4:12	15AUG79:04:56
DCPDCCMO	7106	VECBWM	15AUG79:11:15	15AUG79:11:15	11:18	15AUG79:11:25
DCPIMSDB	7219	VECCLT	15AUG79:11:53	15AUG79:11:53	11:56	15AUG79:13:30
DCPIMSDY	7454	VECCLT	15AUG79:12:46	15AUG79:12:46	12:46	15AUG79:13:38

Daily Network System Performance Analysis
3 am Wednesday, August 15, 1984 thru 3 am Thursday, August 16, 1984
DETAIL JOB SUMMARY

Execute Time HH:MM	Print Queue HH:MM	CWU	IWT CHG	IN	PRN	Remote PUN	REQ	Urgency /	REC	Term Code	Cond Code
0:10	0:00	12.75		0	0	0	4:00	/	0:00	RTRN	0004
0:08	0:00	20.88	R	0	0	0	4:00	/	0:00	RTRN	0004
0:05	0:00	12.51		0	0	0	4:00	/	0:00	RTRN	0004
0:04	0:02	5.38	R	0	0	0	4:00	/	0:00	RTRN	0004
0:13	0:00	10.15		0	0	0	0:15	/	0:00		
0:12	0:00	11.41	R	0	0	0	0:15	/	0:00		
0:17	0:00	12.97		0	0	0	0:15	/	0:00		
0:07	0:00	40.59		0	0	0	1:00	/	0:00		
0:03	0:00	4.24		0	0	0	1:00	/	0:00		
0:05	0:06	4.01		0	0	0	1:00	/	0:02		
0:02	0:01	4.71		0	0	0	1:00	/	0:03		
0:01	0:00	3.59		0	0	0	1:00	/	0:00		
0:03	0:00	3.63		0	0	0	1:00	/	0:01		
0:02	0:07	3.47		0	0	0	1:00	/	0:01		
0:03	0:04	3.58		0	0	0	1:00	/	0:03		
0:14	0:16	33.83		0	0	0	0:15	/	0:00		
0:02	0:03	2.67		0	0	0	1:00	/	0:03		
1:29	0:00	161.23		0	196	0	1:00	/	0:02		
0:05	0:02	6.24	D	0	0	0	1:00	/	0:00		

TSO PERFORMANCE ANALYSIS SYSTEM

Data from Morino Associates' product TSO/MON are used for this primary management report on TSO service objective. Columns represent the 8 response time buckets and pairs of rows quantify management's needs: what percentage of transactions received service in 2, 3, 4, and so forth seconds; and how many transactions were serviced. TSO commands are categorized as trivial and nontrivial based on a table of command names, and long commands are programs executed by the TSO CALL command. The bottom half of the report provides further qualification to management of the size of the TSO workload and shows that this 3033 had a maximum of 94 logged-on users during the day.

This report is a good example of the problem of using average response as a service objective. For the trivial commands, note that although the average response of all 27,817 commands was 2.5 seconds, over 90% of the commands had a response of under 2 seconds. More error is seen when the average response for nontrivial transactions of 6.7 seconds is compared to the distribution statistics. Over 85% of the transactions were serviced in less than the average response time. A small number of large response times causes the average value not to be representative of the users' perception.

Daily Network System Performance Analysis
3 am Wednesday, August 15, 1984 thru 3 am Thursday, August 16, 1984
TSO Performance Analysis System

Daily Response Time Distribution Report

		2 sec	3 sec	4 sec	5 sec	8 sec	15 sec	30 sec	over 30 sec	Average	Total
Trivial	cum%	90	92	94	95	96	98	99	100	2.5	27817
Commands	count	24947	722	406	248	480	391	302	321	Seconds	
											22808
Nontrivial	cum%	69	77	81	85	90	94	97	100	6.7	
Commands	count	15831	1719	1026	702	1143	1093	684	610	Seconds	2196
Long	cum%	77	81	83	86	90	96	98	100	3.7	52821
Commands	count	1699	88	43	59	93	120	55	39	Seconds	
All	cum%	80	85	88	90	93	96	98	100	4.4	
Commands	count	42477	2529	1475	1009	1716	1604	1041	970	Seconds	

Prime Time (7am-4pm)

Command CPU Time	2:02:47.98	Number of User Logons	697
Command Residency Time	42:03:39.55	Average Number of Users	70
Commands per Hour	5869	Maximum Number of Users	94
Command CPU Time per Hour	0:13:38.66	Terminal Connect Hours	555:12:31.18

CICS PERFORMANCE

The management level report for CICS, like all management level reports, is a single page report. Columns are the response in seconds from Performance Analyzer II or CMF, with the CICS transactions categorized into fast, medium, and long based on transaction resources (see chapter twenty-one), and transactions flagged as delayed (for example, the CICS short on storage event) are tabulated as a separate group. Percentage of transactions meeting service and count of transactions provide the how good and how much characteristic of management reports. The second half of the report answered end user's complaints about inconsistency. For each hour, number and average response are calculated. The stability of the response across the entire day for both fast and medium show that MVS can provide consistent CICS response time. (The 4.4 second average for hour 13 was later determined to be the result of a very long running transaction that did no I/O and was falsely classified as a fast transaction.) This CICS system consistency was achieved through fencing sufficient real memory, sufficiently high dispatching priority (even though this CICS was below an IMS subsystem), and especially through I/O isolation so that no other workloads contended for the CICS DASD volumes.

CICS Performance Reports for Wednesday, August 15, 1984
Cumulative Response Percentage Report by Transaction Category

Group	Trans Count	0-1 secs	1-2 secs	2-3 secs	3-4 secs	4-5 secs	5-10 secs	10-15 secs	15-20 secs	20+ secs
Fast	20812	39.97	78.97	93.44	96.79	97.61	98.57	99.44	99.94	0.06
Medium	27413	1.62	35.21	76.43	88.32	91.16	92.73	94.98	99.03	0.97
Long	2300	0.35	9.13	47.17	74.83	85.91	94.83	96.52	99.13	0.87
Delay	161	3.73	25.47	59.63	76.40	81.99	92.55	94.41	94.41	5.59

Hourly Profile of Average CICS Response Time for Wednesday, August 15, 1984

Hour	Fast Transactions Num	Fast Transactions Resp	Medium Transactions Num	Medium Transactions Resp	Long Transactions Num	Long Transactions Resp	Delayed Transactions Num	Delayed Transactions Resp
8	1512	1.4	1782	4.1	114	3.8		
9	2487	1.5	2805	3.9	198	3.5		
10	2042	1.7	3191	3.9	244	4.4	5	3.2
11	1684	1.5	2515	3.5	242	13.0		
12	2249	1.2	3077	3.4	321	3.6		
13	2385	4.4	3561	3.5	270	3.7	19	5.7
14	2293	1.5	3015	3.0	284	9.3		
15	1773	1.8	1827	3.6	174	4.5		
16	1743	2.2	1896	2.7	134	3.3		
17	983	0.9	1654	2.4	143	4.3	2	265.9
18	864	1.1	1291	2.7	105	8.3	94	3.5

CWUs BY HOUR, SYSTEM, AND SUBSYSTEM

The RMF data in the PDB is the backbone of strategic and tactical CPE function reporting. The CWU delivered to each performance group is summarized by work type and system. For any hour, total CWU is reported, and it is easy to see what was executing where. When a response problem is reported, reference to this report can identify if the poor response resulted from an unexpected workload during the hour in question. The total CWU reported is the total captured in the type 72 performance group records and does not include or reflect the MVS overhead.

CRU's by Hour, System, and Subsystem
From Midnight to Midnight
Wednesday, August 15, 1984

Hour	System	Batch	TSO	TCAM	JES2	IMS CTL	IMS BMP	IMS MSG	CICS	TP2K	VTAM	Wylbur	Misc	Total
0	B1	277	12		6	0	0				0	0	17	313
0	B2	1619			8								24	1650
0	01	111	1	27	27	1		0		5			17	189
	Total	2007	13	27	41	1	0	0		5	0	0	58	2152
1	B1	389	11		7		0				0	0	13	421
1	B2	1654			9								17	1679
1	01	161	4	27	28	0	62	0		6			13	302
	Total	2203	16	27	44	0	63	0		6	0	0	43	2402
2	B1	17	4		17	0	0				0	0	12	50
2	B2	631			9								15	705
2	01	184	0	27	29	0	73	0		5			13	331
	Total	881	4	27	54	0	73	0		5	0	0	40	1085
3	B1	546	1		12	0	0					0	14	573
3	B2	324			6								13	344
3	01	814		27	29	0		0		6			13	889
	Total	1684	1	27	48	0	0	0		6		0	40	1806

CPU AND PAGING ACTIVITY BY HOUR

In another report that needs 2 pages here, the hourly RMF data from type 70, 71, 72, and 73 records are merged to profile these resources. CPU utilizations from type 70 and 72 records are combined to report total CPU busy and the percentage in the 3 possible states: TCB busy, SRB busy (both captured at the performance group level), and the OVHD (or CPU busy not captured in the performance group data). The SIO activity rate from the type 73 and the paging and swapping measures provide diagnostic measures. Note that rates or percentages rather than absolute values are generally reported. The data are from an MP that supported IMS, CICS, associated batch, and a small TSO system.

Network System Performance Analysis
CPU and Paging Activity by Hour
Wednesday, August 15, 1984

Hour	System	Pct. CPU Busy	Pct. TCB	Non-TCB CPU		Total SIO Rate
				SRB	OVHD	
0	01	23	4	1	18	87
1	01	30	9	2	19	99
2	01	27	8	2	18	106
3	01	58	39	1	18	117
4	01	39	18	1	20	134
5	01	45	21	2	21	167
6	01	59	35	2	22	165
7	01	76	33	5	38	282
8	01	65	20	3	42	221
9	01	64	19	2	43	225
10	01	63	22	3	38	214
11	01	48	12	2	33	184
12	01	57	8	1	38	173
13	01	61	9	3	49	239
14	01	61	12	3	46	221
15	01	66	21	4	41	193
16	01	42	9	2	31	165

Network System Performance Analysis
CPU and Paging Activity by Hour
Wednesday, August 15, 1984

Paging Rates						Swap Rates			TSO	System
Paging (PTR)	Demand (DPR)	Total (PAGRT)	Swap (SPR)	Local (PFR)	System (PFR)	Batch	TSO	TSO TI	Swaps/ Tran	Up Time
0.1	0.0	0.7	0.6	0.1	0.0	0.00	0.02	0.02	1.01	0:59
0.1	0.1	0.9	0.8	0.1	0.0	0.00	0.03	0.02	1.02	1:00
0.0	0.0	0.3	0.3	0.0	0.0	0.00	0.00	0.00	0.78	1:00
0.3	0.0	0.8	0.7	0.3	0.0	0.00	0.00	0.00	0.75	0:59
0.2	0.0	0.6	0.6	0.1	0.0	0.00		0.00		1:00
0.1	0.0	0.3	0.3	0.1	0.0	0.00		0.00		1:00
1.6	0.9	5.4	4.4	1.4	0.2	0.00	0.13	0.12	0.98	1:00
4.3	3.5	9.7	6.2	3.6	0.8	0.03	0.07	0.06	0.97	1:00
6.7	5.9	17.1	11.2	5.3	1.4	0.05	0.23	0.19	0.97	0:59
8.8	9.6	23.2	13.6	6.8	2.1	0.04	0.30	0.26	1.00	1:00
9.4	9.8	24.4	14.5	7.3	2.1	0.06	0.28	0.23	0.99	0:59
3.8	3.3	10.3	7.0	3.2	0.6	0.01	0.16	0.13	0.97	1:00
4.4	4.0	12.9	8.9	3.8	0.6	0.00	0.24	0.18	0.93	0:59
10.3	12.5	23.7	11.2	7.2	3.1	0.00	0.25	0.22	0.92	1:00
9.5	10.3	25.8	15.5	6.9	2.6	0.02	0.37	0.33	0.95	0:59
6.7	7.7	15.3	7.6	4.5	2.2	0.00	0.13	0.12	0.97	1:00
2.8	3.5	6.4	2.9	2.0	0.9	0.01	0.07	0.07	0.96	0:59

MEMORY INFORMATION BY HOUR

The memory frame counts of significant storage areas are reported in a tactical/strategic level report. Abrupt changes in paging rates frequently result from changes in memory allocation. These changes can be identified in this report, which is written using type 71 data.

Network System Performance Analysis
Memory Information by Hour
Wednesday, August 15, 1984

Hour	System	Avg AFC	SPA + CSA			SQA			Private			Total		
			Min	Max	Avg	Min	Max	Avg	Min	Max	Avg	Min	Max	Avg
0	B1	132	83	89	83	139	143	139	37	94	51	324	425	355
1	B1	132	83	89	83	135	143	139	35	96	55	324	425	365
2	B1	151	83	89	83	135	143	135	32	96	33	313	425	316
3	B1	301	83	90	83	135	139	135	32	171	62	313	510	376
4	B1	296	83	92	84	135	139	137	32	199	89	313	561	420
5	B1	177	83	100	90	137	141	139	32	209	76	332	561	407
6	B1	177	83	104	94	137	144	141	32	209	89	335	559	430
7	B1	200	92	104	94	141	147	143	77	192	104	395	579	467
8	B1	187	94	104	95	141	158	148	77	192	101	400	620	488
9	B1	187	94	104	94	146	158	151	79	163	91	403	620	479
10	B1	206	94	102	96	151	157	151	79	153	86	416	585	461
11	B1	194	96	104	96	151	157	151	79	146	84	414	548	455
12	B1	194	96	104	96	150	155	150	80	118	86	414	555	468
13	B1	203	96	104	96	150	157	150	79	118	87	420	556	482
14	B1	182	96	105	96	150	160	151	79	126	91	423	565	488
15	B1	182	96	105	96	151	162	155	79	126	91	423	574	488
16	B1	203	96	104	96	154	162	154	81	125	85	407	574	443
17	B1	261	83	103	83	149	160	149	35	114	38	330	527	346
18	B1	346	83	100	83	147	154	147	35	90	36	328	459	341
19	B1	317	83	87	83	147	150	147	35	67	39	328	386	343

PHYSICAL CHANNEL USAGE (PERCENT BUSY)

Physical channel utilization measures are often not as useful as I/O delays, but the reporting must meet the needs of the recipient and the tactical CPE user often prefers to see utilizations of the channels. Each row in the report represents one physical channel attached to one CPU; each column an hour of the day. The CPU number is included so that multiprocessors are reported with two lines per channel, one for each CPU. Each column reports channel utilizations for that hour, and a row shows the utilization of that channel during the entire day. These data are from type 73 data. A similar report can be used to report paging data set busy by listing the page data set name instead of channel and CPU.

Network System Performance Analysis
Physical Channel Usage (Percent Busy) Report
Wednesday, August 15, 1984

Channel	CPU	00	01	02	03	04	05	06	07	08	09	10	11	12	13	14	15	16	17	18	19	20	21	22
0	0																							
1	0	17	34	1	8	21	15	11	13	9	9	9	6	9	10	8	11	7	3	2	1	2	2	1
2	0	6	15	0	10	8	4	6	10	14	12	10	8	11	13	15	13	6	3	2	4	2	2	1
3	0	21	12	1	10	22	16	6	14	15	18	12	10	13	18	19	17	10	4	4	3	2	2	1
4	0						1	0	11	12	12	6	1	0										
5	0	0			9	14	5	17	16	0			4	1	6	0								
6	0																							
7	0	22	12	1	10	22	15	6	13	16	17	13	10	14	18	18	18	10	3	4	3	2	1	1
8	0	7	13	3	5	9	9	5	16	25	25	17	15	20	28	28	26	12	7	9	11	7	3	2
9	0	19	39	1	9	22	12	11	13	10	10	8	6	7	9	9	11	5	2	2	2	2	1	1
A	0	37	63	4	21	48	49	41	13	0														
B	0	0			1	6	1	1	2	0														
C	0																							
D	0	8	13	3	5	10	8	5	17	26	25	19	15	21	28	28	26	13	7	9	10	7	3	2
E	0	5	14	0	11	8	5	5	11	14	12	11	8	11	12	15	13	6	3	3	3	2	2	1
F	0	36	44	1	4	31	8	10	1	0														

DAILY COMPUTER CENTER IMS PERFORMANCE MEASUREMENT

The final management single page report shows how well and how much IMS was delivered. Because IMS is made up of two separate services, queuing and service, the report is divided into two parts. The upper report provides statistics on IMS service time (transaction execution time after selection from the queue) by categorizing each IMS transaction based on resources (the IMS work unit, IWU) or by transaction name for the credit card verification transaction. Each category has a separate service goal, in seconds, which is listed after transaction volume, and the percentage of those transactions meeting one-half the goal, meeting the goal, and meeting twice the goal provide a measure of how good and reduces the amount of data to view. (Compare this report to the TSO and CICS reports, shown earlier, which tabulate eight rather than three response values.) The lower report categorizes transactions by input class since that is how transactions are selected, and it also presents the goal, the half-goal, and twice-goal values.

Daily Computer Center IMS Performance Measurement Report
Wednesday, August 15, 1984

Service Time

Category	Volume(%)	Goal	Half Goal	The Goal	Twice Goal
Credit Card	19826 (47.4%)	1.0	83.9%	95.9%	99.1%
00-04.9 IWU	5825 (13.9%)	1.0	93.4%	99.0%	99.8%
05-09.9 IWU	10639 (25.4%)	1.5	90.6%	98.9%	99.8%
10-19.9 IWU	2651 (6.3%)	4.0	88.4%	98.1%	99.6%
20-39.9 IWU	1774 (4.2%)	6.5	85.9%	96.7%	99.4%
40-59.9 IWU	336 (0.8%)	12.0	84.5%	96.7%	98.2%
60 plus IWU	768 (1.8%)				
Total	41819 (100.0%)		87.4%	97.3%	99.4%

Input Queue Time

Class	Volume (%)	Goal	Half Goal	The Goal	Twice Goal
001	2240 (5.4%)	0.5	95.8%	98.2%	99.6%
002	9773 (23.4%)	1.0	98.7%	99.7%	99.9%
003	6845 (16.4%)	4.0	87.2%	91.9%	96.0%
004	314 (0.8%)				
005	2822 (6.7%)	4.0	82.2%	88.1%	94.2%
006	19825 (47.4%)	1.0	95.4%	98.0%	99.3%
Total	41819 (100.0%)		93.9%	96.7%	98.5%

SYSTEM OUTAGE

The detail report of IPLs is not directed to management but is provided to operations. Although SMF provides a record of each IPL and since the length of the outage can be estimated from SMF (see chapter twenty-five), this report is intended to validate the manual reporting system within operations. Since the data do not tell whether the IPL was planned, this report should not be sent to management. Rather, the operations department uses these data to ensure that operators are properly reporting outages.

Network System Performance Analysis
System Outage Report
Wednesday, August 15, 1984

System	Time of Last SMF Record	Time of IPL	Length of Outage
B2	15AUG79:06:03:50.11	15AUG79:06:08:03.61	0:04:13.50
B2	15AUG79:06:17:37.83	15AUG79:06:19:52.48	0:02:14.65
B2	15AUG79:07:33:45.17	15AUG79:07:35:49.61	0:02:04.44
S1	14AUG79:21:48:56.98	15AUG79:07:17:48.39	9:28:51.41

chapter thirty-seven

Neat Features and Tricks with the SAS System for CPE

This chapter describes a collection of neat features of the SAS System that are useful to the performance analyst, and it points out some considerations that can affect the performance of the SAS System itself.

Table 37.1
Time Conversion Tables

Seconds and Smaller

Seconds	Milli-seconds	Micro-seconds	Nano-seconds	Equivalent frequency
1.0	1,000	1,000,000	1,000,000,000	1 Hz - audio
.1	100	100,000	100,000,000	10 Hz - audio
.01	10	10,000	10,000,000	100 Hz - audio
.001	1	1,000	1,000,000	1 KHz - audio
.0001	.1	100	100,000	10 KHz - audio
.00001	.01	10	10,000	100 KHz - long wave
.000001	.001	1	1,000	1 MHz - AM broadcast
	.0001	.1	100	10 MHz - short wave
	.00001	.01	10	100 MHz - VHF TV
		.001	1	1 GHz - radar
		.0001	.1	10 GHz - microwave
			.01	100 GHz - millimeter

Note that 0.01 nanoseconds or 10 picoseconds is the switching time of the Josephson junction, which operates only at very cold temperatures near absolute zero.

Note also that light travels one foot (actually, 11.77 inches) in 1 nanosecond in a vacuum. In a typical coaxial cable, the velocity of light is slowed to about ⅔ of its vacuum value, or about 8 inches in 1 nanosecond.

Table 37.2
Time Conversion Tables

Seconds and Larger

Century	Years	Weeks	Days	Hours	Minutes	Seconds
1	100+	5203	36,521	876,504	52,590,240	3,155,414,400
	1	52	365	8,760	525,600	31,536,000
		1	7	168	10,080	604,800
			1	24	1,440	86,400
				1	60	3,600
					1	60

Microcentury

Dr. Gernot Metze, the author's major professor at the University of Illinois at Urbana, described a microcentury as being about 52 minutes, or about the time of a typical college class hour.

SAS Comparison Operator (=:)

In the SAS language, if two character strings are compared with =: syntax, the comparison length is set by the shorter string. Thus, to find all jobs beginning with a string, use

```
IF JOB=:'AA' THEN...
```

Truncated Datetime Formats

SAS datetime formats are truncated on the right when the field length is under-specified. Since most procedures with a BY statement use the formatted value of the variable to group observations, this truncation can be exploited. To count jobs read in by date without creating a new variable, try

```
PROC FREQ DATA=PDB.JOBS;
    TABLES READTIME;
    FORMAT READTIME DATETIME7.;
```

which tabulates by date, printing READTIME as, say, 20FEB84.

To count jobs read in by date and hour, specify the format as DATETIME10., and READTIME prints 20FEB84:01. Daily is DATETIME7., hourly is DATETIME10., minutely is DATETIME13., and secondly is DATETIME16.

PROC FORMAT To Build a Format for Data Selection

With no table lookup facility in the SAS System, PROC FORMAT can be used to build a very effective lookup table that uses a binary search technique. For example, if a user asks for an analysis of a long list of job names, one choice is to use the TSO editor to make an IF statement with an expression for each name in the list:

```
IF JOB='A' OR JOB='B' OR JOB='C' .....
```

Even though this will work, when the list is long, it can be expensive to execute because all expressions in the IF statement are evaluated before any expression is tested. PROC FORMAT provides a much more effective method of selection because of its binary search. First, build a format named $TEST and assign the formatted value of '99' to the desired job names:

```
PROC FORMAT;
    VALUE $TEST
        'VECBWMJJ'='99'
        'ZEXACMSU'='99'
    ;
```

Once the format is created, it can be used as the lookup table with the PUT statement, as follows:

```
DATA FOUND;
    SET PDB.JOBS;
    CHAR=PUT(JOB,$TEST.);
    IF CHAR='99';
```

The PUT function stores the formatted value '99' in variable CHAR if the JOB value for an observation in PDB.JOBS is given a formatted value of '99' by PROC FORMAT. If the JOB variable is not found in format $TEST., CHAR contains the original value of the JOB variable. Thus, the formatted value must be set to a value that cannot occur in the data. (Use a numeric character for the formatted value of a field that must begin with a character, like job name.)

Under TSO, formats are slightly more complex because you must allocate two files for PROC FORMAT:

```
ALLOC F(SASLIB) DA(SASLIB) TRK SPACE(10) DIR(10)
ALLOC F(LIBRARY) DA(SASLIB)
```

Do not use a secondary extent on the allocation because the SAS System abends when it tries to find a format in the second extent. Repeated use of PROC FORMAT under TSO can fill the SASLIB data set and cause a D37 ABEND. In that case, compress SASLIB or scratch and reallocate.

Using SAS Formats To Store Data and Reduce Data Library Size

The CICS supplement to the original *Merrill's Guide* marked the first time that PROC FORMAT was used with Merrill's code to build SAS formats. Even though this raised the complexity of the system slightly, it was worthwhile, and the use of formats is now standard in MXG software because it reduces the size of the stored data. The use of formats for data storage is a power of the SAS System that should be fully understood and exploited wherever possible in your own SAS programs. However, you do not even have to understand formats to use them. The only additional requirement for using formats for data storage is that a SASLIB DD must point to the SASLIB data set built in the installation process. Without the SASLIB, a SAS error message, "FORMAT NOT FOUND" can result.

The following tutorial on formats describes how the author has chosen to name, build, and use formats to store data values. First, look at the SAS code to create a typical format:

```
PROC FORMAT;
VALUE $MG110TT
  A='A:AUTO INITIATED'
  C='C:CONVERSATIONAL'
  D='D:TRANSIENT DATA'
  T='T:NORMAL TERMINAL STARTED'
  Z='Z:PSEUDO CONVERSATIONAL'
;
```

The naming convention on all formats produced by MXG software begins (after the obligatory $ for formats with character variables) with the letters MG, followed by the three-position descriptor of the source record for which this format stores data. The final two positions of the format name, which must never end in a numeral are attempted acronyms (TT for transaction type in this example from the type 110 SMF record from CICS monitor factility). Note that in the value statement there is no period, but all format items must have a period when referenced. The format is named $MG110TT. in this example. The formatted value is constructed by concatenating the unformatted value with an explanation of that unformatted value. In this example, the unformatted value 'D' is assigned the formatted value 'D:TRANSIENT DATA'. This convention helps in communications when the actual value is needed. In addition, this practice makes it easy to test for specific values since the value is printed as the first character of the formatted value. If a data value that was not assigned a formatted value is encountered, then the unformatted value is printed. You assign a defined format to a variable (for example, TRANTYPE) with a FORMAT statement in the program that creates the variable TRANTYPE:

```
FORMAT TRANTYPE $MG110TT.;
```

Thereafter, when the variable TRANTYPE is printed, its formatted value is printed.

What has this accomplished? In the SAS data set, the length of the variable TRANTYPE is 1 byte, but whenever that variable is printed, you see the complete description of the encoded value of transaction type. Had you created a SAS variable to contain the decoded value of trantype instead, you would have a variable 25 bytes long in every transaction record on the SAS data base. With only 50,000 transactions a day, that would take over 65 tracks of 3350 space for that 1 variable. Instead, the formatted value can be stored in a format library that is built once, and the SAS data set has only 1 byte for the variable TRANTYPE.

In summary, using formats for storing common data is clearly justified in the savings of space in the SAS data libraries. Whenever you want to provide easily-read descriptions for certain values of SAS variables, PROC FORMAT should be used.

Note: the default destination of the format produced by PROC FORMAT is the load library that PDS pointed to by the LIBRARY DD. Close examination of the SAS JCL procedure shows that the LIBRARY DD is a temporary PDS that is also concatenated to the STEPLIB DD. PROC FORMAT writes the format to the temporary library; when the format is needed, the SAS System first searches any SASLIB DDs and then searches the STEPLIB.

Performance Considerations That Affect SAS Processing Costs

SAS processor utilization is extremely low; that is why you can afford to process millions of SMF records each week (or day, at large sites) and still provide cost-effective performance analysis. However, as with any large, comprehensive system, some options (GEN= and BLKSIZE=) exist that can cripple performance of MXG code, in particular, and most SAS code, in general; one option exists that seems valuable enough to be the default (SASLPA).

GEN=   The GEN= option sets the number of generations of SAS source kept in the SAS data library directory. When the SAS System creates a data set and GEN is nonzero, the SAS statements used to build the data set are written to the directory and can be seen with PROC CONTENTS. This is extremely valuable for many applications. For example, the pharmaceutical industry uses this feature to keep the data and analysis programs together. Globally, the SAS System does not permit the GEN= option to be reduced below 1. However, in programs like BUILDPDB, where several SAS data sets are merged as input to create more data sets as output, many tracks of SAS data library space can be eaten up with the source. For every data set built in the merged DATA step, the source for each of the merging SAS data sets is written when GEN=1 is specified. If GEN=2 is specified, the source that built each of the prior data sets is written, and so forth for larger GEN values. Any SAS execution, especially BUILDPDB, that uses

MERGE, UPDATE, or builds multiple SAS data sets from multiple SAS data sets, should use GEN=0 as an option in the EXEC statement. For a benchmark of the costs, see chapter thirty-two.

BLKSIZE=   The SAS BLKSIZE default is the only other option that causes CPU problems, and only then because it is specified too small. You can find the value in effect by executing PROC OPTIONS; remember to execute it once in batch mode and once under TSO because two separate default option lists exist. When you set the BLKSIZE= option equal to 0, the SAS System uses the device dependent values set by PROC SETINIT. SAS data libraries are sequential in access (although defined as RECFM=U to the operating system), and, thus, the recommendations offered in the second section of chapter forty-two for half-track blocking of sequential data on 3380s (blocksize of 23440) are appropriate. Note that this also makes more effective use of 3380 tracks than does the possible 32760 byte blocksize.

SASLPA   Install the SASLPA version of the SAS System. Check with the systems programmer who installed the SAS System at your installation and find out if the step to install the nonoverlaid version of the SAS supervisor was a part of the install process (it is flagged in the documentation as optional). If it was not done, insist that it be completed at least to the extent that a nonoverlaid supervisor (SASLPA) exists in your normal SAS base library if not in SYS1.LPALIB. Typical reductions on the order of 30% in both CPU and I/Os can be expected, although some tests have indicated reductions in CPU time of 60 to 70%, with similar reductions in the number of I/Os performed against the STEPLIB. Whereas it is perfectly possible to run MXG with the overlaid SAS supervisor, you should try the nonoverlaid version SASLPA.

chapter thirty-eight

Bibliography

SMF manual:

IBM. "MVS/Extended Architecture System Programming Library: System Management Facilities (SMF)." GC28-1153-1, modified by TNL GN28-0859 and TNL GN28-0885.

RMF manual:

IBM. "MVS/Extended Architecture Resource Measurement Facility (RMF) Reference and User's Guide." LC28-1138-0, for Licensed Program Number 5665-274, Version 3, Release 1.

CICS/VS monitor facilities:

IBM. "CICS/VS System Programmer's Guide." SC33-0071-2.

VM accounting records:

Denning, P. J. 1970. "Virtual Memory." *Computing Surveys*, vol. 2, no. 3.

DOS/VSE POWER:

IBM. "VSE/POWER Installation and Operations Guide." SH12-5379-3.

IMS:

Scholz, W. 1983. "Annotated IMS/VS Performance Reports." IBM, GG24-1559-1.

Queuing theory and statistics:

Allen O. 1978. *Probability, Statistics, and Queuing Theory with Computer Science Applications*. Academic Press. (Also stocked by IBM, SR29-0301-0.)

IBM. "Independent Study Program, Capacity Planning; Basic Models." SR20-7340-0. (Ghost authored by Dr. Arnold Allen.)

Sub-second response time:

Doherty, W. J., and R. P. Kelisky. 1979. "Managing VM/CMS Systems for User Effectiveness." IBM Systems Journal, vol. 18, no. 1.

Lambert, G.N. 1980. "Sub-second Response Time Study within an I.S. Environment." Internal IBM Report. This report can be obtained from:

G. N. Lambert
CAS Cycle Controller Manager, F24-5820
IBM Information Services Limited
Post Office Box 39
North Harbour, Portsmouth, PO6 3AA
United Kingdom

_____. 1984. "A Comparative Study of System Response Time on Program Developer Productivity." IBM System Journal, G321-0075, vol. 23, no 1.

Thadhani, A.J. 1981. "Interactive User Productivity." IBM System Journal, vol. 20, no. 4.

IBM. "The Economic Value of Rapid Response Time." GE20-0752-0.

IBM. 1983. "Interactive Computing: VM/CMS at IBM's Thomas J. Watson Research Center." G320-0080-0.

I/O paging:

Beretvas, T. "Page/Swap Configuration," *Proceedings of the CMG XIV International Conference.* This document can be obtained from:

Computer Measurement Group, Inc.
Post Office Box 26063
Phoenix, Arizona 85068

Bernardo, E. 1982. "MVS Performance Comparing 3880-11, 3380, and 3350 Paging Configurations." IBM, GG22-9266-0.

Candle Computer Company. 1982. *Candle Computer Report*, vol. 4, no. 8.

_____. 1984. *Candle Computer Report*, vol. 5, no. 9. Both reports can be obtained from:

Candle Corporation
10880 Wilshire Boulevard
Suite 2404
Los Angeles, Ca. 90024

Friesenborg, S. E. "DASD Path and Device Contention." IBM, GG22-2861-0.

————. 1981. "DASD Access Method Performance Considerations." IBM, GG22-9264-00.

Henning, P. J. "Using Data Facility Device Support for DASD Space Management." *Washington Systems Center Technical Bulletin.* IBM, GG22-9306-0.

Benchmark measurement techniques and numeric comparisons:

Bauer, T., P. Dorn, and R. Wicks. 1983. "Comparison of MVS/SP Version 1 Release 3 (MVS/370) to MVS/SP Version 2 Release 1.0 (MVS/XA) on the IBM 3081K." IBM, GG22-9325-00.

Capacity planning:

Bronner, L. 1980. "Capacity Planning Basic Hand Analysis." IBM, GG22-9344-00.

Wicks, R. J. 1982. "Balanced Systems and Capacity Planning." IBM, GG22-9299-0.

Conversion:

IBM. 1983. "MVS/Extended Architecture Conversion Notebook." GC28-1143-1.

Initialization and tuning:

IBM. 1984. "MVS/Extended Architecture System Programming Library: Initialization and Tuning." GC28-1149-1 and TNL GN28-0912.

IBM. "MVS Conversion Guide." GC78-0689-6.

chapter thirty-nine

SAS Primer

This primer's purpose is to explain the SAS code in this book. Statements of the language are not exhaustively described; for more information about the SAS language, consult the *SAS User's Guide: Basics,* which is available from SAS Institute.

Two logical states While the SAS System is executing, it is in one of two states. Either it is building a SAS data set, or it is analyzing a SAS data set with a SAS procedure, which could also build a new SAS data set.

The DATA statement signals the beginning of building a data set; the PROC statement signals the beginning of analyzing a data set.

A logical piece of work to the SAS System consists of all SAS statements between a DATA or PROC statement and the next DATA or PROC statement. One SAS System interprets those statements when it encounters the second DATA or PROC statement and performs the requested functions at that time. Then the SAS System continues to scan the statements for the next DATA or PROC statement, and the process continues until all the DATA and PROC steps in the job have been completed.

SAS statements All SAS statements are free-form. Columns 1 through 80 are scanned (columns 1 through 72 of line-numbered records), and a semicolon delimits each statement. There is no continuation symbol; the absence of a semicolon indicates a continued statement. The SAS System permits multiple statements on a single line, and blank lines can be inserted with no effect. Blanks must separate keywords and names, but they are not required between special characters and keywords or names. Where a single blank is permitted, any number of blanks can occur.

SAS names Names of data sets, files, variables, and so forth are limited to eight characters and must begin with an alphabetic character or underscore. Unlike languages such as PL/1, the same name can be used repeatedly in a SAS program for different purposes. For example, the name can be the same for a SAS data set, a SAS variable within that data set, and a label in the program.

SAS data sets The SAS System stores its data in direct-access **BDAM OS** data sets on disk or in **BSAM OS** data sets on tape. A single **OS** data set used by the SAS System (called a SAS data library) can contain a number of SAS data sets. Each SAS data set is a collection of **observations**, which may be regarded as rows of a matrix. Each observation of a data set is a collection of **variables**, with names assigned by the user, and each variable can be regarded as a column of a matrix. The number of variables is constant for all observations, although some observations can have missing values for some variables.

An Example DATA Step

```
DATA TYPE434(KEEP=JOB READTIME CPUTI);
   LENGTH DEFAULT=4 READTIME 8;
   FORMAT READTIME DATETIME19.2 CONDCODE HEX3.;
   INFILE SMF STOPOVER LENGTH=LEN COL=COL
          RECFM=VBS LRECL=32756;
   INPUT @2 ID PIB1. @3 SMFTIME SMFSTAMP8.
          @23 READDATE PD4. @16 JOB $8. @;
   IF ID=34 OR ID=4;
   IF ID=4 THEN DO;
      EXCPTOT=SUM(EXCP2314,EXCP3330,EXCP3350);
      RIGHTBIT=MOD(BYTE,2);
      LEFTBIT=FLOOR(BYTE/128);
      END;
   OUTPUT TYPE434;
```

DATA step   A SAS DATA step takes input data, which could be an OS data set on tape or disk, a previously built SAS data set, or any combination of any number of OS or SAS data sets, and builds one or more new data sets. The statements above, although not a complete DATA step, are examples of typical SAS statements used to read an SMF data set and build a single data set. Each statement is described below.

```
DATA TYPE434(KEEP=JOB READTIME CPUTI);
```

DATA statement   The DATA statement tells the SAS System to invoke the SAS compiler and names the SAS data set to be built (TYPE434). Additionally, options can be stated through the parenthetical expression. In this example, the KEEP= option is used, which causes only the variables JOB, READTIME, and CPUTI to be kept in data set TYPE434.

```
LENGTH DEFAULT=4 READTIME 8;
```

LENGTH statement   SAS numeric variables are stored as floating-point numbers. The default length is 8 bytes (double precision); however, in SMF applications, there is seldom a need for that accuracy, and significant disk space can be saved by using the LENGTH statement. Here, the default for all numeric variables being built in this DATA step is changed to 4. At the same time, however, the READTIME variable is kept at a length of 8 because the date and time (to hundredths of a second) require a full 8 bytes.

```
FORMAT READTIME DATETIME19.2 CONDCODE HEX3.;
```

FORMAT statement   You can associate formats for output from SAS variables at the time the data set is built, and these formats are then used unless overridden by another FORMAT statement. The SAS System has an extensive collection of date, time, and datetime formats, as well as a series of functions for constructing dates and times. In this FORMAT statement, the DATETIME19.2 format converts the value of READTIME, which is the number of seconds since January 1, 1960, to print out as

```
04JUL79:12:23:02.34
```

```
INFILE SMF STOPOVER LENGTH=LEN COL=COL
   RECFM=VBS LRECL=32756;
```

INFILE statement   The INFILE statement names the DD (input file name or Data Definition) containing the data to be read. In addition, several options can be specified. The name SMF refers to the DD statement in the JCL that describes the OS data set to the operating system.

STOPOVER   The SAS System permits a user to read more than one logical record with one INPUT statement. This can occur if an incomplete record is written to SMF. The STOPOVER option causes the SAS System to stop processing if it is directed to read beyond the present logical record, and it causes the bad record to be printed on the SAS log.

LENGTH= option   The LENGTH= option allows the user to specify a variable name (here, LEN) that contains the length of the logical record being processed. The LENGTH= option is needed to process some SMF records because the user must know the length in order to identify which release of the operating system wrote the record; there are often field relocations between releases.

COL= option   The COL= option allows the user to specify a variable name (here, COL) that will contain the current position of the pointer to the input record (that is, the current column). This feature is needed in SMF processing to take care of different releases and to prevent STOPOVER errors from occurring.

RECFM= and LRECL= options   The DCB attributes of the input file can be specified on the INFILE statement, in the DD statement in the JCL, or in the data set label on the tape or disk SMF file. However, since the attributes may not be correct on the data set, the correct attributes are also specified here using RECFM= and LRECL= options.

```
INPUT @2 ID PIB1. @3 SMFTIME SMFSTAMP8.
      @23 READDATE PD4. @16 JOB $8. @;
```

INPUT statement   The INPUT statement extracts data from the OS records based on the input format specified for each variable and stores them in SAS variables created by the INPUT statement. The @ symbol sends the pointer to the desired column. The variable ID is then named, and its format on the OS record is given (PIB1., for positive integer binary of length 1 byte). Similarly, the variable SMFTIME is found starting in the third column or byte of the OS record, and a special format, SMFSTAMP8., converts the 4-byte date and 4-byte time into a SAS datetime value. At column 23, the read date, with an OS packed decimal format of length 4, is stored in the READDATE variable. And at column 16, the JOB variable, with a character string of length 8, is picked up. The last item in the INPUT statement, a trailing @ sign, causes the SAS system to remain on the same input record for the next INPUT statement.

```
IF ID=34 or ID=4;
```

Subsetting IF statement   The IF statement is a shorthand form of the IF-THEN statement (see below). If the expression is true, execution continues. If the expression is not true, no further processing occurs for the current record, it is not added to the data set being built, and the SAS program returns to get the next input record.

```
IF ID=4 THEN DO;
   EXCPTOT=SUM(EXCP2314,EXCP3330,EXCP3350);
   RIGHTBIT=MOD(BYTE,2);
   LEFTBIT=FLOOR(BYTE/128);
   END;
```

IF-THEN statement   The IF-THEN statement controls the logic flow of a SAS DATA step. With Boolean connectives (AND, OR, NOT), the expression tested can be highly complex and yet compact. In the example above, the result of a true expession (ID=4) is the execution of a DO-group. The expression can be any SAS expression, and the statement can be any executable statement. The SAS System permits both the spelled-out Boolean connectives (AND, OR, NOT), as well as their symbols from the sixty-four-character set (&, |, ¬), and the symbols and characters can be intermixed. Furthermore, the SAS System supports bounded expressions such as

```
IF 70 < = ID < = 79 THEN TYPE='RMF';
```

DO group   A DO group is a sequence of SAS statements preceded by

```
DO;
```

and terminated by

```
END;
```

The statements within the DO group are sequentially executed when the DO statement is executed, and DO groups are most commonly executed conditionally, as the earlier example shows.

```
EXCPTOT=SUM(EXCP2314,EXCP3330,EXCP3350);
```

SUM function   The SUM function is used to add variables that might have missing values. For example, if the number of EXCPs to 2314s could be missing, the statement

```
EXCPTOT=EXCP2314+EXCP3330+EXCP3350;
```

would cause EXCPTOT to have a missing value each time one or more of the three values are missing. If the SUM function is used, the value of EXCPTOT is the sum of the nonmissing values. If the statement is written

```
EXCPTOT=SUM(EXCP2314,EXCP3330,EXCP3350,0);
```

EXCPTOT would be zero rather than missing, even if all three EXCPs are missing.

```
RIGHTBIT=MOD(BYTE,2);
```

MOD function   The MOD function returns the modulo (remainder) of the first argument when the first argument is divided by the second argument. The example causes RIGHTBIT to have the value 1 if BYTE is odd and the value of 0 if BYTE is even.

```
LEFTBIT=FLOOR(BYTE/128);
```

FLOOR function   The FLOOR function returns the largest integer that is less than or equal to the argument. In the example above, LEFTBIT has the value

1 if BYTE is greater than 127 and less than 256 (assuming BYTE is read in with a format of PIB1.) and the value 0 if BYTE is less than or equal to 127. The FLOOR function is also used to truncate the fraction portion of a numeric value. The FLOOR function was extensively used for bit testing before BIT literal values were available in the SAS System.

```
OUTPUT TYPE434;
```

OUTPUT statement   The OUTPUT statement permits the user to tell the SAS System when to add the current observation to the SAS data set being built. In the case of multiple output data sets, the OUTPUT statement names the SAS data set to which the observation is added. If a SAS program contains no OUTPUT statement, each observation is automatically added to the SAS data set when the last statement is executed or when a RETURN statement is encountered.

Other SAS Statements and Features

RETURN statement   The RETURN statement has two distinct uses in the SAS System. When a LINK statement has been executed and a RETURN statement is encountered, the SAS System returns to the statement following the LINK statement. When no LINK statement has been executed, the RETURN statement causes the SAS System to return to get the next record. In addition, when no OUTPUT statements appear in the SAS program, the RETURN statement causes the SAS System to add the current observation to the SAS data set being built. Internally, a RETURN statement is automatically added as the last statement of each SAS program.

```
X = . ;
```

Missing values   The concept of a missing value of a variable is quite important in the SAS System and especially important in SMF analysis, where missing values are frequent. In the SAS System, there is a distinction made between a zero value and a nonexistent value. For example, an initiation time of zero would have a missing value. Internally, numeric missing values have the value of the smallest possible negative value.

To prevent incorrect statistics, the SAS System also ensures integrity in arithmetic operations. Arithmetic operations on missing values result in a missing value. Therefore, you must be aware of the possibility of missing values. If a numeric value can be missing and it appears in an arithmetic statement, you must take other steps; for example, use the SUM function.

The symbol for setting or testing missing variables is the period:

```
IF X=. THEN MISS='YES';
```

Note that the period is not enclosed in quotes; to do so would be to make the test a character test for period rather than a numeric test for a missing value. For character variables, the missing value is a blank character string.

RETAIN statement   At the beginning of execution of each SAS DATA step, the SAS System sets all variables to missing values and then begins to input or assign values. Therefore, a value read in is not inadvertently retained from one observation to the next. If, however, you want to retain the value of a variable from one observation to the next, name the variable in a RETAIN statement.

Date, time, and datetime values and functions   The SAS System provides extensive facilities for reading and manipulating dates, times, and datetime values. Dates are stored as the number of days since January 1, 1960; through formats, the date can be printed. For date comparisons and tests, the desired test values must be converted into SAS dates via SAS functions. In addition, in SMF, most dates are contained as Julian dates in a packed decimal field, requiring a conversion into SAS internal dates. Two methods are used in MSG code:

```
INPUT DATE PD4.;
IF DATE=79034;
```

or

```
INPUT DATE PD4.;
SASDATE=DATEJUL(DATE);
IF SASDATE=MDY(02,03,1979);
```

SAS time values are stored internally as seconds, and a number of formats to print them is provided. There are also functions for conversion:

```
INPUT TIME HHMM5.;      (input value would be 10:15)
IF TIME=HMS(10,15,0);
```

SAS datetime values are stored as the number of seconds since January 1, 1960. Since many of the time functions or formats operate on a modulo 24-hour basis, many are applicable to datetime values as well. However, the date functions are not constructed to handle the date portion of a SAS datetime value directly, so two special functions exist for partitioning datetime values:

```
DATE=DATEPART(DATETIME);
TIME=TIMEPART(DATETIME);
```

Finally, there is a generating function that allows the user to create a SAS date-time value:

```
DATETIME=DHMS(MDY(02,03,1984),10,15,0);
```

to create a datetime value. When printed with the DATETIME13. format, the value printed is

```
02FEB84:10:15.
```

Since the date and time formats truncate from the right (rather than round) when the format underspecifies the field, storing the SMF time and date combinations as SAS datetime values and then using SAS formats to control BY grouping is useful. Specifically, if a datetime value is formatted DATETIME7., the data can be clustered by date, without loss of the full datetime value.

The SMFSTAMP8. input format was created for reading SMF data. The SMFSTAMP8. format reads the Julian date from four packed decimal bytes and then reads the time of day from the next four bytes and converts the eight bytes directly into a SAS datetime value. You must associate the format DATETIME19.2 with the variable to print its complete value.

A final observation on dates, times, and datetimes: in handling SMF data, dates and times can be stored in variables with a length (using the LENGTH statement) of 4 bytes. For a datetime value, however, the value is truncated unless a length of 8 bytes is specified. Therefore, all LENGTH statements use DEFAULT=4 and then list the datetime variables that are to have a length of 8.

SET statement   The SET statement is like the INPUT statement except that its input is from a previously built SAS data set rather than raw OS records. In addition, multiple SAS data sets can be brought together through the SET statement. There are two ways to combine multiple data sets using a SET statement, depending on whether a BY statement is present:

```
DATA ALL;
    SET DAILY WEEKLY MONTHLY;
```

Data set ALL contains all observations of DAILY, followed by all observations of WEEKLY, and finally observations of MONTHLY. Without a BY statement, the SET statement concatenates the SAS data sets in the order listed.

```
DATA ALLJOBS;
    SET LASTWEEK THISWEEK;
    BY READTIME;
```

The new data set ALLJOBS is the interleaved combination of LASTWEEK and THISWEEK, sorted by READTIME (both LASTWEEK and THISWEEK must already be sorted by READTIME).

Following the SET (or BY statement, if used), other SAS statements can be used to subset the data.

The real power of the SET statement (and also the MERGE statement, below) lies in the special variables that can be established by the user. Consider this example:

```
DATA OK535S OK434S;
  SET TYPE535(IN=IN535) TYPE434(IN=IN434);
  BY READTIME JOB;
  IF FIRST.JOB THEN DO;
    FOUNDJOB=0;
    RETAIN FOUNDJOB;
    IF IN535 THEN FOUNDJOB=1;
  END;
  IF FOUNDJOB THEN DO;
    IF IN434 THEN OUTPUT OK434S;
    IF IN535 THEN OUTPUT OK535S;
  END;
  ELSE PUT JOB= READTIME= ' DID NOT HAVE A JOB RECORD ';
```

Two new data sets (OK535S and OK434S) are built using the two data sets TYPE535 and TYPE434 as input. The IN= option is used in the SET statement to create two new variables (IN535 and IN434) that are associated with the two data sets: the variable is set to 1 (true) if the current values of the BY variable are contained in its associated data set, and it is set to 0 (false) otherwise.

The statement following the BY statement exposes another class of special variables, the FIRST. and LAST. variables. FIRST. or LAST. variables are associated with every variable in the BY statement, and they are used to determine whether an observation is the first or last occurrence of the value of that BY variable. In this example, observations are output to OK434S and OK535S only if the first observation encountered was a JOB (5 or 35) record by storing and retaining a 1 in variable FOUNDJOB. (Note that FIRST.JOB is logically true if the READTIME variable changes so that only the last variable needs to be tested.)

MERGE statement   Depending on your computer background, you may or may not consider the MERGE statement correctly named. The MERGE statement is syntactically similar to the SET statement, and it is used to combine multiple SAS data sets into one or more new data sets. However, it does not function like the merge in Sort/Merge; that facility of interleaving records is done with the SET statement and a BY statement in the SAS program.

The MERGE statement in the SAS program takes observations from several input SAS data sets that have common values of BY variables and creates one observation containing all the variables in the input SAS data sets. Therefore, the function of the MERGE statement is to merge variables from several data sets into one data set. The IN= option and the FIRST. and LAST. variables can be used like they are with the SET statement. The following example demonstrates the results with the MERGE statement in a typical application.

SAS data set JOBS			SAS data set STEPS		
JOB	ACCOUNT		JOB	PROGRAM	CPUTCBTM
a	123456789		a	SAS	10:30.02
b	234567890		a	IEDCAMS	:20.01
d	456789012		b	IEBGENER	:15.03
e	467890123		c	TESTPGM	:02.00
			d	DEBE	:01.00

```
DATA PFMACCTS;
  MERGE JOBS(IN=INJ)STEPS(IN=INS);
  BY JOB;
  IF INJ AND INS THEN OUTPUT;
```

SAS data set PGMACCTS

JOB	ACCOUNT	PROGRAM	CPUTCBTM
a	123456789	SAS	10:30.02
a	123456789	IEDCAMS	:20.01
b	234567890	IEBGENER	:13.03
d	456789012	DEBE	:01.00

SAS data set PGMACCTS (no IF statement)

JOB	ACCOUNT	PROGRAM	CPUTCBTM
a	123456789	SAS	10:30.02
a	123456789	IEDCAMS	:20.01
b	234567890	IEBGENER	:13.03
c		TESTPGM	:02.00
d	456789012	DEBE	:02.00
e	467890123		

Procedure step The PROC step (as differentiated from the DATA step) is signified by the presence of a PROC statement that requests the SAS System to execute a particular load module. The procedure step is the statistical power of the SAS System, just as the DATA step is the data-handling power. Several statistical procedures are used heavily in handling SMF. A discussion of the statistical routines is presented below to assist in reading the code in this book.

PROC statement   The PROC statement varies slightly between procedures, but generally it has the following features:

```
PROC procname DATA=input OUT=outputoptions
```

The procname is the load module that is linked to (a true link is issued, and, thus, non-SAS modules can be accessed via a PROC statement). The DATA= option, if supplied, specifies the SAS data set to be processed by the procedure (if the DATA= option is not present, then the most recently created SAS data set is used). The OUT= option applies to some procedures that build output data sets, and it permits you to name the new data set.

For each procedure there are options that can be specified. A common option for many procedures is NOPRINT, which suppresses printed output of the procedure, and usually accompanies an OUT= option when a procedure is used to create a new data set.

BY statement   The BY statement can be used with all procedures and is a very powerful tool for clustering observations. It causes the procedure to be invoked for each group of BY variables that has common values. For example, the statements

```
PROC PLOT;
   PLOT TIME*VALUE;
   BY DATE;
```

produce a separate plot (graph) for each value of DATE encountered.

VAR (VARIABLES) statement   You can restrict the SAS System to certain variables in the data set being processed by using the VAR statement.

FORMAT statement   The same FORMAT statement described under the DATA step can be associated with a procedure execution. The difference is that when a format is associated with a variable in the PROC step, the format association exists only for the life of the procedure and does not permanently alter the variable's format. FORMAT statements are used heavily with the FREQ and PRINT procedures.

PRINT procedure   The PRINT procedure is the most frequently used SAS procedure in SMF analysis. It prints all the variables in a SAS data set (or those variables specified in a VAR statement). A commonly used option is the PAGE option, which, when a BY statement is used, causes each new BY-group to start on a new page:

```
PROC PRINT PAGE DATA=TYPE535;
  BY ACCOUNT;
  VAR CPUTCBTM CPUSRBTM JOB READTIME;
```

The PRINT procedure formats the page based on the device you are using. (For example, if you print to a 3270-type TSO terminal with 80 positions, the SAS System knows the line width, formats the output appropriately, and attempts to make the printed page as readable as possible. In fact, if the variable names are long and the data values short, the SAS System prints the variable names vertically so that all the data fit on a single line. Most printed reports are produced with simple PROC PRINTs.

SAS release 82 offered major enhancements to report writing with PROC PRINT by allowing users to replace the variable name with the variable's label as the column heading. SAS variable labels are created with the LABEL statement, either when the data set is built or when the PROC is executed. If an asterisk (*) is properly located in the label itself and if the PROC PRINT statement specifies that the asterisk is to be used as the split character, the label is split into three lines of column heading on the report:

```
PROC PRINT SPLIT='*';
  LABEL READTIME='TSO*LOGON*TIMEOFDAY';
```

SORT procedure The SORT procedure is used to rearrange the observations in a data set in order of values of some variable.

```
PROC SORT DATA=IN OUT=OUT;
  BY JOB DESCENDING DATE;
```

In the absence of the OUT= option, the SAS System sorts and restores the data in the input data set. The BY statement describes the sort fields, and the option DESCENDING (since it is nine characters long, there can be no ambiguity with a variable name) describes those variables that are to be sorted in descending order instead of default ascending order.

MEANS procedure The MEANS procedure provides univariate statistics and can also build an output data set. The statements

```
PROC MEANS DATA=IN NOPRINT;
  VAR CPU EXCPS ELAPSED;
  OUTPUT OUT=STATS
    SUM=SUMCPU SUMEXCPS SUMELAP
    MAX=MAXCPU MAXEXCPS MAXELAP;
```

produce a new data set named STATS, which contains a single observation (since there is no BY statement) with six variables. The choice of statistics output by the MEANS procedure is determined by the keywords used in the OUTPUT statement. The SUM= option gives, in left-to-right order, the new variable names containing the sum of the values of the variables in the VAR statement. Therefore, the position of the variables in the VAR statement and the OUTPUT statement must match exactly. Similarly, the three variables MAXCPU, MAXEXCPS, and MAXELAP contain the maximum value of the three corresponding variables.

FREQ procedure   The FREQ procedure is used to produce frequency distributions and crosstabulations. It is heavily used for the early scanning of data to determine anomalies, but it is also used to produce tabulations. Since it used the format of the variable to cluster its observations, it is also very flexible. The statements

```
PROC FREQ;
   TABLES READTIME;
   FORMAT READTIME DATETIME7.;
```

produce a tabulation of the read-in time for jobs. The count of jobs read in each day is given, as well as the percentages and cumulative frequencies of job counts. With the WEIGHT statement however, the FREQ procedure weights each observation by the value of the WEIGHT variable; therefore, the statements

```
PROC FREQ;
   TABLES READTIME;
   FORMAT READTIME DATETIME7.;
   WEIGHT CPUTM;
```

provide the distribution of CPU time used for each date on which jobs were read in.

Crosstabulation is very useful in determining who is doing what since it displays the occurrences of each value of the crosstabulated variables. Crosstabulation is invoked by connecting the variables with an asterisk in the TABLES statement. For example, the statements

```
PROC FREQ;
   TABLES JOBCLASS*ACCOUNT;
```

provide a table showing which accounts used which job classes.

PLOT procedure   The PLOT procedure provides a simple tool for producing graphs and plots of data:

```
PROC PLOT;
   PLOT CPUTCBTM*SELAPSTM;
```

Other procedures are also useful for analyzing SMF data. For more information about them, refer to the *SAS User's Guide: Basics* and *SAS User's Guide: Statistics*.

chapter forty

Description and Contents of SAS Data Sets Built by MXG

Each MXG data set that is built from raw data records is described in complete detail in this chapter. This chapter, with its expanded descriptions, is a complete rewrite of the appendices in the original *Merrill's Guide*. The material is arranged in sections, and the data sets are in alphabetical order. Each section is similar in structure. First the data set is described, and then details of observations built and variables created in each data set are discussed. There are many tutorials in these sections, and frequent examples of how these data can be used to answer management questions are presented.

Every CPE analyst should read this chapter in its entirety just to comprehend the wide range of events described in the data sources available to MXG. The time spent will pay high dividends for the one-time investment of the reading time.

Of course its universal purpose is to describe what data are contained in what variable and in what data set, and, where necessary, to expound on the use or meaning of various data values that variables might have. Every variable that is kept in every MXG data set (built from raw OS-read infile) is described here; the chapter was built by SAS code after the execution of JCLTEST, using UTILXREF to build a data set of descriptions of the SAS variables and their data sets. The text descriptions were matched with the cross-reference data set to ensure that every variable was documented and created by MXG software.

Other data sets built by MXG software (usually from previously built MXG data sets) are described in this chapter.

The sections of this chapter are listed below.

Data Set	Type Title	Source
TYPE0	IPL	0
TYPE0203	Dump Program Header or Trailer	2,3
TYPE434	TSO/JOB Step Termination	4,34
TYPE535	Job Termination/Session Logoff	5,35
TYPE6	Output Writer	6

TYPE7	Lost SMF Data	7
TYPE8911	Devices On-line at IPL or Varied On- or Off-line	8,9,11
TYPE10	Allocation Recovery	10
TYPE1415	Non-VSAM Data Set Activity	14,15
TYPE16	Sort or Merge Statistics	16
TYPE1718	Non-VSAM Data Set Scratch or Rename	17,18
TYPE19	DASD Volume	19
TYPE20	Job TSO Initiation	20
TYPE21	Tape Error Statistics by Volume (ESV)	21
TYPE22_1	CPU Configuration	22
TYPE22_2	MVS/370 Physical Channel Configuration	22
TYPE22_3	Storage Configuration	22
TYPE22_4	MSS Configuration at IPL	22
TYPE22_5	Configuration at VARY ONLINE, S	22
TYPE22_6	Configuration at VARY OFFLINE, S	22
TYPE22_7	Channel Path Configuration	22
TYPE22_8	Reconfigured Channel Path	22
TYPE23	SMF Buffer Statistics	23
TYPE25	JES3 Device Allocation	25
TYPE26J2	JES2 Purge Record	26
TYPE26J3	JES3 Purge Record	26
TYPE30_1	TYPE30 Job Initiation	30
TYPE30_4	Work Termination	30
TYPE30_5	TYPE30 Job or Session Job Termination	30
TYPE30_6	TYPE30 System Address Space	30
TYPE30_D	DD Segment Detail	30
TYPE30_V	Interval Accounting	30
TYPE31	TSO Initialization	31
TYPE32	TSO Command Record	32
TYPE38EX	Exception Statistics	38
TYPE38IN	Interval Resource Statistics	38
TYPE38NC	NCP Resource Statistics	38

TYPE40	Dynamic Allocation	40
TYPE43PC	VSPC Start/Modify/Stop	43
TYPE4345	JES2 Start/Stop	43,45
TYPE47PC	VSPC User Logon	47
TYPE4789	Remote Job Entry Session	47,48,49
TYPE48PC	VSPC User Logoff	48
TYPE49PC	VSPC Security	49
TYPE50	VTAM Tuning Statistics	50
TYPE5234	Remote Job Entry Session (JES2 SNA)	52,53,54
TYPE5568	Network Job Entry Accounting	55,56,58
TYPE57J2	JES2 Network SYSOUT Transmission	57
TYPE57J3	JES3 Network SYSOUT Transmission	57
TYPE60	Updated VSAM Volume Data Set	60
TYPE6156	Integrated Catalog Facility (ICF) Activity	61,65,66
TYPE62	VSAM Component or Cluster Opened	62
TYPE6367	VSAM Entry Defined or Deleted	63,67
TYPE64	VSAM Component or Cluster Status	64
TYPE68	VSAM Entry Renamed	68
TYPE69	VSAM Data Space Defined, Extended, or Deleted	69
TYPE70	RMF CPU Activity and Address Space Statistics	70
TYPE71	RMF Paging and Swapping Activity	71
TYPE72	RMF Workload Activity	72
TYPE73	MVS/XA Physical Channels Activity	73
TYPE73L	MVS/370 Logical Channel Activity	73
TYPE73P	MVS/370 Physical Channel Activity	73
TYPE74	RMF Device Activity	74
TYPE75	RMF Page and Swap Data Set Activity	75
TYPE76	Trace Record	76
TYPE77	Enqueue Records	77
TYPE78	MVS/XA Device Queuing Statistics	78

TYPE78CF	MVS/XA Device Configuration	78
TYPE78PA	MVS/XA Virtual Storage (Private Area) Statistics	78
TYPE78SP	MVS/XA Virtual Storage (Private Area Subpool) Statistics	78
TYPE78VS	MVS/XA Virtual Storage Statistics	78
TYPE79	RMF Monitor II Activity	79
TYPE80	RACF Processing Record	80
TYPE81	RACF Initialization Record	81
TYPE82	Security (CRYPTO Facility) Record	82
TYPE90	Operator Commands Record	90
CICSACCT	CICS CMF Accounting Record	110
CICSEXCE	CICS CMF Exception Record	110
CICSTRAN	CICS CMF Transaction Resource and Response	110
CICSYSTM	CICS CMF Global Performance	110
CIMSTRAN	CONTROL/IMS Transaction Response and Resources	C/IMS
CIMSPROG	CONTROL/IMS Program Resources	C/IMS
CIMSDBDS	CONTROL/IMS Data Base Call Activity	C/IMS
TSOMSYST	TSO/MON System User Interval Response and Resources	TSO/MON
TSOMCALL	TSO/MON Program Call and Command Response and Resources	TSO/MON
DOSJOBS	DOS/VSE POWER Job Step Execution Resources	VSE/POWER
DOSLIST	DOS/VSE POWER Printing Resources	VSE/POWER
DOSPUNCH	DOS/VSE POWER Punch Resources	VSE/POWER
DOSREAD	DOS/VSE POWER Read-in Resources	VSE/POWER
DOSRJE	DOS/VSE POWER Bisync Remote Job Entry Resources	VSE/POWER
DOSSNA	DOS/VSE POWER SNA Remote Job Entry Resources	VSE/POWER
VMDEVICE	VM Device Attach	VMACCT
VMDISK	VM Failed Disk Attach	VMACCT

VMLINK	VM Failed Link	VMACCT
VMLOGON	VM Failed Log On	VMACCT
VMSESSN	VM Virtual Machine Session Resources	VMACCT
VMUSRDAT	VM User Created Data	VMACCT
VMVCNA	VM VCNA Session	VMACCT

CICSACCT
CICS CMF Account Record

The CICSACCT data set contains one observation for each accounting class record from a type 110 record. Accounting data are accumulated for each combination of transaction name (TRANNAME), terminal identification (TERMINAL), and operator identification (OPERATOR). The accumulated accounting data include only the message counts, transaction counts, and number of abending transactions. Since the records contain no other resource data, their use is questionable. Furthermore, they contain only the ending time of the interval being reported.

Variable	Type	Length	Format	Label
APPLID	CHAR	8		VTAM*APPLICATION*NAME

VTAM application identification.

| INMSGCNT | NUM | 4 | | INPUT*MESSAGE*COUNT |

number of input messages.

| OPERATOR | CHAR | 3 | | OPERATOR*NAME*CODE |

operator identification.

| SMFTIME | NUM | 8 | DATETIME19.2 | SMF*RECORD*TIME STAMP |

time stamp at which type 110 SMF record containing observation was written. It is the same for all observations contained in the same SMF record.

| SYSTEM | CHAR | 4 | 4. | SYSTEM*ID |

identification of system on which CICS was executing.

| TERMINAL | CHAR | 4 | | TERMINAL*NAME |

terminal identification.

| TRANABND | NUM | 4 | | TRANSACTION*ABENDING*COUNT |

number of transaction abends.

| TRANCNT | NUM | 4 | | TRANSACTION*COUNT |

number of transactions.

| TRANNAME | CHAR | 4 | | TRANSACTION*NAME |

transaction name.

Variable	Type	Length	Format	Label
TRANTYPE	CHAR	8	MG110TT25.	TRANSACTION*TYPE

transaction type:
    A=A:auto initiated
    C=C:conversational
    D=D:transient data
    T=T:normal terminal started
    Z=Z:pseudo conversational.

Variable	Type	Length	Format	Label
USRCNT	NUM	4		USER*COUNT*FIELD

user count field. Zero unless filled in by installation modification.

CICSEXCE
CICS CMF Exception Record

The CICSEXCE data set contains one observation for each exception class record from a type 110 record and provides data on specific exceptional conditions raised by a transaction: VSAM queuing, ISAM overflow file waits, or temporary storage waits. The transaction causing the exception record can be selected from the CICSTRAN data set by the common value of TASKNR. More than one exception record can be produced for a single transaction, and all have the same value of TASKNR in both CICSEXCE and DIDSTRAN data sets.

Variable	Type	Length	Format	Label
APPLID	CHAR	8		VTAM*APPLICATION*NAME

VTAM application identification.

ISAMFILE	CHAR	8		FILE NAME*WITH ISAM*OVERFLOW

name of file with ISAM overflow records.

MSREQWT	NUM	4		GETMAIN*REQUESTED*AND WAITED

total amount of main storage requested but waited.

MSWAITCN	NUM	4		GETMAIN*WAITS

number of waits for main storage.

MSWAITTM	NUM	4	TIME12.2	GETMAIN*WAIT*DURATION

main storage wait time.

OPERATOR	CHAR	3		OPERATOR*NAME*CODE

operator identification.

SMFTIME	NUM	8	DATETIME19.2	SMF*RECORD*TIME STAMP

time stamp at which type 110 SMF record containing observation was written. It is the same for all observations contained in the same SMF record.

SYSTEM	CHAR	4	4.	SYSTEM*ID

identification of system on which CICS was executing.

TASEXCNR	NUM	4		EXCEPTION*NUMBER*FOR THIS TASK

number of exception record for task (1st, 2nd, and so forth exception).

TASKNR	NUM	4		TASK*NUMBER

task sequence identification number. This number is TCAKCTTA value from the TCA. This value can be matched to the same named variable in the SAS data set CICSTRAN so the transaction causing this exception can be examined.

Variable	Type	Length	Format	Label
TERMINAL	CHAR	4		TERMINAL*NAME

terminal identification.

Variable	Type	Length	Format	Label
TRANNAME	CHAR	4		TRANSACTION*NAME

transaction name.

Variable	Type	Length	Format	Label
TRANTYPE	CHAR	8	MG110TT25.	TRANSACTION*TYPE

transaction type:
   A=A:auto initiated
   C=C:conversational
   D=D:transient data
   T=T:normal terminal started
   Z=Z:pseudo conversational.

Variable	Type	Length	Format	Label
TSREQWT	NUM	4		TEMP STORAGE*REQUESTED*AND WAITED

total amount of temporary storage requested.

Variable	Type	Length	Format	Label
TSWAITCN	NUM	4		TEMP*STORAGE*WAITS

number of temporary storage waits.

Variable	Type	Length	Format	Label
TSWAITTM	NUM	4	TIME12.2	TEMP STORAGE*WAIT*DURATION

temporary storage wait time.

Variable	Type	Length	Format	Label
VSAMFILE	CHAR	8		FILE NAME*WITH VSAM*STRING WAIT

name of file waiting for VSAM string.

Variable	Type	Length	Format	Label
VSWAITCN	NUM	4		VSAM*STRING*WAITS

number of VSAM file waits.

Variable	Type	Length	Format	Label
VSWAITTM	NUM	4	TIME12.2	VSAM STRING*WAIT*DURATION

VSAM file wait time.

CICSTRAN
CICS CMF Transaction Resource and Response

The CICSTRAN data set contains one observation for each performance class record (with TYPEREC=1) from a type 110 record. Each observation is the result of the completion of a CICS transaction and contains the response time, terminal, operator, system, application ID, and so forth. This data set is the backbone of CICS transaction reporting and analysis since it permits crosstabulation and investigation of response, resources, and sources of CICS transactions. Since the data set contains one observation per CICS transaction, it can be relatively large (for 50,000 transactions, it requires 20 cyl on 3350 space).

Variable	Type	Length	Format	Label
APPLID	CHAR	8		VTAM*APPLICATION*NAME

VTAM application identification.

BMSINCN	NUM	4		BMS*IN*COUNT

basic mapping support in count.

BMSMAPCN	NUM	4		BMS*MAP*COUNT

basic mapping support map count.

BMSOTHCN	NUM	4		BMS*OTHER*COUNT

basic mapping support other count.

BMSOUTCN	NUM	4		BMS*OUT*COUNT

basic mapping support out count.

ELAPSTM	NUM	4	TIME12.2	ELAPSED*DURATION

elapsed time of transaction. It is calculated by subtracting STRTTIME from ENDTIME. This time is not the internal response time measurement because ELAPSTM includes the think time between user interactions. See IRESP for the actual internal response metric.

ENDTIME	NUM	8	DATETIME19.2	END TIME

detach time of transaction.

FCADDCN	NUM	4		FILE*CONTROL*ADDS

file control add count.

FCAMCNT	NUM	4		FILE*CONTROL*AMCTS

file control access method calls count.

Variable	Type	Length	Format	Label
FCBROCN	NUM	4		FILE*CONTROL*BROWSES

file control browse count. This field was originally two bytes long but was modified by PTF to be four bytes.

| FCDELCN | NUM | 4 | | FILE*CONTROL*DELETES |

file control delete count.

| FCGETCN | NUM | 4 | | FILE*CONTROL*GETS |

file control get count.

| FCOTHCN | NUM | 4 | | FILE*CONTROL*OTHERS |

file control other count.

| FCPUTCN | NUM | 4 | | FILE*CONTROL*PUTS |

file control put count.

| ICPUTCN | NUM | 4 | | INTERVAL*CONTROL*PUTS/INITS |

interval control put/initiate count.

| IRESPTM | NUM | 4 | | INTERNAL*RESPONSE*DURATION |

internal response time of transaction. It is calculated by subtracting TCWAITTM from the ELAPSTM of the transaction to exclude user think time. It does not include the time to send or receive data to and from the terminal (external perceived response time). A better estimate of external response time is made from this IRESPTM by adding line transmission time as described in chapter twenty-one.

| JCPUTCN | NUM | 4 | | JOURNAL*CONTROL*PUTS/WRITES |

journal control put or write count.

| MAXTASK | CHAR | 1 | | MAX*TASK*DELAY |

value of Y if the maximum-task (MXT) condition occurred during life of this transaction.

| OPERATOR | CHAR | 3 | | OPERATOR*NAME*CODE |

operator identification.

| PAGEINS | NUM | 4 | | TOTAL*PAGE-INS |

number of page-ins while dispatched.

| PCLINKCN | NUM | 4 | | PROGRAM*CONTROL*LINKS |

program control link count.

| PCLOADCN | NUM | 4 | | PROGRAM*CONTROL*LOADS |

program control load count.

Variable	Type	Length	Format	Label
PCXCTLCN	NUM	4		PROGRAM*CONTROL*XCTLS

program control XCTL count.

PRIINCHR	NUM	4		PRIMARY*INPUT*CHARACTERS

count of primary input message characters.

PRIOUCHR	NUM	4		PRIMARY*OUTPUT*CHARACTERS

count of primary output message characters.

PROGRAM	CHAR	8		PROGRAM*NAME

program name from PPT at task attach.

PROGSTOR	NUM	4		PROGRAM*STORAGE*USED

amount of program storage used by task.

SCGETCN	NUM	4		STORAGE*CONTROL*USER GETS

storage control user get count.

SECINCHR	NUM	4		SECONDARY*INPUT*CHARACTERS

count of secondary input message characters.

SECOUCHR	NUM	4		SECONDARY*OUTPUT*CHARACTERS

count of secondary output message characters.

SHRTSTOR	CHAR	1		SHORT*ON*STORAGE

value is Y if short-on-storage (SOS) condition occurred during life of this transaction.

SMFTIME	NUM	8	DATETIME19.2	SMF*RECORD*TIME STAMP

time stamp at which type 110 SMF record containing observation was written. It is the same for all observations that were contained in the same SMF record.

STORHWMK	NUM	4		MAXIMUM*STORAGE*ALLOCATED

maximum (high-water mark) storage allocated.

STRTTIME	NUM	8	DATETIME19.2	START*TRANSACTION*TIME STAMP

attach time of transaction.

SUSPNDCN	NUM	4		TASK*SUSPENDS

number of task suspends.

SUSPNDTM	NUM	4	TIME12.2	SUSPEND*DURATION

total duration on suspend chain.

Variable	Type	Length	Format	Label
SYNPTCN	NUM	4		SYNC*POINTS

sync point count.

| SYSTEM | CHAR | 4 | 4. | SYSTEM*ID |

identification of system on which CICS was executing.

| TASCPUTM | NUM | 4 | TIME12.2 | TASK*CPU TCB*TIME |

task CPU TCB processor time.

| TASDSPCN | NUM | 4 | | TASK*DISPATCHES |

number of task dispatches.

| TASDSPTM | NUM | 4 | TIME12.2 | TASK*DISPATCH*DURATION |

task dispatch time.

| TASERRFG | NUM | 4 | MG110ER36. | TASK*ERROR*FLAG |

task error flags. Transactions with nonzero values can have invalid time stamps and data:

internal	formatted value
02X	02X:BAD STORAGE CHAIN
04X	04X:INTERNAL ERROR IN CMF
08X	08X:MVE OR MLTCNT BAD ORIGIN ADDRESS
10X	10X:INTERNAL ERROR IN CMF
20X	20X:USER CLOCK OR COUNT BEYOND MCT
40X	40X:INVALID CLOCK OPERATION

| TASEXRN | NUM | 4 | | EXCEPTION*RECORDS*GENERATED |

number of exception class records generated by this transaction. The exception records, which are in the SAS data set CICSEXCE, can be matched to this observation by the value of the TASKNR variable, which is common to both observations.

| TASKNR | NUM | 4 | | TASK*NUMBER |

task sequence identification number. This number is the TCAKCTTA value from TCA.

| TCALOCCN | NUM | 4 | | TERMINAL*CONTROL*OTHER SYS ALLOCATES |

number of TCTTE allocates—other CICS SYS.

| TCINPRCN | NUM | 4 | | TERMINAL*CONTROL*INPUT PRIMARY |

terminal control input count-primary.

Variable	Type	Length	Format	Label
TCINSECN	NUM	4		TERMINAL*CONTROL*INPUT SECONDARY

terminal control input count-secondary.

| TCOUPRCN | NUM | 4 | | TERMINAL*CONTROL*OUTPUT PRIMARY |

terminal control output count-primary.

| TCOUSECN | NUM | 4 | | TERMINAL*CONTROL*OUTPUT SECONDARY |

terminal control output count-secondary.

| TDGETCN | NUM | 4 | | TRANSIENT*DATA*GETS |

transient data get count.

| TDPURCN | NUM | 4 | | TRANSIENT*DATA*PURGES |

transient data purge count.

| TDPUTCN | NUM | 4 | | TRANSIENT*DATA*PUTS |

transient data put count.

| TERMINAL | CHAR | 4 | | TERMINAL*NAME |

terminal identification.

| TRANNAME | CHAR | 4 | | TRANSACTION*NAME |

transaction name.

| TRANTYPE | CHAR | 8 | MG110TT25. | TRANSACTION*TYPE |

transaction type:
A=A:auto initiated
C=C:conversational
D=D:transient data
T=T:normal terminal started
Z=Z:pseudo conversational.

| TRMCHRCN | NUM | 4 | | CHARACTERS*SENT*TO/FROM |

total number of characters sent to and from terminal.

| TSGETCN | NUM | 4 | | TEMPORARY*STORAGE*GETS |

temporary storage get count.

| TSPUTACN | NUM | 4 | | TEMPORARY*STORAGE*PUT AUX |

temporary storage put auxiliary count.

Variable	Type	Length	Format	Label
TSPUTMCN	NUM	4		TEMPORARY*STORAGE*PUT MAIN

temporary storage put main count.

| USERCHAR | CHAR | 20 | | OPTIONAL*USER FIELD*(CHARACTER) |

up to 100 bytes of user (installation) defined character field. Often used to store the account to which the transaction is to be charged.

| WTFCIOCN | NUM | 4 | | FILE*CONTROL*IO WAITS |

number of file control I/O waits.

| WTFCIOTM | NUM | 4 | TIME12.2 | FILE*CONTROL*IO WAIT TIME |

total wait time for file control I/O.

| WTJCIOCN | NUM | 4 | | JOURNAL*CONTROL*IO WAITS |

number of journal control I/O waits.

| WTJCIOTM | NUM | 4 | TIME12.2 | JOURNAL*CONTROL*IO WAIT TIME |

total wait time for journal control I/O.

| WTTCIOCN | NUM | 4 | | TERMINAL*CONTROL*IO WAITS |

number of terminal control I/O waits.

| WTTCIOTM | NUM | 4 | TIME12.2 | TERMINAL*CONTROL*IO WAIT TIME |

total wait time for terminal control I/O.

| WTTSIOCN | NUM | 4 | | TEMPORARY*STORAGE*IO WAITS |

number of temporary storage I/O waits.

| WTTSIOTM | NUM | 4 | TIME12.2 | TEMPORARY*STORAGE*IO WAIT TIME |

total wait time for temporary storage I/O.

CICSYSTM
CICS CMF Global Performance

The CICSYSTM data set contains one observation for each performance class record (with TYPEREC=2) from a type 110 record, the global system data produced at user chosen intervals on the entire CICS system.

Variable	Type	Length	Format	Label
AMXT	NUM	4		AMXT*MAXIMUM*TASKS

current value of AMXT, the maximum number of active tasks CICS permits in this system; a critical performance value. If it is too high, too many tasks compete for CICS and MVS resources, resulting in excessive waits and paging. If it is too low, tasks are forced to wait within the CICS region rather than being dispatched CICS. This is the CICS equivalent of the maximum multiprogramming level, used by the MVS SRM. See also MAXT.

APPLID	CHAR	8		VTAM*APPLICATION*NAME

VTAM application identification.

CPUSRBTM	NUM	4	TIME12.2	INTERVAL*CPU SRB*TIME

total SRB CPU time during this interval.

CPUTCBTM	NUM	4	TIME12.2	INTERVAL*CPU TCB*TIME

total TCB CPU time during this interval (sum of JCCPUTM, KCCPUTM, TCCPUTM, USRCPUTM).

DSAHWMK	NUM	4		DSA*HIGH*WATERMARK

maximum amount (high-water mark) of dynamic storage area used.

ENDTIME	NUM	8	DATETIME19.2	END TIME

time stamp of interval end time.

ICV	NUM	4		ICV*VALUE

interval control value at end of interval.

ICVTSD	NUM	4		ICVTSD*VALUE

current value of ICVTSD.

JCCPUTM	NUM	4	TIME12.2	JOUR CONTROL*CPU TCB*DURATION

journal control CPU TCB time.

JCDSPCN	NUM	4		JOUR CONTROL*DISPATCH*COUNT

number of times journal control was dispatched.

Variable	Type	Length	Format	Label
JCDSPTM	NUM	4	TIME12.2	JOUR CONTROL*DISPATCH* DURATION

journal control dispatched time.

KCCPUTM	NUM	4	TIME12.2	TASK CONTROL*CPU TCB*DURATION

task control CPU TCB time.

KCDSPCN	NUM	4		TASK CONTROL*DISPATCH*COUNT

number of times task control was dispatched.

KCDSPTM	NUM	4	TIME12.2	TASK CONTROL*DISPATCH* DURATION

task control dispatched time.

MAXT	NUM	4		MAXT*MAXIMUM*TASKS

current value of MAXT. The total number of tasks CICS permits anywhere in its system (both in execution or in any waiting queues). It can be conceptualized as the maximum number of initiators CICS tasks can use. See AMAXT, a far more important variable.

NRTASKS	NUM	4		NUMBER*OF TASKS*ACTIVE

current number of tasks in this CICS system.

OSWAITTM	NUM	4	TIME12.2	OS WAIT*DISPATCH*DURATION

total elapsed time for which CICS/VS issues operating system wait.

OSWTCPTM	NUM	4	TIME12.2	OS WAIT*CPU TCB*DURATION

total processor time during which CICS/VS issues operating system wait.

PAGEINS	NUM	4		TOTAL*PAGE-INS

number of page-ins during this interval.

PAGEOUTS	NUM	4		TOTAL*PAGE-OUTS

number of page-outs during this interval.

PROGCOMP	NUM	4		PROGRAM*STORAGE*COMPRESSION

amount of storage deleted by program-compression mechanism. CICS deletes inactive application programs from dynamic storage if system storage resources become overloaded; this is called program compression.

SIT	CHAR	2		SIT*TABLE*USED

suffix of current SIT (system initialization table).

SMFTIME	NUM	8	DATETIME19.2	SMF*RECORD*TIME STAMP

time stamp at which type 110 SMF record containing observation is written. It is the same for all observations that are contained in the same SMF record.

Variable	Type	Length	Format	Label
STRTTIME	NUM	8	DATETIME19.2	START*TRANSACTION*TIME STAMP

time stamp of interval start time.

| SYSTEM | CHAR | 4 | 4. | SYSTEM*ID |

identification of system on which CICS was executing.

| TCCPUTM | NUM | 4 | TIME12.2 | TERM CONTROL*CPU TCB*DURATION |

terminal control TCP CPU time.

| TCDSPCN | NUM | 4 | | TERM CONTROL*DISPATCH COUNT |

number of times terminal control was dispatched.

| TCDSPTM | NUM | 4 | TIME12.2 | TERM CONTROL*DISPATCH DURATION |

terminal control dispatched time.

| USRCPUTM | NUM | 4 | TIME12.2 | USER*CPU TCB*DURATION |

total user TCB CPU time.

| USRDSPCN | NUM | 4 | | USER*DISPATCH*COUNT |

number of times user dispatched.

| USRDSPTM | NUM | 4 | TIME12.2 | USER*DISPATCH*DURATION |

user dispatched time.

CIMSDBDS
CONTROL/IMS Data Base Call Activity

The CIMSDBDS data set contains one observation for every data base data (DBD) segment in a CONTROL/IMS transaction record. The observation contains the DL/I call activity and the I/O activity for each DBD accessed by an IMS transaction, and it includes information on the transaction (and its program) that accessed this DBD.

Variable	Type	Length	Format	Label
ARRVTIME	NUM	8	DATETIME19.2	TRANSACTION*ARRIVAL*TIME STAMP

time this transaction was submitted (arrived) for processing by IMS. This is the beginning of the input queue duration, INPQUETM. For a message switch transaction, it is the arrival time of the message switch itself.

CALLDBDL	NUM	4		DATA BASE*DELETE*COUNT

number of times a delete was requested by this transaction.

CALLDBGN	NUM	4		DATA BASE*GET NEXT*COUNT

number of times a get next was requested by this transaction.

CALLDBGU	NUM	4		DATA BASE*GET UNIQUE*COUNT

number of times a get unique was requested by this transaction.

CALLDBIN	NUM	4		DATA BASE*INSERT*COUNT

number of times an insert was requested by this transaction.

CALLDBOT	NUM	4		DATA BASE*OTHER*COUNT

number of times a system service call was issued against this data base by this transaction.

CALLDBRP	NUM	4		DATA BASE*REPLACE*COUNT

number of times a replace was requested by this transaction.

DBDNAME	CHAR	8		DBD*NAME

name of data base to which these statistics apply. If the maximum number of DBD segments (defined by CIMSPARM DBT parameter) is exceeded by a particular transaction, this name will be OTHERS.

DBDSEQNR	NUM	4		DBD*SEQUENCE*NUMBER

sequence number of this DBD segment within this transaction.

DBORG	CHAR	8	MGIMSOR32.	DATA BASE*ORGANIZATION*TYPE

type of organization used for this data base. The coded values are formatted to the following possible values:

Variable	Type	Length	Format	Label
				1: HDAM
				2: HIDAM
				3: HISAM
				4: HISAM-CASE2
				5: HSAM
				6: SSAM
				7: ROOT-INDEX
				D: DEDB
				J: MSDB, NONRELATED, KEY IN SEGMENT
				A: MSDB, NONRELATED, LTERM KEY
				C: MSDB, RELATED, FIXED
				G: MSDB, RELATED, DYNAMIC.

DMBPOLSZ   NUM   4   DMB POOL*SIZE*(BYTES)

amount of DMB buffer pool space required by this data base (in bytes).

ENDTIME   NUM   8   DATETIME19.2   TRANSACTION*END*TIME STAMP

time when processing of this transaction ended.

IMSRECNR   NUM   4   INFILE*RECORD*NUMBER

physical record number in IMSLOG file of transaction record containing this DBD activity.

IOKYRD   NUM   4   IO*KEY*READS

number of reads issued to ISAM or key sequence data area in satisfying DL/I requests. These are physical I/O reads for keyed I/O.

IOKYWRT   NUM   4   IO*KEY*WRITES

number of writes issued to ISAM or key sequence data areas in satisfying DL/I requests. These are physical I/O writes for keyed I/O.

IONKYRD   NUM   4   IO*NONKEY*READS

number of reads issued to OSAM or entry sequence data area in satisfying DL/I requests. These are physical I/O reads for nonkeyed I/O.

IONKYWRT   NUM   4   IO*NONKEY*WRITES

number of writes issued to OSAM or entry sequence data areas in satisfying DL/I requests. These are physical I/O writes for nonkeyed I/O.

IONOIN   NUM   4   IO READS*FOUND*IN BUFFER

number of times requested input data were found in the I/O buffer. These represent DL/I calls satisfied without physical reads.

Variable	Type	Length	Format	Label
IONOOU	NUM	4		IO ALTERS*FOUND*IN BUFFER

number of ALTERS to buffered data for this data base. These represent DL/I calls satisfied without physical writes.

| LTERM | CHAR | 8 | | LOGICAL*TERMINAL*NAME |

name of logical terminal used to submit this transaction.

| PROGRAM | CHAR | 8 | | PROGRAM*NAME |

name of program (PSB) that processed this transaction.

| RECSTAT | CHAR | 1 | | RECORD*STATUS |

identifies type of transaction record. Value is 1 for a single record.

| REGIONID | CHAR | 8 | | REGION*ID |

name assigned to initiator used to schedule program into a message region.

| STRTTIME | NUM | 8 | DATETIME19.2 | TRANSACTION*START*TIME STAMP |

time when processing of this transaction started. This ends the INPQUETM and begins the SERVICTM durations.

| SYSTEM | CHAR | 4 | | SYSTEM*IDENTIFICATION |

SMF identification code (from SMCA) on which this transaction was processed.

| TRANSACT | CHAR | 8 | | TRANSACTION*NAME |

transaction name identifying this message or transaction.

CIMSPROG
CONTROL/IMS Program Resources

The CIMSPROG data set contains one observation for every program that was terminated after one or more IMS transactions executed that program. The observation contains statistics on the DL/I activity of this program, including three measures of CPU usage that are not recorded at the transaction level: CPU time to schedule and terminate transactions that used this program, control region CPU time due to overhead functions such as MFS and queuing, and message region CPU time due to overhead functions.

Variable	Type	Length	Format	Label
ABENDSYS	NUM	4		SYSTEM*ABEND*CODE

system abend incurred by this program.

ABENDUSR	NUM	4		USER*ABEND*CODE

user abend forced by this program.

AMFSYSID	CHAR	1		AMF*SYSTEM*ID

identification code (AMF) for computing system on which this program was processed.

APLGRPNM	CHAR	8		APPLICATION*GROUP*NAME

application group name assigned by security system.

BUFDMBSZ	NUM	4		DMB BUFFER*POOL SIZE*(BYTES)

amount of DMB buffer pool space required by this program expressed in bytes.

BUFPSBSZ	NUM	4		PSB BUFFER*POOL SIZE*(BYTES)

amount of PSB buffer pool space required by this program expressed in bytes.

CALLMSGN	NUM	4		MESSAGE*GET NEXT*COUNT

number of message get nexts issued by the program in processing transactions.

CALLMSGU	NUM	4		MESSAGE*GET UNIQUE*COUNT

number of message get uniques issued by the program in processing transactions.

CALLMSIN	NUM	4		MESSAGE*INSERT*COUNT

number of message inserts issued by program in processing transactions.

CALLMSOT	NUM	4		MESSAGE*OTHER*COUNT

number of other message calls, including system service calls, issued by program in processing transactions.

Variable	Type	Length	Format	Label

CALLMSPU NUM 4 MESSAGE*PURGE*COUNT
number of message purges issued by program in processing transactions.

COREALOC NUM 4 CORE*ALLOCATED
size of message region, in 2K units, available at initial scheduling.

COREUSED NUM 4 CORE*USED
amount of message region, in 2K units, program used (linkedit length) of available message region core.

CPUCOVTM NUM 4 TIME12.2 CONTROL*OVERHEAD*CPU TIME
CPU overhead time in control region since last program record. This time is not attributable to only this program as it includes the time for such functions as MFS and queuing.

CPUMOVTM NUM 4 TIME12.2 MESSAGE*OVERHEAD*CPU TIME
CPU overhead time in dependent (message) region since last program record.

CPUMSKTM NUM 4 TIME12.2 MESSAGE*SKED AND TERM*CPU TIME
amount of CPU time used by this program in scheduling and terminating message processing.

ENDTIME NUM 8 DATETIME19.2 TRANSACTION*END*TIME STAMP
time when processing of this transaction ended.

FPBUFHWM NUM 4 FAST PATH*BUFFERS*HIGH WATER MARK
maximum number of fast path buffers used for all transactions processed during this scheduling.

IMSID CHAR 4 IMS*SYSTEM*ID
identification code for the IMS system (IMSID).

IMSLEVEL CHAR 4 IMS*LEVEL
IMS/VS version and PTF level.

IMSRECNR NUM 4 INFILE*RECORD*NUMBER
physical record number in IMSLOG file of transaction record containing this DBD activity.

NBA NUM 4 NORMAL*BUFFER*ALLOCATION
normal buffer allocation (NBA) value from JCL if this program was scheduled in a region that supported fast path data base access.

OBA NUM 4 OVERFLOW*BUFFER*ALLOCATION
overflow buffer allocation (OBA) value from JCL if this program was scheduled in a region that supported fast path data base access.

Variable	Type	Length	Format	Label
OPERSYS	CHAR	3		OPERATING*SYSTEM

operating system (MVS, SVS, VS1) on which IMV/VS executed.

PGMLOGID	NUM	4		PROGRAM*LOGGING*IDENTIFIER

identifier of IMF module that logged this program record.

PROGRAM	CHAR	8		PROGRAM*NAME

name of program (PSB) that processed these transactions.

PROGTYPE	CHAR	8	MGIMSPT30.	PROGRAM*TYPE

program type. Formatted to the program type of this program. The coded values are formatted to the following possible values:

> C: CONVERSATIONAL
>
> B: BMP
>
> M: NORMAL TP PROGRAM
>
> S: SPECIAL
>
> F: FAST PATH MESSAGE_DRIVEN
>
> N: FAST PATH NON_MESSAGE DRIVEN
>
> U: FAST PATH UTILITY

PSTNUMBR	NUM	4		PST*NUMBER

PST associated with region in which this program was scheduled.

REGIONID	CHAR	8		REGION*ID

name assigned to initiator used to schedule program into a message region.

STRTTIME	NUM	8	DATETIME19.2	TRANSACTION* START*TIME STAMP

time when processing of this transaction started. This ends the INPQUETM and begins the SERVICTM durations.

SYSTEM	CHAR	4		SYSTEM*IDENTIFICATION

SMF identification code (from SMCA) on which this transaction was processed.

CIMSTRAN
CONTROL/IMS Transaction Response and Resources

The CIMSTRAN data set contains one observation for every transaction record produced by CONTROL/IMS. The observation contains transaction response time, queue time for and service time in execution, I/O counts caused by this transaction (both real I/O and I/O found in the buffer), and seven measures of CPU time used in the control and message regions.

Variable	Type	Length	Format	Label
AMFSYSID	CHAR	1		AMF*SYSTEM*ID

identification code (AMF) for computing system on which this program was processed.

APLGRPNM	CHAR	8		APPLICATION*GROUP*NAME

application group name assigned by security system.

ARRVTIME	NUM	8	DATETIME19.2	TRANSACTION*ARRIVAL*TIME STAMP

time this transaction was submitted (arrived) for processing by IMS. This marks the beginning of the input queue duration, INPQUETM. For a message switch transaction, it is the arrival time of the message switch itself.

BALGPQUE	NUM	4		BALANCING*GROUP*Q-COUNT

for a message-driven transaction, number of transactions queued on same balancing group when this transaction went through sync point processing.

CALLDBDL	NUM	4		DATA BASE*DELETE*COUNT

number of times a delete was requested by this transaction.

CALLDBGN	NUM	4		DATA BASE*GET NEXT*COUNT

number of times a get next was requested by this transaction.

CALLDBGU	NUM	4		DATA BASE*GET UNIQUE*COUNT

number of times a get unique was requested by this transaction.

CALLDBIN	NUM	4		DATA BASE*INSERT*COUNT

number of times an insert was requested by this transaction.

CALLDBOT	NUM	4		DATA BASE*OTHER*COUNT

number of times a system service call was issued against this data base by this transaction.

CALLDBRP	NUM	4		DATA BASE*REPLACE*COUNT

number of times a replace was requested by this transaction.

Variable	Type	Length	Format	Label
CALLMSGN	NUM	4		MESSAGE*GET NEXT*COUNT

number of message get nexts issued by program in processing transactions.

CALLMSGU	NUM	4		MESSAGE*GET UNIQUE*COUNT

number of message get uniques issued by program in processing transactions.

CALLMSIN	NUM	4		MESSAGE*INSERT*COUNT

number of message inserts issued by program in processing transactions.

CALLMSOT	NUM	4		MESSAGE*OTHER*COUNT

number of other message calls, including system service calls issued by program in processing transactions.

CALLMSPU	NUM	4		MESSAGE*PURGE*COUNT

number of message purges issued by program in processing transactions.

CHRALTRM	NUM	4		ALT TERM*OUTPUT*CHAR COUNT

number of characters output for this transaction to a logical terminal (LTERM) other than originating LTERM.

CHRIN	NUM	4		INPUT*CHARACTER*COUNT

number of characters input from specified LTERM in processing this transaction.

CHRMSGSW	NUM	4		MESSAGE*SWITCH*CHAR COUNT

number of characters output to message input queue as a result of message switch by this transaction.

CHROUT	NUM	4		OUTPUT*CHARACTER*COUNT

number of characters output to originating logical terminal in processing this transaction.

CHRSPAIN	NUM	4		SPA INPUT*CHARACTER*COUNT

number of characters input for this transaction from a scratch pad area in processing this transaction.

CHRSPAOU	NUM	4		SPA OUTPUT*CHARACTER*COUNT

number of characters output to a scratch pad area in processing this transaction.

COREALOC	NUM	4		CORE*ALLOCATED

size of message region, in 2K units, available at initial scheduling.

COREUSED	NUM	4		CORE*USED

amount of message region, in 2K units, program used (linkedit length) of available message region core.

Variable	Type	Length	Format	Label

CPUCBFTM   NUM   4   TIME12.2   CONTROL*BUFFER*CPU TIME

amount of control region CPU time used by buffer handler module during processing of this transaction. This is zero if the buffer handler option is turned off.

CPUCDLTM   NUM   4   TIME12.2   CONTROL*DLI*CPU TIME

amount of control region CPU time used by DL/I analyzer to process transaction. This does not include buffer handling or open and close time. However, if the buffer handler option is turned off, this time includes the buffer handling CPU time.

CPUCOPTM   NUM   4   TIME12.2   CONTROL*OPEN CLOSE*CPU TIME

amount of control region CPU time used by DL/I analyzer to open and close required data bases while processing this transaction.

CPUMBFTM   NUM   4   TIME12.2   MESSAGE*BUFFER*CPU TIME

amount of dependent (message) region CPU time used by buffer handler module during processing of this transaction. This value is zero if the buffer handler option is turned off.

CPUMDLTM   NUM   4   TIME12.2   MESSAGE*DLI*CPU TIME

amount of dependent (message) region CPU time used by DL/I analyzer to process transaction. This value does not include buffer handling or open and close time. However, if the buffer handler option is turned off, this time includes the buffer handling CPU time.

CPUMOPTM   NUM   4   TIME12.2   MESSAGE*OPEN CLOSE*CPU TIME

amount of dependent (message) region CPU time used by DL/I analyzer to open and close required data bases while processing this transaction. Only fast path DEDBs are opened from the message region.

CPUMSGTM   NUM   4   TIME12.2   MESSAGE*REGION*CPU TIME

amount of message region CPU time used by program to process this transaction. This is the CPU time of the application.

ENDTIME   NUM   8   DATETIME19.2   TRANSACTION*END*TIME STAMP

time when processing of this transaction ended.

FASTPATH   CHAR   8   MGIMSFP27.   FAST*PATH*FLAT

identifies fast path characteristics of this transaction, provided it accessed fast path data bases. If this transaction waited for the overflow buffer allocation (OBA) buffer latch, its value is formatted to:

W: WAIT FOR OBA BUFFER LATCH

FLGSPECL   CHAR   8   MGIMSLS11.   SPECIAL*PROCESSING*FLAG

special processing characteristics for this transaction. If this is a local storage options transaction, its value is formatted to:

L: LSO TRANS

Variable	Type	Length	Format	Label
FLGTIMER	CHAR	1		TIMER*ERROR*FLAG

flag to indicate when an error is detected in CPU timing services.

FPBFWAIT	NUM	4		FAST PATH*WAIT FOR*BUFFERS

number of times this transaction had to wait for a fast path buffer to become available.

FPCICONT	NUM	4		FAST PATH*CI*CONTENTIONS

number of fast path control interval contentions that occurred in transaction sync interval.

FSTPTHBF	NUM	4		FAST PATH*BUFFERS*USED

contains number of fast path buffers that were actually used if this transaction accessed fast path data bases.

IMSID	CHAR	4		IMS*SYSTEM*ID

identification code for IMS system (IMSID).

IMSLEVEL	CHAR	4		IMS*LEVEL

IMS/VS version and PTF level.

IMSRECNR	NUM	4		INFILE*RECORD*NUMBER

physical record number in IMSLOG file of transaction record containing this DBD activity.

INPQUETM	NUM	4	TIME12.2	INPUT*QUEUE*DURATION

duration from ARRVTIME to STRTTIME, time on the input queue. In addition to reflecting scheduling conflicts for transactions, stopped data bases and transactions cause transactions to wait for long periods on the input queue. When added to SERVICTM, transaction response RESPONSTM is measured.

INPUTCLS	CHAR	1		INPUT*CLASS

identification of class used to assign program to a specific message region by an initiator.

IOKYRD	NUM	4		IO*KEY*READS

number of reads issued to ISAM or key sequence data area in satisfying DL/I requests. These are physical I/O reads for keyed I/O.

IOKYWRT	NUM	4		IO*KEY*WRITES

number of writes issued to ISAM or key sequence data areas in satisfying DL/I requests. These are physical I/O writes for keyed I/O.

IONKYRD	NUM	4		IO*NONKEY*READS

number of reads issued to OSAM or entry sequence data area in satisfying DL/I requests. These are physical I/O reads for nonkeyed I/O.

Variable	Type	Length	Format	Label
IONKYWRT	NUM	4		IO*NONKEY*WRITES

number of writes issued to OSAM or entry sequence data areas in satisfying DL/I requests. These are physical I/O writes for nonkeyed I/O.

| IONOIN | NUM | 4 | | IO READS*FOUND*IN BUFFER |

number of times requested input data was found in I/O buffer. These represent DL/I calls satisfied without physical reads.

| IONOOU | NUM | 4 | | IO ALTERS*FOUND*IN BUFFER |

number of alters to buffered data for this data base. These represent DL/I calls satisfied without physical writes.

| LINENR | NUM | 4 | | PHYSICAL*LINE*NUMBER |

line number of physical terminal from which this transaction was submitted.

| LTERM | CHAR | 8 | | LOGICAL*TERMINAL*NAME |

name of logical terminal used to submit this transaction.

| NBA | NUM | 4 | | NORMAL*BUFFER*ALLOCATION |

normal buffer allocation (NBA) value from JCL if this program was scheduled in a region that supported fast path data base access.

| NRDBD | NUM | 4 | | NUMBER*OF DBD*SEGMENTS |

number of DBD segments accessed by this transaction, up to maximum number allowed by DBT parameter in CIMSPARM. If a transaction uses more than the maximum allowed number of segments, no counts are lost since they are all accumulated together in a single bucket with DBDNAME OTHERS.

| OBA | NUM | 4 | | OVERFLOW*BUFFER*ALLOCATION |

if this program was scheduled in a region that supported fast path data base access, this is the overflow buffer allocation (OBA) value from JCL.

| OPERSYS | CHAR | 3 | | OPERATING*SYSTEM |

operating system (MVS,SVS,VS1) on which IMV/VS executed.

| PROGRAM | CHAR | 8 | | PROGRAM*NAME |

name of program (PSB) that processed this transaction.

| PROGTYPE | CHAR | 8 | MGIMSPT30. | PROGRAM*TYPE |

program type. Formatted to the program type of this program. The coded values are formatted to the following possible values:

        C: CONVERSATIONAL

        B: BMP

        M: NORMAL TP PROGRAM

Variable	Type	Length	Format	Label
				S: SPECIAL
				F: FAST PATH MESSAGE_DRIVEN
				N: FAST PATH NON_MESSAGE DRIVEN
				U: FAST PATH UTILITY
PSTNUMBR	NUM	4		PST*NUMBER

PST associated with region in which this program was scheduled.

RECSTAT	CHAR	1		RECORD*STATUS

identifies type of transaction record. The value is 1 for a single record.

REGIONID	CHAR	8		REGION*ID

name assigned to initiator used to schedule program into a message region.

RESPNSTM	NUM	4	TIME12.2	TOTAL*(QUEUE + SERVICE)*RESPONSE

transaction response time. This is the duration from ARRVTIME to ENDTIME, which is also the sum of INPQUETM and SERVICETM.

ROUTECDE	CHAR	8		ROUTING*CODE

routing code used to schedule this transaction for fast path message-driven region.

SECUID	CHAR	8		SECURITY*USER*ID

user identification supplied by security system.

SERVICTM	NUM	4	TIME12.2	EXECUTION*SERVICE*DURATION

transaction's execution or service duration from STRTTIME to ENDTIME. It represents the duration to execute after the transaction was started. When added to INPQUETM, total response (RESPNSTM) results.

STRTTIME	NUM	8	DATETIME19.2	TRANSACTION*START*TIME STAMP

time when processing of this transaction started. This ends the INPQUETM and begins the SERVICTM durations.

SYNCRTRN	NUM	4	HEX4.	SYNC POINT*RETURN*CODE

result of sync point processing for a transaction that accessed fast path data bases.

SYSTEM	CHAR	4		SYSTEM*IDENTIFICATION

SMF identification code (from SMCA) on which this transaction was processed.

TERMNR	NUM	4		PHYSICAL*TERMINAL*NUMBER

terminal number of physical terminal from which this transaction was submitted.

Variable	Type	Length	Format	Label
TRANSACT	CHAR	8		TRANSACTION*NAME

transaction name identifying this message or transaction.

TRNLOGID	CHAR	4		TRANSACTION*LOGGING*IDENTIFIER

identifier of CONTROL/IMS module that logged this transaction record.

USERAREA	CHAR	16		RESERVED*FOR*USER

area reserved for and accessed by user functions, frequently used to capture accounting information through user modifications to IMS.

VTAMTERM	CHAR	8		VTAM*TERMINAL*NAME

VTAM node name of physical terminal from which this transaction was submitted (if it is a VTAM terminal). It is not filled in for fast path message-driven transactions.

DOSJOBS
DOS/VSE POWER Job Step Execution Resources

There is one observation in data set DOSJOBS for every execution account record created by POWER under DOS/VSE, created for each VSE job step (or phase) executed. The observation contains accounting information passed by the VSE job accounting interface plus information produced by the VSE/POWER accounting routing, such as CPU time, I/O activity, and so forth. This record is equivalent to the steps record in an MVS environment, and it provides the primary source of resource data on job step execution under VSE.

Variable	Type	Length	Format	Label
APLICATN	CHAR	8	MGDOSAP19.	BUSINESS*ELEMENT

character string decoded from job name which is then associated with format $MGDOSAP in member FORMATS to allow DOSJOBS to be summarized by business element (that is, application). Sample reports in member ANALDOS use this formatted variable. The code in TYPEDOS must be examined, and an algorithm to map job name to application must be coded by the MXG user, and then the $MGDOSAP format must be changed to agree with the values of this variable in order for it all to work as designed. Only the MXG summary report by business element is affected by this created variable.

CLASSJOB	CHAR	1		JOB*CLASS

class of job.

CPUHOURS	NUM	4		CPU*HOURS

processor time used, in hours, for simple tabulations.

CPUTM	NUM	4	TIME8.	CPU*ACTIVE*DURATION

processor time used, with full resolution to .0033 second units. This is the real CPU time used by the step.

DATE	NUM	4	DATE7.	START*EXECUTION*DATE

date of start of execution (STARTIME) for reporting purposes.

DCANCODE	NUM	4	MGDOSDC30.	VSE*CANCEL*CODE

DOS cancel code. The formatted values are:

000X= '00X:UNKNOWN HEX 00'

019X= '19X:OPER CANCEL AFTER IO ERROR'

01AX= '1AX:IO ERROR'

020X= '20X:PROGRAM CHECK'

023X= '23X:CANCEL MACRO ISSUED'

024X= '24X:CANCEL BY OPER REQUEST'

Variable	Type	Length	Format	Label

025X= '25X:INVALID VIRTUAL ADDR'

027X= '27X:UNDEFINED LOGICAL UNIT'

02BX= '2BX:IO ERROR FROM CIL'

09AX= '9AX:UNKNOWN HEX 9A'

0A3X= 'A3X:UNKNOWN HEX A3'

0A4X= 'ARX:UNKNOWN HEX A4'

0FFX= 'FFX:UNKNOWN HEX FF'

010X= '10X:FLUSHED'.

DEVICES	NUM	4		TOTAL*DEVICES*USED

total number of devices used by this step.

ELAPSTM	NUM	4	TIME8.	PHASE*ELAPSED*DURATION

elapsed execution (wall clock) time of this step.

FROMRMOT	NUM	4		FROM*REMOTE*ID

FROM remote id.

JOB	CHAR	8		VSE*JOB*NAME

job name from // JOB card.

JOBNR	NUM	4		POWER*JOB*NUMBER

job number assigned by VSE/POWER.

JOBSEQNR	NUM	8		JOB*SEQUENCE*NUMBER

job sequence number as processed by MXG software.

MEMPAGES	NUM	4		MEMORY*PAGES

number of memory pages.

NDEVCH0	NUM	4		CHAN 0*DEVICES*USED

number of devices on channel zero that were used.

NDEVCH1	NUM	4		CHAN 1*DEVICES*USED

number of devices on channel one that were used.

NDEVCH2	NUM	4		CHAN 2*DEVICES*USED

number of devices on channel two that were used.

NDEVCH3	NUM	4		CHAN 3*DEVICES*USED

number of devices on channel three that were used.

Variable	Type	Length	Format	Label

NDEVCH4 NUM 4 CHAN 4*DEVICES*USED

number of devices on channel four that were used.

NDEVCH5 NUM 4 CHAN 5*DEVICES*USED

number of devices on channel five that were used.

OVERDEVS CHAR 1 TOO*MANY*DEV?

if more devices were used by this step than were specified by the SYSGEN option, value is Y; it is blank otherwise.

OVERTM NUM 4 TIME8. CPU*OVERHEAD*DURATION

overhead CPU time. This is the time for various activities that cannot be charged to a specific program or partition. For example, the time for the calling routine, error recovery, paging activities, or from the start of the $JBOACCT routine to the EXEC command. All SVCs are calculated to the active processor time of the step. These times are divided by the number of active partitions.

PARTION CHAR 2 PARTITION*ID

partition identification number.

PCANCODE NUM 4 MGDOSPC12. POWER*CANCEL*CODE

VSE/POWER cancel code. The value is formatted to the following possible values:

'10X:NORMAL' although no abnormal termination occurred, the VSE jobs associated with the queue entry could have been canceled via VSE.

'20X:PCANCEL' PCANCEL command was issued.

'30X:PSTOP' PSTOP command was issued. However, the PSTOP cancel code is not stored in an account record if the EOJ option was specified in the PSTOP command.

'40X:PFLUSH' PFLUSH command was issued.

'50X:PDELETE' PDELETE command was issued.

'60X:PFLUSH' VSE/POWER job was flushed via RDREXIT.

'70X:IO ERROR' VSE/POWER job canceled due to I/O error.

PHASE CHAR 8 PHASE*NAME

phase name, taken from // EXEC card.

PHASENR NUM 8 PHASE*WITHIN*JOB

sequence number of this phase within its job as phase records (steps) were processed by MXG software.

POWERJB CHAR 8 POWER*JOB*NAME

current VSE/POWER job name or AUTONAME. This is not the job name by which the job is usually referred.

Variable	Type	Length	Format	Label
PRTYJOB	NUM	4		PRTY

job scheduling priority.

| RECTYPE | CHAR | 8 | MGDOSRC11. | RECORD*TYPE |

type of phase record. It is formatted to:

> L: LAST STEP
> S: JOB STEP

| SHIFT | CHAR | 8 | MGDOSHF7. | SHIFT*AT*START |

shift of start of execution. Defined in TYPEDOS and set to P if start was between 8 a.m. and 4 p.m., Monday through Friday, or to N otherwise. The $MGDOSHF format produces the following values:

> EVENING
> PRIME

| SIOCHAN0 | NUM | 4 | | CHAN 0*SIO*COUNT |

count of SIOs to devices on channel zero.

| SIOCHAN1 | NUM | 4 | | CHAN 1*SIO*COUNT |

count of SIOs to devices on channel one.

| SIOCHAN2 | NUM | 4 | | CHAN 2*SIO*COUNT |

count of SIOs to devices on channel two.

| SIOCHAN3 | NUM | 4 | | CHAN 3*SIO*COUNT |

count of SIOs to devices on channel three.

| SIOCHAN4 | NUM | 4 | | CHAN 4*SIO*COUNT |

count of SIOs to devices on channel four.

| SIOCHAN5 | NUM | 4 | | CHAN 5*SIO*COUNT |

count of SIOs to devices on channel five.

| SIOCOUNT | NUM | 4 | | TOTAL*SIO*COUNT |

count of SIOs to devices on all channels.

| SPOLCARD | NUM | 4 | | CARDS*SPOOLED |

number of cards spooled (zero for VSE/POWER-E.A.R.).

| SPOLINES | NUM | 4 | | LINES*SPOOLED |

number of lines written to spool (zero for VSE/POWER-E.A.R.). This does not mean the lines were actually printed, as the job could have been canceled or multiple copies could be printed from the spooling operation. Printing is described in the DOSLIST data set.

Variable	Type	Length	Format	Label
SPOLPAGE	NUM	4		PAGES*SPOOLED

number of pages written to spool (zero for VSE/POWER-E.A.R.).

STARTIME	NUM	8	DATETIME16.	START*TIME STAMP

start of execution of this phase.

STOPTIME	NUM	8	DATETIME16.	END*TIME STAMP

end of execution of this phase.

TORMOT	NUM	4		TO*REMOTE*ID

to remote identification.

USRINFO1	CHAR	16		USER*INFORMATION*($$ JOB CARD)

sixteen bytes of user information from * $$ JOB card.

USRINFO2	CHAR	16		USER*INFORMATION*(// JOB CARD)

sixteen bytes of user information from // JOB card.

WAITTM	NUM	4	TIME8.	ALL-BOUND*(WAITING)*DURATION

all-bound time. This is the wait time of the total system. No system activities have been performed. The all-bound time is divided by the number of active partitions, based on the percentage of the used processor time.

DOSLIST
DOS/VSE POWER Printing Resources

There is one observation in the DOSLIST data set for every list account record created by DOS/VSE POWER, for each list queue entry that is processed by a list task. It is a copy of the first 72 bytes of the corresponding queue record and provides data on printing activity.

Variable	Type	Length	Format	Label
CLASSPRT	CHAR	1		PRINTED*OUTPUT*CLASS

printed output class.

| COPIES | NUM | 4 | | PRINTED*COPIES |

number of printed copies. If more than one, the statistics are totals for all copies.

| EXTRALIN | NUM | 4 | | EXTRA*LINES*PRINTED |

number of extra records printed due to PRESTART, PSETUP, separator lines, or extra copies.

| EXTRAPAG | NUM | 4 | | EXTRA*PAGES*PRINTED |

number of extra pages printed due to PRESTART, PSETUP, separator cards, or extra copies.

| FORMPRNT | CHAR | 4 | | PRINT*FORM*IDENTIFICATION |

print forms identification.

| FROMRMOT | NUM | 4 | | FROM*REMOTE* ID |

FROM remote identification.

| JOBNR | NUM | 4 | | POWER*JOB*NUMBER |

job number assigned by VSE/POWER.

| PAGESPRT | NUM | 4 | | PAGES*PRINTED |

number of pages printed (skips to channel one or page filled, see also EXTRAPAG).

| PCANCODE | NUM | 4 | MGDOSPC12. | POWER*CANCEL*CODE |

VSE/POWER cancel code. The value is formatted to the following possible values:

'10X:NORMAL'   although no abnormal termination occurred, the VSE jobs associated with the queue entry could have been canceled via VSE.

'20X:PCANCEL' PCANCEL command was issued.

'30X:PSTOP'   PSTOP command was issued. However, the PSTOP cancel code is not stored in an account record if the EOJ option was specified in the PSTOP command.

Variable	Type	Length	Format	Label
	'40X:PFLUSH'			PFLUSH command was issued.
	'50X:PDELETE'			PDELETE command was issued.
	'60X:PFLUSH'			VSE/POWER job was flushed via RDREXIT.
	'70X:IO ERROR'			VSE/POWER job canceled due to I/O error.

POWERJB   CHAR   8   POWER*JOB*NAME

current VSE/POWER job name or AUTONAME. This is not the job name by which the job is usually referred.

PRTADDR   CHAR   3   PRINTER*DEVICE*ADDRESS

printer device address, SNA, GSP, or line address (cuu).

PRTYPRT   CHAR   1   PRINTED*OUTPUT*PRIORITY

printed output priority number.

STARTIME   NUM   8   DATETIME16.   START*TIME STAMP

start time of list operation.

STOPTIME   NUM   8   DATETIME16.   END*TIME STAMP

stop time of list operation.

SUFFIX   CHAR   1   HEX2.   JOB*SUFFIX*NUMBER

job suffix number assigned by VSE/POWER. (This value is X '00' for only segment of a job. Bit 0 is on for the last segment.)

TORMOT   NUM   4   TO*REMOTE*ID

TO remote identification.

TRACKS   NUM   4   TRACKS OR*FBA BLOCKS*USED

number of tracks for output storage. If the data file resides on an FBA device, the field contains the number of FBA blocks used instead of tracks.

USRINFO1   CHAR   16   USER*INFORMATION*($$ JOB CARD)

sixteen bytes of user information from * $$ JOB card.

DOSPUNCH
DOS/VSE POWER Punch Resources

There is one observation in data set DOSPUNCH for each punch account record created by DOS/VSE POWER, created for each punch-queue entry that is processed by a punch task. It is a copy of the first 68 bytes of the corresponding queue record, and it provides data on punch activity.

Variable	Type	Length	Format	Label
CLASSPUN	CHAR	1		PUNCHED*OUTPUT*CLASS

punched output class.

| EXTRAPUN | NUM | 4 | | EXTRA*CARDS*PUNCHED |

number of extra records punched due to RESTART, separator lines, or extra copies.

| FORMPUNC | CHAR | 4 | | PUNCH*FORM*IDENTIFICATION |

punch forms identification.

| FROMRMOT | NUM | 4 | | FROM*REMOTE*ID |

FROM remote identification.

| JOBNR | NUM | 4 | | POWER*JOB*NUMBER |

job number assigned by VSE/POWER.

| PCANCODE | NUM | 4 | MGDOSPC12. | POWER*CANCEL*CODE |

VSE/POWER cancel code. The value is formatted to the following possible values:

'10X:NORMAL'   although no abnormal termination occurred, the VSE jobs associated with the queue entry could have been canceled via VSE.

'20X:PCANCEL' PCANCEL command was issued.

'30X:PSTOP'   PSTOP command was issued. However, the PSTOP cancel code is not stored in an account record if the EOJ option was specified in the PSTOP command.

'40X:PFLUSH'   PFLUSH command was issued.

'50X:PDELETE' PDELETE command was issued.

'60X:PFLUSH'   VSE/POWER job was flushed via RDREXIT.

'70X:IO ERROR' VSE/POWER job canceled due to I/O error.

| POWERJB | CHAR | 8 | | POWER*JOB*NAME |

current VSE/POWER job name or AUTONAME. This is not the job name by which the job is usually referred.

Variable	Type	Length	Format	Label
PRTYPUN	CHAR	1		PUNCHED*OUTPUT*PRIORITY

punched output priority number.

| PUNADDR | CHAR | 3 | | PUNCH*DEVICE*ADDRESS |

punch device address, SNA, GSP, or line address (cuu).

| PUNCHES | NUM | 4 | | CARDS*PUNCHED |

number of records punched. See also EXTRAPUN.

| STARTIME | NUM | 8 | DATETIME16. | START*TIME STAMP |

start time of punch operation.

| STOPTIME | NUM | 8 | DATETIME16. | END*TIME STAMP |

end time of punch operation.

| SUFFIX | CHAR | 1 | HEX2. | JOB*SUFFIX*NUMBER |

job suffix number assigned by VSE/POWER. (This value is X '00' for only segment of a job. Bit 0 is on for the last segment.)

| TORMOT | NUM | 4 | | TO*REMOTE*ID |

TO remote identification.

| TRACKS | NUM | 4 | | TRACKS OR*FBA BLOCKS*USED |

number of tracks for output storage. If the data file resides on an FBA device, the field contains the number of FBA blocks used instead of tracks.

| USRINFO1 | CHAR | 16 | | USER*INFORMATION*($$ JOB CARD) |

sixteen bytes of user information from * $$ JOB card.

DOSREAD
DOS/VSE POWER Read-in Resources

There is one observation in data set DOSREAD for each reader account record created by DOS/VSE POWER, created for each read-queue entry that is entered into the VS/POWER system. Whether or not the queue entry has been placed in the queue file is indicated by the VSE/POWER cancel code (PCANCODE). The record is copied from the first 58 bytes of the corresponding queue record. Reader account records are not created for a writer-only partition.

Variable	Type	Length	Format	Label
CARDSRDR	NUM	4		CARDS*READ

number of records read (including record added or deleted by a reader exit routine).

CLASSRDR	CHAR	1		INPUT*CLASS

punched output class.

FROMRMOT	NUM	4		FROM*REMOTE*ID

FROM remote identification.

JOBNR	NUM	4		POWER*JOB*NUMBER

job number assigned by VSE/POWER.

PCANCODE	NUM	4	MGDOSPC12.	POWER*CANCEL*CODE

VSE/POWER cancel code. The value is formatted to the following possible values:

'10X:NORMAL'	although no abnormal termination occurred, the VSE jobs associated with the queue entry could have been canceled via VSE.
'20X:PCANCEL'	PCANCEL command was issued.
'30X:PSTOP'	PSTOP command was issued. However, the PSTOP cancel code is not stored in an account record if the EOJ option was specified in the PSTOP command.
'40X:PFLUSH'	PFLUSH command was issued.
'50X:PDELETE'	PDELETE command was issued.
'60X:PFLUSH'	VSE/POWER job was flushed via RDREXIT.
'70X:IO ERROR'	VSE/POWER job canceled due to I/O error.

POWERJB	CHAR	8		POWER*JOB*NAME

current VSE/POWER job name or AUTONAME. This is not the job name by which the job is usually referred.

Variable	Type	Length	Format	Label
PRTYRDR	CHAR	1		INPUT*PRIORITY

input priority number.

Variable	Type	Length	Format	Label
RDRADDR	CHAR	3		READER*DEVICE*ADDRESS

reader device address, SNA, PSP with PUTSPOOL, or line address (cuu).

STARTIME	NUM	8	DATETIME16.	START*TIME STAMP

start time of read operation.

STOPTIME	NUM	8	DATETIME16.	END*TIME STAMP

stop time of read operation.

TORMOT	NUM	4		TO*REMOTE*ID

TO remote identification.

TRACKS	NUM	4		TRACKS OR*FBA BLOCKS*USED

number of tracks for output storage. If the data file resides on an FBA device, the field contains the number of FBA blocks used instead of tracks.

USRINFO1	CHAR	16		USER*INFORMATION*($$ JOB CARD)

sixteen bytes of user information from the * $$ JOB card.

DOSRJE
DOS/VSE POWER Bisync Remote Job Entry Resources

There is one observation in data set DOSRJE for each account record created by DOS/VSE POWER for a remote job entry session that used bisynchronous communications protocol. An RJE BSC user session creates these account records when sign off or line stop is processed. It is a copy of the first 62 bytes of the line control block.

Variable	Type	Length	Format	Label
BSCOFFCD	NUM	4	MGDOSBS35.	BSC*SIGNOFF*REASON

SIGNOFF code. The value is formatted to:

01X:NORMAL SIGNOFF

02X:SIGNOFF FORCED DUE TO PSTOP CUU

04X:SIGNOFF FORCED DUE EXCESSIVE IDLE TIME

08X:SIGNOFF FORCED DUE UNRECOVERABLE I/O ERROR

10X:SIGNOFF FORCED DUE TO PEND OR PSTOP CUU,EOJ

20X:SIGNOFF FORCED DUE TO REAL STORAGE SHORTAGE

40X:SIGNOFF FORCED DUE PSTOP CUU,KILL

80X:DISASTROUS ERROR OCCURRED.

Variable	Type	Length	Format	Label
DOSREMOT	NUM	4		REMOTE*IDENTIFIER

remote identifier.

Variable	Type	Length	Format	Label
ERRCOUNT	NUM	4		ERROR*COUNT

error count for the session.

Variable	Type	Length	Format	Label
INVLRESP	NUM	4		INVALID*RESPONSE*COUNT

number of invalid responses during transmission.

Variable	Type	Length	Format	Label
LINEADDR	CHAR	3		LINE*ADDRESS

line address.

Variable	Type	Length	Format	Label
LINEPWRD	CHAR	8		LINE*PASSWORD

line password.

Variable	Type	Length	Format	Label
STARTIME	NUM	8	DATETIME16.	START*TIME STAMP

time RJE user signed on.

Variable	Type	Length	Format	Label
STOPTIME	NUM	8	DATETIME16.	END*TIME STAMP

time RJE user signed off.

TERMERRS	NUM	4		TERMINAL*ERROR*COUNT

terminal error count.

TIMEOUTS	NUM	4		TIMEOUT*COUNT

timeout count per session.

USRINFO1	CHAR	16		USER*INFORMATION*($$ JOB CARD)

sixteen bytes of user information from the * $$ JOB card.

XMSNCNT	NUM	4		TRANSMISSION*COUNT

transmission count per session.

DOSSNA
DOS/VSE POWER SNA Remote Job Entry Resources

There is one observation in DOSSNA for every DOS RJE session using SNA protocol. The record is written when the session terminates, and it is a copy of bytes 32-79 of the SNA unit control block.

Variable	Type	Length	Format	Label
DOSREMOT	NUM	4		REMOTE*IDENTIFIER
INVLRESP	NUM	4		INVALID*RESPONSE*COUNT
LUNAME	CHAR	8		LOGICAL*UNIT*NAME
SNAOFFCD	NUM	4	MGDOSSN24.	SNA*SIGNOFF*REASON
STARTIME	NUM	8	DATETIME16.	START*TIME STAMP
STOPTIME	NUM	8	DATETIME16.	END*TIME STAMP
USRINFO1	CHAR	16		USER*INFORMATION*($$ JOB CARD)

DOSREMOT NUM 4 REMOTE*IDENTIFIER
    remote identifier.

INVLRESP NUM 4 INVALID*RESPONSE*COUNT
    number of invalid responses during transmission.

LUNAME CHAR 8 LOGICAL*UNIT*NAME
    logical unit name.

SNAOFFCD NUM 4 MGDOSSN24. SNA*SIGNOFF*REASON
    01X= '01X:NORMAL TERMINATION'
    02X= '02X:ABNORMAL TERMINATION'.

STARTIME NUM 8 DATETIME16. START*TIME STAMP
    time of SIGNON.

STOPTIME NUM 8 DATETIME16. END*TIME STAMP
    time of SIGNOFF.

USRINFO1 CHAR 16 USER*INFORMATION*($$ JOB CARD)
    sixteen bytes of user information from * $$ JOB card.

TSOMCALL
TSO/MON Program Call, Command Response, and Resources

There is one observation in data set TSOMCALL for every TSO/MON command record, written each time a TSO user issues a selected command or subcommand. The installation selects commands that require recording by specifying C or P in the commands table entry in TSO/MON. C indicates that a command record with no program information is to be generated. P indicates that a command record containing program name and, optionally, the data set name from which the program was called are to be generated. The command record documents resource usage, response, and swap statistics for each selected command.

Normally, the command record is created for each call command, and for each program called, the response of all interactions during that call are recorded in the TSO/MON response buckets. For example, when the SAS System is called or when the SASCP command procedure is marked for command recording in TSO/MON, an observation in TSOMCALL describes each execution of the SAS System under TSO, and the response of each of the interactions with the SAS System is recorded in the TRIV*n*, NTRIV*n*, and LONG*n* response buckets. The TSOMCALL data can also be used to track usage of proprietary programs under TSO to justify their continued expense.

Variable	Type	Length	Format	Label
ASID	NUM	4		ADDRESS*SPACE*ID
address space identification number.				
COMND	CHAR	8		TSO/MON*COMMAND*CODE
abbreviated command name of this call.				
CPUSRBTM	NUM	4	TIME12.2	TASK*CPU SRB*TIME
CPU SRB time during this call.				
CPUTCBTM	NUM	4	TIME12.2	TASK*CPU TCB*TIME
CPU TCB time during this call.				
CPUTM	NUM	4	TIME12.2	TASK*TOTAL CPU*TIME
total CPU time during this call.				
DSNAME	CHAR	44		DATA SET*NAME OF*CALLED LIBRARY
optional data set name from which program was called.				

Variable	Type	Length	Format	Label
ELAPSTM	NUM	4	TIME12.2	ELAPSED*DURATION

elapsed duration of call.

| EXCPDASD | NUM | 4 | | EXCP*COUNT*DASD |

EXCP count caused by this program.

| INITTIME | NUM | 8 | DATETIME19.2 | STEP*INITIATE*EVENT |

beginning of execution of call.

| JOB | CHAR | 8 | | JOB NAME*OR*TSO USER |

job name or TSO user issuing call.

| LONGTM | NUM | 4 | TIME12.2 | ALL LONG*COMMANDS*DURATION |

total response time for all LONG interactions during call.

| LONG1 | NUM | 4 | | LONG*COMMANDS*FIRST |

number of LONG interactions completed during first LONG response interval.

| LONG2 | NUM | 4 | | LONG*COMMANDS*SECOND |

number of LONG interactions completed during second LONG response interval.

| LONG3 | NUM | 4 | | LONG*COMMANDS*THIRD |

number of LONG interactions completed during third LONG response interval.

| LONG4 | NUM | 4 | | LONG*COMMANDS*FOURTH |

number of LONG interactions completed during fourth LONG response interval.

| LONG5 | NUM | 4 | | LONG*COMMANDS*FIFTH |

number of LONG interactions completed during fifth LONG response interval.

| LONG6 | NUM | 4 | | LONG*COMMANDS*SIXTH |

number of LONG interactions completed during sixth LONG response interval.

| LONG7 | NUM | 4 | | LONG*COMMANDS*SEVENTH |

number of LONG interactions completed during seventh LONG response interval.

| LONG8 | NUM | 4 | | LONG*COMMANDS*EIGHTH |

number of LONG interactions completed during eighth LONG response interval.

| MAXRSPTM | NUM | 4 | TIME12.2 | MAXIMUM*RESPONSE*DURATION |

maximum response time of any interaction during this call.

Variable	Type	Length	Format	Label
NRLONG	NUM	4		NUMBER*OF LONG*COMMANDS

total number of LONG interactions during this call.

| NRNTRIV | NUM | 4 | | NUMBER OF*NONTRIVIAL* COMMANDS |

total number of nontrivial interactions during call.

| NRTRIV | NUM | 4 | | NUMBER OF*TRIVIAL*COMMANDS |

total number of trivial interactions during call.

| NTRIVTM | NUM | 4 | TIME12.2 | ALL NONTRIVIAL*COMMANDS* DURATION |

total response time for all nontrivial interactions during call.

| NTRIV1 | NUM | 4 | | NONTRIVIAL*COMMANDS*FIRST |

number of nontrivial interactions completed in first nontrivial response interval.

| NTRIV2 | NUM | 4 | | NONTRIVIAL*COMMANDS*SECOND |

number of nontrivial interactions completed in second nontrivial response interval.

| NTRIV3 | NUM | 4 | | NONTRIVIAL*COMMANDS*THIRD |

number of nontrivial interactions completed in third nontrivial response interval.

| NTRIV4 | NUM | 4 | | NONTRIVIAL*COMMANDS*FOURTH |

number of nontrivial interactions completed in fourth nontrivial response interval.

| NTRIV5 | NUM | 4 | | NONTRIVIAL*COMMANDS*FIFTH |

number of nontrivial interactions completed in fifth nontrivial response interval.

| NTRIV6 | NUM | 4 | | NONTRIVIAL*COMMANDS*SIXTH |

number of nontrivial interactions completed in sixth nontrivial response interval.

| NTRIV7 | NUM | 4 | | NONTRIVIAL*COMMANDS*SEVENTH |

number of nontrivial interactions completed in seventh nontrivial response interval.

| NTRIV8 | NUM | 4 | | NONTRIVIAL*COMMANDS*EIGHTH |

number of nontrivial interactions completed in eighth nontrivial response interval.

| PERFGRP | NUM | 4 | | PERFORMANCE*GROUP |

performance group of TSO user.

| PROGRAM | CHAR | 8 | | PROGRAM*NAME |

program name.

Variable	Type	Length	Format	Label
READTIME	NUM	8	DATETIME19.2	READ-IN*OR LOGON*EVENT

job read-in (TSO LOGON) time of this job or user.

| RESIDTM | NUM | 4 | TIME12.2 | RESIDENT*IN REAL*STORAGE |

duration that command was resident in real memory.

| SERVUNIT | NUM | 4 | | SERVICE*UNITS |

service units consumed by command.

| SMFTIME | NUM | 8 | DATETIME19.2 | SMF*RECORD*TIME STAMP |

time stamp of SMF record describing this event.

| SWPDELTM | NUM | 4 | TIME12.2 | SWAP-IN*DELAY |

swap-in delay time, measured from user ready to swap-in start.

| SWPINTM | NUM | 4 | TIME12.2 | SWAP-IN*TIME |

swap-in time, measured from swap-in start to restore complete.

| SYSTEM | CHAR | 4 | 4. | SYSTEM*ID |

system identification.

| TERMTIME | NUM | 8 | | TERMINATION*TIME STAMP |

termination time of this command.

| TGETCHAR | NUM | 4 | | TOTAL*TGET*CHARS |

number of characters transferred during TGET.

| TGETS | NUM | 4 | | TOTAL*TGET*COUNT |

number of TGETS issued.

| TPUTCHAR | NUM | 4 | | TOTAL*TPUT*CHARS |

number of characters transferred during TPUT.

| TPUTS | NUM | 4 | | TOTAL*TPUT*COUNT |

number of TPUTS issued.

| TRIVTM | NUM | 4 | TIME12.2 | ALL TRIVIAL*COMMANDS*DURATION |

total response time for all trivial interactions during call.

| TRIV1 | NUM | 4 | | TRIVIAL*COMMANDS*FIRST |

number of trivial interactions completed in first trivial response interval.

Variable	Type	Length	Format	Label
TRIV2	NUM	4		TRIVIAL*COMMANDS*SECOND

number of trivial interactions completed in second trivial response interval.

TRIV3	NUM	4		TRIVIAL*COMMANDS*THIRD

number of trivial interactions completed in third trivial response interval.

TRIV4	NUM	4		TRIVIAL*COMMANDS*FOURTH

number of trivial interactions completed in fourth trivial response interval.

TRIV5	NUM	4		TRIVIAL*COMMANDS*FIFTH

number of trivial interactions completed in fifth trivial response interval.

TRIV6	NUM	4		TRIVIAL*COMMANDS*SIXTH

number of trivial interactions completed in sixth trivial response interval.

TRIV7	NUM	4		TRIVIAL*COMMANDS*SEVENTH

number of trivial interactions completed in seventh trivial response interval.

TRIV8	NUM	4		TRIVIAL*COMMANDS*EIGHTH

number of trivial interactions completed in eighth trivial response interval.

TSOMSYST
TSO/MON System User Interval Response and Resources

There is 1 observation in TSOMSYST for each logged on TSO user for each TSO/MON installation-defined monitor interval (typically 15 to 30 minutes). The TSO user's resources consumed and responses received during that interval are captured by the TSO/MON product and the response times are reported in 8 distribution values (for example, 1, 2, 3, 4, 8, 15, 30, and >30 seconds). TSO transactions are categorized as trivial or nontrivial, based either on service units consumed or by the command name; CALL, TEST, and other commands are categorized as LONG. Thus, the response received is described by variables TRIV1-8, NTRIV1-8, and LONG1-8.

Variable	Type	Length	Format	Label
ASID	NUM	4		ADDRESS*SPACE*ID
				address space identification of this TSO user.
CONECTTM	NUM	4	TIME12.2	CONNECT*DURATION
				duration of connect time for this session during this interval.
CPUSRBTM	NUM	4	TIME12.2	TASK*CPU SRB*TIME
				CPU SRB time for this user for this interval.
CPUTCBTM	NUM	4	TIME12.2	TASK*CPU TCB*TIME
				CPU TCB time for this user for this interval.
CPUTM	NUM	4	TIME12.2	TASK*TOTAL CPU*TIME
				total CPU time for this user for this interval.
ENDTIME	NUM	8	DATETIME19.2	END TIME
				end time of this interval.
EXCPDASD	NUM	4		EXCP*COUNT*DASD
				EXCP count to DASD devices.
INTRVTM	NUM	4	TIME12.2	TSO/MON*INTERVAL*DURATION
				TSO/MON interval duration.
JOB	CHAR	8		JOB NAME*OR*TSO USER
				job name (batch); user ID (TSO).

Variable	Type	Length	Format	Label
LOGFLAG	CHAR	3		LOGON*LOGOFF*FLAG

flag that user logged on, off, or both during interval. The values are:

ON - user logged on during this interval

OFF - user logged off during this interval

ONF - user logged on and off during this interval.

| LONGTM | NUM | 4 | TIME12.2 | ALL LONG*COMMANDS*DURATION |

total response time for all LONG interactions during call.

| LONG1 | NUM | 4 | | LONG*COMMANDS*FIRST |

number of LONG interactions completed in first LONG response interval.

| LONG2 | NUM | 4 | | LONG*COMMANDS*SECOND |

number of LONG interactions completed in second LONG response interval.

| LONG3 | NUM | 4 | | LONG*COMMANDS*THIRD |

number of LONG interactions completed in third LONG response interval.

| LONG4 | NUM | 4 | | LONG*COMMANDS*FOURTH |

number of LONG interactions completed in fourth LONG response interval.

| LONG5 | NUM | 4 | | LONG*COMMANDS*FIFTH |

number of LONG interactions completed in fifth LONG response interval.

| LONG6 | NUM | 4 | | LONG*COMMANDS*SIXTH |

number of LONG interactions completed in sixth LONG response interval.

| LONG7 | NUM | 4 | | LONG*COMMANDS*SEVENTH |

number of LONG interactions completed in seventh LONG response interval.

| LONG8 | NUM | 4 | | LONG*COMMANDS*EIGHTH |

number of LONG interactions completed in eighth LONG response interval.

| MAXUSERS | NUM | 4 | | MAXIMUM*USERS*LOGGED ON |

maximum number of users during this interval.

| NRCMDS | NUM | 4 | | UNIQUE*COMMANDS*(ABBREV NAME) |

number of unique abbreviated commands executed by this user during this interval. This value is not the number of transactions that resulted, only the count of unique transactions.

| NRFCBS | NUM | 4 | | UNIQUE*COMMANDS*(FULL NAME) |

number of full command name commands executed by this user during this interval.

Variable	Type	Length	Format	Label
NRSWAPS	NUM	4		NUMBER*OF*SWAP-OUTS

number of swap-outs for this user for this interval.

NRSWPDEL	NUM	4		NUMBER*SWAP*DELAYS

number of swap delays for this user for this interval.

NRSWPIN	NUM	4		NUMBER*USER*SWAP-INS

number of swap-ins for this user for this interval.

NRTHINK	NUM	4		NUMBER*OF USER*THINKS

number of user thinks for this interval.

NRTRANS	NUM	4		NUMBER*OF*TRANS ENDED

number of transactions counted by SRM. Although this number matches the transaction counts recorded in TYPE72 data, the definitions of an SRM transaction and a TSO/MON (or TSO user's) transaction are quite different.

NTRIVTM	NUM	4	TIME12.2	ALL NONTRIVIAL*COMMANDS* DURATION

total response time for all nontrivial interactions during the call.

NTRIV1	NUM	4		NONTRIVIAL*COMMANDS*FIRST

number of nontrivial interactions completed in first nontrivial response interval.

NTRIV2	NUM	4		NONTRIVIAL*COMMANDS*SECOND

number of nontrivial interactions completed in second nontrivial response interval.

NTRIV3	NUM	4		NONTRIVIAL*COMMANDS*THIRD

number of nontrivial interactions completed in third nontrivial response interval.

NTRIV4	NUM	4		NONTRIVIAL*COMMANDS*FOURTH

number of nontrivial interations completed in fourth nontrivial response interval.

NTRIV5	NUM	4		NONTRIVIAL*COMMANDS*FIFTH

number of nontrivial interactions completed in fifth nontrivial response interval.

NTRIV6	NUM	4		NONTRIVIAL*COMMANDS*SIXTH

number of nontrivial interactions completed in sixth nontrivial response interval.

NTRIV7	NUM	4		NONTRIVIAL*COMMANDS*SEVENTH

number of nontrivial interactions completed in seventh nontrivial response interval.

Variable	Type	Length	Format	Label
NTRIV8	NUM	4		NONTRIVIAL*COMMANDS*EIGHTH

number of nontrivial interactions completed in eighth nontrivial response interval.

| PERFGRP | NUM | 4 | | PERFORMANCE*GROUP |

performance group of this TSO user at end of interval.

| READTIME | NUM | 8 | DATETIME19.2 | READ-IN*OR LOGON*EVENT |

job read-in (TSO LOGON) time of this user. This field will be constant across the multiple intervals from the same TSO session.

| RESIDTM | NUM | 4 | TIME12.2 | RESIDENT*IN REAL*STORAGE |

duration user was in real memory during this interval.

| SERVUNIT | NUM | 4 | | SERVICE*UNITS |

service units consumed by user during this interval.

| SMFTIME | NUM | 8 | DATETIME19.2 | SMF*RECORD*TIME STAMP |

time stamp when record was written to SMF.

| STRTTIME | NUM | 8 | DATETIME19.2 | START*TRANSACTION*TIME STAMP |

time stamp at beginning of interval.

| SWAPHIGH | NUM | 4 | | SWAP*HIGHWATER*MARK (2K BLKS) |

swap high-water mark. The greatest number of 2K blocks swapped during the interval.

| SWAPSIZE | NUM | 4 | | SWAP SIZE*TOTAL*(2K BLKS) |

total number of bytes swapped during interval in 2K blocks.

| SWPDELTM | NUM | 4 | TIME12.2 | SWAP-IN*DELAY |

swap-in delay time, measured from user-ready to swap-in start.

| SWPINTM | NUM | 4 | TIME12.2 | SWAP-IN*TIME |

swap-in time, measured from swap-in start to restore complete.

| SYSTEM | CHAR | 4 | 4. | SYSTEM*ID |

identification of system on which this user executed.

| TGETCHAR | NUM | 4 | | TOTAL*TGET*CHARS |

total characters transferred via TGET in interval.

| TGETS | NUM | 4 | | TOTAL*TGET*COUNT |

number of TGETS completed during interval.

Variable	Type	Length	Format	Label
THINKTM	NUM	4	TIME12.2	TOTAL*THINK*TIME

total user think time for this interval.

| TPUTCHAR | NUM | 4 | | TOTAL*TPUT*CHARS |

total characters transferred via TPUTS in interval.

| TPUTS | NUM | 4 | | TOTAL*TPUT*COUNT |

number of TPUTS completed during interval.

| TRIVTM | NUM | 4 | TIME12.2 | ALL TRIVIAL*COMMANDS*DURATION |

total response time for all trivial interactions from this user during this interval.

| TRIV1 | NUM | 4 | | TRIVIAL*COMMANDS*FIRST |

number of trivial interactions completed in first trivial response interval.

| TRIV2 | NUM | 4 | | TRIVIAL*COMMANDS*SECOND |

number of trivial interactions completed in second trivial response interval.

| TRIV3 | NUM | 4 | | TRIVIAL*COMMANDS*THIRD |

number of trivial interactions completed in third trivial response interval.

| TRIV4 | NUM | 4 | | TRIVIAL*COMMANDS*FOURTH |

number of trivial interactions completed in fourth trivial response interval.

| TRIV5 | NUM | 4 | | TRIVIAL*COMMANDS*FIFTH |

number of trivial interactions completed in fifth trivial response interval.

| TRIV6 | NUM | 4 | | TRIVIAL*COMMANDS*SIXTH |

number of trivial interactions completed in sixth trivial response interval.

| TRIV7 | NUM | 4 | | TRIVIAL*COMMANDS*SEVENTH |

number of trivial interactions completed in seventh trivial response interval.

| TRIV8 | NUM | 4 | | TRIVIAL*COMMANDS*EIGHTH |

number of trivial interactions completed in eighth trivial response interval.

VMDEVICE
VM Device Attach

There is one observation in data set VMDEVICE for every successful attach of a VM device.

Variable	Type	Length	Format	Label
ACCOUNT	CHAR	8		ACCOUNT*NUMBER

eight-byte VM account field for this session.

BLOCKS	NUM	4		NUMBER*OF*BLOCKS

number of blocks allocated on device.

CONECTTM	NUM	4	TIME9.	SESSION*CONNECT*TIME

duration device was attached to this user's session.

CYLINDER	NUM	4		TEMPORARY*DISK*CYLINDERS

number of cylinders of temporary allocation on this device.

DEVICECL	CHAR	8		DEVICE*CLASS

device class of this device.

DEVICETY	NUM	4	HEX2.	DEVICE*TYPE*CODE

device type of this device.

FEATURE	NUM	4	HEX2.	DEVICE*FEATURE*CODE

device feature code of this device.

MODEL	NUM	4	HEX2.	DEVICE*MODEL

device model number.

STARTIME	NUM	8	DATETIME19.2	START TIME*OF*INTERVAL

start time of attachment.

USER	CHAR	8		USER*ID

user identification.

VMID	CHAR	2		RECORD*ID

record ID of this device record.

VMDISK
VM Failed Disk Attach

There is one observation in data set VMDISK for every VM account record describing a failed attempt to attach a VM minidisk.

Variable	Type	Length	Format	Label
ACCOUNT	CHAR	8		ACCOUNT*NUMBER
eight-byte VM account field for this session.				
ACCTTIME	NUM	8	DATETIME16.	TIME STAMP*OF THIS*RECORD
time stamp when this record was written.				
MINIADDR	NUM	4	HEX6.	MINI*DISK*ADDRESS
address of mini disk on which attaching was attempted.				
OWNERID	CHAR	8		OWNER*ID
id of owner of disk being attached.				
TERMADDR	NUM	4	HEX6.	TERMINAL*ADDRESS
terminal address of user attempting attach.				
USER	CHAR	8		USER*ID
user identification.				

VMLINK
VM Failed Link

There is one observation in data set VMLINK for every VM account record describing a failed attempt to link.

Variable	Type	Length	Format	Label
ACCOUNT	CHAR	8		ACCOUNT*NUMBER
				eight-byte VM account field for this session.
ACCTTIME	NUM	8	DATETIME16.	TIME STAMP*OF THIS*RECORD
				time stamp when this record was written.
BADPASSW	CHAR	8		BAD*PASSWORD
				bad password, which caused LINK to fail.
JPSLNKAR	NUM	4		JPSLNKAR
				JPSLNKAR.
MINIADDR	NUM	4	HEX6.	MINI*DISK*ADDRESS
				address of mini disk involved.
OWNERID	CHAR	8		OWNER*ID
				user id of owner of resource being LINKed.
PWCOUNT	NUM	4		PWCOUNT
				PWCOUNT.
TERMADDR	NUM	4	HEX6.	TERMINAL*ADDRESS
				terminal address being used by this user.
USER	CHAR	8		USER*ID
				user identification.

VMLOGON
VM Failed Log On

There is one observation in data set VMLOGON for every VM account record describing a failed log on attempt.

Variable	Type	Length	Format	Label
ACCOUNT	CHAR	8		ACCOUNT*NUMBER
				eight-byte VM account field for this session.
ACCTTIME	NUM	8	DATETIME16.	TIME STAMP*OF THIS*RECORD
				time stamp when this record was written.
BADPASSW	CHAR	8		BAD*PASSWORD
				bad password, which caused failure.
JPDLOGAR	NUM	4		JPDLOGAR
				JPDLOGAR.
PWCOUNT	NUM	4		PWCOUNT
				PWCOUNT.
TERMADDR	NUM	4	HEX6.	TERMINAL*ADDRESS
				terminal address of this user.
USER	CHAR	8		USER*ID
				user identification.

VMSESSN
VM Virtual Machine Session Resources

There is one observation in data set VMSESSN for every VM account record for each user. Normally, a session account record is written at log off, and these observations would correspond to a TSO session record. However, VM allows you to issue automatic commands. If this automatic command facility is used to invoke the ACCOUNT ALL command every hour, session records that describe the resources consumed by each VM machine can be created for hourly intervals. The hourly session account observations can be summed to provide total hourly resources consumed on the VM hardware, and profiles of usage by department and machine can easily be generated. See chapter six for more information.

Variable	Type	Length	Format	Label
ACCOUNT	CHAR	8		ACCOUNT*NUMBER

eight-byte VM account field for this session.

| CONECTTM | NUM | 4 | TIME9. | SESSION*CONNECT*TIME |

duration of this session (or this account interval). It is not possible to identify if the user logged off or if the record was created by the ACCOUNT ALL facility.

| CPUCPTM | NUM | 4 | TIME13.3 | CP*(TTIME−VTIME)*CPU TIME |

CPU time consumed by CP on behalf of this virtual machine. This is the overhead services of CP as the result of requests by this virtual machine (SIO, paging, and so forth). This is the difference between the CPUVMTM and CPUVIRTM recorded by VM. It is equivalent to the MVS overhead consumed in managing a task, but in MVS the value is not recorded.

| CPUVIRTM | NUM | 4 | TIME13.3 | VIRTUAL*MACHINE*CPU TIME |

CPU time consumed by this virtual machine in virtual machine execution itself. This loosely represents the utilization of that virtual machine (or CMS session) due to its application. In VM circles, this is referred to as the VTIME. See also CPUVMTM and CPUCPTM.

| CPUVMTM | NUM | 4 | TIME13.3 | TOTAL*(CP+VM)*CPU TIME |

total CPU time consumed by and caused by this virtual machine. This is the sum of CPUCPTM and CPUVIRTM, and in VM circles, this is referred to as the TTIME.

| EXCPPGIN | NUM | 4 | | NUMBER*OF PAGE*READS |

count of SIOs issued for page-ins.

| EXCPPGOU | NUM | 4 | | NUMBER*OF PAGE*WRITES |

count of SIOs issued for page-outs.

Variable	Type	Length	Format	Label
EXCPSIO	NUM	4		NUMBER*OF*START IO

count of SIOs issued for virtual machine I/O.

| SPOOLCRD | NUM | 4 | | CARDS*READ*FROM SPOOL |

count of cards read from VM spool.

| SPOOLINE | NUM | 4 | | LINES*SPOOLED*TO PRINT |

count of print lines sent to VM spool.

| SPOOLPUN | NUM | 4 | | CARDS*SPOOLED*TO PUNCH |

count of punch images sent to VM spool.

| STARTIME | NUM | 8 | DATETIME19.2 | START TIME*OF*INTERVAL |

beginning time stamp of this session record. The end time of the interval is
STARTIME + CONECTTM.

| USER | CHAR | 8 | | USER*ID |

user identification.

VMUSRDAT
VM User Created Data

There is one observation in data VMUSRDAT for each VM account record created by the optional user interface routine.

Variable	Type	Length	Format	Label
USER	CHAR	8		USER*ID
user identification.				
USERDATA	CHAR	70		USER*FORMATTED*DATA
user data written to VM account file.				

VMVCNA
VM VCNA Session

There is one observation in VMVCNA for every VM user session that originated at a VTAM terminal. This session record describes the interactions between VTAM and the VM user session. There is a separate observation in VMSESSN corresponding to this communication session observation.

Variable	Type	Length	Format	Label
ACCOUNT	CHAR	8		ACCOUNT*NUMBER
eight-byte VM account field for this session.				
CONSOUT	NUM	4		CONSOLE*OUTPUT*LINES
output lines sent to console.				
COPYREQ	NUM	4		COPY*REQUESTS
number of copy requests.				
ENDTIME	NUM	8	DATETIME19.2	END*INTERNAL*TIME STAMP
time stamp of log off.				
INBYTES	NUM	4		TOTAL*INPUT*BYTES
total input bytes.				
INPUTRU	NUM	4		INPUT*REQUEST*UNITS
number of input request units.				
OUTBYTES	NUM	4		TOTAL*OUTPUT*BYTES
total bytes output.				
OUTPUTRU	NUM	4		OUTPUT*REQUEST*UNITS
number of output request units.				
STARTIME	NUM	8	DATETIME19.2	START TIME*OF*INTERVAL
time stamp of log on.				
USER	CHAR	8		USER*ID
user identification.				

TYPE0
IPL

Data set TYPE0 contains one observation for each type 0 SMF record, written when the operator enters the command to IPL the system. The TYPE0 data set is useful for tracking system uptime since an IPL signifies the complete start-up of the system, usually because the system crashed. IBM CE diagnostics executed during Preventive Maintenance occasionally write over the clock area, and occasionally IPLs during these PM periods contain incorrect dates and times.

Variable	Type	Length	Format	Label
DOWNTM	NUM	4		ESTIMATED*SYSTEM*DOWNTIME

duration from SMF record that immediately preceded this record, if preceding record was written on same system as this record. This is an estimate of downtime of the operating system, but is valid only if the SMF data were processed in the same order as they were created.

IPLTIME	NUM	4	DATETIME19.2	SMF*RECORD*TIME STAMP

datetime stamp of the IPL. The date and time when the operator entered the command to IPL the system.

OPTDSETS	CHAR	3		CREATE*DATA SET/DASD*RECORDS?

data set accounting option. If selected, SMF record types 14, 15, 17, 18, 62, 63, 67, or 68 may be written.

value	meaning
NO	option not chosen
YES	option chosen.

OPTVOL	CHAR	3		CREATE*VOLUME*RECORDS(19/69)?

data set accounting option. If selected, SMF record types 10 or 69 may be written.

value	meaning
NO	option not chosen
YES	option chosen.

REALSIZE	NUM	4		REAL*MEMORY*SIZE(KBYTES)

real memory size, in 1024 (1K) bytes. Not necessarily correct in a multi- or dyadic-processor environment prior to 308x series. It seems to reflect the installed real memory, minus the part taken by the SP operating system.

REC	CHAR	4		TEMPORARY*SCRATCHES*(PERM/ALL)?

SMF generation parameter. It should scratch records for temporary data sets to be written. REC(PERM) is suggested because it reduces the volume of SMF type 17 records written.

Variable	Type	Length	Format	Label

There seems to be little need for a record confirming that a temporary data set was scratched.

old value	suppress SMF scratch records for:
0	17 (temporary only)
2	none
new value	**write SMF scratch records for:**
PERM	permanent data sets only
ALL	all (permanent and temporary) data set scratches.

SMCAJWTM   NUM   4   TIME12.   JOB WAIT*(ABEND 522)*LIMIT

Job Wait Time (JWT) parameter. How long a task can remain in a wait state before being canceled by the operating system with a system abend 522.

SMFBUFF   NUM   4   SMF*BUFFER*SIZE(BYTES)

SMF buffer size, in bytes. The blocksize of the records written to the SYS1.MANx data set is half this value.

SYSTEM   CHAR   4   4.   SYSTEM*ID

identification of the IPLed system.

VIRTSIZE   NUM   4   VIRTUAL*MEMORY*SIZE

virtual memory size, in 1024 (1K) bytes.

TYPE0203
Dump Program Header or Trailer

Data set TYPE0203 contains one observation for each type 2 or 3 SMF record. A type 2 SMF record is written at the beginning of the execution of the IFASMFDP program (when it specifies DUMP and CLEAR). A type 3 SMF record is written at the end of the execution of this SMF dump program.

Variable	Type	Length	Format	Label
DUMP	CHAR	7		SMF*DUMP*EVENT

event causing this record.

value	meaning
HEADER	beginning of dump of SMF file
TRAILER	end of dump of SMF file.

SMFTIME	NUM	8	DATETIME19.2	SMF*RECORD*TIME STAMP

datetime stamp of the record.

SYSTEM	CHAR	4	4.	SYSTEM*ID

identification of system on which the dump program executed. Note that this is not necessarily the system identification of the system being dumped since the SMF data from a system that is down for maintenance (down system) can be dumped from a different system. In that case, the dumped data records would contain the down system's ID, but the type 2 and 3 records would be written with the up system's ID. This is why type 2 and 3 records need to be excluded when testing to see if SMF records are written in sequence; that they are not in the dumped data in datetime sequence.

TYPE434
TSO/JOB Step Termination

Data set TYPE434 contains one observation for each type 4 (batch step) or type 34 (TSO step) record.

It permits resource consumption to be classified according to users, jobs, programs, time of day, and so forth. Because there are so few differences between batch steps and TSO steps (only a few variables are different), type 4 and type 34 records are grouped together.

Type 4 and 34 records are written for each step that terminated or was flushed, except steps terminating after an operator CANCEL command.

The basic SMF record consists of:

- a fixed portion, containing job and step identification information; step event time stamps; and step resources
- a variable portion, containing device information: one entry per DD statement that includes the unit address and unit type allocated to DD, plus the EXCP count for the DD
- another variable portion, containing step accounting information; this information is rarely used since most installations do accounting at the job level rather than at the step level
- a fixed portion with paging statistics.

The handling of the variable-length device portion is a matter of choice. To maximize the useful information and minimize the size of the TYPE434 data set, device information from the DD segments is consolidated by device type. Thus the TYPE434 data set contains the total EXCP count for each device type (for example, TAPE, 3330, 3380, VIO, and so forth) for the step. In addition, the number of mountable tape and 3330 disk drives allocated is counted. The device portion is handled in the installation-dependent macro, IMACCHAN.

The new TYPE30_4 data set, built from the type 30, subtype 4 record on MVS/SE2 (or MVS/SP1) and later operating systems, contains all the information in TYPE434 and more (for example, I/O connect time in MVS/XA is not carried in the TYPE434 data).

Variable	Type	Length	Format	Label
ABEND	CHAR	6		COMPLETION*ABEND*INDICATOR

step completion indicator. A description of how and why this step ended. For abnormal completions, see the variable CONDCODE for amplification of the reason for termination.

Variable	Type	Length	Format	Label

value	meaning
blank	normal completion.
CANCEXIT	step was canceled by an SMF exit. The variable CONDCODE contains the exit that did the canceling.
FLUSH	step was flushed (because a previous step had failed).
OTHER	step abended for unknown reason. The variable CONDCODE contains the value in register 15 at time of the abend. This value is set when the step abend bit is on, but the numerical contents of abend code are inconsistent with SMF documentation.
RESTART	step was restarted. Any subsequent restart will have program name of IEFRSTRT.
RETURN	step completed with nonzero condition code. CONDCODE contains the returned value.
SYSTEM	step completed with system abnormal end (abend). The variable CONDCODE contains the abend code.
USER	step completed with an abend issued by a user program rather than by the operating system itself. Any programmer can choose to issue a user abend rather than a return code (for example, the SAS System issues a USER ABEND 999 when ERRORABEND is specified and an error occurs). The variable CONDCODE contains the abend code.

ACCOUNT1   CHAR   53   FIRST*ACCOUNT*FIELD

first step account field specified on the EXEC statement. Step accounting is rarely used since most installations use accounting at the job level (in which case the account number is in the TYPE535 data set variable of the same name). See NRACCTFL to determine if any account fields were specified and LENACCT1 to determine the length of the first field.

ACCOUNT2   CHAR   10   SECOND*ACCOUNT*FIELD

second step account field specified on the EXEC statement.

ACCOUNT3   CHAR   4   THIRD*ACCOUNT*FIELD

third step account field specified on the EXEC statement.

Variable	Type	Length	Format	Label

ACCOUNT4   CHAR   4   FOURTH*ACCOUNT*FIELD

fourth step account field specified on the EXEC statement.

ACCOUNT5   CHAR   4   FIFTH*ACCOUNT*FIELD

fifth step account field specified on the EXEC statement.

ACCOUNT6   CHAR   4   SIXTH*ACCOUNT*FIELD

sixth step account field specified on the EXEC statement.

ACCOUNT7   CHAR   4   SEVENTH*ACCOUNT*FIELD

seventh step account field specified on the EXEC statement.

ACCOUNT8   CHAR   4   EIGHTH*ACCOUNT*FIELD

eighth step account field specified on the EXEC statement.

ACCOUNT9   CHAR   4   NINTH*ACCOUNT*FIELD

ninth step account field specified on the EXEC statement.

ACTIVETM   NUM   4   TIME12.2   TASK*ACTIVE*TIME

step active time. Duration that the System Resource Manager (SRM) defined the task as active. A task is made active when the SRM decides the task should be given service. The SRM then notifies the ASM to bring in the task (if the task is swapped out). The difference between EXECTM and ACTIVETM is the duration that the task was swapped out or was not-ready or was waiting for mount to complete. See also RESIDTM.

ALOCTIME   NUM   8   DATETIME19.2   START OF*ALLOCATION*EVENT

allocation time stamp. This is the second event in the lifetime of a step and signifies the beginning of allocation of the correct device for each DD card in the step. If this field is missing, it means that the step never entered allocation, usually for some type of execution JCL error (such as, data set not found in the catalog). See LOADTIME and ALOCTM.

ALOCTM   NUM   4   TIME12.2   ALLOCATION*DELAY*DURATION

step allocation time. Duration required for the operating system to allocate all devices. This is LOADTIME minus ALOCTIME. It is missing if the step never entered allocation or if the job entered allocation but failed to complete it, usually because of device unavailability. For example, if sufficient tape drives were unavailable and the operator replied cancel to the allocation recovery message, the LOADTIME and this field would both be missing.

AVGWKSET   NUM   4   5.   AVERAGE*WORKING*SET (PAGES)

average working set size, in pages (one page is 4096 bytes). This value is the result of dividing the page-seconds by the CPU (TCB time only since page-seconds are pages times TCB seconds) to get an estimate of the real storage working set of this program. It is considerably less repeatable than other resource measures for the same program, especially if the TCB seconds are less than a few seconds; it often varies by 30% and sometimes by much more. However, it is still the best indication of the real memory used by a task.

Variable	Type	Length	Format	Label
COMPAGIN	NUM	4		COMMON*AREA*PAGE-INS

common area page-ins.

| COMRECLM | NUM | 4 | | COMMON*AREA*RECLAIMS |

common area page-reclaims.

| CONDCODE | NUM | 4 | HEX4. | COMPLETION*CONDITION*CODE |

condition code. This variable amplifies the meaning of abend. It is internally a binary number but is formatted to display as hex so that testing for a specific condition uses this syntax:

IF ABEND= 'SYSTEM' AND CONDCODE=0322X THEN ...

ABEND *value contents of* CONDCODE

	value	canceled by
CANCEXIT	4	IEFUJI (job initiation)
CANCEXIT	2	IEFUSI (step initiation)
CANCEXIT	1	IEFACTRT (step termination)
OTHER		completion code value
RETURN		return code value
SYSTEM		system abend code
USER		user abend code.

| CPUSRBTM | NUM | 4 | TIME12.2 | TASK*CPU SRB*TIME |

duration that the CPU was executing instructions under a Service Request Block (SRB) for this task.

| CPUTCBTM | NUM | 4 | TIME12.2 | TASK*CPU TCB*TIME |

duration that the CPU was executing instructions under the Task Control Block (TCB) for this task.

| CPUTM | NUM | 4 | TIME12.2 | TASK*TCB+SRB*TIME |

duration that the CPU was executing instructions for this task. Sum of CPUSRBTM and CPUTCBTM.

| CPUUNITS | NUM | 4 | | CPU TCB*SERVICE*UNITS |

SRM recorded TCB CPU service units consumed by this task. A TCB CPU service unit is defined as the number of TCB CPU seconds times the installation-specified CPUCOEFF coefficient (specified in the IEAIPSxx member of PARMLIB and reported in SAS data set TYPE72) times a machine-dependent constant (which is set at IPL time based on the CPU model and CPU version). SOURCLIB member TYPE7072 provides one source of the value

Variable	Type	Length	Format	Label

of the machine-dependent constant, called SU_SEC, since it sets the number of service units generated by one second of CPU time.

| DPRTY | NUM | 4 | HEX2. | DISPATCH*PRIORITY |

dispatching priority at step termination.

| DSENQTM | NUM | 4 | TIME12.2 | DATA SET*ENQUEUE*DELAY |

duration of step between initiation and beginning of allocation. So named because for the first step of a job, the wait for data set enqueue occurs in this interval.

| D3330DRV | NUM | 4 | | MOUNTABLE*3330 DRIVES*ALLOCATED |

number of different 3330 mountable disk drives allocated to this step, where mountable is defined by an explicit list of unit addresses in the IMAC3330 member.

| ELAPSTM | NUM | 4 | TIME12.2 | ELAPSED*DURATION |

duration of step between initiation and termination, the step elapsed time. During this duration, the step owned the initiator. It is the sum of DSENQTM, ALOCTM, and EXECTM.

| EXCPCOMM | NUM | 4 | | EXCPS*COUNT*COMM |

EXCPs (blocks of data) to communication devices.

| EXCPDASD | NUM | 4 | | EXCPS*COUNT*DASD |

sum of EXCPs to 2305, 3330, 3340, 3350, 3375, and 3380 devices.

| EXCPGRAF | NUM | 4 | | EXCPS*COUNT*GRAPHICS |

EXCPs (blocks of data) to graphics devices.

| EXCPMSS | NUM | 4 | | EXCPS*COUNT*MSS |

EXCPs (blocks of data) to mass storage volume.

| EXCPTAPE | NUM | 4 | | EXCPS*COUNT*TAPE |

EXCPs (blocks of data) to tape volumes.

| EXCPTODD | NUM | 4 | | TOTAL EXCPS*IN ALL*DD SEGMENTS |

total EXCPs to all DDs in this step.

| EXCPUREC | NUM | 4 | | EXCPS*COUNT*UNITREC |

EXCPs to unit record devices that were allocated directly to the step. This value does not include EXCPs to the JES spool devices.

| EXCPVIO | NUM | 4 | | EXCPS*COUNT*VIO |

EXCPs to virtual I/O.

Variable	Type	Length	Format	Label
EXCP2305	NUM	4		EXCPS*COUNT*2305

EXCPs (blocks of data) to 2305 devices.

EXCP3330	NUM	4		EXCPS*COUNT*3330

EXCPs (blocks of data) to 3330 devices.

EXCP3340	NUM	4		EXCPS*COUNT*3340

EXCPs (blocks of data) to 3340 devices.

EXCP3350	NUM	4		EXCPS*COUNT*3350

EXCPs (blocks of data) to 3350 devices.

EXCP3375	NUM	4		EXCPS*COUNT*3375

EXCPs (blocks of data) to 3375 devices.

EXCP3380	NUM	4		EXCPS*COUNT*3380

EXCPs (blocks of data) to 3380 devices.

EXECTM	NUM	4	TIME12.2	EXECUTION*DURATION*TIME

duration of step between load time and termination, the step execution time. It is only during this duration that the program can actually execute instructions (and often not even for all of this time). See ACTIVETM and RESIDTM.

ID	NUM	2		RECORD*ID

SMF record type.

value	meaning
4	batch step
34	TSO step.

INITTIME	NUM	8	DATETIME19.2	STEP*INITIATE*EVENT

initiation time stamp.

IOUNITS	NUM	4		IO*SERVICE*UNITS

SRM recorded I/O service units consumed by this task. In MVS/370, an I/O service unit is defined as the number of EXCP times the installation-specified IOCCOEFF coefficient (specified in the IEAIPSxx member of PARMLIB and reported in SAS data set TYPE72). In MVS/XA, the IOUNITS can be based on either EXCPs or Device Connect Time (IOTM). It is not possible to tell from an MVS/XA step record which resource (EXCP or IOTM) was the basis of I/O service measurement.

JOB	CHAR	8		JOB NAME*OR*TSO USER

job name (batch); user ID (TSO).

Variable	Type	Length	Format	Label
LENACCT1	NUM	4		LENGTH*ACCOUNT*ONE

length of the first account field on the EXEC JCL card.

| LENACCT2 | NUM | 4 | | LENGTH*ACCOUNT*TWO |

length of the second account field on the EXEC JCL card.

| LENACCT3 | NUM | 4 | | LENGTH*ACCOUNT*THREE |

length of the third account field on the EXEC JCL card.

| LENACCT4 | NUM | 4 | | LENGTH*ACCOUNT*FOUR |

length of the fourth account field on the EXEC JCL card.

| LENACCT5 | NUM | 4 | | LENGTH*ACCOUNT*FIVE |

length of the fifth account field on the EXEC JCL card.

| LENACCT6 | NUM | 4 | | LENGTH*ACCOUNT*SIX |

length of the sixth account field on the EXEC JCL card.

| LENACCT7 | NUM | 4 | | LENGTH*ACCOUNT*SEVEN |

length of the seventh account field on the EXEC JCL card.

| LENACCT8 | NUM | 4 | | LENGTH*ACCOUNT*EIGHT |

length of the eighth account field on the EXEC JCL card.

| LENACCT9 | NUM | 4 | | LENGTH*ACCOUNT*NINE |

length of the ninth account field on the EXEC JCL card.

| LOADTIME | NUM | 8 | DATETIME19.2 | PROGRAM*FETCH*EVENT |

load (problem program start) time stamp. This event is the third one in the lifetime of a step and signifies the loading of the program from the library into real memory. If this field is missing, it means the program was never completely loaded into memory by PROGRAM FETCH (that part of the operating system that loads programs). Only after the program is loaded into real memory does the program begin to execute its instructions, open its files, and so forth.

| LOCLINFO | CHAR | 8 | | LOCAL*INSTALLATION*FIELD |

locally-defined field. The field is filled in by the installation's SMF exit routines.

| LPAGINS | NUM | 4 | | LPA*AREA*PAGE-INS |

link pack area page-ins.

| LPARECLM | NUM | 4 | | LPA*AREA*RECLAIMS |

link pack area reclaims.

Variable	Type	Length	Format	Label
MAXADRSP	NUM	4		MAXIMUM*VIRTUAL*STORAGE(K)

address space (memory if VIRTREAL= 'R') used. Sum of PVTTOP and PVTBOT.

| MSOUNITS | NUM | 4 | | MEMORY*SERVICE*UNITS |

SRM recorded memory service units consumed by this task. A memory service unit is defined as the number of page seconds (real pages times CPU TCB seconds) times the installation- specified MSOCOEFF (specified in the IEAIPSxx member of PARMLIB and reported in SAS data set TYPE72) times a constant of one-fiftieth (to normalize memory service to that of CPU and I/O).

| NDASDDD | NUM | 4 | | NUMBER*DASD*DD CARDS |

number of DD statements that allocated DASD devices.

| NRACCTFL | NUM | 4 | | NUMBER*ACCOUNT*FIELDS |

number of account fields specified on the EXEC JCL card.

| NTAPEDD | NUM | 4 | | NUMBER*TAPE*DD CARDS |

number of DD statements that allocated TAPE devices.

| NUMDD | NUM | 4 | | NUMBER*ALL*DD CARDS |

total number of DD statements in this step. Note that NUMDD−(NDASDD+NTAPEDD) equals the number of DDs for JES, VIO, MSS, COMM, UREC, and graphics allocations.

| PAGEINS | NUM | 4 | | TOTAL*PAGE-INS |

number of page-ins.

| PAGEOUTS | NUM | 4 | | TOTAL*PAGE-OUTS |

number of page-outs.

| PAGESECS | NUM | 4 | | MEMORY*PAGESECS*(PER TCB) |

page-seconds of real memory used by this step. This value, when divided by the CPUTCBTM (seconds), gives the AVGWKSET value.

| PAGESTOL | NUM | 4 | | PAGES*STOLEN*AWAY |

pages stolen from this step.

| PERFGRP | NUM | 4 | | PERFORMANCE*GROUP |

performance group in which this step was at termination.

| PKEY | NUM | 4 | HEX2. | PROTECT*KEY |

storage-protect key.

Variable	Type	Length	Format	Label

PROGRAM   CHAR   8   PROGRAM*NAME

program name (PGM=) from EXEC statement. If backward reference was used, the PROGRAM value is *.DD. If the current step is a restarted step, its PROGRAM value and that of all subsequent steps will be IEFRSTRT.

PVTAREA   NUM   4   SIZE OF*PRIVATE*AREA

if VIRTREAL= 'V' (virtual storage was specified), the PVTAREA value is the size of the private area in 1024 (1K) bytes. The private area is constant in size, set at IPL, and is the maximum address space that a task can request. If VIRTREAL= 'R' (real storage was specified), the PVTAREA value is the REGION requested in K-bytes.

PVTBOT   NUM   4   GETMAIN*SIZE*FROM BOTTOM

if VIRTREAL= 'V' (virtual storage was specified), the PVTBOT value is the address space used (in K-bytes) from the bottom of the private area (that is, subpools 0-127, 251, and 252). If VIRTREAL= 'R', the PVTBOT value is the amount of contiguous real storage used, in K-bytes.

PVTTOP   NUM   4   GETMAIN*SIZE*FROM TOP

if VIRTREAL= 'V' (virtual storage was specified), the PVTTOP value is the address space used, in K-bytes, from the top of the private area, that is, subpools 229, 239, 236-237, 253-255, the LSQA and SWA. If VIRTREAL= 'R' (real storage was specified), the PVTTOP value is the amount of storage in K-bytes used that was not from the contiguous storage reserved for the program.

READTIME   NUM   8   DATETIME19.2   READ-IN*OR LOGON*EVENT

job read-in (TSO LOGON) time stamp.

RECLAIMS   NUM   4   PAGES*RECLAIMED

pages reclaimed. See TYPE71 appendix for discussion.

REGREQST   NUM   4   REGION*REQUESTED*IN JCL

region size established, in 1K units taken from REGION= parameter in JCL, and rounded up to 4K boundary. If V=R, this is the amount of contiguous real storage reserved for the program. If the region requested was greater than 16 megabytes, the region established resides above 16 megabytes, and this field contains a minimum value of 32 megabytes.

RESIDTM   NUM   4   TIME12.2   RESIDENT*IN REAL*STORAGE

duration that the step was resident in real storage. This value is accumulated by the SRM and represents the absolute maximum duration that the program could have executed instructions. The difference between RESIDTM and CPUTM is the duration that the task was in memory but not dispatched and represents wait for CPU and wait for I/O completion, among other waits while in memory.

Variable	Type	Length	Format	Label
SERVUNIT	NUM	4		TOTAL*SERVICE*UNITS

total SRM service units consumed by this step. It is the sum of CPUUNITS, SRBUNITS, IOUNITS, and MSOUNITS.

SRBUNITS	NUM	4		CPU SRB*SERVICE*UNITS

SRM recorded SRB CPU service units consumed by this task. An SRB CPU service unit is defined as the number of SRB CPU seconds times the installation-specified SRBCOEFF coefficient (specified in the IEAIPS*xx* member of PARMLIB and reported in SAS data set TYPE72) times a machine-dependent constant, which is set at IPL time based on the CPU model and CPU version. SOURCLIB member TYPE7072 provides one source of the value of the machine-dependent constant, called SU_SEC, since it sets the number of service units generated by one second of CPU time.

STEPNAME	CHAR	8		STEP*NAME

step name that appeared on the EXEC PGM= statement. Note that if this step executed a JCL procedure instead, this step name is not the one on that EXEC statement; rather it is the step name on the EXEC PGM= card within that JCL procedure. Also, for a TSO session, the step name is the TSO procedure name, either the default from UADS or the user-supplied PR(name) value.

STEPNR	NUM	4		STEP*NUMBER

step number. This number is reset to one when a job is canceled and restarted, so it is possible for the same job to have steps with duplicate values.

SWAPS	NUM	4		TIMES*TASK WAS*SWAPPED OUT

number of times this step was swapped out.

SWPAGINS	NUM	4		PAGE-INS*TO SWAP*TASK IN

number of pages swapped in.

SWPAGOUT	NUM	4		PAGE-OUTS*TO SWAP*TASK OUT

number of pages swapped out.

SYSINCNT	NUM	4		CARD IMAGES*READ*BY PROGRAM

number of card-image records in DD DATA and DD * data sets read by the reader for this step.

SYSTEM	CHAR	4	4.	SYSTEM*ID

identification of system on which step executed.

TAPEDRVS	NUM	4		TAPE*DRIVES*ALLOCATED

number of different tape drives allocated to this step. Note that in MVS/370, the IMACCHAN member must describe the installation's two-channel switches if the number of tape drives is to be counted correctly.

Variable	Type	Length	Format	Label
TERMTIME	NUM	8	DATETIME19.2	STEP*TERMINATION*EVENT

step termination time stamp. This event is the fourth and last time stamp in the lifetime of a step.

TGETS	NUM	4		TERMINAL*READS*(TGETS)

TSO only. The number of terminals TGETS satisfied; that is, the number of times that the TSO user pushed the ENTER key.

TPUTS	NUM	4		TERMINAL*WRITES*(TPUTS)

TSO only. The number of terminal TPUTS issued; that is, the number of times that output lines were sent to the terminal.

VIOPAGIN	NUM	4		VIO*PAGE-INS

virtual I/O page-ins.

VIOPAGOU	NUM	4		VIO*PAGE-OUTS

virtual I/O page-outs.

VIORECLM	NUM	4		VIO*RECLAIMS

virtual I/O page reclaims.

VIRTREAL	CHAR	1		VIRTUAL*OR*REAL?

type of address space requested.

value	requested
R	real storage (ADDRSPC=R specified)
V	virtual storage.

TYPE535
Job Termination/Session Logoff

The TYPE535 data set contains one observation for each type 5 record (batch job termination) or type 35 SMF record (TSO session termination).

Type 5 and 35 records are written at job termination. Note, however, that a restarted job has more than one execution and, thus, more than one type 5 record; each type 5 record corresponds to a single execution of the job.

The basic type 5 or type 35 record contains a fixed portion followed by a variable accounting portion. Since the design and usage of the account field on the JOB statement are installation-dependent, use the IMACACCT member of SOURCLIB to define how many account fields you want to keep for your installation. (For TSO users, only one account field is allowed.)

Variable	Type	Length	Format	Label
ABEND	CHAR	6		COMPLETION*ABEND*INDICATOR

job completion indicator. A description of how or why the last step of this job ended. For abnormal completions, see the variable CONDCODE for amplification of the reason for termination.

value	meaning
blank	normal completion.
CANCEXIT	last step was canceled by an SMF exit. The variable CONDCODE contains the exit that did the canceling.
FLUSH	last step was flushed (because a previous step had failed).
OTHER	last step abended for unknown reason. The variable CONDCODE contains the value in register 15 at time of the abend. This value is set when the step abend bit is on, but the numerical contents of abend code are inconsistent with SMF documentation.
RESTART	last step was restarted. Any subsequent restart has program name of IEFRSTRT.
RETURN	last step completed with nonzero condition code. CONDCODE contains the returned value.
SYSTEM	last step completed with system abnormal end (abend). The variable CONDCODE contains the abend code.

Variable	Type	Length	Format	Label

| | | USER | | last step completed with an abend issued by a user program rather than by the operating system itself. Any programmer can choose to issue a user abend rather than a return code (for example, the SAS System issues a USER ABEND 999 when ERRORABEND is specified and an error occurs). The variable CONDCODE contains the abend code. |

ACCOUNT1   CHAR   53   FIRST*ACCOUNT*FIELD

first job account field specified on JOB statement. Job level accounting is the predominate method of assigning account numbers to jobs although account numbers can be provided on the EXEC cards if step level accounting is desired. Accounting at the job level involves charging all steps in the job to the same account. NRACCTFL counts the number of account fields specified by the user, and LENACCTn variables contain the length of the nth account field. SOURCLIB member IMACACCT defines how many account numbers are to be kept and their maximum length.

ACCOUNT2   CHAR   10   SECOND*ACCOUNT*FIELD

second job account field specified on JOB statement.

ACCOUNT3   CHAR   4   THIRD*ACCOUNT*FIELD

third job account field specified on JOB statement.

ACCOUNT4   CHAR   4   FOURTH*ACCOUNT*FIELD

fourth job account field specified on JOB statement.

ACCOUNT5   CHAR   4   FIFTH*ACCOUNT*FIELD

fifth job account field specified on JOB statement.

ACCOUNT6   CHAR   4   SIXTH*ACCOUNT*FIELD

sixth job account field specified on JOB statement.

ACCOUNT7   CHAR   4   SEVENTH*ACCOUNT*FIELD

seventh job account field specified on JOB statement.

ACCOUNT8   CHAR   4   EIGHTH*ACCOUNT*FIELD

eighth job account field specified on JOB statement.

ACCOUNT9   CHAR   4   NINTH*ACCOUNT*FIELD

ninth job account field specified on JOB statement.

CONDCODE   NUM   4   HEX4.   COMPLETION*CONDITION*CODE

condition code. This variable amplifies the meaning of abend for the last step. It is internally a binary number but is formatted to display as hex so that testing for a specific

Variable	Type	Length	Format	Label

condition uses this syntax:
IF ABEND='SYSTEM' AND CONDCODE=0322X THEN ...
ABEND *value contents of* CONDCODE

	value	**canceled by**
CANCEXIT	1	IEFUSI (step initiation)
CANCEXIT	2	IEFUJI (job initiation)
CANCEXIT	4	IEFUJV (job validation)
OTHER	completion code value	
RETURN	return code value	
SYSTEM	system abend code	
USER	user abend code.	

CPUSRBTM   NUM   4   TIME12.2   TASK*CPU SRB*TIME

duration that CPU was executing instructions under a Service Request Block (SRB) for this job.

CPUTCBTM   NUM   4   TIME12.2   TASK*CPU TCB*TIME

duration that CPU was executing instructions under Task Control Block (TCB) for this job.

CPUTM   NUM   4   TIME12.2   TASK*TCB+SRB*TIME

duration that CPU was executing instructions for this task. Sum of CPUSRBTM and CPUTCBTM.

ELAPSTM   NUM   4   TIME12.2   ELAPSED*DURATION

duration of step between initiation and termination (the step elapsed time). During this duration, the step owned the initiator. It is the sum of DSENQTM, ALOCTM, and EXECTM.

ENQTIME   NUM   8   DATETIME19.2   ENQUEUE ON*SYS1.UADS*EVENT

TSO only. Time when logon process enqueues on SYS1.UADS data set. This time has been used to calculate the time it takes to log on to TSO:
(LOGONTM=ENQTIME−READTIME) .
This time is very close to the actual time the user sees READY.

JACTIVTM   NUM   4   TIME12.2   JOB TOTAL*SRM ACTIVE*DURATION

sum of step ACTIVETMs for this execution. See TYPE434 documentation.

JCPUNITS   NUM   4   JOB TOTAL*CPU TCB*SERVICE UNITS

sum of step CPUUNITS for this execution. See TYPE434 documentation.

JINITIME   NUM   8   DATETIME19.2   JOB*INITIATION*EVENT

job initiation time stamp for this execution.

Variable	Type	Length	Format	Label

JIOUNITS   NUM   4   JOB TOTAL*IO*SERVICE UNITS
sum of step IOUNITS for this execution. See TYPE434 documentaion.

JMSOUNIT   NUM   4   JOB TOTAL*MEMORY*SERVICE UNITS
sum of step MSOUNITS for this execution. See TYPE434 documentation.

JOB   CHAR   8   JOB NAME*OR*TSO USER
job name (batch); user ID (TSO).

JOBCLASS   CHAR   1   JOB*CLASS
job class.

JOBPRTY   NUM   4   MVS JOB*PRIORITY*(NOT USEFUL)
job priority after job was passed from JES to MVS. Does not relate to job scheduling
priority in the type 26 record.

JOBSERV   NUM   4   JOB TOTAL*SERVICE*UNITS
sum of step SERVUNIT for this execution. See TYPE434 documentation.

JPERFGRP   NUM   4   JOB*PERFORMANCE*GROUP
performance group at job termination.

JPKEY   NUM   4   HEX2.   JOB*PROTECT*KEY
storage-protect key.

JRESIDTM   NUM   4   TIME12.2   JOB*RESIDENCY*DURATION
sum of step RESIDTM for this execution. See TYPE434 documentaion.

JSRBUNIT   NUM   4   JOB*SRB SERVICE*UNITS
sum of step SRBUNITS for this execution. See TYPE434 documentation.

JTRMTIME   NUM   8   DATETIME19.2   JOB*TERMINATION*EVENT
termination time stamp of this execution.

LENACCT1   NUM   4   LENGTH*ACCOUNT*ONE
length of first account field on JOB JCL card.

LENACCT2   NUM   4   LENGTH*ACCOUNT*TWO
length of second account field on JOB JCL card.

LENACCT3   NUM   4   LENGTH*ACCOUNT*THREE
length of third account field on JOB JCL card.

Variable	Type	Length	Format	Label
LENACCT4	NUM	4		LENGTH*ACCOUNT*FOUR

length of fourth account field on JOB JCL card.

Variable	Type	Length	Format	Label
LENACCT5	NUM	4		LENGTH*ACCOUNT*FIVE

length of fifth account field on JOB JCL card.

LENACCT6	NUM	4		LENGTH*ACCOUNT*SIX

length of sixth account field on JOB JCL card.

LENACCT7	NUM	4		LENGTH*ACCOUNT*SEVEN

length of seventh account field on JOB JCL card.

LENACCT8	NUM	4		LENGTH*ACCOUNT*EIGHT

length of eighth account field on JOB JCL card.

LENACCT9	NUM	4		LENGTH*ACCOUNT*NINE

length of ninth account field on JOB JCL card.

LOCLINFO	CHAR	8		LOCAL*INSTALLATION*FIELD

locally-defined field; filled in by installation-written SMF exit routine.

NRACCTFL	NUM	4		NUMBER*ACCOUNT*FIELDS

number of account fields specified on JOB JCL card.

NRTRANS	NUM	4		NUMBER*OF*TRANSACTIONS

TSO only. Number of transactions as counted by the SRM.

NSTEPS	NUM	4		NUMBER*OF*STEPS

number of steps in this execution.

PGMRNAME	CHAR	20		PROGRAMMER*NAME*FIELD

programmer name field from JOB statement.

RDRDEVCL	NUM	4	HEX2.	READER*CLASS

reader class.

RDRDEVTY	NUM	4	HEX2.	READER*TYPE

reader type.

RDRTM	NUM	4	TIME12.2	READER*EVENT*DURATION

duration MVS reader was active while reading this job. For a job read in through RJE, this value indicates how long the job took to be transmitted. The TYPE26 record for this job identifies the remote (INROUTE) from which the job was read and the number of cards (SPOOLCRD) processed.

Variable	Type	Length	Format	Label
READER	CHAR	8		INTERNAL*READER*USED?

values are INTERNAL if this job was processed by the internal reader; otherwise, it is blank.

| READTIME | NUM | 8 | DATETIME19.2 | READ-IN*OR LOGON*EVENT |

job read-in (TSO LOGON) time stamp.

| SYSINCNT | NUM | 4 | | CARD IMAGES*READ*BY PROGRAM |

batch only. Number of card-image records in DD DATA and DD * data sets read by the reader for this execution. This value is less than SPOOLCRD in the TYPE26 data.

| SYSTEM | CHAR | 4 | 4. | SYSTEM*ID |

identification of system on which this job executed.

| TGETS | NUM | 4 | | TERMINAL*READS*(TGETS) |

TSO only. The number of terminal TGETs satisfied (that is, essentially the number of times the user pressed ENTER) in this session.

| TPUTS | NUM | 4 | | TERMINAL*WRITES*(TPUTS) |

TSO only. The number of terminals TPUTs issued (that is, the number of times one or more lines were sent to the screen) in this session.

TYPE6
Output Writer

The TYPE6 data set contains one observation for each type 6 SMF record, written after processing of printed or punched output by JES or by an external writer.

JES2, JES3, and the external writer each write a type 6 SMF record for each job output element. There will be one observation in TYPE6 for each job's error-free output processing with the same node, remote identification, SYSOUT class, form number, FCB, and UCS. In addition, for 3800 printers, a separate observation occurs for any change in the number of copies in a copy group, character arrangement tables, copy modification module, or forms overlay.

The type 6 record is written at the completion of each printing event, which normally occurs after job completion. However, if FREE=CLOSE is specified in the SYSOUT DD statement (as is usually the case for TSO printed SYSOUT), the printing or punching occurs when the file is closed, and, thus, type 6 records may exist with time stamps prior to the job termination time.

The TYPE6 data set contains information about SYSOUT class and records processed. It does not explicitly contain the device type to which the SYSOUT was directed; by decoding the device name (OUTDEVCE), a SAS variable is created that identifies the SYSOUT as print or punch. This decoding assumes that your installation follows the normal conventions in naming JES remote devices.

The actual number of lines printed or punched is contained in the TYPE6 data set. If multiple copies are printed (as opposed to multi-part forms that are printed only once), the total lines of all copies actually printed are available. If printing is canceled, only the actual number of lines printed is counted.

The number of pages printed can be estimated but is not accurately measured. The PAGECNT variable has different meanings in JES2 and in JES3. In JES2 all skip to channel operations are counted as a page, whereas in JES3 only skip to channel one operations are counted as a page. (JES2 installations can easily modify JES to change the value of PAGECNT to count only skip to channel one, which is more accurate.) Furthermore, many programs print many pages with only one skip to channel one at the beginning of printing. You may want to improve the estimated page count by creating an estimated page count based on the maximum number of lines per page your installation uses. For example, if you chose 96 lines per page as the maximum, an improved estimate of the number of pages printed can be obtained with the statement:

```
PAGECNT= MAX (PAGECNT, NRLINES/96);
```

Variable	Type	Length	Format	Label

BURST   CHAR   3   WAS 3800*OUTPUT*BURST?

3800 printer only.

	value	meaning
	YES	output was burst into sheets.

CONTRIND   CHAR   21   OUTPUT*CONTROL*INDICATORS

control indicators. The possible values are blank or:

for JES2 or JES3	meaning
SPIN DATA SETS	record represents spin data sets
OPR TERMINATED	operator terminated this data group
OPR RESTARTED	operator restarted this data group
INTERPRETED	punch output was interpreted (3525 only).

for JES2 only	meaning
OPER INTERRUPTED	operator interrupted this data group
CONTINUATION	record represents continuation of interrupted data group
OPR OVERRODE	operator overrode programmed carriage control (printer only).

for JES3 only	meaning
RESTART WITH DEST	operator restarted data set with destination
RECVD OPR RESTART	received operator restarted data set
OPR STRT SINGLE SPACE	operator started with single space.

COPIES   NUM   4   3800*COPIES*PRINTED

3800 printer only. Total number of copies printed.

COPYMODF   CHAR   4   COPY*MODIFICATION*MODULE

3800 printer only. Names of the copy modification module used to modify the data.

DATAERRS   CHAR   14   POSSIBLE*DATA*ERRORS

JES3 only. Data format error indicators. These bits are set when a data set is completed or restarted.

	CNTRL CHAR ERR	some first character control data is bad; default used.

DCTCHAR1   CHAR   4   CHARACTER*ARRANGEMENT*TABLE
(DCT) 1

3800 printer only. Name of the first character arrangement table that defines the characters used in printing.

Variable	Type	Length	Format	Label
DCTCHAR2	CHAR	4		CHARACTER*ARRANGEMENT*TABLE (DCT) 2

3800 printer only. Name of the second character arrangement table that defines the characters used in printing.

DCTCHAR3	CHAR	4		CHARACTER*ARRANGEMENT*TABLE (DCT) 3

3800 printer only. Name of the third character arrangement table that defines the characters used in printing.

DCTCHAR4	CHAR	4		CHARACTER*ARRANGEMENT*TABLE (DCT) 4

3800 printer only. Name of the fourth character arrangement table that defines the characters used in printing.

DEVICE	CHAR	7		DEVICE*TYPE

JES2 only. Type of device used. Assumes installation has used standard JES2 naming conventions for devices. The possible values are:

value	meaning
EXT WTR	external writer created this record
PRINTER	device is named like a printer
PUNCH	device is named like a punch.

DOCLENFT	NUM	4		DOCUMENT*LENGTH*(FEET)

number of feet of document printed.

FCB	CHAR	4		FCB*IMAGE*IDENTIFICATION

FCB image identification.

FLASH	CHAR	4		FORMS*OVERLAY*(FLASH)

3800 printer only. Name of the forms overlay printed (flashed) on the copies.

FLASHCPY	NUM	4		NUMBER*COPIES*FLASHED

3800 printer only. Number of copies on which the forms overlay was printed.

FONTLOAD	NUM	4		NUMBER*OF FONTS*LOADED

number of fonts loaded.

FONTUSED	NUM	4		NUMBER*OF FONTS*USED

number of fonts used.

Variable	Type	Length	Format	Label

FORM   CHAR   4   FORM*NUMBER
form number.

FORMDEFS   NUM   4   NUMBER*FORMDEFS*USED
number of FORMDEFs used.

IOSTATUS   CHAR   14   ERROR*STATUS*INDICATOR
MVS/370 JES2 only. I/O status indicators.

value	meaning
DATABUFF ERROR	data buffer read error
CNTLBUFF ERROR	control buffer read error.

JESNR   NUM   4   JES*NUMBER
job number assigned by JES.

JOB   CHAR   8   JOB NAME*OR*TSO USER
job name (batch); user ID (TSO).

LOCLINFO   CHAR   8   LOCAL*INSTALLATION*FIELD
locally-defined field, filled in by installation-written SMF exit routine.

NODE   NUM   4   NODE
JES2 NJE only. If routing section is present, this is the node number of the JES2 NJE node to which this remote is connected.

NRDSETS   NUM   4   NUMBER*DATA SETS*PROCESSED
number of data sets processed (if multiple copies are produced, each copy is counted).

NRLINES   NUM   4   LINES*ACTUALLY*PRINTED
number of logical records actually physically processed (that is, punched, printed, and so forth), including JOBLOG and multiple copies printed.

OPTCD   CHAR   1   3800*OPTCD*J?
3800 printer only. The possible value is:

value	meaning
J	DCB subparameter OPTCD=J was specified. Each output data line contained a table reference character that selected the character arrangement table used when printing that line.

OUTCLASS   CHAR   1   SYSOUT*CLASS
SYSOUT class; blank for non-SYSOUT data sets.

Variable	Type	Length	Format	Label
OUTDEVCE	CHAR	8		OUTPUT*DEVICE*NAME

output device name.

| OUTPRTY | NUM | 4 | | OUTPUT*PRIORITY |

JES3 only. Output priority.

| OVLYLOAD | NUM | 4 | | NUMBER*OVERLAYS*LOADED |

number of overlays loaded.

| OVLYUSED | NUM | 4 | | NUMBER*OVERLAYS*USED |

number of overlays used.

| PAGECNT | NUM | 4 | | APPROX*PAGE*COUNT |

for printer, approximate page count; for JES3 punch, number of cards punched.

| PAGEDEFS | NUM | 4 | | NUMBER*PAGEDEFS*USED |

number of PAGEDEFs used.

| PGSGLOAD | NUM | 4 | | NUMBER*PAGE SEGMENTS*LOADED |

number of page segments loaded.

| PGSGUSED | NUM | 4 | | NUMBER*PAGE SEGMENTS*USED |

number of page segments used.

| PRENTIME | NUM | 8 | DATETIME19.2 | PRINTING*ENDED*EVENT |

print or punch ended time stamp. For the 3800 printer, this is the time the burst page is at the stacker. As long as the 3800 printer is continually printing, this value is valid, but for the last job of a series that printed on a 3800, this time is when the operator manually ejected (moved) the print to the stacker.

| PRINTIME | NUM | 8 | DATETIME19.2 | START*PRINTING*EVENT |

print or punch started time stamp.

| READTIME | NUM | 8 | DATETIME19.2 | READ-IN*OR LOGON*EVENT |

job read-in (TSO LOGON) time stamp.

| RMOTID | NUM | 4 | | REMOTE*(ROUTE)*NUMBER |

JES2 only. Remote ID number at which printing or punching occurred.

| SUBSYS | CHAR | 4 | | SUB*SYSTEM |

subsystem value. The value may be either JES2 or JES3.

Variable	Type	Length	Format	Label
SUPGROUP	CHAR	8		OUTPUT*DEVICE*GROUP

JES3 only. Logical output device group name.

| SYSTEM | CHAR | 4 | 4. | SYSTEM*ID |

identification of system on which this job executed.

| UCS | CHAR | 4 | | UCS*IMAGE*ID |

UCS image identification.

TYPE7
Lost SMF Data

The TYPE7 data set contains one observation for each type 7 SMF record, written at the end of an SMF data lost event when both SVS1.MANX and SYS1.MANY have filled with SMF records.

When data fill the active SMF data set, the system automatically switches to the next defined SMF data set and notifies the operator to dump the SMF data set. If all defined SMF data sets are filled, SMF stops recording. When recording is restarted after the operator DUMPs the data to make more room, the type 7 SMF record is written.

The type 7 record should never occur. By properly sizing the MANX/MANY data sets and by providing operators with adequate instruction on how and when to dump SMF, space should always be available in either MANX or MANY for records. The only purpose served by the existence of observations in the TYPE7 data set is to point out some deficiency in operations or in sizing of the MANX/MANY data sets.

The type 7 record is written whenever an SMF data set (MANX or MANY) becomes available for writing again. Other than a console message at the time MANX and MANY were both filled, you get no SMF information until after the problem has been fixed.

Variable	Type	Length	Format	Label
LOSSTIME	NUM	8	DATETIME19.2	BEGINNING OF*SMF DATA LOSS*EVENT

time when loss of SMF recording began. All SMF data sets were full at this time, thus, a console message was generated telling the operator that SMF was no longer recording data.

Variable	Type	Length	Format	Label
LOSTRECS	NUM	4		NUMBER OF*SMF RECORDS*LOST

number of records lost.

Variable	Type	Length	Format	Label
SMFTIME	NUM	8	DATETIME19.2	SMF*RECORD*TIME STAMP

end-of-data-loss time stamp. An SMF data set was dumped, and it became the active data set at this time.

Variable	Type	Length	Format	Label
SYSTEM	CHAR	4	4.	SYSTEM*ID

identification of system that lost data.

TYPE8911
Devices On-line at IPL or Varied On- or Off-line

The TYPE8911 data set contains observations for each type 8, 9, or 11 SMF record. A type 8 SMF record, written at the completion of each IPL, contains all the devices on-line at that time. A type 9 SMF record, written for each VARY ONLINE command issued by an operator, contains all devices affected by that command.

A type 11 SMF record, written for each VARY OFFLINE command issued by an operator, contains all devices affected by that command.

The TYPE8911 data set is useful for tracking operator-issued changes in the I/O configuration. (Note that a device varied on-line in response to an allocation recovery is recorded in the type 10 record contained in data set TYPE10.) Since the volume serial number on the device is not included in the SMF record, tracking of direct access mountable volumes is impossible.

Variable	Type	Length	Format	Label
DEVICE	CHAR	7		DEVICE*TYPE

device type (for example, 3330, 3350, and so forth). Decoded from UCB type by the VMACUCB member of SOURCLIB.

DEVNR	NUM	4	HEX4.	DEVICE*NUMBER

number of device. Formerly the unit address in MVS/370. The unique number or address of the device.

LCU	NUM	4	HEX2.	LOGICAL*CONTROL*UNIT

logical control unit number to which this device is connected.

REASON	CHAR	14		REASON

reason that record was written:

value	meaning
IPL	device was on-line at IPL
ONLINE	vary on-line command was issued
OFFLINE	vary off-line command was issued.

SMFTIME	NUM	8	DATETIME19.2	SMF*RECORD*TIME STAMP

event time stamp.

SYSTEM	CHAR	4	4.	SYSTEM*ID

identification of system from which command was issued.

Variable	Type	Length	Format	Label
UNITADR	NUM	4	HEX3.	UNIT*ADDRESS

unit address of device.

TYPE10
Allocation Recovery

Data set TYPE10 contains one observation for each type 10 SMF record, written after any allocation recovery event that was successful because the operator replied with a unit address to be varied on-line. The type 10 record is not written if the operator replies WAIT or CANCEL to the allocation recovery message. Thus, the utility of the TYPE10 data set depends on the operator's instructions in dealing with allocation recoveries.

A better approach for analyzing allocation recovery delays is described in chapter fourteen, Resource Measurement-Tapes and Tape Drives.

Variable	Type	Length	Format	Label
DEVICE	CHAR	7		DEVICE*TYPE

device type (for example, 3330, 3350, and so forth). Decoded from UCB type by the VMACUCB member of SOURCLIB.

DEVNR	NUM	4	HEX4.	DEVICE*NUMBER

device number of device. Formerly the Unit Address in MVS/370. The unique number or address of the device that is supplied by the operator and varied on-line.

JOB	CHAR	8		JOB NAME*OR*TSO USER

job name (batch); user ID (TSO).

LCU	NUM	4		LOGICAL*CONTROL*UNIT

logical control unit number to which this device is connected.

LOCLINFO	CHAR	8		LOCAL*INSTALLATION*FIELD

locally-defined field, filled in by an installation-written SMF exit.

READTIME	NUM	8	DATETIME19.2	READ-IN*OR LOGON*EVENT

job-read-in (TSO LOGON) time stamp.

SMFTIME	NUM	8	DATETIME19.2	SMF*RECORD*TIME STAMP

allocation-recovery-completed time stamp. This occurs when the operator replies with the device address (DEVNR) of an off-line device, which is then varied on-line and given to this job.

SYSTEM	CHAR	4	4.	SYSTEM*ID

system identification on which allocation recovery occurs.

UNITADR	NUM	4	HEX3.	UNIT*ADDRESS

unit address of device. This address is supplied by the operator and varied on-line.

TYPE1415
Non-VSAM Data Set Activity

The TYPE1415 data set contains almost everything you want to know about how your data sets are being used and by whom. It is the basis for analysis of data set blocksize, data set placement, data set usage, media selection for data sets, program usage of data, and so forth.

Data set TYPE1415 contains one or more observations for each type 14 or 15 SMF record. The type 14 and 15 records are written for all non-VSAM DASD or TAPE data sets defined by DD statements (excluding DD *, DD DATA, and SYSOUT) that are opened by a problem program. The records are written when the file is closed, either by an explicit close, or by end-of-volume processing for multiple volume and concatenated sequential files. The type 14 record is written for files opened for INPUT or RDBACK, whereas the type 15 is written for files opened for OUTPUT, INOUT, or OUTIN.

Usually there is one observation in TYPE1415 for each type 14 or 15 SMF record. However, there are two occurrences in which multiple observations are created for single SMF records:

1. If concatenated data sets are accessed by BPAM (Basic Partitioned Access Method), there will be one observation for each UCB segment in the type 14 or 15 record. A typical example of concatenated BPAM accessed data is the STEPLIB DD. For concatenated BPAM accessed data, SMF writes only a single record for the concatenation. The only data set name contained in this SMF record is the DSNAME of the first data set in the concatenation, but the record does contain the UCB (DEVNR) and VOLSER of the other concatenations, as well as the EXCPs to those data sets. As a result, you will not know the data set name of the second and subsequent data sets. However, data set TYPE1415 identifies the existence of this environment by building a data set name 'UNKNOWN - CONCATENATED BPAM n' (where n is the concatenation number) for the second and subsequent concatenations. Note that this absence of the data set name opened applies ONLY to BPAM-accessed concatenations. As a matter of clarification about BPAM-accessed data sets, note that whenever the JCL (or ALLOCATE command under TSO) contains a member name, the access is never BPAM but instead is either BSAM or QSAM.

2. If ISAM data sets are involved, there are three observations in TYPE1415 for each SMF record, since there are three UCB segments for an ISAM file. The data set name in TYPE1415 for these segments is fabricated by adding -INDEX, -PRIMARY, or -OVERFLOW, as appropriate, to the end of the existing DSNAME variable. If necessary, this addition is truncated so the real DSNAME plus addition is only 44 bytes.

Type 14 and 15 records are written at each close; no information about data set usage is recorded for steps that are active when the system crashes. Files can be opened multiple times in the same step. The EXCP count in any type 14 or 15 record is accumulated by DDNAME and DEVNR (UNITADR) within each step for each open. Thus, multiple opened data sets and/or data sets on devices with two channel switches (and hence two UNITADRs for real I/O) will have multiple SMF records and multiple observations in TYPE1415. Furthermore, EXCPs are accumulated across these multiple opens, so you cannot simply sum the EXCPs in TYPE1415 to get true EXCPs.

There are other difficulties. Concatenated sequential (that is, QSAM or BSAM) files have blank DDnames for the second and subsequent concatenations. If a step has multiple concatenations, it is impossible to associate the concatenations correctly. Probably the most serious omission affects concatenated BPAM data sets: a single record is written for the entire concatenation, giving only the first data set's name; however, the record does contain the UCBs for each of the concatenations.

In spite of these problems, the information in the TYPE1415 data set is of significant value in performance measurement. Member DBANAL of SOURCLIB uses TYPE1415 and other SAS data sets to perform data set analysis; see the discussion in chapter thirteen, Resource Management - I/O and Data Set Activity, for more information.

Variable	Type	Length	Format	Label
ACCESS	CHAR	5		ACCESS*METHOD

access method used during this OPEN.

value	meaning
BDAM	Basic Direct Access Method
BDSAM	either BDAM or BSAM (cannot distinguish between them)
BISAM	Basic Indexed Sequential Access Method
BPSAM	either BPAM or BSAM (cannot distinguish between them)
BSAM	Basic Sequential Access Method
EXCP	Execute Channel Program
QISAM	Queued Indexed Sequential Access Method
QSAM	Queued Sequential Access Method
blank	unknown.

Variable	Type	Length	Format	Label
AVGBLK	NUM	4		AVERAGE*BLOCK*LENGTH

average data block length (from JFCBDRLH+171). Although it appears useful, it is zero too frequently to be considered an important variable.

| BLKCNT | NUM | 4 | | TAPE*BLOCK*COUNT |

tape only. Block count for this volume sequence number.

| BLKSIZE | NUM | 4 | | PHYSICAL*BLOCK SIZE*(BYTES) |

blocksize. The number of bytes of data in each physical block. For a variable length record format, the blocksize is the maximum number of bytes in a record. Depending on the access method and how the I/O routines that opened this file were written, it may be inaccurate or zero. Following are some known examples that illustrate the problem:

1. If the access method is EXCP (usually the SORTWORK files of most SORT programs), the SMF record contains a zero for the blocksize, unless the programmer who wrote the EXCP logic copied the blocksize value into the control block used by the SMF record. Because EXCP does not need the blocksize in that control block, the blocksize is seldom nonzero.

2. If the data set was opened more than once and the I/O programmer changed the blocksize, that change is often not recorded. The COBOL compiler, for example, opens SYSUT1 with a blocksize of 500, reads in the input, and then closes and re-opens SYSUT1 with a much larger blocksize (full track, if BUF and SIZE defaults are correct. See also chapter twenty-seven on COBOL). The second TYPE1415 observation still has the blocksize of 500.

3. Open type J allows the I/O programmer to do strange and wonderful things, but rarely provides the correct blocksize in TYPE1415.

4. Concatenated sequential files have a blocksize of zero for second and subsequent records. In summary, use the blocksize from TYPE1415 with caution. If you think you have identified a file with poor blocksize, look first at the file's actual attributes (using IEHLIST, SPF, or LISTD) before you suspect a poor blocksize.

| BUFFLEN | NUM | 4 | | BUFFER*LENGTH*(BYTES) |

buffer length.

| BUFNO | NUM | 4 | | NUMBER*DATA*BUFFERS |

formerly number of buffers, now zero. See JFCBUFNO.

| BUFTEK | NUM | 4 | HEX2. | BUFFERING*TECHNIQUE*(JFCBFTEK) |

JFCBFTEK control byte (buffering technique).

| CRDATE | NUM | 4 | | CREATION*DATE*(YYDDD) |

data set creation date (yyddd).

| CYLINDEX | NUM | 4 | | ISAM INDEX*AREA SIZE*(CYLINDERS) |

ISAM only. Number of cylinders in the independent index area.

Variable	Type	Length	Format	Label
CYLOFLO	NUM	4		ISAM OVERFLOW*AREA SIZE*(CYLINDERS)

ISAM only. Number of cylinders in the independent overflow area.

CYLOFULL	NUM	4		ISAM CYLINDER*AREAS WHICH*ARE FULL

ISAM only. Number of full cylinder areas.

CYLPRIME	NUM	4		ISAM PRIME*DATA AREA*(CYLINDERS)

ISAM only. Number of cylinders in the prime data area.

DCBOFLGS	NUM	4	HEX2.	OPEN*ROUTINE*FLAGS

flags used by open routine; these vary depending on the access method.

DCBOPTCD	NUM	4	HEX2.	DCB*OPTIONS*CODES

DCB option codes. These vary with the access method. These options may also be set in the JFCBOPCD variable. If the bit is on, the option was specified. Note that this first bit is one, whereas IBM calls the first bit zero.

For BPAM/BSAM/
QSAM/EXCP:

bit	OPTCD	(explanation)
1	W	(write verify check) very expensive, in terms of performance, since it requires a second full revolution of the disk device after every write to verify the data are correctly written. Although it was needed for the early disk devices, hardware reliability has supplemented this software verification. Therefore, it is no longer necessary and should be eliminated from the program that wrote these data.
2	U	(allow data ck[1403])
3	C	(chained scheduling)
4		(1288/DOS options)
5		(ASCII translation)
6	Z	(TAPE - use reduced error recovery)
6	Z	(DASD - use search direct)
7		(user totaling)
8	J	(3800 printer)

Variable	Type	Length	Format	Label

For BISAM/QISAM:

bit	OPTCD	(explanation)
1	W	(write verify check)
2	M	(full track index write)
3	M	(master indexes)
4	I	(independent overflow)
5	Y	(cylinder overflow)
6		
7	L	(delete option)
8	R	(reorg criteria)

For BDAM:

bit	OPTCD	(explanation)
1	W	(write verify check)
2		
3	E	(extended search)
4	F	(feedback)
5	A	(actual addressing)
6		(dynamic buffering)
7		(read exclusive)
8	R	(relative block addressing)

DDNAME	CHAR	8		DD NAME

DDname used to access the data set. Blank for concatenated files.

DEBOFLGS	NUM	4	HEX2.	DATA SET*STATUS*FLAGS

data set status flags (offset 8 in DEB). Bits 1 to 2 are decoded to create variable DISP. If the bit is on, this indicates the status was set. Note that this first bit is one, whereas IBM calls the first bit zero.

bit	status set
3	EOF encountered
4	DASD: RLSE specified
4	TAPE: short blocks permitted
5	DCB modification
6	DASD: split cylinder
6	TAPE: emulator 7-track

Variable	Type	Length	Format	Label
		7		nonstandard labels
		8		DASD: concatenated PO processed with BPAM
		8		TAPE: use reduced error recovery
DEBOPATB	NUM	4	HEX2.	DEB*FLAGS*AT EOV

DEB flags indicating method of I/O processing and disposition when EOV occurs. Note that this first bit is one, whereas IBM calls the first bit zero.

bits	meaning	
1	ABEND SYSABEND/SYSUDUMP data set	
3-4	positioning flags:	
	01	reread
	11	leave
5-8	I/O accessing being done:	
	0000	INPUT
	1111	OUTPUT
	0011	INOUT
	0111	OUTIN
	0001	RDBACK
	0100	UPDAT.

Variable	Type	Length	Format	Label
DEBVLSEQ	NUM	4		VOLUME*SEQUENCE*NUMBER

volume sequence number. For disks this is relative to the first volume in the data set; for tapes it is relative to the first volume processed.

DEN	NUM	4		TAPE*DENSITY

tape only. Density 200, 556, 800, 1600, or 6250 bytes per inch.

DEVICE	CHAR	7		DEVICE*TYPE

device type (for example, 3330, 3350, and so forth). Decoded from UCB type by the VMACUCB member of SOURCLIB.

DEVNR	NUM	4	HEX4.	DEVICE*NUMBER

device number of device. Formerly the Unit Address in MVS/370. The unique number or address of the device.

DISP	CHAR	3		DISPOSITION

disposition of data set: MOD, NEW, OLD, OTHR, SHR.

Variable	Type	Length	Format	Label

DSNAME   CHAR   44   DATA SET NAME

data set name. See the discussion at the beginning of this member concerning concatenated BPAM and ISAM data sets.

DSORG   CHAR   2   .   DATA SET*ORGANIZATION

data set organization:

value	meaning
blank	unknown
DA	direct access
IS	indexed sequential
PO	partitioned organization (member not specified)
PS	physical sequential (includes use of member of PDS if member name was included in JCL)
VI	virtual I/O.

DSSEQCNT   NUM   4   TAPE*SEQUENCE*COUNT

tape only. Data set sequence count.

DSSEQNR   NUM   4   TAPE*SEQUENCE*NUMBER

tape only. Data set sequence number.

EROPT   CHAR   3   ERROR*OPTION

action to be taken (due to EROPT option) if I/O error occurs:

value	action
ABE	abend
ACC	accept the error and continue
SKP	skip this record and continue.

EXCPCNT   NUM   4   RECORD*EXCP*COUNT

EXCP count accumulated to this DDname on this DEVNR at the time of this close. In general, this number has no meaning since you must know if there were preceding type 14 or 15 records created for this DDname/DEVNR in this step. If there is only one TYPE1415 observation for this DDname, then this is the EXCP count to that file. See chapter thirteen and the discussion at the beginning of this section.

EXCPOFLO   NUM   4   ISAM OVERFLOW*EXCPS NOT*IN 1ST CHAIN

ISAM only. EXCPs to overflow records that are not first in a chain of overflow records.

EXPDT   NUM   4   EXPIRATION*DATE*(YYDDD)

expiration date of data set (0 if not date-protected).

Variable	Type	Length	Format	Label

EXTINDEX   NUM   4   ISAM*INDEX*EXTENTS

ISAM only. Number of extents in the independent index area.

EXTOFLO   NUM   4   ISAM*OVERFLOW*EXTENTS

ISAM only. Number of extents in the independent overflow area.

EXTPRIME   NUM   4   ISAM*PRIME*EXTENTS

ISAM only. Number of extents in the prime data area.

EXTREL   NUM   4   DASD*EXTENTS*RELEASED

DASD only. Number of extents released (RLSE).

FILESEQ   NUM   4   TAPE*FILE*SEQUENCE

tape only. File sequence number (that is, position on tape volume if more than one data set is on the same volume. This position is the same as the first position of the label parameter).

ID   NUM   2   RECORD*ID

record ID.

value	meaning
14	opened for INPUT or RDBACK
15	opened for OUTPUT, UPDAT, INOUT, or OUTIN.

JESIO   CHAR   1   JES*IO*?

Was I/O issued by JES.

blank	no
y	yes

JFCBCTRI   NUM   4   HEX2.   JFCBCTRI*SPACE*CODE

space parameters (DASD only). Note that this first bit is one, whereas IBM calls the first bit zero.

bit	meaning
1-2	space requested units
00	ABSTR
01	AVG BLOCK LENGTH
10	TRK request
11	CYL request
3	MSVGP (Mass Storage Volume Group) request
5	CONTIG request

Variable	Type	Length	Format	Label
		6	MXIG request	
		7	ALX request	
		8	ROUND request.	
JFCBOPCD	NUM	4	HEX2.	JFCBOPCT*OPTION*CODE

JFCB option codes. Vary with access method. These options may also be set in DCBOPTCD variable. If the bit is on, the option was specified. Note that this first bit is one, whereas IBM calls the first bit zero.

For BPAM/BSAM/
    QSAM/EXCP:

bit	OPTCD	(explanation)
1	W	(write verify check) very expensive, in terms of performance, since it requires a second full revolution of the disk device after every write to verify the data are correctly written. Although it was needed for the early disk devices, hardware reliability has supplemented this software verification. Therefore, it is no longer necessary and should be eliminated from the program that wrote these data.
2	U	(allow data check [1403]).
3	C	(chained scheduling).
4		(bypass DOS checkpoint).
5		(ASCII translation).
6	Z	(TAPE - use reduced error recovery).
6	Z	(DASD - use search direct).
7		(user totaling).
8	J	(3800 printer).

For BISAM/QISAM:

bit	OPTCD	(explanation)
1	W	(write verify check). See above under BPAM.
2		(track overflow).

Variable	Type	Length	Format	Label
		3	M	(master indexes).
		4	I	(independent overflow).
		5	Y	(cylinder overflow).
		6		
		7	L	(delete option).
		8	R	(reorg criteria).

For BDAM:

	bit	OPTCD	(explanation)
	1	W	(write verify check). See above under BPAM.
	2		
	3	E	(extended search).
	4	F	(feedback).
	5	A	(actual addressing).
	6		(dynamic buffering).
	7		(read exclusive).
	8	R	(relative block addressing).

JFCBUFNO   NUM   4   NUMBER*OF*BUFFERS

number of buffers. Will be zero unless actually specified on the DD card. See also chapter thirteen.

JFCFLGS1   NUM   4   HEX2.   JFCFLGS1*FLAG*CODE

flag byte (offset 159 decimal in JFCB). Note that this first bit is one, whereas IBM calls the first bit zero.

bit	meaning
1	VS: delete when extending JOBQUEUE or SPOOL
2	tape data set has been opened
3	automatic data set protection indicator
5	CHKPT=EOV specified
6	VIO data set
8	UNIT=AFF specified.

JOB   CHAR   8   JOB NAME*OR*TSO USER

job name (batch); User ID (TSO).

Variable	Type	Length	Format	Label
KEEP	CHAR	5		DATA SET*CATALOG*STATUS

data set catalog status:

value	action
blank	not cataloged
CATLG	data set is a cataloged data set.

Variable	Type	Length	Format	Label
KEYLEN	NUM	4		DASD*KEY*LENGTH

DASD only. Key length if data set has keys.

Variable	Type	Length	Format	Label
LABEL	CHAR	3		DATA*SET*LABEL

data set label (second position of JCL LABEL parameter):

value	meaning
blank	unknown label
AL	American National Standard
AUL	American User National Standard
BLP	Bypass Label Processing
LTM	Leading Tape Mark (DOS-created unlabeled)
NL	Non-Labeled
NSL	Nonstandard Label
SL	IBM Standard Label
SUL	Standard User Label.

Variable	Type	Length	Format	Label
LCU	NUM	4	HEX2.	LOGICAL*CONTROL*UNIT

logical control unit number to which this device is connected.

Variable	Type	Length	Format	Label
LIMCT	NUM	4		DASD BDAM*SEARCH*LIMIT

DASD direct access only. BDAM search limit.

Variable	Type	Length	Format	Label
LOCATION	CHAR	5		MOVABILITY*OF*DATA SET

data set movability. This is indicated by a blank or UNMOV if this data set is unmovable.

Variable	Type	Length	Format	Label
LOCLINFO	CHAR	8		LOCAL*INSTALLATION*FIELD

locally-defined field, filled in by an installation-written SMF exit.

Variable	Type	Length	Format	Label
LRECL	NUM	4		LOGICAL*RECORD*LENGTH

logical record length. Many of the cautions (above) about blocksize may apply to LRECL also.

Variable	Type	Length	Format	Label
MEMBER	CHAR	8		PDS*MEMBER*NAME

PDS only. Member name (if specified on JCL).

| MSSCVOLI | NUM | 4 | | MASS STORAGE*VOLUME*SELECTION INDEX |

Mass Storage System Communicator (MSSC) volume selection index.

| NEXTENT | NUM | 4 | | NUMBER*OF*EXTENTS |

number of extents in the data set.

| NRLEVELS | NUM | 4 | | ISAM*INDEX*LEVELS |

ISAM only. Number of index levels.

| NRVOLS | NUM | 4 | | NUMBER*OF*VOLUMES |

number of volume serial numbers (JFCBNVOL+118) in the data set. Only the first five volume serials are ever contained in the type 14 or 15 record.

| NUCB | NUM | 4 | | NUMBER*OF*UCB SEGMENTS |

number of UCB segments. Usually one, but will be more for ISAM (one index, one overflow extent, and one per volume for primary), and for concatenated BPAM there is one per data set. Note that there is one observation per UCB for type 14 or 15 records.

| OPEN | CHAR | 7 | | TYPE*OF*OPEN |

type of OPEN. Possible values are:

value	meaning
INOUT	open initially for input, but data can be written to without reopen.
INPUT	open only for input. Data cannot be written.
OTHER	unknown open type. Report occurrence to author.
OUTIN	open initially for output, but data set can be read without reopen. Data can be written.
OUTPUT	open for output. Data can be written.
RDBACK	open for read-back. Data cannot be written, but can be read backwards.
UPDATE	open for update. Data can be written.

| OPENTIME | NUM | 8 | DATETIME19.2 | TIME*OF*OPEN |

time stamp when this observation from this data set was opened.

Variable	Type	Length	Format	Label
OPTCODE	CHAR	1		SEARCH*DIRECT*IF =Z

search direct (OPTCD=Z) specified. (See DCBOPTCD and JFCBOPCD.) This was previously a performance option, but it is now the default with SAM/E (SU 9).

value	meaning
blank	not specified
Z	OPTCD=Z specified.

PRIALOC	NUM	4		PRIMARY*ALLOCATION*SIZE

DASD only. Size of primary allocation (see SPACE).

READTIME	NUM	8	DATETIME19.2	READ-IN*OR LOGON*EVENT

job read-in (TSO LOGON) time stamp.

RECFM	CHAR	4		RECORD*FORMAT

record format. This is a constructed character variable that can have several combinations:

position	value	meaning
1-4	OTHR	unknown record format
1	F	fixed length records
1	U	undefined records
1	V	variable length records
2	B	records are blocked
3	T	track overflow permitted
3	S	records are spanned across blocks
4	T	VBS records track overflow.

Typical combinations usually encountered are F, FB, V, VB, VBS.

RECIND	NUM	4	HEX2.	RECORD*DATA SET*INDICATOR

record and data set indicator. Note that this first bit is one, whereas IBM calls the first bit zero.

bit	meaning
1	record written by EOV (End of Volume processing)
2	DASD device
3	temporary data set
4	DCBDSORG=DA (data set organization is direct access)
5	DCBDSORG=IS and DCBMACRF is not EXCP

Variable	Type	Length	Format	Label
		6		JFCDSORG=IS (data set organization is indexed sequentially)
		7		VIO data set.
RECOFLOW	NUM	4		ISAM LOGICAL*RECORDS IN*OVERFLOW AREA

ISAM only. Number of logical records in the overflow area.

RECPRIME	NUM	4		ISAM LOGICAL*RECORDS IN*PRIME AREA

ISAM only. Number of logical records in the prime area.

RELGDG	CHAR	8		RELATIVE*GDG DATA SET*REFERENCE

generation data group only. Relative generation number if the data set was specified by a relative number, (for example, DSN= GDG [-2]).

RLSE	CHAR	4		RLSE IF*SPACE*RELEASED

DASD only. Space was released:

value	meaning
blank	not specified
RLSE	RLSE options specified.

SECALOC	NUM	4		SIZE OF*SECONDARY*ALLOCATION

DASD only. Size of secondary allocation (see also SPACE).

SMFTIME	NUM	8	DATETIME19.2	SMF*RECORD*TIME STAMP

time stamp of close (and time when record was written).

SPACE	CHAR	3		SPACE*ALLOCATION*UNITS

DASD only. SPACE allocation units (see PRIALOC and SECALOC).

value	meaning
ABS	absolute track address specified
BLK	blocks
CYL	cylinders
MSS	mass storage allocation
TRK	tracks.

SYSTEM	CHAR	4	4.	SYSTEM*ID

identification of system on which this job executed.

Variable	Type	Length	Format	Label

TEMP   CHAR   4   TEMP*OR*PERM

temporary data set. The values are either PERM or TEMP.

TIOELINK   NUM   4   HEX2.   TIOELINK*FLAG*CODE

TIOT flag byte (offset 27 decimal in TIOT). Note that this first bit is one, whereas IBM calls the first bit zero.

bit	meaning
1	SYSOUT data set containing data
3	device is a terminal
4	DYNAM coded on DD statement
6	VS/1: entry for spooled SYSIN data set
7	VS/1: entry for spooled SYSOUT data set
7	VS/2: entry for a subsystem data set
8	entry for a remote device.

TIOESTTA   NUM   4   HEX2.   TIOESTTA*STATUS*CODE A

TIOT status byte A (offset 25 decimal in TIOT). Note that this first bit is one, whereas IBM calls the first bit zero.

bit	meaning
1	nonstandard label (see LABEL)
2	no unallocation necessary (at termination)
3	rewind but no unloading (at termination)
4	JOBLIB indicator. This is a JOBLIB DDname
5	DADSM allocation necessary
6	labeled tape (see LABEL)
7	TAPE: REWIND/UNLOAD the tape volume
7	DASD: d~~taa~~ data set is on a private volume
8	TAPE: rewind the tape volume
8	DASD: data set is on a public volume.

TIOESTTC   NUM   4   HEX2.   TIOESTTC*STATUS*CODE C

TIOT status byte C (offset 39 decimal in TIOT). Unfortunately, used only at allocation, and reset to zero by the time the data set is closed, which is when this record is written.

TIOEWTCT   NUM   4   HEX2.   NUMBER*DEVICES*REQUESTED

number of devices requested for this data set.

Variable	Type	Length	Format	Label
TRKREL	NUM	4		TRACKS*RELEASED

DASD only. Tracks are released at close.

TRKSALOC	NUM	4		TRACKS*ALLOCATED

DASD only. Number of tracks allocated to this data set on this device.

TRKSLEFT	NUM	4		ISAM OVERFLOW*TRACKS* REMAINING

ISAM only. Number of tracks (whole or partial) remaining in the overflow area.

TRTCH	NUM	4	HEX2.	TAPE*RECORDING*TECHNIQUE

tape recording technique.

TTRN	NUM	4	HEX8.	LAST RECORD*TRACK AND*RECORD NR

physical and partitioned only. Track (TT), record (R) number, and concatenation number (N) for concatenated BPAM of the last record processed.

UCBSTAB	NUM	4	HEX2.	UCBSTAB*VOLUME*STATUS

volume status (UCB offset 34 decimal). Note that this first bit is·one, whereas IBM calls the first bit zero.

bit	meaning
1	DASD: volume is being demounted by data management routine
1	TAPE: device is not being shared among several CPUs
2	UCB is open and being used as a page file
3	DASD: used during volume attribute processing
3	TAPE: additional volume label processing
4	private volume use status
5	public volume use status
6	DASD: storage volume use status
6	TAPE: American National Standard Label
7	volume being shared among job steps
8	DASD: control volume. This volume contains a catalog.

UNITADR	NUM	4	HEX3.	UNIT*ADDRESS

unit address of this UCB segment.

Variable	Type	Length	Format	Label
VOLSEQ	NUM	4		VOLUME*SEQUENCE*NUMBER

volume sequence number (JFCBVLSQ+70).

| VOLSER | CHAR | 6 | | VOLUME*SERIAL*NUMBER |

volume serial number of this volume.

| VOLSER1 | CHAR | 6 | | FIRST*VOLUME*SERIAL |

volume serial number of first volume of multivolume data set. Only the first five VOLSERs exist in the TYPE1415 data (the other VOLSERs are contained in an extension of the JFCB, which is not moved into the type 14 or 15 records).

| VOLSER2 | CHAR | 6 | | SECOND*VOLUME*SERIAL |

volume serial number of second volume of multivolume data set.

| VOLSER3 | CHAR | 6 | | THIRD*VOLUME*SERIAL |

volume serial number of third volume of multivolume data set.

| VOLSER4 | CHAR | 6 | | FOURTH*VOLUME*SERIAL |

volume serial number of fourth volume of multivolume data set.

| VOLSER5 | CHAR | 6 | | FIFTH*VOLUME*SERIAL |

volume serial number of fifth volume of multivolume data set.

TYPE16
Sort or Merge Statistics

Data set TYPE16 contains one observation for each type 16 SMF record, created for each execution of the Sort/Merge Program Product (5740-SMI), when requested by initialization options. The SORT/MERGE product's installation options allow you to select whether no record, a complete record, or a short record (with no record length statistics variables RECINT01-RECINT16) will be created.

Variable	Type	Length	Format	Label
BYTESORT	NUM	4		TOTAL*BYTES*SORTED

number of bytes sorted (sum of record lengths).

| FIELDLEN | NUM | 4 | | SORT*FIELD*LENGTH |

total control field length. The number of bytes actually compared by the sort.

| INBLKSIZ | NUM | 4 | | INPUT*BLOCK*SIZE |

maximum input blocksize. This field is set to zero if the input data set is not present.

| INRECLEN | NUM | 4 | | INPUT*RECORD*LENGTH |

specified input record length.

| INVOKED | CHAR | 7 | | INVOKED*SORT*? |

sort was dynamically or explicitly invoked. The possible values are either blank or DYNAMIC.

| JOB | CHAR | 8 | | JOB NAME*OR*TSO USER |

job name (batch); user ID (TSO).

| LOCLINFO | CHAR | 8 | | LOCAL*INSTALLATION*FIELD |

locally-defined field. The field is filled in by an installation-written SMF exit routine.

| OUBLKSIZ | NUM | 4 | | OUTPUT*BLOCK*SIZE |

output blocksize. The value is zero for VSAM data sets and if output data set is not present.

| READTIME | NUM | 8 | DATETIME19.2 | READ-IN*OR LOGON*EVENT |

job-read-in (TSO LOGON) time stamp.

| RECFM | CHAR | 4 | | RECORD*FORMAT |

record format. The possible values are:

value	meaning
F	fixed length records (F or FB)
V	variable length non-spanned records (V or VB)

Variable	Type	Length	Format	Label
	VS			variable length spanned records (VS or VBS).
RECINT01	NUM	4		RECORDS*IN 1ST*INTERVAL

number of records sorted that were in first interval of record length. At initialization of ICEMAN, sixteen intervals of record lengths are defined. These variables provide the distribution of actual lengths encountered in the sort. Note that if the data being sorted are fixed length (RECFM=F), these variables have missing values. If ICEMAN initialization specifies short records to be created (SORTRECD=S), the value of these variables also is missing.

RECINT02	NUM	4		RECORDS*IN 2ND*INTERVAL

number of records sorted that were in second interval of record length.

RECINT03	NUM	4		RECORDS*IN 3RD*INTERVAL

number of records sorted that were in third interval of record length.

RECINT04	NUM	4		RECORDS*IN 4TH*INTERVAL

number of records sorted that were in fourth interval of record length.

RECINT05	NUM	4		RECORDS*IN 5TH*INTERVAL

number of records sorted that were in fifth interval of record length.

RECINT06	NUM	4		RECORDS*IN 6TH*INTERVAL

number of records sorted that were in sixth interval of record length.

RECINT07	NUM	4		RECORDS*IN 7TH*INTERVAL

number of records sorted that were in seventh interval of record length.

RECINT08	NUM	4		RECORDS*IN 8TH*INTERVAL

number of records sorted that were in eighth interval of record length.

RECINT09	NUM	4		RECORDS*IN 9TH*INTERVAL

number of records sorted that were in ninth interval of record length.

RECINT10	NUM	4		RECORDS*IN 10TH*INTERVAL

number of records sorted that were in tenth interval of record length.

RECINT11	NUM	4		RECORDS*IN 11TH*INTERVAL

number of records sorted that were in eleventh interval of record length.

RECINT12	NUM	4		RECORDS*IN 12TH*INTERVAL

number of records sorted that were in twelfth interval of record length.

Variable	Type	Length	Format	Label
RECINT13	NUM	4		RECORDS*IN 13TH*INTERVAL

number of records sorted that were in thirteenth interval of record length.

RECINT14	NUM	4		RECORDS*IN 14TH*INTERVAL

number of records sorted that were in fourteenth interval of record length.

RECINT15	NUM	4		RECORDS*IN 15TH*INTERVAL

number of records sorted that were in fifteenth interval of record length.

RECINT16	NUM	4		RECORDS*IN 16TH*INTERVAL

number of records sorted that were in sixteenth interval of record length.

RECORDS	NUM	4		TOTAL*RECORDS*SORTED

total number of records sorted.

SMFTIME	NUM	8	DATETIME19.2	SMF*RECORD*TIME STAMP

time stamp of record when sort ended.

SORTCPTM	NUM	4	TIME12.2	SORT*CPU TCB*USED

CPU TCB time taken by sort. This CPU time also is included in the CPUTCBTM of the job step that executed the sort.

SORTOPTN	CHAR	8		SORT*OPTION*USED

sort technique used. The possible values are: BLOCKSET, PEERAGE, VALE, or MERGE (for conventional sort and merge).

SORTWORK	NUM	4		SORT WORK*DATA SETS*ALLOCATED

number of sort work data sets allocated.

STEPNAME	CHAR	8		STEP*NAME

name of step that invoked sort (from the EXEC=PGM JCL statement). Note that if this step executed a JCL procedure instead, this is not the step name on that EXEC statement, but rather it is the step name on the EXEC PGM= card within that JCL procedure. Note further that for a TSO session, the step name is the TSO procedure name, either the default from UADS, or the user-supplied PR(name) value.

STEPNR	NUM	4		STEP*NUMBER

number of step that invoked sort.

SYSTEM	CHAR	4	4.	SYSTEM*ID

system identification on which step executed.

WORKTRKS	NUM	4		SORT WORK*TRACKS*USED

total number of tracks of SORTWORK used. Unfortunately, there is no information about whether this is a 3330, 3350 or 3380.

TYPE1718
Non-VSAM Data Set Scratch or Rename

The TYPE1718 data set contains observations for every type 17 or 18 SMF record. A type 17 SMF record is written whenever a non-VSAM data set is scratched. For a multivolume data set, there will be one observation in TYPE1718 for each volume. (Note that the SMF option REC(ALL) must be specified if scratch records are to be written for temporary data sets. The usefulness of scratch records for temporary data sets is limited, and, thus, REC(PERM) should be specified so that scratch records are produced only for non-temporary data sets.) A type 18 SMF record is written whenever a non-VSAM data set specified by a DD statement is renamed. For a multivolume data set, there will be one observation in TYPE1718 for each volume. Type 17 and 18 records are written only when an entire PDS is scratched or renamed.

Data set TYPE1718 is most useful for tracking lost data sets.

Variable	Type	Length	Format	Label
DSNAME	CHAR	44		DATA SET NAME

original data set name that was scratched or renamed.

| ID | NUM | 2 | | RECORD*ID |

record identification.

	value	meaning
	17	SCRATCH
	18	RENAME

| JOB | CHAR | 8 | | JOB NAME*OR*TSO USER |

job name (batch); user ID (TSO).

| LOCLINFO | CHAR | 8 | | LOCAL*INSTALLATION*FIELD |

locally-defined field, filled in by installation-written SMF exit.

| NEWNAME | CHAR | 44 | | NAME*AFTER*RENAME |

new data set name (blank for scratch).

| NRVOLS | NUM | 4 | | NUMBER*OF*VOLUMES |

number of volumes in data set. This is the number of observations in TYPE1718 for this SMF record.

Variable	Type	Length	Format	Label

OPEN   CHAR   7   TYPE*OF*OPEN

type of action. This variable name was chosen because TYPE1718 and TYPE1415 data are often selected together to identify what happened (that is, who interfered with your data set).

value	meaning
SCRATCH	data set was scratched. This means only that the pointer to the data set in the VTOC was removed. The actual data still exist on the track where the data was, and a resourceful person could read that data, if their space has not been reallocated and rewritten by a new data set. Thus, to ensure absolute removal of data, it is necessary to over-write the data set with blanks and then scratch the data set. (VSAM offers the ERASE option to accomplish this task, and IBM is considering developing a similar option.)
RENAME	data set was renamed. Both the old name and new name are provided. When investigating suspicious data set disappearances, look for a rename and then a scratch, not just a scratch. Someone may have used a rename and scratch to circumvent RACF.

READTIME   NUM   8   DATETIME19.2   READ-IN*OR LOGON*EVENT

job read-in (TSO LOGON) time stamp.

SMFTIME   NUM   8   DATETIME19.2   SMF*RECORD*TIME STAMP

scratch or rename time stamp.

SYSTEM   CHAR   4   4.   SYSTEM*ID

identification of system on which data set was scratched or renamed.

TEMP   CHAR   4   TEMP*OR*PERM

temporary or permanent data set. The data set name is parsed for a pattern of SYS*nnnnn*.T*nnnnn* (where *nnnnn* is a numeric field) and the value set to TEMP if that pattern is found, or is set to PERM otherwise. This system will work as long as IBM does not change its naming convention for temporary data sets.

VOLSER   CHAR   6   VOLUME*SERIAL*NUMBER

volume serial number on which data set is located. See also NRVOLS (above).

TYPE19
DASD Volume

The TYPE19 data set contains one observation for each type 19 SMF record, written for every DASD device that is on-line at IPL, HALT EOD, or SWITCH SMF; or when a volume defined by a DD statement is dismounted.

TYPE19 information includes space usage on the DASD volume and a flag that possible VTOC errors exist on the volume. The usefulness of TYPE19 information is limited. Member BUILDPDB contains some code that can assist in DASD management.

Variable	Type	Length	Format	Label
CYLAVAIL	NUM	4		NUMBER OF*UNALLOCATED* CYLINDERS

number of unallocated cylinders on this volume.

DEVICE	CHAR	7		DEVICE*TYPE

device type (for example, 3330, 3350, and so forth). The device type is decoded from the UCB type by the VMACUCB member of SOURCLIB.

DEVNR	NUM	4	HEX4.	DEVICE*NUMBER

device number of device. Formerly the Unit Address in MVS/370. The unique number or address of the device.

DSCBERR	CHAR	1		FMT5 DSCB*MISSING*OR ERROR

format 5 DSCBs are missing or erroneous. The volume should be investigated immediately. The value is either blank (no) or Y (yes).

DSCBFIX	CHAR	1		BAD DSCB 5/6*HAVE BEEN*CORRECTED

format 5 DSCB error has been fixed. A prior record contained a value for variable DSCBERR of Y for this volume. The error condition was corrected at that time.

INDXVTOC	CHAR	1		INDEXED*VTOC*VOLUME

volume has an indexed VTOC. Note that indexed VTOCs are found to reduce I/O to the VTOC by 80 to 90 percent. The value is either blank (no) or Y (yes).

LCU	NUM	4	HEX2.	LOGICAL*CONTROL*UNIT

logical control unit number to which device is connected.

MAXCYLS	NUM	4		MAX CONTIGUOUS*UNALLOCATED* CYLINDERS

number of contiguous cylinders in largest unallocated extent on this volume.

Variable	Type	Length	Format	Label
MAXTRKS	NUM	4		MAX CONTIGUOUS*UNALLOCATED*TRACKS

number of contiguous tracks in largest unallocated extent on this volume.

| MODULID | NUM | 4 | | MODULE*IDENTIFICATION*(SENSE BYTE 4) |

module identification (drive number). Taken from bits 2-7 of sense byte 4 for the device. Note that this first bit is one, whereas IBM calls the first bit zero.

| NRALTRKS | NUM | 4 | | UNUSED*ALTERNATE*TRACKS |

number of unused alternate tracks on this volume. If this number is zero, the volume could cause serious I/O problems, since not having alternate tracks causes permanent I/O errors when an alternate track is needed.

| NRDSCBS | NUM | 4 | | TOTAL*NUMBER*OF DSCBS |

total number of DSCBs defined on this volume. This calculated number is based on the number of tracks in the VTOC times the number of DSCBs per track on this device.

| NRDSCB0 | NUM | 4 | | NUMBER*AVAILABLE*DSCBS |

number of available DSCBs (that is, count of DSCB0s). Since each new data set requires a DSCB, this quantifies how many more data sets can be placed on a volume before the VTOC must be expanded.

| NRUNEXTS | NUM | 4 | | NUMBER*UNALLOCATED*EXTENTS |

number of unallocated extents on this volume. This is the number of "spaces" on the volume that could be allocated.

| SMFTIME | NUM | 8 | DATETIME19.2 | SMF*RECORD*TIME STAMP |

event (IPL, HALT EOD, SWITCH SMF, or dismount) time stamp.

| SYSTEM | CHAR | 4 | 4. | SYSTEM*ID |

identification of system on which this event occurred.

| TRKAVAIL | NUM | 4 | | NUMBER OF*UNALLOCATED*TRACKS |

total number of unallocated tracks on this volume.

| UCBTYP | NUM | 4 | | ENTIRE*UNIT*CONTROL BLOCK |

unit control block type (all four bytes).

| UNITADR | NUM | 4 | HEX3. | UNIT*ADDRESS |

unit address of this device.

| VOLOWNER | CHAR | 10 | | VOLUME*OWNER*IDENTIFICATION |

volume owner identification, normally filled in when volume was first labeled.

Variable	Type	Length	Format	Label
VOLSER	CHAR	6		VOLUME*SERIAL*NUMBER

volume serial number on this device at this event.

VTOCADDR	NUM	4	HEX10.	ADDRESS*OF VOLUME*TABLE OF CONTENTS

address on the volume of the VTOC.

VTOCERR	CHAR	1		POSSIBLE*VTOC ERROR*IF NOT INDEXED VTOC

possible VTOC or VTOC index error. This flag of a potential VTOC error cannot be believed if the volume has an indexed VTOC (indicated by variable INDXVTOC). If this is not an indexed VTOC volume, this flag suggests that you scan this pack because this flag is set when there is a strong potential exposure. For example, if a system had crashed while a reserve was posted for this VTOC, the error condition would be flagged. The value is either blank (no) or Y (yes).

VTOCFIX	CHAR	1		VTOC ERROR*HAS BEEN*FIXED

VTOC error has been fixed. A prior record contained a value for variable VTOCERR of Y for this volume. The error condition was corrected at this time.

VTOCIND	NUM	4	HEX2.	VTOC*INDICATOR*BYTE

VTOC indicator. The variables with names that end with the letters ERR and FIX are decodes of this byte.

bit	meaning
1	format 5 DSCBs are missing or erroneous (DSCBERR set to Y).
2-3	reserved.
4	VTOC does not begin on record 1 (VTOCLOC1 set to Y).
5	format 5 and 6 DSCBs are now accurate. Bit 1 was set back to 0 (VTOCFIX set to Y).
6	possible VTOC or VTOC index error (VTOCERR set to Y).
7	VTOC error has been fixed. Bit 6 was set to 0 (VTOCFIX set to Y).
8	indexed VTOC (INDXVTOC set to Y).

VTOCLOC1	CHAR	1		VTOC DOES*NOT BEGIN*ON RECORD 1

VTOC does not begin on record 1.

TYPE20
Job/TSO Initiation

Data set TYPE20 contains one observation for each type 20 SMF record. A type 20 SMF record is written at each job initiation or TSO LOGON, and it contains the initiation time of the job or session and accounting information. TYPE20 is normally not very important since most of the information is repeated in TYPE535, written at job or session termination. However, for jobs or sessions that were active when the system crashed, TYPE20 was the only source of accounting information.

The information in the type 20 record is also contained in the type 30, subtype 1 record along with other information, so you may not need to write the type 20 record. (Check with your accounting system first to see if they need this record for old programs.)

Variable	Type	Length	Format	Label
ACCOUNT1	CHAR	53		FIRST*ACCOUNT*FIELD

first job account field specified on JOB statement. Job level accounting is the predominate method of assigning account numbers to jobs, although account numbers can be provided on EXEC statements if step level accounting is desired. With accounting at the job level, all steps in the job are charged to the same account. NRACCTFL counts the number of account fields specified by the user, and LENACCTn contains the length of the nth account field. SOURCLIB member IMACACCT defines how many account numbers are kept and their maximum length.

ACCOUNT2	CHAR	10		SECOND*ACCOUNT*FIELD

second job account field specified on JOB statement.

ACCOUNT3	CHAR	4		THIRD*ACCOUNT*FIELD

third job account field specified on JOB statement.

ACCOUNT4	CHAR	4		FOURTH*ACCOUNT*FIELD

fourth job account field specified on JOB statement.

ACCOUNT5	CHAR	4		FIFTH*ACCOUNT*FIELD

fifth job account field specified on JOB statement.

ACCOUNT6	CHAR	4		SIXTH*ACCOUNT*FIELD

sixth job account field specified on JOB statement.

ACCOUNT7	CHAR	4		SEVENTH*ACCOUNT*FIELD

seventh job account field specified on JOB statement.

Variable	Type	Length	Format	Label
ACCOUNT8	CHAR	4		EIGHTH*ACCOUNT*FIELD

eighth job account field specified on JOB statement.

ACCOUNT9	CHAR	4		NINTH*ACCOUNT*FIELD

ninth job account field specified on JOB statement.

JOB	CHAR	8		JOB NAME*OR*TSO USER

job name (batch); user ID (TSO).

LENACCT1	NUM	4		LENGTH*ACCOUNT*ONE

length of first account field on JOB JCL statement.

LENACCT2	NUM	4		LENGTH*ACCOUNT*TWO

length of second account field on JOB JCL statement.

LENACCT3	NUM	4		LENGTH*ACCOUNT*THREE

length of third account field on JOB JCL statement.

LENACCT4	NUM	4		LENGTH*ACCOUNT*FOUR

length of fourth account field on JOB JCL statement.

LENACCT5	NUM	4		LENGTH*ACCOUNT*FIVE

length of fifth account field on JOB JCL statement.

LENACCT6	NUM	4		LENGTH*ACCOUNT*SIX

length of sixth account field on JOB JCL statement.

LENACCT7	NUM	4		LENGTH*ACCOUNT*SEVEN

length of seventh account field on JOB JCL statement.

LENACCT8	NUM	4		LENGTH*ACCOUNT*EIGHT

length of eighth account field on JOB JCL statement.

LENACCT9	NUM	4		LENGTH*ACCOUNT*NINE

length of ninth account field on JOB JCL statement.

LOCLINFO	CHAR	8		LOCAL*INSTALLATION*FIELD

locally-defined field. This field is filled in by an installation-written SMF exit routine.

NRACCTFL	NUM	4		NUMBER*ACCOUNT*FIELDS

number of account fields specified on JOB JCL statement.

Variable	Type	Length	Format	Label

PGMRNAME   CHAR   20   PROGRAMMER*NAME*FIELD
programmer name field from JOB statement.

RACFGRUP   CHAR   8   RACF*GROUP*IDENTIFICATION
RACF group identification (zero if RACF is not enabled).

RACFTERM   CHAR   8   RACF/VTAM*TERMINAL*NAME USED
RACF terminal name used. This is the VTAM terminal name used by this TSO session. If
you use RACF or a security package that enables RACF exits, this variable will be non-
blank and can be used to identify and quantify VTAM terminal usage. The VTAM terminal
name is associated with the physical port address on the control unit so that recabling
terminals can change the physical terminal that has this VTAM terminal name.

RACFUSER   CHAR   8   RACF*USER*IDENTIFICATION
RACF user identification (blank if RACF is not enabled).

READTIME   NUM   8   DATETIME19.2   READ-IN*OR LOGON*EVENT
job read-in (TSO LOGON) time stamp.

SMFTIME   NUM   8   DATETIME19.2   SMF*RECORD*TIME STAMP
initiation time stamp of this job. Jobs that initiate multiple times (for example, if canceled
and requeued due to data set enqueue conflict with the $EJ command) create multiple
observations in TYPE20 for the same logical job (that is, same READTIME and JOB
values).

SYSTEM   CHAR   4   4.   SYSTEM*ID
identification of system on which job or session was initiated.

TYPE21
Tape Error Statistics by Volume (ESV)

Data set TYPE21 contains one observation for each type 21 SMF record. A type 21 SMF record is written for every dismount of a tape volume (actually, every dismount following a successful mount; if an incorrect volume is mounted and rejected by the system, there is no corresponding type 21 record). TYPE21 contains statistics on the tape errors and I/O counts for each volume. Unfortunately, you cannot tell whether errors were caused by the device, control unit, or channel or by defects in the tape media itself. Furthermore, neither the name of the job that used the tape nor the length of time it took to mount it is contained in the record.

However, the TYPE21 analysis is of considerable value in tracking and identifying bad tape volumes and drives. See chapter fourteen, Resource Management-Tapes and Tape Drives, for examples of using TYPE21 data.

TYPE21 data are included in BUILDPDB code.

Variable	Type	Length	Format	Label
BLKSIZE	NUM	4		PHYSICAL*BLOCK SIZE*(BYTES)

blocksize. Zero if recorded format is unblocked, record length is variable, or access method is EXCP.

CLEAN	NUM	4		READ*CLEANER*ACTIONS

number of cleaner actions during read. A CLEAN is a backspace of four physical blocks, followed by a read forward of five blocks. Its purpose is to remove the loose oxide flakes and particulate matter that often cause read errors. When a read error is detected, four attempts are made to reread, and then a CLEAN is attempted. This sequence can be repeated up to nine times. An error that clears is marked as a temporary read error. Otherwise, the error is marked as a permanent read error.

DENSITY	CHAR	4		TAPE*DENSITY

tape density. The possible values are 200, 556, 800, 1600, or 6250.

DEVNR	NUM	4	HEX4.	DEVICE*NUMBER

device number of device; the unique number or address of the device. Formerly the Unit Address in MVS/370.

ERASE	NUM	4		WRITE*ERASE*ACTIONS

number of erase actions during write. An ERASE is a forward space of 3½ inches of tape to skip over a defective area (a crimp or scrape, for example) of the tape media. Up to 14 ERASEs can be issued before the error is reclassified from temporary to permanent.

Variable	Type	Length	Format	Label
ERRORS	NUM	4		TOTAL*TAPE*ERRORS

total errors. The sum of PERMREAD, PERMWRIT, NOISE, ERASE, and the maximum of CLEAN or TEMPREAD. This is simply a gross estimate of the error activity during this mount of this volume.

LCU	NUM	4	HEX2.	LOGICAL*CONTROL*UNIT

logical control unit number to which this device is connected.

NOISE	NUM	4		NOISE*BLOCKS*DETECTED

number of noise blocks detected. These are always the result of a hardware failure rather than a media problem.

PERMREAD	NUM	4		PERMANENT*READ*ERRORS

number of permanent read errors. Normally a permanent error causes the task using the tape to abend, but options such as ACC (accept any error) and SKP (skip any error) permit processing of the volume to continue even after permanent errors are encountered.

PERMWRIT	NUM	4		PERMANENT*WRITE*ERRORS

number of permanent write errors. See PERMREAD, above.

SIOCOUNT	NUM	4		START-IO*UNT

number of I/O actions attempted (SIOs issued).

SMFTIME	NUM	8	DATETIME19.2	SMF*RECORD*TIME STAMP

dismount time stamp.

SYSTEM	CHAR	4	4.	SYSTEM*ID

identification of system on which tape was dismounted.

TEMPREAD	NUM	4		TEMPORARY*READ*ERRORS

number of temporary read errors. See CLEAN, above.

TEMPWRIT	NUM	4		TEMPORARY*WRITE*ERRORS

number of temporary write errors. See ERASE, above.

UCBTYPE	NUM	4	HEX8.	UCB*TYPE

all four bytes of Unit Control Block Type for this device.

UNITADR	NUM	4	HEX3.	UNIT*ADDRESS

unit address of this device.

VOLSER	CHAR	6		VOLUME*SERIAL*NUMBER

volume serial number of dismounted tape. Blank for nonlabeled tape and for tapes that failed volume verification (that is, wrong tape mounted by operator).

TYPE22_1
CPU Configuration

The TYPE22_1 data set contains one observation for each type 22 SMF record with a subtype 1 (CPU) section, created at each IPL and after a CONFIG CPU operator command. The record describes the processors that are on-line after the event.

Variable	Type	Length	Format	Label
CPUID	NUM	4		PROCESSOR*NUMBER

processor id number. Prior to 303x series processors, UP processors were 0, and the AP or MP processor was 1. With 308x series, however, the dyadic processors are numbered 0 and 2, and the 3083 series UPs are numbered 2. The processors in the 3084 are numbered 0, 1, 2, and 3.

Variable	Type	Length	Format	Label
CPUTYPE	CHAR	2	HEX4.	CPU*MODEL*NUMBER

CPU model number (168, 3033, and so forth). Note that there is no CPU version number by which the actual model (3033 model U, N or S, 3081 model D, G, or K) can be identified in this record. The CPU version is contained only in the TYPE70 data set in MVS/XA.

Variable	Type	Length	Format	Label
REASON	CHAR	14		REASON

reason record was written. The possible values are:

>   IPL
>   VARY ONLINE
>   VARY OFFLINE

Variable	Type	Length	Format	Label
SMFTIME	NUM	8	DATETIME19.2	SMF*RECORD*TIME STAMP

time stamp of reason event.

Variable	Type	Length	Format	Label
SYSTEM	CHAR	4	4.	SYSTEM*ID

identification of system on which event occurred.

TYPE22_2
MVS/370 Physical Channel Configuration

The TYPE22_2 data set contains one observation for each type 22 SMF record with a subtype 2 (MVS/370 Physical Channel) section, created at each IPL and after a VARY ONLINE or VARY OFFLINE operator command. The record describes the physical channels that are on-line after the event.

Variable	Type	Length	Format	Label
CHAN	NUM	4	HEX2.	CHANNEL*NUMBER

physical channel number.

CHANMODL	NUM	4	HEX2.	CHANNEL*MODEL*NUMBER

channel model number.

CHANSET	NUM	4		CHANNEL*SET*ID

channel set identification.

CHANTYPE	CHAR	9		CHANNEL*TYPE

channel type. The values are BYTE, MUX, BLOCK MUX, or SELECTOR.

CPUID	NUM	4		PROCESSOR*NUMBER

processor id number. Prior to 303x series processors, UP processors were 0, and the AP or MP processor was 1. With 308x series, however, the dyadic processors are numbered 0 and 2 and the 3083 series UPs are numbered 2. The processors in the 3084 are numbered 0, 1, 2, and 3.

REASON	CHAR	14		REASON

reason record was written. The possible values are:

> IPL
>
> VARY ONLINE
>
> VARY OFFLINE

SMFTIME	NUM	8	DATETIME19.2	SMF*RECORD*TIME STAMP

time stamp of reason event.

SYSTEM	CHAR	4	4.	SYSTEM*ID

identification of system on which event occurred.

TYPE 22_3
Storage Configuration

The TYPE22_3 data set contains one observation for each type 22 SMF record with a subtype 3 (storage) section, created at each IPL and after a VARY ONLINE or VARY OFFLINE operator command. The record describes the storage that is on-line after the event.

Variable	Type	Length	Format	Label
INTERLEV	CHAR	1		REAL STORAGE*FRAMES* INTERLEAVED?

real storage frames are interleaved. The values are either blank (no) or Y (yes).

| LOWADDR | NUM | 4 | | LOWEST REAL*CONTIGUOUS*PAGE ADDRESS |

address (31-bits in MVS/XA) of lowest page in real contiguous storage (taken from the CONFIG STOR command).

| NRPAGES | NUM | 4 | | NUMBER PAGES*IN REAL*STORAGE |

number of pages (frames) in real contiguous storage (taken from the CONFIG STOR command). Each page (frame) is 4K and is 4096 bytes.

| REASON | CHAR | 14 | | REASON |

reason record was written. The possible values are:

> IPL

> VARY ONLINE

> VARY OFFLINE

| SMFTIME | NUM | 8 | DATETIME19.2 | SMF*RECORD*TIME STAMP |

time stamp of reason event.

| SYSTEM | CHAR | 4 | 4. | SYSTEM*ID |

identification of system on which event occurred.

TYPE 22_4
MSS Configuration at IPL

The TYPE22_4 data set contains one observation for each type 22 SMF record with subtype 4, created at each Initial Program Load (IPL). The record describes the MSS units on-line at IPL.

Variable	Type	Length	Format	Label
DRC0400	CHAR	1		MSF 0*DRC 400*ON-LINE

MSF 0 Device Recording Control 400 is on-line.

DRC0401	CHAR	1		MSF 0*DRC 401*ON-LINE

MSF 0 Device Recording Control 401 is on-line.

DRC0402	CHAR	1		MSF 0*DRC 402*ON-LINE

MSF 0 Device Recording Control 402 is on-line.

DRC0403	CHAR	1		MSF 0*DRC 403*ON-LINE

MSF 0 Device Recording Control 403 is on-line.

DRC1410	CHAR	1		MSF 1*DRC 410*ON-LINE

MSF 1 Device Recording Control 410 is on-line.

DRC1411	CHAR	1		MSF 1*DRC 411*ON-LINE

MSF 1 Device Recording Control 411 is on-line.

DRC1412	CHAR	1		MSF 1*DRC 412*ON-LINE

MSF 1 Device Recording Control 412 is on-line.

DRC1413	CHAR	1		MSF 1*DRC 413*ON-LINE

MSF 1 Device Recording Control 413 is on-line.

DRD0200	CHAR	1		MSF 0*DRD 200*ON-LINE

MSF 0 Data Recording Device 200 is on-line.

DRD0201	CHAR	1		MSF 0*DRD 201*ON-LINE

MSF 0 Data Recording Device 201 is on-line.

DRD0202	CHAR	1		MSF 0*DRD 202*ON-LINE

MSF 0 Data Recording Device 202 is on-line.

DRD0203	CHAR	1		MSF 0*DRD 203*ON-LINE

MSF 0 Data Recording Device 203 is on-line.

Variable	Type	Length	Format	Label
DRD0204	CHAR	1		MSF 0*DRD 204*ON-LINE
MSF 0 Data Recording Device 204 is on-line.				
DRD0205	CHAR	1		MSF 0*DRD 205*ON-LINE
MSF 0 Data Recording Device 205 is on-line.				
DRD0206	CHAR	1		MSF 0*DRD 206*ON-LINE
MSF 0 Data Recording Device 206 is on-line.				
DRD0207	CHAR	1		MSF 0*DRD 207*ON-LINE
MSF 0 Data Recording Device 207 is on-line.				
DRD1210	CHAR	1		MSF 1*DRD 210*ON-LINE
MSF 1 Data Recording Device 210 is on-line.				
DRD1211	CHAR	1		MSF 1*DRD 211*ON-LINE
MSF 1 Data Recording Device 211 is on-line.				
DRD1212	CHAR	1		MSF 1*DRD 212*ON-LINE
MSF 1 Data Recording Device 212 is on-line.				
DRD1213	CHAR	1		MSF 1*DRD 213*ON-LINE
MSF 1 Data Recording Device 213 is on-line.				
DRD1214	CHAR	1		MSF 1*DRD 214*ON-LINE
MSF 1 Data Recording Device 214 is on-line.				
DRD1215	CHAR	1		MSF 1*DRD 215*ON-LINE
MSF 1 Data Recording Device 215 is on-line.				
DRD1216	CHAR	1		MSF 1*DRD 216*ON-LINE
MSF 1 Data Recording Device 216 is on-line.				
DRD1217	CHAR	1		MSF 1*DRD 217*ON-LINE
MSF 1 Data Recording Device 217 is on-line.				
MSF0101	CHAR	1		MSF 0*SSID 101*ON-LINE
MSF 0 SSID 101 is on-line.				
MSF0102	CHAR	1		MSF 0*SSID 102*ON-LINE
MSF 0 SSID 102 is on-line.				

Variable	Type	Length	Format	Label
MSF1111	CHAR	1		MSF 1*SSID 111*ON-LINE

MSF 1 SSID 111 is on-line.

MSF1112	CHAR	1		MSF 1*SSID 112*ON-LINE

MSF 1 SSID 112 is on-line.

REASON	CHAR	14		REASON

reason record was written. The possible values are: MSS AT IPL.

SDGA050	CHAR	1		SDG 10*SSID 050*ON-LINE

Staging Data Group 10 SSID 050 is on-line.

SDGA051	CHAR	1		SDG 10*SSID 051*ON-LINE

Staging Data Group 10 SSID 051 is on-line.

SDGA052	CHAR	1		SDG 10*SSID 052*ON-LINE

Staging Data Group 10 SSID 052 is on-line.

SDGA053	CHAR	1		SDG 10*SSID 053*ON-LINE

Staging Data Group 10 SSID 053 is on-line.

SDGA054	CHAR	1		SDG 10*SSID 054*ON-LINE

Staging Data Group 10 SSID 054 is on-line.

SDGA055	CHAR	1		SDG 10*SSID 055*ON-LINE

Staging Data Group 10 SSID 055 is on-line.

SDGA056	CHAR	1		SDG 10*SSID 056*ON-LINE

Staging Data Group 10 SSID 056 is on-line.

SDGA057	CHAR	1		SDG 10*SSID 057*ON-LINE

Staging Data Group 10 SSID 057 is on-line.

SDGB05A	CHAR	1		SDG 11*SSID 05A*ON-LINE

Staging Data Group 11 SSID 05A is on-line.

SDGB05B	CHAR	1		SDG 11*SSID 05B*ON-LINE

Staging Data Group 11 SSID 05B is on-line.

SDGB05C	CHAR	1		SDG 11*SSID 05C*ON-LINE

Staging Data Group 11 SSID 05C is on-line.

Variable	Type	Length	Format	Label
SDGB05D	CHAR	1		SDG 11*SSID 05D*ON-LINE
Staging Data Group 11 SSID 05D is on-line.				
SDGB05E	CHAR	1		SDG 11*SSID 05E*ON-LINE
Staging Data Group 11 SSID 05E is on-line.				
SDGB05F	CHAR	1		SDG 11*SSID 05F*ON-LINE
Staging Data Group 11 SSID 05F is on-line.				
SDGB058	CHAR	1		SDG 11*SSID 058*ON-LINE
Staging Data Group 11 SSID 058 is on-line.				
SDGB059	CHAR	1		SDG 11*SSID 059*ON-LINE
Staging Data Group 11 SSID 059 is on-line.				
SDGC060	CHAR	1		SDG 12*SSID 060*ON-LINE
Staging Data Group 12 SSID 060 is on-line.				
SDGC061	CHAR	1		SDG 12*SSID 061*ON-LINE
Staging Data Group 12 SSID 061 is on-line.				
SDGC062	CHAR	1		SDG 12*SSID 062*ON-LINE
Staging Data Group 12 SSID 062 is on-line.				
SDGC063	CHAR	1		SDG 12*SSID 063*ON-LINE
Staging Data Group 12 SSID 063 is on-line.				
SDGC064	CHAR	1		SDG 12*SSID 064*ON-LINE
Staging Data Group 12 SSID 064 is on-line.				
SDGC065	CHAR	1		SDG 12*SSID 065*ON-LINE
Staging Data Group 12 SSID 065 is on-line.				
SDGC066	CHAR	1		SDG 12*SSID 066*ON-LINE
Staging Data Group 12 SSID 066 is on-line.				
SDGC067	CHAR	1		SDG 12*SSID 067*ON-LINE
Staging Data Group 12 SSID 067 is on-line.				
SDGD06A	CHAR	1		SDG 13*SSID 06A*ON-LINE
Staging Data Group 13 SSID 06A is on-line.				

Variable	Type	Length	Format	Label
SDGD06B	CHAR	1		SDG 13*SSID 06B*ON-LINE

Staging Data Group 13 SSID 06B is on-line.

Variable	Type	Length	Format	Label
SDGD06C	CHAR	1		SDG 13*SSID 06C*ON-LINE

Staging Data Group 13 SSID 06C is on-line.

| SDGD06D | CHAR | 1 | | SDG 13*SSID 06D*ON-LINE |

Staging Data Group 13 SSID 06D is on-line.

| SDGD06E | CHAR | 1 | | SDG 13*SSID 06E*ON-LINE |

Staging Data Group 13 SSID 06E is on-line.

| SDGD06F | CHAR | 1 | | SDG 13*SSID 06F*ON-LINE |

Staging Data Group 13 SSID 06F is on-line.

| SDGD068 | CHAR | 1 | | SDG 13*SSID 068*ON-LINE |

Staging Data Group 13 SSID 068 is on-line.

| SDGD069 | CHAR | 1 | | SDG 13*SSID 069*ON-LINE |

Staging Data Group 13 SSID 069 is on-line.

| SDGE070 | CHAR | 1 | | SDG 14*SSID 070*ON-LINE |

Staging Data Group 14 SSID 070 is on-line.

| SDGE071 | CHAR | 1 | | SDG 14*SSID 071*ON-LINE |

Staging Data Group 14 SSID 071 is on-line.

| SDGE072 | CHAR | 1 | | SDG 14*SSID 072*ON-LINE |

Staging Data Group 14 SSID 072 is on-line.

| SDGE073 | CHAR | 1 | | SDG 14*SSID 073*ON-LINE |

Staging Data Group 14 SSID 073 is on-line.

| SDGE074 | CHAR | 1 | | SDG 14*SSID 074*ON-LINE |

Staging Data Group 14 SSID 074 is on-line.

| SDGE075 | CHAR | 1 | | SDG 14*SSID 075*ON-LINE |

Staging Data Group 14 SSID 075 is on-line.

| SDGE076 | CHAR | 1 | | SDG 14*SSID 076*ON-LINE |

Staging Data Group 14 SSID 076 is on-line.

Variable	Type	Length	Format	Label
SDGE077	CHAR	1		SDG 14*SSID 077*ON-LINE
	Staging Data Group 14 SSID 077 is on-line.			
SDGF07A	CHAR	1		SDG 15*SSID 07A*ON-LINE
	Staging Data Group 15 SSID 07A is on-line.			
SDGF07B	CHAR	1		SDG 15*SSID 07B*ON-LINE
	Staging Data Group 15 SSID 07B is on-line.			
SDGF07C	CHAR	1		SDG 15*SSID 07C*ON-LINE
	Staging Data Group 15 SSID 07C is on-line.			
SDGF07D	CHAR	1		SDG 15*SSID 07D*ON-LINE
	Staging Data Group 15 SSID 07D is on-line.			
SDGF07E	CHAR	1		SDG 15*SSID 07E*ON-LINE
	Staging Data Group 15 SSID 07E is on-line.			
SDGF07F	CHAR	1		SDG 15*SSID 07F*ON-LINE
	Staging Data Group 15 SSID 07F is on-line.			
SDGF078	CHAR	1		SDG 15*SSID 078*ON-LINE
	Staging Data Group 15 SSID 078 is on-line.			
SDGF079	CHAR	1		SDG 15*SSID 079*ON-LINE
	Staging Data Group 15 SSID 079 is on-line.			
SDGG080	CHAR	1		SDG 16*SSID 080*ON-LINE
	Staging Data Group 16 SSID 080 is on-line.			
SDGG081	CHAR	1		SDG 16*SSID 081*ON-LINE
	Staging Data Group 16 SSID 081 is on-line.			
SDGG082	CHAR	1		SDG 16*SSID 082*ON-LINE
	Staging Data Group 16 SSID 082 is on-line.			
SDGG083	CHAR	1		SDG 16*SSID 083*ON-LINE
	Staging Data Group 16 SSID 083 is on-line.			
SDGG084	CHAR	1		SDG 16*SSID 084*ON-LINE
	Staging Data Group 16 SSID 084 is on-line.			

Variable	Type	Length	Format	Label
SDGG085	CHAR	1		SDG 16*SSID 085*ON-LINE

Staging Data Group 16 SSID 085 is on-line.

SDGG086	CHAR	1		SDG 16*SSID 086*ON-LINE

Staging Data Group 16 SSID 086 is on-line.

SDGG087	CHAR	1		SDG 16*SSID 087*ON-LINE

Staging Data Group 16 SSID 087 is on-line.

SDGH08A	CHAR	1		SDG 17*SSID 08A*ON-LINE

Staging Data Group 17 SSID 08A is on-line.

SDGH08B	CHAR	1		SDG 17*SSID 08B*ON-LINE

Staging Data Group 17 SSID 08B is on-line.

SDGH08C	CHAR	1		SDG 17*SSID 08C*ON-LINE

Staging Data Group 17 SSID 08C is on-line.

SDGH08D	CHAR	1		SDG 17*SSID 08D*ON-LINE

Staging Data Group 17 SSID 08D is on-line.

SDGH08E	CHAR	1		SDG 17*SSID 08E*ON-LINE

Staging Data Group 17 SSID 08E is on-line.

SDGH08F	CHAR	1		SDG 17*SSID 08F*ON-LINE

Staging Data Group 17 SSID 08F is on-line.

SDGH088	CHAR	1		SDG 17*SSID 088*ON-LINE

Staging Data Group 17 SSID 088 is on-line.

SDGH089	CHAR	1		SDG 17*SSID 089*ON-LINE

Staging Data Group 17 SSID 089 is on-line.

SDGI090	CHAR	1		SDG 18*SSID 090*ON-LINE

Staging Data Group 18 SSID 090 is on-line.

SDGI091	CHAR	1		SDG 18*SSID 091*ON-LINE

Staging Data Group 18 SSID 091 is on-line.

SDGI092	CHAR	1		SDG 18*SSID 092*ON-LINE

Staging Data Group 18 SSID 092 is on-line.

Variable	Type	Length	Format	Label
SDGI093	CHAR	1		SDG 18*SSID 093*ON-LINE
Staging Data Group 18 SSID 093 is on-line.				
SDGI094	CHAR	1		SDG 18*SSID 094*ON-LINE
Staging Data Group 18 SSID 094 is on-line.				
SDGI095	CHAR	1		SDG 18*SSID 095*ON-LINE
Staging Data Group 18 SSID 095 is on-line.				
SDGI096	CHAR	1		SDG 18*SSID 096*ON-LINE
Staging Data Group 18 SSID 096 is on-line.				
SDGI097	CHAR	1		SDG 18*SSID 097*ON-LINE
Staging Data Group 18 SSID 097 is on-line.				
SDGJ09A	CHAR	1		SDG 19*SSID 09A*ON-LINE
Staging Data Group 19 SSID 09A is on-line.				
SDGJ09B	CHAR	1		SDG 19*SSID 09B*ON-LINE
Staging Data Group 19 SSID 09B is on-line.				
SDGJ09C	CHAR	1		SDG 19*SSID 09C*ON-LINE
Staging Data Group 19 SSID 09C is on-line.				
SDGJ09D	CHAR	1		SDG 19*SSID 09D*ON-LINE
Staging Data Group 19 SSID 09D is on-line.				
SDGJ09E	CHAR	1		SDG 19*SSID 09E*ON-LINE
Staging Data Group 19 SSID 09E is on-line.				
SDGJ09F	CHAR	1		SDG 19*SSID 09F*ON-LINE
Staging Data Group 19 SSID 09F is on-line.				
SDGJ098	CHAR	1		SDG 19*SSID 098*ON-LINE
Staging Data Group 19 SSID 098 is on-line.				
SDGJ099	CHAR	1		SDG 19*SSID 099*ON-LINE
Staging Data Group 19 SSID 099 is on-line.				
SDGK0A0	CHAR	1		SDG 20*SSID 0A0*ON-LINE
Staging Data Group 20 SSID 0A0 is on-line.				

Variable	Type	Length	Format	Label
SDGK0A1	CHAR	1		SDG 20*SSID 0A1*ON-LINE

Staging Data Group 20 SSID 0A1 is on-line.

SDGK0A2	CHAR	1		SDG 20*SSID 0A2*ON-LINE

Staging Data Group 20 SSID 0A2 is on-line.

SDGK0A3	CHAR	1		SDG 20*SSID 0A3*ON-LINE

Staging Data Group 20 SSID 0A3 is on-line.

SDGK0A4	CHAR	1		SDG 20*SSID 0A4*ON-LINE

Staging Data Group 20 SSID 0A4 is on-line.

SDGK0A5	CHAR	1		SDG 20*SSID 0A5*ON-LINE

Staging Data Group 20 SSID 0A5 is on-line.

SDGK0A6	CHAR	1		SDG 20*SSID 0A6*ON-LINE

Staging Data Group 20 SSID 0A6 is on-line.

SDGK0A7	CHAR	1		SDG 20*SSID 0A7*ON-LINE

Staging Data Group 20 SSID 0A7 is on-line.

SDGL0AA	CHAR	1		SDG 21*SSID 0AA*ON-LINE

Staging Data Group 21 SSID 0AA is on-line.

SDGL0AB	CHAR	1		SDG 21*SSID 0AB*ON-LINE

Staging Data Group 21 SSID 0AB is on-line.

SDGL0AC	CHAR	1		SDG 21*SSID 0AC*ON-LINE

Staging Data Group 21 SSID 0AC is on-line.

SDGL0AD	CHAR	1		SDG 21*SSID 0AD*ON-LINE

Staging Data Group 21 SSID 0AD is on-line.

SDGL0AE	CHAR	1		SDG 21*SSID 0AE*ON-LINE

Staging Data Group 21 SSID 0AE is on-line.

SDGL0AF	CHAR	1		SDG 21*SSID 0AF*ON-LINE

Staging Data Group 21 SSID 0AF is on-line.

SDGL0A8	CHAR	1		SDG 21*SSID 0A8*ON-LINE

Staging Data Group 21 SSID 0A8 is on-line.

Variable	Type	Length	Format	Label
SDGL0A9	CHAR	1		SDG 21*SSID 0A9*ON-LINE
Staging Data Group 21 SSID 0A9 is on-line.				
SDGM0B0	CHAR	1		SDG 22*SSID 0B0*ON-LINE
Staging Data Group 22 SSID 0B0 is on-line.				
SDGM0B1	CHAR	1		SDG 22*SSID 0B1*ON-LINE
Staging Data Group 22 SSID 0B1 is on-line.				
SDGM0B2	CHAR	1		SDG 22*SSID 0B2*ON-LINE
Staging Data Group 22 SSID 0B2 is on-line.				
SDGM0B3	CHAR	1		SDG 22*SSID 0B3*ON-LINE
Staging Data Group 22 SSID 0B3 is on-line.				
SDGM0B4	CHAR	1		SDG 22*SSID 0B4*ON-LINE
Staging Data Group 22 SSID 0B4 is on-line.				
SDGM0B5	CHAR	1		SDG 22*SSID 0B5*ON-LINE
Staging Data Group 22 SSID 0B5 is on-line.				
SDGM0B6	CHAR	1		SDG 22*SSID 0B6*ON-LINE
Staging Data Group 22 SSID 0B6 is on-line.				
SDGM0B7	CHAR	1		SDG 22*SSID 0B7*ON-LINE
Staging Data Group 22 SSID 0B7 is on-line.				
SDGN0BA	CHAR	1		SDG 23*SSID 0BA*ON-LINE
Staging Data Group 23 SSID 0BA is on-line.				
SDGN0BB	CHAR	1		SDG 23*SSID 0BB*ON-LINE
Staging Data Group 23 SSID 0BB is on-line.				
SDGN0BC	CHAR	1		SDG 23*SSID 0BC*ON-LINE
Staging Data Group 23 SSID 0BC is on-line.				
SDGN0BD	CHAR	1		SDG 23*SSID 0BD*ON-LINE
Staging Data Group 23 SSID 0BD is on-line.				
SDGN0BE	CHAR	1		SDG 23*SSID 0BE*ON-LINE
Staging Data Group 23 SSID 0BE is on-line.				

Variable	Type	Length	Format	Label
SDGN0BF	CHAR	1		SDG 23*SSID 0BF*ON-LINE

Staging Data Group 23 SSID 0BF is on-line.

SDGN0B8	CHAR	1		SDG 23*SSID 0B8*ON-LINE

Staging Data Group 23 SSID 0B8 is on-line.

SDGN0B9	CHAR	1		SDG 23*SSID 0B9*ON-LINE

Staging Data Group 23 SSID 0B9 is on-line.

SDGO0C0	CHAR	1		SDG 24*SSID 0C0*ON-LINE

Staging Data Group 24 SSID 0C0 is on-line.

SDGO0C1	CHAR	1		SDG 24*SSID 0C1*ON-LINE

Staging Data Group 24 SSID 0C1 is on-line.

SDGO0C2	CHAR	1		SDG 24*SSID 0C2*ON-LINE

Staging Data Group 24 SSID 0C2 is on-line.

SDGO0C3	CHAR	1		SDG 24*SSID 0C3*ON-LINE

Staging Data Group 24 SSID 0C3 is on-line.

SDGO0C4	CHAR	1		SDG 24*SSID 0C4*ON-LINE

Staging Data Group 24 SSID 0C4 is on-line.

SDGO0C5	CHAR	1		SDG 24*SSID 0C5*ON-LINE

Staging Data Group 24 SSID 0C5 is on-line.

SDGO0C6	CHAR	1		SDG 24*SSID 0C6*ON-LINE

Staging Data Group 24 SSID 0C6 is on-line.

SDGO0C7	CHAR	1		SDG 24*SSID 0C7*ON-LINE

Staging Data Group 24 SSID 0C7 is on-line.

SDGP0CA	CHAR	1		SDG 25*SSID 0CA*ON-LINE

Staging Data Group 25 SSID 0CA is on-line.

SDGP0CB	CHAR	1		SDG 25*SSID 0CB*ON-LINE

Staging Data Group 25 SSID 0CB is on-line.

SDGP0CC	CHAR	1		SDG 25*SSID 0CC*ON-LINE

Staging Data Group 25 SSID 0CC is on-line.

Variable	Type	Length	Format	Label
SDGP0CD	CHAR	1		SDG 25*SSID 0CD*ON-LINE
Staging Data Group 25 SSID 0CD is on-line.				
SDGP0CE	CHAR	1		SDG 25*SSID 0CE*ON-LINE
Staging Data Group 25 SSID 0CE is on-line.				
SDGP0CF	CHAR	1		SDG 25*SSID 0CF*ON-LINE
Staging Data Group 25 SSID 0CF is on-line.				
SDGP0C8	CHAR	1		SDG 25*SSID 0C8*ON-LINE
Staging Data Group 25 SSID 0C8 is on-line.				
SDGP0C9	CHAR	1		SDG 25*SSID 0C9*ON-LINE
Staging Data Group 25 SSID 0C9 is on-line.				
SDGQ0D0	CHAR	1		SDG 26*SSID 0D0*ON-LINE
Staging Data Group 26 SSID 0D0 is on-line.				
SDGQ0D1	CHAR	1		SDG 26*SSID 0D1*ON-LINE
Staging Data Group 26 SSID 0D1 is on-line.				
SDGQ0D2	CHAR	1		SDG 26*SSID 0D2*ON-LINE
Staging Data Group 26 SSID 0D2 is on-line.				
SDGQ0D3	CHAR	1		SDG 26*SSID 0D3*ON-LINE
Staging Data Group 26 SSID 0D3 is on-line.				
SDGQ0D4	CHAR	1		SDG 26*SSID 0D4*ON-LINE
Staging Data Group 26 SSID 0D4 is on-line.				
SDGQ0D5	CHAR	1		SDG 26*SSID 0D5*ON-LINE
Staging Data Group 26 SSID 0D5 is on-line.				
SDGQ0D6	CHAR	1		SDG 26*SSID 0D6*ON-LINE
Staging Data Group 26 SSID 0D6 is on-line.				
SDGQ0D7	CHAR	1		SDG 26*SSID 0D7*ON-LINE
Staging Data Group 26 SSID 0D7 is on-line.				
SDGR0DA	CHAR	1		SDG 27*SSID 0DA*ON-LINE
Staging Data Group 27 SSID 0DA is on-line.				

Variable	Type	Length	Format	Label
SDGR0DB	CHAR	1		SDG 27*SSID 0DB*ON-LINE
Staging Data Group 27 SSID 0DB is on-line.				
SDGR0DC	CHAR	1		SDG 27*SSID 0DC*ON-LINE
Staging Data Group 27 SSID 0DC is on-line.				
SDGR0DD	CHAR	1		SDG 27*SSID 0DD*ON-LINE
Staging Data Group 27 SSID 0DD is on-line.				
SDGR0DE	CHAR	1		SDG 27*SSID 0DE*ON-LINE
Staging Data Group 27 SSID 0DE is on-line.				
SDGR0DF	CHAR	1		SDG 27*SSID 0DF*ON-LINE
Staging Data Group 27 SSID 0DF is on-line.				
SDGR0D8	CHAR	1		SDG 27*SSID 0D8*ON-LINE
Staging Data Group 27 SSID 0D8 is on-line.				
SDGR0D9	CHAR	1		SDG 27*SSID 0D9*ON-LINE
Staging Data Group 27 SSID 0D9 is on-line.				
SDG0000	CHAR	1		SDG 0*SSID 000*ON-LINE
Staging Data Group 0 SSID 000 is on-line.				
SDG0001	CHAR	1		SDG 0*SSID 001*ON-LINE
Staging Data Group 0 SSID 001 is on-line.				
SDG0002	CHAR	1		SDG 0*SSID 002*ON-LINE
Staging Data Group 0 SSID 002 is on-line.				
SDG0003	CHAR	1		SDG 0*SSID 003*ON-LINE
Staging Data Group 0 SSID 003 is on-line.				
SDG0004	CHAR	1		SDG 0*SSID 004*ON-LINE
Staging Data Group 0 SSID 004 is on-line.				
SDG0005	CHAR	1		SDG 0*SSID 005*ON-LINE
Staging Data Group 0 SSID 005 is on-line.				
SDG0006	CHAR	1		SDG 0*SSID 006*ON-LINE
Staging Data Group 0 SSID 006 is on-line.				

Variable	Type	Length	Format	Label
SDG0007	CHAR	1		SDG 0*SSID 007*ON-LINE
Staging Data Group 0 SSID 007 is on-line.				
SDG100A	CHAR	1		SDG 1*SSID 00A*ON-LINE
Staging Data Group 1 SSID 00A is on-line.				
SDG100B	CHAR	1		SDG 1*SSID 00B*ON-LINE
Staging Data Group 1 SSID 00B is on-line.				
SDG100C	CHAR	1		SDG 1*SSID 00C*ON-LINE
Staging Data Group 1 SSID 00C is on-line.				
SDG100D	CHAR	1		SDG 1*SSID 00D*ON-LINE
Staging Data Group 1 SSID 00D is on-line.				
SDG100E	CHAR	1		SDG 1*SSID 00E*ON-LINE
Staging Data Group 1 SSID 00E is on-line.				
SDG100F	CHAR	1		SDG 1*SSID 00F*ON-LINE
Staging Data Group 1 SSID 00F is on-line.				
SDG1008	CHAR	1		SDG 1*SSID 008*ON-LINE
Staging Data Group 1 SSID 008 is on-line.				
SDG1009	CHAR	1		SDG 1*SSID 009*ON-LINE
Staging Data Group 1 SSID 009 is on-line.				
SDG2010	CHAR	1		SDG 2*SSID 010*ON-LINE
Staging Data Group 2 SSID 010 is on-line.				
SDG2011	CHAR	1		SDG 2*SSID 011*ON-LINE
Staging Data Group 2 SSID 011 is on-line.				
SDG2012	CHAR	1		SDG 2*SSID 012*ON-LINE
Staging Data Group 2 SSID 012 is on-line.				
SDG2013	CHAR	1		SDG 2*SSID 013*ON-LINE
Staging Data Group 2 SSID 013 is on-line.				
SDG2014	CHAR	1		SDG 2*SSID 014*ON-LINE
Staging Data Group 2 SSID 014 is on-line.				

Variable	Type	Length	Format	Label
SDG2015	CHAR	1		SDG 2*SSID 015*ON-LINE
Staging Data Group 2 SSID 015 is on-line.				
SDG2016	CHAR	1		SDG 2*SSID 016*ON-LINE
Staging Data Group 2 SSID 016 is on-line.				
SDG2017	CHAR	1		SDG 2*SSID 017*ON-LINE
Staging Data Group 2 SSID 017 is on-line.				
SDG301A	CHAR	1		SDG 3*SSID 01A*ON-LINE
Staging Data Group 3 SSID 01A is on-line.				
SDG301B	CHAR	1		SDG 3*SSID 01B*ON-LINE
Staging Data Group 3 SSID 01B is on-line.				
SDG301C	CHAR	1		SDG 3*SSID 01C*ON-LINE
Staging Data Group 3 SSID 01C is on-line.				
SDG301D	CHAR	1		SDG 3*SSID 01D*ON-LINE
Staging Data Group 3 SSID 01D is on-line.				
SDG301E	CHAR	1		SDG 3*SSID 01E*ON-LINE
Staging Data Group 3 SSID 01E is on-line.				
SDG301F	CHAR	1		SDG 3*SSID 01F*ON-LINE
Staging Data Group 3 SSID 01F is on-line.				
SDG3018	CHAR	1		SDG 3*SSID 018*ON-LINE
Staging Data Group 3 SSID 018 is on-line.				
SDG3019	CHAR	1		SDG 3*SSID 019*ON-LINE
Staging Data Group 3 SSID 019 is on-line.				
SDG4020	CHAR	1		SDG 4*SSID 020*ON-LINE
Staging Data Group 4 SSID 020 is on-line.				
SDG4021	CHAR	1		SDG 4*SSID 021*ON-LINE
Staging Data Group 4 SSID 021 is on-line.				
SDG4022	CHAR	1		SDG 4*SSID 022*ON-LINE
Staging Data Group 4 SSID 022 is on-line.				

Variable	Type	Length	Format	Label
SDG4023	CHAR	1		SDG 4*SSID 023*ON-LINE
Staging Data Group 4 SSID 023 is on-line.				
SDG4024	CHAR	1		SDG 4*SSID 024*ON-LINE
Staging Data Group 4 SSID 024 is on-line.				
SDG4025	CHAR	1		SDG 4*SSID 025*ON-LINE
Staging Data Group 4 SSID 025 is on-line.				
SDG4026	CHAR	1		SDG 4*SSID 026*ON-LINE
Staging Data Group 4 SSID 026 is on-line.				
SDG4027	CHAR	1		SDG 4*SSID 027*ON-LINE
Staging Data Group 4 SSID 027 is on-line.				
SDG502A	CHAR	1		SDG 5*SSID 02A*ON-LINE
Staging Data Group 5 SSID 02A is on-line.				
SDG502B	CHAR	1		SDG 5*SSID 02B*ON-LINE
Staging Data Group 5 SSID 02B is on-line.				
SDG502C	CHAR	1		SDG 5*SSID 02C*ON-LINE
Staging Data Group 5 SSID 02C is on-line.				
SDG502D	CHAR	1		SDG 5*SSID 02D*ON-LINE
Staging Data Group 5 SSID 02D is on-line.				
SDG502E	CHAR	1		SDG 5*SSID 02E*ON-LINE
Staging Data Group 5 SSID 02E is on-line.				
SDG502F	CHAR	1		SDG 5*SSID 02F*ON-LINE
Staging Data Group 5 SSID 02F is on-line.				
SDG5028	CHAR	1		SDG 5*SSID 028*ON-LINE
Staging Data Group 5 SSID 028 is on-line.				
SDG5029	CHAR	1		SDG 5*SSID 029*ON-LINE
Staging Data Group 5 SSID 029 is on-line.				
SDG6030	CHAR	1		SDG 6*SSID 030*ON-LINE
Staging Data Group 6 SSID 030 is on-line.				

Variable	Type	Length	Format	Label
SDG6031	CHAR	1		SDG 6*SSID 031*ON-LINE
Staging Data Group 6 SSID 031 is on-line.				
SDG6032	CHAR	1		SDG 6*SSID 032*ON-LINE
Staging Data Group 6 SSID 032 is on-line.				
SDG6033	CHAR	1		SDG 6*SSID 033*ON-LINE
Staging Data Group 6 SSID 033 is on-line.				
SDG6034	CHAR	1		SDG 6*SSID 034*ON-LINE
Staging Data Group 6 SSID 034 is on-line.				
SDG6035	CHAR	1		SDG 6*SSID 035*ON-LINE
Staging Data Group 6 SSID 035 is on-line.				
SDG6036	CHAR	1		SDG 6*SSID 036*ON-LINE
Staging Data Group 6 SSID 036 is on-line.				
SDG6037	CHAR	1		SDG 6*SSID 037*ON-LINE
Staging Data Group 6 SSID 037 is on-line.				
SDG703A	CHAR	1		SDG 7*SSID 03A*ON-LINE
Staging Data Group 7 SSID 03A is on-line.				
SDG703B	CHAR	1		SDG 7*SSID 03B*ON-LINE
Staging Data Group 7 SSID 03B is on-line.				
SDG703C	CHAR	1		SDG 7*SSID 03C*ON-LINE
Staging Data Group 7 SSID 03C is on-line.				
SDG703D	CHAR	1		SDG 7*SSID 03D*ON-LINE
Staging Data Group 7 SSID 03D is on-line.				
SDG703E	CHAR	1		SDG 7*SSID 03E*ON-LINE
Staging Data Group 7 SSID 03E is on-line.				
SDG703F	CHAR	1		SDG 7*SSID 03F*ON-LINE
Staging Data Group 7 SSID 03F is on-line.				
SDG7038	CHAR	1		SDG 7*SSID 038*ON-LINE
Staging Data Group 7 SSID 038 is on-line.				

Variable	Type	Length	Format	Label
SDG7039	CHAR	1		SDG 7*SSID 039*ON-LINE
Staging Data Group 7 SSID 039 is on-line.				
SDG8040	CHAR	1		SDG 8*SSID 040*ON-LINE
Staging Data Group 8 SSID 040 is on-line.				
SDG8041	CHAR	1		SDG 8*SSID 041*ON-LINE
Staging Data Group 8 SSID 041 is on-line.				
SDG8042	CHAR	1		SDG 8*SSID 042*ON-LINE
Staging Data Group 8 SSID 042 is on-line.				
SDG8043	CHAR	1		SDG 8*SSID 043*ON-LINE
Staging Data Group 8 SSID 043 is on-line.				
SDG8044	CHAR	1		SDG 8*SSID 044*ON-LINE
Staging Data Group 8 SSID 044 is on-line.				
SDG8045	CHAR	1		SDG 8*SSID 045*ON-LINE
Staging Data Group 8 SSID 045 is on-line.				
SDG8046	CHAR	1		SDG 8*SSID 046*ON-LINE
Staging Data Group 8 SSID 046 is on-line.				
SDG8047	CHAR	1		SDG 8*SSID 047*ON-LINE
Staging Data Group 8 SSID 047 is on-line.				
SDG904A	CHAR	1		SDG 9*SSID 04A*ON-LINE
Staging Data Group 9 SSID 04A is on-line.				
SDG904B	CHAR	1		SDG 9*SSID 04B*ON-LINE
Staging Data Group 9 SSID 04B is on-line.				
SDG904C	CHAR	1		SDG 9*SSID 04C*ON-LINE
Staging Data Group 9 SSID 04C is on-line.				
SDG904D	CHAR	1		SDG 9*SSID 04D*ON-LINE
Staging Data Group 9 SSID 04D is on-line.				
SDG904E	CHAR	1		SDG 9*SSID 04E*ON-LINE
Staging Data Group 9 SSID 04E is on-line.				

Variable	Type	Length	Format	Label
SDG904F	CHAR	1		SDG 9*SSID 04F*ON-LINE

Staging Data Group 9 SSID 04F is on-line.

SDG9048	CHAR	1		SDG 9*SSID 048*ON-LINE

Staging Data Group 9 SSID 048 is on-line.

SDG9049	CHAR	1		SDG 9*SSID 049*ON-LINE

Staging Data Group 9 SSID 049 is on-line.

SMFTIME	NUM	8	DATETIME19.2	SMF*RECORD*TIME STAMP

time stamp of reason event.

STA08A0	CHAR	1		STAGING ADAPTER*SSID 8A0*ON-LINE

Staging Adapter SSID 8A0 is on-line.

STA08B0	CHAR	1		STAGING ADAPTER*SSID 8B0*ON-LINE

Staging Adapter SSID 8B0 is on-line.

STA08C0	CHAR	1		STAGING ADAPTER*SSID 8C0*ON-LINE

Staging Adapter SSID 8C0 is on-line.

STA08D0	CHAR	1		STAGING ADAPTER*SSID 8D0*ON-LINE

Staging Adapter SSID 8D0 is on-line.

STA08E0	CHAR	1		STAGING ADAPTER*SSID 8E0*ON-LINE

Staging Adapter SSID 8E0 is on-line.

STA08F0	CHAR	1		STAGING ADAPTER*SSID 8F0*ON-LINE

Staging Adapter SSID 8F0 is on-line.

STA0800	CHAR	1		STAGING ADAPTER*SSID 800*ON-LINE

Staging Adapter SSID 800 is on-line.

STA0810	CHAR	1		STAGING ADAPTER*SSID 810*ON-LINE

Staging Adapter SSID 810 is on-line.

STA0820	CHAR	1		STAGING ADAPTER*SSID 820*ON-LINE

Staging Adapter SSID 820 is on-line.

STA0830	CHAR	1		STAGING ADAPTER*SSID 830*ON-LINE

Staging Adapter SSID 830 is on-line.

Variable	Type	Length	Format	Label
STA0840	CHAR	1		STAGING ADAPTER*SSID 840*ON-LINE
Staging Adapter SSID 840 is on-line.				
STA0850	CHAR	1		STAGING ADAPTER*SSID 850*ON-LINE
Staging Adapter SSID 850 is on-line.				
STA0860	CHAR	1		STAGING ADAPTER*SSID 860*ON-LINE
Staging Adapter SSID 860 is on-line.				
STA0870	CHAR	1		STAGING ADAPTER*SSID 870*ON-LINE
Staging Adapter SSID 870 is on-line.				
STA0880	CHAR	1		STAGING ADAPTER*SSID 880*ON-LINE
Staging Adapter SSID 880 is on-line.				
STA0890	CHAR	1		STAGING ADAPTER*SSID 890*ON-LINE
Staging Adapter SSID 890 is on-line.				
SYSTEM	CHAR	4	4.	SYSTEM*ID
identification of system on which event occurred.				

TYPE22_5
Configuration at VARY ONLINE, S

Data set TYPE22_5 contains one observation for each type 22 SMF record with subtype 5, created at each VARY ONLINE, S operator command.

Variable	Type	Length	Format	Label
REASON	CHAR	14		REASON

reason record was written. The possible values are:
VARY ONLINE, S

SMFTIME	NUM	8	DATETIME19.2	SMF*RECORD*TIME STAMP

time stamp of reason event.

SUBSYSID	CHAR	3	HEX6.	SUB*SYSTEM*ID

subsystem identification of device that was varied.

SYSTEM	CHAR	4	4.	SYSTEM*ID

identification of system on which event occurred.

TYPE22_6
Configuration at VARY OFFLINE, S

Data set TYPE22_6 contains one observation for each type 22 SMF record with subtype 6, created at each VARY OFFLINE, S operator command.

Variable	Type	Length	Format	Label
REASON	CHAR	14		REASON

    reason record was written. The possible values are:

        VARY OFFLINE, S

SMFTIME	NUM	8	DATETIME19.2	SMF*RECORD*TIME STAMP

    time stamp of reason event.

SUBSYSID	CHAR	3	HEX6.	SUB*SYSTEM*ID

    subsystem identification of device varied.

SYSTEM	CHAR	4	4.	SYSTEM*ID

    identification of system on which event occurred.

TYPE22_7
Channel Path Configuration

The TYPE22_7 data set contains one or more observations for each type 22 SMF record with subtype 7, written at each IPL. The record describes the channel paths that are on-line after the event. For each subtype 7 section, TYPE22_7 contains one observation for each valid CHPID.

Variable	Type	Length	Format	Label
CHONLINE	CHAR	1		CHANNEL*PATH*ON-LINE?

channel path on-line status. The values are either blank (no) or Y (yes).

CHOWNED	CHAR	1		CHANNEL*PATH*OWNED?

channel path ownership status. Whether CPID is owned by this system. The values are either blank (no) or Y (yes).

CHPID	NUM	4	HEX2.	CHANNEL*PATH*ID

channel path identification.

REASON	CHAR	14		REASON

reason record was written. The possible value is: IPL.

SMFTIME	NUM	8	DATETIME19.2	SMF*RECORD*TIME STAMP

time stamp of reason event.

SYSTEM	CHAR	4	4.	SYSTEM*ID

identification of system on which event occurred.

TYPE22_8
Reconfigured Channel Path

Data set TYPE22_8 contains one or more observations for each type 22 SMF record with subtype 8, written when channel paths are reconfigured (CONFIG CHP operator command). The record describes the channel paths that are on-line after the event. For each subtype 8 section, TYPE22_8 contains one observation for each reconfigured CHPID.

Variable	Type	Length	Format	Label
CHPID	NUM	4	HEX2.	CHANNEL*PATH*ID

    channel path identification.

REASON	CHAR	14		REASON

    reason record was written. The possible values are:
        VARY CHANNEL PATH

SMFTIME	NUM	8	DATETIME19.2	SMF*RECORD*TIME STAMP

    time stamp of reason event.

SYSTEM	CHAR	4	4.	SYSTEM*ID

    identification of system on which event occurred.

TYPE23
SMF Buffer Statistics

The TYPE23 data set contains one observation for each type 23 SMF record written at user-specified intervals. The record describes the number of SMF records written during the interval and identifies any delays due to insufficient SMF buffers.

The redesign of SMF in MVS/XA places SMF in its own address space, and the number of buffers now is limited only by the virtual storage size of the SMF task. Thus, the need for TYPE23 data is reduced in MVS/XA.

Variable	Type	Length	Format	Label
INTERVAL	NUM	4	TIME12.2	TYPE23*INTERVAL*(HHMMSS)

interval (HHMMSS) at which records are written. The interval is set by the status keyword of SMFPRM*xx* member of SYS1.PARMLIB. The default value is hourly.

MAXBUFF	NUM	4		MAXIMUM*SMF BUFFERS*FILLED

maximum number of buffers used at any one time during this interval.

NBUFWRIT	NUM	4		NUMBER*BUFFERS*WRITTEN

number of buffers (physical blocks) actually written to MAN data set(s) during the interval.

NRECWRIT	NUM	4		NUMBER*LRECS*WRITTEN

number of SMF logical records in the (NBUFWRIT) physical records that were written during the interval.

NRSUSPND	NUM	4		TIMES*SMF RECORDING*SUSPENDED

number of times SMF recording was suspended due to insufficient buffers during interval.

MVS/370:

if nonzero, it suggests that the number of buffers defined in SMFPRM*xx* is not sufficient for this system's workload. MAXBUFF identifies how many buffers are being used; the default maximum should be raised above MAXBUFF until no delay is encountered. You must increase the size of CSA virtual storage by 4096 bytes for each additional SMF buffer to gain this improved SMF performance.

MVS/XA:

the number of buffers is limited only by the amount of virtual storage below 16 megabytes in the SMF address space. At initialization, MVS/XA starts with 100 SMF buffers, and it gets more as SMF activity increases. As a result of this redesign, suspend of SMF due to buffer shortage should not occur in MVS/XA.

Variable	Type	Length	Format	Label
PRODUCT	CHAR	8		PRODUCT*NAME
RELEASE	CHAR	4		OPERATING*SYSTEM*RELEASE
SMFTIME	NUM	8	DATETIME19.2	SMF*RECORD*TIME STAMP
SUBTYPE	NUM	4		SUBTYPE*ID
SYSTEM	CHAR	4	4.	SYSTEM*ID
VERSION	CHAR	2		VERSION*NUMBER

PRODUCT CHAR 8 PRODUCT*NAME
product name that produced this record.

RELEASE CHAR 4 OPERATING*SYSTEM*RELEASE
operating system release number.

SMFTIME NUM 8 DATETIME19.2 SMF*RECORD*TIME STAMP
time this record was written to SMF.

SUBTYPE NUM 4 SUBTYPE*ID
subtype id. The value is 0.

SYSTEM CHAR 4 4. SYSTEM*ID
identification of this system.

VERSION CHAR 2 VERSION*NUMBER
record version number.

TYPE25
JES3 Device Allocation

The TYPE25 data set contains one observation for each type 25 SMF record. One type 25 record per job is written by JES3 for all device allocations that result from DD statements; additional type 25 records are written for each group of JES3 allocations for private catalogs, and a type 25 is written for each MDS dynamic allocation request.

TYPE25 contains the count of volumes fetched and mounted by JES3 and time stamps of fetch processing, manual start setup, first volume mount time, and device verification. It is very useful for tracking usage of devices and analysis of fetch or setup queue delays.

Variable	Type	Length	Format	Label
ALLOCATN	CHAR	5		DEVICE*ALLOCATION*SOURCE

source of device allocation:

value	meaning
AUTO	automatic allocation by JES3
CATLG	catalog allocation by JES3
DYNAM	dynamic allocation
MANL	manual allocation by operator
NOCAT	noncataloged allocation by JES3
USER	allocation by user DD statement.

Variable	Type	Length	Format	Label
DISKMNTS	NUM	4		DISK*VOLUMES*MOUNTED

number of disk volumes mounted for the job.

Variable	Type	Length	Format	Label
DSKFETCH	NUM	4		DISK*VOLUMES*FETCHED

number of disk volumes fetched for the job.

Variable	Type	Length	Format	Label
FETCTIME	NUM	8	DATETIME19.2	FETCH*PROCESSING*END TIME

fetch processing start time stamp.

Variable	Type	Length	Format	Label
JOB	CHAR	8		JOB NAME*OR*TSO USER

job name (batch); user ID (TSO).

Variable	Type	Length	Format	Label
LOCLINFO	CHAR	8		LOCAL*INSTALLATION*FIELD

locally-defined field, filled in by installation-written SMF exit routine.

Variable	Type	Length	Format	Label
MNTTIME	NUM	8	DATETIME19.2	FIRST VOLUME*MOUNT MSG* TIME STAMP

first volume mount message time stamp. (If no mounts are required, MNTTIME contains the time of JES3 allocation.)

MSSALOCS	NUM	4		MASS STORAGE*VOLUMES* ALLOCATED

number of mass storage volume requests allocated.

READTIME	NUM	8	DATETIME19.2	READ-IN*OR LOGON*EVENT

job read-in (TSO LOGON) time stamp.

SMFTIME	NUM	8	DATETIME19.2	SMF*RECORD*TIME STAMP

event time stamp.

STRTTIME	NUM	8	DATETIME19.2	LAST VOLUME*MOUNT MESSAGE*TIME STAMP

start setup time stamp (missing if automatic allocation).

SYSTEM	CHAR	4	4.	SYSTEM*ID

identification of system on which record was written.

TAPEMNTS	NUM	4		TAPE*VOLUMES*MOUNTED

number of tape volumes mounted.

TAPFETCH	NUM	4		TAPE*VOLUMES*FETCHED

number of tape volumes fetched.

VERFTIME	NUM	8	DATETIME19.2	DEVICE*VERIFICATION*TIME STAMP

device verification time stamp.

TYPE26J2
JES2 Purge Record

The TYPE26J2 data set contains one observation for each type 26 written by JES2. A type 26 SMF record is written when all SYSOUT for a job is processed at this node, when a job is purged by the operator-issued purge ($P) command, or when a job is transmitted from one node to another by NJE (either for execution at the next node or for printing SYSOUT at that node).

Multiple purge records can occur for the same job in an NJE environment. The purge record that describes the actual execution phase of the job (as opposed to NJE transmit or receive actions for input or SYSOUT processing) has a non-blank value for the SYSEXEC variable. At each node where a purge record is created, the SMF record is written on the CPU where the purge event occurred, which is not necessarily the CPU on which the job executed. In a node with multiple CPUs, the SMF data from all CPUs must be combined to reconstruct a composite job record accurately since the job can be read in, converted, executed, printed, and purged on different CPUs within the node.

TYPE26J2 contains the starting time stamp and duration of a job on each JES2 processor (reader, converter, execution, output, and purge), as well as the system identification of the CPU where each JES2 event occurred. It is the source of JES2 priorities when the job was read in, executed, and printed, and the only source of I/O counts processed to the spool on behalf of the job or session.

TYPE26J2 is very important for analysis of job scheduling. See chapter nineteen.

Variable	Type	Length	Format	Label
ACCT	CHAR	4		PROGRAMMER*ACCOUNTING*NUMBER

programmer accounting number. This four-byte field has no connection with the account variables on the job card (see TYPE535 or TYPE30_5), and is seldom useful.

| ACTBYTES | NUM | 4 | | ACTUAL*BYTES*PRINTED |

actual bytes printed by JES2.

| ACTPAGES | NUM | 4 | | ACTUAL*PAGES*PRINTED |

actual pages printed by JES2.

| CANCELED | CHAR | 1 | | CANCELED*BY*OPERATOR |

job canceled by an operator command.

| CONVRTTM | NUM | 4 | TIME12.2 | CONVERTER*DURATION |

Variable	Type	Length	Format	Label

duration job was in converter. The duration should be very short; therefore, it has seldom been a serious performance bottleneck.

| CVTRPROC | CHAR | 8 | | CONVERTER*PROCEDURE*NAME |

name of the JES2 converter. Procedure used for JCL conversion.

| DEVNAME | CHAR | 8 | | NJE JOB*TRANSMITTER*DEVICE NAME |

NJE only. Job transmitter device name.

| ENDPRTY | NUM | 4 | | OUTPUT*SELECTION*PRIORITY |

output selection priority when output was selected.

| ESTBYTES | NUM | 4 | | ESTIMATED*BYTES TO BE*PRINTED |

estimated bytes to be printed. See also ACTBYTES.

| ESTELPTM | NUM | 4 | TIME12.2 | ESTIMATED*ELAPSED*TIME |

estimated elapsed time. A console message is issued when this time has been exceeded by the job.

| ESTPAGES | NUM | 4 | | ESTIMATED*PAGES TO BE*PRINTED |

estimated pages to be printed. See also ACTPAGES.

| ESTPRINT | NUM | 4 | | ESTIMATED*PRINT*LINES |

estimated output lines. Jobs exceeding this value are usually terminated with a 722 abend, although that is an installation choice.

| ESTPUNCH | NUM | 4 | | ESTIMATED*PUNCH*LINES |

estimated output punched cards. Jobs exceeding this value are usually terminated with a 722 abend, although that is an installation choice.

| EXECNODE | CHAR | 8 | | NJE*EXECUTION*NODE NAME |

NJE only. Execution node name.

| EXECSTAT | CHAR | 8 | | EXECUTION*STATUS*OF JOB |

NJE only. Execution status of NJE job. Indicates whether it has yet executed and if it executed at this node.

value	meaning
nodename	job was executed at this nodename
AFTER	job had executed prior to arrival at this node
BEFORE	job had not executed prior to arrival at this node
UNKNOWN	unable to decipher.

Variable	Type	Length	Format	Label

INDEVICE   CHAR   8   INPUT*DEVICE*NAME

input device name:

value	meaning
INTRDR	job was read in through internal reader
TSOINRDR	TSO session
R*rrr*.RD*n*	job read in from reader number *n* at remote (RJE) number *rrr* (for example, R196.RD1).
READER*n*	job read in through local reader number *n* (for example, READER3).

INPRTY   NUM   4   INPUT*PRIORITY

JES job selection priority at read-in time. See also ONPRTY, below.

INREASON   CHAR   8   REASON*JOB*ARRIVED

NJE only. Indicates why job arrived at this node.

value	meaning
JR	job received for execution or transmission
SR	job received for SYSOUT processing
blank	job not received, but originated here (SOURCE is blank also).

INROUTE   NUM   4   INPUT*REMOTE*NUMBER

input remote number. Zero for local readers, for jobs submitted from TSO sessions, or for the TSO session purge record.

INTRDR   CHAR   1   INTERNAL*READER*USED?

job was read in through an internal reader. Values are blank (no) or Y (yes).

JCNVTIME   NUM   8   DATETIME19.2   CONVERTER*START TIME

converter start time stamp. This event should immediately follow end of job read-in (JRDRTIME). If the job was canceled while still being read in or before the converter was invoked, this time stamp will be a missing value.

JENDTIME   NUM   8   DATETIME19.2   END OF EXECUTION*PROCESSOR

execution-processor end time stamp. This occurs when MVS returns the job to JES, usually at normal termination of the job for output processing. If the job was active when the MVS operating system crashed or if the job was FORCEd or EXITd from MVS, this time stamp is missing. When a job is canceled and requeued for execution (for example, via the $E command), this time stamp will be filled in with the time of cancel. If the job is subsequently released and restarted, the JENDTIME is not overwritten until the subsequent execution terminates. Thus, if a restarted job is active during an MVS crash, FORCE or

Variable	Type	Length	Format	Label

EXIT, it has a nonmissing JENDTIME that is less than (or earlier than) the JSTRTIME job start execution time stamp.

JESNR   NUM   4   JES*NUMBER

JES-assigned JOB/TSU/STC number. Three separate unique counters are maintained for job numbers for JOB, TSO, and system tasks by JES.

JFINTIME   NUM   8   DATETIME19.2   END OF OUTPUT*PROCESSOR

output-processor-stop time stamp. All output to be processed by JES2 is now available for printing or punching. This time stamp is the beginning of print or punch queuing for this job's output files (except for print or punch files specifying FREE=CLOSE, which were available for earlier printing, and except for held printed output, which is not printed until released from hold).

JOB   CHAR   8   JOB NAME*OR*TSO USER

job name (batch); user ID (TSO).

JOBCLASS   CHAR   1   JOB*CLASS

job class. For TSO, it prints as a blank, but contains the hex value E0, which is a nonprintable character between R and S.

JPRNTIME   NUM   8   DATETIME19.2   BEGIN OF OUTPUT*PROCESSOR

output-processor start time stamp. This begins the output processor, but it does not signify beginning of print queue time. The JES output processor re-sets the JOEs (Job Output Elements) created by this job to make them available for print or punch services, but it is the end of output processor (JFINTIME) that signifies the beginning of print queue time for each print or punch file.

JPURTIME   NUM   8   DATETIME19.2   PURGE TIME

job purge time stamp. All printing or punching for the job or session has been completed (or for NJE, this node has completed all requested processing for this job at this node).

JRDRTIME   NUM   8   DATETIME19.2   LAST-CARD-READ

time stamp when this processor recognized last card read for this job. This event immediately precedes JCNVTIME. All card images for the job have now been copied to the JES spool. If the job had an error in the job card (or a JCL error that was detected by the reader), the JCL error occurs immediately after this time. See also RDRTM, below.

JSTRTIME   NUM   8   DATETIME19.2   BEGIN OF EXECUTION*PROCESSOR

execution-processor start time stamp. This occurs when JES2 sends the job to be executed by MVS because an initiator of the correct class is available, and the job is the highest priority job for that job class in the execution processor's queue. If the job is canceled prior to execution, has a JCL error in the reader, or has a syntax error that was caught in the converter, the time stamp is missing. When a job is canceled and requeued for execution (for example, via the $E command), this time stamp contains the time when the job was

Variable	Type	Length	Format	Label

started prior to the cancel. If the job is subsequently released and restarted, the JSTRTIME is overwritten with the new start time of execution. See also JENDTIME, above.

LASTNODE   CHAR   8   LAST*NODE*NAME

NJE only. Last node name, that is, the node from which this job came before it entered this node.

LINPERPG   NUM   4   LINES*PER*PAGE

lines per page to be printed.

LOCLINFO   CHAR   8   LOCAL*INSTALLATION*FIELD

locally-defined field, filled in by an installation-written SMF exit routine.

MSGCLASS   CHAR   1   MESSAGE*CLASS

output message class for SYSMSG, from JOB statement or default.

NETACCT   CHAR   8   NETWORK*ACCOUNT*NUMBER

NJE only. Network accounting number.

NEXTNODE   CHAR   8   NEXT*NODE*NAME

NJE only. Next node name; that is, the name of the next node to which this job is sent for further processing.

NJETRANS   CHAR   8   TRANSMIT*JOB FOR*EXECUTION?

NJE only. Indicates whether the job was transmitted for execution.

value	meaning
blank	not transmitted for execution
nodename	job sent to this node.

ONPRTY   NUM   4   EXECUTION*SELECTION*PRIORITY

JES job selection priority at JSTRTIME. If aging is used, this is the actual aged priority. Note that for simplicity and to avoid confusion, the FLOOR function is used to keep only the integer part of the priority value. The actual internals of priority aging by JES2 are as follows:

The priority at read-in time (INPRTY) is stored in the left nybble of the priority byte. Aging is specified to JES as the number of minutes between priority increases of 1 unit, but the number of minutes is actually divided by 16 to get a delta, and for every delta minute, a binary 1 is added to the right nybble of the priority byte. After 16 deltas, the right nybble overflows into the left nybble, incrementing priority by 1 full (integer) unit. The SMF record field contains the 1 byte, which is processed as

ONPRTY=FLOOR(ONPRTY/16);

Variable	Type	Length	Format	Label

to shift right and present as an integer (similar to what the operator sees when $DJ is issued). If you really want the priority as a fraction, remove the FLOOR and associated parenthesis.

OPTEXBAT   CHAR   1   EXECUTION*BATCHING?

indicates whether execution batching option was specified. The values are either blank (no) or Y (yes).

OPTJBLOG   CHAR   1   JOB*LOG?

indicates whether the no job log option was specified. The values are either blank (no) or Y (yes, no job log was specified).

OPTJOURN   CHAR   1   JOURNALING?

indicates whether the no journal option was specified. The values are either blank (no) or Y (yes, no journaling was specified).

OPTOUTPT   CHAR   1   OUTPUT*OPTION?

indicates whether the no output option was specified. The values are either blank (no) or Y (yes, no output was specified).

ORIGJBID   CHAR   8   ORIGINAL*JOB*IDENTIFICATION

NJE only. Original job identification (see JOBID).

ORIGNODE   CHAR   8   ORIGIN*NODE*NAME

NJE only. Original node name.

OUTFORM   CHAR   8   SYSMSG*FORM*NUMBER

output form number for the SYSMSG output, either from the job accounting fields or the system default if not specified in the job's accounting fields.

PGMRNAME   CHAR   20   PROGRAMMER*NAME*FIELD

programmer name field from job statement.

PRNTCOPY   NUM   4   PRINT*COPIES

print copies, either from the job accounting fields or the system default, if not specified in the job's accounting fields.

PRPRTY   NUM   4   PRINT*PRIORITY

selection priority when the output was selected for printing or punching. See also ONPRTY.

PRROUTE   NUM   4   PRINT*REMOTE*DESTINATION

remote number to which SYSMSG printing is routed from the ROUTE PRINT JES control card or default.

Variable	Type	Length	Format	Label

PRTYCARD   CHAR   1   PRIORITY*CARD?

priority statement present or PRTY parameter specified on JOB statement. The values are either blank (no) or Y (yes).

PUROUTE   NUM   4   PUNCH*REMOTE*DESTINATION

remote number to which punching is routed from the ROUTE PUNCH JES control card or default.

RDRTM   NUM   4   READER*EVENT*DURATION

duration the MVS reader was active while reading this job. For a job read in via RJE, it indicates how long the job took to be transmitted. The remote from which this job was read is INROUTE, and the number of cards processed is in SPOOLCRD.

READTIME   NUM   8   DATETIME19.2   READ-IN*OR LOGON*EVENT

job read-in (TSO LOGON) time stamp.

RERUN   CHAR   1   RERUN*BY*JES?

job was rerun by JES. The values are either blank (not rerun) or Y (yes, rerun).

RESTART   CHAR   1   RESTART?

RESTART=Y was specified. The values are either blank (no) or Y (yes).

ROOM   CHAR   4   PROGRAMMER*ROOM*NUMBER

programmer's room number.

SETUP   CHAR   1   SETUP*CARD?

SETUP card(s) were present. The values are either blank (no) or Y (yes).

SOURCE   CHAR   8   SOURCE*OF NJE*JOB

NJE only. Indicates whether this job was read in at this node or received from another node.

value	meaning
blank	job was read in at 'this' node. (Unfortunately, the name of 'this' node is not available.)
nodename	job was received from this node.

SPOOLCRD   NUM   4   INPUT*CARDS*SPOOLED

number of input card images (JCL and SYSIN) read from the input device and put on the spool by JES reader. See also RDRTM.

SPOOLINE   NUM   4   OUTPUT*LINES*SPOOLED

number of print lines written to spool. These lines may be printed many times (multiple copies printed) or may not be actually printed at all (if canceled before print).

Variable	Type	Length	Format	Label
SPOOLPUN	NUM	4		PUNCH*CARDS*SPOOLED

number of punched cards put on the spool. See also SPOOLINE.

Variable	Type	Length	Format	Label
SUBSYS	CHAR	4		SUB*SYSTEM

JES2.

Variable	Type	Length	Format	Label
SYSCVRT	CHAR	4		CONVERTER*PROCESSOR*SYSTEM ID

system identification of system on which job was converted.

Variable	Type	Length	Format	Label
SYSEXEC	CHAR	4		EXECUTION*PROCESSOR*SYSTEM ID

system identification of system on which this job was executed.
Note 1. For NJE networks, this is non-blank only in the type 26 record written on the execution processor, which is the purge record needed by BUILDPDB; BUILDPDB is the real purge record containing the priorities, spool cards, and so forth of real interest.
Note 2. This is the last system on which the job executed. If a job is restarted (for example, $EJ), there have been job and step termination records already written (which could be on a different system, if the job began execution on a different system). However, there is only one purge record written at the execution node, and it has the system id of the (last) execution processor.

Variable	Type	Length	Format	Label
SYSOUTP	CHAR	4		OUTPUT*PROCESSOR*SYSTEM ID

system identification of which system the output processor executed (see JPRNTIME and JFINTIME). This is not related to the system on which the printing eventually occurred (see TYPE6 for the system id that actually printed each file).

Variable	Type	Length	Format	Label
SYSOUTPR	CHAR	3		SYSOUT*PROCESSED*HERE?

NJE only. Indicates whether SYSOUT was processed at this node.

value	meaning
blank	SYSOUT was not processed at this node.
YES	SYSOUT was processed at this node.

Variable	Type	Length	Format	Label
SYSREAD	CHAR	4		READ-IN*PROCESSOR*SYSTEM ID

identification of system that read in this job. This is the system on which the RJE station is connected to JES2.

Variable	Type	Length	Format	Label
SYSTEM	CHAR	4	4.	SYSTEM*ID

identification of system that purged in this job. This is also the system on which the purge record is actually written by JES2.

Variable	Type	Length	Format	Label
SYSTRANS	CHAR	4		JOB*TRANSMITTER*SYSTEM ID

NJE only. Job transmitter system ID.

Variable	Type	Length	Format	Label

TYPETASK   CHAR   4   TYPE*OF*TASK

type of task. This is the first four characters of the JES job identification. The possible values are:

value	meaning
JOB	batch job
TSU	TSO session
STC	started (system) task.

TYPRUN   CHAR   4   TYPE*OF*RUN

TYPRUN parameter from job card. This is the action JES is to take when it receives this job. The possible values are:

value	meaning
blank	normal
COPY	copy run
HOLD	job is to be held
SCAN	scan JCL for syntax errors, but do not execute the job.

XMENTIME   NUM   8   DATETIME19.2   END OF JOB*TRANSMISSION*TIME

time stamp at end of job transmission.

XMITTIME   NUM   8   DATETIME19.2   START OF JOB*TRANSMISSION*TIME

time stamp at beginning of job transmission.

TYPE26J3
JES3 Purge Record

The TYPE26J3 data set contains one observation for each type 26 written by JES3 for each job or session at purge time when all SYSOUT for the job is processed at this node or when the job is purged by the operator-issued Purge ($P) command.

TYPE26J3 contains the starting time stamp and duration of the job on each JES3 processor (reader, converter, execution, output, and purge), as well as the system identification of the CPU where the JES3 events occurred. It is the only source of the number of card images, print lines, and punched cards read to or from the JES3 spool. Unlike the JES2 purge record, the JES3 record provides the account fields from the JOB statement.

Variable	Type	Length	Format	Label
ACCOUNT1	CHAR	53		FIRST*ACCOUNT*FIELD

first job account field specified on the JOB statement. NRACCTFL counts the number of account fields specified by the user. LENACCTn variables contain the length of the nth account field. SOURCLIB member IMACACCT defines how many account numbers are kept and their maximum length.

ACCOUNT2	CHAR	10		SECOND*ACCOUNT*FIELD

second job account field specified on JOB statement.

ACCOUNT3	CHAR	4		THIRD*ACCOUNT*FIELD

third job account field specified on JOB statement.

ACCOUNT4	CHAR	4		FOURTH*ACCOUNT*FIELD

fourth job account field specified on JOB statement.

ACCOUNT5	CHAR	4		FIFTH*ACCOUNT*FIELD

fifth job account field specified on JOB statement.

ACCOUNT6	CHAR	4		SIXTH*ACCOUNT*FIELD

sixth job account field specified on JOB statement.

ACCOUNT7	CHAR	4		SEVENTH*ACCOUNT*FIELD

seventh job account field specified on JOB statement.

ACCOUNT8	CHAR	4		EIGHTH*ACCOUNT*FIELD

eighth job account field specified on JOB statement.

Variable	Type	Length	Format	Label
ACCOUNT9	CHAR	4		NINTH*ACCOUNT*FIELD

ninth job account field specified on JOB statement.

| CANCELED | CHAR | 1 | | CANCELED*BY*OPERATOR |

job was canceled by operator command. The values are either blank (no) or Y (yes, if it was canceled).

| CLASS | CHAR | 8 | | JOB*CLASS*ON MAIN |

job class, taken from CLASS= on a MAIN statement or the default JES3 job class (JS3BATCH). See JOBCLASS.

| CONVRTTM | NUM | 4 | TIME12.2 | CONVERTER*DURATION |

duration the job was in the converter.

| CVTRPROC | CHAR | 8 | | CONVERTER*PROCEDURE*NAME |

converter procedure name (DDname) used for JCL conversion. Taken from PROC= parameter on a MAIN statement, or the default.

| DEADLMET | CHAR | 1 | | DEADLINE*MET? |

whether job met scheduled deadline time. The values are Y if met, blank otherwise.

| DEADLREQ | CHAR | 1 | | DEADLINE*REQUESTED? |

deadline scheduling requested (that is, DEADLINE specified). The values are either blank or Y if yes.

| DEADLTYP | CHAR | 1 | | DEADLINE*TYPE |

deadline schedule type, if DEADLINE specified on MAIN statement. (The valid types are A through Z and 0 through 9.)

| DLNETIME | NUM | 8 | DATETIME19.2 | DEADLINE*SCHEDULING*TIME STAMP |

deadline schedule time, taken from DEADLINE parameter on the JES3 MAIN card.

| ENTERDJ | CHAR | 1 | | ENTERED*VIA*DJ? |

job entered system via DJ (dump job) processing. The values are either Y if yes or blank.

| ENTERNJP | CHAR | 1 | | ENTERED*VIA*NJP? |

job entered system via NJP (network job processing). The values are either Y if yes or blank.

| ESTELPTM | NUM | 4 | TIME12.2 | ESTIMATED*ELAPSED*TIME |

estimated elapsed duration, from JOB card or default.

| ESTPRINT | NUM | 4 | | ESTIMATED*PRINT*LINES |

estimated output lines, taken from LINES= on MAIN statement or 1000*JOBLINES default in TVT.

Variable	Type	Length	Format	Label
ESTPUNCH	NUM	4		ESTIMATED*PUNCH*LINES

estimated punched cards output, taken from CARDS= on MAIN statement or 100*JOBCARDS default in TVT.

| INDEVICE | CHAR | 8 | | INPUT*DEVICE*NAME |

input device name from which this job was read in:

for job from	input device name contains
JES3 device	JES3 logical input device name
NJP	line name
TSO	user identification

| INPRTY | NUM | 4 | | INPUT*PRIORITY |

JES3 job selection priority when job was initially read in. Taken from PRTY= on JOB statement, class default priority from main processor job class priority table, or default priority from TVT.

| INTRDR | CHAR | 1 | | INTERNAL*READER*USED? |

job was entered via the internal reader. The values are either Y if yes or blank.

| JCNVTIME | NUM | 8 | DATETIME19.2 | CONVERTER*START TIME |

converter-processor start time.

| JENDTIME | NUM | 8 | DATETIME19.2 | END OF EXECUTION*PROCESSOR |

execution-processor end time stamp.

| JESNR | NUM | 4 | | JES*NUMBER |

JES3-assigned job number.

| JFINTIME | NUM | 8 | DATETIME19.2 | END OF OUTPUT*PROCESSOR |

output-processor stop time stamp. The time stamp is filled in when an RQ is removed from the writer queue, when all output OSEs are deleted/released, or when a request from the SYSOUT interface is processed. It does not correspond to the printing for the job, but rather it is the start of print queue time.

| JOB | CHAR | 8 | | JOB NAME*OR*TSO USER |

job name (batch); user ID (TSO).

| JOBCLASS | CHAR | 1 | | JOB*CLASS |

job class, taken from CLASS= on JOB statement. This characteristic is blank if class is taken from default or if CLASS= is specified on MAIN statement. If blank, actual class is in variable CLASS.

Variable	Type	Length	Format	Label

JPRNTIME   NUM   8   DATETIME19.2   BEGIN OF OUTPUT*PROCESSOR

output-processor start time stamp. Filled in when output service starts to process the job's data sets for later printing. See JFINTIME.

JPURTIME   NUM   8   DATETIME19.2   PURGE TIME

job purge time stamp. All SYSOUT processing has been completed and the job or session is purged.

JRDRTIME   NUM   8   DATETIME19.2   LAST-CARD-READ

job reader stop time stamp. (READTIME is the start time stamp.)

JSTRTIME   NUM   8   DATETIME19.2   BEGIN OF EXECUTION*PROCESSOR

execution-processor start time stamp.

LEFTDJ   CHAR   1   LEFT*VIA*DJ?

job left this system via DJ (dump job) processing. The values are either Y if yes or blank.

LEFTNJP   CHAR   1   LEFT*VIA*NJP?

job left this system via NJP (network job processing). The values are either Y if yes or blank.

LENACCT1   NUM   4   LENGTH*ACCOUNT*ONE

length of first account field on JOB JCL card.

LENACCT2   NUM   4   LENGTH*ACCOUNT*TWO

length of second account field on JOB JCL card.

LENACCT3   NUM   4   LENGTH*ACCOUNT*THREE

length of third account field on JOB JCL card.

LENACCT4   NUM   4   LENGTH*ACCOUNT*FOUR

length of fourth account field on JOB JCL card.

LENACCT5   NUM   4   LENGTH*ACCOUNT*FIVE

length of fifth account field on JOB JCL card.

LENACCT6   NUM   4   LENGTH*ACCOUNT*SIX

length of sixth account field on JOB JCL card.

LENACCT7   NUM   4   LENGTH*ACCOUNT*SEVEN

length of seventh account field on JOB JCL card.

Variable	Type	Length	Format	Label
LENACCT8	NUM	4		LENGTH*ACCOUNT*EIGHT

length of eighth account field on JOB JCL card.

LENACCT9	NUM	4		LENGTH*ACCOUNT*NINE

length of ninth account field on JOB JCL card.

LNJPTERM	CHAR	8		LOCAL*NJP*TERMINAL

name of local NJP terminal supplied by JES3 initialization deck.

LOCLINFO	CHAR	8		LOCAL*INSTALLATION*FIELD

locally-defined field, filled in by an installation-written SMF exit routine.

MSGCLASS	CHAR	1		MESSAGE*CLASS

message class (taken from MSGCLASS= on JOB card).

NETCARD	CHAR	1		NET*STATEMENT?

dependent job (that is, NET statement was processed). The values are either Y if yes or blank.

NETNAME	CHAR	8		JOB NET*FROM*NET STATEMENT

name of dependent job net to which this job belongs (taken from NET statement).

NJEACCT	CHAR	8		NETWORKING*ACCOUNT*NUMBER

networking account number (for job transmitted to JES3 via NJE).

NJEBLDG	CHAR	8		NJE*BUILDING*NUMBER

programmer's building number (for job transmitted to JES3 via NJE).

NJEDEPT	CHAR	8		NJE*DEPARTMENT*NUMBER

programmer's department number (for job transmitted to JES3 via NJE).

NJEJOBNM	CHAR	8		NJE*JOB*NAME

job name of NJE job (for job transmitted to JES3 via NJE).

NJEJOBNO	NUM	4		NJE JOB*NUMBER*(ORIGINAL)

original job number on originating node (for job transmitted to JES3 via NJE).

NJEPRGMR	CHAR	20		NJE*PROGRAMMER*NAME

programmer's name (for job transmitted to JES3 via NJE).

NJEROOM	CHAR	8		NJE*ROOM*NUMBER

programmer's room number (for job transmitted to JES3 via NJE).

Variable	Type	Length	Format	Label
NJEUSRID	CHAR	8		NJE*USER*ID

origin or notify user identification (for job transmitted to JES3 via NJE).

NJEXEQNM	CHAR	8		NJE*EXECUTION*NODE

execution node name (for job transmitted to JES3 via NJE).

NJEXEQU	CHAR	8		NJE*EXECUTION*USER ID

execution user identifier (for job transmitted to JES3 via NJE).

NRACCTFL	NUM	4		NUMBER*ACCOUNT*FIELDS

number of account fields specified on the EXEC JCL card.

ONPRTY	NUM	4		EXECUTION*SELECTION*PRIORITY

JES3 job selection priority when this job was selected for execution processor.

PGMRNAME	CHAR	20		PROGRAMMER*NAME*FIELD

programmer name field from JOB statement.

PROCESS	CHAR	1		PROCESS*CARD?

process job (that is, PRTOCESS statement processed). The values are either Y if yes or blank.

PRTYCARD	CHAR	1		PRIORITY*CARD?

job scheduling priority was specified via PRTY= on JOB statement. The values are either Y if yes or blank.

READTIME	NUM	8	DATETIME19.2	READ-IN*OR LOGON*EVENT

job read-in (TSO LOGON) time stamp.

RERUN	CHAR	1		RERUN*BY*JES?

job was re-run on an ASP or JES3 reader. The values are either Y if yes or blank.

SETUP	CHAR	1		SETUP*CARD?

job was processed by pre-execution setup. The values are either Y if yes or blank.

SPOOLCRD	NUM	4		INPUT*CARDS*SPOOLED

number of input lines placed on JES3 spool; includes JCL and SYSIN lines.

SPOOLINE	NUM	4		OUTPUT*LINES*SPOOLED

number of output lines placed on JES3 spool.

SPOOLPUN	NUM	4		PUNCH*CARDS*SPOOLED

number of punched cards placed on JES3 spool.

Variable	Type	Length	Format	Label
SUBSYS	CHAR	4		SUB*SYSTEM

subsystem name. The value is JES3.

SYSCVRT	CHAR	4		CONVERTER*PROCESSOR*SYSTEM ID

system identification of conversion processor.

SYSEXEC	CHAR	4		EXECUTION*PROCESSOR*SYSTEM ID

system identification of execution processor.

SYSOUTP	CHAR	4		OUTPUT*PROCESSOR*SYSTEM ID

system identification of output processor.

SYSREAD	CHAR	4		READ-IN*PROCESSOR*SYSTEM ID

system identification of input processor.

SYSTEM	CHAR	4	4.	SYSTEM*ID

system identification of the purging system.

TONJPSYS	CHAR	8		SYSTEM*TO WHICH*JOB SENT

name of system to which job is sent via NJP.

TYPETASK	CHAR	4		TYPE*OF*TASK

type of task. This specifies the first four characters of the JES job identification. The possible values are:

value	meaning
JOB	batch job
TSU	TSO session
STC	started (system) task.

TYPRUN	CHAR	4		TYPE*OF*RUN

type of run. TYPRUN=HOLD is specified on JOB statement. The values are either HOLD if yes or blank.

TYPE30_1
TYPE30 Job Initiation

The TYPE30_1 data set contains one observation for each type 30 SMF record with subtype 1, written at the initiation of a batch job step, a TSO session, or a started task.

The information in TYPE30_1 is repeated in TYPE30_5, written at termination of a job or session. However, for sessions active when the system crashed, TYPE30_1 and TYPE20 are the only sources of accounting information.

Since all of the information in the type 20 record and more is contained in the type 30, subtype 1 record, you may want to supress writing the type 20 record. (Check with your accounting system first since they may need this record for old SMF processing programs.)

Variable	Type	Length	Format	Label
ACCOUNT1	CHAR	53		FIRST*ACCOUNT*FIELD

first job account field specified on the JOB statement. Job level accounting is the predominate method of assigning account numbers to jobs, although account numbers can be provided on the EXEC cards if step level accounting is desired. With accounting at the job level, all steps in the job are charged to the same account. NRACCTFL counts the number of account fields specified by the user, and LENACCTn variables contain the length of the nth account field. SOURCLIB member IMACACCT defines how many account numbers are to be kept and their maximum length.

ACCOUNT2	CHAR	10		SECOND*ACCOUNT*FIELD

second job account field specified on JOB statement.

ACCOUNT3	CHAR	4		THIRD*ACCOUNT*FIELD

third job account field specified on JOB statement.

ACCOUNT4	CHAR	4		FOURTH*ACCOUNT*FIELD

fourth job account field specified on JOB statement.

ACCOUNT5	CHAR	4		FIFTH*ACCOUNT*FIELD

fifth job account field specified on JOB statement.

ACCOUNT6	CHAR	4		SIXTH*ACCOUNT*FIELD

sixth job account field specified on JOB statement.

ACCOUNT7	CHAR	4		SEVENTH*ACCOUNT*FIELD

seventh job account field specified on JOB statement.

Variable	Type	Length	Format	Label
ACCOUNT8	CHAR	4		EIGHTH*ACCOUNT*FIELD

eighth job account field specified on JOB statement.

ACCOUNT9	CHAR	4		NINTH*ACCOUNT*FIELD

ninth job account field specified on JOB statement.

ENQTIME	NUM	8	DATETIME19.2	TSO LOGON*ENQUEUE ON UADS*TIME STAMP

TSO only. Time when LOGON process enqueues on SYS1.UADS data set. This time has been used to calculate the time it takes to logon to TSO (LOGONTM=ENQTIME-READTIME) because it is very close to the actual time the user sees READY.

INPRTY	NUM	4		INPUT*PRIORITY

JES job selection priority at read-in time.

JESNR	NUM	4		JES*NUMBER

JES-assigned JOB/TSO/STC number. Three unique counters are maintained for JOB, TSO, and system tasks by JES.

JINTTIME	NUM	8	DATETIME19.2	JOB*INITIATE*TIME

job initiate time stamp. Since there can be multiple type 30, subtype 1 records, this may be the first, last, or an in-between initiation.

JOB	CHAR	8		JOB NAME*OR*TSO USER

job name (batch); user ID (TSO).

JOBCLASS	CHAR	1		JOB*CLASS

job class.

LENACCT1	NUM	4		LENGTH*ACCOUNT*ONE

length of first account field on JOB JCL card.

LENACCT2	NUM	4		LENGTH*ACCOUNT*TWO

length of second account field on JOB JCL card.

LENACCT3	NUM	4		LENGTH*ACCOUNT*THREE

length of third account field on JOB JCL card.

LENACCT4	NUM	4		LENGTH*ACCOUNT*FOUR

length of fourth account field on JOB JCL card.

LENACCT5	NUM	4		LENGTH*ACCOUNT*FIVE

length of fifth account field on JOB JCL card.

Variable	Type	Length	Format	Label
LENACCT6	NUM	4		LENGTH*ACCOUNT*SIX

length of sixth account field on JOB JCL card.

| LENACCT7 | NUM | 4 | | LENGTH*ACCOUNT*SEVEN |

length of seventh account field on JOB JCL card.

| LENACCT8 | NUM | 4 | | LENGTH*ACCOUNT*EIGHT |

length of eighth account field on JOB JCL card.

| LENACCT9 | NUM | 4 | | LENGTH*ACCOUNT*NINE |

length of ninth account field on JOB JCL card.

| LOCLINFO | CHAR | 8 | | LOCAL*INSTALLATION*FIELD |

locally-defined field; filled in by the installation's SMF exit routines.

| NRACCTFL | NUM | 4 | | NUMBER*ACCOUNT*FIELDS |

number of account fields specified on JOB JCL card.

| PERFGRP | NUM | 4 | | PERFORMANCE*GROUP |

performance group this step was in at termination.

| PGMRNAME | CHAR | 20 | | PROGRAMMER*NAME*FIELD |

programmer name field from JOB statement.

| PRODUCT | CHAR | 8 | | PRODUCT*NAME |

product name that produced this record.

| RACFGRUP | CHAR | 8 | | RACF*GROUP*IDENTIFICATION |

RACF group identification (zero if RACF is not enabled).

| RACFTERM | CHAR | 8 | | RACF/VTAM*TERMINAL*NAME USED |

RACF terminal name used. This indicates the VTAM terminal name used by this TSO session. If you use RACF or a security package that enables the RACF exits, this variable is non-blank and can be used to identify and quantify VTAM terminal usage. The VTAM terminal name is actually associated with the physical port address on the control unit so that recabling terminals can change the physical terminal that has this VTAM terminal name.

| RACFUSER | CHAR | 8 | | RACF*USER*IDENTIFICATION |

RACF user identification (blank if RACF is not enabled).

| RDRTM | NUM | 4 | | READER*EVENT*DURATION |

duration the MVS reader was active while reading this job. For a job read-in via RJE, the duration is how long the job took to be transmitted. The TYPE26 record for this job

Variable	Type	Length	Format	Label

identifies the remote (INROUTE) from which the job was read, and the number of cards (SPOOLCRD) processed.

| READTIME | NUM | 8 | DATETIME19.2 | READ-IN*OR LOGON*EVENT |

job read-in (TSO LOGON) time stamp. Time stamp when record was written.

| SUBSYS | CHAR | 4 | | SUB*SYSTEM |

subsystem. The value may be either JES2 or JES3.

| SYSTEM | CHAR | 4 | 4. | SYSTEM*ID |

identification of the system on which the step executed.

| TYPETASK | CHAR | 4 | | TYPE*OF*TASK |

type of task. This is indicated by the first four characters of the JES job identification. The possible values are:

value	meaning
JOB	batch job
TSU	TSO session
STC	started (system) task.

| VERSION | CHAR | 2 | | VERSION*NUMBER |

record version number.

TYPE30_4
Work Termination

The TYPE30_4 data set contains one observation for each type 30 SMF record with subtype 4, written for each step that terminated normally or abnormally except those subsequent to an operator-issued CANCEL command.

The TYPE30_4 data set is sometimes considered the backbone of SMF analysis, since it classifies resource consumption according to users, jobs, programs, time of day, and so forth.

The handling of the variable-length device portion is a matter of choice. To maximize information and minimize the size of the TYPE30_4 data set, device information from the DD segments is consolidated by device type into a variable-length portion. Thus, the TYPE30_4 data set contains the total EXCP count for each device type (for example, EXCPTAPE, EXCP3330, EXCP3380, EXCPVIO, and so forth) used by the step. The data set also contains the number of mountable tape and 3330 disk drives allocated.

In MVS/370, update the Installation Macro IMACCHAN to identify the multiple channel paths so that the tape drive count is correct. In MVS/370, if UNIT=AFF is used (and it should be used wherever possible) to reduce the number of tape drives allocated, there will be multiple DD segments for the same UCB. However, they will not necessarily contain the same UCB address. When MVS/370 completes an I/O, it keeps track of the actual physical path to the device, and the last path ends up as the Unit Address. Thus a single tape drive with two addresses, 181 and 381, is counted as two tape drives. By updating IMACCHAN, you provide the mapping so that 381 is recognized and changed to 181 before counting. If you have not updated IMACCHAN, the variables TAPEDRVS and D3330DRV are usually too large. This exception does not exist in MVS/XA because the DD segment contains the unique device number and not the unit address.

Installation Macro IMAC3330 must be updated in order to count mountable 3330 devices. Specify the exact unit address or device number of mountable 3330s.

Variable	Type	Length	Format	Label
ABEND	CHAR	6		COMPLETION*ABEND*INDICATOR

step completion indicator. A description of how or why this step ended. For non-normal completions, see variable CONDCODE for amplification of the termination reason.

Variable	Type	Length	Format	Label

		value	**meaning**	
		blank	normal completion.	
		CANCEXIT	step was canceled by an SMF exit; variable CONDCODE contains the exit that did the canceling.	
		FLUSH	step was flushed (because a previous step had failed).	
		OTHER	step abended for unknown reason. Variable CONDCODE contains the value in register 15 at time of the abend. This value is set when the step ABEND bit is on but the numerical contents of ABEND code are inconsistent with SMF documentation.	
		RESTART	step was restarted; subsequent restart has program name of IEFRSTRT.	
		RETURN	step completed with nonzero condition code. CONDCODE contains the returned value.	
		SYSTEM	step completed with system abnormal end (abend). The variable CONDCODE contains the abend code.	
		USER	step completed with an abend issued by a user program, rather than by the operating system itself. Any programmer can choose to issue a USER ABEND rather than a return code (for example, the SAS System issues a USER ABEND 999 when ERRORABEND is specified and an error occurs). The variable CONDCODE contains the abend code.	

ACTIVETM   NUM   4   TIME12.2   TASK*ACTIVE*TIME

step active time. This indicates the duration that the SRM (system resource manager) defined the task as active. A task is made active when the SRM decides the task should be given service. The SRM then notifies the ASM to bring in the task (if the task is swapped out). The difference between EXECTM and ACTIVETM is the duration that the task was swapped out or was not-ready or was waiting for mount to complete. See also RESIDTM.

ALOCTIME   NUM   8   DATETIME19.2   START OF*ALLOCATION*EVENT

allocation time stamp. This is the second event in the lifetime of a step, and it signifies the beginning of allocation of the correct device for each DD card in the step. If this field is missing, it means that the step never entered allocation, usually for some type of execution JCL error (such as data set not found in the catalog). See also LOADTIME and ALOCTM.

Variable	Type	Length	Format	Label

ALOCTM   NUM   4   ALLOCATION*DELAY*DURATION

step allocation time. Duration required for the operating system to allocate all devices. This is LOADTIME minus ALOCTIME. It is missing if the step never entered allocation or if the job entered allocation but failed to complete, usually because of device unavailability. For example, if sufficient tape drives are unavailable and the operator replied "cancel" to the allocation recovery message, the LOADTIME and this field both would be missing.

AVGWKSET   NUM   4   5.   AVERAGE*WORKING*SET (PAGES)

average working set size, in pages (one page is 4096 bytes). This value is the result of dividing the page-seconds by the CPU (TCB time only, since page-seconds are pages times TCB seconds) to get an estimate of the real storage working set of this program. It is considerably less repeatable than other resource measures for the same program, especially if the TCB seconds are less than a few seconds, often varying by 30 percent and sometimes by much more. It is still the best indication of the real memory used by a task.

COMPAGIN   NUM   4   COMMON*AREA*PAGE-INS

common area page-ins.

COMRECLM   NUM   4   COMMON*AREA*RECLAIMS

common area page-reclaims.

CONDCODE   NUM   4   HEX4.   COMPLETION*CONDITION*CODE

condition code. This variable amplifies the meaning of abend. It is internally a binary number but is formatted to display as hex so that testing for a specific condition uses this syntax:

```
IF ABEND= 'SYSTEM' AND CONDCODE=0322X THEN ...
```

ABEND *value contents* of CONDCODE

	value	**canceled by**
CANCEXIT	4	IEFUJI (job initiation)
CANCEXIT	2	IEFUSI (step initiation)
CANCEXIT	1	IEFACTRT (step termination)
OTHER		completion code value
RETURN		return code value
SYSTEM		system ABEND code
USER		user ABEND code.

CPISRBTM   NUM   4   TIME12.2   INITIATOR*CPU SRB*TIME

duration that the central processor (CPU) was executing instructions under a Service Request Block (SRB) under the initiator. This CPU time occurs in the process of initiation

Variable	Type	Length	Format	Label

and termination and is not included in the SRB CPU time reported in this job's performance group in RMF, but instead in the uncaptured or MVS overhead CPU state.

CPITCBTM   NUM   4   TIME12.2   INITIATOR*CPU TCB*TIME

duration that the central processor (CPU) was executing instructions under a Task Control Block (TCB) under the initiator. This CPU time occurs in the process of initiation and termination and is not included in the TCB CPU time reported in this job's performance group in RMF, but instead in the uncaptured or MVS overhead CPU state.

CPUSRBTM   NUM   4   TIME12.2   TASK*CPU SRB*TIME

duration that the central processor (CPU) was executing instructions under a Service Request Block (SRB) for this task.

CPUTCBTM   NUM   4   TIME12.2   TASK*CPU TCB*TIME

duration that the central processor (CPU) was executing instructions under the Task Control Block (TCB) for this task.

CPUTM   NUM   4   TIME12.2   TOTAL*CPU*TIME

duration that the central processor (CPU) was executing instructions for this task. The duration is the sum of CPUSRBTM and CPUTCBTM.

CPUUNITS   NUM   4   CPU TCB*SERVICE*UNITS

SRM recorded TCB CPU service units consumed by this task. A TCB CPU service unit is defined as the number of TCB CPU seconds times the installation-specified CPUCOEFF coefficient (specified in the IEAIPSxx member of PARMLIB and reported in SAS data set TYPE72) times a machine-dependent constant (which is set at IPL time based on the CPU Model and CPU Version). SOURCLIB member TYPE7072 provides one source of the value of the machine-dependent constant, called SU_SEC, since it sets the number of service units generated by one second of CPU time.

DASNMNTS   NUM   4   SCRATCH*DASD*MOUNTS

DASD volumes mounted for nonspecific requests. This is a mount of a scratch volume since no specific volume serial number was requested. Only mount requests actually satisfied by volume verification are counted. If the wrong volume is mounted, this count is not incremented until the correct volume is verified.

DASSMNTS   NUM   4   PRIVATE*DASD*MOUNTS

DASD volumes mounted for specific volume requests. This is a mount of a private volume since the specific volume serial number was requested. Only mount requests actually satisfied by volume verification are counted. If the wrong volume is mounted, this count is not incremented until the correct volume is verified.

DPRTY   NUM   4   DISPATCH*PRIORITY

dispatching priority at step termination.

Variable	Type	Length	Format	Label
DSENQTM	NUM	4		DATA SET*ENQUEUE*DELAY

duration of step between initiation and beginning of allocation. So named because for the first step of a job, the wait for data set enqueue occurs in this interval.

D3330DRV	NUM	4		MOUNTABLE*3330 DRIVES* ALLOCATED

number of different 3330 mountable disk drives that are allocated to this step, where mountable is defined by an explicit list of unit addresses in the IMAC3330 member.

ENQTIME	NUM	8	DATETIME19.2	TSO LOGON*ENQUEUE ON UADS*TIME STAMP

TSO only. The time when LOGON process enqueues on SYS1.UADS data set. This time has been used to calculate the time it takes to logon to TSO:
(LOGONTM = ENQTIME − READTIME).
This time is very close to the actual time the user sees READY.

EXCPCOMM	NUM	4		EXCPS*COUNT*COMMUNICATIONS

EXCPs (blocks of data) to communication devices.

EXCPDASD	NUM	4		EXCPS*COUNT*DASD

sum of EXCPs to 2305, 3330, 3340, 3350, 3375, and 3380 devices.

EXCPGRAF	NUM	4		EXCPS*COUNT*GRAPHICS

EXCPs (blocks of data) to graphics devices.

EXCPMSS	NUM	4		EXCPS*COUNT*MSS

EXCPs (blocks of data) to mass storage volumes.

EXCPNODD	NUM	4		EXCPS*NOT IN*ANY DD SEGMENT

total EXCPs not recorded to a DD. This is EXCPTOTL minus EXCPTODD and represents EXCPs to catalogs and linklist data sets; in JES2 it includes the physical EXCPs to the spool on behalf of this step.

EXCPRMF	NUM	4		EXCPS*COUNT*BY RMF

EXCPs delivered to this task, as counted by RMF. Note that this number does not come from the normal SMF data (that is, the TIOT), but rather it is calculated from the I/O Service Units that were measured by RMF. It is calculated by dividing the actual I/O Service Units in this record by the IOCCOEFF from the preceding type 72 record. This is completely safe if all systems have the same IOCCOEFF, but it can lead to miscalculation if different IOCCOEFF are used for different systems and if the type 30 record being examined is from a different system than the preceding type 72 (it is missing if no type 72 record was encountered before this type 30 record). Finally, if you have specified (MVS/XA only) for I/O service units to be based on the I/O Device Connect time, this is not EXCPs but raw IOTM instead.

Variable	Type	Length	Format	Label
EXCPTAPE	NUM	4		EXCPS*COUNT*TAPE

EXCPs (blocks of data) to tape volumes.

Variable	Type	Length	Format	Label
EXCPTODD	NUM	4		TOTAL EXCPS*IN ALL*DD SEGMENTS

total EXCPs to all DD segments in this step.

Variable	Type	Length	Format	Label
EXCPTOTL	NUM	4		TOTAL*EXCPS*COUNT

total EXCPs issued by this step. This is also called the total address space EXCP count. It represents SMF's count of how many blocks of data were transferred to or from this address space during this step.

Variable	Type	Length	Format	Label
EXCPUREC	NUM	4		EXCPS*COUNT*UNIT RECORD

EXCPs to unit record devices that were allocated directly to the step. This does not include EXCPs to the JES spool devices.

Variable	Type	Length	Format	Label
EXCPVIO	NUM	4		EXCPS*COUNT*VIO

EXCPs to virtual I/O.

Variable	Type	Length	Format	Label
EXCP2305	NUM	4		EXCPS*COUNT*2305

EXCPs (blocks of data) to 2305 devices.

Variable	Type	Length	Format	Label
EXCP3330	NUM	4		EXCPS*COUNT*3330

EXCPs (blocks of data) to 3330 devices.

Variable	Type	Length	Format	Label
EXCP3340	NUM	4		EXCPS*COUNT*3340

EXCPs (blocks of data) to 3340 devices.

Variable	Type	Length	Format	Label
EXCP3350	NUM	4		EXCPS*COUNT*3350

EXCPs (blocks of data) to 3350 devices.

Variable	Type	Length	Format	Label
EXCP3375	NUM	4		EXCPS*COUNT*3375

EXCPs (blocks of data) to 3375 devices.

Variable	Type	Length	Format	Label
EXCP3380	NUM	4		EXCPS*COUNT*3380

EXCPs (blocks of data) to 3380 devices.

Variable	Type	Length	Format	Label
EXECTM	NUM	4	TIME12.2	EXECUTION*DURATION

duration of step between load time and termination, known as step execution time. It is only during this duration that the program can actually execute instructions (and often not even for all of this time). See also ACTIVETM and RESIDTM.

Variable	Type	Length	Format	Label
EXTRADD	NUM	4		EXTRA*DD*RECORD?

if nonzero, there were extra DD segments in a subsequent type 30, subtype 4 record for this step. The type 30 can contain only about 1534 DD segments (which should be enough), but long-running, dynamically allocating tasks could exceed that number of DD segments.

Variable	Type	Length	Format	Label
INITTIME	NUM	8	DATETIME19.2	STEP*INITIATE*EVENT

initiation time stamp.

| INPRTY | NUM | 4 | | INPUT*PRIORITY |

JES job selection priority at read-in time.

| IOTMCOMM | NUM | 4 | TIME12.2 | CONNECT*TIME*COMMUNICATIONS |

IOTM (device connect time) to communication devices.

| IOTMDASD | NUM | 4 | TIME12.2 | CONNECT*TIME*DASD |

sum of IOTM to 2305, 3330, 3340, 3350, 3375, and 3380 devices.

| IOTMERR | CHAR | 1 | | CONNECT*TIME*IN ERROR? |

device connect time (IOTM) may be incorrect. If this flag is set, the SRM disabled the
channel measurement while the job was executing and device connect time (IOTM) was not
captured. Some or all of the IOTM variables contain less than the true device connect
duration.

value	meaning
blank	no error flagged
Y	IOTMs may be incorrect.

| IOTMGRAF | NUM | 4 | TIME12.2 | CONNECT*TIME*GRAPHICS |

IOTM (device connect time) to graphics devices.

| IOTMMSS | NUM | 4 | TIME12.2 | CONNECT*TIME*MSS |

IOTM (device connect time) to mass storage volume.

| IOTMNODD | NUM | 4 | TIME12.2 | TOTAL CONNECT*TIME NOT IN*ANY DD SEGMENT |

total IOTM (device connect time) not recorded to a DD. This is IOTMTOTL minus
IOTMTODD and represents IOTM to catalogs and to linklist data sets; in JES2 it includes
the physical IOTM to the spool on behalf of this step.

| IOTMTAPE | NUM | 4 | TIME12.2 | CONNECT*TIME*TAPE |

IOTM (device connect time) to tape volumes.

| IOTMTODD | NUM | 4 | TIME12.2 | TOTAL CONNECT*TIME IN ALL*DD SEGMENTS |

total IOTM (device connect time) to all DDs in this step.

| IOTMTOTL | NUM | 4 | TIME12.2 | TOTAL*CONNECT*TIME |

total IOTM (device connect time) measured for this step. This is also called the total
address space IOTM count. It represents SMF's count of how many seconds data transfer
was occurring to or from this address space during this step.

Variable	Type	Length	Format	Label
IOTMUREC	NUM	4	TIME12.2	CONNECT*TIME*UNIT RECORD

IOTM (device connect time) to unit record devices that were allocated directly to the step. This does not include IOTMs to the JES spool devices.

IOTM2305	NUM	4	TIME12.2	CONNECT*TIME*2305

IOTM (device connect time) to 2305 devices.

IOTM3330	NUM	4	TIME12.2	CONNECT*TIME*3330

IOTM (device connect time) to 3330 devices.

IOTM3340	NUM	4	TIME12.2	CONNECT*TIME*3340

IOTM (device connect time) to 3340 devices.

IOTM3350	NUM	4	TIME12.2	CONNECT*TIME*3350

IOTM (device connect time) to 3350 devices.

IOTM3375	NUM	4	TIME12.2	CONNECT*TIME*3375

IOTM (device connect time) to 3375 devices.

IOTM3380	NUM	4	TIME12.2	CONNECT*TIME*3380

IOTM (device connect time) to 3380 devices.

IOUNITS	NUM	4		IO*SERVICE*UNITS

SRM recorded I/O service units consumed by this task. In MVS/370, an I/O service unit is defined as the number of EXCPS times the installation-specified IOCCOEFF coefficient (specified in the IEAIPSxx member of PARMLIB and reported in SAS data set TYPE72). In MVS/XA, the IOUNITS can be based on either EXCPs or Device Connect Time (IOTM). It is not possible to tell from an MVS/XA step record which resource (EXCP or IOTM) was the basis of I/O service measurement.

JESNR	NUM	4		JES*NUMBER

job number assigned by JES.

JOB	CHAR	8		JOB NAME*OR*TSO USER

job name (batch); user ID (TSO).

JOBCLASS	CHAR	1		JOB*CLASS

job class.

LOADTIME	NUM	8	DATETIME19.2	PROGRAM*FETCH*EVENT

load (problem program start) time stamp. This is the third event in the lifetime of a step, and it signifies the loading of the program from the library into real memory. If this field is missing, it means that the program was never completely loaded into memory by PROGRAM FETCH (that part of the operating system that loads programs). Only after the

Variable	Type	Length	Format	Label

program is loaded into real memory does the program begin to execute its instructions, open its files, and so forth.

LOCLINFO   CHAR   8   LOCAL*INSTALLATION*FIELD

locally-defined field; filled in by installation's SMF exit routines.

LPAGINS   NUM   4   LPA*AREA*PAGE-INS

link pack area page-ins.

LPARECLM   NUM   4   LPA*AREA*RECLAIMS

link pack area reclaims.

LSQSZHI   NUM   4   LSQA+SWA*SUBPOOLS*ABOVE 16MB

maximum virtual storage in bytes allocated from LSQA and SWA subpools above 16 megabytes.

LSQSZLOW   NUM   4   LSQA+SWA*SUBPOOLS*BELOW 16MB

maximum virtual storage in bytes allocated from LSQA and SWA subpools below 16 megabytes.

MSOUNITS   NUM   4   MEMORY*SERVICE*UNITS

SRM recorded memory service units consumed by this task. A memory service unit is defined as the number of page seconds (real pages times CPU TCB seconds) times the installation-specified MSOCOEFF (specified in the IEAIPS*xx* member of PARMLIB and reported in SAS data set TYPE72) times a constant of one-fiftieth (to normalize memory service to that of CPU and I/O).

MSSNMNTS   NUM   4   SCRATCH*MSS*MOUNTS

MSS volumes mounted for nonspecific requests. This is a mount of a scratch volume since no specific volume serial number was requested.

MSSSMNTS   NUM   4   PRIVATE*MSS*MOUNTS

DASD volumes mounted for specific volume requests. This is a mount of a private volume since the specific volume serial number was requested.

NDASDDD   NUM   4   NUMBER*DASD*DD CARDS

number of DD statements that allocated DASD devices.

NRTRANS   NUM   4   NUMBER*OF*TRANSACTIONS

TSO only. Number of transactions as counted by the SRM.

NTAPEDD   NUM   4   NUMBER*TAPE*DD CARDS

number of DD statements that allocated TAPE devices.

Variable	Type	Length	Format	Label
NUMDD	NUM	4		NUMBER*ALL*DD CARDS

total number of DD statements in this step. Note that

```
NUMDD-(NDASDD+NTAPEDD)
```

equals the number of DDs for JES, VIO, MSS, COMM, UREC, and graphics allocations.

PAGEINS	NUM	4		TOTAL*PAGE-INS

number of page-ins.

PAGEOUTS	NUM	4		TOTAL*PAGE-OUTS

number of page-outs.

PAGESECS	NUM	4		MEMORY*PAGESECS*(PER TCB)

page-seconds of real memory used by this step. This value, when divided by the CPUTCBTM (seconds), gives the AVGWKSET value.

PAGESTOL	NUM	4		PAGES*STOLEN*AWAY

pages stolen from this step.

PERFGRP	NUM	4		PERFORMANCE*GROUP

performance group where step was at termination.

PGMRNAME	CHAR	20		PROGRAMMER*NAME*FIELD

programmer name field from JOB statement.

PKEY	NUM	4	HEX2.	PROTECT*KEY

storage-protect key.

PRODUCT	CHAR	8		PRODUCT*NAME

product name that produced this record.

PROGRAM	CHAR	8		PROGRAM*NAME

program name (PGM=) from EXEC statement. If backward reference was used, the PROGRAM value is *.DD. If the current step is a restarted step, its PROGRAM value and that of all subsequent steps is IEFRSTRT.

PVTAREA	NUM	4		SIZE OF*PRIVATE*AREA

if VIRTREAL= 'V' (virtual storage was specified), PVTAREA value is size of private area in 1024 (1K) bytes. The private area is constant in size, set at IPL, and is the maximum address space that a task can request. If VIRTREAL= 'R' (real storage was specified), the PVTAREA value is the REGION requested in K-bytes.

Variable	Type	Length	Format	Label

PVTBOT NUM 4 GETMAIN*SIZE*FROM BOTTOM

if VIRTREAL= 'V' (virtual storage was specified), PVTBOT value is address space used (in K-bytes) from bottom of private area (that is, subpools 0-127, 251, and 252). If VIRTREAL= 'R', the PVTBOT value is the amount of contiguous real storage used, in K-bytes.

PVTSZHI NUM 4 PRIVATE*AREA SIZE*ABOVE 16MB

private area size, in bytes, above 16 megabytes.

PVTSZLOW NUM 4 PRIVATE*AREA SIZE*BELOW 16MB

private area size, in bytes, below 16 megabytes.

PVTTOP NUM 4 GETMAIN*SIZE*FROM TOP

if VIRTREAL= 'V' (virtual storage was specified), PVTTOP value is address space used, in K-bytes, from top of private area (that is, subpools 229, 239, 236-237, 253-255, the LSQA, and SWA). If VIRTREAL= 'R' (real storage was specified), the PVTTOP value is the amount of storage in K-bytes used that was not from the contiguous storage reserved for the program.

RACFGRUP CHAR 8 RACF*GROUP*IDENTIFICATION

RACF group identification (zero if RACF is not enabled).

RACFTERM CHAR 8 RACF/VTAM*TERMINAL*NAME USED

RACF terminal name used. This indicates the VTAM terminal name used by this TSO session. If you use RACF or a security package that enables the RACF exits, this variable is non-blank and can be used to identify and quantify VTAM terminal usage. The VTAM terminal name is actually associated with the physical port address on the control unit, so that recabling terminals can change the physical terminal that has this VTAM terminal name.

RACFUSER CHAR 8 RACF*USER*IDENTIFICATION

RACF user identification (blank if RACF is not enabled).

RDRDEVCL NUM 4 HEX2. READER*DEVICE*CLASS

reader class.

RDRDEVTY NUM 4 HEX2. READER*DEVICE*TYPE

reader type.

RDRTM NUM 4 READER*EVENT*DURATION

duration MVS reader was active while reading this job. For a job read-in via RJE, the duration is how long the job took to be transmitted. The TYPE26 record for this job identifies the remote (INROUTE) from which the job was read, and the number of cards (SPOOLCRD) processed.

Variable	Type	Length	Format	Label

READTIME NUM 8 DATETIME19.2 READ-IN*OR LOGON*EVENT

job read-in (TSO LOGON) time stamp.

RECLAIMS NUM 4 PAGES*RECLAIMED

pages reclaimed. See also TYPE71 for discussion.

REGREQST NUM 4 REGION*REQUESTED*IN JCL

region size established, in 1K units taken from REGION= parameter in JCL, and rounded up to a 4K boundary. If V=R, this is the amount of contiguous real storage reserved for the program. If the region requested was greater than 16 megabytes, the region established resides above 16 megabytes, and this field will contain a minimum value of 32 megabytes.

RESIDTM NUM 4 TIME12.2 RESIDENT*IN REAL*STORAGE

duration that the step resided in real storage. This value is accumulated by the SRM and represents the absolute maximum duration that the program could have executed instructions. The difference between RESIDTM and CPUTM is the duration that the task was in memory but not dispatched, and it represents wait for CPU and wait for I/O completion, among other waits while in memory.

SELAPSTM NUM 4 TIME12.2 STEP*ELAPSED*DURATION

duration of step between initiation and termination, known as the step elapsed time. During this duration, the step owned the initiator. It is the sum of DSENQTM, ALOCTM, and EXECTM.

SERVUNIT NUM 4 TOTAL*SERVICE*UNITS

total SRM service units consumed by this step. It is the sum of CPUUNITS, SRBUNITS, IOUNITS, and MSOUNITS.

SKIPFLAG CHAR 1 TYPE 30*INTERVAL*SKIPPED?

previous interval record was not written because an error occurred. The cumulative resource counts may be in error because the counters were cleared. This is decode of SMF30ISK.

SRBUNITS NUM 4 CPU SRB*SERVICE*UNITS

SRM recorded SRB CPU service units consumed by this task. An SRB CPU service unit is defined as the number of SRB CPU seconds times the installation-specified SRBCOEFF coefficient (specified in the IEAIPSxx member of PARMLIB and reported in SAS data set TYPE72) times a machine-dependent constant (which is set at IPL time based on the CPU model and CPU version). SOURCLIB member TYPE7072 provides one source of the value of the machine-dependent constant, called SU_SEC, since it sets the number of service units generated by one second of CPU time.

STEPNAME CHAR 8 STEP*NAME

step name appearing on the EXEC PGM= statement. Note that if this step executed a JCL procedure instead, this is not the stepname on that EXEC statement, but rather it is the stepname on the EXEC PGM= card within that JCL procedure. Note further that for a

Variable	Type	Length	Format	Label

TSO session, the stepname is the TSO procedure name, either the default from UADS or the user-supplied PR(name) value.

STEPNR   NUM   4   STEP*NUMBER

step number. This number is reset to 1 when a job is canceled and restarted so that it is possible for the same job to have steps with duplicate values.

SUBSYS   CHAR   4   SUB*SYSTEM

subsystem. The value may be either JES2 or JES3.

SWAPS   NUM   4   TIMES*TASK WAS*SWAPPED OUT

number of times this step was swapped out.

SWPAGINS   NUM   4   SWAP*PAGE*INS

number of pages swapped in.

SWPAGOUT   NUM   4   PAGE-OUTS*TO SWAP*TASK OUT

number of pages swapped out.

SYSINCNT   NUM   4   CARD IMAGES*READ*BY PROGRAM

number of card-image records in DD DATA and DD * data sets read by the reader for this step.

SYSTEM   CHAR   4   4.   SYSTEM*ID

identification of the system on which the step executed.

TAPEDRVS   NUM   4   TAPE*DRIVES*ALLOCATED

number of tape drives allocated to this step. Note that in MVS/370, the IMACCHAN member must describe the installation's two-channel switches if the number of tape drives is to be counted correctly.

TAPNMNTS   NUM   4   SCRATCH*TAPE*MOUNTS

TAPE volumes mounted for nonspecific requests. This is a mount of a scratch volume since no specific volume serial number was requested. Only mount requests actually satisfied by volume verification are counted. If the wrong volume was mounted, this count is not incremented until the correct volume is verified.

TAPSMNTS   NUM   4   PRIVATE*TAPE*MOUNTS

TAPE volumes mounted for specific volume requests. This is a mount of a private volume since the specific volume serial number was requested. Only mount requests actually satisfied by volume verification are counted. If the wrong volume was mounted, this count is not incremented until the correct volume is verified.

Variable	Type	Length	Format	Label
TERMTIME	NUM	8	DATETIME19.2	TERMINATION*EVENT*TIME STAMP

step termination time stamp. This is the fourth and last time stamp in the lifetime of a step.

| TGETS | NUM | 4 | | TERMINAL*READS*(TGETS) |

TSO only. The number of terminals TGETS satisfied (that is, the number of times that the TSO user pushed the ENTER key).

| TPUTS | NUM | 4 | | TERMINAL*WRITES*(TPUTS) |

TSO only. The number of terminal TPUTS issued (that is, the number of times that output lines were sent to the terminal).

| TYPETASK | CHAR | 4 | | TYPE*OF*TASK |

type of task. This is indicated by the first four characters of the JES job identification. The possible values are:

value	meaning
JOB	batch job
TSU	TSO session (acronym is for TSO User)
STC	started (system) task.

| USRSZHI | NUM | 4 | | USER*SUBPOOLS*ABOVE 16MB |

maximum virtual storage in bytes allocated from user subpools above 16 megabytes.

| USRSZLOW | NUM | 4 | | USER*SUBPOOLS*BELOW 16MB |

maximum virtual storage in bytes allocated from user subpools below 16 megabytes.

| VERSION | CHAR | 2 | | VERSION*NUMBER |

record version number.

| VIOPAGIN | NUM | 4 | | VIO*PAGE-INS |

virtual I/O page-ins.

| VIOPAGOU | NUM | 4 | | VIO*PAGE-OUTS |

virtual I/O page-outs.

| VIORECLM | NUM | 4 | | VIO*RECLAIMS |

virtual I/O page reclaims.

Variable	Type	Length	Format	Label
VIRTREAL	CHAR	1		VIRTUAL*OR*REAL?

type of address space requested.

value	requested
R	real storage (ADDRSPC=R specified)
V	virtual storage.

TYPE30_5
TYPE30 Job or Session Termination

Data set TYPE30_5 contains one observation for each type 30 SMF record with subtype 5 written at the termination of the last step of a batch job, a TSO session, or a started task. Restarted jobs have more than one execution and, thus, more than one type 30 subtype 5 record. Multiple records for the same job have the same READTIME and JOB variables.

The type 30, subtype 5 record contains a variable accounting portion extracted from the JOB card account fields. The IMACACCT member of SOURCLIB must define how many account fields your installation keeps. For TSO sessions, only one account field is allowed.

Variable	Type	Length	Format	Label
ABEND	CHAR	6		COMPLETION*ABEND*INDICATOR

job completion indicator. A description of how or why the last step of this job ended. For non-normal completions, see variable CONDCODE for amplification of the termination reason.

value	meaning
blank	normal completion.
CANCEXIT	last step was canceled by an SMF exit; variable CONDCODE contains the exit that did the canceling.
FLUSH	last step was flushed (because a previous step had failed).
OTHER	last step abended for unknown reason. Variable CONDCODE contains the value in register 15 at time of the abend. This value is set when the job abend bit is on, but the numerical contents of abend code are inconsistent with SMF documentation.
RESTART	last step was restarted; subsequent restart has program name of IEFRSTRT.
RETURN	last step completed with nonzero condition code. CONDCODE contains the returned value.
SYSTEM	last step completed with system abnormal end (ABEND). The variable CONDCODE contains the abend code.
USER	last step completed with an abend issued by a user program rather than by the operating

Variable	Type	Length	Format	Label

system itself. Any programmer can choose to issue a USER ABEND rather than a return code (for example, the SAS System issues a USER ABEND 999 when ERRORABEND is specified and an error occurs). The variable CONDCODE contains the abend code.

ACCOUNT1   CHAR   53   FIRST*ACCOUNT*FIELD

first job account field specified on the JOB statement. Job level accounting is the predominate method of assigning account numbers to jobs, although account numbers can be provided on the EXEC cards if step level accounting is desired. With accounting at the job level, all steps in the job are charged to the same account. NRACCTFL counts the number of account fields specified by the user, and LENACCTn variables contain the length of the nth account field. SOURCLIB member IMACACCT defines how many account numbers are to be kept and their maximum length.

ACCOUNT2   CHAR   10   SECOND*ACCOUNT*FIELD

second job account field specified on JOB statement.

ACCOUNT3   CHAR   4   THIRD*ACCOUNT*FIELD

third job account field specified on JOB statement.

ACCOUNT4   CHAR   4   FOURTH*ACCOUNT*FIELD

fourth job account field specified on JOB statement.

ACCOUNT5   CHAR   4   FIFTH*ACCOUNT*FIELD

fifth job account field specified on JOB statement.

ACCOUNT6   CHAR   4   SIXTH*ACCOUNT*FIELD

sixth job account field specified on JOB statement.

ACCOUNT7   CHAR   4   SEVENTH*ACCOUNT*FIELD

seventh job account field specified on JOB statement.

ACCOUNT8   CHAR   4   EIGHTH*ACCOUNT*FIELD

eighth job account field specified on JOB statement.

ACCOUNT9   CHAR   4   NINTH*ACCOUNT*FIELD

ninth job account field specified on JOB statement.

ACTIVETM   NUM   4   TIME12.2   TASK*ACTIVE*TIME

sum of step active times. This indicates the duration that the System Resource Manager (SRM) defined the task as active. A task is made active when the SRM decides the task should be given service. The SRM then notifies the ASM to bring in the task (if the task is swapped out). The difference between EXECTM and ACTIVETM is the duration that the task was swapped out, not-ready, or waiting for mount to complete. See also RESIDTM.

Variable	Type	Length	Format	Label
AVGWKSET	NUM	4	5.	AVERAGE*WORKING*SET (PAGES)

average working set size, in pages (one page is 4096 bytes). This value is the result of dividing the page-seconds by the CPU (TCB time only since page-seconds are pages times TCB seconds) to get an estimate of the real storage working set of this program. It is considerably less repeatable than other resource measures for the same program, especially if the TCB and seconds are less than a few seconds, often varying by 30% and sometimes by much more. It is still the best indication of the real memory used by a task.

COMPAGIN	NUM	4		COMMON*AREA*PAGE-INS

common area page-ins.

COMRECLM	NUM	4		COMMON*AREA*RECLAIMS

common area page-reclaims.

CONDCODE	NUM	4	HEX4.	COMPLETION*CONDITION*CODE

condition code. This variable amplifies the meaning of ABEND. It is internally a binary number but formatted to display as hex so that testing for a specific condition uses this syntax:

    IF ABEND= 'SYSTEM' AND CONDCODE=0322X THEN ...

ABEND value contents of CONDCODE

value		canceled by
CANCEXIT	4	IEFUJI (job initiation)
CANCEXIT	2	IEFUSI (step initiation)
CANCEXIT	1	IEFACTRT (step termination)
OTHER		completion code value
RETURN		return code value
SYSTEM		system ABEND code
USER		user ABEND code.

CPISRBTM	NUM	4	TIME12.2	INITIATOR*CPU SRB*TIME

duration that the central processor (CPU) was executing instructions under a Service Request Block (SRB) under the initiator. This CPU time occurs in the process of initiation and termination and is not included in the SRB CPU time reported in this job's performance group in RMF; instead, it is included in the uncaptured or MVS overhead CPU state.

CPITCBTM	NUM	4	TIME12.2	INITIATOR*CPU TCB*TIME

duration that the central processor (CPU) was executing instructions under a Task Control Block (TCB) under the initiator. This CPU time occurs in the process of initiation and

Variable	Type	Length	Format	Label

termination and is not included in the TCB CPU time reported in this job's performance group in RMF; instead, it is included in the uncaptured or MVS overhead CPU state.

CPUSRBTM	NUM	4	TIME12.2	TASK*CPU SRB*TIME

duration that the central processor (CPU) was executing instructions under a Service Request Block (SRB) for this job.

CPUTCBTM	NUM	4	TIME12.2	TASK*CPU TCB*TIME

duration that the central processor (CPU) was executing instructions under the Task Control Block (TCB) for this job.

CPUTM	NUM	4	TIME12.2	TOTAL*CPU*TIME

duration that the central processor (CPU) was executing instructions for this task. The duration is the sum of CPUSRBTM and CPUTCBTM.

CPUUNITS	NUM	4		CPU TCB*SERVICE*UNITS

SRM recorded TCB CPU service units consumed by this job. A TCB CPU service unit is defined as the number of TCB CPU seconds times the installation-specified CPUCOEFF coefficient (specified in the IEAIPS*xx* member of PARMLIB and reported in SAS data set TYPE72) times a machine-dependent constant (which is set at IPL time based on the CPU model and CPU version). SOURCLIB member TYPE7072 provides one source of the value of the machine-dependent constant, called SU_SEC, since it sets the number of service units generated by one second of CPU time.

DASNMNTS	NUM	4		SCRATCH*DASD*MOUNTS

DASD volumes mounted for nonspecific requests. This is a mount of a scratch volume since no specific volume serial number was requested. Only mount requests actually satisfied by volume verification are counted. If the wrong volume is mounted, this count is not incremented until the correct volume is verified.

DASSMNTS	NUM	4		PRIVATE*DASD*MOUNTS

DASD volumes mounted for specific volume requests. This is a mount of a private volume since the specific volume serial number was requested. Only mount requests actually satisfied by volume verification are counted. If the wrong volume is mounted, this count is not incremented until the correct volume is verified.

DPRTY	NUM	4		DISPATCH*PRIORITY

dispatching priority at job termination.

D3330DRV	NUM	4		MOUNTABLE*3330 DRIVES*ALLOCATED

number of different 3330 mountable disk drives that are allocated to this job, where mountable is defined by an explicit list of unit addresses in the IMAC3330 member.

Variable	Type	Length	Format	Label
ENQTIME	NUM	8	DATETIME19.2	TSO LOGON*ENQUEUE ON UADS*TIME STAMP

TSO only. The time when LOGON process enqueues on SYS1.UADS data set. This time has been used to calculate the time it takes to logon to TSO:
(LOGONTM = ENQTIME − READTIME).
This time is very close to the actual time the user sees READY.

EXCPTOTL	NUM	4		TOTAL*EXCPS*COUNT

total EXCPs issued by this job. This is also called the total address space EXCP count. It represents SMF's count of how many blocks of data were transferred to or from this address space during this job.

INPRTY	NUM	4		INPUT*PRIORITY

JES job selection priority at read-in time.

IOTMTOTL	NUM	4	TIME12.2	TOTAL*CONNECT*TIME

total IOTM (device connect time) measured for this job. This is also called the total address space IOTM count. It represents SMF's count of how many seconds data transfer was occurring to or from this address space during this job.

IOUNITS	NUM	4		IO*SERVICE*UNITS

SRM recorded I/O service units consumed by this job. In MVS/370, an I/O service unit is defined as the number of EXCPS times the installation specified IOCCOEFF coefficient (specified in the IEAIPSxx member of PARMLIB and reported in SAS data set TYPE72). In MVS/XA, the IOUNITS can be based on either EXCPs or Device Connect Time (IOTM). It is not possible to tell from an MVS/XA job record which resource (EXCP or IOTM) was the basis of I/O service measurement.

JELAPSTM	NUM	4	TIME12.2	JOB*ELAPSED*DURATION

job elapsed time for this execution.

JESNR	NUM	4		JES*NUMBER

job number assigned by JES.

JINITIME	NUM	8	DATETIME19.2	JOB*INITIATION*EVENT

job initiation time stamp for this execution.

JOB	CHAR	8		JOB NAME*OR*TSO USER

job name (batch); user ID (TSO).

JOBCLASS	CHAR	1		JOB*CLASS

job class.

Variable	Type	Length	Format	Label
JTRMTIME	NUM	8	DATETIME19.2	JOB*TERMINATION*EVENT

termination time stamp of this execution.

| LENACCT1 | NUM | 4 | | LENGTH*ACCOUNT*ONE |

length of first account field on JOB JCL card.

| LENACCT2 | NUM | 4 | | LENGTH*ACCOUNT*TWO |

length of second account field on JOB JCL card.

| LENACCT3 | NUM | 4 | | LENGTH*ACCOUNT*THREE |

length of third account field on JOB JCL card.

| LENACCT4 | NUM | 4 | | LENGTH*ACCOUNT*FOUR |

length of fourth account field on JOB JCL card.

| LENACCT5 | NUM | 4 | | LENGTH*ACCOUNT*FIVE |

length of fifth account field on JOB JCL card.

| LENACCT6 | NUM | 4 | | LENGTH*ACCOUNT*SIX |

length of sixth account field on JOB JCL card.

| LENACCT7 | NUM | 4 | | LENGTH*ACCOUNT*SEVEN |

length of seventh account field on JOB JCL card.

| LENACCT8 | NUM | 4 | | LENGTH*ACCOUNT*EIGHT |

length of eighth account field on JOB JCL card.

| LENACCT9 | NUM | 4 | | LENGTH*ACCOUNT*NINE |

length of ninth account field on JOB JCL card.

| LOCLINFO | CHAR | 8 | | LOCAL*INSTALLATION*FIELD |

locally-defined field; filled in by installation's SMF exit routines.

| LPAGINS | NUM | 4 | | LPA*AREA*PAGE-INS |

link pack area page-ins.

| LPARECLM | NUM | 4 | | LPA*AREA*RECLAIMS |

link pack area reclaims.

| LSQSZHI | NUM | 4 | | LSQA+SWA*SUBPOOLS*ABOVE 16MB |

maximum virtual storage in bytes allocated from LSQA and SWA subpools above 16 megabytes.

Variable	Type	Length	Format	Label
LSQSZLOW	NUM	4		LSQA+SWA*SUBPOOLS*BELOW 16MB

maximum virtual storage in bytes allocated from LSQA and SWA subpools below 16 megabytes.

MSOUNITS	NUM	4		MEMORY*SERVICE*UNITS

SRM recorded memory service units consumed by this task. A memory service unit is defined as the number of page seconds (real pages times CPU TCB seconds) times the installation-specified MSOCOEFF (specified in the IEAIPS*xx* member of PARMLIB and reported in SAS data set TYPE72) times a constant of one-fiftieth (to normalize memory service to that of CPU and I/O).

MSSNMNTS	NUM	4		SCRATCH*MSS*MOUNTS

MSS volumes mounted for nonspecific requests. This is a mount of a scratch volume since no specific volume serial number was requested.

MSSSMNTS	NUM	4		PRIVATE*MSS*MOUNTS

DASD volumes mounted for specific volume requests. This is a mount of a private volume since the specific volume serial number was requested.

NRACCTFL	NUM	4		NUMBER*ACCOUNT*FIELDS

number of account fields specified on the JOB JCL card.

NRTRANS	NUM	4		NUMBER*OF*TRANSACTIONS

TSO only. Number of transactions as counted by the SRM.

PAGEINS	NUM	4		TOTAL*PAGE-INS

number of page-ins.

PAGEOUTS	NUM	4		TOTAL*PAGE-OUTS

number of page-outs.

PAGESECS	NUM	4		MEMORY*PAGESECS*(PER TCB)

page-seconds of real memory used by this job. This value, when divided by the CPUTCBTM (seconds), gives the AVGWKSET value.

PAGESTOL	NUM	4		PAGES*STOLEN*AWAY

pages stolen from this step.

PERFGRP	NUM	4		PERFORMANCE*GROUP

performance group where job was at termination.

PGMRNAME	CHAR	20		PROGRAMMER*NAME*FIELD

programmer name field from JOB statement.

Variable	Type	Length	Format	Label

PKEY   NUM   4   HEX2.   PROTECT*KEY

storage-protect key.

PRODUCT   CHAR   8   PRODUCT*NAME

product name that produced this record.

PVTAREA   NUM   4   SIZE OF*PRIVATE*AREA

if VIRTREAL= 'V' (virtual storage was specified), the PVTAREA value is size of private area in 1024 (1K) bytes. The private area is constant in size, set at IPL, and is the maximum address space that a task can request. If VIRTREAL= 'R' (real storage was specified), the PVTAREA value is the REGION requested in K-bytes.

PVTBOT   NUM   4   GETMAIN*SIZE*FROM BOTTOM

if VIRTREAL= 'V' (virtual storage was specified), PVTBOT value is address space used (in K-bytes) from bottom of private area (that is, subpools 0-127, 251, and 252). If VIRTREAL= 'R', the PVTBOT value is the amount of contiguous real storage used in K-bytes.

PVTSZHI   NUM   4   PRIVATE*AREA SIZE*ABOVE 16MB

private area size, in bytes, above 16 megabytes.

PVTSZLOW   NUM   4   PRIVATE*AREA SIZE*BELOW 16MB

private area size, in bytes, below 16 megabytes.

PVTTOP   NUM   4   GETMAIN*SIZE*FROM TOP

if VIRTREAL= 'V' (virtual storage was specified), PVTTOP value is address space used, in K-bytes, from top of private area (that is, subpools 229, 239, 236-237, 253-255, the LSQA, and SWA). If VIRTREAL= 'R' (real storage was specified), the PVTTOP value is the amount of storage in K-bytes used that was not from the contiguous storage reserved for the program.

RACFGRUP   CHAR   8   RACF*GROUP*IDENTIFICATION

RACF group identification (zero if RACF is not enabled).

RACFTERM   CHAR   8   RACF/VTAM*TERMINAL*NAME USED

RACF terminal name used. This indicates the VTAM terminal name used by this TSO session. If you use RACF or a security package that enables the RACF exits, this variable is non-blank and can be used to identify and quantify VTAM terminal usage. The VTAM terminal name is actually associated with the physical port address on the control unit so that recabling terminals can change the physical terminal that has this VTAM terminal name.

RACFUSER   CHAR   8   RACF*USER*IDENTIFICATION

RACF user identification (blank if RACF is not enabled).

Variable	Type	Length	Format	Label
RDRDEVCL	NUM	4	HEX2.	READER*DEVICE*CLASS

reader class.

| RDRDEVTY | NUM | 4 | HEX2. | READER*DEVICE*TYPE |

reader type.

| RDRTM | NUM | 4 | | READER*EVENT*DURATION |

duration MVS reader was active while reading this job. For a job read-in via RJE, the duration is how long the job took to be transmitted. The TYPE26 record for this job identifies the remote (INROUTE) from which the job was read and the number of cards (SPOOLCRD) processed.

| READTIME | NUM | 8 | DATETIME19.2 | READ-IN*OR LOGON*EVENT |

job read-in (TSO LOGON) time stamp.

| RECLAIMS | NUM | 4 | | PAGES*RECLAIMED |

pages reclaimed. See the TYPE71 discussion below.

| REGREQST | NUM | 4 | | REGION*REQUESTED*IN JCL |

region size established, in 1K units taken from REGION= parameter in JCL, and rounded up to a 4K boundary. If V=R, this is the amount of contiguous real storage reserved for the program. If the region requested was greater than 16 megabytes, the region established resides above 16 megabytes, and this field will contain a minimum value of 32 megabytes.

| RESIDTM | NUM | 4 | TIME12.2 | RESIDENT*IN REAL*STORAGE |

duration that the job was resident in real storage. This value is accumulated by the SRM and represents the absolute maximum duration that the program could have executed instructions. The difference between RESIDTM and CPUTM is the duration that the task was in memory but not dispatched and represents wait for CPU and wait for I/O completion, among other waits while in memory.

| SERVUNIT | NUM | 4 | | TOTAL*SERVICE*UNITS |

total SRM service units consumed by this job. It is the sum of CPUUNITS, SRBUNITS, IOUNITS, and MSOUNITS. A previous interval record was not written because an error occurred. The cumulative resource counts may be in error because the counters were cleared. This is decode of SMF30ISK.

| SRBUNITS | NUM | 4 | | CPU SRB*SERVICE*UNITS |

SRM recorded SRB CPU service units consumed by this job. A SRB CPU service unit is defined as the number of SRB CPU seconds times the installation-specified SRBCOEFF coefficient (specified in the IEAIPSxx member of PARMLIB and reported in SAS data set TYPE72) times a machine-dependent constant (which is set at IPL time based on the CPU model and CPU version). SOURCLIB member TYPE7072 provides one source of the value of the machine-dependent constant, called SU_SEC, since it sets the number of service units generated by one second of CPU time.

Variable	Type	Length	Format	Label

STEPNR   NUM   4   STEP*NUMBER

maximum step number for this execution. It is set to one when a job is canceled and restarted so that it is possible for the same job to have steps with duplicate values.

SUBSYS   CHAR   4   SUB*SYSTEM

subsystem. The value may be either JES2 or JES3.

SWAPS   NUM   4   TIMES*TASK WAS*SWAPPED OUT

number of times this job was swapped out.

SWPAGINS   NUM   4   SWAP*PAGE*INS

number of pages swapped in.

SWPAGOUT   NUM   4   PAGE OUTS*TO SWAP*TASK OUT

number of pages swapped out.

SYSINCNT   NUM   4   CARD IMAGES*READ*BY PROGRAM

number of card-image records in DD DATA and DD * data sets read by the reader for this job.

SYSTEM   CHAR   4   4.   SYSTEM*ID

identification of the system on which the job executed.

TAPEDRVS   NUM   4   TAPE*DRIVES*ALLOCATED

number of tape drives allocated to this job. Note that in MVS/370, the IMACCHAN member must describe the installation's two-channel switches if the number of tape drives is to be counted correctly.

TAPNMNTS   NUM   4   SCRATCH*TAPE*MOUNTS

TAPE volumes mounted for nonspecific requests. This is a mount of a scratch volume since no specific volume serial number was requested. Only mount requests actually satisfied by volume verification are counted. If the wrong volume was mounted, this count is not incremented until the correct volume is verified.

TAPSMNTS   NUM   4   PRIVATE*TAPE*MOUNTS

TAPE volumes mounted for specific volume requests. This is a mount of a private volume since the specific volume serial number was requested. Only mount requests actually satisfied by volume verification are counted. If the wrong volume was mounted, this count is not incremented until the correct volume is verified.

TGETS   NUM   4   TERMINAL*READS*(TGETS)

TSO only. The number of terminals TGETS satisfied (that is, the number of times that the TSO user pushed the ENTER key).

Variable	Type	Length	Format	Label

TPUTS   NUM   4   TERMINAL*WRITES*(TPUTS)

TSO only. The number of terminal TPUTS issued (that is, the number of times that output lines were sent to the terminal).

TYPETASK   CHAR   4   TYPE*OF*TASK

type of task. This is indicated by the first four characters of the JES job identification. The possible values are:

value	meaning
JOB	batch job
TSU	TSO session (acronym is for TSO "U"ser)
STC	started (system) task.

USRSZHI   NUM   4   USER*SUBPOOLS*ABOVE 16MB

maximum virtual storage in bytes allocated from user subpools above 16 megabytes.

USRSZLOW   NUM   4   USER*SUBPOOLS*BELOW 16MB

maximum virtual storage in bytes allocated from user subpools below 16 megabytes.

VERSION   CHAR   2   VERSION*NUMBER

record version number.

VIOPAGIN   NUM   4   VIO*PAGE-INS

virtual I/O page-ins.

VIOPAGOU   NUM   4   VIO*PAGE-OUTS

virtual I/O page-outs.

VIORECLM   NUM   4   VIO*RECLAIMS

virtual I/O page reclaims.

VIRTREAL   CHAR   1   VIRTUAL*OR*REAL?

type of address space requested.

value	requested
R	real storage (ADDRSPC=R specified)
V	virtual storage.

TYPE30_6
TYPE30 System Address Space

Data set TYPE30_6 contains one observation for each type 30 SMF record with subtype 6, written at the expiration of an interval for system address spaces (data only address spaces). The resource values are cumulative and indicate data collected since initialization of the system address space.

Variable	Type	Length	Format	Label

ACTIVETM   NUM   4   TIME12.2   TASK*ACTIVE*TIME

> sum of step active times. This value indicates the duration that the System Resource Manager (SRM) defined the task as active. A task is made active when the SRM decides the task should be given service. The SRM then notifies the ASM to bring in the task (if the task is swapped out). The difference between EXECTM and ACTIVETM is the duration that the task was swapped out, not-ready, or waiting for mount to complete. See also RESIDTM.

AVGWKSET   NUM   4   5.   AVERAGE*WORKING*SET (PAGES)

> average working set size, in pages (one page is 4096 bytes). This value is the result of dividing the page-seconds by the CPU (TCB time only since page-seconds are pages times TCB seconds) to get an estimate of the real storage working set of this program. It is considerably less repeatable than other resource measures for the same program, especially if the TCB seconds are less than a few seconds, often varying by 30% and sometimes by much more. It is still the best indication of the real memory used by a task.

COMPAGIN   NUM   4   COMMON*AREA*PAGE-INS

> common area page-ins.

COMRECLM   NUM   4   COMMON*AREA*RECLAIMS

> common area page reclaims.

CPISRBTM   NUM   4   TIME12.2   INITIATOR*CPU SRB*TIME

> duration that the central processor (CPU) was executing instructions under a Service Request Block (SRB) under the initiator. This CPU time occurs in the process of initiation and termination and is not included in the SRB CPU time reported in this job's performance group in RMF; instead, it is included in the uncaptured or MVS overhead CPU state.

CPITCBTM   NUM   4   TIME12.2   INITIATOR*CPU TCB*TIME

> duration that the central processor (CPU) was executing instructions under a Task Control Block (TCB) under the initiator. This CPU time occurs in the process of initiation and termination and is not included in the TCB CPU time reported in this job's performance group in RMF; instead, it is included in the uncaptured or MVS overhead CPU state.

Variable	Type	Length	Format	Label
CPUSRBTM	NUM	4	TIME12.2	TASK*CPU SRB*TIME

duration that the central processor (CPU) was executing instructions under a Service Request Block (SRB) for this job.

CPUTCBTM	NUM	4	TIME12.2	TASK*CPU TCB*TIME

duration that the central processor (CPU) was executing instructions under the Task Control Block (TCB) for this job.

CPUTM	NUM	4	TIME12.2	TOTAL*CPU*TIME

duration that the central processor (CPU) was executing instructions for this task. The duration is the sum of CPUSRBTM and CPUTCBTM.

CPUUNITS	NUM	4		CPU TCB*SERVICE*UNITS

SRM recorded TCB CPU service units consumed by this job. A TCB CPU service unit is defined as the number of TCB CPU seconds times the installation-specified CPUCOEFF coefficient (specified in the IEAIPSxx member of PARMLIB and reported in SAS data set TYPE72) times a machine-dependent constant (which is set at IPL time based on the CPU model and CPU version). SOURCLIB member TYPE7072 provides one source of the value of the machine-dependent constant, called SU_SEC, since it sets the number of service units generated by one second of CPU time.

DPRTY	NUM	4		DISPATCH*PRIORITY

dispatching priority at job termination.

IOTMTOTL	NUM	4	TIME12.2	TOTAL*CONNECT*TIME

total IOTM (device connect time) measured for this step. This is also called the total address space IOTM count. It represents SMF's count of how many seconds data transfer was occurring to or from this address space during this step.

IOUNITS	NUM	4		IO*SERVICE*UNITS

SRM recorded I/O service units consumed by this job. In MVS/370, an I/O service unit is defined as the number of EXCPS times the installation-specified IOCCOEFF coefficient (specified in the IEAIPSxx member of PARMLIB and reported in SAS data set TYPE72). In MVS/XA, the IOUNITS can be based on either EXCPs or Device Connect Time (IOTM). It is not possible to tell from an MVS/XA job record which resource (EXCP or IOTM) was the basis of I/O service measurement.

JESNR	NUM	4		JES*NUMBER

job number assigned by JES.

JOB	CHAR	8		JOB NAME*OR*TSO USER

job name (batch); user ID (TSO).

Variable	Type	Length	Format	Label
LOCLINFO	CHAR	8		LOCAL*INSTALLATION*FIELD

locally-defined field; filled in by installation's SMF exit routines.

LPAGINS	NUM	4		LPA*AREA*PAGE-INS

link pack area page-ins.

LPARECLM	NUM	4		LPA*AREA*RECLAIMS

link pack area reclaims.

LSQSZHI	NUM	4		LSQA+SWA*SUBPOOLS*ABOVE 16MB

maximum virtual storage in bytes allocated from LSQA and SWA subpools above 16 megabytes.

LSQSZLOW	NUM	4		LSQA+SWA*SUBPOOLS*BELOW 16MB

maximum virtual storage in bytes allocated from LSQA and SWA subpools below 16 megabytes.

MSOUNITS	NUM	4		MEMORY*SERVICE*UNITS

SRM recorded memory service units consumed by this task. A memory service unit is defined as the number of page seconds (real pages times CPU TCB seconds) times the installation-specified MSOCOEFF (specified in the IEAIPSxx member of PARMLIB and reported in SAS data set TYPE72) times a constant of one-fiftieth (to normalize memory service to that of CPU and I/O).

PAGEINS	NUM	4		TOTAL*PAGE-INS

number of page-ins.

PAGEOUTS	NUM	4		TOTAL*PAGE-OUTS

number of page-outs.

PAGESECS	NUM	4		MEMORY*PAGESECS*(PER TCB)

page-seconds of real memory used by this job. This value, when divided by the CPUTCBTM (seconds), gives the AVGWKSET value.

PAGESTOL	NUM	4		PAGES*STOLEN*AWAY

pages stolen from this step.

PERFGRP	NUM	4		PERFORMANCE*GROUP

performance group where job was at termination.

PRODUCT	CHAR	8		PRODUCT*NAME

product name that produced this record.

Variable	Type	Length	Format	Label
PVTSZHI	NUM	4		PRIVATE*AREA SIZE*ABOVE 16MB

private area size, in bytes, above 16 megabytes.

| PVTSZLOW | NUM | 4 | | PRIVATE*AREA SIZE*BELOW 16MB |

private area size, in bytes, below 16 megabytes.

| READTIME | NUM | 8 | DATETIME19.2 | READ-IN*OR LOGON*EVENT |

job read-in (TSO LOGON) time stamp.

| RECLAIMS | NUM | 4 | | PAGES*RECLAIMED |

pages reclaimed. See the TYPE71 discussion below.

| REGREQST | NUM | 4 | | REGION*REQUESTED*IN JCL |

region size established, in 1K units taken from REGION= parameter in JCL, and rounded up to a 4K boundary. If V=R, this is the amount of contiguous real storage reserved for the program. If the region requested was greater than 16 megabytes, the region established resides above 16 megabytes, and this field will contain a minimum value of 32 megabytes.

| RESIDTM | NUM | 4 | TIME12.2 | RESIDENT*IN REAL*STORAGE |

duration that the job was resident in real storage. This value is accumulated by the SRM and represents the absolute maximum duration that the program could have executed instructions. The difference between RESIDTM and CPUTM is the duration that the task was in memory but not dispatched and represents wait for CPU and wait for I/O completion among other waits while in memory.

| SERVUNIT | NUM | 4 | | TOTAL*SERVICE*UNITS |

total SRM service units consumed by this job. It is the sum of CPUUNITS, SRBUNITS, IOUNITS, and MSOUNITS. A previous interval record was not written because an error occurred. The cumulative resource counts may be in error because the counters were cleared. This is decode of SMF30ISK.

| SMFTIME | NUM | 8 | DATETIME19.2 | SMF*RECORD*TIME STAMP |

time stamp when record was written.

| SRBUNITS | NUM | 4 | | CPU SRB*SERVICE*UNITS |

SRM recorded SRB CPU service units consumed by this job. A SRB CPU service unit is defined as the number of SRB CPU seconds times the installation-specified SRBCOEFF coefficient (specified in the IEAIPSxx member of PARMLIB and reported in SAS data set TYPE72) times a machine-dependent constant (which is set at IPL time based on the CPU model and CPU version). SOURCLIB member TYPE7072 provides one source of the value of the machine-dependent constant, called SU_SEC, since it sets the number of service units generated by one second of CPU time.

Variable	Type	Length	Format	Label
SUBSYS	CHAR	4		SUB*SYSTEM

subsystem. The value may be either JES2 or JES3.

SWAPS	NUM	4		TIMES*TASK WAS*SWAPPED OUT

number of times this job was swapped out.

SWPAGINS	NUM	4		SWAP*PAGE*INS

number of pages swapped in.

SWPAGOUT	NUM	4		PAGE OUTS*TO SWAP*TASK OUT

number of pages swapped out.

SYSTEM	CHAR	4	4.	SYSTEM*ID

identification of the system on which the job executed.

TYPETASK	CHAR	4		TYPE*OF*TASK

type of task. This is indicated by the first four characters of the JES job identification. The possible values are:

value	meaning
JOB	batch job
TSU	TSO session (acronym is for TSO "U"ser)
STC	started (system) task.

USRSZHI	NUM	4		USER*SUBPOOLS*ABOVE 16MB

maximum virtual storage, in bytes, allocated from user subpools above 16 megabytes.

USRSZLOW	NUM	4		USER*SUBPOOLS*BELOW 16MB

maximum virtual storage, in bytes, allocated from user subpools below 16 megabytes.

VERSION	CHAR	2		VERSION*NUMBER

record version number.

VIOPAGIN	NUM	4		VIO*PAGE-INS

virtual I/O page-ins.

VIOPAGOU	NUM	4		VIO*PAGE-OUTS

virtual I/O page-outs.

VIORECLM	NUM	4		VIO*RECLAIMS

virtual I/O page reclaims.

TYPE30_D
DD Segment Detail

Data set TYPE30_D may contain one observation for each DD segment in each Type 30, subtype 4 SMF record, written at the termination of a step. The total step resources in the subtype 4 record are contained in data set TYPE30_4 where the EXCP count and IOTM device connect times are accumulated by device time. However, the actual subtype 4 record contains a segment for each DD statement in the step. The TYPE30_D data set allows examination of the detailed EXCP count and IOTM device connect time for selected DD segments from selected type 30, subtype 4 records.

The TYPE30_D data set is always created but has zero observations unless your installation changes member IMAC30DD to select and output desired DD segments. Note that there may be more than one DD segment for each DD in the step since DD segments are consolidated in the type 30, subtype 4 record. If the DDNAME, DEVICE (device class and device type), and DEVNR are the same in entries in the TCTTIOT for the task, there is only one DD segment for all activity to that DDNAME-DEVICE-DEVNR combination. A common example of this consolidation is the STEPLIB DD. If several STEPLIB data sets on the same volume are concatenated, there is only a single DD segment for those data sets on that volume.

Variable	Type	Length	Format	Label
BLKSIZE	NUM	4		BLOCK*SIZE

largest blocksize of this data set.

| DDNAME | CHAR | 8 | | DD*NAME |

DDname used to access data set.

| DEVICE | CHAR | 7 | | DEVICE*TYPE |

device type (for example, 3330, 3350, and so forth). Decoded from UCB type by the VMACUCB member of SOURCLIB.

| DEVNR | NUM | 4 | | DEVICE*NUMBER |

device number of device. Formerly the Unit Address in MVS/370. The unique number or address of the device.

| EXCPCNT | NUM | 4 | | DD*SEGMENT*EXCPS |

count of blocks issued for device against the data set.

Variable	Type	Length	Format	Label

INITTIME NUM 8 DATETIME19.2 STEP*INITIATE*EVENT
initiation time stamp.

IOTM NUM 4 TIME12.2 DD*CONNECT*TIME
device connect time for this data set.

JESNR NUM 4 JES*NUMBER
job number assigned by JES.

JOB CHAR 8 JOB NAME*OR*TSO USER
job name (batch); user ID (TSO).

MULTSIZE CHAR 1 MULTIPLE*BLOCKSIZE*FLAG?
indicates if blocksize was changed for the data set (that is, not only if there were multiple opens, but if the blocksize changed between opens). The values are blank (no) or Y (yes). Note if MULTSIZE=Y, BLKSIZE is the maximum value for any open in this step.

MVSXA NUM 2 MVS*XA?
indicates whether these data are from MVS/370 or MVS/XA. The values are blank (no) or Y (yes). This is included to make comparisons by DDname easier if both MVS/370 and MVS/XA SMF records are processed together.

PROGRAM CHAR 8 PROGRAM*NAME
program name (PGM=) from EXEC statement. If backward reference was used, the PROGRAM value is *.DD. If the current step is a restarted step, its PROGRAM value and that of all subsequent steps are IEFRSTRT.

READTIME NUM 8 DATETIME19.2 READ-IN*OR LOGON*EVENT
job read-in (TSO LOGON) time stamp.

SMFTIME NUM 8 DATETIME19.2 SMF*RECORD*TIME STAMP
datetime stamp of the record. This indicates the termination time of this step.

STEPNAME CHAR 8 STEP*NAME
step name that appeared on the EXEC PGM= statement. Note that if this step executed a JCL procedure instead, this is not the stepname on that EXEC statement, but rather is the stepname on the EXEC PGM= card within that JCL procedure. Note further that for a TSO session, the stepname is the TSO procedure name, either the default from UADS, or the user-supplied PR (name) value.

STEPNR NUM 4 STEP*NUMBER
step number. This number is reset to 1 when a job is canceled and restarted, so that it is possible for the same job to have steps with duplicate values.

Variable	Type	Length	Format	Label
SUBTYPE	NUM	4		RECORD*SUBTYPE

record subtype number. The possible values are:

value	meaning
2	interval record
3	interval between last interval and step termination
4	step termination
5	job termination
6	system address space (may not ever occur).

Variable	Type	Length	Format	Label
SYSTEM	CHAR	4	4.	SYSTEM*ID

identification of system on which step executed.

TYPE30_V
Interval Accounting

Data set TYPE30_V may contain one observation for each type 30 SMF record with subtype 2 or 3. Member IMACINTV defines the criteria for creating an observation. A type 30, subtype 2 SMF record, written at the termination of an accounting interval, contains the resources consumed in that interval. A type 30, subtype 3 SMF record, written at the termination of a step, contains the resources consumed in the interval between the last subtype 2 record and the step termination. A subtype 3 record is always created if interval accounting is specified, even if the step elapsed time is less than required to produce a subtype 2 interval record.

Interval accounting lets you recover resources consumed by long-running jobs, sessions, or tasks prior to a system failure. See also the discussion of the TYPE30_4 data set.

Interval records also provide performance statistics on each address space for the interval since the interval records contain the same resources reported in the step termination record. Thus, performance metrics such as the average paging rate of a CICS system or an IMS message or control region can be calculated from the interval records.

The duration of the interval is specified in the SMFPRM*xx* member of SYS1.PARMLIB as the INTERVAL subparameter of the SYS or SUBSYS keywords. Thus a separate duration can be requested for each subsystem (JOB/TSU/STC). Currently, there is no time stamp for the beginning of the interval in the interval records. Although you could use the defined INTERVAL value (above) for the nonswappable tasks, the swappable tasks will not necessarily create a record every INTERVAL minutes, since a task will not be swapped back in just to write the interval record. Only by sorting all interval records for a job by SMFTIME and then creating the beginning time stamp (INTBTIME) can the actual interval duration be determined. (This is done in BUILDPDB to process the TYPE30_V data set.)

The intervals are not aligned with RMF data. The interval starts when the step initiates and records are created every INTERVAL minutes. Thus, correlation with other performance measures may be difficult. It may be possible (especially for nonswappable tasks) to align these TYPE30_V records with corresponding RMF intervals by starting these on-line systems (such as CICS) exactly on the hour, but this would be difficult for operations to accomplish.

TYPE30_V does not always contain an observation for every interval record encountered. To minimize processing of unnecessary data, only records that meet the criteria specified in member IMACINTV create observations. You can select interval records you want by job name, performance group, job class, and so forth. The data set has zero observations unless IMACINT**V** is modified to select the desired records.

Variable	Type	Length	Format	Label

ACTIVETM   NUM   4   TIME12.2   TASK*ACTIVE*TIME

step active time. Duration that the SRM (system resource manager) defined the task as active. A task is made active when the SRM decides the task should be given service. The SRM then notifies the ASM to bring in the task (if the task is swapped out). The difference between EXECTM and ACTIVETM is the duration that the task was swapped out, was not ready, or was waiting for mount to complete. See also RESIDTM.

ALOCTIME   NUM   8   DATETIME19.2   START OF*ALLOCATION*EVENT

allocation time stamp. This indicates the second event in the lifetime of a step, and signifies the beginning of allocation of the correct device for each DD card in the step. If this field is missing, it means the step never entered allocation, usually for some type of execution JCL error (such as, data set not found in the catalog). See also LOADTIME and ALOCTM.

ALOCTM   NUM   4   ALLOCATION*DELAY*DURATION

step allocation time. Duration required for the operating system to allocate all devices. This is LOADTIME minus ALOCTIME. It is missing if the step never entered allocation, or if the job entered allocation but failed to complete, usually because of device unavailability. For example, if sufficient tape drives are unavailable, and the operator replied "cancel" to the allocation recovery message, the LOADTIME and this field both would be missing.

AVGWKSET   NUM   4   5.   AVERAGE*WORKING*SET (PAGES)

average working set size, in pages (one page is 4096 bytes). This value is the result of dividing the page-seconds by the CPU (TCB time only, since page-seconds are pages times TCB seconds) to get an estimate of the real storage working set of this program. It is considerably less repeatable than other resource measures for the same program, especially if the TCB seconds are less than a few seconds, often varying by 30 percent and sometimes by much more. It is still the best indication of the real memory used by a task.

COMPAGIN   NUM   4   COMMON*AREA*PAGE-INS

common area page-ins.

COMRECLM   NUM   4   COMMON*AREA*RECLAIMS

common area page-reclaims.

CPISRBTM   NUM   4   TIME12.2   INITIATOR*CPU SRB*TIME

duration that the central processor (CPU) was executing instructions under a Service Request Block (SRB) under the initiator. This CPU time occurs in the process of initiation and termination and is not included in the SRB CPU time reported in this job's performance group in RMF, but instead in the uncaptured or MVS overhead CPU state.

CPITCBTM   NUM   4   TIME12.2   INITIATOR*CPU TCB*TIME

duration that the central processor (CPU) was executing instructions under a Task Control Block (TCB) under the initiator. This CPU time occurs in the process of initiation and termination and is not included in the TCB CPU time reported in this job's performance group in RMF, but instead is in the uncaptured or MVS overhead CPU state.

Variable	Type	Length	Format	Label

CPUSRBTM   NUM   4   TIME12.2   TASK*CPU SRB*TIME

duration that the central processor (CPU) was executing instructions under a Service Request Block (SRB) for this task.

CPUTCBTM   NUM   4   TIME12.2   TASK*CPU TCB*TIME

duration that the central processor (CPU) was executing instructions under the Task Control Block (TCB) for this task.

CPUTM   NUM   4   TIME12.2   TOTAL*CPU*TIME

duration that the central processor (CPU) was executing instructions for this task. The duration is the sum of CPUSRBTM and CPUTCBTM.

CPUUNITS   NUM   4   CPU TCB*SERVICE*UNITS

SRM recorded TCB CPU service units consumed by this task. A TCB CPU service unit is defined as the number of TCB CPU seconds times the installation-specified CPUCOEFF coefficient (specified in the IEAIPSxx member of PARMLIB and reported in SAS data set TYPE72) times a machine-dependent constant (which is set at IPL time based on the CPU Model and CPU Version). SOURCLIB member TYPE7072 provides one source of the value of the machine-dependent constant, called SU_SEC, since it sets the number of service units generated by one second of CPU time.

DASNMNTS   NUM   4   SCRATCH*DASD*MOUNTS

DASD volumes mounted for nonspecific requests. This is a mount of a scratch volume, since no specific volume serial number was requested. Only mount requests that are actually satisfied by volume verification are counted. If the wrong volume is mounted, this count is not incremented until the correct volume is verified.

DASSMNTS   NUM   4   PRIVATE*DASD*MOUNTS

DASD volumes mounted for specific volume requests. This is a mount of a private volume, since the specific volume serial number was requested. Only mount requests actually satisfied by volume verification are counted. If the wrong volume is mounted, this count is not incremented until the correct volume is verified.

DPRTY   NUM   4   DISPATCH*PRIORITY

dispatching priority at step termination.

DSENQTM   NUM   4   DATA SET*ENQUEUE*DELAY

duration of step between initiation and beginning of allocation. So named because for the first step of a job, the wait for data set enqueue occurs in this interval.

D3330DRV   NUM   4   MOUNTABLE*3330
DRIVES*ALLOCATED

number of different 3330 mountable disk drives allocated to this step, where mountable is defined by an explicit list of unit addresses in the IMAC3330 member.

Variable	Type	Length	Format	Label
ENQTIME	NUM	8	DATETIME19.2	TSO LOGON*ENQUEUE ON UADS* TIME STAMP

TSO only. The time when LOGON process enqueues on SYS1.UADS data set. This time has been used to calculate the time it takes to logon to TSO (LOGONTM=ENQTIME-READTIME) because it is very close to the actual time the user sees READY.

| EXCPCOMM | NUM | 4 | | EXCPS*COUNT*COMMUNICATIONS |

EXCPs (blocks of data) to communication devices.

| EXCPDASD | NUM | 4 | | EXCPS*COUNT*DASD |

sum of EXCPs to 2305, 3330, 3340, 3350, 3375, and 3380 devices.

| EXCPGRAF | NUM | 4 | | EXCPS*COUNT*GRAPHICS |

EXCPs (blocks of data) to graphics devices.

| EXCPMSS | NUM | 4 | | EXCPS*COUNT*MSS |

EXCPs (blocks of data) to mass storage volumes.

| EXCPNODD | NUM | 4 | | EXCPS*NOT IN*ANY DD SEGMENT |

total EXCPs not recorded to a DD. This is EXCPTOTL minus EXCPTODD and represents EXCPs to catalogs and linklist data sets; in JES2 it includes the physical EXCPs to the spool on behalf of this step.

| EXCPRMF | NUM | 4 | | EXCPS*COUNT*BY RMF |

EXCPs delivered to this task, as counted by RMF. Note that this number does not come from the normal SMF data (that is, the TIOT), but rather is calculated from the I/O Service Units that were measured by RMF. It is calculated by dividing the actual I/O Service Units in this record by the IOCCOEFF from the preceding type 72 record. This is completely safe if all systems have the same IOCCOEFF, but can lead to miscalculation if different IOCCOEFF are used for different systems, and if the type 30 record being examined is from a different system than the preceding type 72 (it is missing if no type 72 record was encountered before this type 30 record). Finally, if you have specified (MVS/XA only) for I/O service units to be based on the I/O Device Connect time, this is not EXCPs but IOTM instead.

| EXCPTAPE | NUM | 4 | | EXCPS*COUNT*TAPE |

EXCPs (blocks of data) to tape volumes.

| EXCPTODD | NUM | 4 | | TOTAL EXCPS*IN ALL*DD SEGMENTS |

total EXCPs to all DD segements in this step.

| EXCPTOTL | NUM | 4 | | TOTAL*EXCPS*COUNT |

total EXCPs issued by this step. This is also called the total address space EXCP count. It represents SMF's count of how many blocks of data were transferred to or from this address space during this step.

Variable	Type	Length	Format	Label

EXCPUREC   NUM   4   EXCPS*COUNT*UNIT RECORD

EXCPs to unit record devices that were allocated directly to the step. This does not include EXCPs to the JES spool devices.

EXCPVIO   NUM   4   EXCPS*COUNT*VIO

EXCPs to virtual I/O.

EXCP2305   NUM   4   EXCPS*COUNT*2305

EXCPs (blocks of data) to 2305 devices.

EXCP3330   NUM   4   EXCPS*COUNT*3330

EXCPs (blocks of data) to 3330 devices.

EXCP3340   NUM   4   EXCPS*COUNT*3340

EXCPs (blocks of data) to 3340 devices.

EXCP3350   NUM   4   EXCPS*COUNT*3350

EXCPs (blocks of data) to 3350 devices.

EXCP3375   NUM   4   EXCPS*COUNT*3375

EXCPs (blocks of data) to 3375 devices.

EXCP3380   NUM   4   EXCPS*COUNT*3380

EXCPs (blocks of data) to 3380 devices.

EXECTM   NUM   4   TIME12.2   EXECUTION*DURATION

duration of step between load time and termination, known as step execution time. It is only during this duration that the program can actually execute instructions (and often not even for all of this time). See also ACTIVETM and RESIDTM.

EXTRADD   NUM   4   EXTRA*DD*RECORD?

if nonzero, there were extra DD segments in a subsequent type 30, subtype 4 record for this step. The type 30 can contain only about 1534 DD segments (which should be enough), but long-running, dynamically allocating tasks could exceed that number of DD segments.

INITTIME   NUM   8   DATETIME19.2   STEP*INITIATE*EVENT

initiation time stamp.

INPRTY   NUM   4   INPUT*PRIORITY

JES job selection priority at read-in time.

INTBTIME   NUM   8   DATETIME19.2   INTERVAL*BEGIN*EVENT

interval begin time. Unfortunately, this time does not currently exist in the SMF record, and it is set to missing. It can be constructed by sorting all interval records in sequence and assigning the begin time of this interval to the end time of the preceding record.

Variable	Type	Length	Format	Label
INTETIME	NUM	8	DATETIME19.2	INTERVAL*END*EVENT

interval ending time. This is the SMF record time stamp. Note that the actual interval can be much longer than was specified since a task that is swapped out when it's accounting interval ends is not swapped back in just to write the interval record. When the task is swapped back in to do work, the interval record is written and reflects an interval longer by the swapped-out duration.

| INTRVLTM | NUM | 4 | TIME12.2 | ACTUAL*INTERVAL*DURATION |

actual duration of the interval from INTBTIME to INTETIME.

| IOTMCOMM | NUM | 4 | TIME12.2 | CONNECT*TIME*COMMUNICATIONS |

IOTM (device connect time) to communication devices.

| IOTMDASD | NUM | 4 | TIME12.2 | CONNECT*TIME*DASD |

sum of IOTM to 2305, 3330, 3340, 3350, 3375, and 3380 devices.

| IOTMERR | CHAR | 1 | | CONNECT*TIME*IN ERROR? |

device connect time (IOTM) may be incorrect. If this flag is set, the SRM disabled the channel measurement while the job was executing, and device connect time (IOTM) was not captured. Some or all of the IOTM variables contain less than the true device connect duration.

value	meaning
blank	no error flagged
Y	IOTMs may be incorrect.

| IOTMGRAF | NUM | 4 | TIME12.2 | CONNECT*TIME*GRAPHICS |

IOTM (device connect time) to graphics devices.

| IOTMMSS | NUM | 4 | TIME12.2 | CONNECT*TIME*MSS |

IOTM (device connect time) to mass storage volume.

| IOTMNODD | NUM | 4 | TIME12.2 | TOTAL CONNECT*TIME NOT IN*ANY DD SEGMENT |

total IOTM (device connect time) not recorded to a DD. This is IOTMTOTL minus IOTMTODD, and it represents ITOM to catalogs, to linklist data sets; in JES2 it includes the physical IOTM to the spool on behalf of this step.

| IOTMTAPE | NUM | 4 | TIME12.2 | CONNECT*TIME*TAPE |

IOTM (device connect time) to tape volumes.

| IOTMTODD | NUM | 4 | TIME12.2 | TOTAL CONNECT*TIME IN ALL*DD SEGMENTS |

total IOTM (device connect time) to all DDs in this step.

Variable	Type	Length	Format	Label
IOTMTOTL	NUM	4	TIME12.2	TOTAL*CONNECT*TIME

total IOTM (device connect time) measured for this step. This is also called the total address space IOTM count. It represents SMF's count of how many seconds data transfer was occurring to or from this address space during this step.

| IOTMUREC | NUM | 4 | TIME12.2 | CONNECT*TIME*UNIT RECORD |

IOTM (device connect time) to unit record devices that were allocated directly to the step. This does not include IOTMs to the JES spool devices.

| IOTM2305 | NUM | 4 | TIME12.2 | CONNECT*TIME*2305 |

IOTM (device connect time) to 2305 devices.

| IOTM3330 | NUM | 4 | TIME12.2 | CONNECT*TIME*3330 |

IOTM (device connect time) to 3330 devices.

| IOTM3340 | NUM | 4 | TIME12.2 | CONNECT*TIME*3340 |

IOTM (device connect time) to 3340 devices.

| IOTM3350 | NUM | 4 | TIME12.2 | CONNECT*TIME*3350 |

IOTM (device connect time) to 3350 devices.

| IOTM3375 | NUM | 4 | TIME12.2 | CONNECT*TIME*3375 |

IOTM (device connect time) to 3375 devices.

| IOTM3380 | NUM | 4 | TIME12.2 | CONNECT*TIME*3380 |

IOTM (device connect time) to 3380 devices.

| IOUNITS | NUM | 4 | | IO*SERVICE*UNITS |

SRM recorded I/O service units consumed by this task. In MVS/370, an I/O service unit is defined as the number of EXCPS times the installation-specified IOCCOEFF coefficient (specified in the IEAIPSxx member of PARMLIB and reported in SAS data set TYPE72). In MVS/XA, the IOUNITS can be based on either EXCPs or Device Connect Time (IOTM). It is not possible to tell from an MVS/XA step record which resource (EXCP or IOTM) was the basis of I/O service measurement.

| JESNR | NUM | 4 | | JES*NUMBER |

job number assigned by JES.

| JOB | CHAR | 8 | | JOB NAME*OR*TSO USER |

job name (batch); user ID (TSO).

| JOBCLASS | CHAR | 1 | | JOB*CLASS |

job class.

Variable	Type	Length	Format	Label
LOADTIME	NUM	8	DATETIME19.2	PROGRAM*FETCH*EVENT

load (problem program start) time stamp. This is the third event in the lifetime of a step, and it signifies the loading of the program from the library into real memory. If this field is missing, it means that the program was never completely loaded into memory by PROGRAM FETCH (that part of the operating system that loads programs). Only after the program is loaded into real memory does the program begin to execute its instructions, open its files, and so forth.

LOCLINFO	CHAR	8		LOCAL*INSTALLATION*FIELD

locally-defined field; filled in by installation's SMF exit routines.

LPAGINS	NUM	4	LPA*AREA*PAGE-INS

link pack area page-ins.

LPARECLM	NUM	4	LPA*AREA*RECLAIMS

link pack area reclaims.

LSQSZHI	NUM	4	LSQA+SWA*SUBPOOLS*ABOVE 16MB

maximum virtual storage in bytes allocated from LSQA and SWA subpools above 16 megabytes.

LSQSZLOW	NUM	4	LSQA+SWA*SUBPOOLS*BELOW 16MB

maximum virtual storage in bytes allocated from LSQA and SWA subpools below 16 megabytes.

MSOUNITS	NUM	4	MEMORY*SERVICE*UNITS

SRM recorded memory service units consumed by this task. A memory service unit is defined as the number of page seconds (real pages times CPU TCB seconds) times the installation specified MSOCOEFF (specified in the IEAIPS*xx* member of PARMLIB and reported in SAS data set TYPE72) times a constant of one-fiftieth (to normalize memory service to that of CPU and I/O).

MSSNMNTS	NUM	4	SCRATCH*MSS*MOUNTS

MSS volumes mounted for nonspecific requests. This is a mount of a scratch volume, since no specific volume serial number was requested.

MSSSMNTS	NUM	4	PRIVATE*MSS*MOUNTS

DASD volumes mounted for specific volume requests. This is a mount of a private volume, since the specific volume serial number was requested.

NDASDDD	NUM	4	NUMBER*DASD*DD CARDS

number of DD statements that allocated DASD devices.

Variable	Type	Length	Format	Label
NRTRANS	NUM	4		NUMBER*OF*TRANSACTIONS

TSO only. The number of transactions as counted by the SRM.

NTAPEDD	NUM	4		NUMBER*TAPE*DD CARDS

number of DD statements that allocated TAPE devices.

NUMDD	NUM	4		NUMBER*ALL*DD CARDS

total number of DD statements in this step. Note that

NUMDD-(NDASDD+NTAPEDD)

equals the number of DDs for JES, VIO, MSS, COMM, UREC, and graphics allocations.

PAGEINS	NUM	4		TOTAL*PAGE-INS

number of page-ins.

PAGEOUTS	NUM	4		TOTAL*PAGE-OUTS

number of page-outs.

PAGESECS	NUM	4		MEMORY*PAGESECS*(PER TCB)

page-seconds of real memory used by this step. This value, when divided by the CPUTCBTM (seconds), gives the AVGWKSET value.

PAGESTOL	NUM	4		PAGES*STOLEN*AWAY

pages stolen from this step.

PERFGRP	NUM	4		PERFORMANCE*GROUP

performance group where this step was at termination.

PGMRNAME	CHAR	20		PROGRAMMER*NAME*FIELD

programmer name field from JOB statement.

PKEY	NUM	4	HEX2.	PROTECT*KEY

storage-protect key.

PRODUCT	CHAR	8		PRODUCT*NAME

product name that produced record.

PROGRAM	CHAR	8		PROGRAM*NAME

program name (PGM=) from EXEC statement. If backward reference was used, the PROGRAM value is *.DD. If the current step is a restarted step, its PROGRAM value and that of all subsequent steps is IEFRSTRT.

PVTAREA	NUM	4		SIZE OF*PRIVATE*AREA

if VIRTREAL= 'V' (virtual storage was specified), PVTAREA value is size of private area in 1024 (1K) bytes. The private area is constant in size, set at IPL, and is the maximum

Variable	Type	Length	Format	Label

address space that a task can request. If VIRTREAL= 'R' (real storage was specified), the PVTAREA value is the REGION requested in K-bytes.

PVTBOT	NUM	4		GETMAIN*SIZE*FROM BOTTOM

if VIRTREAL= 'V' (virtual storage was specified), PVTBOT value is address space used (in K-bytes) from bottom of private area (that is, subpools 0-127, 251, and 252). If VIRTREAL= 'R', the PVTBOT value is the amount of contiguous real storage used, in K-bytes.

PVTSZHI	NUM	4		PRIVATE*AREA SIZE*ABOVE 16MB

private area size, in bytes, above 16 megabytes.

PVTSZLOW	NUM	4		PRIVATE*AREA SIZE*BELOW 16MB

private area size, in bytes, below 16 megabytes.

PVTTOP	NUM	4		GETMAIN*SIZE*FROM TOP

if VIRTREAL= 'V' (virtual storage was specified), PVTTOP value is address space used, in K-bytes, from top of private area (that is, subpools 229, 239, 236-237, 253-255, the LSQA, and SWA). If VIRTREAL= 'R' (real storage was specified), the PVTTOP value is the amount of storage in K-bytes used that was not from the contiguous storage reserved for the program.

RACFGRUP	CHAR	8		RACF*GROUP*IDENTIFICATION

RACF group identification (zero if RACF is not enabled).

RACFTERM	CHAR	8		RACF/VTAM*TERMINAL*NAME USED

RACF terminal name used. This indicates the VTAM terminal name used by this TSO session. If you use RACF or a security package that enables the RACF exits, this variable is non-blank and can be used to identify and quantify VTAM terminal usage. The VTAM terminal name is actually associated with the physical port address on the control unit, so that recabling terminals can change the physical terminal that has this VTAM terminal name.

RACFUSER	CHAR	8		RACF*USER*IDENTIFICATION

RACF user identification (blank if RACF is not enabled).

RDRDEVCL	NUM	4	HEX2.	READER*DEVICE*CLASS

reader class.

RDRDEVTY	NUM	4	HEX2.	READER*DEVICE*TYPE

reader type.

RDRTM	NUM	4		READER*EVENT*DURATION

duration the MVS reader was active while reading this job. For a job read-in via RJE, the duration is how long the job took to be transmitted. The TYPE26 record for this job

Variable	Type	Length	Format	Label

identifies the remote (INROUTE) from which the job was read, and the number of cards (SPOOLCRD) processed.

READTIME   NUM   8   DATETIME19.2   READ-IN*OR LOGON*EVENT

job read-in (TSO LOGON) time stamp.

RECLAIMS   NUM   4   PAGES*RECLAIMED

pages reclaimed. See also TYPE71 appendix for discussion.

REGREQST   NUM   4   REGION*REQUESTED*IN JCL

region size established, in 1K units taken from REGION= parameter in JCL, and rounded up to a 4K boundary. If V=R, this is the amount of contiguous real storage reserved for the program. If the region requested was greater than 16 megabytes, the region established resides above 16 megabytes, and this field will contain a minimum value of 32 megabytes.

RESIDTM   NUM   4   TIME12.2   RESIDENT*IN REAL*STORAGE

duration step was resident in real storage. This value is accumulated by the SRM and it represents the absolute maximum duration that the program could have executed instructions. The difference between RESIDTM and CPUTM is the duration that the task was in memory but not dispatched, and it represents wait for CPU and wait for I/O completion, among other waits while in memory.

SERVUNIT   NUM   4   TOTAL*SERVICE*UNITS

total SRM service units consumed by this step. It is the sum of CPUUNITS, SRBUNITS, IOUNITS, and MSOUNITS.

SKIPFLAG   CHAR   1   TYPE 30*INTERVAL*SKIPPED?

a previous interval record was not written because an error occurred. The cumulative resource counts may be in error because the counters were cleared. This is decode of SMF30ISK.

SRBUNITS   NUM   4   CPU SRB*SERVICE*UNITS

SRM recorded SRB CPU service units consumed by this task. An SRB CPU service unit is defined as the number of SRB CPU seconds times the installation-specified SRBCOEFF coefficient (specified in the IEAIPSxx member of PARMLIB and reported in SAS data set TYPE72) times a machine-dependent constant (which is set at IPL time based on the CPU model and CPU version). SOURCLIB member TYPE7072 provides one source of the value of the machine-dependent constant, called SU_SEC, since it sets the number of service units generated by one second of CPU time.

STEPNAME   CHAR   8   STEP*NAME

step name appearing on the EXEC PGM= statement. Note that if this step executed a JCL procedure instead, this is not the stepname on that EXEC statement, but rather it is the stepname on the EXEC PGM= card within that JCL procedure. Note further that for a TSO session, the stepname is the TSO procedure name, either the default from UADS, or the user-supplied PR(name) value.

Variable	Type	Length	Format	Label
STEPNR	NUM	4		STEP*NUMBER

step number. This number is reset to 1 when a job is canceled and restarted, so that it is possible for the same job to have steps with duplicate values.

SUBSYS	CHAR	4		SUB*SYSTEM

subsystem. The value may be either JES2 or JES3.

SUBTYPE	NUM	4		RECORD*SUBTYPE

record subtype number. The possible values are:

value	meaning
2	interval record
3	interval between last interval and step termination
4	step termination
5	job termination
6	system address space (may not ever occur).

SWAPS	NUM	4		TIMES*TASK WAS*SWAPPED OUT

number of times this step was swapped out.

SWPAGINS	NUM	4		SWAP*PAGE*INS

number of pages swapped in.

SWPAGOUT	NUM	4		PAGE OUTS*TO SWAP*TASK OUT

number of pages swapped out.

SYSINCNT	NUM	4		CARD IMAGES*READ*BY PROGRAM

number of card-image records in DD DATA and DD * data sets read by the reader for this step.

SYSTEM	CHAR	4	4.	SYSTEM*ID

identification of the system on which the step executed.

TAPEDRVS	NUM	4		TAPE*DRIVES*ALLOCATED

number of tape drives allocated to this step. Note that in MVS/370, the IMACCHAN member must describe the installation's two-channel switches if the number of tape drives is to be counted correctly.

TAPNMNTS	NUM	4		SCRATCH*TAPE*MOUNTS

TAPE volumes mounted for nonspecific requests. This is a mount of a scratch volume since no specific volume serial number was requested. Only mount requests actually satisfied by volume verification are counted. If the wrong volume was mounted, this count is not incremented until the correct volume is verified.

Variable	Type	Length	Format	Label
TAPSMNTS	NUM	4		PRIVATE*TAPE*MOUNTS

TAPE volumes mounted for specific volume requests. This is a mount of a private volume since the specific volume serial number was requested. Only mount requests actually satisfied by volume verification are counted. If the wrong volume was mounted, this count is not incremented until the correct volume is verified.

| TGETS | NUM | 4 | | TERMINAL*READS*(TGETS) |

TSO only. The number of terminals TGETS satisfied (that is, the number of times that the TSO user pushed the ENTER key).

| TPUTS | NUM | 4 | | TERMINAL*WRITES*(TPUTS) |

TSO only. The number of terminal TPUTS issued (that is, the number of times that output lines were sent to the terminal).

| TYPETASK | CHAR | 4 | | TYPE*OF*TASK |

type of task. This is indicated by the first four characters of the JES job identification. The possible values are:

value	meaning
JOB	batch job
TSU	TSO session (acronym is for TSO "User")
STC	started (system) task.

| USRSZHI | NUM | 4 | | USER*SUBPOOLS*ABOVE 16MB |

maximum virtual storage in bytes allocated from user subpools above 16 megabytes.

| USRSZLOW | NUM | 4 | | USER*SUBPOOLS*BELOW 16MB |

maximum virtual storage in bytes allocated from user subpools below 16 megabytes.

| VERSION | CHAR | 2 | | VERSION*NUMBER |

record version number.

| VIOPAGIN | NUM | 4 | | VIO*PAGE-INS |

virtual I/O page-ins.

| VIOPAGOU | NUM | 4 | | VIO*PAGE-OUTS |

virtual I/O page-outs.

| VIORECLM | NUM | 4 | | VIO*RECLAIMS |

virtual I/O page reclaims.

Variable	Type	Length	Format	Label
VIRTREAL	CHAR	1		VIRTUAL*OR*REAL?

type of address space requested.

value	requested
R	real storage (ADDRSPC=R specified)
V	virtual storage.

TYPE31
TSO Initialization

The TYPE31 data set contains one observation for each type 31 SMF record, written when TSO is started. TYPE31 contains several TSO option values that are important to TSO performance.

Variable	Type	Length	Format	Label
BUFFSIZE	NUM	4		TSB*BUFFER*SIZE

size of the time-sharing buffer in bytes.

LWAITHI	NUM	4		LWAITHI*BUFFERS

maximum number of input buffers allowed per terminal before the LWAIT event. LWAIT results in the terminal's keyboard locking because the terminal user filled all the available input buffers. The user LWAITs until LWAITLO (see below) is reached.

LWAITLO	NUM	4		LWAITLO*BUFFERS

RESTART threshold. The number of input buffers that must be freed (for example, by reading in the data) so the user can be freed from LWAIT.

MINBUFF	NUM	4		BUFFERS*ON THE*FREE QUEUE

number of buffers reserved on the free queue. If fewer than this number of buffers are available, the entire TSO system must LWAIT.

NRBUFFER	NUM	4		NUMBER*TSB*BUFFERS

number of time-sharing buffers.

OWAITHI	NUM	4		OWAITHI*BUFFERS

maximum number of output buffers allowed per terminal before the OWAIT event. OWAIT results in the program suspending during I/O processing to the terminal because no output buffers were available. The user must OWAIT until OWAITLO (see below) is reached.

OWAITLO	NUM	4		OWAITLO*BUFFERS

OWAIT threshold. The number of output buffers that must be freed (for example, by putting the data to the terminal) so the user can be freed from OWAIT.

SMFTIME	NUM	8	DATETIME19.2	SMF*RECORD*TIME STAMP

MODIFY TCAM command event time stamp.

SYSTEM	CHAR	4	4.	SYSTEM*ID

identification of system on which TSO was started.

Variable	Type	Length	Format	Label
TSBSIZE	NUM	4		SIZE*OF*TSB

  size of timesharing buffers in bytes.

TYPE32
TSO Command Record

The TYPE32 data set contains one observation for each command segment in each type 32 SMF record. An SMF type 32 record is written at the normal or abnormal end of a TSO session or at the end of an accounting interval if interval accounting was requested for the TSO subsystem in SMFPRM*xx*. There is a command segment for each command used in each session or interval. Type 32 records are written only if TSO/E is installed in MVS/XA.

Type 32 records can be created with the count of commands by command name and, if DETAIL is specified, to create CPU and I/O measures by command name. There is no measure of response time available in the type 32 data. TSO commands issued from a batch job do not create type 32 records.

The session end record (subtype 2 or 4) contains all resources in this session. The interval records (subtype 1 or 3), like the type 30 interval records, contain only the resources used in the interval and do not contain a start of interval time stamp.

The data for the type 32 record are kept in CSA, and it has been determined that the type 32 record consumes a great deal of CSA space per user. Since the command segment itself is 40 bytes per command, a large TSO system could require significant virtual storage for these data. It would be best to quantify the virtual storage cost at your own installation since it is the number of unique commands issued by each user that drives up the virtual storage cost, and that number cannot be predicted. You might want to collect and analyze one day's type 32 data before deciding whether or not to create type 32 records everyday.

Although there are good data in the type 32, the absence of response measures makes its use relatively infrequent. The variable SUBTYPE identifies whether the observation is a session or interval record and whether or not DETAIL was specified.

Variable	Type	Length	Format	Label
ALOCTIME	NUM	8	DATETIME19.2	START OF*ALLOCATION*EVENT

allocation time stamp of TSO session.

Variable	Type	Length	Format	Label
CMDCOUNT	NUM	4		COUNT*OF*COMMANDS

count of times command was issued during this interval or session. Note that this value differs from the number of transactions as counted by the SRM, which will be in the type 72 RMF record. See SRMTRANS for that count.

Variable	Type	Length	Format	Label
COMMAND	CHAR	8		COMMAND*NAME

name of the command or alias executed. For example:

LOGON	contains all resources from the start of a session until the first command is obtained
**OTHER	counts commands not included in CSECT IEEMB846
EXEC	counts invalid or unknown commands.

Variable	Type	Length	Format	Label
CPUSRBTM	NUM	4	TIME12.2	TASK*CPU SRB*TIME

duration that the CPU was executing instructions under a Service Request Block (SRB) during this interval or session. Missing if DETAIL is not specified.

Variable	Type	Length	Format	Label
CPUTCBTM	NUM	4	TIME12.2	TASK*CPU TCB*TIME

duration that the CPU was executing instructions under the Task Control Block (TCB) during this interval or session. Missing if DETAIL is not specified.

Variable	Type	Length	Format	Label
CPUTM	NUM	4	TIME12.2	TOTAL*CPU*TIME

duration that the CPU was executing instructions for this interval or session. Sum of CPUSRBTM and CPUTCBTM. Missing if DETAIL is not specified.

Variable	Type	Length	Format	Label
EXCPS	NUM	4		EXCP*COUNT

EXCPs issued by this command during this interval or session. Missing if DETAIL is not specified.

Variable	Type	Length	Format	Label
INITTIME	NUM	8	DATETIME19.2	STEP*INITIATE*EVENT

initiation time stamp of this TSO session.

Variable	Type	Length	Format	Label
INPRTY	NUM	4		INPUT*PRIORITY

job selection priority at LOGON time.

Variable	Type	Length	Format	Label
IOTMTOTL	NUM	4	TIME12.2	CONNECT*TIME*ALL DEVICES

total IOTM (device connect time) measured for this interval or session. This value is also called the total address space IOTM count. It represents SMF's count of how many seconds data transfer was occurring to or from this TSO session during this interval or session. Missing if DETAIL is not specified.

Variable	Type	Length	Format	Label
JESNR	NUM	4		JES*NUMBER

JES-assigned TSU number.

Variable	Type	Length	Format	Label
JOB	CHAR	8		JOB NAME*OR*TSO USER

TSO user ID.

Variable	Type	Length	Format	Label

LOADTIME   NUM   8   DATETIME19.2   PROGRAM*FETCH*EVENT
load (problem program start) time stamp of this session.

LOCLINFO   CHAR   8   LOCAL*INSTALLATION*FIELD
locally-defined field, filled in by an installation-written SMF exit routine.

PERFGRP   NUM   4   PERFORMANCE*GROUP
performance group where this command executed.

PGMRNAME   CHAR   20   PROGRAMMER*NAME*FIELD
programmer name field of TSO session.

PRODUCT   CHAR   8   PRODUCT*NAME
product name that produced this record.

PROGRAM   CHAR   8   PROGRAM*NAME
program name (PGM=) from EXEC statement. IKJEFT01 is the normal TSO TMP
program name.

RACFGRUP   CHAR   8   RACF*GROUP*IDENTIFICATION
RACF group identification (zero if RACF is not active).

RACFTERM   CHAR   8   RACF/VTAM*TERMINAL*NAME USED
RACF terminal name used. This value indicates the VTAM terminal name used by this
TSO session. If you use RACF or a security package that enables the RACF exits, this
variable is non-blank and can be used to identify and quantify VTAM terminal usage. The
VTAM terminal name is actually associated with the physical port address on the control
unit so that recabling terminals can change the physical terminal that has this VTAM
terminal name.

RACFUSER   CHAR   8   RACF*USER*IDENTIFICATION
RACF user identification.

READTIME   NUM   8   DATETIME19.2   READ-IN*OR LOGON*EVENT
TSO logon time stamp.

SMFTIME   NUM   8   DATETIME19.2   SMF*RECORD*TIME STAMP
time this record was written to SMF, either end of session or end of interval. Since there is
no beginning of interval time stamp, if this value is an interval record, then it becomes the
end time of one interval and the start time of the next one. See SUBTYPE.

SRMTRANS   NUM   4   TRANSACTION*COUNT*BY SRM
SRM transactions counted for this command. This value differs from the number of times
the command name was entered. See CMDCOUNT. Missing if DETAIL is not specified.

Variable	Type	Length	Format	Label

STEPNAME   CHAR   8   STEP*NAME

step name of the step executing these commands (from the EXEC=PGM JCL statement). Note that if this step executed a JCL procedure instead, this value is not the step name on that EXEC statement; rather, it is the step name on the EXEC PGM= card within that JCL procedure. Also, for a TSO session, the step name is the TSO procedure name, either the default from UADS or the user-supplied PR(name) value.

STEPNR   NUM   4   STEP*NUMBER

step number of this step within this TSO session. The number is usually one.

SUBSYS   CHAR   4   SUB*SYSTEM

subsystem name, for example, TSO.

SUBTYPE   NUM   4   SUBTYPE*ID

type of command record:

value	meaning
1	interval record, no DETAIL statistics
2	total session record, no DETAIL statistics
3	interval record with DETAIL statistics
4	total session record with DETAIL statistics.

SYSTEM   CHAR   4   4.   SYSTEM*ID

identification of the system on which the job executed.

TGETS   NUM   4   TERMINAL*READS*(TGETS)

number of terminals GETS satisfied (that is, the number of times the TSO user pushed the ENTER key) during this interval or session. DETAIL must be specified to obtain this count. Missing if DETAIL is not specified.

TPUTS   NUM   4   TERMINAL*WRITES*(TPUTS)

number of terminal PUTS issued (that is, the number of times one or more lines were sent to the terminal) during this interval or session. DETAIL must be specified to obtain this count. Missing if DETAIL is not specified.

TYPETASK   CHAR   4   TYPE*OF*TASK

type of task. This information is indicated by the first four characters of the JES job identification. The possible values are:

value	meaning
JOB	batch job
TSU	TSO session (acronym is for TSO "U"ser)
STC	started (system) task.

Variable	Type	Length	Format	Label
VERSION	CHAR	2		VERSION*NUMBER

record version number.

TYPE38EX
Exception Statistics

The TYPE38EX data set contains one observation for each type 38 SMF record containing exception statistics, written by the Network Performance Analyzer Field Developed Program after an NPA interval with an exceeded exception threshold. Data sets TYPE38IN and TYPE38NC are also created from type 38 SMF records

Variable	Type	Length	Format	Label

NPAADDR　　CHAR　2　HEX4.　　　　　ADDRESS

　　　resource network address from the Resource Resolution Table.

NPADATA　　NUM　4　MG038DA32.　　EXCEPTION*EVENT

　　　exception event that created data. The internal and formatted values are:

value	formatted value
04X	004X:NEGATIVE POLL RATE/MIN
08X	008X:POSITIVE POLL RATE/MIN
0CX	00CX:MESSAGES/MINUTE
10X	010X:BYTES/SEC
14X	014X:LINE UTILIZATION (PERCENT)
18X	018X:ERROR COUNT
1CX	01CX:PERCENT FREE BUFFERS
20X	02CX:3705 UTILIZATION (PERCENT)
24X	024X:OUTBOUND QUEUE LENGTH
28X	028X:PERCENT OF TIME IN SLOWDOWN.

NPAFWDTM　NUM　4　TIME12.2　　　　FORWARD*TO VTAM*TIME STAMP

　　　time when forward RU was sent to NCP to collect data.

NPAINTCT　　NUM　4　　　　　　　　INTERVAL*COUNT

　　　if a totals record, indicates the number of intervals accumulated in this record. This value times LOGINTTM is the expected collection time for this record.

NPAINTTM　　NUM　4　TIME12.2　　　　INTERVAL*DURATION

　　　expected interval time. Expected NPA interval size (duration).

NPALOWER　　NUM　4　　　　　　　　LOWER*THRESHOLD*VALUE

　　　minimum or low criteria for this exception. Compare this threshold value to NPAMONVL.

Variable	Type	Length	Format	Label
NPALSPRF	NUM	4		RECEIVE*SPEED*(BITS PER SECOND)

receiving line speed in bits per second.

Variable	Type	Length	Format	Label
NPALSPSF	NUM	4		SEND*SPEED*(BITS PER SECOND)

sending line speed in bits per second.

Variable	Type	Length	Format	Label
NPAMMXF	NUM	4		MAXIMUM*FREE*BUFFERS

maximum number of free buffers. This field existed in earlier versions of NPA but is not documented in SB21-2479. It is used only to calculate the percentage of free buffers.

Variable	Type	Length	Format	Label
NPAMONVL	NUM	4		MONITORED*EXCEPTION*VALUE

actual value measured that caused this exception. The actual exception is described in the NPADATA value.

Variable	Type	Length	Format	Label
NPANAME	CHAR	8		VTAM*NAME

resource network name.

Variable	Type	Length	Format	Label
NPANCPNM	CHAR	8		NCP*NAME

name of the NCP for this resource.

Variable	Type	Length	Format	Label
NPANTYPE	NUM	4	MG038NT31.	TYPE OF*NETWORK*RESOURCE

type of network resource. The formatted and internal values are:

value	formatted value
81X	081X:SDLC-3705/NCP RESOURCE
80X	080X:BSC -3705/NCP RESOURCE
43X	043X:SDLC NPA PSEUDO LINK
41X	041X:SDLC-LINK
40X	040X:BSC -LINE
21X	021X:SDLC-PHYSICAL UNIT
20X	020X:BSC -CLUSTER
11X	011X:SDLC-LOGICAL UNIT
10X	010X:BSC -TERMINAL
09X	009X:SDLC-COMPONENT
08X	008X:BSC -COMPONENT
04X	004X:SDLC-SWITCHED RESOURCE
03X	003X:SDLC-NPA PSEUDO DEVICE
02X	002X:NPA PSEUDO DEVICE.

Variable	Type	Length	Format	Label
NPAQUE	NUM	4		INTERVAL*NUMBER*OF THIS DATA

interval number for this collection.

Variable	Type	Length	Format	Label
NPATM	NUM	4	TIME12.2	ACTUAL*COLLECTION*TIME STAMP

time (HH:MM:SS) of this log record.

Variable	Type	Length	Format	Label
NPATODTM	NUM	4	TIME12.2	TIME*OF*DAY

time (HH:MM:SS) the record was moved from VTAM to SMF.

Variable	Type	Length	Format	Label
NPATYPE	NUM	4	MG038TY23.	TYPE*OF LOG*RECORD

type of network resource. The formatted and internal values are:

value	formatted value
81X	081X:SDLC-3705/NCP RESOURCE
80X	080X:BSC -3705/NCP RESOURCE
43X	043X:SDLC NPA PSEUDO LINK
41X	041X:SDLC-LINK
40X	040X:BSC -LINE
21X	021X:SDLC-PHYSICAL UNIT
20X	020X:BSC -CLUSTER
11X	011X:SDLC-LOGICAL UNIT
10X	010X:BSC -TERMINAL
09X	009X:SDLC-COMPONENT
08X	008X:BSC -COMPONENT
04X	004X:SDLC-SWITCHED RESOURCE
03X	003X:SDLC-NPA PSEUDO DEVICE
02X	002X:NPA PSEUDO DEVICE.

Variable	Type	Length	Format	Label
NPAUPPER	NUM	4		UPPER*THRESHOLD*VALUE

maximum or upper criteria for this exception. Compare this threshold value with
NPAMONVL.

Variable	Type	Length	Format	Label
SMFTIME	NUM	8	DATETIME19.2	SMF*RECORD*TIME STAMP

time stamp when record was actually written by SMF.

Variable	Type	Length	Format	Label
STARTIME	NUM	8	DATETIME19.2	START OF*INTERVAL

start time of this NPA interval. The value is calculated by subtracting the interval
NPAINTTM from sending time NPAFWDTM and assuming they occurred on the same
date as SMFTIME.

Variable	Type	Length	Format	Label
SYSTEM	CHAR	4	4.	SYSTEM*ID

identification of system on which this record was written and system on which this NCP/VTAM executed.

TYPE38IN
Interval Resources Statistics

The TYPE38IN data set contains one observation for each type 38 SMF record, containing interval resource statistics on lines, clusters, and terminals. A type 38 SMF interval resource record is written by the Network Performance Analyzer Field Developed Program after each NPA interval. The record describes the utilization and queuing of the line or link, the Physical Unit (PU) or cluster, or the Logical Unit (LU) or terminal for which NPA monitoring was requested. The data allow analysis of the percent of time data bytes were in transit to and from the device/cluster/line (PCTBUSY), the total message traffic (NPATPS and NPATPR), and the total bytes sent and received in these messages (NPATBS and NPATBR). Data sets TYPE38EX and TYPE38NC are also created from type 38 SMF records.

Variable	Type	Length	Format	Label
NPAADDR	CHAR	2	HEX4.	ADDRESS

resource network address from the Resource Resolution Table.

NPAERR	NUM	4		ERROR*COUNT

error count during this interval.

NPAFWDTM	NUM	4	TIME12.2	FORWARD*TO VTAM*TIME STAMP

time when forward RU was sent to NCP to collect data.

NPAINTCT	NUM	4		INTERVAL*COUNT

if a totals record, the number of intervals accumulated in this record. This value times LOGINTTM is the expected collection time for this record.

NPAINTTM	NUM	4	TIME12.2	INTERVAL*DURATION

expected NPA interval size (duration).

NPALSPRF	NUM	4		RECEIVE*SPEED*(BITS PER SECOND)

receiving line speed in bits per second.

NPALSPSF	NUM	4		SEND*SPEED*(BITS PER SECOND)

sending line speed in bits per second.

NPANAME	CHAR	8		VTAM*NAME

resource network name.

Variable	Type	Length	Format	Label
NPANCPNM	CHAR	8		NCP*NAME

name of the NCP for this resource.

Variable	Type	Length	Format	Label
NPANTYPE	NUM	4	MG038NT31.	TYPE OF*NETWORK*RESOURCE

type of network resource. The formatted and internal values are:

value	formatted value
81X	081X:SDLC-3705/NCP RESOURCE
80X	080X:BSC -3705/NCP RESOURCE
43X	043X:SDLC NPA PSEUDO LINK
41X	041X:SDLC-LINK
40X	040X:BSC -LINE
21X	021X:SDLC-PHYSICAL UNIT
20X	020X:BSC -CLUSTER
11X	011X:SDLC-LOGICAL UNIT
10X	010X:BSC -TERMINAL
09X	009X:SDLC-COMPONENT
08X	008X:BSC -COMPONENT
04X	004X:SDLC-SWITCHED RESOURCE
03X	003X:SDLC-NPA PSEUDO DEVICE
02X	002X:NPA PSEUDO DEVICE.

Variable	Type	Length	Format	Label
NPAPPC	NUM	4		POSITIVE*POLL*COUNT

positive poll count during this interval.

Variable	Type	Length	Format	Label
NPAQUE	NUM	4		INTERVAL*NUMBER*OF THIS DATA

interval number for this collection.

Variable	Type	Length	Format	Label
NPARBC	NUM	4		RETRANSMIT*PIU*COUNT

retransmitted byte count.

Variable	Type	Length	Format	Label
NPAROQ	NUM	4		RESOURCE*OUTBOUNT*QUEUE

resource outbound queue length.

Variable	Type	Length	Format	Label
NPARPC	NUM	4		RETRANSMIT*PIU*COUNT

retransmit PIU count.

Variable	Type	Length	Format	Label
NPATBR	NUM	4		TOTAL*BYTES*RECEIVED

total bytes received.

Variable	Type	Length	Format	Label
NPATBS	NUM	4		TOTAL*BYTES*SENT

total bytes sent.

| NPATM | NUM | 4 | TIME12.2 | ACTUAL*COLLECTION*TIME STAMP |

time (HH:MM:SS) of this log record.

| NPATODTM | NUM | 4 | TIME12.2 | TIME*OF*DAY |

time (HH:MM:SS) record was moved from VTAM to SMF.

| NPATPC | NUM | 4 | | TOTAL*POLL*COUNT |

total poll count during this interval.

| NPATPR | NUM | 4 | | TOTAL*MESSAGES*RECEIVED |

total messages received during this interval.

| NPATPS | NUM | 4 | | TOTAL*MESSAGES*SENT |

total messages sent during this interval.

| NPATYPE | NUM | 4 | MG038TY23. | TYPE*OF LOG*RECORD |

type of log record. Internal and formatted values are:

value	formatted value
01X	01X:START COLLECT RECORD
04X	04X:INTERVAL RECORD
08X	08X:TOTAL RECORD
0CX	0CX:EXCEPTION RECORD
0FX	0FX:STOP COLLECT RECORD.

| PCTBUSY | NUM | 4 | | PERCENT*BUSY |

percent line/cluster/terminal was actually busy with data. This value is calculated from bytes sent and received and line speed, and it does not necessarily include all communications to or from the line/cluster/terminal (such as modem turnaround time for HDX).

| SMFTIME | NUM | 8 | DATETIME19.2 | SMF*RECORD*TIME STAMP |

time stamp when record was actually written by SMF.

| STARTIME | NUM | 8 | DATETIME19.2 | START OF*INTERVAL |

start time of this NPA interval. Calculated by subtracting the interval NPAINTTM from sending time NPAFWDTM and assuming they occurred on the same date as SMFTIME.

| SYSTEM | CHAR | 4 | 4. | SYSTEM*ID |

identification of system on which this record was written.

TYPE38NC
NCP Resource Statistics

The TYPE38NC data set contains one observation for each type 38 SMF record containing NCP resource statistics, written by the Network Performance Analyzer Field Developed Program after each NPA interval. The record describes the utilization and queuing of the NCP itself.

Of special interest are PCTBUSY, the percent of the time the NCP was busy, and PCTSLOW, the percent of time the NCP was overloaded and had entered slowdown. These data are an excellent, first-level source of performance and capacity data for the NCP program in the 37xx processor. Data sets TYPE38EX and TYPE38IN are also created from type 38 SMF records.

Variable	Type	Length	Format	Label
NPAADDR	CHAR	2	HEX4.	ADDRESS

resource network address from the Resource Resolution Table.

NPACHQ	NUM	4		HOLD*QUEUE*LENGTH

NCP channel hold queue length.

NPACIQ	NUM	4		INTERMEDIATE*QUEUE*LENGTH

NCP channel intermediate queue length.

NPAFBH	NUM	4		MAXIMUM*FREE*BUFFERS

free buffer high water mark.

NPAFBL	NUM	4		MINIMUM*FREE*BUFFERS

free buffer low water mark.

NPAFBQ	NUM	4		FREE*BUFFER*QUEUE

free buffer queue length.

NPAFCCTM	NUM	4	TIME12.2	FREE*CYCLE*DURATION

free cycle time (duration).

NPAFWDTM	NUM	4	TIME12.2	FORWARD*TO VTAM*TIME STAMP

time when forward RU was sent to NCP to collect data.

NPAINTCT	NUM	4		INTERVAL*COUNT

if a totals record, the number of intervals accumulated in this record. This value times LOGINTTM is the expected collection time for this record.

Variable	Type	Length	Format	Label
NPAINTTM	NUM	4	TIME12.2	INTERVAL*DURATION

expected NPA interval size (duration).

| NPALSPRF | NUM | 4 | | RECEIVE*SPEED*(BITS PER SECOND) |

receiving line speed in bits per second.

| NPALSPSF | NUM | 4 | | SEND*SPEED*(BITS PER SECOND) |

sending line speed in bits per second.

| NPAMXF | NUM | 4 | | MAXIMUM*AVAILABLE*NCP BUFFERS |

maximum available NCP buffers.

| NPANAME | CHAR | 8 | | VTAM*NAME |

resource network name.

| NPANCPNM | CHAR | 8 | | NCP*NAME |

name of the NCP for this resource.

| NPANTYPE | NUM | 4 | MG038NT31. | TYPE OF*NETWORK*RESOURCE |

type of network resource. The formatted and internal values are:

value	formatted value
81X	081X:SDLC-3705/NCP RESOURCE
80X	080X:BSC -3705/NCP RESOURCE
43X	043X:SDLC NPA PSEUDO LINK
41X	041X:SDLC-LINK
40X	040X:BSC -LINE
21X	021X:SDLC-PHYSICAL UNIT
20X	020X:BSC -CLUSTER
11X	011X:SDLC-LOGICAL UNIT
10X	010X:BSC -TERMINAL
09X	009X:SDLC-COMPONENT
08X	008X:BSC -COMPONENT
04X	004X:SDLC-SWITCHED RESOURCE
03X	003X:SDLC-NPA PSEUDO DEVICE
02X	002X:NPA PSEUDO DEVICE.

| NPAQUE | NUM | 4 | | INTERVAL*NUMBER*OF THIS DATA |

interval number for this collection.

Variable	Type	Length	Format	Label
NPASLHTM	NUM	4	TIME12.2	DURATION*NCP IN*SLOWDOWN

slowdown duration. This value is a performance degradation since NCP enters slowdown whenever it cannot handle all requests.

NPASLM	NUM	4		FREE BUFFERS*WHEN ENTERED*SLOWDOWN

number of free buffers when NCP entered slowdown.

NPATM	NUM	4	TIME12.2	ACTUAL*COLLECTION*TIME STAMP

time (HH:MM:SS) of this log record.

NPATODTM	NUM	4	TIME12.2	TIME*OF*DAY

time (HH:MM:SS) record was moved from VTAM to SMF.

NPATYPE	NUM	4	MG038TY23.	TYPE*OF LOG*RECORD

type of log record. Internal and formatted values are:

value	formatted value
01X	01X:START COLLECT RECORD
04X	04X:INTERVAL RECORD
08X	08X:TOTAL RECORD
0CX	0CX:EXCEPTION RECORD
0FX	0FX:STOP COLLECT RECORD.

PCTBUSY	NUM	4		PERCENT*BUSY

percent of interval during which NCP was busy, that is, executing.

PCTSLOW	NUM	4		PERCENT*IN*SLOWDOWN

percent of the interval during which NCP was in slowdown.

SMFTIME	NUM	8	DATETIME19.2	SMF*RECORD*TIME STAMP

time stamp when record was actually written by SMF.

STARTIME	NUM	8	DATETIME19.2	START OF*INTERVAL

start time of this NPA interval. Calculated by subtracting the interval NPAINTTM from sending time NPAFWDTM and assuming they occurred on the same date as SMFTIME.

SYSTEM	CHAR	4	4.	SYSTEM*ID

identification of system on which this record was written and system on which this NCP/VTAM executed.

TYPE40
Dynamic Allocation

The TYPE40 data set contains one observation for each type 40 SMF record, written for each dynamic allocation that is freed (unallocated), concatenated, or deconcatenated. TYPE40 contains observations for jobs as well as for TSO sessions since both tasks can issue dynamic allocation.

Type 40 is necessary if type 4 records are used for step data to account for all EXCPs, especially for TSO sessions. When a dynamic allocation is freed, the EXCPs to that allocation are contained in TYPE40. When any dynamic allocation is deconcatenated, all EXCPs thus far are written out in the type 40 record and the TIOT (from which type 4/34 is written) EXCP counters are zeroed. Thus, it is necessary to sum the EXCPs in TYPE40 with the EXCPs in TYPE434 to get total EXCPs for a task. Note: in type 30 data, dynamic EXCPs are captured and EXCP counters are not zeroed. Thus there is little value in the type 40 record now, provided your accounting and performance are based (as they must be in the future) on type 30 records.

Variable	Type	Length	Format	Label
DYNAM	CHAR	6		TYPE*DYNAMIC*EVENT

type of event.

value	meaning
CONCAT	concatenation
DECAT	deconcatenation
UNALOC	unallocation.

Variable	Type	Length	Format	Label
D3330DRV	NUM	4		MOUNTABLE*3330 DRIVES*ALLOCATED

number of different 3330 mountable disk drives allocated to this DD in this single dynamic allocation, where mountable is defined by an explicit list of unit addresses in the IMAC3330 member. This value could be a poor measure since there may be repeated dynamic allocations to the same device, yet separate observations in TYPE40 will show a count of one. It will identify allocations to the devices in IMAC3330, but it cannot be summed across the job to get an accurate count.

Variable	Type	Length	Format	Label
ERROR	CHAR	13		EXCP*COUNT*ERROR?

possible error in EXCP count. The values are blank or EXCPCNT WRONG.

Variable	Type	Length	Format	Label
EXCPCOMM	NUM	4		EXCPS*COUNT*COMMUNICATIONS

EXCPs to communications devices.

Variable	Type	Length	Format	Label
EXCPDASD	NUM	4		EXCPS*COUNT*DASD

sum of EXCPs to 2305, 3330, 3340, 3350, 3375, and 3380 devices.

| EXCPGRAF | NUM | 4 | | EXCPS*COUNT*GRAPHICS |

EXCPs to graphics devices.

| EXCPMSS | NUM | 4 | | EXCPS*COUNT*MSS |

EXCPs to mass storage volumes.

| EXCPTAPE | NUM | 4 | | EXCPS*COUNT*TAPE |

EXCPs to tape devices.

| EXCPTODD | NUM | 4 | | TOTAL EXCPS*IN ALL*DD SEGMENTS |

total EXCPs to all UCB segments in this dynamic allocation.

| EXCPUREC | NUM | 4 | | EXCPS*COUNT*UNIT RECORD |

EXCPs to unit record devices directly allocated to the tasks that issued this dynamic allocation (that is, does not include EXCPs to JES devices since they are not dynamically allocated).

| EXCPVIO | NUM | 4 | | EXCPS*COUNT*VIO |

EXCPs to virtual I/O.

| EXCP2305 | NUM | 4 | | EXCPS*COUNT*2305 |

EXCPs to 2305 devices.

| EXCP3330 | NUM | 4 | | EXCPS*COUNT*3330 |

EXCPs to 3330 devices.

| EXCP3340 | NUM | 4 | | EXCPS*COUNT*3340 |

EXCPs to 3340 devices.

| EXCP3350 | NUM | 4 | | EXCPS*COUNT*3350 |

EXCPs to 3350 devices.

| EXCP3375 | NUM | 4 | | EXCPS*COUNT*3375 |

EXCPs to 3375 devices.

| EXCP3380 | NUM | 4 | | EXCPS*COUNT*3380 |

EXCPs to 3380 devices.

| JOB | CHAR | 8 | | JOB NAME*OR*TSO USER |

job name (batch); user ID (TSO).

Variable	Type	Length	Format	Label
NDASDDD	NUM	4		NUMBER*DASD*DD CARDS

number of DASD devices allocated in this dynamic allocation.

| NTAPEDD | NUM | 4 | | NUMBER*TAPE*DD CARDS |

number of tape devices allocated in this dynamic allocation.

| NUMDD | NUM | 4 | | NUMBER*ALL*DD CARDS |

total number of devices allocated in this dynamic allocation.

| READTIME | NUM | 8 | DATETIME19.2 | READ-IN*OR LOGON*EVENT |

job read-in (TSO LOGON) time stamp.

| SMFTIME | NUM | 8 | DATETIME19.2 | SMF*RECORD*TIME STAMP |

event time stamp.

| STEPNR | NUM | 4 | | STEP*NUMBER |

step number.

| SYSTEM | CHAR | 4 | 4. | SYSTEM*ID |

identification of system on which dynamic allocation occurred.

| TAPEDRVS | NUM | 4 | | TAPE*DRIVES*ALLOCATED |

number of different tape drives allocated in this dynamic allocation.

TYPE43PC
VSPC Start/Modify/Stop

The TYPE43PC data set contains one observation for each type 43, 44, or 45 SMF record written by the interactive system, Virtual Storage Personal Computing (VSPC) Program Product. Note that other subsystems write type 43 and 45 records; these are described in other appendices.

A type 43 record is written whenever VSPC is started; a type 44 when VSPC is modified; and type 45 when VSPC terminates abnormally or by a HALT VSPC command.

These records are useful in tracking availability of that on-line system.

Variable	Type	Length	Format	Label
EVENT	CHAR	16		EVENT*WHICH*OCCURRED

event for which record was written. The possible values are:

	STARTUP	VSPC
	MODIFY	VSPC
	TERMINATION	VSPC

Variable	Type	Length	Format	Label
HALTUSER	NUM	4		USER*ISSUING*HALT

user identification of the user issuing HALT.

Variable	Type	Length	Format	Label
NRLOGDON	NUM	4		NR VSPC*USERS*LOGGED ON

number of users logged on at start of termination.

Variable	Type	Length	Format	Label
OPTIONS	CHAR	73		VSPC*OPTIONS

VSPC options at start or modify. See VSPC source module ASUIOP to decode.

Variable	Type	Length	Format	Label
SMFTIME	NUM	8	DATETIME19.2	SMF*RECORD*TIME STAMP

time this event occurred.

Variable	Type	Length	Format	Label
SYSTEM	CHAR	4	4.	SYSTEM*ID

identification of the system on which VSPC executed.

Variable	Type	Length	Format	Label
TERMREAS	CHAR	10		REASON*VSPC*STOPPED

reason VSPC terminated. The possible values are:

        ABNORMAL
    HALT/NOSAVE
        HALTED
        STOPPED

Variable	Type	Length	Format	Label
VSPCPROC	CHAR	8		VSPC*PROCEDURE*NAME

procedure name started or modified.

TYPE4345
JES2 Start/Stop

The TYPE4345 data set contains one observation for each type 43 or 45 SMF record written by JES2 or JES3. (Other subsystems, such as VSPC, write type 43 and 45 records and are included in other sections of chapter forty.

A type 43 SMF record is written by JES2 when:

- an S JES2 command is issued to MVS to start JES2
- a $E SYS command is issued to JES to reclaim the job processing that was being done on the named system in a multi-access spool complex.

A type 43 SMF record is written by JES3 when JES3 is initialized.

A type 45 SMF record is written by JES2 when:

- a $P JES2 command is issued to JES2 to withdraw JES2 from the system
- an abnormal termination of JES2 occurs, provided JES2 retains control long enough to write the record.

A type 45 SMF record is written by JES3 when JES3 is terminated.

TYPE4345 contains options and descriptions that are useful when tracking subsystem availability, JES reliability, and operator activity in starting and stopping JES.

Variable	Type	Length	Format	Label
AUTOINIT	CHAR	1		JES*AUTOMATIC*INITIATOR?

JES2 only. Start option. Request automatic initiator. The values are either blank (no) or Y (yes).

Variable	Type	Length	Format	Label
CMD	NUM	4	MG043CM21.	COMMAND*ISSUED*(FORMATTED)

command or event causing the record. This variable is formatted with an MG format in SASLIB.

internal value	formatted value
1	1:$P (STOP) JES2
2	2:JES2 ABENDED
3	3:$E (RECLAIM) JES2
4	4:$S (START) JES2
5	5:P (STOP) JES3
6	6:JES3 ABENDED

Variable	Type	Length	Format	Label
		7		7:INTERCHANGE SYSTEMS
		8		8:S (START) JES3.

COLDSTRT   CHAR   1   JES*COLD*START?

JES start option. Cold start (that is, all present work is lost.) The values are either blank (no) or Y (yes).

CONDCODE   NUM   4   HEX4.   COMPLETION*CONDITION*CODE

JES2 only. Completion code when JES2 terminates abnormally.

FORMAT   CHAR   1   FORMAT*THE JES*SPOOL?

JES2 only. Start option. Format the spool (that is, wipe out all unexecuted input and unprinted output). This step should not be taken lightly. The values are blank (no) or Y (yes).

HOTSTRT   CHAR   1   JES*HOT*START?

JES3 only. Start option. Hot start (that is, quick recovery). The values are blank (no) and Y (yes).

INITDECK   CHAR   1   JES*INITDECK*OPTION

JES3 only. JES3 initialization deck origin type (taken from operator's response to WTOR macro). See MEMBER.

value	meaning	MEMBER contains
N	JCL in JES3 procedure	member name
M	data set in JES3 procedure	member name
U	unit at specified address	unit address.

LISTCARD   CHAR   1   JES*LISTCARD*OPTION?

JES2 only. Start option. List replacement card option. The values are blank (no) or Y (yes).

MEMBER   CHAR   8   PDS*MEMBER*NAME

JES3 only. JES3 initialization deck origin location. See INITDECK variable for description of contents.

PROCESOR   CHAR   11   JES*PROCESSOR*TYPE

JES3 only. Processor:

value	meaning
JES3 GLOBAL	JES3 global processor
JES3 LOCAL	JES3 local processor
LOCAL RESET	local processor is being reset to global.

Variable	Type	Length	Format	Label
PROCNAME	CHAR	4		JES*PROCEDURE*NAME

JES3 only. JES3 procedure name.

| QUEUEANL | CHAR | 1 | | JES*QUEUE*ANALYSIS? |

JES3 only. Start is with JES3 queue analysis. Values are blank (no) or Y (yes).

| RECLMSYS | CHAR | 4 | | SYSTEM*BEING*RECLAIMED |

JES2 only. Identification of system whose job processing is to be reclaimed (that is, CMD is $E SYS).

| SMFTIME | NUM | 8 | DATETIME19.2 | SMF*RECORD*TIME STAMP |

event time stamp.

| SUBSYS | CHAR | 4 | | SUB*SYSTEM |

subsystem, including JES2 or JES3.

| SYSTCODE | NUM | 4 | HEX3. | JES*SYSTEM*ABEND |

JES3 only. Abend only. System completion code.

| SYSTEM | CHAR | 4 | 4. | SYSTEM*ID |

system identification of processor on which this record was written.

| USERCODE | NUM | 4 | HEX3. | JES*USER*ABEND |

JES3 only. Abend only. User completion code.

| WRMSTRT | CHAR | 1 | | JES*WARM*START? |

JES3 only. Start option. Warm start specified. Values are blank (no) or Y (yes).

TYPE47PC
VSPC User Logon

The TYPE47PC data set contains one observation for each type 47 record written
by the VSPC subsystem. A type 47 record is written whenever a VSPC user successfully logs on or when the VSPC Service Program ACCOUNT control statement is executed. These data are needed to determine the duration of VSPC
sessions by matching with TYPE48PC.

Variable	Type	Length	Format	Label
JOBENTID	CHAR	6		JOB*ENTRY*ID CODE
LANGATTR	NUM	4		LANGUAGE*ATTRIBUTE*ASSIGNED
LIBRPROJ	NUM	4		PROJECT*LIBRARY*ID NUMBER
LIBRTYPE	NUM	4		LIBRARY*TYPE*CODE
LOGOFF	CHAR	10		STATUS OF*PREVIOUS*LOGOFF

JOBENTID job entry ID code.

LANGATTR language attribute assigned.

LIBRPROJ project library identification number.

LIBRTYPE library type code.

LOGOFF status of previous logoff. The possible values are:

NOT OFF	service program account: not logged off from last session
LOCKED	service program account: user locked
ACCT REC	service program account: this is a record from account
CONTINUE	workspace was saved during last normal logoff.

Variable	Type	Length	Format	Label
PLIBYTES	NUM	4		DASD BYTES*IN PROJECT/PUBLIC*LIBRARIES
PRIVCLAS	NUM	4		PRIVILEGED*CLASS*INDICATORS
SMFTIME	NUM	8	DATETIME19.2	SMF*RECORD*TIME STAMP

PLIBYTES bytes of DASD space in the project or public libraries.

PRIVCLAS privileged class indicators.

SMFTIME time of logon.

Variable	Type	Length	Format	Label
SYSTEM	CHAR	4	4.	SYSTEM*ID

identification of system on which VSPC executed.

Variable	Type	Length	Format	Label
ULIBYTES	NUM	4		DASD BYTES*IN THIS*USERS LIBRARY

bytes of DASD space in this user's library.

Variable	Type	Length	Format	Label
VSPCUSER	NUM	4		VSPC USER*IDENTIFICATION*NUMBER

user identification number.

TYPE4789
Remote Job Entry Session

The TYPE4789 data set contains one observation for each type 47, 48, or 49 SMF record written by JES2 or JES3. The VSPC subsystem also writes type 47, 48, and 49 records, which are described elsewhere in this chapter.

JES2 type 47, 48, and 49 records are written only for actions on Binary Synchronous Communications (BSC) protocol. Similar JES2 actions for System Network Architecture (SNA) protocol are in type 52, 53, and 54 SMF records in the TYPE5234 data set.

JES3 type 47, 48, and 49 records are written for actions on both BSC and SNA protocol.

JES2 actions that create a type 47 SMF record are:

- $S LNEn command is issued to JES2 to start a BSC line
- $E LNEn command is issued to JES2 to restart a BSC line
- BSC SIGNON from a remote user (RJE) is processed.

JES3 actions that create a type 47 SMF record are:

- BSC line is started
- BSC SIGNON from a remote user (RJE) is processed
- SNA LOGON is processed.

JES2 actions that create a type 48 SMF record are:

- $P LNEn command is issued to JES2 to stop a BSC line
- BSC SIGNOFF from a remote user (RJE) is processed.

JES3 actions that create a type 48 SMF record are:

- BSC line is stopped
- BSC SIGNOFF from a remote user (RJE) is processed
- SNA LOGOFF is processed.

JES2 action that creates a type 49 SMF record is:

- BSC SIGNON is attempted with an invalid password.

JES3 actions that create a type 49 SMF record are:

- BSC SIGNON is attempted with an invalid password
- SNA LOGON is attempted with an invalid password.

The TYPE4789 data set contains the line name and statistics on EXCPs and error conditions. It is extremely valuable in RJE environments since the sign-on and sign-off records can be matched to determine connect time of RJE/RJP users and an analysis of line usage can be made. Complaints from remote users about poor batch service often turn out to be failure of the remote site to activate RJE in time to retrieve printed output from the host. By analyzing these data, the host can determine the validity of a particular remote user's complaint. Furthermore, since the records for each RJE site contain the line name used, analysis of incorrect line usage (for example, dial back up lines being used in lieu of dedicated lines) can be detected. In addition, the EXCP statistics provide some measure of utilization and various error conditions can be detected.

The resource counts are session totals for records that describe a Signoff or Logoff. For $P LNE actions, counts are for the total duration of the connection (which may include many sessions).

Variable	Type	Length	Format	Label
EXCPCNT	NUM	4		TOTAL*EXCPS*COUNT

JES2 and JES3. BSC only. Count of EXCPs issued by JES.

LINENAME	CHAR	8		JES*LINE*NAME

line name for BSC lines, logical unit (LU) name for SNA lines.

LINERRS	NUM	4		LINE*ERROR*COUNT

JES3 only. BSC only. Number of line errors.

NRBUSCKS	NUM	4		NUMBER*BUS-OUT*CHECKS

JES3 only. BSC only. Number of bus-out checks.

NRCMDREJ	NUM	4		NUMBER*COMMANDS*REJECTED

JES3 only. BSC only. Number of command rejects.

NRDATACK	NUM	4		NUMBER*DATA*CHECKS

JES2 and JES3. BSC only. Number of data checks (to read text in JES2).

NREQUPCK	NUM	4		NUMBER*EQUIPMENT*CHECKS

JES3 only. BSC and SNA. Number of equipment checks.

NRINTVRQ	NUM	4		NUMBER*INTERVENTIONS*REQUIRED

JES3 only. SNA only. Number of interventions required.

NRLOSTDT	NUM	4		NUMBER*LOST DATA*EVENTS

JES3 only. BSC only. Number of lost data events.

NRNEGAK	NUM	4		NUMBER*NEGATIVE*ACKS

JES2 and JES3. BSC only. Number of negative acknowledgments to write text.

NROTHR	NUM	4		NUMBER*OTHER*ERRORS

JES2 only. BSC only. Sum of all errors other than those specifically counted in NRNEGAK, NRDATACK, and NRTIMEOT.

Variable	Type	Length	Format	Label
NROVERUN	NUM	4		NUMBER*DATA*OVERRUNS

JES3 only. BSC only. Number of data overruns.

NRTIMEOT	NUM	4		NUMBER*TIME-OUTS*TO READ TEXT

JES2 and JES3. BSC only. Number of time-outs to read text.

PASSWORD	CHAR	8		INVALID*PASSWORD*ATTEMPTED

JES2 and JES3. BSC and SNA. Password. (If event is INVALID PASSWORD, this variable contains the invalid password.)

RECVCNT	NUM	4		SNA*RECEIVE*COUNT

JES3 only. SNA only. Receive count.

RECVNEG	NUM	4		SNA*RECEIVE*NEG COUNT

JES3 only. SNA only. Receive negative response count.

RECVPOS	NUM	4		SNA*RECEIVE*POS COUNT

JES3 only. SNA only. Receive positive response count.

REMOTE	CHAR	8		REMOTE*(ROUTE)*NUMBER

remote number.

RJEVENT	CHAR	20		RJE*EVENT

event creating this observation. The possible values are:

value	created by
BSC INVALID PASSWORD	JES2 and JES3
BSC LINE ALREADY ON	JES3 only
BSC SIGNOFF	JES2 and JES3
BSC SIGNON	JES2 and JES3
BSC START LINE	JES2 and JES3
BSC STOP LINE	JES2 and JES3
BSC TERM ALREADY ON	JES3 only
BSC UNDEFINED TERM	JES3 only
SNA BIND FAILED	JES3 only
SNA SIGNOFF	JES3 only
SNA SIGNON	JES3 only
SNA INVALID PASSWORD	JES3 only
SNA LIMIT EXCEEDED	JES3 only
SNA UNDEFINED WKSTN	JES3 only.

Variable	Type	Length	Format	Label
RSVDJES3	CHAR	8		RESERVED*FOR*JES3

JES3 only. BSC only. Reserved field for JES3.

RSVDUSER	CHAR	4		RESERVED*FOR*JES3 USER

JES3 only. BSC only. Reserved field for user.

SENDCNT	NUM	4		SNA*SEND*COUNT

JES3 only. SNA only. SEND count.

SENDNEG	NUM	4		SNA*SEND*NEG COUNT

JES3 only. SNA only. SEND negative response count.

SENDPOS	NUM	4		SNA*SEND*POS COUNT

JES3 only. SNA only. SEND positive response count.

SIGNON	CHAR	36		TEXT*OF*SIGNON

message text (columns 35-70) of the SIGNON line.

SMFTIME	NUM	8	DATETIME19.2	SMF*RECORD*TIME STAMP

event time stamp.

SUBSYS	CHAR	4		SUB*SYSTEM

subsystem; either JES2 or JES3.

SYSTEM	CHAR	4	4.	SYSTEM*ID

identification of system on which this event occurred.

UCBNAME	CHAR	3		LINE*ADAPTER*ADDRESS

JES2 and JES3. BSC only. Line adapter number.

TYPE48PC
VSPC User Logoff

The TYPE48PC data set contains one observation for each type 48 record written by the VSPC subsystem.

A type 48 SMF record is written by VSPC whenever:

- a user issues the OFF command
- an interpreter foreground processor issues a TOFF
- a user is disconnected by line-drop or telephone hang-up
- a STOP is issued by the system console operator against VSPC
- a VSPC HALT command is issued
- at LOGON, VSPC recognized that the previous session was incomplete
- the VSPC Service Program ACCOUNT command is issued.

TYPE48PC is the accounting record for VSPC users and contains resource consumption data describing this session as well as the total resources by this user since creation.

Variable	Type	Length	Format	Label
AVGWKSET	NUM	4	5.	AVERAGE*WORKING*SET (PAGES)

average working set size for this session, in pages (4096 bytes).

CPUTCBTM	NUM	4	TIME12.2	TASK*CPU TCB*TIME

CPU time recorded for this session.

ELAPSTM	NUM	4	TIME12.2	ELAPSED*DURATION

elapsed time in this record.

EXCPCOMM	NUM	4		EXCPS*COUNT*COMMUNICATIONS

EXCP counts to teleprocessing (communications) device during this session.

EXCPDASD	NUM	4		EXCPS*COUNT*DASD

EXCP count to DASD devices during this session.

LOGFLG	NUM	2	HEX2.	LOGOFF*FLAGS

logoff flags.

LOGOFF	CHAR	10		STATUS OF*PREVIOUS*LOGOFF

logoff indicator. The possible values are:

INCOMPLETE	record for a previously incomplete session
CANCEL	CANCEL issued
CONT/SAVE	CONTINUE, workspace saved in this logoff

Variable	Type	Length	Format	Label
	CONT/PURG		CONTINUE, purged in this logoff	
	HALT/STOP		HALT or STOP issued	
	LOCKED		user locked.	
PAGESECS	NUM	4		MEMORY*PAGESECS*(PER TCB)

memory space-time usage (K byte-seconds).

| PLIBYTES | NUM | 4 | | DASD BYTES*IN PROJECT/PUBLIC*LIBRARIES |

bytes of DASD space in the project or public libraries.

| PRNTPAGE | NUM | 4 | | PAGES*SENT TO*PRINTER |

number of pages sent to hardcopy device during this session.

| SMFTIME | NUM | 8 | DATETIME19.2 | SMF*RECORD*TIME STAMP |

time of logoff event.

| SYSTEM | CHAR | 4 | 4. | SYSTEM*ID |

identification of system on which VSPC executed.

| TOTCPUTM | NUM | 4 | TIME12.2 | VSPC USER*TOTAL CPU TIME*TO DATE |

total CPU time to date for this user.

| TOTELPTM | NUM | 4 | TIME12.2 | VSPC USER*CONNECT TIME*TO DATE |

accumulated (total to date) elapsed time in this record.

| TOTEXCPC | NUM | 4 | | VSPC USER*TELEPROC EXCPS*TO DATE |

total communications (teleprocessing) EXCPs to date for this user.

| TOTEXCPD | NUM | 4 | | VSPC USER*DASD EXCPS*TO DATE |

total DASD EXCPs to date for this user.

| TOTPAGSC | NUM | 4 | | VSPC USER*PAGE SECONDS*TO DATE |

total memory space-time usage (page seconds) to date for this user.

| TOTPRNT | NUM | 4 | | VSPC USER*HARDCOPY PAGES*TO DATE |

total hardcopy pages to date for this user.

| ULIBYTES | NUM | 4 | | DASD BYTES*IN THIS*USERS LIBRARY |

bytes of DASD space in this user's library.

Variable	Type	Length	Format	Label
VSPCUSER	NUM	4		VSPC USER*IDENTIFICATION*NUMBER

user identification number.

TYPE49PC
VSPC Security

The TYPE49PC data set contains one observation for each type 49 SMF record written by the VSPC subsystem.

A type 49 record is written whenever a VSPC user incorrectly specifies a password at logon or at access to a VSPC file.

Variable	Type	Length	Format	Label
FILENAME	CHAR	11		FILE NAME*ATTEMPTED*TO ACCESS

name of file for which access was attempted (blank if logon event).

FILEOWNR	NUM	4		FILE OWNERS*VSPC USER*ID NUMBER

VSPC user identification number of file owner.

LIBRNUM	NUM	4		LIBRARY*NUMBER*OF FILE

library number of accessed file.

SMFTIME	NUM	8	DATETIME19.2	SMF*RECORD*TIME STAMP

time of this event.

SYSTEM	CHAR	4	4.	SYSTEM*ID

identification of system on which VSPC executed.

VSPCUSER	NUM	4		VSPC USER*IDENTIFICATION*NUMBER

user identification of violator.

TYPE50
VTAM Tuning Statistics

The TYPE50 data set contains one observation for each type 50 SMF record.

A type 50 SMF record is written by VTAM at the end of the VTAM tuning statistics interval specified by the user, if tuning statistics were specified.

The type 50 record provides the only source of statistics on VTAM activity and is quite useful in determining if you have defined enough VTAM buffers.

Variable	Type	Length	Format	Label
CONTROLR	CHAR	8		INTELLIGENT*CONTROLLER*NAME

intelligent controller name.

DLRCOUNT	NUM	4		DUMP-LOAD*RESTART*REQUESTS(MAX)

maximum dump-load-restart requests during this interval.

INPIOS	NUM	4		INBOUND*PIUS

number of inbound PIUs during this interval.

NCPSLOWS	NUM	4		TIMES NCP*ENTERED*SLOWDOWN

number of times NCP entered slowdown during this interval.

NRATTNS	NUM	4		ATTENTIONS*RECEIVED

total number of attentions received during this interval.

NREADATN	NUM	4		READ*CHANNEL*ATTENTIONS

number of attentions on ending status of READ channel programs during this interval.

NRREADS	NUM	4		READ*CHANNEL*PROGRAMS

count of READ channel programs during this interval.

NRWRITES	NUM	4		WRITE*CHANNEL*PROGRAMS

count of WRITE channel programs during this interval.

OUTPIOS	NUM	4		OUTBOUND*PIUS

number of outbound PIUs during this interval.

RDBUFUSE	NUM	4		READ*BUFFERS*USED

total number of read buffers used during this interval.

SMFTIME	NUM	8	DATETIME19.2	SMF*RECORD*TIME STAMP

time stamp at end of this interval.

Variable	Type	Length	Format	Label
SYSTEM	CHAR	4	4.	SYSTEM*ID

identification of system on which this record was written.

TYPE5234
Remote Job Entry Session (JES2 SNA)

The TYPE5234 data set contains one observation for each type 52, 53, or 54 SMF record written by JES2 for actions on System Network Architecture (SNA) protocol. JES2 actions for BSC protocol are in type 47, 48, and 49 SMF records in the TYPE4789 data set.

JES2 actions that create a type 52 SMF record are:

- $S LNEn command is issued to JES2 to start an SNA line
- SNA LOGON from a remote user (RJE) is processed.

JES2 actions that create a type 53 SMF record are:

- $P LNEn command is issued to JES2 to stop an SNA line
- SNA LOGOFF from a remote user (RJE) is processed.

JES2 action that creates a type 54 SMF record is:

- remote user (RJE) attempts to sign on with an invalid password.

Variable	Type	Length	Format	Label
LINEIDNT	CHAR	3		LINE*IDENTIFIER
line type identifier - SNA (LOGOFF/$P LNE only).				
LINENAME	CHAR	8		LINE*NAME
line name.				
LINEPWRD	CHAR	8		LINE*PASSWORD
line password.				
NBIDREJ	NUM	4		BID*REJECTS
number of bid rejects (LOGOFF/$P LNE only).				
NEXCRESP	NUM	4		EXCEPTION*RESPONSES
number of exception responses (LOGOFF/$P LNE only).				
NLUSTATS	NUM	4		LUSTATS*RECEIVED
number of LUSTATs received (LOGOFF/$P LNE only).				
NTEMPERR	NUM	4		TEMPORARY*ERRORS
number of temporary errors (LOGOFF/$P LNE only).				
NVTAMREQ	NUM	4		VTAM*REQUESTS*PROCESSED
number of VTAM requests processed (LOGOFF/$P LNE only).				

Variable	Type	Length	Format	Label
REMOTE	CHAR	8		REMOTE*(ROUTE)*NUMBER

remote number (LOGON/LOGOFF only).

RJEVENT	CHAR	20		RJE*EVENT

RJE event that created this observation. The possible values are:

value	meaning
SNA LOGON	SNA session has started
SNA START LINE	line has been started
SNA LOGOFF	SNA session has ended
SNA STOP LINE	line has been stopped
SNA INVALID PASSWORD	invalid password was given.

SMFTIME	NUM	8	DATETIME19.2	SMF*RECORD*TIME STAMP

time this event occurred.

SUBSYS	CHAR	4		SUB*SYSTEM

subsystem that created this event. The possible value is: JES2.

SYSTEM	CHAR	4	4.	SYSTEM*ID

identification of system to which JES line involved in this event was connected.

VERSN52	NUM	4		VERSION*NUMBER

record version number.

TYPE5568
Network Job Entry Accounting

The TYPE5568 data set contains one observation for each type 55, 56, or 58 SMF record.

A type 55 SMF record is written at each node in a JES2 network when a start-networking command is executed. The initial sign-on is recorded at the node to which the sign-on was sent, and the response sign-on is recorded at the node that originated the initial sign-on. A type 58 record is similarly written at each node when a networking session is terminated.

A type 56 SMF record is written whenever an attempt to sign on contains an invalid password.

Thus, TYPE5568 is important for accounting the passage of jobs through an NJE network.

Variable	Type	Length	Format	Label
LINENAME	CHAR	8		LINE*NAME

line name.

LINEPWRD	CHAR	8		LINE*PASSWORD

line password.

MEMBERNR	NUM	4		NJE*MEMBER*NUMBER

member number.

NJEVENT	CHAR	15		NJE*EVENT

event that created this observation. The possible values are:

value	meaning
INVALID RESPONSE	SIGNON was rejected by destination
INVALID SIGNON	SIGNON was rejected by origination
SIGNOFF	session terminated normally
SIGNON	SIGNON issued to start networking
SIGNON RESPONSE	SIGNON was accepted and session is in progress.

NODENAME	CHAR	8		NJE*NODE*NAME

node name.

NODEPWRD	CHAR	8		NJE*NODE*PASSWORD

node password (contains the invalid password if NJEVENT is INVALID SIGNON or INVALID RESPONSE).

Variable	Type	Length	Format	Label
SMFTIME	NUM	8	DATETIME19.2	SMF*RECORD*TIME STAMP

event time stamp on this system.

| SUBSYS | CHAR | 4 | | SUB*SYSTEM |

subsystem that created this event. The possible value is: JES2.

| SYSTEM | CHAR | 4 | 4. | SYSTEM*ID |

identification of system on which this event record was written.

TYPE57J2
JES2 Network SYSOUT Transmission

The TYPE57J2 data set contains one observation for each type 57 SMF record written by JES2. Note that type 57 SMF records written by JES3 are described and kept in data set TYPE57J3. A type 57 SMF record is written in an NJE environment for each SYSOUT transmission through the network.

TYPE57J2 contains start and stop times and a count of records transmitted and is useful in tracking NJE usage. There is no accounting information from the job that caused the SYSOUT transmission except the 8-byte network account number (assuming it was filled in by your NJE system). Furthermore, there is not enough information in the record to match the observation with its job since the job's read-in time and date are not provided.

Variable	Type	Length	Format	Label
DEVNAME	CHAR	8		NJE JOB*TRANSMITTER*DEVICE NAME

SYSOUT transmitter device name.

NJEACCT	CHAR	8		NETWORKING*ACCOUNT*NUMBER

network account number. Note that this value is not the accounting information from the JOB card, but it is the 8-byte field network field, which may or may not contain useful data.

NJEJOBID	CHAR	8		CURRENT*JOB*IDENTIFICATION

JES job identification at the current node (that is, the node at which this record was written). The job identification provides the type of task (JOB/TSU/STC) and the JES2-assigned job number. (In the TYPE26J2 data set, it is decoded into two variables, TYPETASK and JESNR). This value may have no relationship to the original job number assigned by JES2 when the job was created; however, if the original number is not currently in use on this system, the original number is used by JES here.

NJENJORG	CHAR	8		NJE*JOB*ORIGIN

original node name.

NJENJPTH	CHAR	8		NJE*TRANSMISSION*PATH

next node name.

NJEORGID	CHAR	8		ORIGINAL*JOB*IDENTIFICATION

JES job identification at originating node of this job. The job identification provides the type of task (JOB/TSU/STC) and the JES2-assigned job number. (In the TYPE26J2 data set, it is decoded into two variables, TYPETASK and JESNR).

NJERECDS	NUM	4		NJE*RECORD*COUNT

count of logical SYSOUT (teleprocessing records) transmitted.

Variable	Type	Length	Format	Label
NJEXEQNM	CHAR	8		NJE*EXECUTION*NODE

execution node name.

Variable	Type	Length	Format	Label
SMFTIME	NUM	8	DATETIME19.2	SMF*RECORD*TIME STAMP

event time stamp at completion of SYSOUT transmission.

Variable	Type	Length	Format	Label
SUBSYS	CHAR	4		SUB*SYSTEM

subsystem that created this event. The possible value is: JES2.

Variable	Type	Length	Format	Label
SYSOUTP	CHAR	4		OUTPUT*PROCESSOR*SYSTEM ID

system identification of SYSOUT transmitter system.

Variable	Type	Length	Format	Label
SYSTEM	CHAR	4	4.	SYSTEM*ID

identification of system on which this record was written.

Variable	Type	Length	Format	Label
XMENTIME	NUM	8	DATETIME19.2	END OF JOB*TRANSMISSION*TIME

SYSOUT transmitter stop (end) time stamp.

Variable	Type	Length	Format	Label
XMITTIME	NUM	8	DATETIME19.2	START OF JOB*TRANSMISSION*TIME

SYSOUT transmitter start time stamp.

TYPE57J3
JES3 Network SYSOUT Transmission

The TYPE57J3 data set contains one observation for each type 57 SMF record written by JES3. Note that type 57 SMF records written by JES2 are described and kept in data set TYPE57J2.

TYPE57J3 contains start and stop times and a count of records transmitted and is useful in tracking NJE usage. There is no accounting information from the job that caused the SYSOUT transmission except the 8-byte network account number (presuming it was filled in by your NJE system). Furthermore, there is not enough information in the record to match the observation with its job since the job's read-in time and date are not provided.

Variable	Type	Length	Format	Label
JESNR	NUM	4		CURRENT*JOB*JES NUMBER

JES job number at current node (that is, the node at which this record was written). This value may have no relationship to the original job number assigned by JES2 when the job was created; however, if the original number is not currently in use on this system, the original number is used here by JES.

JOB	CHAR	8		JOB*NAME

job name.

NJEACCT	CHAR	8		NETWORKING*ACCOUNT*NUMBER

network account number. Note that this value is not the accounting information from the JOB card, but it is the 8-byte field network field, which may or may not contain useful data.

NJEBLDG	CHAR	8		NJE*BUILDING*NUMBER

building number.

NJEBUFFS	NUM	4		TRANSMISSION*BUFFER*COUNT

count of buffers transmitted.

NJEBYTES	NUM	4		COMPRESSED*BYTE*COUNT

compressed byte count.

NJEDEPT	CHAR	8		NJE*DEPARTMENT*NUMBER

department number.

NJEJBTYP	CHAR	6		NJE*JOB*TYPE

job type indicator for this transmission. The possible values are:

value	meaning
JOB	job or jobstream to be executed or transmitted

Variable	Type	Length	Format	Label
	SYSOUT			SYSOUT being transmitted for ultimate printing.

NJEJOBNO NUM 4 NJE JOB*NUMBER*(ORIGINAL)

JES job identification at originating node of this job. The job identification provides the type of task (JOB/TSU/STC) and the JES2-assigned job number. (In the TYPE26J2 data set, it is decoded into two variables, TYPETASK and JESNR).

NJENJDST CHAR 8 DESTINATION*NODE*NAME

destination node name.

NJENJORG CHAR 8 NJE*JOB*ORIGIN

original node name.

NJENJPTH CHAR 8 NJE*TRANSMISSION*PATH

next node name.

NJENJRMT CHAR 8 SECONDARY*JOB*ORIGIN

secondary job origin node name.

NJEPRGMR CHAR 20 NJE*PROGRAMMER*NAME

programmer name field, from original JOB card.

NJERECDS NUM 4 NJE*RECORD*COUNT

count of logical SYSOUT (teleprocessing records) transmitted.

NJEROOM CHAR 8 NJE*ROOM*NUMBER

room number, from original JOB card.

NJEUSRID CHAR 8 NJE*USER*ID

origin or notify USER identification. This value indicates the destination of the NOTIFY message sent back to the origin node.

NJEXEQNM CHAR 8 NJE*EXECUTION*NODE

execution node name.

NJEXEQU CHAR 8 NJE*EXECUTION*USER ID

execution user identification.

SMFTIME NUM 8 DATETIME19.2 SMF*RECORD*TIME STAMP

event time stamp.

SUBSYS CHAR 4 SUB*SYSTEM

subsystem that created this event. The possible value is: JES3.

Variable	Type	Length	Format	Label
SYSTEM	CHAR	4	4.	SYSTEM*ID

identification of system on which this record was written.

Variable	Type	Length	Format	Label
XMENTIME	NUM	8	DATETIME19.2	END OF JOB*TRANSMISSION*TIME

SYSOUT transmitter stop (end) time stamp.

Variable	Type	Length	Format	Label
XMITTIME	NUM	8	DATETIME19.2	START OF JOB*TRANSMISSION*TIME

SYSOUT transmitter start time stamp.

TYPE60
Updated VSAM Volume Data Set

The TYPE60 data set contains one observation for each type 60 SMF record, written whenever a VSAM Volume Record (VVR) is inserted, updated, or deleted from a VSAM Volume Data Set (VVDS). For example, when a VSAM cluster is defined, closed, or deleted, one type 60 record is written for each VVR that is written or deleted.

The VVDS in which the VVR was altered, the new, updated or deleted VVR, and the job that altered the VVR are identified.

Variable	Type	Length	Format	Label
ACTION	CHAR	8		ACTION*REQUESTED

action taken to this VVR (and hence the reason this observation exists). The possible values are:

value	meaning
INSERT	record was inserted (for example, a new record)
UPDATED	record was changed
DELETED	record was deleted.

Variable	Type	Length	Format	Label
ENTRNAME	CHAR	44		ENTRY*NAME

entry name.

| ENTTYPID | CHAR | 1 | | ENTRY*TYPE*IDENTIFIER |

type of entry.

| JOB | CHAR | 8 | | JOB NAME*OR*TSO USER |

job name (batch) or user ID (TSO) that updated the VVR.

| LOCLINFO | CHAR | 8 | | LOCAL*INSTALLATION*FIELD |

locally-defined field filled in by installation-written SMF exit routine.

| READTIME | NUM | 8 | DATETIME19.2 | READ-IN*OR LOGON*EVENT |

job read-in (TSO LOGON) time stamp.

| SMFTIME | NUM | 8 | DATETIME19.2 | SMF*RECORD*TIME STAMP |

event time stamp when the VVR was updated.

| SYSTEM | CHAR | 4 | 4. | SYSTEM*ID |

identification of system from which the VVR was updated.

Variable	Type	Length	Format	Label
VVDSNAME	CHAR	44		VVDS NAME*IN WHICH*ENTRY IS MADE

VSAM Volume Data Set (VVDS) that was updated (because it contains this VVR).

Variable	Type	Length	Format	Label
VVR	CHAR	100	HEX200.	FIRST 100 BYTES*OF VSAM VOLUME*RECORD

first 100 bytes of VVR. (If necessary, the VVR is decoded into its parts in a later release.)

Variable	Type	Length	Format	Label
VVRLEN	NUM	4		VVR*LENGTH

actual length of VVR.

TYPE6156
Integrated Catalog Facility(ICF) Activity

The TYPE6156 data set contains one observation for each type 61, 65, or 66 SMF record, written when the ICF catalog is changed by the Access Method Services commands DEFINE, DELETE, or ALTER or by a data set extend operation. A type 61 record is written for each ICF catalog record that is inserted or updated as the result of an Access Method Services (AMS) DEFINE command. A type 65 record is written for each ICF catalog record that is updated or deleted during the processing of an AMS DELETE command. A type 66 record is written for each ICF catalog record that is updated or deleted during the processing of an AMS ALTER command or during a data set extend operation.

The variable FUNCTION contains the record types and flags and describes which AMS function was performed on the variable ENTRNAME (the 'data set' in the catalog. Thus, only one data set is needed for all three SMF records that record ICF activity.

TYPE6156 data are useful in identifying who is using and abusing the catalog. In addition, after a hardware failure such as a head crash, the ICF records for the affected volume can be examined to identify data sets that were created or deleted since the last backup of the volume since these data sets must be re-created by the user. The ICF records can also be examined to identify data sets that were deleted after the last backup since those data sets will not require restoration. Thus, the recovery from a catastrophe like a head crash can be mitigated with the knowledge from TYPE6156 data.

Variable	Type	Length	Format	Label
ACTION	CHAR	8		ACTION*REQUESTED

action taken to this VVR (that is, to the catalog record). The possible values are:

value	meaning
INSERT	record was inserted (that is, a new record)
UPDATED	record was changed
DELETED	record was deleted.

BUFSIZE	NUM	4		DATA/INDEX*BUFFER*SIZE

buffer size. Applies only if this is a data or index record.

CATENTRY	CHAR	44		ENTRY*NAME IN*CATALOG

entry name in catalog record. This term is the same as ENTRNAME.

Variable	Type	Length	Format	Label
CATNAME	CHAR	44		CATALOG*NAME

name of catalog in which component or cluster is defined.

CINUM	NUM	4		CI NUMBER*OF THIS*CATALOG RECORD

control internal number of this catalog record.

CLUST	CHAR	9		TYPE*OF*CLUSTER

type of cluster. This value applies only to cluster record.

value	meaning
blank	not a cluster record
PAGESPACE	cluster describes a page space
SWAPSPACE	cluster describes a swap space.

COMP	CHAR	11		COMPONENT*NOT*USABLE?

component usable status. Data or index only.

value	meaning
blank	N/A
NOT USABLE	component is not usable.

CRADEVT	NUM	4	HEX8.	CRA*DEVICE*TYPE

CRA device type (zeros if catalog is not recoverable or if there is no associated CRA volume).

CRADTIME	NUM	8	DATETIME19.2	DATA/INDEX*CREATION*EVENT

creation time stamp. Data or index only.

CRAIDNO	NUM	4		CRA*CI*NUMBER

CRA control internal number (zeros if catalog is not recoverable or if there is no associated CRA volume).

CRATIME	NUM	4	HHMM8.2	CRA*CREATION*EVENT

CRA creation time. Data or index only.

CRAVOL	CHAR	6		CRA*VOLUME*SERIAL

CRA volume serial (zeros if catalog is not recoverable or if there is no associated CRA volume).

DSCRDT	NUM	4		CLUSTER/DATA*CREATION*DATE

cluster or data set creation date (YYDDD).

Variable	Type	Length	Format	Label
DSET	CHAR	8		INTERNAL*SYSTEM*DATA SET?

internal system data set flag. Data or index only.

Variable	Type	Length	Format	Label

	value	meaning
	blank	not an internal system data set
	INTERNAL	an internal system data set.

DSEXTD   NUM   4   CLUSTER/DATA*EXPIRATION*DATE

cluster or data set expiration date (YYDDD).

ENTRNAME   CHAR   44   ENTRY*NAME

name of data set, component, cluster being affected.

ENTTYPID   CHAR   1   ENTRY*TYPE*IDENTIFIER

type of entry.

ERASED   CHAR   1   INDEX*OVERWRITTEN*IF DELETED?

option to erase the entry when that entry is deleted.

	value	meaning
	blank	option was not specified. The actual data still exist on the volume since delete only breaks the pointer to the data. It is possible to access the original data until that track is overwritten by a subsequent entry.
	Y	ERASE option was specified. The actual data are overwritten to erase its contents.

FUNCTION   CHAR   7   DELETE*FUNCTION*PERFORMED

function performed by AMS command or function. The possible values are:

	value	meaning
	ALTER	catalog entry was changed, but not renamed (AMS ALTER)
	CATALOG	only catalog entries were modified; data set was not scratched (AMS DELETE)
	DEFINE	data set was cataloged (AMS DEFINE)
	RENAME	data set was renamed (AMS ALTER)
	SCRATCH	data set was scratched and catalog record changed (AMS DELETE).

GDGDELET   CHAR   1   GDG*DELETE*ACTION

generation data group deletion action to be taken when GDGLIMIT is exceeded:

Variable	Type	Length	Format	Label

		value	meaning	
		A	delete all generations from catalog	
		O	delete only the oldest generation from catalog.	

GDGLIMIT   NUM   4   GDG*LEVELS*MAXIMUM

maximum number of GDG levels allowed. See GDGDELET and GDGSCRAT

GDGSCRAT   CHAR   1   GDG*SCRATCH*ACTION

generation data group scratch action to be taken when GDGLIMIT is exceeded:

		value	meaning	
		D	do not scratch DSCB-1 of deleted data sets	
		S	scratch DSCB-1 of deleted data sets.	

GENLVLS   NUM   4   GENERATION*LEVEL*DIFFERENCE

generation level difference string.

HARBADS   NUM   4   HIGHEST*ALLOCATED*RBA

high allocated RBA of data set or index. Data or index only.

HURBADS   NUM   4   HIGHEST*USED*RBA

high used RBA of data set or index. Data or index only.

INHIBIT   CHAR   1   UPDATE*INHIBITED*?

data set attribute. Data or index only.

		value	meaning	
		blank	attribute not specified	
		Y	if update of data set or index is inhibited.	

JOB   CHAR   8   JOB NAME*OR*TSO USER

job name (batch) or user ID (TSO) that opened the cluster or component.

LOCLINFO   CHAR   8   LOCAL*INSTALLATION*FIELD

locally-defined field filled in by installation-written SMF exit routine.

LRECL   NUM   4   LOGICAL*RECORD*LENGTH

logical record size of data set. Data only.

NEWNAME   CHAR   44   NEW ENTRY NAME* (RENAME ONLY)

new entry name (is ENTRNAME in next record) after rename.

Variable	Type	Length	Format	Label
OPEN	CHAR	7		TYPE*OF*OPEN

type of OPEN. Data or index only. The possible values are:

value	meaning
blank	not data or index
INPUT	opened for input
OUTPUT	opened for output.

| OWNERID | CHAR | 8 | | OWNER*OF*DATA SET |

owner of data set (specified when data set was defined).

| PRIALOC | NUM | 4 | | PRIMARY*SPACE*ALLOCATION |

volume of primary space allocation for data set or index (specified when data set or index was defined). See SPACE for units. Data or index only.

| RACFPROT | CHAR | 1 | | RACF*PROTECTED? |

RACF-protected entry.

value	meaning
blank	not protected by RACF
Y	protected by RACF (or by other security systems as well if they use the RACF structure, exits, and turns on the RACF protection bit).

| READTIME | NUM | 8 | DATETIME19.2 | READ-IN*OR LOGON*EVENT |

job read-in (TSO LOGON) time stamp.

| RECOVRBL | CHAR | 1 | | RECOVERABLE*CATALOG*? |

catalog recoverability attribute. Data or index only.

value	meaning
blank	attribute not set
Y	this catalog is recoverable.

| RELIND | NUM | 4 | | VSAM*RELEASE*INDICATOR |

VSAM release indicator :

value	meaning
0	nonenhanced VSAM
1	enhanced VSAM.

| REUSABLE | CHAR | 1 | | REUSABLE*CLUSTER? |

reusability attribute. Data or index only.

Variable	Type	Length	Format	Label

value	meaning
blank	attribute not set
Y	cluster associated with this component is reusable.

SECALOC   NUM   4   SECONDARY*SPACE*ALLOCATION

secondary space allocation for data set or index (specified when data set or index is defined). See SPACE for units. Data or index only.

SHARING   CHAR   10   DATA SET*SHARING*ATTRIBUTES

data set sharing attributes. Data or index only.

value	meaning
READ OR	data set can be shared by READ users or it can be used by one UPDATE/OUTPUT user
READ AND	data set can be shared by READ users and one UPDATE/OUTPUT user
FULLY	data set can be fully shared
FULLY WITH	data set can be fully shared, with assistance supplied by VSAM.

SMFTIME   NUM   8   DATETIME19.2   SMF*RECORD*TIME STAMP

event time stamp.

SPACE   CHAR   3   SPACE*REQUEST*UNITS

units in which space is allocated. See PRIALOC and SECALOC. Data or index only.

value	meaning
CYL	space request specified in cylinders
TRK	space request specified in tracks.

SPEED   CHAR   1   DO NOT*PREFORMAT*?

Data set SPEED attribute. Data or index only.

value	meaning
blank	not specified
Y	DASD device for the data set or index is not preformatted before records are written.

SYSTEM   CHAR   4   4.   SYSTEM*ID

identification of this system.

Variable	Type	Length	Format	Label
TEMPXPOR	CHAR	1		TEMPORARY*EXPORT*COPY?

data set temporary export attribute. Data or index only.

value	meaning
blank	not specified
Y	temporary export (that is, the original copy of this data set or index is not to be deleted although another copy of it exists elsewhere).

Variable	Type	Length	Format	Label
TRKOVFLO	CHAR	1		TRACK*OVERFLOW*?

data set track overflow attribute. Data or index only.

value	meaning
blank	not specified
Y	track overflow specified.

Variable	Type	Length	Format	Label
UNIQUE	CHAR	1		UNIQUE*DATA SET*?

data set unique attribute. Data or index only.

value	meaning
blank	not specified.
Y	unique VSAM data set (that is, data set or index must reside in its own data space).

Variable	Type	Length	Format	Label
XSYSSHR	CHAR	10		CROSS*SYSTEM*SHARING

data set sharing across systems. Data or index only.

value	meaning
FULLY	data set can be fully shared
FULLY WITH	data set can be fully shared with assistance supplied by VSAM.

TYPE62
VSAM Component or Cluster Opened

The TYPE62 data set contains one or more observations for each type 62 SMF record, written when a VSAM component or cluster is opened, regardless of whether or not the open is successful. A type 62 record is not written when the open is issued by a system task. If the component or cluster being opened contains more than one volume, there will be one observation for each VOLSER.

TYPE62 contains information about the job or session that opened the component or cluster and about the volumes involved. Thus, it is useful in tracking VSAM usage since it gives the time when the open was issued. By matching with TYPE64, the duration that VSAM data sets are open can be determined.

Variable	Type	Length	Format	Label
CATNAME	CHAR	44		CATALOG*NAME

name of catalog in which component or cluster is defined.

| CATVOL | CHAR | 6 | | CATALOG*VOLUME |

volume serial number of volume containing catalog.

| DEVICE | CHAR | 7 | | DEVICE*TYPE |

device type of volume containing component or cluster (for example, 3330, 3350, and so forth). Decoded from UCB type by the VMACUCB code.

| ENTRNAME | CHAR | 44 | | ENTRY*NAME |

name of component or cluster being opened.

| JOB | CHAR | 8 | | JOB NAME*OR*TSO USER |

job name (batch) or user ID (TSO) that opened the cluster or component.

| LOCLINFO | CHAR | 8 | | LOCAL*INSTALLATION*FIELD |

locally-defined field filled in by installation-written SMF exit routine.

| NRVOLS | NUM | 4 | | NUMBER*OF*VOLUMES |

number of on-line volumes containing component or cluster. TYPE62 contains this number of observations for each type 62 SMF record describing a multivolume cluster or component.

| READTIME | NUM | 8 | DATETIME19.2 | READ-IN*OR LOGON*EVENT |

job read-in (TSO LOGON) time stamp.

Variable	Type	Length	Format	Label
SMFTIME	NUM	8	DATETIME19.2	SMF*RECORD*TIME STAMP

open time stamp.

| STATUS | CHAR | 6 | | IO*STATUS |

open status.

value	meaning
SUCCESSFUL	component or cluster was opened successfully
FAILED	security violation (invalid password).

| SYSTEM | CHAR | 4 | 4. | SYSTEM*ID |

identification of system on which open was issued.

| UCBTYPE | NUM | 4 | HEX8. | UCB*TYPE |

UCB type control block for this VOLSER.

| VOLSEQNR | NUM | 4 | | VOLUME*SEQUENCE*NUMBER |

sequence number of this VOLSER.

| VOLSER | CHAR | 6 | | VOLUME*SERIAL*NUMBER |

volume serial number of volume containing component or cluster.

TYPE6367
VSAM Entry Defined or Deleted

The TYPE6367 data set contains one observation for each type 63 or type 67 SMF record written when a VSAM catalog entry (that is, a component, cluster, catalog, alternate index, path, or non-VSAM data set) is defined or altered. Examples of altering an entry include when VSAM extends the entries by VSAM EOV with new space allocation and changes caused by the ALTER AMS command. If the change is to rename the entry, a type 68 SMF record (data set TYPE68) is written instead. A type 67 SMF record is written for each VSAM catalog entry that is deleted. For example, when an indexed cluster is deleted, three records are written: one for the index, another for the data component, and a third for the relationship between the components of the cluster.

TYPE6367 observations describe the job causing the action and the affected VSAM entry and provide the old catalog record for deletions and alterations and the new catalog record for definitions and alterations. The catalog record (new for type 63 and old for type 67) is decoded and many variables in TYPE6367 come from the catalog record portion of these SMF records.

TYPE6367 is useful in tracking usage and alterations of VSAM data sets, especially for audit trails of creation and deletion. Note that resource usage (for example, EXCPs) is contained in the TYPE64 data set.

The catalog record is documented separately by IBM in publication SYS26-3826-3.

Variable	Type	Length	Format	Label
ACTION	CHAR	8		ACTION*REQUESTED

action causing this observation.

value	meaning
NEW DEFN	new definition
ALT DEFN	definition was altered
ALT PATH	alternate path defined
ALT INDX	alternate index defined
UNCATLG	uncataloged
SCRATCH	scratched
UNCATSCR	uncataloged and scratched
PATHDEL	path deleted
ALTINDX	alternate index deleted.

Variable	Type	Length	Format	Label
BUFSIZE	NUM	4		DATA/INDEX*BUFFER*SIZE

buffer size. Applies only if this value is a data or index record.

CATENTRY	CHAR	44		ENTRY*NAME IN*CATALOG

entry name in catalog record. Same as ENTRNAME.

CATNAME	CHAR	44		CATALOG*NAME

name of catalog in which component or cluster is defined.

CATRECSZ	NUM	4		SIZE OF*CATALOG*RECORD

size of new catalog records.

CINUM	NUM	4		CI NUMBER*OF THIS*CATALOG RECORD

control internal number of this catalog record.

CLUST	CHAR	9		TYPE*OF*CLUSTER

type of cluster. Applies only to cluster record.

value	meaning
blank	not a cluster record
PAGESPACE	cluster describes a page space
SWAPSPACE	cluster describes a swap space.

COMP	CHAR	11		COMPONENT*NOT*USABLE?

component usable status. Data or index only.

value	meaning
blank	N/A
NOT USABLE	the component is not usable.

COMPONT	CHAR	9		TYPE*OF*COMPONENT

type of component being processed.

value	meaning
ALIAS	alias
CATLG	VSAM catalog
CLUSTER	VSAM cluster
DATA COMP	VSAM data component
GEN GDG	generation data group
INDX COMP	VSAM index component
NON VSAM	non-VSAM data set.

Variable	Type	Length	Format	Label
CRADEVT	NUM	4	HEX8.	CRA*DEVICE*TYPE

CRA device type (zeros if catalog is not recoverable or if there is no associated CRA volume).

CRADTIME	NUM	8	DATETIME19.2	DATA/INDEX*CREATION*EVENT

creation time stamp. Data or index only.

CRAIDNO	NUM	4		CRA*CI*NUMBER

CRA control internal number (zeros if catalog is not recoverable or if there is no associated CRA volume).

CRATIME	NUM	4	HHMM8.2	CRA*CREATION*EVENT

CRA creation time. Data or index only.

CRAVOL	CHAR	6		CRA*VOLUME*SERIAL

CRA volume serial (zeros if catalog is not recoverable or if there is no associated CRA volume).

DSCRDT	NUM	4		CLUSTER/DATA*CREATION*DATE

cluster or data set creation date (YYDDD).

DSET	CHAR	8		INTERNAL*SYSTEM*DATA SET?

internal system data set flag. Data or index only.

value	meaning
blank	not an internal system data set
INTERNAL	an internal system data set.

DSEXTD	NUM	4		CLUSTER/DATA*EXPIRATION*DATE

cluster or data set expiration date (YYDDD).

ENTRNAME	CHAR	44		ENTRY*NAME

name of component or cluster being opened.

ENTTYPID	CHAR	1		

type of entry.

ERASED	CHAR	1		INDEX*OVERWRITTEN*IF DELETED?

option to erase entry when that entry is deleted.

value	meaning
blank	option was not specified. The actual data still exist on the volume since delete only breaks the pointer to the data. A resourceful person could

Variable	Type	Length	Format	Label
				access the original data until that track is overwritten by a subsequent entry.
		Y		ERASE option was specified. The actual data are overwritten to erase its contents.
GDGDELET	CHAR	1		GDG*DELETE*ACTION

generation data group deletion action to be taken when GDGLIMIT is exceeded:

	value	meaning
	A	delete all generations from catalog
	O	delete only the oldest generation from catalog.

Variable	Type	Length	Format	Label
GDGLIMIT	NUM	4		GDG*LEVELS*MAXIMUM

maximum number of GDG levels allowed. See GDGDELET and GDGSCRAT.

Variable	Type	Length	Format	Label
GDGSCRAT	CHAR	1		GDG*SCRATCH*ACTION

generation data group scratch action to be taken when GDGLIMIT is exceeded:

	value	meaning
	D	do not scratch DSCB-1 of deleted data sets
	S	scratch DSCB-1 of deleted data sets.

Variable	Type	Length	Format	Label
GENLVLS	NUM	4		GENERATION*LEVEL*DIFFERENCE

generation level difference string.

Variable	Type	Length	Format	Label
HARBADS	NUM	4		HIGHEST*ALLOCATED*RBA

high allocated RBA of data set or index. Data or index only.

Variable	Type	Length	Format	Label
HURBADS	NUM	4		HIGHEST*USED*RBA

high used RBA of data set or index. Data or index only.

Variable	Type	Length	Format	Label
INHIBIT	CHAR	1		UPDATE*INHIBITED*?

data set attribute. Data or index only.

	value	meaning
	blank	attribute not specified
	Y	if update of data set or index is inhibited.

Variable	Type	Length	Format	Label
JOB	CHAR	8		JOB NAME*OR*TSO USER

job name (batch) or user ID (TSO) that opened the cluster or component.

Variable	Type	Length	Format	Label
LOCLINFO	CHAR	8		LOCAL*INSTALLATION*FIELD

locally-defined field filled in by installation-written SMF exit routine.

Variable	Type	Length	Format	Label
LRECL	NUM	4		LOGICAL*RECORD*LENGTH

logical record size of data set. Data only.

Variable	Type	Length	Format	Label
OLDRECSZ	NUM	4		OLD*CATALOG*RECORD SIZE

size of old catalog record before alteration.

Variable	Type	Length	Format	Label
OPEN	CHAR	7		TYPE*OF*OPEN

type of OPEN. Data or index only. The possible values are:

value	meaning
blank	not data or index
INPUT	opened for input
OUTPUT	opened for output.

Variable	Type	Length	Format	Label
OWNERID	CHAR	8		OWNER*OF*DATA SET

owner of data set (specified when data set was defined).

Variable	Type	Length	Format	Label
PRIALOC	NUM	4		PRIMARY*SPACE*ALLOCATION

volume of primary space allocation for data set or index (specified when data set or index was defined). See SPACE for units. Data or index only.

Variable	Type	Length	Format	Label
RACFPROT	CHAR	1		RACF*PROTECTED?

RACF-protected entry.

value	meaning
blank	not protected by RACF
Y	protected by RACF (or by other security systems as well, if they use the RACF structure, exits, and turns on the RACF protection bit).

Variable	Type	Length	Format	Label
READTIME	NUM	8	DATETIME19.2	READ-IN*OR LOGON*EVENT

job read-in (TSO LOGON) time stamp.

Variable	Type	Length	Format	Label
RECOVRBL	CHAR	1		RECOVERABLE*CATALOG*?

catalog recoverability attribute. Data or index only.

value	meaning
blank	attribute not set
Y	catalog is recoverable.

Variable	Type	Length	Format	Label
RELIND	NUM	4		VSAM*RELEASE*INDICATOR

VSAM release indicator:

Variable	Type	Length	Format	Label

		value	meaning	
		0	nonenhanced VSAM	
		1	enhanced VSAM.	

| REUSABLE | CHAR | 1 | | REUSABLE*CLUSTER? |

reusability attribute. Data or index only.

	value	meaning
	blank	attribute not set
	Y	the cluster associated with this component is reusable.

| SECALOC | NUM | 4 | | SECONDARY*SPACE*ALLOCATION |

secondary space allocation for data set or index (specified when data set or index was defined). See SPACE for units. Data or index only.

| SHARING | CHAR | 10 | | DATA SET*SHARING*ATTRIBUTES |

data set sharing attributes. Data or index only.

	value	meaning
	READ OR	data set can be shared by READ users or it can be used by one UPDATE/OUTPUT user
	READ AND	data set can be shared by READ users and one UPDATE/OUTPUT user
	FULLY	data set can be fully shared
	FULLY WITH	data set can be fully shared, with assistance supplied by VSAM.

| SMFTIME | NUM | 8 | DATETIME19.2 | SMF*RECORD*TIME STAMP |

event time stamp.

| SPACE | CHAR | 3 | | SPACE*REQUEST*UNITS |

units in which space is allocated. See PRIALOC and SECALOC. Data or index only.

	value	meaning
	CYL	space request specified in cylinders
	TRK	space request specified in tracks.

| SPEED | CHAR | 1 | | DO NOT*PREFORMAT*? |

data set SPEED attribute. Data or index only.

Variable	Type	Length	Format	Label

		value	meaning
		blank	not specified
		Y	DASD device for data set or index is not preformatted before records are written.

SYSTEM   CHAR   4   4.   SYSTEM*ID

identification of this system.

TEMPXPOR   CHAR   1   TEMPORARY*EXPORT*COPY?

data set temporary export attribute. Data or index only.

		value	meaning
		blank	not specified
		Y	temporary export (that is, the original copy of this data set or index is not to be deleted, although another copy of it exists elsewhere).

TRKOVFLO   CHAR   1   TRACK*OVERFLOW*?

data set track overflow attribute. Data or index only.

		value	meaning
		blank	not specified
		Y	track overflow specified.

UNIQUE   CHAR   1   UNIQUE*DATA SET*?

data set unique attribute. Data or index only.

		value	meaning
		blank	not specified
		Y	unique VSAM data set (that is, data set or index must reside in its own data space).

XSYSSHR   CHAR   10   CROSS*SYSTEM*SHARING

data set sharing across systems. Data or index only.

		value	meaning
		FULLY	data set can be fully shared
		FULLY WITH	data set can be fully shared with assistance supplied by VSAM.

TYPE64
VSAM Component or Cluster Status

The TYPE64 data set contains one observation for each type 64 SMF record, written when

- a VSAM component or cluster is closed
- VSAM switches to another volume to continue reading or writing
- no more space is available for writing.

When a cluster is closed, a separate type 64 record is written for each component in the cluster.

TYPE64 contains a description of the VSAM component or cluster and accounting statistics such as number of records, deletes, EXCPs, and so forth. The statistics are presented as the total counts since creation, and the change in the total due to this job's use of the VSAM component or cluster. TYPE64 is the only source of EXCP statistics for VSAM files by name (although EXCP counts are also contained in the step records). Furthermore, since the data also contain the control interval size, the EXCP counts at each interval size can be tabulated from TYPE64. For example, the SAS step below tabulates the distribution of EXCPs by CISIZE for each job name, giving the number of times buffers of each size are being used.

```
PROC FREQ DATA=TYPE64;
TABLES JOB*CISIZE;
WEIGHT EXCPS;
```

This step counts the distribution of EXCPs by CISIZE for each jobname, and it can be very useful for jobs like IMS that may have many VSAM data sets opened and those that offer an option (for IMS, through the DFSVSAMP DD option) to pool VSAM buffers. The above program tells how many times the buffers of each size are being used. Other information, such as number of CI splits, can be used to identify potential VSAM performance problems, making the TYPE64 data set important in the analysis of VSAM-related performance problems.

Variable	Type	Length	Format	Label
ACCASPLT	NUM	4		CA SPLITS*SINCE*CREATION

accumulated number of control areas split in component since creation to this open.

ACCDELET	NUM	4		DELETES*SINCE*CREATION

accumulated number of records deleted from component since creation to this open.

Variable	Type	Length	Format	Label
ACCEXCPS	NUM	4		EXCPS*SINCE*CREATION

accumulated number of EXCPs since creation to this open.

| ACCINSRT | NUM | 4 | | INSERTS*SINCE*CREATION |

accumulated number of records inserted in components since creation to this open.

| ACCISPLT | NUM | 4 | | CI SPLITS*SINCE*CREATION |

accumulated number of control intervals split in components since creation to this open.

| ACCLEVEL | NUM | 4 | | INDEX LEVELS*SINCE*CREATION |

accumulated number of levels in index since creation to this open.

| ACCNEXTS | NUM | 4 | | EXTENTS*SINCE*CREATION |

accumulated number of extents since creation to this open.

| ACCNRECS | NUM | 4 | | RECORDS*SINCE*CREATION |

accumulated number of records in component since creation to this open.

| ACCRETRV | NUM | 4 | | RETRIEVALS*SINCE*CREATION |

number of records retrieved from component since creation to this open.

| ACCUNUCI | NUM | 4 | | UNUSED CI*SINCE*CREATION |

number of unused control intervals in components since creation to this open.

| ACCUPDAT | NUM | 4 | | UPDATES*SINCE*CREATION |

number of records updated in component since creation to this open.

| BEGCCHH1 | NUM | 4 | HEX8. | EXTENT 1*CCHH*ADDR |

beginning cylinder and tracks (where CC is cylinder number and HH, for head, is track number) of first extent.

| BEGCCHH2 | NUM | 4 | HEX8. | EXTENT 2*CCHH*ADDR |

beginning cylinder and tracks (where CC is cylinder number and HH, for head, is track number) of second extent.

| BEGCCHH3 | NUM | 4 | HEX8. | EXTENT 3*CCHH*ADDR |

beginning cylinder and tracks (where CC is cylinder number and HH, for head, is track number) of third extent.

| BLKSIZE | NUM | 4 | | PHYSICAL*BLOCK SIZE*(BYTES) |

physical blocksize.

Variable	Type	Length	Format	Label
CASPLITS	NUM	4		CA SPLITS*THIS*OPEN

number of control areas in this component split during this open.

| CATNAME | CHAR | 44 | | CATALOG*NAME |

name of catalog in which component is defined.

| CISIZE | NUM | 4 | | CONTROL*INTERVAL*SIZE |

control interval size.

| CISPLITS | NUM | 4 | | CI SPLITS*THIS*OPEN |

number of control intervals split in component during this open.

| COMPONT | CHAR | 9 | | TYPE*OF*COMPONENT |

component being processed.

value	meaning
DATA COMP	data component
INDEX	index component.

| DDNAME | CHAR | 8 | | DDNAME |

DDname used. (Zeros for catalog or catalog recovery area; blank if concatenated.)

| DELETES | NUM | 4 | | DELETES*THIS*OPEN |

number of records deleted from this component during this open.

| DEVICE1 | CHAR | 7 | | EXTENT 1*DEVICE*TYPE |

device type of first extent (for example, 3330, 3350, and so forth). Decoded from UCB type by VMACUCB member of SOURCLIB.

| DEVICE2 | CHAR | 7 | | EXTENT 2*DEVICE*TYPE |

device type of second extent (for example, 3330, 3350, and so forth). Decoded from UCB type by VMACUCB member of SOURCLIB.

| DEVICE3 | CHAR | 7 | | EXTENT 3*DEVICE*TYPE |

device type of third extent (for example, 3330, 3350, and so forth). Decoded from UCB type by the VMACUCB member of SOURCLIB.

| DEVNR1 | NUM | 4 | HEX4. | EXTENT 1*DEVICE*NUMBER |

device number of first extent device. Formerly the unit address in MVS/370. The unique number or address of this device.

| DEVNR2 | NUM | 4 | HEX4. | EXTENT 2*DEVICE*NUMBER |

device number of second extent device. Formerly the unit address in MVS/370. The unique number or address of this device.

Variable	Type	Length	Format	Label
DEVNR3	NUM	4	HEX4.	EXTENT 3*DEVICE*NUMBER

device number of third extent device. Formerly the unit address in MVS/370. The unique number or address of this device.

| ENDCCHH1 | NUM | 4 | HEX8. | EXTENT 1*END*CCHH |

ending cylinder and track of first extent.

| ENDCCHH2 | NUM | 4 | HEX8. | EXTENT 2*END*CCHH |

ending cylinder and track of second extent.

| ENDCCHH3 | NUM | 4 | HEX8. | EXTENT 3*END*CCHH |

ending cylinder and track of third extent.

| ENTRNAME | CHAR | 44 | | ENTRY*NAME |

name of component being processed.

| EXCPS | NUM | 4 | | EXCPS*THIS*OPEN |

number of EXCPs to or from this component during this open.

| HIGHRBA | NUM | 4 | | HIGHEST*RBA*USED |

highest used relative byte address (RBA) of component.

| INDXLVLS | NUM | 4 | | LEVELS*THIS*OPEN |

change in number of levels in index during this open.

| INSERTS | NUM | 4 | | INSERTS*THIS*OPEN |

number of records inserted in component during this open.

| JOB | CHAR | 8 | | JOB NAME*OR*TSO USER |

job name (batch); user ID (TSO).

| KEYLEN | NUM | 4 | | DASD*KEY*LENGTH |

key length.

| LCU1 | NUM | 4 | HEX2. | EXTENT*ONE*LCU |

logical control unit number to which device with first extent is connected.

| LCU2 | NUM | 4 | HEX2. | EXTENT*TWO*LCU |

logical control unit number to which device with second extent is connected.

| LCU3 | NUM | 4 | HEX2. | EXTENT*THREE*LCU |

logical control unit number to which device with third extent is connected.

Variable	Type	Length	Format	Label
LOCLINFO	CHAR	8		LOCAL*INSTALLATION*FIELD

locally-defined field, filled in by installation-written SMF exit routine.

| MAXLRECL | NUM | 4 | | MAXIMUM*LOGICAL*RECORD |

maximum logical record size.

| NREXTENT | NUM | 4 | | NUMBER*OF*EXTENTS |

number of extents in this component.

| NREXTNTS | NUM | 4 | | EXTENTS*THIS*OPEN |

change in number of extents during this open.

| READTIME | NUM | 8 | DATETIME19.2 | READ-IN*OR LOGON*EVENT |

job read-in (TSO LOGON) time stamp.

| RECORDS | NUM | 4 | | RECORDS*THIS*OPEN |

change in number of records in component during this open.

| RETRVALS | NUM | 4 | | RETRIEVALS*THIS*OPEN |

number of records retrieved during this open.

| SITUATN | CHAR | 16 | | SITUATION |

situation description (reason record was written). Note that these descriptions are assumed to be mutually exclusive in the decoding. Please advise the author if this is found to be not true.

value	meaning
ABEND PROCESS	record written during ABEND processing
CAT OR CRA REC	record is a catalog or CRA record
CLOSED TYPE=T	component closed, TYPE=T
COMPONENT CLOSED	component closed
NO SPACE AVAIL	no space available
VOL SWITCHED	volume switched
VVDS OR ICF	VVDS or ICF catalog being opened as a data set.

| SMFTIME | NUM | 8 | DATETIME19.2 | SMF*RECORD*TIME STAMP |

event time stamp.

| SPINDLE1 | NUM | 4 | HEX4. | EXTENT*ONE*SPINDLE |

spindle identification of first extent.

Variable	Type	Length	Format	Label
SPINDLE2	NUM	4	HEX4.	EXTENT*TWO*SPINDLE

spindle identification of second extent.

Variable	Type	Length	Format	Label
SPINDLE3	NUM	4	HEX4.	EXTENT*THREE*SPINDLE

spindle identification of third extent.

Variable	Type	Length	Format	Label
SYSTEM	CHAR	4	4.	SYSTEM*ID

system identification.

Variable	Type	Length	Format	Label
TRKNOTAL	NUM	4		REQUESTED*TRACKS NOT*ALLOCATED

number of tracks requested, but could not be allocated.

Variable	Type	Length	Format	Label
UCBTYPE1	NUM	4	HEX8.	EXTENT 1*UCB*TYPE

UCB type of first extent.

Variable	Type	Length	Format	Label
UCBTYPE2	NUM	4	HEX8.	EXTENT 2*UCB*TYPE

UCB type of second extent.

Variable	Type	Length	Format	Label
UCBTYPE3	NUM	4	HEX8.	EXTENT 3*UCB*TYPE

UCB type of third extent.

Variable	Type	Length	Format	Label
UNITADR1	NUM	4	HEX3.	EXTENT 1*UNIT*ADDR

unit address of first extent.

Variable	Type	Length	Format	Label
UNITADR2	NUM	4	HEX3.	EXTENT 2*UNIT*ADDR

unit address of second extent.

Variable	Type	Length	Format	Label
UNITADR3	NUM	4	HEX3.	EXTENT 3*UNIT*ADDR

unit address of third extent.

Variable	Type	Length	Format	Label
UNUSEDCI	NUM	4		UNUSED CI*THIS*OPEN

change in number of unused control intervals during this open.

Variable	Type	Length	Format	Label
UPDATES	NUM	4		UPDATES*THIS*OPEN

number of records updated during this open.

Variable	Type	Length	Format	Label
VOLSER1	CHAR	6		EXTENT 1*VOLSER

volume serial number of first extent.

Variable	Type	Length	Format	Label
VOLSER2	CHAR	6		EXTENT 2*VOLSER

volume serial number of second extent.

Variable	Type	Length	Format	Label
VOLSER3	CHAR	6		EXTENT 3*VOLSER

volume serial number of third extent.

TYPE68
VSAM Entry Renamed

The TYPE68 data set contains one observation for each type 68 SMF record, written whenever a VSAM catalog entry (that is, component, cluster, catalog, alternate index, path, or non-VSAM data set) is renamed.

The TYPE68 observation identifies the job that renamed the entry and describes the entry, including the old and new names. TYPE68 is important in constructing an audit trail of VSAM usage.

Variable	Type	Length	Format	Label
CATNAME	CHAR	44		CATALOG*NAME
				name of catalog in which entry is defined.
ENTRNAME	CHAR	44		ENTRY*NAME
				entry name (data set name) before rename.
JOB	CHAR	8		JOB NAME*OR*TSO USER
				job name (batch); user ID (TSO).
LOCLINFO	CHAR	8		LOCAL*INSTALLATION*FIELD
				locally-defined field, filled in by installation-written SMF exit routine.
NEWNAME	CHAR	44		NAME*AFTER*RENAME
				entry name (data set name) after rename.
READTIME	NUM	8	DATETIME19.2	READ-IN*OR LOGON*EVENT
				job read-in (TSO LOGON) time stamp.
SMFTIME	NUM	8	DATETIME19.2	SMF*RECORD*TIME STAMP
				rename event time stamp.
SYSTEM	CHAR	4	4.	SYSTEM*ID
				identification of system on which rename occurred.

TYPE69
VSAM Data Space Defined, Extended, or Deleted

The TYPE69 data set contains one observation for each type 69 SMF record, written whenever a VSAM data space is defined, extended, or deleted. (A type 69 record is not written when a catalog or a unique data set is defined or deleted; see data sets TYPE6156 and TYPE6367.)

The TYPE69 observation contains a description of the job causing this event and a description of the volume on which the data space was (or is) allocated. Unfortunately, TYPE69 contains no information to identify the event as a definition, extension, or deletion; however, it may be possible to infer which event occurred from the amount of free space after the event is given.

Variable	Type	Length	Format	Label
CATNAME	CHAR	44		CATALOG*NAME

name of catalog in which data space is defined.

DEVNR	NUM	4	HEX4.	DEVICE*NUMBER

device number. Formerly unit address in MVS/370. Unique number or address of the device.

JOB	CHAR	8		JOB NAME*OR*TSO USER

job name (batch); user ID (TSO).

LCU	NUM	4	HEX2.	LOGICAL*CONTROL*UNIT

logical control unit number to which this device is connected.

LOCLINFO	CHAR	8		LOCAL*INSTALLATION*FIELD

locally-defined field, filled in by installation-written SMF exit routine.

NRCYL	NUM	4		CONTIGUOUS*UNALLOCATED*CYLINDERS(MAX)

number of cylinders in largest contiguous unallocated area in any data space on volume.

NRFREEXT	NUM	4		FREE DATA SPACE*EXTENTS*ON VOLUME

number of free data space extents on affected volume after this event.

NRTRK	NUM	4		CONTIGUOUS*UNALLOCATED*TRACKS(MAX)

number of tracks (in addition to number of cylinders) in largest contiguous unallocated area in any data space on volume.

NRUNCYL	NUM	4		UNALLOCATED*CYLINDERS*IN DATA SPACE

number of unallocated cylinders in all data spaces on volume.

Variable	Type	Length	Format	Label
NRUNTRK	NUM	4		UNALLOCATED*TRACKS*IN DATA SPACE

number of unallocated tracks (in addition to number of unallocated cylinders) in all data spaces on volume.

READTIME	NUM	8	DATETIME19.2	READ-IN*OR LOGON*EVENT

job read-in (TSO LOGON) time stamp.

SMFTIME	NUM	8	DATETIME19.2	SMF*RECORD*TIME STAMP

event time stamp.

SPINDLE	NUM	4	HEX4.	SPINDLE*IDENTIFICATION

spindle identification.

SYSTEM	CHAR	4	4.	SYSTEM*ID

identification of system on which event occurred.

UNITADR	NUM	4	HEX3.	UNIT*ADDRESS

unit address of this volume.

VOLSER	CHAR	6		VOLUME*SERIAL*NUMBER

volume serial number.

TYPE70
RMF CPU Activity and Address Space Statistics

The TYPE70 data set contains one observation for each type 70 SMF record written at the end of each RMF INTERVAL and whenever an RMF session is terminated.*Only one record is written, even on systems with multiple processors (engines).

Data in TYPE70 are required for almost every evaluation you will ever make. The data set contains not only CPU active data but also measures of workload, states of tasks, and I/O interrupts serviced and delayed in MVS/XA.

CPU Measures

The CPU measurement in TYPE70 is equivalent to the CPU measured by a hardware monitor. The type 70 record actually contains the CPU wait time for each engine or processor in a multiengine system, not the CPU active. By subtracting this CPU wait time from the duration the record represents (DURATM), the percent CPU busy is calculated as a whole (PCTCPUBY) and for each engine separately (PCTCPBY1-PCTCPBY4).

Status variables for each processor contain the CPU serial number and flags if the processor was varied on or off during the interval. (If the processor was varied on or off, CPU wait and, hence, CPU busy calculations will be invalid.)

Two critical variables are the CPU model (CPUTYPE 3033, 3081, and so forth) and the CPU version (CPUVERSN, new with MVS/XA, differentiates between a 3081 D, G, K, and so forth). When a type 72 record is processed, CPU service units are converted into CPU seconds in order to compare delivered CPU time (TYPE72) with total CPU time (TYPE70) to calculate MVS overhead. To make the conversion, you must know the processor being used. MVS guarantees that type 70 records will precede type 72 records, so CPUTYPE and CPUVERSN can be used to look up the value of SU_SEC, the hardware-dependent constant that converts CPU service units to CPU seconds. The value of SU_SEC is set by the Nucleus Initialization Program (NIP) when you Initial Program Loaded (IPL) and stored in the RMCT control block. Its purpose is to make service units constant across processors; therefore, it is an excellent measure of the relative speed of different processors.

Note that the value has been changed by software Program Temporary Fix (PTFs, IBM's acronym for patches to errors between releases). They have been published both in the Initialization and Tuning Guides, in the Performance Notebook, and in the MVS Conversion Notebook.

---

* The TYPE70 data set built by the earlier version of *Merrill's Guide* contained one observation for each processor in a type 70 SMF record. In the new TYPE70 data set, separate variables rather than separate observations describe the CPU busy of each processor.

Or, if you have the TSO TEST command available, you can log on to TSO on the new processor and retrieve the value in your machine by using the following procedure:

```
TEST 'SYS1.LINKLIB(IEFBR14)'
```

```
L 10.%+25C%+40 F                    if you are on MVS/370, or
```

```
L 10.?+25C?+40 F                    if you are on MVS/XA.
```

(You have just asked the system to list the contents of +40 into the RMCT pointed to by the address at offset +25C into the CVT, with absolute address 10.)

The TEST command responds with:

HHHHHH. NNNNNN

where *HHHHHH* is the actual address of the data, and *NNNNNN* is a number. If you divide *NNNNNN* into 16,000,000 (a scaling factor), you get the Service Units generated from one second of CPU active:

```
SU_SEC = 16000000 / NNNNNN;
```

ASID Count by State Measures

TYPE70 contains statistics on six states in which address spaces were found during its sampling. The states recorded are:

variable name begins with	state	descriptions
IN	IN	tasks in real memory on the SRM IN queue including tasks that are IN READY.
READY	IN-READY	tasks in real memory and READY to execute.
OUT	OUT-READY	tasks not in real memory but physically swapped out yet ready to execute. This variable always indicates poor performance. Note that OUT READY tasks held out by the Response Time Objective (RTO) delay are not included.
WAIT	OUT-WAIT	tasks not in real memory that are waiting (for example, for the user to type in a TSO command).
LRDY	LOGICAL OUT-READY	tasks logically swapped out, but not yet physically swapped out, that are now READY. Interactive users pass through this state after they press ENTER to get their next screen of

		data, if they were sufficiently interactive to avoid the physical Terminal-Input swap out.
LWAIT	LOGICAL OUT-WAIT	tasks logically swapped out and physically swapped in that are waiting. This is where you spend some time as you read your screen of data before you are physically swapped out.

The minimum, maximum, and mean numbers of address spaces in each state are provided. In addition, for each state there are 12 intervals (buckets) containing the percentage of time that the number of tasks were in a particular state (for example, the percentage of the RMF interval with 0 READY users, 1-2 READY users, and so forth) in this MVS system. The variable names for these 12 buckets are suffixed from 0 to 11 (OUT0-OUT11), and the variable's label describes the range of each bucket. The average, minimum, and maximum values are suffixed with AVG, MIN, and MAX, respectively.

ASID Count by Type Measures

TYPE70 contains statistics on the number of logged on or initiated address spaces of each type. MVS recognizes 3 types of users: batch jobs, TSO users, and started tasks. For each type, the minimum, maximum, and average numbers during the interval are provided. For 12 intervals, the percentage of time that a particular number of users was on the system is provided. For example, the percentage of time (0, 1-2, 3-4, 5-6, and so forth) that TSO users were logged on to the system is available. Unfortunately, these intervals are not very useful for large systems since the maximum interval value is 36. When MVS was developed, this value was considered big! The average value, however, is still valid and is the best source of data on the number of TSO users and batch jobs during the RMF interval. The variable names for these intervals and statistics begin with BATCH, TSO, or STC and follow the naming convention described above.

I/O Interrupt Rate Measures (MVS/XA ONLY)

TYPE70 contains statistics on the number of I/O interrupts handled by each engine. The CPU record contains I/O measures since in MVS/XA, a multiengine system, the SRM would like to disable one or more of its engines for I/O interrupts. If you could operate with only one processor handling all I/O interrupts, you would get better throughput and higher delivered MIPS because the handling of I/O interrupts disturbs the smooth delivery of instructions to your program. MVS/XA does that. Whenever the I/O interrupt rate is low enough, XA disables one or more engines for I/O interrupts to maximize delivery of processor power. If too many I/O interrupts are being delayed, however, the engine is re-enabled. The decision is dynamic, lasts for 10 to 20 seconds, and is based on the number of I/O interrupts handled by TPI (Test Pending Interrupt).

Normally, I/O interrupts are handled by the Second Level Interrupt Handler (SLIH). In MVS/XA, after an interrupt has been serviced by the SLIH, he checks for any unhandled interrupts. If they occur, the second interrupt is handled by TPI, which saves some time over a return and re-entry into SLIH. However, any I/O interrupt handled via TPI was delayed; had another processor been enabled, it would have processed the interrupt via SLIH. TYPE70 contains the total (SLIH plus TPI) interrupt rate and the I/O rate for each processor in the IORATE variables.

TYPE70 also contains the percentage of total I/O interrupts that were handled by TPI and the percentage handled for each processor in the PCTTPI variables. This percentage is used by the SRM to decide whether or not to disable. The default threshold enables when 30% are being delayed and disables when only 10% of I/O interrupts are being delayed.

Variable	Type	Length	Format	Label
BATCHAVG	NUM	4	5.1	AVERAGE*INITIATORS*ACTIVE

average number of batch initiators over RMF interval. Note that this statistic (and all of the BATCH variables) counts all batch initiators, including those containing IMS Message Regions because they are really batch jobs to MVS; ADABAS and MODEL204 nucleus if read in as batch jobs; and other system tasks that happen to execute in a real batch initiator. This value is an excellent measure of the batch multiprogramming level and, hence, the number of initiators in use, provided you have accounted for the batch initiators that you do not call batch and can subtract them out of the average.

BATCHMAX	NUM	4	5.1	MAXIMUM*INITIATORS*ACTIVE

maximum number of batch initiators over the RMF interval.

BATCHMIN	NUM	4	5.1	MINIMUM*INITIATORS*ACTIVE

minimum number of batch initiators over the RMF interval.

BATCH00	NUM	4	5.1	PERCENT*WHEN 0*INITS

percentage of time when there were no batch initiators active.

BATCH01	NUM	4	5.1	PERCENT*WHEN 1-2*INITS

percentage of time when there were one or two batch initiators active.

BATCH02	NUM	4	5.1	PERCENT*WHEN 3-4*INITS

percentage of time when there were three or four batch initiators active.

BATCH03	NUM	4	5.1	PERCENT*WHEN 5-6*INITS

percentage of time when there were five or six batch initiators active.

Variable	Type	Length	Format	Label
BATCH04	NUM	4	5.1	PERCENT*WHEN 7-8*INITS

percentage of time when there were seven or eight batch initiators active.

BATCH05	NUM	4	5.1	PERCENT*WHEN 9-10*INITS

percentage of time when there were nine or ten batch initiators active.

BATCH06	NUM	4	5.1	PERCENT*WHEN 11-15*INITS

percentage of time when there were eleven to fifteen batch initiators active.

BATCH07	NUM	4	5.1	PERCENT*WHEN 16-20*INITS

percentage of time when there were sixteen to twenty batch initiators active.

BATCH08	NUM	4	5.1	PERCENT*WHEN 21-25*INITS

percentage of time when there were twenty-one to twenty-five batch initiators active.

BATCH09	NUM	4	5.1	PERCENT*WHEN 26-30*INITS

percentage of time when there were twenty-six to thirty batch initiators active.

BATCH10	NUM	4	5.1	PERCENT*WHEN 31-35*INITS

percentage of time when there were thirty-one to thirty-five batch initiators active.

BATCH11	NUM	4	5.1	PERCENT*WHEN OVER 35*INITS

percentage of time when there were thirty-six or more batch initiators active.

CAI0	CHAR	1	HEX2.	ON-LINE*STATUS*CPU 0

configuration activity indicator for CPU 0.

value	meaning
1	CPU is currently on-line at end of interval.
2	CPU was varied on- or off-line during measurement interval. CPU wait data for this engine are invalid.
3	CPU was varied on- or off-line during the measurement interval and is currently off-line at end of the interval. CPU wait data for this engine are invalid.

CAI1	CHAR	1	HEX2.	ON-LINE*STATUS*CPU 1

configuration activity indicator for CPU 1. See CAI0.

CAI2	CHAR	1	HEX2.	ON-LINE*STATUS*CPU 2

configuration activity indicator for CPU 2. See CAI0.

Variable	Type	Length	Format	Label

CAI3   CHAR   1   HEX2.   ON-LINE*STATUS*CPU 3

configuration activity indicator for CPU 3. See CAI0.

CPUSER0   CHAR   3   HEX6.   SERIAL*NUMBER*CPU 0

serial number of CPU 0. Previously, the serial number was on a removable card. The first byte of the serial number on the 308*x* family contains the CPU number (that is, 00, 01, 02, and so forth).

CPUSER1   CHAR   3   HEX6.   SERIAL*NUMBER*CPU 1

serial number of CPU 1. See CPUSER0.

CPUSER2   CHAR   3   HEX6.   SERIAL*NUMBER*CPU 2

serial number of CPU 2. See CPUSER0.

CPUSER3   CHAR   3   HEX6.   SERIAL*NUMBER*CPU 3

serial number of CPU 3. See CPUSER0.

CPUTYPE   CHAR   2   HEX4.   CPU*MODEL*NUMBER

CPU model number. Note that the value is actually a character value formatted to print hex. If you want to test for a specific value, like a 3083, remember to use the syntax for a hex literal character:

    IF CPUTYPE='3083'X THEN ...

See also CPUVERSN, below.

CPUVERSN   CHAR   1   HEX2.   CPU*VERSION*NUMBER

CPU version number. MVS/XA only. This field describes the model of processor within CPUTYPE. The currently known values are:

value	CPUTYPE	processor
01	3083	3083-E
03	3081	3081-D
11	3083	3083-B
13	3081	3081-G
21	3083	3083-J
23	3081	3081-K

CPUWAITM   NUM   4   TIME12.2   TOTAL*CPU WAIT*DURATION

total processor wait time for all processors (engines) during interval. This value is the sum of the wait time for each of the processors and is the time that all processors were not executing instructions. Invalid if CAI0-CAI3 are not one.

Variable	Type	Length	Format	Label
CPUWAIT0	NUM	4	TIME12.3	CPU WAIT*DURATION*CPU 0

processor 0 wait time. Invalid if CAI0 is not one.

CPUWAIT1	NUM	4	TIME12.3	CPU WAIT*DURATION*CPU 1

processor 1 wait time. Invalid if CAI1 is not one.

CPUWAIT2	NUM	4	TIME12.3	CPU WAIT*DURATION*CPU 2

processor 2 wait time. Invalid if CAI2 is not one.

CPUWAIT3	NUM	4	TIME12.3	CPU WAIT*DURATION*CPU 3

processor 3 wait time. Invalid if CAI3 is not one.

CYCLE	NUM	4		SAMPLE*CYCLE*TIME(MS)

RMF sample cycle time (in milliseconds). Every CYCLE, a sampling observation is made.

DURATM	NUM	4	TIME12.2	DURATION*OF*INTERVAL

duration of this RMF interval. This usually is very close to the specified value of INTERVAL in IEAIPS member of PARMLIB. It can vary slightly because RMF may not have been in control exactly at the end of interval and can vary substantially if RMF is terminated.

INAVG	NUM	4	5.1	AVERAGE*IN*USERS

average number of IN tasks over the RMF interval.

INMAX	NUM	4	5.1	MAXIMUM*IN*USERS

maximum number of IN tasks over the RMF interval.

INMIN	NUM	4	5.1	MINIMUM*IN*USERS

minimum number of IN tasks over the RMF interval.

IN00	NUM	4	5.1	PERCENT*WHEN 0*IN USERS

percent of time when the number of IN tasks was zero. An IN user is in real storage on the SRM IN QUEUE. This includes the tasks that are IN READY (variables READY).

IN01	NUM	4	5.1	PERCENT*WHEN 1-2*IN USERS

percentage of time when number of IN tasks was one or two.

IN02	NUM	4	5.1	PERCENT*WHEN 3-4*IN USERS

percentage of time when number of IN tasks was three or four.

IN03	NUM	4	5.1	PERCENT*WHEN 5-6*IN USERS

percentage of time when number of IN tasks was five or six.

Variable	Type	Length	Format	Label
IN04	NUM	4	5.1	PERCENT*WHEN 7-8*IN USERS

percentage of time when number of IN tasks was seven or eight.

IN05	NUM	4	5.1	PERCENT*WHEN 9-10*IN USERS

percentage of time when number of IN tasks was nine or ten.

IN06	NUM	4	5.1	PERCENT*WHEN 11-15*IN USERS

percentage of time when number of IN tasks was eleven to fifteen.

IN07	NUM	4	5.1	PERCENT*WHEN 16-20*IN USERS

percentage of time when number of IN tasks was sixteen to twenty.

IN08	NUM	4	5.1	PERCENT*WHEN 21-25*IN USERS

percentage of time when number of IN tasks was twenty-one to twenty-five.

IN09	NUM	4	5.1	PERCENT*WHEN 26-30*IN USERS

percentage of time when number of IN tasks was twenty-six to thirty.

IN10	NUM	4	5.1	PERCENT*WHEN 31-35*IN USERS

percentage of time when number of IN tasks was thirty-one to thirty-five.

IN11	NUM	4	5.1	PERCENT*WHEN OVER 35*IN USERS

percentage of time when number of IN tasks was thirty-six or more.

IORATE	NUM	4		TOTAL IO*INTERRUPT*RATE

total I/O interrupt rate (per second) for all interrupts (SLIH and TPI) on all processors during interval.

IORATE0	NUM	4		CPU 0 IO*INTERRUPT*RATE

total I/O interrupt rate (per second) for all interrupts (SLIH and TPI) on processor 0 during interval.

IORATE1	NUM	4		CPU 1 IO*INTERRUPT*RATE

total I/O interrupt rate (per second) for all interrupts (SLIH and TPI) on processor 1 during interval.

IORATE2	NUM	4		CPU 2 IO*INTERRUPT*RATE

total I/O interrupt rate (per second) for all interrupts (SLIH and TPI) on processor 2 during interval.

IORATE3	NUM	4		CPU 3 IO*INTERRUPT*RATE

total I/O interrupt rate (per second) for all interrupts (SLIH and TPI) on processor 3 during interval.

Variable	Type	Length	Format	Label
LRDYAVG	NUM	4	5.1	AVERAGE*LOGICAL*OUT READY

average number of LOGICAL OUT READY tasks over RMF interval.

| LRDYMAX | NUM | 4 | 5.1 | MAXIMUM*LOGICAL*OUT READY |

maximum number of LOGICAL OUT READY tasks over RMF interval.

| LRDYMIN | NUM | 4 | 5.1 | MINIMUM*LOGICAL*OUT READY |

minimum number of LOGICAL OUT READY tasks over RMF interval.

| LRDY00 | NUM | 4 | 5.1 | PERCENT*WHEN 0*LOGICAL OUT READY |

percentage of time when the number of LOGICAL OUT READY tasks was zero. A task is LOGICAL OUT READY when it is on the SRM OUT queue and is physically in real storage but is logically swapped out of real storage and is ready to execute.

| LRDY01 | NUM | 4 | 5.1 | PERCENT*WHEN 1-2*LOGICAL OUT READY |

percentage of time when number of LOGICAL OUT READY tasks was one or two.

| LRDY02 | NUM | 4 | 5.1 | PERCENT*WHEN 3-4*LOGICAL OUT READY |

percentage of time when number of LOGICAL OUT READY tasks was three or four.

| LRDY03 | NUM | 4 | 5.1 | PERCENT*WHEN 5-6*LOGICAL OUT READY |

percentage of time when number of LOGICAL OUT READY tasks was five or six.

| LRDY04 | NUM | 4 | 5.1 | PERCENT*WHEN 7-8*LOGICAL OUT READY |

percentage of time when number of LOGICAL OUT READY tasks was seven or eight.

| LRDY05 | NUM | 4 | 5.1 | PERCENT*WHEN 9-10*LOGICAL OUT READY |

percentage of time when number of LOGICAL OUT READY tasks was nine or ten.

| LRDY06 | NUM | 4 | 5.1 | PERCENT*WHEN 11-15*LOGICAL OUT READY |

percentage of time when number of LOGICAL OUT READY tasks was eleven to fifteen.

| LRDY07 | NUM | 4 | 5.1 | PERCENT*WHEN 16-20*LOGICAL OUT READY |

percentage of time when number of LOGICAL OUT READY tasks was sixteen to twenty.

Variable	Type	Length	Format	Label
LRDY08	NUM	4	5.1	PERCENT*WHEN 21-25*LOGICAL OUT READY

percentage of time when number of LOGICAL OUT READY tasks was twenty-one to twenty-five.

LRDY09	NUM	4	5.1	PERCENT*WHEN 26-30*LOGICAL OUT READY

percentage of time when number of LOGICAL OUT READY tasks was twenty-six to thirty.

LRDY10	NUM	4	5.1	PERCENT*WHEN 31-35*LOGICAL OUT READY

percentage of time when number of LOGICAL OUT READY tasks was thirty-one to thirty-five.

LRDY11	NUM	4	5.1	PERCENT*WHEN OVER 35*LOGICAL OUT READY

percentage of time when number of LOGICAL OUT READY tasks was thirty-six or more.

LWAITAVG	NUM	4	5.1	AVERAGE*LOGICAL*OUT WAIT

average number of LOGICAL OUT WAIT tasks over RMF interval.

LWAITMAX	NUM	4	5.1	MAXIMUM*LOGICAL*OUT WAIT

maximum number of LOGICAL OUT WAIT tasks over RMF interval.

LWAITMIN	NUM	4	5.1	MINIMUM*LOGICAL*OUT WAIT

minimum number of LOGICAL OUT WAIT tasks over RMF interval.

LWAIT00	NUM	4	5.1	PERCENT*WHEN 0*LOGICAL OUT WAIT

percentage of time when number of LOGICAL OUT WAIT users was zero. A task is LOGICAL OUT WAIT when it is on the SRM WAIT queue, physically in real storage, logically swapped out, and not ready to execute.

LWAIT01	NUM	4	5.1	PERCENT*WHEN 1-2*LOGICAL OUT WAIT

percentage of time when number of LOGICAL OUT WAIT tasks was one or two.

LWAIT02	NUM	4	5.1	PERCENT*WHEN 3-4*LOGICAL OUT WAIT

percentage of time when number of LOGICAL OUT WAIT tasks was three or four.

LWAIT03	NUM	4	5.1	PERCENT*WHEN 5-6*LOGICAL OUT WAIT

percentage of time when number of LOGICAL OUT WAIT tasks was five or six.

Variable	Type	Length	Format	Label
LWAIT04	NUM	4	5.1	PERCENT*WHEN 7-8*LOGICAL OUT WAIT

percentage of time when number of LOGICAL OUT WAIT tasks was seven or eight.

LWAIT05	NUM	4	5.1	PERCENT*WHEN 9-10*LOGICAL OUT WAIT

percentage of time when number of LOGICAL OUT WAIT tasks was nine or ten.

LWAIT06	NUM	4	5.1	PERCENT*WHEN 11-15*LOGICAL OUT WAIT

percentage of time when number of LOGICAL OUT WAIT tasks was eleven to fifteen.

LWAIT07	NUM	4	5.1	PERCENT*WHEN 16-20*LOGICAL OUT WAIT

percentage of time when number of LOGICAL OUT WAIT tasks was sixteen to twenty.

LWAIT08	NUM	4	5.1	PERCENT*WHEN 21-25*LOGICAL OUT WAIT

percentage of time when number of LOGICAL OUT WAIT tasks was twenty-one to twenty-five.

LWAIT09	NUM	4	5.1	PERCENT*WHEN 26-30*LOGICAL OUT WAIT

percentage of time when number of LOGICAL OUT WAIT tasks was twenty-six to thirty.

LWAIT10	NUM	4	5.1	PERCENT*WHEN 31-35*LOGICAL OUT WAIT

percentage of time when number of LOGICAL OUT WAIT tasks was thirty-one to thirty-five.

LWAIT11	NUM	4	5.1	PERCENT*WHEN OVER 35*LOGICAL OUT WAIT

percentage of time when number of LOGICAL OUT WAIT tasks was thirty-six or more.

NRCPUS	NUM	4		NUMBER*OF*CPUS

number of CPUs on-line at end of interval that had no VARY activity.

NRSAMPLE	NUM	4		NUMBER*OF*SAMPLES

number of samples in RMF interval. (Samples are taken at CYCLE intervals.)

OUTAVG	NUM	4	5.1	AVERAGE*OUT READY*USERS

average number of OUTREADY tasks over RMF interval.

Variable	Type	Length	Format	Label
OUTMAX	NUM	4	5.1	MAXIMUM*OUT READY*USERS

maximum number of OUTREADY tasks over RMF interval.

Variable	Type	Length	Format	Label
OUTMIN	NUM	4	5.1	MINUMUM*OUT READY*USERS

minimum number of OUTREADY tasks over RMF interval.

Variable	Type	Length	Format	Label
OUT00	NUM	4	5.1	PERCENT*WHEN 0*OUT READY USERS

percentage of time when number of OUTREADY tasks was zero. A task is OUTREADY when it is on the SRM OUT queue, physically swapped out of real storage, and is ready to execute. Note that tasks that are OUTREADY because they are being held out by the Response Time Objective (RTO) delay are not included in this value.

Variable	Type	Length	Format	Label
OUT01	NUM	4	5.1	PERCENT*WHEN 1-2*OUT READY USERS

percentage of time when number of OUT READY tasks was one or two.

Variable	Type	Length	Format	Label
OUT02	NUM	4	5.1	PERCENT*WHEN 3-4*OUT READY USERS

percentage of time when number of OUT READY tasks was three or four.

Variable	Type	Length	Format	Label
OUT03	NUM	4	5.1	PERCENT*WHEN 5-6*OUT READY USERS

percentage of time when number of OUT READY tasks was five or six.

Variable	Type	Length	Format	Label
OUT04	NUM	4	5.1	PERCENT*WHEN 7-8*OUT READY USERS

percentage of time when number of OUT READY tasks was seven or eight.

Variable	Type	Length	Format	Label
OUT05	NUM	4	5.1	PERCENT*WHEN 9-10*OUT READY USERS

percentage of time when number of OUT READY tasks was nine or ten.

Variable	Type	Length	Format	Label
OUT06	NUM	4	5.1	PERCENT*WHEN 11-15*OUT READY USERS

percentage of time when number of OUT READY tasks was eleven to fifteen.

Variable	Type	Length	Format	Label
OUT07	NUM	4	5.1	PERCENT*WHEN 16-20*OUT READY USERS

percentage of time when number of OUT READY tasks was sixteen to twenty.

Variable	Type	Length	Format	Label
OUT08	NUM	4	5.1	PERCENT*WHEN 21-25*OUT READY USERS

percentage of time when number of OUT READY tasks was twenty-one to twenty-five.

Variable	Type	Length	Format	Label
OUT09	NUM	4	5.1	PERCENT*WHEN 26-30*OUT READY USERS

percentage of time when number of OUT READY tasks was twenty-six to thirty.

| OUT10 | NUM | 4 | 5.1 | PERCENT*WHEN 31-35*OUT READY USERS |

percentage of time when number of OUT READY tasks was thirty-one to thirty-five.

| OUT11 | NUM | 4 | 5.1 | PERCENT*WHEN OVER 35*OUT READY USERS |

percentage of time when number of OUT READY tasks was thirty-six or more.

| PCTCPBY0 | NUM | 4 | | CPU 0*PERCENT*BUSY |

percentage of DURATM in which CPU number zero was executing instructions (that is, CPU was busy).

| PCTCPBY1 | NUM | 4 | | CPU 1*PERCENT*BUSY |

percentage of DURATM in which CPU number one was executing instructions.

| PCTCPBY2 | NUM | 4 | | CPU 2*PERCENT*BUSY |

percentage of DURATM in which CPU number two was executing instructions (that is, CPU was busy).

| PCTCPBY3 | NUM | 4 | | CPU 3*PERCENT*BUSY |

percentage of DURATM in which CPU number three was executing instructions.

| PCTCPUBY | NUM | 4 | | ALL CPUS*PERCENT*BUSY |

percentage of time when all available CPUs were busy. If a CPU is reconfigured during the interval (CAIn=2 or 3) or is off-line (CAIn=0), this measure will not be valid.

| PCTTPI | NUM | 4 | | TOTAL % IO*INTERRUPTS*DELAYED (TPI) |

percentage of all I/O interrupts from all processors handled by Test Pending Interrupt (TPI) during interval.

| PCTTPI0 | NUM | 4 | | CPU0 % IO*INTERRUPTS*DELAYED (TPI) |

percentage of I/O interrupts from CPU 0 handled by the Test Pending Interrupt (TPI) during interval.

| PCTTPI1 | NUM | 4 | | CPU1 % IO*INTERRUPTS*DELAYED (TPI) |

percentage of I/O interrupts from CPU 1 handled by the Test Pending Interrupt (TPI) during interval.

Variable	Type	Length	Format	Label
PCTTPI2	NUM	4		CPU2 % IO*INTERRUPTS*DELAYED (TPI)

percentage of I/O interrupts from CPU 2 handled by the Test Pending Interrupt (TPI) during interval.

| PCTTPI3 | NUM | 4 | | CPU3 % IO*INTERRUPTS*DELAYED (TPI) |

percentage of I/O interrupts from CPU 3 handled by the Test Pending Interrupt (TPI) during interval.

| READYAVG | NUM | 4 | 5.1 | AVERAGE*IN READY*USERS |

average number of IN READY tasks over RMF interval.

| READYMAX | NUM | 4 | 5.1 | MAXIMUM*IN READY*USERS |

maximum number of IN READY tasks over RMF interval.

| READYMIN | NUM | 4 | 5.1 | MINIMUM*IN READY*USERS |

minimum number of IN READY tasks over RMF interval.

| READY00 | NUM | 4 | 5.1 | PERCENT*WHEN 0*IN READY |

percentage of time when number of IN READY tasks was zero. A task is IN READY when it is in real storage and is ready to execute.

| READY01 | NUM | 4 | 5.1 | PERCENT*WHEN 1*IN READY |

percentage of time when number of IN READY tasks was one.

| READY02 | NUM | 4 | 5.1 | PERCENT*WHEN 2*IN READY |

percentage of time when number of IN READY tasks was two.

| READY03 | NUM | 4 | 5.1 | PERCENT*WHEN 3*IN READY |

percentage of time when number of IN READY tasks was three.

| READY04 | NUM | 4 | 5.1 | PERCENT*WHEN 4*IN READY |

percentage of time when number of IN READY tasks was four.

| READY05 | NUM | 4 | 5.1 | PERCENT*WHEN 5*IN READY |

percentage of time when number of IN READY tasks was five.

| READY06 | NUM | 4 | 5.1 | PERCENT*WHEN 6*IN READY |

percentage of time when number of IN READY tasks was six.

| READY07 | NUM | 4 | 5.1 | PERCENT*WHEN 7*IN READY |

percentage of time when number of IN READY tasks was seven.

Variable	Type	Length	Format	Label
READY08	NUM	4	5.1	PERCENT*WHEN 8*IN READY

percentage of time when number of IN READY tasks was eight.

READY09	NUM	4	5.1	PERCENT*WHEN 9*IN READY

percentage of time when number of IN READY tasks was nine.

READY10	NUM	4	5.1	PERCENT*WHEN 10*IN READY

percentage of time when number of IN READY tasks was ten.

READY11	NUM	4	5.1	PERCENT*WHEN 11*IN READY

percentage of time when number of IN READY tasks was eleven.

READY12	NUM	4	5.1	PERCENT*WHEN 12*IN READY

percentage of time when number of IN READY tasks was twelve.

READY13	NUM	4	5.1	PERCENT*WHEN 13*IN READY

percentage of time when number of IN READY tasks was thirteen.

READY14	NUM	4	5.1	PERCENT*WHEN 14*IN READY

percentage of time when number of IN READY tasks was fourteen.

READY15	NUM	4	5.1	PERCENT*WHEN 15*IN READY

percentage of time when number of IN READY tasks was fifteen or more.

RELEASE	CHAR	4		OPERATING*SYSTEM*RELEASE

operating system release number and level (for example, 0380 for Release 3 Level 8, or 3.8).

SMFTIME	NUM	8	DATETIME19.2	SMF*RECORD*TIME STAMP

approximate ending time stamp of RMF interval. Actually, this is when the record was moved to the buffer.

STARTIME	NUM	8	DATETIME19.2	START OF*INTERVAL

beginning of RMF interval time stamp.

STCAVG	NUM	4	5.1	AVERAGE*STC*USERS

average number of STARTED TASKS over RMF interval.

STCMAX	NUM	4	5.1	MAXIMUM*STC*USERS

maximum number of STARTED TASKS over RMF interval.

STCMIN	NUM	4	5.1	MINIMUM*STC*USERS

minimum number of STARTED TASKS over RMF interval.

Variable	Type	Length	Format	Label
STC00	NUM	4	5.1	PERCENT*WHEN 0*STC USERS

percentage of time when there were no STARTED TASKS active.

| STC01 | NUM | 4 | 5.1 | PERCENT*WHEN 1-2*STC USERS |

percentage of time when there were one or two STARTED TASKS active.

| STC02 | NUM | 4 | 5.1 | PERCENT*WHEN 3-4*STC USERS |

percentage of time when there were three or four STARTED TASKS active.

| STC03 | NUM | 4 | 5.1 | PERCENT*WHEN 5-6*STC USERS |

percentage of time when there were five or six STARTED TASKS active.

| STC04 | NUM | 4 | 5.1 | PERCENT*WHEN 7-8*STC USERS |

percentage of time when there were seven or eight STARTED TASKS active.

| STC05 | NUM | 4 | 5.1 | PERCENT*WHEN 9-10*STC USERS |

percentage of time when there were nine or ten STARTED TASKS active.

| STC06 | NUM | 4 | 5.1 | PERCENT*WHEN 11-15*STC USERS |

percentage of time when there were eleven to fifteen STARTED TASKS active.

| STC07 | NUM | 4 | 5.1 | PERCENT*WHEN 16-20*STC USERS |

percentage of time when there were sixteen to twenty STARTED TASKS active.

| STC08 | NUM | 4 | 5.1 | PERCENT*WHEN 21-25*STC USERS |

percentage of time when there were twenty-one to twenty-five STARTED TASKS active.

| STC09 | NUM | 4 | 5.1 | PERCENT*WHEN 26-30*STC USERS |

percentage of time when there were twenty-six to thirty STARTED TASKS active.

| STC10 | NUM | 4 | 5.1 | PERCENT*WHEN 31-35*STC USERS |

percentage of time when there were thirty-one to thirty-five STARTED TASKS active.

| STC11 | NUM | 4 | 5.1 | PERCENT*WHEN OVER 35*STC USERS |

percentage of time when there were thirty-six or more STARTED TASKS active.

| SUPATERN | CHAR | 14 | HEX28. | SELECTABLE*UNIT*BIT PATTERN |

bit pattern for installed selectable units. High order bit is SU0 (Initial System).

| SYSTEM | CHAR | 4 | 4. | SYSTEM*ID |

identification of this system.

Variable	Type	Length	Format	Label
TSOAVG	NUM	4	5.1	AVERAGE*TSO*USERS

average number of TSO users logged on over RMF interval.

TSOMAX	NUM	4	5.1	MAXIMUM*TSO*USERS

maximum number of TSO users logged on over RMF interval.

TSOMIN	NUM	4	5.1	MINIMUM*TSO*USERS

minimum number of TSO users logged on over RMF interval.

TSO00	NUM	4	5.1	PERCENT*WHEN 0*TSO USERS

percentage of time when there were no TSO users logged on.

TSO01	NUM	4	5.1	PERCENT*WHEN 1-2*TSO USERS

percentage of time when there were one or two TSO users logged on.

TSO02	NUM	4	5.1	PERCENT*WHEN 3-4*TSO USERS

percentage of time when there were three or four TSO users logged on.

TSO03	NUM	4	5.1	PERCENT*WHEN 5-6*TSO USERS

percentage of time when there were five or six TSO users logged on.

TSO04	NUM	4	5.1	PERCENT*WHEN 7-8*TSO USERS

percentage of time when there were seven or eight TSO users logged on.

TSO05	NUM	4	5.1	PERCENT*WHEN 9-10*TSO USERS

percentage of time when there were nine or ten TSO users logged on.

TSO06	NUM	4	5.1	PERCENT*WHEN 11-15*TSO USERS

percentage of time when there were eleven to fifteen TSO users logged on.

TSO07	NUM	4	5.1	PERCENT*WHEN 16-20*TSO USERS

percentage of time when there were sixteen to twenty TSO users logged on.

TSO08	NUM	4	5.1	PERCENT*WHEN 21-25*TSO USERS

percentage of time when there were twenty-one to twenty-five TSO users logged on.

TSO09	NUM	4	5.1	PERCENT*WHEN 26-30*TSO USERS

percentage of time when there were twenty-six to thirty TSO users logged on.

TSO10	NUM	4	5.1	PERCENT*WHEN 31-35*TSO USERS

percentage of time when there were thirty-one to thirty-five TSO users logged on.

Variable	Type	Length	Format	Label

TSO11   NUM   4   5.1   PERCENT*WHEN OVER 35*TSO USERS

percentage of time when there were thirty-six or more TSO users logged on.

VERSION   CHAR   2   VERSION*NUMBER

record version number.

value	meaning
01	MF/1
02	RMF Version 1
03	RMF Version 2 Release 1 or 2
04	RMF Version 2 Release 2 with MVS/SE Release 1
05	RMF Version 2 Release 2 with MVS/SE Release 2, or RMF Version 2 Release 3
06	RMF Version 2 Release 3 with MVS/SP 1
07	RMF Version 2 Release 4 with MVS/SP 2
08	RMF Version 2 Release 4 enhancements with MVS/SP3
31	RMF Version 3 Release 1
32	RMF Version 3 Release 2.

WAITAVG   NUM   4   5.1   AVERAGE*OUT WAIT*TASKS

average number of OUT WAIT tasks over the RMF interval.

WAITMAX   NUM   4   5.1   MAXIMUM*OUT WAIT*TASKS

maximum number of OUT WAIT tasks over the RMF interval.

WAITMIN   NUM   4   5.1   MINIMUM*OUT WAIT*TASKS

minimum number of OUT WAIT tasks over the RMF interval.

WAIT00   NUM   4   5.1   PERCENT*WHEN 0*OUT WAIT

percentage of time when the number of OUT WAIT tasks was zero.

WAIT01   NUM   4   5.1   PERCENT*WHEN 1-2*OUT WAIT

percentage of time when the number of OUT WAIT tasks was one or two.

WAIT02   NUM   4   5.1   PERCENT*WHEN 3-4*OUT WAIT

percentage of time when the number of OUT WAIT tasks was three or four.

WAIT03   NUM   4   5.1   PERCENT*WHEN 5-6*OUT WAIT

percentage of time when the number of OUT WAIT tasks was five or six.

Variable	Type	Length	Format	Label
WAIT04	NUM	4	5.1	PERCENT*WHEN 7-8*OUT WAIT

percentage of time when the number of OUT WAIT tasks was seven or eight.

Variable	Type	Length	Format	Label
WAIT05	NUM	4	5.1	PERCENT*WHEN 9-10*OUT WAIT

percentage of time when the number of OUT WAIT tasks was nine or ten.

Variable	Type	Length	Format	Label
WAIT06	NUM	4	5.1	PERCENT*WHEN 11-15*OUT WAIT

percentage of time when the number of OUT WAIT tasks was eleven to fifteen.

Variable	Type	Length	Format	Label
WAIT07	NUM	4	5.1	PERCENT*WHEN 16-20*OUT WAIT

percentage of time when the number of OUT WAIT tasks was sixteen to twenty.

Variable	Type	Length	Format	Label
WAIT08	NUM	4	5.1	PERCENT*WHEN 21-25*OUT WAIT

percentage of time when the number of OUT WAIT tasks was twenty-one to twenty-five.

Variable	Type	Length	Format	Label
WAIT09	NUM	4	5.1	PERCENT*WHEN 26-30*OUT WAIT

percentage of time when the number of OUT WAIT tasks was twenty-six to thirty.

Variable	Type	Length	Format	Label
WAIT10	NUM	4	5.1	PERCENT*WHEN 31-35*OUT WAIT

percentage of time when the number of OUT WAIT tasks was thirty-one to thirty-five.

Variable	Type	Length	Format	Label
WAIT11	NUM	4	5.1	PERCENT*WHEN OVER 35*OUT WAIT

percentage of time when the number of OUT WAIT tasks was thirty-six or more.

TYPE71
RMF Paging and Swapping Activity

The TYPE71 data set contains one observation for every type 71 SMF record written at the end of each RMF interval or when RMF is stopped.

The type 71 records contain statistics on paging activity and memory usage, and they track swap management by the SRM. TYPE71 is important in resource analysis since it can identify whether or not real memory is limiting performance and whether the IPS is properly specified by analysis of swap types and rates.

Swap Count by Reason

The primary control mechanism used by the SRM to deal with resource shortage is swapping. Swapping-out is the removal from real memory of an entire address space (that is, a batch job or a TSO user). All recently referenced changed pages are written out to the swap data set (if one exists) and the page data sets as one logical I/O activity (though in fact it takes several I/O operations since an address space typically contains thirty to forty pages in a swap operation, and only twelve are usually written in one physical swap I/O operation). Thus, the physical I/O resulting from a swap-out or swap-in is the movement of many pages in one logical I/O operation.

In addition to managing resource overcommitment by swapping out tasks, there are a number of other situations that require a swap. TYPE71 contains variables (beginning with the letters SWAP) that represent a count of the swap rate for each of the thirteen types of swaps that can occur. Of particular interest are SWAPDW, SWAPEX, and SWAPUS, which are described below.

Memory Usage by Memory Area

The real memory can be subdivided into 5 areas: Common Storage Area (CSA), Link Pack Area (LPA), System Queue Area (SQA), Local System Queue Area (LSQA), and Private (or Local) Area. Within these areas, the frames (as pages are frequently called) can be further subdivided into fixed or pageable frames. For each of the above combination of area and type of frame, RMF records 3 statistics per interval: the mean (average), minimum, and maximum numbers of frames. In MVS/XA, the number of fixed frames below the 16 Megabyte Real Memory line is also provided. Thus, TYPE71 contains 33 variables per interval that describe the number of frames in use:

Area	Variable names for fixed frames (avg, min, and max)	Variable names for pageable frames (avg, min, and max)
CSA	CSAFXAV, MN, MX	CSAPGAV, MN, MX
LPA	LPAFXAV, MN, MX	LPAPGAV, MN, MX
LSQA	LSQFXAV, MN, MX	n/a (LSQA is fixed)
SQA	SQAFXAV, MN, MX	n/a (SQA is fixed)
Private	PRVFXAV, MN, MX	PRVPGAV, MN, MX
Total	FIXEDAV, MN, MX	PAGBLAV, MN, MX
Below 16MB	FIXLOAV, MN, MX	does not apply

These values are best used for tracking, although their absolute magnitude is also important, especially for the variables that measure fixed frames. For example, these statements

```
PROC PLOT DATA=WEEK.TYPE71
    PLOT (CSAFXAV,LPAGXAV,LSQFXAV,SQAFXAV,PRVFXAV,
        FIXEDAV, FIXLOAV) * STARTIME;
```

show when abrupt changes occurred. The steps that initiated and terminated (TYPE30_4 data set variables INITTIME and TERMTIME) during those RMF intervals can be selected for identification of the culprit task. The above PLOT also identifies the more insidious memory problem of slow erosion over hours or days. Although TYPE71 can show that erosion is occurring, it can provide little help in the cause. The TYPE78VS, TYPE78PA, and TYPE78SP data sets, although actually recording only virtual storage requirements, can be very useful tactical tools for this problem of memory erosion. Typical causes have been design errors in software (like the LOGREC component GETMAINing IF6 bytes but freeing only IF0 bytes for every record) that are tedious to locate and fix.

Paging Rates

Paging is the event in a virtual memory system that attempts to optimize dynamically real memory by keeping in real memory only the pages that are currently needed. When there is insufficient real memory, paging increases, and it is necessary to track paging rates to measure the effect of memory on performance. For paging, the source of the page is subdivided into four areas: CSA, LPA, Private VIO, and Private non-VIO . For each area, TYPE71 provides the number of pages read in from auxiliary storage (a page-in), the number of pages written out to auxiliary storage (a page-out), and the number of pages previously stolen from an address space but reclaimed by that address space before being reassigned to another (a reclaim). The variables are:

Area	Page-in rate variable	Page reclaim variable	Page-out variable
CSA	PVTCAIN	PVTCAREC	PVTCAOUT
LPA	LPAGINS	LPARECLM	never
Private: VIO	PVTVAMI	PVTVAMR	PVTVAMO
non-VIO	PVTNPIN	PVTNPREC	PVTNPOUT

A page that has never been changed does not need to be written out since it already exists on the page or swap data set. Thus, there are never any LPA page-outs since the LPA must be reentrant, which, by definition, can never be changed.

The SRM calculates several variables from the paging rates and uses them to determine overcommitment. These variables are the primary paging performance indicators:

Variable	Equation	Description
PFRATE	PVTNPIN + PVTNPREC	non-VIO page fault rate
PAGING	PVTNPIN + PVTNPOUT	non-VIO paging I/O load
SPR	PVTSPIN + PVTSPOUT	swap paging rate
PTR	PVTNPIN + PVTNPREC	PTR paging rate - RMF Demand Paging
DPR	PVTNPIN + PVTNPOUT	DPR paging rate
VIO	PVTVAMI + PVTVAMO	VIO paging rate
PAGRT	DPR + SPR + VIO	total paging rate
SYSPFR	PVTCAIN + PVTCAREC + LPAGINS	system area page fault rate
LCLPFR	PVTNPIN + PVTNPREC - SYSPFR	local area page fault rate

Note that paging means physical I/O was necessary to move a page in or out of real memory, but paging does not necessarily cause any task to delay. On the other hand, a page fault means that an in-memory task requires an additional page that is not in real memory, and the task must wait while the page is brought in by I/O (or located by reclaim). Thus, page fault rates are always a better measure than paging since page faults always cause a delay.

Variable	Type	Length	Format	Label
ASMNVSC	NUM	4		LOCAL SLOTS*ALLOCATED*NON-VIO

number of local page data set slots allocated to non-VIO private area pages.

| ASMSLOTS | NUM | 4 | | LOCAL SLOTS*DEFINED |

total number of local page data set slots.

| ASMSLOTX | NUM | 4 | | LOCAL SLOTS*UNALLOCATED |

number of local page data set slots not allocated.

| ASMVSC | NUM | 4 | | LOCAL SLOTS*ALLOCATED*TO VIO |

number of local page data set slots allocated to VIO private area pages.

| CSAPGAV | NUM | 4 | | CSA PAGEABLE*FRAMES*AVERAGE |

average number of CSA pageable frames.

| CSAPGMN | NUM | 4 | | CSA PAGEABLE*FRAMES*MINIMUM |

minimum number of CSA pageable frames.

| CSAPGMX | NUM | 4 | | CSA PAGEABLE*FRAMES*MAXIMUM |

maximum number of CSA pageable frames.

| CSLPFXAV | NUM | 4 | | CSA/LPA FIXED*FRAMES*AVERAGE |

average number of CSA+LPA fixed frames.

| CSLPFXMN | NUM | 4 | | CSA/LPA FIXED*FRAMES*MINIMUM |

minimum number of CSA+LPA fixed frames.

| CSLPFXMX | NUM | 4 | | CSA/LPA FIXED*FRAMES*MAXIMUM |

maximum number of CSA+LPA fixed frames.

| CYCLE | NUM | 4 | | SAMPLE*CYCLE*TIME(MS) |

sample cycle length (in milliseconds). At each CYCLE, a sampling observation is made.

| DPR | NUM | 4 | 5.1 | DEMAND*PAGING*RATE(DPR) |

Demand Paging Rate (DPR). Introduced as a calculated measure used by the SRM as one of the happy values in MVS/SE1, it is actually the number of non-VIO pages read or written, even though pages written out are not demanded. Note that in the RMF reports, the field marked demand pages is not this value, but rather the page fault rate (PTR) variable, which is described below.

| DURATM | NUM | 4 | TIME12.2 | DURATION*OF*INTERVAL |

duration of this RMF interval. At the end of each DURATM, all data gathered and sampled are written to SMF.

Variable	Type	Length	Format	Label
FIXEDAV	NUM	4		TOTAL FIXED*FRAMES*AVERAGE

average number of private area fixed frames.

FIXEDMN	NUM	4		TOTAL FIXED*FRAMES*MINIMUM

minimum number of private area fixed frames.

FIXEDMX	NUM	4		TOTAL FIXED*FRAMES*MAXIMUM

maximum number of private area fixed frames.

FIXLOAV	NUM	4		FRAMES FIXED*BELOW 16MB*AVERAGE

MVS/XA only. Average number of fixed frames below the 16 megabyte real memory line. Since some pages can only exist below the 16 meagbyte real memory line, MVS/XA keeps track of how many fixed frames are in this area, which is more restrictive.

FIXLOMN	NUM	4		FRAMES FIXED*BELOW 16MB*MINIMUM

MVS/XA only. Minimum number of fixed frames below the 16 megabyte real memory line.

FIXLOMX	NUM	4		FRAMES FIXED*BELOW 16MB*MAXIMUM

MVS/XA only. Maximum number of fixed frames below the 16 megabyte real memory line.

FRAMES	CHAR	8		RECORD*CONTAINS*DATA FOR

MVS/370 only. Flag that this record tracks total or pageable frames.

LCLPFR	NUM	4	5.1	PRIVATE AREA*PAGE FAULT*RATE

local area page fault rate. A very strong metric since each page fault means an in-memory task waited this page. See also SYSPFR.

LPAFXAV	NUM	4		LPA-TCB FIXED*FRAMES*AVERAGE

average number of LPA fixed frames.

LPAFXMN	NUM	4		LPA-TCB FIXED*FRAMES*MINIMUM

minimum number of LPA fixed frames.

LPAFXMX	NUM	4		LPA-TCB FIXED*FRAMES*MAXIMUM

maximum number of LPA fixed frames.

LPAGINS	NUM	4	5.1	LPA*AREA*PAGE-INS

non-VIO, nonswap page-in rate (per second) in the LPA.

Variable	Type	Length	Format	Label
LPAPGAV	NUM	4		LPA-TCB PAGEABLE*FRAMES*AVERAGE

average number of LPA pageable frames.

| LPAPGMN | NUM | 4 | | LPA-TCB PAGEABLE*FRAMES*MINIMUM |

minimum number of LPA pageable frames.

| LPAPGMX | NUM | 4 | | LPA-TCB PAGEABLE*FRAMES*MAXIMUM |

maximum number of LPA pageable frames.

| LPARECLM | NUM | 4 | 5.1 | LPA*AREA*RECLAIMS |

non-VIO, nonswap reclaim rate (per second) in the LPA.

| LPSWRCLM | NUM | 4 | 5.1 | LPA NON-VIO*SWAP*RECLAIM RATE |

MVS/370 only. Non-VIO swap reclaim rate (per second) in the the LPA.

| LSQAFXAV | NUM | 4 | | LSQA FIXED*FRAMES*AVERAGE |

average number of LSQA fixed frames.

| LSQAFXMN | NUM | 4 | | LSQA FIXED*FRAMES*MINIMUM |

minimum number of LSQA fixed frames.

| LSQAFXMX | NUM | 4 | | LSQA FIXED*FRAMES*MAXIMUM |

maximum number of LSQA fixed frames.

| LSWBEG | NUM | 4 | | LOGICAL*SWAP-OUTS*AT BEGIN |

number of logical swap-outs at the beginning of the interval.

| LSWEND | NUM | 4 | | LOGICAL*SWAP-OUTS*AT END |

number of logical swap-outs at the end of the interval.

| NRSAMPLE | NUM | 4 | | NUMBER*OF*SAMPLES |

number of samples taken in this RMF interval. (Samples are taken at cycle intervals.)

| PAGBLAV | NUM | 4 | | TOTAL PAGEABLE*FRAMES*AVERAGE |

average number of private area pageable frames.

| PAGBLMN | NUM | 4 | | TOTAL PAGEABLE*FRAMES*MINIMUM |

minimum number of private area pageable frames.

Variable	Type	Length	Format	Label
PAGBLMX	NUM	4		TOTAL PAGEABLE*FRAMES*MAXIMUM

maximum number of private area pageable frames.

| PAGING | NUM | 4 | 5.1 | TOTAL PAGING*(NON-VIO NON-SWAP)*RATE |

total paging rate (per second). This rate includes non-VIO nonswap page-ins plus page-outs.

| PAGRT | NUM | 4 | 5.1 | TOTAL*PAGING*RATE(PAGRT) |

total paging I/O load. The sum of DPR, SPR, and VIO page rates.

| PCTLSWAP | NUM | 4 | 5.1 | PCT LOGICAL*SWAPS WHICH*SWAPPED |

percentage of logical swaps that were physically swapped.

| PFRATE | NUM | 4 | 5.1 | TOTAL PAGE FAULT*(NON-VIO NON-SWAP)*RATE |

total page fault rate (per second). This rate includes non-VIO nonswap page-ins plus reclaims.

| PRVFXAV | NUM | 4 | | PRIVATE FIXED*FRAMES*AVERAGE |

average number of private area fixed frames.

| PRVFXMN | NUM | 4 | | PRIVATE FIXED*FRAMES*MINIMUM |

minimum number of private area fixed frames.

| PRVFXMX | NUM | 4 | | PRIVATE FIXED*FRAMES*MAXIMUM |

maximum number of private area fixed frames.

| PRVPGAV | NUM | 4 | | PRIVATE PAGEABLE*FRAMES* AVERAGE |

average number of private area pageable frames.

| PRVPGMN | NUM | 4 | | PRIVATE PAGEABLE*FRAMES* MINIMUM |

minimum number of private area pageable frames.

| PRVPGMX | NUM | 4 | | PRIVATE PAGEABLE*FRAMES* MAXIMUM |

maximum number of private area pageable frames.

| PTR | NUM | 4 | 5.1 | PRIVATE*PAGE*RATE(PTR) |

PTR private paging rate. Introduced as a calculated measure used by the SRM as one of the happy values in MVS/SE1, it is actually the page fault rate for non-VIO pages. Note that in the RMF reports, this is the value reported as demand pages. In fact, it is one of the most

Variable	Type	Length	Format	Label

important metrics since it does quantify the paging operations (a page fault) that cause a task to wait.

PVTAFC	NUM	4		AVAILABLE*FRAME COUNT*AT END

number of available page frames in real storage at end of interval.

PVTAFCAV	NUM	4		AVAILABLE*REAL FRAMES*AVERAGE

average number of unused page frames.

PVTAFCMN	NUM	4		AVAILABLE*REAL FRAMES*MINIMUM

minimum number of unused page frames.

PVTAFCMX	NUM	4		AVAILABLE*REAL FRAMES*MAXIMUM

maximum number of unused page frames.

PVTCAIN	NUM	4	5.1	COMMON AREA*PAGE-IN*RATE

non-VIO page-in rate (per second) in CSA.

PVTCAOUT	NUM	4	5.1	COMMON AREA*PAGE-OUTS*RATE

non-VIO page-out rate (per second) in CSA.

PVTCAREC	NUM	4	5.1	COMMON AREA*RECLAIMS*RATE

non-VIO reclaim rate (per second) in CSA.

PVTFPFN	NUM	4		REAL STORAGE*FRAMES*IN NUCLEUS

number of page frames defined in nucleus.

PVTMVCLC	NUM	4		PAGES MOVED*BETWEEN*V=R AND RECONFIG

MVS/370 only, and only if more than 16MB real memory is on this system. Pages moved between V=R and reconfigurable area.

PVTMVDWN	NUM	4		PAGES MOVED*BELOW 16MB*LINE (VERY BAD)

MVS/370 only, and only if more than 16MB real memory is on this system. Pages moved below 16MB line (very bad for performance in MVS/370 because pages below the 16MB line are more restrictive than pages above the line).

PVTMVTOT	NUM	4		TOTAL*PAGES*MOVED

MVS/XA. Total pages moved from above the 16MB real memory line to below or from below to above. Applies only if more than 16MB of real memory exists on this system. Whereas MVS/370 has four measures of page traffic above and below the 16MB real memory line, MVS/XA has only this single measure. Since MVS/XA has addressed much of the virtual storage constraint problem by moving MVS control blocks above the 16MB line

Variable	Type	Length	Format	Label

(provided you have more than 16MB of real memory), the page traffic above and below just is not the performance problem it was in MVS/370.

PVTMVUP0   NUM   4

PAGES MOVED UP*NOT LIKELY*TO MOVE AGAIN

MVS/370 only, and only if more than 16MB real memory is on this system. Pages moved up that are not likely to move again.

PVTMVUP1   NUM   4

PAGES MOVED UP*LIKELY*TO MOVE AGAIN

MVS/370 only, and only if more than 16MB real memory is on this system. Pages moved up that are likely to move again.

PVTNPIN   NUM   4   5.1

PAGE-IN*(NON-VIO NONSWAP)*RATE

total non-VIO nonswap page-in rate (per second). This includes page-ins required through page faults, specific page requests, and page fixes. It excludes page reclaims, VIO, and swaps.

PVTNPOUT   NUM   4   5.1

PAGE-OUT*(NON-VIO NONSWAP)*RATE

total non-VIO nonswap page-out rate (per second).

PVTNPREC   NUM   4   5.1

RECLAIMS*(NON-VIO NONSWAP)*RATE

total non-VIO page reclaim rate (per second).

PVTPOOL   NUM   4

REAL STORAGE*FRAMES*BEYOND NUCLEUS

number of page frames defined in real storage. This does not include frames occupied by the nucleus (see PVTFPFN) or frames marked as bad or off-line.

PVTSPIN   NUM   4   5.1

SWAP-IN*PAGE-IN*RATE

total swap-in page rate (per second) including LSQA, fixed pages, and active pages when swapped in. Excludes reclaims.

PVTSPOUT   NUM   4   5.1

SWAP-OUT*PAGE-OUT*RATE

total swap-out page rate (per second).

PVTVAMI   NUM   4   5.1

PAGE-IN*(VIO)*RATE

VIO page-in rate (per second).

PVTVAMO   NUM   4   5.1

PAGE-OUT*(VIO)*RATE

VIO page-out rate (per second).

PVTVAMR   NUM   4   5.1

RECLAIM*(VIO)*RATE

VIO reclaim rate (per second).

Variable	Type	Length	Format	Label
RELEASE	CHAR	4		OPERATING*SYSTEM*RELEASE

operating system release number and level (for example, 0370 for Release 3 level 7, or 3.7).

SLOTLOMN	NUM	4		TOTAL LOCAL*SLOTS*MINIMUM

minimum total number of local page data set slots.

SLOTLOMX	NUM	4		TOTAL LOCAL*SLOTS*MAXIMUM

maximum total number of local page data set slots.

SLOTNGAV	NUM	4		UNUSABLE*SLOTS*AVERAGE

average number of unusable local page data set slots.

SLOTNGMN	NUM	4		UNUSABLE*SLOTS*MINIMUM

minimum number of unusable local page data set slots.

SLOTNGMX	NUM	4		UNUSABLE*SLOTS*MAXIMUM

maximum number of unusable local page data set slots.

SLOTNVAV	NUM	4		ALLOCATED*NON-VIO SLOTS*AVERAGE

average number of local page data set slots allocated to non-VIO private area pages.

SLOTNVMN	NUM	4		ALLOCATED*NON-VIO SLOTS*MINIMUM

minimum number of local page data set slots allocated to non-VIO private area pages.

SLOTNVMX	NUM	4		ALLOCATED*NON-VIO SLOTS*MAXIMUM

maximum number of local page data set slots allocated to non-VIO private area pages.

SLOTUNAV	NUM	4		UNALLOCATED*NON-VIO SLOTS*AVERAGE

average number of local page data set slots that are not allocated.

SLOTUNMN	NUM	4		UNALLOCATED*NON-VIO SLOTS*MINIMUM

minimum number of local page data set slots that are not allocated.

SLOTUNMX	NUM	4		UNALLOCATED*NON-VIO SLOTS*MAXIMUM

maximum number of local page data set slots that are not allocated.

SLOTVIAV	NUM	4		ALLOCATED*VIO SLOTS*AVERAGE

average number of local page data set slots that are allocated to VIO.

Variable	Type	Length	Format	Label
SLOTVIMN	NUM	4		ALLOCATED*VIO SLOTS*MINIMUM

minimum number of local page data set slots that are allocated to VIO.

| SLOTVIMX | NUM | 4 | | ALLOCATED*VIO SLOTS*MAXIMUM |

maximum number of local page data set slots that are allocated to VIO.

| SMFTIME | NUM | 8 | DATETIME19.2 | SMF*RECORD*TIME STAMP |

approximate interval end time stamp (actually, the time the record was moved to the buffer).

| SPR | NUM | 4 | 5.1 | SWAP*PAGING*RATE |

swap paging rate. Total paging rate of all pages moved in and out as a result of all swapping.

| SQAFXAV | NUM | 4 | | SQA FIXED*FRAMES*AVERAGE |

average number of SQA fixed frames.

| SQAFXMN | NUM | 4 | | SQA FIXED*FRAMES*MINIMUM |

minimum number of SQA fixed frames.

| SQAFXMX | NUM | 4 | | SQA FIXED*FRAMES*MAXIMUM |

maximum number of SQA fixed frames.

| STARTIME | NUM | 8 | DATETIME19.2 | START OF*INTERVAL |

beginning of RMF interval time stamp.

| SWAPAS | NUM | 4 | 5.1 | AUXILIARY*STORAGE*SWAP RATE |

number of swap-outs because 70% of all local page slots are allocated (that is, auxiliary storage shortage). Note that when this occurs the user acquiring auxiliary storage at the greatest rate is swapped out. This is so serious (because you have not defined enough slots on the page or swap data sets) that it usually happens only once and is not a normal occurrence.

| SWAPDW | NUM | 4 | 5.1 | DETECTED* WAIT*SWAP RATE |

number of swap-outs because of detected wait (that is, address space waited longer than 8 SRM seconds in a wait state without issuing the WAIT, LONG=YES macro). This usually is an indication that something is causing unexpected delays. Such things as reserves and enqueues have caused these swaps, and some systems (particularly ADABAS-like systems that communicate between address spaces via an SVC and then wait for data to come back) seem to breed these swaps.

| SWAPEX | NUM | 4 | 5.1 | EXCHANGE*SWAP*RATE |

number of exchange swaps. This occurs when one user in a domain is swapped out to allow another user in the same domain with a higher workload level to be swapped in. The SRM here is basically unable to provide services to both tasks so it switches back and forth. Thus,

Variable	Type	Length	Format	Label

these generally also indicate an overcommitted system, though not so overcommitted that the tasks are swapped out unilaterally (SWAPUS).

SWAPLGPY   NUM   4   5.1   LOGICAL*ACTUALLY*SWAPPED RATE

number of logically swapped-out address spaces that had to be physically swapped out before they were ready to execute again. This happens when the user is not really interactive enough to be kept in real memory or when there is not enough real memory immediately available to permit logical swapping.

SWAPNQ   NUM   4   5.1   ENQUEUE*SWAP*RATE

number of swap-outs required to swap-in a user who is enqueued on a needed system resource. The idea is that the SRM wants to swap in the task that is currently swapped out and holding the resource on which someone just enqueued. If the task holding can be swapped in and is given a burst of service (the amount is set by the ERV IPS parameter), then the holder of the contending resource may finish and release the enqueue so the second task can get service. This can reflect performance problems.

SWAPNS   NUM   4   5.1   NONSWAP*SWAP*RATE

number of swap-outs because an address space has been made nonswappable. What really happens is that the task is brought in memory, and only then does the SRM know that it needs to be nonswappable. The SRM wants to bring nonswappable tasks into preferred memory and swaps out to relocate the nonswappable task better. This is not usually a performance problem.

SWAPRATE   NUM   4   5.1   TOTAL*SWAP*RATE

total swap sequence rate. A swap sequence is the swap-out and the swap-in of an address space.

SWAPRS   NUM   4   5.1   REAL*STORAGE*SWAP RATE

number of swap-outs due to a shortage of real pageable frames. When this occurs, the swappable user with the most fixed pages is swapped. This is a serious problem, so serious it almost never happens (unless you try to IPL in a 2Meg machine).

SWAPSHRT   NUM   4   5.1   LOGICAL*CANDIDATE*SWAP RATE

number of logical swap-outs. These are not physical swaps, but they are candidates for physical swaps if they do not become active (that is, for a TSO user, press enter) soon enough. If they continue to wait rather than do something, they will then be physically swapped out. See SWAPLGPY.

SWAPTI   NUM   4   5.1   TERMINAL*INPUT*SWAP RATE

number of logical swap-out candidates due to a terminal waiting for input.

SWAPTO   NUM   4   5.1   TERMINAL*OUTPUT*SWAP RATE

number of logical swap-out candidates due to a terminal waiting for output buffers.

Variable	Type	Length	Format	Label

SWAPUS   NUM   4   5.1   UNILATERAL* SWAP OUT*RATE

number of unilateral swaps (that is, swap because the SRM decided the system is overcommitted and has begun to reduce the multiprogramming level for a domain that is over its target multiprogramming level). This is the best indicator of the SRM voting overcommitment. However, just because the SRM voted that the system is overcommitted does not necessarily mean the system is actually overcommitted. If you have mis-set your IPS happy values, you can make the SRB vote (think it is) overcommitted when it is not. Compare the actual resources used with the SWAPUS rate to confirm that the SRM is really detecting an overcommitment. Whether the system is really overcommitted or the SRM just thinks it is overcommitted, appreciable unilateral swap rate is a serious performance degradation.

SWAPVR   NUM   4   5.1   V=R*SWAP*RATE

number of swap-outs because V=R or nonswappable was specified in the Program Properties Table. Like SWAPNS above, the SRM has to determine you want to be V=R first.

SWAPWT   NUM   4   5.1   LONG WAIT*SWAP*RATE

number of swap-outs caused by user request wait states. This is desirable since it indicates the software's knowledge that there would be a wait for a response (for example, if you are going to issue a WTOR, it is appropriate to WAIT LONG instead of tying up memory for several seconds).

SYSPFR   NUM   4   5.1   SYSTEM AREAS*PAGE FAULT*RATE

system area page fault rate. A very strong metric since each of these page faults means that an in-memory task had to wait on this page. See also LCLPFR.

SYSTEM   CHAR   4   4.   SYSTEM*ID

identification of this system.

VERSION   CHAR   2   VERSION*NUMBER

RMF version number. See VERSION in the TYPE70 data set for all possible values.

VIO   NUM   4   5.1   VIO*PAGING*RATE

paging rate for VIO. PVTVAMI plus PVTVAMO.

TYPE72
RMF Workload Activity

The TYPE72 data set contains one observation for each period of each performance group in a type 72 SMF record written at the end of each RMF interval or when RMF is stopped.

Each task (job, TSO user, started task) executes in a performance group chosen by the user (with the PERFORM JCL parameter) or set for the user at read-in time based on the job class userid, job name, or some combination of these. The JESPARM, IEAIPS, and IEAICS members can all be used to define the performance group into which a task is placed. For example, batch jobs in Class A might be in PERFGRP 5, batch jobs in other classes in PERFGRP 4, TSO users in PERFGRP 2, and started tasks in PERFGRP 6. A performance group is defined by the installation and a group's tasks for resource collection by the SRM.

An SRM transaction (for example, a TSO command or a batch job step) can be further subdivided into periods. As the transaction accumulates service units, it changes from period 1 to period 2 when it has received more service units than were specified (in the DUR parameter of IEAIPS). For example, an installation might divide a typical TSO transaction into four periods. The first, for TSO trivial, might have very high dispatching priority for a small amount of service. The second, for TSO nontrivial, might have high priority for more service. The third, for TSO long, might have the same priority as batch for a larger amount of service. The fourth period might be at a priority lower than batch to persuade TSO users to migrate very long work to batch because batch service is much cheaper to deliver than TSO.

For each period of each performance group, TYPE72 contains the total resources consumed during the previous RMF interval. Thus, if you define performance groups according to your business purpose, you can track the hour-by-hour consumption or resources by business element. There appears to be no significant overhead with a large number of performance groups (150-200). The performance groups do not compete with one another, so there is no scanning or queuing that would cause overhead to increase. When a task enters the wait state, the SRM points to that task's performance group bucket and adds the resources. Except for the increase in physical size of the RMF record (quite small at 56 bytes per PERFGRP), using many performance groups is an excellent way to capture hour-by-hour resource consumption of major business elements.

In fact, it is recommended that every on-line task be in its own performance group. For example, each IMS message region, IMS control region, ADABAS, CICS, and started task should be placed in its own performance group. The service given to a performance group is not based on the performance group but on the domain to which the period of the performance group points. Thus, all on-line tasks that need to receive the same level of service can be placed in different performance groups but pointed to the same domain to be treated equally. For example, if you place each IMS message region in its own performance group, the resource growth of the applications that used the different message regions can be tracked. It is usually not as critical to have different performance groups for batch and TSO since SMF reporting is usually adequate to map resources to business element. Capturing the service for each on-line system and started task allows tracking of the resources delivered, which is useful for capacity planning and has permitted detection of a performance problem. An unexpected step increase in the service to a started task or on-line system may be the result of bad maintenance, a new application, or a change in the system's parameters. When each task is isolated in a performance group, tracking such changes is easy.

Report Performance Groups

The preceding discussion dealt only with control performance groups. RMF also offers report performance groups. Care should be taken when using RMF data when report performance groups have been defined since there is double accounting of resources in the TYPE72 data. For example, if control PERFGRP=2 is for TSO, report PERFGRP=80 is for TSO users with the first letter of S, and report PERFGRP=88 is for users ending with HWM or JSM (perhaps a group of people), TSO user SYSTHWM's resources are reported in all three performance groups. Thus, the total of TYPE72 data no longer has meaning when report performance groups are defined, and analysis of TYPE72 data is no longer straightforward. There is a variable (PERFRPGN) that identifies whether a particular observation in TYPE72 is from a control or report performance group, which eases the analysis somewhat. It has been the author's experience that if on-line and started tasks are placed in their own control performance groups, the effect of report performance groups can be achieved without defining them.

CPU Resource Measures

The TYPE72 data set contains CPU service units, not CPU seconds. For both TCB and SRB, CPU service units are calculated by the SRM from the actual CPU seconds delivered. The equation used is:

```
CPUUNITS=CPUTCBTM*CPUCOEFF*SU_SEC     for TCB service units

SRBUNITS=CPUSRBTM*SRBCOEFF*SU_SEC     for SRB service units
```

where CPUCOEFF and SRBCOEFF are coefficients specified by the installation in IEAIPS (and contained in the TYPE72 record). These parameters allow the installation to set the relative impact of CPU on total service units since the SRM manages tasks based only on the total. Note that these

coefficients must be specified as greater than zero
to get nonzero CPU service units.

CPUTCBTM and CPUSRBTM are the actual CPU seconds
consumed under TCB and SRB for tasks in this
performance group.

SU_SEC is the machine-dependent constant described in
the TYPE70 section in this chapter. Because SU_SEC
is dependent on the CPU model and version, the code
that builds TYPE72 also processes TYPE70 data and
determines the SU_SEC by table lookup. Using the
value of SU_SEC from the TYPE70, you can solve for
the CPUTCBTM and CPUSRBTM delivered to each period of
each performance group.

It is important to recognize that the accuracy of the CPUTCBTM and
CPUSRBTM measures in TYPE72 are dependent on the accuracy of SU_SEC
in the TYPE70 hardware record. Also keep in mind that SU_SEC values used
by IBM have been changed by PTF, so you need to verify periodically, as
described in TYPE70, that the SU_SEC value set by the code is the correct value
for your hardware and software configuration.

I/O Resource Measurement

TYPE72 provides a measure of I/O service delivered to each period of each performance group. In MVS/370, the EXCP count is the only raw I/O unit on which
I/O service can be based. In MVS/XA, I/O service can be based on EXCP counts
or on device connect time (IOTM), as specified by the IOSRVC parameter in
IEAIPS, but you cannot determine which. There is no flag in the record; however,
the name of the IPS in effect could be used to identify the basis of I/O service
units. The I/O service units in the TYPE72 record are calculated as:

```
IOUNITS= IOCCOEFF * (raw I/O units)
```

where 1 raw I/O unit equals 1 EXCP if EXCP count is
used or where 1 raw I/O unit equals 65 connect time
units. (A connect time unit is 128 microseconds, so 65
units is 8.32 milliseconds or about half a
revolution at 3600 rpm).

Since IOUNITS and IOCCOEFF are in the TYPE72 record, two calculated
variables (PGPEXCP and PGPIOTM) contain the raw I/O units delivered.

Memory Resource Measurement

TYPE72 also provides a measure of real memory usage through the memory service units. This measure is based on real memory page seconds used and reflects the number of real pages a task used and how long they were held. Because of page stealing and memory isolation, this measure is not as repeatable as other measures and has not been used for cost-recovery or billing purposes. It is susceptible to hardware and software changes. Since it is acquired by sampling only when the task is executing CPU time, it is unrepresentative for tasks that use very little CPU time. The measure has its weaknesses but is the best we have to estimate the average working set size of all tasks in a performance group. The code always calculates the variable AVGWKSET (in K-bytes) from:

```
AVGWKSET=200*MSOUNITS*CPUCOEFF/(MSOCOEFF*CPUUNITS);
```

but if the performance group does not usually accumulate on the order of 30 to 60 CPU seconds in an hour, the value is better set missing than used.

Response Time Measurement

In addition to the resources above, each observation in TYPE72 contains the total elapsed time of all transactions that ended during this period and the total number of transactions that ended. You can estimate the average elapsed time of transactions that ended in a period by calculating:

```
average response = ELAPSTM / TRANS;
```

If you have defined the TSO performance group as described above, you can calculate this average response for PERIOD=1 and report the average response of transactions that ended in that period. Since a transaction that ends in period 1 used less than DUR service units (remember, if it used more than DUR it would have been moved into period 2), you are calculating the response time of all transactions that used less than DUR service units. Although the average response calculation can be made for all periods, it is most useful when applied to first period TSO transactions, usually called the average trivial TSO RMF-measured response. By adding ELAPSTM and TRANS for the entire TSO performance group, the ratio of ELAPSTM and TRANS result in average total TSO RMF-measured response. Note that the SRM definition of a transaction is quite different from what TSO/MON or a real TSO user might count as a transaction. The classification of a transaction into one ending in period 1 or 2 is affected by the service unit equation, which is different on different processors and operating systems. Thus, this measure of TSO response is most useful as a trend measure within the same hardware and software configuration.

Variable	Type	Length	Format	Label
ACTIVETM	NUM	4	TIME12.2	TASK*ACTIVE*TIME

transaction-active duration. This variable includes the total time that each transaction was in real storage plus any swapped-out time that the transaction was not in a long wait state. It does not include time between job steps for batch transactions.

| AVGWKSET | NUM | 4 | | AVG WORKING*SET(K) THIS*PERF GRP PERIOD |

[handwritten annotation: AVGMEMSZ]

average working set size (K-bytes) for performance group during period.

| CPUCOEFF | NUM | 4 | | TCB CPU*SERVICE UNIT*COEFFICIENT |

CPU TCB service definition coefficient from Installation Performance Specification (IPS).

| CPURFC | NUM | 4 | | CPU*RFC*FACTOR |

CPU resource factor coefficient (from IPS).

| CPUSRBTM | NUM | 4 | TIME12.2 | TASK*CPU SRB*TIME |

CPU SRB duration used by this performance group in this period during this RMF interval.

| CPUTCBTM | NUM | 4 | TIME12.2 | TASK*CPU TCB*TIME |

CPU TCB duration used by this performance group in this period during this RMF interval.

| CPUTM | NUM | 4 | TIME12.2 | TASK*TCB+SRB*TIME |

sum of CPUTCBTM and CPUSRBTM.

| CPUTYPE | CHAR | 2 | HEX4. | CPU*MODEL*NUMBER |

CPU model number (such as, 158, 168, 3033, or 3081). Note that this is actually kept from the immediately preceding type 70 record since the CPUTYPE is not contained in the type 72 record. CPUTYPE and CPUVERSN are necessary to convert CPU service units to units of CPU time.

| CPUUNITS | NUM | 4 | | CPU TCB*SERVICE*UNITS |

CPU TCB service units delivered to this performance group in this period during this interval.

Variable	Type	Length	Format	Label

CPUVERSN   CHAR   1   HEX2.   CPU*VERSION*NUMBER

CPU version number. MVS/XA only. This field describes the model of processor within CPUTYPE. The currently known values are:

value	CPUTYPE	processor
01	3083	3083-E
03	3081	3081-D
11	3083	3083-B
13	3081	3081-G
21	3083	3083-J
23	3081	3081-K

CYCLE   NUM   4   SAMPLE*CYCLE*TIME(MS)

sample cycle length (in milliseconds). At each cycle, a sampling observation is made.

DOMAIN   NUM   4   DOMAIN*NUMBER

domain number in which this performance group and period competed for service.

DURATM   NUM   4   TIME12.2   DURATION*OF*INTERVAL

duration of this RMF interval. At the end of each DURATM, all data gathered and sampled are written to SMF.

ELAPSTM   NUM   4   TIME12.2   ELAPSED*DURATION

sum of elapsed duration of all transactions that ended in this performance group period.

ERV   NUM   4   ENQUEUE*RESOURCE*VALUE

ERV resource manager coefficient (from IPS).

FLAGS72   CHAR   1   HEX2.   FLAG*FIELD

flag field. One bit is used to define whether this is a control or report performance group. It is hoped that another bit will eventually be used to identify whether I/O service is based on EXCP or IOTM.

HIGHPG   NUM   4   HIGHEST*PERFGRP*DEFINED

highest performance group number defined in IPS.

ICSNAME   CHAR   8   IEAICSXX*MEMBER*NAME

name of IEAICSxx member (from SYS1.PARMLIB) in effect. If no ICS is defined, the last two bytes of this field can be 6060X.

IOCCOEFF   NUM   4   IO*SERVICE*COEFFICIENT

IOC service definition coefficient (from IPS).

Variable	Type	Length	Format	Label
IOCRFC	NUM	4		IO*RFC*FACTOR

IOC resource factor coefficient (from IPS).

| IOUNITS | NUM | 4 | | IO*SERVICE*UNITS |

I/O service units delivered to this performance group in this period during this interval.

| IPSNAME | CHAR | 8 | | IEAIPSXX*MEMBER*NAME |

name of IEAIPSxx member (from SYS1.PARMLIB) in effect.

| MSOCOEFF | NUM | 4 | | MEMORY*SERVICE UNIT*COEFFICIENT |

main storage service definition coefficient.

| MSOUNITS | NUM | 4 | | MEMORY*SERVICE*UNITS |

main storage service units delivered to this performance group in this period during this interval.

| OBJCTIVE | NUM | 4 | | OBJECTIVE*NUMBER |

performance objective number for this performance group period.

| OPTNAME | CHAR | 8 | | IEAOPTXX*MEMBER*NAME |

name of IEAOPTxx member (from SYS1.PARMLIB) in effect.

| PERFGRP | NUM | 4 | | PERFORMANCE*GROUP |

performance group number.

| PERFRPGN | NUM | 4 | | REPORT*PERFORMANCE*GROUP |

performance group number if this is a report performance group. This value is missing if the observation is for a control performance group.

| PERIOD | NUM | 4 | | PERFORMANCE*GROUP*PERIOD |

period number.

| PGNCLASS | CHAR | 10 | | PERFGRP*CLASS*NAME |

name of class associated with this performance group.

| PGNTRANS | CHAR | 10 | | TRANSACTION*NAME*OF PERFGRP |

name of transaction associated with this performance group.

| PGNUSER | CHAR | 10 | | USER ID*NAME*OF PERFGRP |

name of user identifier associated with this performance group.

Variable	Type	Length	Format	Label
PGPEXCP	NUM	4	8.	EXCPS ISSUED*BY THIS*PERF GROUP PERIOD

contains the total EXCPs delivered to this performance group during this period, if I/O service units are based on EXCP count.

Variable	Type	Length	Format	Label
PGPIOTM	NUM	4	TIME12.2	IO CONNECT TIME*BY THIS*PERF GROUP PERIOD

contains the total IOTM delivered to this performance group during this period, if I/O service units are based on IOTM (device connect time).

Variable	Type	Length	Format	Label
RELEASE	CHAR	4		OPERATING*SYSTEM*RELEASE

operating system release number and level (for example, 0370 for release 3 level 7, or 3.7).

Variable	Type	Length	Format	Label
RESIDTM	NUM	4	TIME12.2	RESIDENT*IN REAL*STORAGE

transaction residency duration. The time the SRM recorded that the task was actually in real memory.

Variable	Type	Length	Format	Label
SERVICE	NUM	4		TOTAL*SERVICE*UNITS

total service units delivered to this performance group in this period during this interval.

Variable	Type	Length	Format	Label
SMFTIME	NUM	8	DATETIME19.2	SMF*RECORD*TIME STAMP

approximate ending time stamp of interval. (Actually, the time the record is moved to SMF.)

Variable	Type	Length	Format	Label
SRBCOEFF	NUM	4		SRB CPU*SERVICE UNIT*COEFFICIENT

SRB service definition coefficient (from IPS).

Variable	Type	Length	Format	Label
SRBUNITS	NUM	4		CPU SRB*SERVICE*UNITS

SRB service units delivered to this performance group in this period during this interval.

Variable	Type	Length	Format	Label
SSQELAP	NUM	4	E9.	SUM OF SQUARES*OF*ELAPSED TIMES

sum of squares of elapsed times of all ended transactions in this PG period. Used to calculate standard deviation in RMF reports.

Variable	Type	Length	Format	Label
STARTIME	NUM	8	DATETIME19.2	START OF*INTERVAL

beginning of RMF interval time stamp.

Variable	Type	Length	Format	Label
SU_SEC	NUM	4		CONVERSION*FACTOR FOR*CPU (SU_SEC)

conversion coefficient set from CPUTYPE to convert CPU and SRB service units to CPU minutes.

Variable	Type	Length	Format	Label
SUBSYS	CHAR	4		SUB*SYSTEM

name of subsystem associated with this performance group.

Variable	Type	Length	Format	Label
SWAPSEQ	NUM	4		NUMBER*OF*SWAPS

number of swap sequences for this performance group in this period during this interval.

| SYSTEM | CHAR | 4 | 4. | SYSTEM*ID |

identification of this system.

| TRANS | NUM | 4 | | SRM*TRANSACTION* COUNT |

number of transactions in performance group period that ended in this interval.

| TSLGROUP | NUM | 4 | | TIME*SLICE*GROUP |

time slice group number.

| VERSION | CHAR | 2 | | VERSION*NUMBER |

RMF version number. See TYPE70 for complete description.

| WKLOAD | NUM | 4 | | WORKLOAD*LEVEL |

workload level of all transactions.

TYPE73
MVS/XA Physical Channel Activity

The TYPE73 data set contains one observation for each channel path (CHPID) in each type 73 SMF record written by MVS/XA at the end of each RMF interval or when RMF is stopped. This data set does not exist in MVS/370. See TYPE73P and TYPE73L data sets.

MVS/XA provides minimal data on physical channel activity. TYPE73 describes each channel path (CHPID) and provides a measure of physical channel busy that uses the results of the store channel path status (STCPS) instruction issued by SRM periodically; the goal is five times a second. In MVS/370, RMF actually sets the sample rate, samples the channel busy, and counts I/O actions. However, in MVS/XA, there is no count of I/O actions on the channel, and the sampling rate is set by the SRM and is unrelated to RMF CYCLE or NRSAMPLE. Although the data are less comprehensive, by using SRM data rather than creating its own, RMF does cost less to run. Even though CYCLE and NRSAMPLE exist in the MVS/XA type 73 record, they are not kept in the TYPE73 data set since they do not apply.

Variable	Type	Length	Format	Label
CHANTYPE	CHAR	9		CHANNEL*TYPE

channel type. There is no longer a selector channel.

value	meaning
BYTE MUX	byte multiplexor channel
BLOCK MUX	block multiplexor channel.

Variable	Type	Length	Format	Label
CHPID	NUM	4	HEX2.	CHANNEL*PATH*IDENTIFICATION

channel path identification.

Variable	Type	Length	Format	Label
DURATM	NUM	4	TIME12.2	DURATION*OF*INTERVAL

duration of this RMF interval. At end of each DURATM, all data gathered and sampled are written to SMF.

Variable	Type	Length	Format	Label
INVALID	CHAR	1		PARTIAL*STATISTICS?

flag that data recorded are invalid because only partial statistics were received.

value	meaning
blank	full statistics received
Y	data are invalid, partial statistics received.

Variable	Type	Length	Format	Label

NRSTCPS   NUM   4   NUMBER*OF STCPS*SAMPLES

number of store channel path status (STCPS) instructions SRB issued to sample channel path busy. The SRM tries to sample every 200 milliseconds, but it is preemptable and can have a lower sample rate.

ONLINE   CHAR   1   CHANNEL*ON-LINE*AT END?

channel is currently on-line at end of RMF interval.

value	meaning
blank	not on-line at end of interval
Y	channel path is on-line at end of interval.

PCHANBY   NUM   4   5.1   PERCENT WHEN*CHANNEL*WAS BUSY

percentage of samples (SRM STCPS) when channel was busy.

RELEASE   CHAR   4   OPERATING*SYSTEM*RELEASE

operating system release number and level (for example, 0370 for release 3, level 7, or 3.7).

SMFTIME   NUM   8   DATETIME19.2   SMF*RECORD*TIME STAMP

approximate ending time stamp of RMF interval. (Actually, the time the record is moved to SMF.)

STARTIME   NUM   8   DATETIME19.2   START OF*INTERVAL

beginning of RMF interval time stamp.

SYSTEM   CHAR   4   4.   SYSTEM*ID

identification of this system.

VARIED   CHAR   1   CHANNEL*VARIED*?

channel was varied during this interval; data are invalid.

value	meaning
blank	channel path was not varied; data are valid
Y	channel path was varied; data are invalid.

VERSION   CHAR   2   VERSION*NUMBER

RMF version number. See TYPE70 data set.

TYPE73L
MVS/370 Logical Channel Activity

The TYPE73L data set contains one observation for each logical channel in each type 73 SMF record written by MVS/370 at the end of each RMF interval, or when RMF is stopped. *

The TYPE73L data are important to MVS/370 installations since they provide the best measure of overall I/O performance. Although data set TYPE73P (physical channel statistics) reports utilizations, TYPE73L data give the actual number of delayed SIOs, the percentage of time a queue exists for the logical channel, and why I/Os are being delayed and queued.

To analyze the TYPE73L data, one must understand a logical channel and what happens when MVS/370 issues an I/O operation.

A logical channel is nothing more than the grouping of one or more physical channels by which a CPU can communicate with a device. It identifies to the input-output supervisor (IOS) which physical channels can reach this device from this CPU. Therefore, a logical channel can consist of one or more physical channels. All devices sharing this same path (for example, a device on the same control unit, or devices on a similarly connected control unit) are on the same logical channel.

When MVS/370 receives an I/O request from a program, it first checks to see if I/O is already scheduled for this device from this CPU. MVS can only handle one I/O to a device at a time, so it first checks the unit control block (UCB) busy bit. If the UCB is busy, then IOS knows that it already has an I/O outstanding to this device, and IOS then queues the new I/O until the prior I/O is completed. This is called a LOGICAL CHANNEL queued request.

If the UCB is not busy, IOS turns on the busy bit and issues a test channel instruction (TCH) to see if one of the physical channels in this logical channel is free. If the first channel checked is busy, the next physical channel is then checked, and so forth, until a free channel is found. If all physical channels in this logical channel are busy, IOS queues this I/O in the PHYSICAL CHANNEL queue. If a channel is free, IOS issues an SIO to the control unit. If the control unit is free, then the SIO is issued to the device itself. If the control unit is busy, the I/O waits in the CONTROL UNIT queue.

If the device is not busy, then the SIO for the data is issued by IOS since the physical channel, control unit, and device were free. If the device itself was busy the I/O is queued in the DEVICE queue. How could the device be busy, if the UCB busy bit was not on? This is precisely what happens in a shared DASD environment when two tasks in different CPUs try to use the same DASD volume (it also happens with string switches).

---

* This data set does not exist for MVS/XA since logical channels no longer exist. Queuing in MVS/XA is at the device rather than the logical channel, and the data are reported in the TYPE78 data set.

The four reasons for queuing an I/O, LOGICAL CHANNEL, PHYSICAL CHANNEL, CONTROL UNIT, and DEVICE are quantified in the TYPE73L data. Note especially:

Reason for defer	Explanation
LOGICAL	IOS knew that an I/O was outstanding from this CPU for this device and, thus, queued this I/O immediately. No extra work was done to queue this I/O.
PHYSICAL CONTROL UNIT DEVICE	In these cases, IOS thought the device was available and scheduled a TCH/SIO, which then failed to complete because the physical channel, control unit, or device was in use. Not only is the original I/O now queued, but IOS actually **had to do an I/O to find out that it could not do an I/O!**

Note that if you must queue an I/O, it is far better to queue it for logical channel than to have it deferred for any other reason. Any deferrals due to control unit or physical channel are the installation's responsibility. Although a user can compete with himself and cause deferrals for both the device and the logical channel, the installation designed the configuration and, thus, is to be blamed for path-induced delays. A goal of each installation should be to minimize deferrals due to physical channel and control unit and concern itself with deferrals due to device and logical channel.

I/O Delay Statistics

TYPE73L records the number and percentage of SIOs delayed on this logical channel by cause of delay:

Reason for deferral	Count of SIOs deferred	Percentage of SIOCOUNT deferred
Total	DEFERED	PCTDEFER
LOGICAL	DEFLCHBY	PCTDEFLC
PHYSICAL	DEFPHYBY	PCTDEFPY
CONTROL UNIT	DEFCUBY	PCTDEFCU
DEVICE	DEFDEVBY	PCTDEFDV

Print the TYPE73L data for the peak hour to identify logical channels (LCHAN) with significant deferred I/Os and to quantify why I/Os are being delayed.

I/O Queuing Statistics

In addition to the count of delayed SIOs, TYPE73L also identifies the percentage of the time there was a queue for the LCHAN. While a high number of SIOs being deferred can be a clear sign of a problem, if they happened during a relatively brief period of time, the impact may be much less than having a constant queue of I/O for this logical channel. QUEUE0 through QUEUE4 variables describe the percentage of the RMF interval for which a queue of length 0, 1, 2, 3, and 4 or more existed and AVGENQUE describes the average number of requests queued. QUEUE0 (or its complement, 100-QUEUE0) provides the best measure for identifying the worst LCHANs.

TYPE73L is the first place to begin investigating I/O delays. After identifying the LCHANs with most of the delays, the devices on those LCHANs can be selected from the TYPE74 data set. While data are available only at the volume level from RMF, a LISTVTOC of the candidate volumes is usually sufficient to identify why I/Os are delayed.

Shared DASD

Even before investigating I/O delays, consider what you might have done to create contention. If you actually use shared DASD, you are increasing the time to do an I/O. Shared DASD should only be used for increased availability and was never designed to improve performance, and defining devices as shared actually increases the average time to do an I/O. The optimal I/O configuration for performance is one with no DASD shared between systems. While it is clearly impossible to achieve this pristine I/O configuration, it should be the objective of your configuration. Volumes like paging and swapping volumes and work packs (temporary disk, sort work, and so forth) should always be used by only one system. While you will want additional paths to these devices in order to make them available in the event of an outage (that is, "shareable"), you should plan your I/O configuration so that they are never used concurrently by two systems, except in the event of a failure. Otherwise, I/O time is increased and overall performance of your installation is degraded.

I/O Queuing Not Reported in TYPE73L

The TYPE73L data set is the place to begin analysis of configuration. One class of I/O servers does not show any queuing in the TYPE73L data set. Remember that these measures are based on queuing after IOS receives the request. The application issuing the I/O could look at the UCB itself, and only give the I/O to IOS when it knew the UCB was free. Such an application would be queuing internally, and the TYPE73L data set would show no queuing statistics. The auxiliary storage manager (ASM), also known as the paging supervisor, manages internal paging and swapping I/O requests. ASM does not pass I/O requests to IOS if the UCB busy bit is on, and you see no queuing of I/O for paging or swapping. (In fact, if you ever see any queuing on your page or swap volumes, someone other than ASM is using that device.) Thus TYPE73L can be used for all I/O delays except those queued internally. There is no direct measure of the queuing within ASM for page and swap logical channels.

Variable	Type	Length	Format	Label
AVGENQUE	NUM	4	5.3	AVERAGE*ENQUEUED*REQUESTS

average number of requests enqueued for this logical channel.

| CHANMAP0 | NUM | 4 | HEX4. | CPU 0 MAP*PHYSICAL*CHANNELS |

bit pattern of physical channels that are included in this logical channel from CPU0. High-order bit is physical channel zero.

| CHANMAP1 | NUM | 4 | HEX4. | CPU 1 MAP*PHYSICAL*CHANNELS |

same as CHANMAP0 for CPU1.

| CYCLE | NUM | 4 | | SAMPLE*CYCLE*TIME(MS) |

sample cycle length (in milliseconds). At each CYCLE, a sampling observation is made.

| C0ANYCH | NUM | 4 | 5.1 | PERCENT WHEN*ANY CHAN BUSY*ON CPU 0 |

percent of samples when any physical channel is busy on CPU0.

| C0BYWT | NUM | 4 | 5.1 | PERCENT WHEN*ANY CHAN BUSY*& CPU 0 WAIT |

percent of samples when any physical channel is busy on CPU0 and CPU0 is in a wait state.

| C1ANYCH | NUM | 4 | 5.1 | PERCENT WHEN*ANY CHAN BUSY*ON CPU 1 |

percent of samples when any physical channel is busy on CPU1.

| C1BYWT | NUM | 4 | 5.1 | PERCENT WHEN*ANY CHAN BUSY*& CPU 1 WAIT |

percent of samples when any physical channel is busy on CPU1 and CPU1 is in a wait state.

| DEFCUBY | NUM | 4 | | IO REQUESTS*DEFERRED*CU BUSY |

number of requests deferred because control unit is busy.

| DEFDEVBY | NUM | 4 | | IO REQUEST*DEFERRED*DEVICE BUSY |

number of requests deferred because device is busy.

| DEFERED | NUM | 4 | | IO REQUEST*DEFERRED*TOTAL |

total deferred requests for this logical channel in this RMF interval.

Variable	Type	Length	Format	Label
DEFLCHBY	NUM	4		IO REQUESTS*DEFERRED*LOGICAL (UCB) BUSY

number of requests deferred because logical channel is busy.

DEFPHYBY	NUM	4		IO REQUESTS*DEFERRED*PHYSICAL CHAN BUSY

number of requests deferred because physical channel is busy.

DURATM	NUM	4	TIME12.2	DURATION*OF*INTERVAL

duration of this RMF interval. At end of each DURATM, all data gathered and sampled are written to SMF.

FQCUBY	NUM	4		FREQ COUNTER*CU BUSY*DEFERRED

frequency counter for control unit busy deferred I/O requests.

FQDEVBY	NUM	4		FREQ COUNTER*DEV BUSY*DEFERRED

frequency counter for device busy deferred I/O requests.

FQLCHRQ	NUM	4		FREQ COUNTER*LOGICAL*DEFERRED

frequency counter for logical channel busy deferred I/O requests.

FQPHYRQ	NUM	4		FREQ COUNTER*PHYSICAL*DEFERRED

frequency counter for physical channel busy deferred I/O requests.

LCHAN	NUM	4	HEX2.	LOGICAL*CHANNEL*NUMBER

logical channel number.

LCI	CHAR	1		LCHAN*CONFIG*CHANGED?

logical channel configuration has changed during the interval. The values are either blank or Y.

NRSAMPLE	NUM	4		NUMBER*OF*SAMPLES

number of samples taken in this RMF interval (samples are taken at LCYCLE intervals).

PCTDEFCU	NUM	4	5.1	PERCENT REQ*DEFERRED*CU BUSY

percent of total SIO count deferred due to control unit busy.

PCTDEFDV	NUM	4	5.1	PERCENT REQ*DEFERRED*DEVICE BUSY

percent of total SIO count deferred due to device busy.

PCTDEFER	NUM	4	5.1	PERCENT REQ*DEFERRED*TOTAL

percent of total SIO count deferred for any reason.

Variable	Type	Length	Format	Label
PCTDEFLC	NUM	4	5.1	PERCENT REQ*DEFERRED*LOGICAL(UCB) BUSY

percent of total SIO count deferred for logical channel busy.

Variable	Type	Length	Format	Label
PCTDEFPY	NUM	4	5.1	PERCENT REQ*DEFERRED*PHYSICAL CHAN BUSY

percent of total SIO count deferred for physical channel busy.

Variable	Type	Length	Format	Label
QUEUE0	NUM	4	5.1	PERCENT WHEN*NO REQUESTS*WERE WAITING

percent of samples when there were no requests queued for this logical channel.

Variable	Type	Length	Format	Label
QUEUE1	NUM	4	5.1	PERCENT WHEN* 1 REQUESTS*WERE WAITING

percent of samples when there was one request queued for this logical channel.

Variable	Type	Length	Format	Label
QUEUE2	NUM	4	5.1	PERCENT WHEN* 2 REQUESTS*WERE WAITING

percent of samples when there were two requests queued for this logical channel.

Variable	Type	Length	Format	Label
QUEUE3	NUM	4	5.1	PERCENT WHEN* 3 REQUESTS*WERE WAITING

percent of samples when there were three requests queued for this logical channel.

Variable	Type	Length	Format	Label
QUEUE4	NUM	4	5.1	PERCENT WHEN*OVER 3 SIO *WERE WAITING

percent of samples when there were four or more requests queued for this logical channel.

Variable	Type	Length	Format	Label
RELEASE	CHAR	4		OPERATING*SYSTEM*RELEASE

operating system release number and level (for example, 0370 for release 3 level 7, or 3.7).

Variable	Type	Length	Format	Label
SIO73CNT	NUM	4		START-IO*(TYPE73)*COUNT

total number of successful start I/Os.

Variable	Type	Length	Format	Label
SMFTIME	NUM	8	DATETIME19.2	SMF*RECORD*TIME STAMP

approximate ending time stamp of RMF interval. (Actually, the time the record is moved to SMF.)

Variable	Type	Length	Format	Label
STARTIME	NUM	8	DATETIME19.2	START OF*INTERVAL

beginning of RMF interval time stamp.

Variable	Type	Length	Format	Label
SYSTEM	CHAR	4	4.	SYSTEM*ID

identification of this system.

Variable	Type	Length	Format	Label
VERSION	CHAR	2		VERSION*NUMBER

RMF version number. See TYPE70.

TYPE73P
MVS/370 Physical Channel Activity

The TYPE73P data set contains one observation for each channel path (CHPID) in each type 73 SMF record written by MVS/XA, written by RMF at the end of each RMF interval, or when RMF is stopped.*

TYPE73P contains the number of start I/Os (SIO count) issued for each channel and the percent of samples when the channel was busy.

At one time, physical channel utilization was very important because there were so many rules of thumb about channel busy; however, the advent of queuing measures in RMF, especially the TYPE73L data on logical delays, generally replaced the need for utilizations. Utilizations are useful as the first phase of measurement because they are so easy to generate, but they only imply delay; they do not measure delay.

Variable	Type	Length	Format	Label
AVGENQUE	NUM	4	5.3	AVERAGE*ENQUEUED*REQUESTS

average number of requests enqueued for this channel.

Variable	Type	Length	Format	Label
AVGPHYNQ	NUM	4	5.3	AVERAGE*PHYSICAL CHAN*ENQUEUES

average number of physical requests enqueued for this channel.

Variable	Type	Length	Format	Label
CHAN	NUM	4	HEX2.	CHANNEL*NUMBER

physical channel number.

Variable	Type	Length	Format	Label
CHANTYPE	CHAR	9		CHANNEL*TYPE

channel type. There is no longer a selector channel.

values	meaning
BYTE MUX	byte multiplexor channel
BLOCK MUX	block multiplexor channel.

Variable	Type	Length	Format	Label
CPUID	NUM	4		CPU ID*FROM WHICH*IO CAME

CPU to which this channel is connected and for which these data apply.

Variable	Type	Length	Format	Label
CYCLE	NUM	4		SAMPLE*CYCLE*TIME(MS)

sample cycle length (in milliseconds). At each CYCLE, a sampling observation is made.

Variable	Type	Length	Format	Label
C0ANYCH	NUM	4	5.1	PERCENT WHEN*ANY CHAN BUSY*ON CPU 0

percent of samples when any physical channel is busy on CPU0.

* This data set does not exist in MVS/XA. See the TYPE73 data sets.

Variable	Type	Length	Format	Label
C0BYWT	NUM	4	5.1	PERCENT WHEN*ANY CHAN BUSY*& CPU 0 WAIT

percent of samples when any physical channel is busy on CPU0 and CPU0 is in wait state.

C1ANYCH	NUM	4	5.1	PERCENT WHEN*ANY CHAN BUSY*ON CPU 1

percent of samples when any physical channel is busy on CPU1.

C1BYWT	NUM	4	5.1	PERCENT WHEN*ANY CHAN BUSY*& CPU 1 WAIT

percent of samples when any physical channel is busy on CPU1 and CPU1 is in wait state.

DURATM	NUM	4	TIME12.2	DURATION*OF*INTERVAL

duration of this RMF interval. At end of each DURAT, all data gathered and sampled are written to SMF.

IDWRONG	CHAR	1		INVALID*CHANNEL*ID?

invalid channel identification (Y or blanks). An error occurred when RMF constructed this record. CHAN is in error and CHANTYPE will be SELECTOR.

NRSAMPLE	NUM	4		NUMBER*OF*SAMPLES

number of samples taken in this RMF interval. (Samples are taken at CYCLE intervals.)

ONLINE	CHAR	1		CHANNEL*ON-LINE*AT END?

channel is currently on-line at end of RMF interval. These values are either blank or Y.

PCHANBY	NUM	4	5.1	PERCENT WHEN*CHANNEL*IS BUSY

percent of samples when channel is busy. This number is always zero for byte multiplexor channels, even though the channel is busy.

PCHANWT	NUM	4	6.2	PERCENT WHEN*CPU WAITING*THIS CHAN BUSY

percent of samples in which this channel is busy and the CPU (CPUID) is in wait state. This number is always zero for byte multiplexor channels also.

QUEUE0	NUM	4	5.1	PERCENT WHEN*NO REQUESTS*WERE WAITING

percent of samples when there were no requests queued for this channel.

QUEUE1	NUM	4	5.1	PERCENT WHEN* 1 REQUEST*WAS WAITING

percent of samples when there was one request queued for this channel.

Variable	Type	Length	Format	Label
QUEUE2	NUM	4	5.1	PERCENT WHEN* 2 REQUESTS*WERE WAITING

percent of samples when there were two requests queued for this channel.

| QUEUE3 | NUM | 4 | 5.1 | PERCENT WHEN* 3 REQUESTS*WERE WAITING |

percent of samples when there were three requests queued for this channel.

| QUEUE4 | NUM | 4 | 5.1 | PERCENT WHEN*OVER 3 SIO *WERE WAITING |

percent of samples when there were four or more requests queued for this channel.

| RELEASE | CHAR | 4 | | OPERATING*SYSTEM*RELEASE |

operating system release number and level (for example, 0370 for release 3 level 7, or 3.7).

| SIO73CNT | NUM | 4 | | START-IO*(TYPE73)*COUNT |

number of successful start I/Os issued to this channel by this CPU during this RMF interval. This number includes redundant successful start I/O fast release instructions but not sense start I/Os.

| SMFTIME | NUM | 8 | DATETIME19.2 | SMF*RECORD*TIME STAMP |

approximate ending time stamp of RMF interval. (Actually, the time the record is moved to SMF.)

| STARTIME | NUM | 8 | DATETIME19.2 | START OF*INTERVAL |

beginning of RMF interval time stamp.

| SYSTEM | CHAR | 4 | 4. | SYSTEM*ID |

identification of this system.

| VARIED | CHAR | 1 | | CHANNEL*VARIED*? |

channel was varied during this interval, and data are invalid. The values are either blank or Y.

| VERSION | CHAR | 2 | | VERSION*NUMBER |

RMF version number. See TYPE70.

TYPE74
RMF Device Activity

The TYPE74 data set contains one observation for each device in each type 74 SMF record written by RMF at the end of each RMF interval or when RMF is stopped. There is one observation in TYPE74 for each device in each type 74 SMF record that had either a nonzero start I/O count, samples in which the device was busy, an average queue length greater than zero, or was allocated during the RMF interval.

Device Queuing Statistics

TYPE74 contains statistics on the start I/O counts to each device, the percentage of requests deferred, and the percentage of time there was a queue for this device. The queuing statistics are provided from two perspectives. The percentage of samples that were 0, 1, 2, 3, or more than 4 requests in the queue is contained in variables QUEUE0 through QUEUE4. In addition, the percentage of time queued for path (PCTQUEPA) and the percentage of time queued for device (PCTQUEDV) are also provided. Note the following relationships.

Percentage of interval that there was a queue:

= QUEUE1 + QUEUE2 + QUEUE3 + QUEUE4
= 100 − QUEUE0
= PCTQUEDV + PCTQUEPA

Device Busy Statistics

Since both physical and logical channels to which this device is connected are reported, TYPE74 is useful for managing channels that are out of balance. The data set identifies heavily used devices on those channels and can identify devices that should be relocated to different channels and control units.

Device State Statistics

TYPE74 also provides statistics on various states of a device during the RMF interval. Some are performance metrics, and others (like PCTALOC) are useful for migrating data from a volume and are more operationally useful.

variable	percentage of time that
PCTALOC	a task was allocated to this device.
PCTRESVD	this CPU had issued a reserve. This variable does not measure a delay on the system; rather it can cause a delay on another system if the device is shared.

PCTDELAY an I/O from this CPU was delayed after IOS thought the device was available. These delays are due to reserves from other systems and delays from string switching (usually minimal when compared to reserve delays).

MOUNT a mount was outstanding.

NOTREADY device was not ready.

DEVBUSY device was busy transferring data or commands.

Variable	Type	Length	Format	Label
AVDSOPEN	NUM	4	5.1	AVERAGE*DATA SETS*OPENED

average number of data sets open on the device.

| AVGCONMS | NUM | 4 | 5.1 | AVERAGE*CONNECT*TIME(MS) |

average I/O connect time (milliseconds) per SSCH. MVS/XA only.

| AVGDISMS | NUM | 4 | 5.1 | AVERAGE*DISCONNECT*TIME(MS) |

average I/O disconnect time (milliseconds) per SSCH. MVS/XA only.

| AVGENQUE | NUM | 4 | 5.3 | AVERAGE*REQUESTS*ENQUEUED |

average number of requests enqueued for this device.

| AVGIOQMS | NUM | 4 | 5.1 | AVERAGE*IOS QUEUE*TIME(MS) |

average I/O queue time (milliseconds) per SSCH. MVS/XA only.

| AVGPNDMS | NUM | 4 | 5.1 | AVERAGE*PENDING*TIME(MS) |

average I/O pending time (milliseconds) per SSCH. MVS/XA only.

| AVGRSPMS | NUM | 4 | 5.1 | AVERAGE*RESPONSE*TIME(MS) |

average I/O response time (milliseconds) per SSCH. This variable matches the similarly named RMF metric. MVS/XA only.

| BASE | CHAR | 1 | | BASE*EXPOSURE*? |

base exposure of multiple-exposure device if nonblank. The values are either blank or Y.

| CMBINVLD | CHAR | 1 | | CONNECT*TIME*INVALID? |

connect time measurement for this device for this interval is invalid if nonblank.

| CUBUSY | NUM | 4 | 5.1 | PERCENT WHEN*CONTROL*UNIT BUSY |

percentage of samples when control unit was busy. For MVS, this value is generally in error, as there were errors in setting the counter. Since MVS/SE1, however, the value is generally regarded as accurate.

Variable	Type	Length	Format	Label
CYCLE	NUM	4		SAMPLE*CYCLE*TIME(MS)

sample cycle length (in milliseconds). At each CYCLE, a sampling observation is made.

| DEFERCUB | NUM | 4 | | NUMBER SIO*DEFERRED*CU BUSY |

number of requests deferred because control unit to which this device is attached was busy.

| DEFERED | NUM | 4 | | IO REQUEST*DEFERRED*TOTAL |

number of requests deferred (queued) because device was busy and control unit was not busy.

| DEFERSVD | NUM | 4 | | NUMBER SIO*DEFERRED WHEN*VOLUME RESERVED |

number of requests deferred because device was reserved by another system (or blocked by head of string switch in this system).

| DEVACTTM | NUM | 4 | TIME12.2 | DEVICE*ACTIVE*DURATION |

duration that device is active during interval.

| DEVBUSY | NUM | 4 | 5.1 | PERCENT WHEN*DEVICE*BUSY |

percentage of samples in which device was busy and control unit was not busy.

| DEVCONTM | NUM | 4 | TIME12.2 | DEVICE*CONNECT*DURATION |

duration that device is connected during interval.

| DEVDISTM | NUM | 4 | TIME12.2 | DEVICE*DISCONNECT*DURATION |

duration that device is disconnected during interval.

| DEVICE | CHAR | 7 | | DEVICE*TYPE |

device type (for example, 3330, 3350, and so forth) from DEVICE macro.

| DEVNR | NUM | 4 | HEX4. | DEVICE*NUMBER |

number of device. Formerly the unit address in MVS/370. The unique number or address of the device.

| DEVPNDTM | NUM | 4 | TIME12.2 | DEVICE*PENDING*DURATION |

duration that device is disconnected during interval.

| DURATM | NUM | 4 | TIME12.3 | DURATION*OF*INTERVAL |

duration of RMF interval. At end of each DURATM, all data gathered and sampled are written to SMF.

| IORATE | NUM | 4 | | IO*ACTIVITY*RATE |

I/O activity (SSCH) rate per second.

Variable	Type	Length	Format	Label
LCHAN	NUM	4		LOGICAL*CHANNEL*NUMBER

logical channel number with which this device is associated.

| LCU | NUM | 4 | HEX2. | LOGICAL*CONTROL*UNIT |

logical control unit to which this device is connected.

| MOUNT | NUM | 4 | 5.1 | PERCENT WHEN*MOUNT*PENDING |

percentage of samples (time) during which mount was pending for this device.

| NOTREADY | NUM | 4 | 5.1 | PERCENT WHEN*DEVICE WAS*NOT READY |

percentage of samples (time) during which this device was not ready.

| NREXPOSR | NUM | 4 | | NUMBER*OF*EXPOSURES |

number of exposures if this is a multiple exposure (for example, drum or drumlike) device.

| NRSAMPLE | NUM | 4 | | NUMBER*OF*SAMPLES |

number of samples taken in RMF interval. (Samples are taken at cycle intervals.)

| ONLINE | CHAR | 1 | | CHANNEL*ON-LINE*AT END? |

device is on-line at end of interval flag. The values are either blank or Y.

| OVERFLOW | NUM | 4 | | TIMER*OVERFLOW*COUNT |

number of requests that detected that hardware timer register containing connect time had overflowed. Early MVS/XA had problems in connect time overflow, so the timer's hardware and microcode were changed. This field should be near zero, but the potential for overflow (and hence incorrect data) still exists.

| PARTIAL | CHAR | 1 | | PARTIAL*DATA? |

flag that only partial statistics are available. The values are either blank or Y. MVS/XA only.

| PCTALOC | NUM | 4 | 5.1 | PERCENT WHEN*DEVICE*ALLOCATED |

percentage of samples (time) during which device was allocated.

| PCTDEFCU | NUM | 4 | 5.1 | PERCENT REQ*DEFERRED*CU BUSY |

percentage of total SIO count deferred due to control unit busy.

| PCTDEFER | NUM | 4 | 5.1 | PERCENT REQ*DEFERRED*TOTAL |

percentage of total SIO count to this device deferred because device was busy and control unit was not.

| PCTDEFRS | NUM | 4 | 5.1 | PERCENT REQ*DEFERRED*RESERVED |

percentage of total SIO count to this device deferred because device was reserved by another system (or head of string).

Variable	Type	Length	Format	Label
PCTDELAY	NUM	4	5.1	PERCENT WHEN*OTHER SYSTEM*HAD RESERVED

percentage of time when this I/O was delayed to this device because device was reserved by another system (or head of string).

PCTDVACT	NUM	4	5.1	PERCENT WHEN*DEVICE*WAS ACTIVE

percentage of interval time when device was active.

PCTDVCON	NUM	4	5.1	PERCENT WHEN*DEVICE*WAS CONNECTED

percentage of interval time when device was connected.

PCTDVDIS	NUM	4	5.1	PERCENT WHEN*DEVICE*WAS DISCONNECTED

percentage of interval time when device was disconnected.

PCTDVPND	NUM	4	5.1	PERCENT WHEN*DEVICE*WAS PENDING

percentage of interval time when device was pending.

PCTDVUSE	NUM	4	5.1	PERCENT WHEN*DEVICE WAS*UTILIZED

percentage of interval time when device was utilized.

PCTQUEDV	NUM	4	5.1	PERCENT WHEN*QUEUED WHEN*DEVICE BUSY

percentage of samples when requests were queued because device was busy. See PCTQUEPA. Note that PCTQUEPA+PCTQUEDV=100−QUEUE0.

PCTQUEPA	NUM	4	5.1	PERCENT WHEN*QUEUED WHEN*PATH BUSY

percentage of samples when requests were queued because path was busy. See PCTQUEDV.

PCTRESVD	NUM	4	5.1	PERCENT WHEN*RESERVED*FROM THIS SYS

percentage of samples when this CPU had reserved the device (that is, potential delay to the other CPU in a shared DASD environment).

QUEUE0	NUM	4	5.1	PERCENT WHEN*NO REQUESTS*WERE WAITING

percentage of samples when there were no requests queued for this device.

QUEUE1	NUM	4	5.1	PERCENT WHEN*1 REQUEST*WAS WAITING

percentage of samples when there was one request queued for this device.

Variable	Type	Length	Format	Label
QUEUE2	NUM	4	5.1	PERCENT WHEN*2 REQUESTS*WERE WAITING

percentage of samples when there were two requests queued for this device.

QUEUE3	NUM	4	5.1	PERCENT WHEN*3 REQUESTS*WERE WAITING

percentage of samples when there were three requests queued for this device.

QUEUE4	NUM	4	5.1	PERCENT WHEN*OVER 3 REQ*WERE WAITING

percent of samples when there were four or more requests queued for this device.

RELEASE	CHAR	4		OPERATING*SYSTEM*RELEASE

operating system release number and level. (For example, 0370 for release 3 level 7, or 3.7.)

SIO74CNT	NUM	4		START-IO*(TYPE74)*COUNT

total number of successful start I/Os for this device.

SMFTIME	NUM	8	DATETIME19.2	SMF*RECORD*TIME STAMP

approximate ending time stamp of RMF interval. (Actually, the time the record is moved to SMF.)

SSCHSAMP	NUM	4		MEASUREMENT*EVENT*COUNT

number of SSCH instructions sampled. RMF calls this the measurement event count, for it is this number of SSCHs for which connect, pending and active times are stored.

STARTIME	NUM	8	DATETIME19.2	START OF*INTERVAL

beginning of RMF interval time stamp.

SYSTEM	CHAR	4	4.	SYSTEM*ID

identification of this system.

UCBTYPE	NUM	4	HEX8.	UCB*TYPE

UCB unit type bytes 1-4. (See DEVICE.)

UNITADR	NUM	4	HEX3.	UNIT*ADDRESS

unit address of this device.

VARY	CHAR	1		DEVICE*VARIED*?

flag that data are invalid because device was varied during this interval. The values are either blank or Y.

VERSION	CHAR	2		VERSION*NUMBER

RMF version number. See TYPE70.

Variable	Type	Length	Format	Label
VOLSER	CHAR	6		VOLUME*SERIAL*NUMBER

volume serial number on this device at end of interval.

TYPE75
RMF Page and Swap Data Set Activity

The TYPE75 data set contains one observation for each page or swap data set in each type 75 SMF record written by RMF at the end of each RMF interval or when RMF is stopped.

TYPE75 contains statistics on the utilization of the page and swap data sets. Unfortunately, only utilizations and not queuing or delays are reported. The data are the best (and the only) available, as seen by the auxiliary storage manager's (ASM) page and swap data set activity. The important metric is the ASM view of data set busy (DSBUSY). You have to fall back to second generation concepts and use a utilization measure and rules of thumb to determine when additional page and swap data sets are required. In addition, TYPE75 contains the number of pages transferred to or from each page data set and the number of used versus allocated slots on each data set. Especially in a virtual storage constrained MVS/370 system, you should not greatly overallocate the page and swap data sets since there is real storage required in CSA for each slot. It may be reasonable to allocate twice as many slots as the maximum that has been used, but more than that wastes CSA space.

Variable	Type	Length	Format	Label
AVGUSED	NUM	4		AVERAGE*SLOTS*USED
				average number of slots or swap set used.
CYCLE	NUM	4		SAMPLE*CYCLE*TIME(MS)
				sample cycle length (in milliseconds). At each CYCLE, a sampling observation is made.
DEVICE	CHAR	7		DEVICE*TYPE
				device type (for example, 3330, 3350, and so forth) from DEVICE macro.
DEVNR	NUM	4	HEX4.	DEVICE*NUMBER
				device number of device. Formerly the unit address in MVS/370. The unique number or address of the device.
DSBUSY	NUM	4	5.1	PERCENT WHEN*DATA SET*WAS BUSY
				percent of samples (time) during which data set was being used by ASM.
DURATM	NUM	4	TIME12.2	DURATION*OF*INTERVAL
				duration of RMF interval. At the end of each DURATM, all data gathered and samples are written to SMF.

Variable	Type	Length	Format	Label
LCU	NUM	4	HEX2.	LOGICAL*CONTROL*UNIT

logical control unit to which device containing this page or swap data set is connected.

| MAXUSED | NUM | 4 | | MAXIMUM*SLOTS*USED |

maximum number of slots or swap set used.

| MINUSED | NUM | 4 | | MINIMUM*SLOTS*USED |

minimum number of slots or swap sets used.

| NRPAGTRF | NUM | 4 | | NUMBER OF*PAGES*TRANSFERRED |

number of pages transferred to or from data set during interval.

| NRSAMPLE | NUM | 4 | | NUMBER*OF*SAMPLES |

number of samples taken in this RMF interval. (Samples are taken at CYCLE intervals.)

| NRSAMREQ | NUM | 4 | | NUMBER OF*REQUESTS |

number of requests for data set observed during RMF sampling.

| PAGEDSN | CHAR | 44 | | PAGE/SWAP*DATA SET*NAME |

name of page or swap data set.

| PAGETYPE | CHAR | 6 | | TYPE*PAGING*DATA SET |

type of paging data set: PLPA, COMMON, DUPLEX, LOCAL, SWAP.

| RELEASE | CHAR | 4 | | OPERATING*SYSTEM*RELEASE |

operating system release number and level. (For example, 0370 for release 3 level 7, or 3.7.)

| SIOCOUNT | NUM | 4 | | START-IO*COUNT |

number of I/O requests for this data set.

| SLOTS | NUM | 4 | | NUMBER*OF SLOTS*DEFINED |

total number of slots or swap sets in this data set.

| SMFTIME | NUM | 8 | DATETIME19.2 | SMF*RECORD*TIME STAMP |

approximate ending time stamp of RMF interval. (Actually, the time the record is moved to SMF.)

| STARTIME | NUM | 8 | DATETIME19.2 | START OF*INTERVAL |

beginning of RMF interval time stamp.

| SYSTEM | CHAR | 4 | 4. | SYSTEM*ID |

identification of this system.

Variable	Type	Length	Format	Label
UCBTYPE	NUM	4	HEX8.	UCB*TYPE

UCB unit type bytes 1-4. (See DEVICE).

| UNITADR | NUM | 4 | HEX4. | UNIT*ADDRESS |

unit address of this device.

| UNUSABLE | CHAR | 1 | | UNUSABLE*DATA SET*? |

flag if this data set is unusable. The values are either blank or Y.

| UNUSLOTS | NUM | 4 | | UNUSABLE*SLOTS |

number of unusable slots or swap sets.

| VARY | CHAR | 1 | | DEVICE*VARIED*? |

flag that data are invalid because device was varied during this interval. The values are either blank or Y.

| VERSION | CHAR | 2 | | VERSION*NUMBER |

RMF version number. See TYPE70.

| VIOALOWD | CHAR | 1 | | VIO*ALLOWED*? |

flag that VIO pages are allowed to exist on this page data set. The values are either blank or Y.

| VOLSER | CHAR | 6 | | VOLUME*SERIAL*NUMBER |

volume serial number of device containing this data set.

TYPE76
Trace Record

The TYPE76 data set contains multiple observations for every type 76 SMF record. Type 76 SMF records are written at the end of each RMF interval when tracing of specific SRM fields was requested, and they are very useful for tracking specific information in the MVS SRM. This is the logical equivalent of GTF data for RMF SYSEVENTS. For each field that is traced, each type 76 SMF record contains multiple segments that contain the value of the traced field. The TYPE76 data set contains one observation for each sample value of each field in each type 76 SMF record. Further information is available in the discussion of the trace option in the *RMF User's Guide*, referenced in chapter thirty-eight.

Variable	Type	Length	Format	Label
CYCLE	NUM	4		SAMPLE*CYCLE*TIME(MS)

sample cycle length (in milliseconds). At each CYCLE, a sampling observation is made.

DURATM	NUM	4	TIME12.2	DURATION*OF*INTERVAL

duration of RMF interval. At the end of each DURAT, all data gathered and sampled are written to SMF.

END	NUM	4		SAMPLE*SET*END VALUE

ending value of traced field in each sample set (in other words, each time of the trace).

FIELDNME	CHAR	8		FIELD*NAME

name of RMF field that this record reports.

INTRVEND	NUM	4		INTERVAL*END*VALUE

value of traced field at end of RMF interval.

INTRVMAX	NUM	4		INTERVAL*MAXIMUM*VALUE

maximum value of traced field during RMF interval.

INTRVMIN	NUM	4		INTERVAL*MINIMUM*VALUE

minimum value of traced field during RMF interval.

INTRVSSQ	NUM	4		INTERVAL*SUM OF SQUARES*VALUE

sum of squared values of traced field during RMF interval.

INTRVSUM	NUM	4		INTERVAL*SUM*VALUE

sum of traced-field values during RMF interval.

Variable	Type	Length	Format	Label
LPBEND	CHAR	1		LPB*TRACE*END?

flag that LPB trace request has ended. The values are either blank or Y. MVS/XA only.

| LPBREQ | CHAR | 1 | | LPB*TRACE*REQUESTED? |

flag that LPB trace was requested. The values are either blank or Y. MVS/XA only.

| MAX | NUM | 4 | | SAMPLE*SET*MAXIMUM |

maximum value of traced field in each sample set (in other words, each line of trace).

| MIN | NUM | 4 | | SAMPLE*SET*MINIMUM |

minimum value of traced field in each sample set (in other words, each line of trace).

| NRSAMPLE | NUM | 4 | | NUMBER*OF*SAMPLES |

number of samples taken in RMF interval.

| NRSETS | NUM | 4 | | NUMBER*SAMPLE*SETS |

number of sample sets (that is, lines of data) in trace.

| OPTNS76 | NUM | 4 | | OPTIONS*SPECIFIED |

options specified for this field name:

bit	meaning when on
1	minimum value requested
2	maximum value requested
3	sum value requested
4	sum of squared values requested
5	end value requested
6	all options requested
7	domain tracing terminated
8	entry is a domain field.

| RELEASE | CHAR | 4 | | OPERATING*SYSTEM*RELEASE |

operating system release number and level (for example, 0370 for release 3 level 7, or 3.7).

| SAMP_LST | NUM | 4 | | SAMPLES*IN*LAST SET |

number of samples in last sample set being built when RMF interval ended.

| SAMP_SET | NUM | 4 | | SAMPLES*IN*SAMPLE SET |

number of samples in each sample set.

Variable	Type	Length	Format	Label
SMFTIME	NUM	8	DATETIME19.2	SMF*RECORD*TIME STAMP

approximate ending time stamp of RMF interval. (Actually, the time the record is moved to SMF.)

SSQ	NUM	4		SAMPLE*SET*SUM OF SQUARES

sum of squared values of traced field in each sample set (in other words, each line of trace).

STARTIME	NUM	8	DATETIME19.2	START OF*INTERVAL

beginning of RMF interval time stamp.

SUM	NUM	4		SAMPLE*SET*SUM

sum of traced-field values in each sample set (in other words, each line of the trace).

SYSTEM	CHAR	4	4.	SYSTEM*ID

identification of this system.

VERSION	CHAR	2		VERSION*NUMBER

RMF version number. See TYPE70.

TYPE77
Enqueue Records

The TYPE77 data set contains multiple observations for every type 77 SMF record, written at the end of each RMF interval or when RMF is stopped.

The TYPE77 data set contains one observation for every resource that was enqueued during the interval. TYPE77 provides statistics on the duration of the enqueue conflict and the current owner and awaiting owners for each of the enqueue events. It is especially valuable in determining those resources for which conflicts are occurring at the enqueue level. By looking at the resource names in TYPE77, unexpected QNAMEs that cause performance degradation will often be discovered.

Variable	Type	Length	Format	Label
CURROWN	NUM	4		NUMBER*CURRENT*OWNERS
number of current owners using enqueued resource.				
CURRWAIT	NUM	4		NUMBER*CURRENT*WAITERS
number of current tasks waiting for resource.				
DURATM	NUM	4	TIME12.2	DURATION*OF*INTERVAL
duration of RMF interval.				
EVENTS	NUM	4		TOTAL*CONTENTION*EVENTS
total number of contention events that occurred in interval.				
JOBOWN1	CHAR	8		NAME OF*CURRENT*OWNER#1
task name of first current owner.				
JOBOWN2	CHAR	8		NAME OF*CURRENT*OWNER#2
task name of second current owner.				
JOBWANT1	CHAR	8		NAME OF*WANTER#1
task name of first wanting (waiting) task.				
JOBWANT2	CHAR	8		NAME OF*WANTER#2
task name of second wanting (waiting) task.				
MAXEXC	NUM	4		MAXIMUM*EXCLUSIVE*REQUESTS
maximum number of exclusive requests.				

Variable	Type	Length	Format	Label
MAXSHR	NUM	4		MAXIMUM*SHARED*REQUESTS

maximum number of shared requests.

| MAXTM | NUM | 4 | TIME12.2 | MAXIMUM*CONTENTION*DURATION |

maximum duration of contention time.

| MINEXC | NUM | 4 | | MINIMUM*EXCLUSIVE*REQUESTS |

minimum number of exclusive requests.

| MINORQCB | NUM | 4 | | MINOR*NAME*LENGTH STAT |

minor name length status.

| MINSHR | NUM | 4 | | MINIMUM*SHARED*REQUESTS |

minimum number of shared requests.

| MINTM | NUM | 4 | TIME12.2 | MINIMUM*CONTENTION*DURATION |

minimum duration of contention time.

| NRSAMPLE | NUM | 4 | | NUMBER*OF*SAMPLES |

number of RMF samples during this interval.

| QNAME | CHAR | 8 | | MAJOR*ENQUEUE*(QNAME) |

major name (QNAME in ENQ macro) of resource for which contention occurred.

| QUEUE1 | NUM | 4 | 5.1 | PERCENT WHEN*1 REQUEST*WAS WAITING |

percentage of samples when there was one request waiting on this resource.

| QUEUE2 | NUM | 4 | 5.1 | PERCENT WHEN*2 REQUESTS*WERE WAITING |

percentage of samples when there were two requests waiting on this resource.

| QUEUE3 | NUM | 4 | 5.1 | PERCENT WHEN*3 REQUESTS*WERE WAITING |

percentage of samples when there were three requests waiting on this resource.

| QUEUE4 | NUM | 4 | 5.1 | PERCENT WHEN*OVER 3 SIO*WERE WAITING |

percentage of samples when there were more than three requests waiting on this resource.

| RELEASE | CHAR | 4 | | OPERATING*SYSTEM*RELEASE |

operating system release and level (for example, 0370 for release 3 level 7, or 3.7).

Variable	Type	Length	Format	Label
RESIND	NUM	4		RESOURCE*INDICATOR*FLAG

resource indicator flag.

bit	value	meaning
1	1	resource still in contention
2	1	scope of systems
2	0	scope of system
3	1	owner has exclusive control
3	0	owner shares the resource
4	1	JOBWAIT1 wants exclusive use
4	0	JOBWAIT1 wants shared use
5	1	JOBWAIT2 wants exclusive use
5	0	JOBWAIT2 wants shared use.

Variable	Type	Length	Format	Label
RNAME	CHAR	44		MINOR*ENQUEUE*(RNAME)

minor name (RNAME in ENQ macro) of resource for which contention occurred.

Variable	Type	Length	Format	Label
SMFTIME	NUM	8	DATETIME19.2	SMF*RECORD*TIME STAMP

approximate ending time stamp of RMF interval. (Actually, the time the record is moved to SMF.)

Variable	Type	Length	Format	Label
STARTIME	NUM	8	DATETIME19.2	START OF*INTERVAL

beginning of RMF interval time stamp.

Variable	Type	Length	Format	Label
STATIND	NUM	4		ENQUEUE*STATUS*INDICATOR

enqueue status indicator

bit	value	meaning
1	1	enqueue summary table full
2	1	specified resource had no contention
3	1	enqueue had bad CPU clock
4	1	enqueue processing event abended
5	1	detailed data requested
	0	summary data requested.

Variable	Type	Length	Format	Label
SYSOWN1	CHAR	8		CURRENT*OWNER#1*SYSTEM

identification of system on which JOBOWN1 is executing.

Variable	Type	Length	Format	Label
SYSOWN2	CHAR	8		CURRENT*OWNER#2*SYSTEM

identification of system on which JOBOWN2 is executing.

| SYSTEM | CHAR | 4 | 4. | SYSTEM*ID |

identification of this system.

| SYSWANT1 | CHAR | 8 | | WANTER#1*SYSTEM |

identification of system on which JOBWANT1 is executing.

| SYSWANT2 | CHAR | 8 | | WANTER#2*SYSTEM |

identification of system on which JOBWANT2 is executing.

| TOTLTM | NUM | 4 | TIME12.2 | TOTAL*CONTENTION*DURATION |

total resource contention duration (seconds).

| VERSION | CHAR | 2 | | VERSION*NUMBER |

RMF version. See TYPE70.

| WAITS | NUM | 4 | | TOTAL*WAITING*REQUESTS |

total number of waiting requests during interval.

TYPE78
MVS/XA Device Queuing Statistics

The TYPE78 data set contains multiple observations for every type 78 SMF record written at the end of each RMF interval or when RMF is stopped.

The type 78 data that describe the configuration are output to data set TYPE78CF. Data from type 78 records that describe device queuing are output to data set TYPE78, which replaces the logical channel queuing data formerly in TYPE73. See the discussion of data set TYPE73 for more information about these data.

Data on virtual storage usage are also written in a type 78 record but are described in sections TYPE78VS, TYPE78PA, and TYPE78SP.

Variable	Type	Length	Format	Label
CYCLE	NUM	4		SAMPLE*CYCLE*TIME(MS)

sample cycle length (in milliseconds). At each CYCLE, a sampling observation is made.

| DURATM | NUM | 4 | TIME12.2 | DURATION*OF*INTERVAL |

duration of RMF interval. At the end of each DURATM, all data gathered and sampled are written to SMF.

| INVALSAM | NUM | 4 | | INVALID*SAMPLES |

count of invalid samples.

| IORATE | NUM | 4 | 8.3 | IO*ACTIVITY*RATE |

rate (per second) of I/O activity to this device.

| LCUID | NUM | 4 | HEX2. | LCU*IDENTIFIER |

logical control unit identifier.

| NOSTCPS | CHAR | 1 | | NO*STCPS*DATA? |

flag that data are invalid because no Store Channel Path Status (STCPS) instruction data were available.

| NOUCBFND | CHAR | 1 | | NO*UCB*FOUND |

flag that data may be invalid because no UCB was found. However, this flag is normally on if IOCDS defines more devices than SYSGEN defined.

| NRATTMPS | NUM | 4 | | INITIAL*SELECTION*ATTEMPTS |

total number of initial selection attempts.

| NRREQENQ | NUM | 4 | | REQUESTS*ENQUEUED*FOR LCU |

total number of requests queued for the logical control unit (accumulated at initial selection time).

Variable	Type	Length	Format	Label
NRSAMPLE	NUM	4		NUMBER*OF*SAMPLES

number of samples taken in RMF interval. (Samples are taken at cycle intervals.)

Variable	Type	Length	Format	Label
PCTALLBY	NUM	4	5.1	PERCENT WHEN*ALL PATHS*WERE BUSY

percentage of time when all channel paths in the logical control unit were busy.

Variable	Type	Length	Format	Label
PCTDEFCU	NUM	4	5.1	PERCENT REQ*DEFERRED*CU BUSY

percentage of initial selection attempts deferred because control unit was busy.

Variable	Type	Length	Format	Label
PCTDEFDV	NUM	4	5.1	PERCENT REQ*DEFERRED*DEVICE BUSY

percentage of initial selection attempts deferred because device was busy.

Variable	Type	Length	Format	Label
PCTDEFER	NUM	4	5.1	PERCENT REQ*DEFERRED*TOTAL

percentage of total SIO count deferred for any reason.

Variable	Type	Length	Format	Label
PCTSUCES	NUM	4	5.1	PERCENT*REQUESTS*SUCCESSFUL

percentage of successful initial selection attempts.

Variable	Type	Length	Format	Label
RELEASE	CHAR	4		OPERATING*SYSTEM*RELEASE

operating system release number and level (for example, 0370 for release 3 level 7, or 3.7).

Variable	Type	Length	Format	Label
SIO78CNT	NUM	4		START IO*(TYPE78)*COUNT

successful SSCH (SIO) count for this device number.

Variable	Type	Length	Format	Label
SMFTIME	NUM	8	DATETIME19.2	SMF*RECORD*TIME STAMP

approximate ending time stamp of RMF interval. (Actually, the time the record is moved to SMF.)

Variable	Type	Length	Format	Label
STARTIME	NUM	8	DATETIME19.2	START OF*INTERVAL

beginning of RMF interval time stamp.

Variable	Type	Length	Format	Label
SYSTEM	CHAR	4	4.	SYSTEM*ID

identification of this system.

Variable	Type	Length	Format	Label
VERSION	CHAR	2		VERSION*NUMBER

RMF version number. See TYPE70.

TYPE78CF
MVS/XA Device Configuration

The TYPE78CF data set contains multiple observations for every type 78 SMF record written at the end of each RMF interval or when RMF is stopped.

TYPE78CF contains type 78 data that describe the configuration. Data from type 78 records that describe device queuing are output in TYPE78. Because I/O configurations are frequently long-lived, the split was made to reduce the data that were actively needed.

Data on virtual storage usage are also written in a type 78 record but is described in sections TYPE78VS, TYPE78PA, and TYPE78SP.

Variable	Type	Length	Format	Label
CHPID	NUM	4	HEX2.	CHANNEL*PATH*IDENTIFIER

channel path identification on which this device is connected.

CU1	NUM	4	HEX4.	FIRST*CONTROL*UNIT

first control unit attached.

CU2	NUM	4	HEX4.	SECOND*CONTROL*UNIT

second control unit attached.

CU3	NUM	4	HEX4.	THIRD*CONTROL*UNIT

third control unit attached.

CU4	NUM	4	HEX4.	FOURTH*CONTROL*UNIT

fourth control unit attached.

CYCLE	NUM	4		SAMPLE*CYCLE*TIME(MS)

sample cycle length (in milliseconds). At each cycle, a sampling observation is made.

DURATM	NUM	4	TIME12.2	DURATION*OF*INTERVAL

duration of RMF interval. At the end of each DURATM, all data gathered and sampled are written to SMF.

INSTALL	CHAR	1		CHANNEL*PATH*INSTALLED?

flag if this channel path is actually installed. The values are either blank or Y.

LCUID	NUM	4	HEX2.	LCU*IDENTIFIER

logical control unit identifier.

Variable	Type	Length	Format	Label
NRCUS	NUM	4		CONTROL* UNITS*ATTACHED

number of control units attached.

| NRSAMPLE | NUM | 4 | | NUMBER*OF*SAMPLES |

number of samples taken in RMF interval.

| ONLINE | CHAR | 1 | | CHANNEL*ON-LINE*AT END? |

device is on-line at end of interval flag. The flag values are either blank or Y.

| RELEASE | CHAR | 4 | | OPERATING*SYSTEM*RELEASE |

operating system release number and level (for example, 0370 for release 3 level 7, or 3.7).

| SMFTIME | NUM | 8 | DATETIME19.2 | SMF*RECORD*TIME STAMP |

approximate ending time stamp of RMF interval. (Actually, the time the record is moved to SMF.)

| STARTIME | NUM | 8 | DATETIME19.2 | START OF*INTERVAL |

beginning of RMF interval time stamp.

| SYSTEM | CHAR | 4 | 4. | SYSTEM*ID |

identification of this system.

| VARIED | CHAR | 1 | | CHANNEL*VARIED* ? |

channel was varied during this interval; data are invalid. The values are either blank or Y.

| VERSION | CHAR | 2 | | VERSION*NUMBER |

RMF version number. See TYPE70.

TYPE78PA
MVS/XA Virtual Storage (Private Area) Statistics

The TYPE78PA data set contains multiple observations for every type 78 SMF record that monitored virtual storage usage in the private area for a task. A type 78 SMF record is written at the end of each RMF interval or when RMF is stopped.

Virtual storage usage is reported in TYPE78VS. If monitoring of the private area for tasks is requested, there is one observation in TYPE78PA for each task monitored. For monitored tasks, their usage of subpools is reported in TYPE78SP.

Variable	Type	Length	Format	Label
GMLIMHI	NUM	4		GETMAIN*LIMIT*ABOVE

GETMAIN limit (in bytes) above 16 megabytes.

GMLIMLOW	NUM	4		GETMAIN*LIMIT*BELOW

GETMAIN limit (in bytes) below 16 megabytes.

JOB	CHAR	8		JOB NAME*OR*TSO USER

name of job whose private area was monitored.

LSQALPG0	NUM	4		LSQA/SWA*PAGES*MIN BELOW

minimum value of pages allocated below 16 MB in LSQA, SWA, and SUBPOOLs 229 and 230.

LSQALPG1	NUM	4	DATETIME19.2	LSQA/SWA*PAGES*MIN BELOW TIME

time when minimum value of LSQA/SWA/229/230 pages allocated below 16 MB occurred.

LSQALPG2	NUM	4		LSQA/SWA*PAGES*MAX BELOW

maximum value of pages allocated below 16 MB in LSQA, SWA, and SUBPOOLs 229 and 230.

LSQALPG3	NUM	4	DATETIME19.2	LSQA/SWA*PAGES*MAX BELOW TIME

time when maximum value of LSQA/SWA/229/230 pages allocated below 16 MB occurred.

LSQALPG4	NUM	4		LSQA/SWA*PAGES*AVERAGE BELOW

average value of pages allocated below 16 MB in LSQA, SWA, and SUBPOOLs 229 and 230.

LSQALPG5	NUM	4		LSQA/SWA*PAGES*MIN ABOVE

minimum value of pages allocated above 16 MB in LSQA, SWA, and SUBPOOLs 229 and 230.

Variable	Type	Length	Format	Label
LSQALPG6	NUM	4		LSQA/SWA*PAGES*MIN ABOVE TIME

time when minimum value of LSQA/SWA/229/230 pages allocated above 16 MB occurred.

| LSQALPG7 | NUM | 4 | | LSQA/SWA*PAGES*MAX ABOVE |

maximum value of pages allocated above 16 MB in LSQA, SWA, and SUBPOOLs 229 and 230.

| LSQALPG8 | NUM | 4 | | LSQA/SWA*PAGES*MAX ABOVE TIME |

time when maximum value of LSQA/SWA/229/230 pages allocated above 16 MB occurred.

| LSQALPG9 | NUM | 4 | | LSQA/SWA*PAGES*AVERAGE ABOVE |

average value of pages allocated above 16 MB in LSQA, SWA, and SUBPOOLs 229 and 230.

| LSQALSZ0 | NUM | 4 | | LSQA/SWA*SIZE*MIN BELOW |

minimum value of allocated area size below 16 MB in LSQA, SWA, and SUBPOOLs 229 and 230.

| LSQALSZ1 | NUM | 4 | DATETIME19.2 | LSQA/SWA*SIZE*MIN BELOW TIME |

time when minimum value of LSQA/SWA/229/230 allocated area size below 16 MB occurred.

| LSQALSZ2 | NUM | 4 | | LSQA/SWA*SIZE*MAX BELOW |

maximum value of allocated area size below 16 MB in LSQA, SWA, and SUBPOOLs 229 and 230.

| LSQALSZ3 | NUM | 4 | DATETIME19.2 | LSQA/SWA*SIZE*MAX BELOW TIME |

time when maximum value of LSQA/SWA/229/230 allocated area size below 16 MB occurred.

| LSQALSZ4 | NUM | 4 | | LSQA/SWA*SIZE*AVERAGE BELOW |

average value of allocated area size below 16 MB in LSQA, SWA, and SUBPOOLs 229 and 230.

| LSQALSZ5 | NUM | 4 | | LSQA/SWA*SIZE*MIN ABOVE |

minimum value of allocated area size above 16 MB in LSQA, SWA, and SUBPOOLs 229 and 230.

| LSQALSZ6 | NUM | 4 | | LSQA/SWA*SIZE*MIN ABOVE TIME |

time when minimum value of LSQA/SWA/229/230 allocated area size above 16 MB occurred.

| LSQALSZ7 | NUM | 4 | | LSQA/SWA*SIZE*MAX ABOVE |

maximum value of allocated area size above 16 MB in LSQA, SWA, and SUBPOOLs 229 and 230.

Variable	Type	Length	Format	Label
LSQALSZ8	NUM	4		LSQA/SWA*SIZE*MAX ABOVE TIME

time when maximum value of LSQA/SWA/229/230 allocated area size above 16 MB occurred.

| LSQALSZ9 | NUM | 4 | | LSQA/SWA*SIZE*AVERAGE ABOVE |

average value of allocated area size above 16 MB in LSQA, SWA, and SUBPOOLs 229 and 230.

| LSQFRPG0 | NUM | 4 | | LSQA/SWA*FREE*MIN BELOW |

minimum value of free pages below 16 MB in LSQA, SWA, and SUBPOOLs 229 and 230.

| LSQFRPG1 | NUM | 4 | DATETIME19.2 | LSQA/SWA*FREE*MIN BELOW TIME |

time when minimum value of LSQA/SWA/229/230 free pages below 16 MB occurred.

| LSQFRPG2 | NUM | 4 | | LSQA/SWA*FREE*MAX BELOW |

maximum value of free pages below 16 MB in LSQA, SWA, and SUBPOOLs 229 and 230.

| LSQFRPG3 | NUM | 4 | DATETIME19.2 | LSQA/SWA*FREE*MAX BELOW TIME |

time when maximum value of LSQA/SWA/229/230 free pages below 16 MB occurred.

| LSQFRPG4 | NUM | 4 | | LSQA/SWA*FREE*AVERAGE BELOW |

average value of free pages below 16 MB in LSQA, SWA, and SUBPOOLs 229 and 230.

| LSQFRPG5 | NUM | 4 | | LSQA/SWA*FREE*MIN ABOVE |

minimum value of free pages above 16 MB in LSQA, SWA, and SUBPOOLs 229 and 230.

| LSQFRPG6 | NUM | 4 | | LSQA/SWA*FREE*MIN ABOVE TIME |

time when minimum value of LSQA/SWA/229/230 free pages above 16 MB occurred.

| LSQFRPG7 | NUM | 4 | | LSQA/SWA*FREE*MAX ABOVE |

maximum value of free pages above 16 MB in LSQA, SWA, and SUBPOOLs 229 and 230.

| LSQFRPG8 | NUM | 4 | | LSQA/SWA*FREE*MAX ABOVE TIME |

time when maximum value of LSQA/SWA/229/230 free pages above 16 MB occurred.

| LSQFRPG9 | NUM | 4 | | LSQA/SWA*FREE*AVERAGE ABOVE |

average value of free pages above 16 MB in LSQA, SWA, and SUBPOOLs 229 and 230.

| LSQLARG0 | NUM | 4 | | LSQA/SWA*LARGEST*MIN BELOW |

minimum value of largest free block below 16 MB in LSQA, SWA, and SUBPOOLs 229 and 230.

Variable	Type	Length	Format	Label
LSQLARG1	NUM	4	DATETIME19.2	LSQA/SWA*LARGEST*MIN BELOW TIME

time when minimum value of LSQA/SWA/229/230 largest free block below 16 MB occurred.

LSQLARG2	NUM	4		LSQA/SWA*LARGEST*MAX BELOW

maximum value of largest free block below 16 MB in LSQA, SWA, and SUBPOOLs 229 and 230.

LSQLARG3	NUM	4	DATETIME19.2	LSQA/SWA*LARGEST*MAX BELOW TIME

time when maximum value of LSQA/SWA/229/230 largest free block below 16 MB occurred.

LSQLARG4	NUM	4		LSQA/SWA*LARGEST*AVERAGE BELOW

average value of largest free block below 16 MB in LSQA, SWA, and SUBPOOLs 229 and 230.

LSQLARG5	NUM	4		LSQA/SWA*LARGEST*MIN ABOVE

minimum value of largest free block above 16 MB in LSQA, SWA, and SUBPOOLs 229 and 230.

LSQLARG6	NUM	4		LSQA/SWA*LARGEST*MIN ABOVE TIME

time when minimum value of LSQA/SWA/229/230 largest free block above 16 MB occurred.

LSQLARG7	NUM	4		LSQA/SWA*LARGEST*MAX ABOVE

maximum value of largest free block above 16 MB in LSQA, SWA, and SUBPOOLs 229 and 230.

LSQLARG8	NUM	4		LSQA/SWA*LARGEST*MAX ABOVE TIME

time when maximum value of LSQA/SWA/229/230 largest free block above 16 MB occurred.

LSQLARG9	NUM	4		LSQA/SWA*LARGEST*AVERAGE ABOVE

average value of largest free block above 16 MB in LSQA, SWA, and SUBPOOLs 229 and 230.

NRPASAMP	NUM	4		NUMBER*PRIVATE AREA*SAMPLES

number of samples taken for this private area.

Variable	Type	Length	Format	Label
PROGRAM	CHAR	8		PROGRAM*NAME

program name of job being monitored.

| READTIME | NUM | 8 | | READ-IN*OR LOGON*EVENT |

read-in time of job being monitored.

| REGABOVE | NUM | 4 | | REGION*BY EXITS*ABOVE |

region above 16 MB that was assigned by exits (in bytes).

| REGBELOW | NUM | 4 | | REGION*BY EXITS*BELOW |

region below 16 MB that was assigned by exits (in bytes).

| REGREQST | NUM | 4 | | REGION*REQUESTED*IN JCL |

region requested in JCL (in bytes).

| R78PAFLG | NUM | 4 | | JOB*STATUS*FLAGS |

flags describing status of job being monitored.

value	meaning
1.......	job active at start of interval
.1......	job terminated during interval
..1.....	GETMAIN limit changed during interval
...1....	data invalid because RMF terminated abnormally while sampling.

| STEPNAME | CHAR | 8 | | STEP*NAME |

name of step that was active when monitoring began.

| USERADHI | NUM | 4 | | USER*ADDRESS*ABOVE |

user region address above 16 MB.

| USERADLO | NUM | 4 | | USER*ADDRESS*BELOW |

user region address below 16 MB.

| USRALPG0 | NUM | 4 | | USER*PAGES*MIN BELOW |

minimum value of user region pages allocated below 16 MB.

| USRALPG1 | NUM | 4 | DATETIME19.2 | USER*PAGES*MIN BELOW TIME |

time when minimum value of user region pages allocated below 16 MB occurred.

| USRALPG2 | NUM | 4 | | USER*PAGES*MAX BELOW |

maximum value of user region pages allocated below 16 MB.

Variable	Type	Length	Format	Label
USRALPG3	NUM	4	DATETIME19.2	USER*PAGES*MAX BELOW TIME

time when maximum value of user region pages allocated below 16 MB occurred.

| USRALPG4 | NUM | 4 | | USER*PAGES*AVERAGE BELOW |

average value of user region pages allocated below 16 MB.

| USRALPG5 | NUM | 4 | | USER*PAGES*MIN ABOVE |

minimum value of user region pages allocated above 16 MB.

| USRALPG6 | NUM | 4 | | USER*PAGES*MIN ABOVE TIME |

time when minimum value of user region pages allocated above 16 MB occurred.

| USRALPG7 | NUM | 4 | | USER*PAGES*MAX ABOVE |

maximum value of user region pages allocated above 16 MB.

| USRALPG8 | NUM | 4 | | USER*PAGES*MAX ABOVE TIME |

time when maximum value of user region pages allocated above 16 MB occurred.

| USRALPG9 | NUM | 4 | | USER*PAGES*AVERAGE ABOVE |

average value of user region pages allocated above 16 MB.

| USRALSZ0 | NUM | 4 | | USER*SIZE*MIN BELOW |

minimum value of user region allocated area size below 16 MB.

| USRALSZ1 | NUM | 4 | DATETIME19.2 | USER*SIZE*MIN BELOW TIME |

time when minimum value of user region allocated area size below 16 MB occurred.

| USRALSZ2 | NUM | 4 | | USER*SIZE*MAX BELOW |

maximum value of user region allocated area size below 16 MB.

| USRALSZ3 | NUM | 4 | DATETIME19.2 | USER*SIZE*MAX BELOW TIME |

time when maximum value of user region allocated area size below 16 MB occurred.

| USRALSZ4 | NUM | 4 | | USER*SIZE*AVERAGE BELOW |

average value of user region allocated area size below 16 MB.

| USRALSZ5 | NUM | 4 | | USER*SIZE*MIN ABOVE |

minimum value of user region allocated area size above 16 MB.

| USRALSZ6 | NUM | 4 | | USER*SIZE*MIN ABOVE TIME |

time when minimum value of user region allocated area size above 16 MB occurred.

Variable	Type	Length	Format	Label
USRALSZ7	NUM	4		USER*SIZE*MAX ABOVE

maximum value of user region allocated area size above 16 MB.

USRALSZ8	NUM	4		USER*SIZE*MAX ABOVE TIME

time when maximum value of user region allocated area size above 16 MB occurred.

USRALSZ9	NUM	4		USER*SIZE*AVERAGE ABOVE

average value of user region allocated area size above 16 MB.

USRFRPG0	NUM	4		USER REGION*FREE*MIN BELOW

minimum value of user region free pages below 16 MB.

USRFRPG1	NUM	4	DATETIME19.2	USER REGION*FREE*MIN BELOW TIME

time when minimum value of user region free pages below 16 MB occurred.

USRFRPG2	NUM	4		USER REGION*FREE*MAX BELOW

maximum value of user region free pages below 16 MB.

USRFRPG3	NUM	4	DATETIME19.2	USER REGION*FREE*MAX BELOW TIME

time when maximum value of user region free pages below 16 MB occurred.

USRFRPG4	NUM	4		USER REGION*FREE*AVERAGE BELOW

average value of user region free pages below 16 MB.

USRFRPG5	NUM	4		USER REGION*FREE*MIN ABOVE

minimum value of user region free pages above 16 MB.

USRFRPG6	NUM	4		USER REGION*FREE*MIN ABOVE TIME

time when minimum value of user region free pages above 16 MB occurred.

USRFRPG7	NUM	4		USER REGION*FREE*MAX ABOVE

maximum value of user region free pages above 16 MB.

USRFRPG8	NUM	4		USER REGION*FREE*MAX ABOVE TIME

time when maximum value of user region free pages above 16 MB occurred.

USRFRPG9	NUM	4		USER REGION*FREE*AVERAGE ABOVE

average value of user region free pages above 16 MB.

USRLARG0	NUM	4		USER*LARGEST*MIN BELOW

minimum value of user region largest free block below 16 MB.

Variable	Type	Length	Format	Label
USRLARG1	NUM	4	DATETIME19.2	USER*LARGEST*MIN BELOW TIME

time when minimum value of user region largest free block below 16 MB occurred.

| USRLARG2 | NUM | 4 | | USER*LARGEST*MAX BELOW |

maximum value of user region largest free block below 16 MB.

| USRLARG3 | NUM | 4 | DATETIME19.2 | USER*LARGEST*MAX BELOW TIME |

time when maximum value of user region largest free block below 16 MB occurred.

| USRLARG4 | NUM | 4 | | USER*LARGEST*AVERAGE BELOW |

average value of user region largest free block below 16 MB.

| USRLARG5 | NUM | 4 | | USER*LARGEST*MIN ABOVE |

minimum value of user region largest free block above 16 MB.

| USRLARG6 | NUM | 4 | | USER*LARGEST*MIN ABOVE TIME |

time when minimum value of user region largest free block above 16 MB occurred.

| USRLARG7 | NUM | 4 | | USER*LARGEST*MAX ABOVE |

maximum value of user region largest free block above 16 MB.

| USRLARG8 | NUM | 4 | | USER*LARGEST*MAX ABOVE TIME |

time when maximum value of user region largest free block above 16 MB occurred.

| USRLARG9 | NUM | 4 | | USER*LARGEST*AVERAGE ABOVE |

average value of user region largest free block above 16 MB.

TYPE78SP
MVS/XA Virtual Storage (Private Area Subpool) Statistics

The TYPE78SP data set contains multiple observations for every type 78 SMF record that monitored virtual storage usage in the private area for a task. A type 78 SMF record is written at the end of each RMF interval or when RMF is stopped.

Virtual storage of the private area is reported in TYPE78PA if monitoring was requested. For each observation in TYPE78PA, there are as many observations in TYPE78SP as there are subpools allocated by the monitored task.

Variable	Type	Length	Format	Label
JOB	CHAR	8		JOB NAME*OR*TSO USER
				name of job whose private area was monitored and allocated to this subpool.
READTIME	NUM	8		READ-IN*OR LOGON*EVENT
				read-in time of job being monitored.
SUBPOOL	NUM	4		SUBPOOL*NUMBER
				subpool number described by this observation.
SUBPOOL0	NUM	4		SUBPOOL*VALUE*MINIMUM
				minimum value of area allocated in this subpool.
SUBPOOL1	NUM	4	DATETIME19.2	SUBPOOL*VALUE*MIN TIME
				time at which minimum value occurred.
SUBPOOL2	NUM	4		SUBPOOL*VALUE*MAXIMUM
				maximum value of area allocated in this subpool.
SUBPOOL3	NUM	4	DATETIME19.2	SUBPOOL*VALUE*MAX TIME
				time at which maximum value occurred.
SUBPOOL4	NUM	4		SUBPOOL*VALUE*AVERAGE
				average value of area allocated in this subpool.

TYPE78VS
MVS/XA Virtual Storage Statistics

The TYPE78VS data set contains one observation for every type 78, subtype 2 RMF record, written at the end of each RMF interval or when RMF is stopped.

Virtual storage usage for the entire system is reported in TYPE78VS. An area of virtual storage is monitored, and five statistics are produced: average, minimum, maximum, and the times of the minimum and maximum values. If the virtual storage area exists both above and below the 16MB line, these statistics are reported for both areas. The CSA area is reported extensively, even to the level of these statistics on each protect key in each of four subpools of CSA. TYPE78VS provides nearly complete descriptions of the shared virtual storage areas of MVS/XA. If additional detail on usage of the private area by individual tasks is required, the task can be monitored and the data reported in TYPE78PA and TYPE78SP.

Variable	Type	Length	Format	Label
CSAADHI	NUM	4		CSA*ADDRESS*ABOVE
				CSA address size above 16 MB.
CSAADLO	NUM	4		CSA*ADDRESS*BELOW
				CSA address size below 16 MB.
CSAALOC0	NUM	4		CSA*ALLOC*MIN BELOW
				minimum value of CSA allocated area size below 16 MB.
CSAALOC1	NUM	4	DATETIME19.2	CSA*ALLOC*MIN BELOW TIME
				time when minimum value of CSA allocated area size below 16 MB occurred.
CSAALOC2	NUM	4		CSA*ALLOC*MAX BELOW
				maximum value of CSA allocated area size below 16 MB.
CSAALOC3	NUM	4	DATETIME19.2	CSA*ALLOC*MAX BELOW TIME
				time when maximum value of CSA allocated area size below 16 MB occurred.
CSAALOC4	NUM	4		CSA*ALLOC*AVERAGE BELOW
				average value of CSA allocated area size below 16 MB.
CSAALOC5	NUM	4		CSA*ALLOC*MIN ABOVE
				minimum value of CSA allocated area size above 16 MB.

Variable	Type	Length	Format	Label
CSAALOC6	NUM	4	DATETIME19.2	CSA*ALLOC*MIN ABOVE TIME

time when minimum value of CSA allocated area size above 16 MB occurred.

| CSAALOC7 | NUM | 4 | | CSA*ALLOC*MAX ABOVE |

maximum value of CSA allocated area size above 16 MB.

| CSAALOC8 | NUM | 4 | DATETIME19.2 | CSA*ALLOC*MAX ABOVE TIME |

time when maximum value of CSA allocated area size above 16 MB occurred.

| CSAALOC9 | NUM | 4 | | CSA*ALLOC*AVERAGE ABOVE |

average value of CSA allocated area size above 16 MB.

| CSAFREE0 | NUM | 4 | | CSA*FREE*MIN BELOW |

minimum value of free CSA below 16 MB.

| CSAFREE1 | NUM | 4 | DATETIME19.2 | CSA*FREE*MIN BELOW TIME |

time when minimum value of free CSA below 16 MB occurred.

| CSAFREE2 | NUM | 4 | | CSA*FREE*MAX BELOW |

maximum value of free CSA below 16 MB.

| CSAFREE3 | NUM | 4 | DATETIME19.2 | CSA*FREE*MAX BELOW TIME |

time when maximum value of free CSA below 16 MB occurred.

| CSAFREE4 | NUM | 4 | | CSA*FREE*AVERAGE BELOW |

average value of free CSA below 16 MB.

| CSAFREE5 | NUM | 4 | | CSA*FREE*MIN ABOVE |

minimum value of free CSA above 16 MB.

| CSAFREE6 | NUM | 4 | DATETIME19.2 | CSA*FREE*MIN ABOVE TIME |

time when minimum value of free CSA above 16 MB occurred.

| CSAFREE7 | NUM | 4 | | CSA*FREE*MAX ABOVE |

maximum value of free CSA above 16 MB.

| CSAFREE8 | NUM | 4 | DATETIME19.2 | CSA*FREE*MAX ABOVE TIME |

time when maximum value of free CSA above 16 MB occurred.

| CSAFREE9 | NUM | 4 | | CSA*FREE*AVERAGE ABOVE |

average value of free CSA above 16 MB.

Variable	Type	Length	Format	Label
CSALARG0	NUM	4		CSA*LARGEST*MIN BELOW

minimum value of largest free block of CSA below 16 MB.

CSALARG1	NUM	4	DATETIME19.2	CSA*LARGEST*MIN BELOW TIME

time when minimum value of free block of CSA below 16 MB occurred.

CSALARG2	NUM	4		CSA*LARGEST*MAX BELOW

maximum value of largest free block of CSA below 16 MB.

CSALARG3	NUM	4	DATETIME19.2	CSA*LARGEST*MAX BELOW TIME

time when maximum value of free block of CSA below 16 MB occurred.

CSALARG4	NUM	4		CSA*LARGEST*AVERAGE BELOW

average value of largest free block of CSA below 16 MB.

CSALARG5	NUM	4		CSA*LARGEST*MIN ABOVE

minimum value of largest free block of CSA above 16 MB.

CSALARG6	NUM	4	DATETIME19.2	CSA*LARGEST*MIN ABOVE TIME

time when minimum value of free block of CSA above 16 MB occurred.

CSALARG7	NUM	4		CSA*LARGEST*MAX ABOVE

maximum value of largest free block of CSA above 16 MB.

CSALARG8	NUM	4	DATETIME19.2	CSA*LARGEST*MAX ABOVE TIME

time when maximum value of free block of CSA above 16 MB occurred.

CSALARG9	NUM	4		CSA*LARGEST*AVERAGE ABOVE

average value of largest free block of CSA above 16 MB.

CSASZHI	NUM	4		CSA*SIZE*ABOVE

CSA size above 16 MB.

CSASZLO	NUM	4		CSA*SIZE*BELOW

CSA size below 16 MB.

CSAUSED0	NUM	4		CSA*USED*MIN BELOW

minimum value of CSA used below 16 MB.

CSAUSED1	NUM	4	DATETIME19.2	CSA*USED*MIN BELOW TIME

time when minimum value of CSA used below 16 MB occurred.

Variable	Type	Length	Format	Label
CSAUSED2	NUM	4		CSA*USED*MAX BELOW
maximum value of CSA used below 16 MB.				
CSAUSED3	NUM	4	DATETIME19.2	CSA*USED*MAX BELOW TIME
time when maximum value of CSA used below 16 MB occurred.				
CSAUSED4	NUM	4		CSA*USED*AVERAGE BELOW
average value of CSA used below 16 MB.				
CSAUSED5	NUM	4		CSA*USED*MIN ABOVE
minimum value of CSA used above 16 MB.				
CSAUSED6	NUM	4	DATETIME19.2	CSA*USED*MIN ABOVE TIME
time when minimum value of CSA used above 16 MB occurred.				
CSAUSED7	NUM	4		CSA*USED*MAX ABOVE
maximum value of CSA used above 16 MB.				
CSAUSED8	NUM	4	DATETIME19.2	CSA*USED*MAX ABOVE TIME
time when maximum value of CSA used above 16 MB occurred.				
CSAUSED9	NUM	4		CSA*USED*AVERAGE ABOVE
average value of CSA used above 16 MB.				
CSAUSE00	NUM	4		CSA USED*KEY 0*MIN BELOW
minimum value of CSA used by key 0 below 16 MB.				
CSAUSE01	NUM	4	DATETIME19.2	CSA USED*KEY 0*MIN BELOW TIME
time when minimum value of CSA used by key 0 below 16 MB occurred.				
CSAUSE02	NUM	4		CSA USED*KEY 0*MAX BELOW
maximum value of CSA used by key 0 below 16 MB.				
CSAUSE03	NUM	4	DATETIME19.2	CSA USED*KEY 0*MAX BELOW TIME
time when maximum value of CSA used by key 0 below 16 MB occurred.				
CSAUSE04	NUM	4		CSA USED*KEY 0*AVERAGE BELOW
average value of CSA used by key 0 below 16 MB.				
CSAUSE05	NUM	4		CSA USED*KEY 0*MIN ABOVE
minimum value of CSA used by key 0 above 16 MB.				

Variable	Type	Length	Format	Label
CSAUSE06	NUM	4	DATETIME19.2	CSA USED*KEY 0*MIN ABOVE TIME

time when minimum value of CSA used by key 0 above 16 MB occurred.

| CSAUSE07 | NUM | 4 | | CSA USED*KEY 0*MAX ABOVE |

maximum value of CSA used by key 0 above 16 MB.

| CSAUSE08 | NUM | 4 | DATETIME19.2 | CSA USED*KEY 0*MAX ABOVE TIME |

time when maximum value of CSA used by key 0 above 16 MB occurred.

| CSAUSE09 | NUM | 4 | | CSA USED*KEY 0*AVERAGE ABOVE |

average value of CSA used by key 0 above 16 MB.

| CSAUSE10 | NUM | 4 | | CSA USED*KEY 1*MIN BELOW |

minimum value of CSA used by key 1 below 16 MB.

| CSAUSE11 | NUM | 4 | DATETIME19.2 | CSA USED*KEY 1*MIN BELOW TIME |

time when minimum value of CSA used by key 1 below 16 MB occurred.

| CSAUSE12 | NUM | 4 | | CSA USED*KEY 1*MAX BELOW |

maximum value of CSA used by key 1 below 16 MB.

| CSAUSE13 | NUM | 4 | DATETIME19.2 | CSA USED*KEY 1*MAX BELOW TIME |

time when maximum value of CSA used by key 1 below 16 MB occurred.

| CSAUSE14 | NUM | 4 | | CSA USED*KEY 1*AVERAGE BELOW |

average value of CSA used by key 1 below 16 MB.

| CSAUSE15 | NUM | 4 | | CSA USED*KEY 1*MIN ABOVE |

minimum value of CSA used by key 1 above 16 MB.

| CSAUSE16 | NUM | 4 | DATETIME19.2 | CSA USED*KEY 1*MIN ABOVE TIME |

time when minimum value of CSA used by key 1 above 16 MB occurred.

| CSAUSE17 | NUM | 4 | | CSA USED*KEY 1*MAX ABOVE |

maximum value of CSA used by key 1 above 16 MB.

| CSAUSE18 | NUM | 4 | DATETIME19.2 | CSA USED*KEY 1*MAX ABOVE TIME |

time when maximum value of CSA used by key 1 above 16 MB occurred.

| CSAUSE19 | NUM | 4 | | CSA USED*KEY 1*AVERAGE ABOVE |

average value of CSA used by key 1 above 16 MB.

Variable	Type	Length	Format	Label
CSAUSE20	NUM	4		CSA USED*KEY 2*MIN BELOW

minimum value of CSA used by key 2 below 16 MB.

CSAUSE21	NUM	4	DATETIME19.2	CSA USED*KEY 2*MIN BELOW TIME

time when minimum value of CSA used by key 2 below 16 MB occurred.

CSAUSE22	NUM	4		CSA USED*KEY 2*MAX BELOW

maximum value of CSA used by key 2 below 16 MB.

CSAUSE23	NUM	4	DATETIME19.2	CSA USED*KEY 2*MAX BELOW TIME

time when maximum value of CSA used by key 2 below 16 MB occurred.

CSAUSE24	NUM	4		CSA USED*KEY 2*AVERAGE BELOW

average value of CSA used by key 2 below 16 MB.

CSAUSE25	NUM	4		CSA USED*KEY 2*MIN ABOVE

minimum value of CSA used by key 2 above 16 MB.

CSAUSE26	NUM	4	DATETIME19.2	CSA USED*KEY 2*MIN ABOVE TIME

time when minimum value of CSA used by key 2 above 16 MB occurred.

CSAUSE27	NUM	4		CSA USED*KEY 2*MAX ABOVE

maximum value of CSA used by key 2 above 16 MB.

CSAUSE28	NUM	4	DATETIME19.2	CSA USED*KEY 2*MAX ABOVE TIME

time when maximum value of CSA used by key 2 above 16 MB occurred.

CSAUSE29	NUM	4		CSA USED*KEY 2*AVERAGE ABOVE

average value of CSA used by key 2 above 16 MB.

CSAUSE30	NUM	4		CSA USED*KEY 3*MIN BELOW

minimum value of CSA used by key 3 below 16 MB.

CSAUSE31	NUM	4	DATETIME19.2	CSA USED*KEY 3*MIN BELOW TIME

time when minimum value of CSA used by key 3 below 16 MB occurred.

CSAUSE32	NUM	4		CSA USED*KEY 3*MAX BELOW

maximum value of CSA used by key 3 below 16 MB.

CSAUSE33	NUM	4	DATETIME19.2	CSA USED*KEY 3*MAX BELOW TIME

time when maximum value of CSA used by key 3 below 16 MB occurred.

Variable	Type	Length	Format	Label
CSAUSE34	NUM	4		CSA USED*KEY 3*AVERAGE BELOW

average value of CSA used by key 3 below 16 MB.

| CSAUSE35 | NUM | 4 | | CSA USED*KEY 3*MIN ABOVE |

minimum value of CSA used by key 3 above 16 MB.

| CSAUSE36 | NUM | 4 | DATETIME19.2 | CSA USED*KEY 3*MIN ABOVE TIME |

time when minimum value of CSA used by key 3 above 16 MB occurred.

| CSAUSE37 | NUM | 4 | | CSA USED*KEY 3*MAX ABOVE |

maximum value of CSA used by key 3 above 16 MB.

| CSAUSE38 | NUM | 4 | DATETIME19.2 | CSA USED*KEY 3*MAX ABOVE TIME |

time when maximum value of CSA used by key 3 above 16 MB occurred.

| CSAUSE39 | NUM | 4 | | CSA USED*KEY 3*AVERAGE ABOVE |

average value of CSA used by key 3 above 16 MB.

| CSAUSE40 | NUM | 4 | | CSA USED*KEY 4*MIN BELOW |

minimum value of CSA used by key 4 below 16 MB.

| CSAUSE41 | NUM | 4 | DATETIME19.2 | CSA USED*KEY 4*MIN BELOW TIME |

time when minimum value of CSA used by key 4 below 16 MB occurred.

| CSAUSE42 | NUM | 4 | | CSA USED*KEY 4*MAX BELOW |

maximum value of CSA used by key 4 below 16 MB.

| CSAUSE43 | NUM | 4 | DATETIME19.2 | CSA USED*KEY 4*MAX BELOW TIME |

time when maximum value of CSA used by key 4 below 16 MB occurred.

| CSAUSE44 | NUM | 4 | | CSA USED*KEY 4*AVERAGE BELOW |

average value of CSA used by key 4 below 16 MB.

| CSAUSE45 | NUM | 4 | | CSA USED*KEY 4*MIN ABOVE |

minimum value of CSA used by key 4 above 16 MB.

| CSAUSE46 | NUM | 4 | DATETIME19.2 | CSA USED*KEY 4*MIN ABOVE TIME |

time when minimum value of CSA used by key 4 above 16 MB occurred.

| CSAUSE47 | NUM | 4 | | CSA USED*KEY 4*MAX ABOVE |

maximum value of CSA used by key 4 above 16 MB.

Variable	Type	Length	Format	Label
CSAUSE48	NUM	4	DATETIME19.2	CSA USED*KEY 4*MAX ABOVE TIME

time when maximum value of CSA used by key 4 above 16 MB occurred.

Variable	Type	Length	Format	Label
CSAUSE49	NUM	4		CSA USED*KEY 4*AVERAGE ABOVE

average value of CSA used by key 4 above 16 MB.

CSAUSE50	NUM	4		CSA USED*KEY 5*MIN BELOW

minimum value of CSA used by key 5 below 16 MB.

CSAUSE51	NUM	4	DATETIME19.2	CSA USED*KEY 5*MIN BELOW TIME

time when minimum value of CSA used by key 5 below 16 MB occurred.

CSAUSE52	NUM	4		CSA USED*KEY 5*MAX BELOW

maximum value of CSA used by key 5 below 16 MB.

CSAUSE53	NUM	4	DATETIME19.2	CSA USED*KEY 5*MAX BELOW TIME

time when maximum value of CSA used by key 5 below 16 MB occurred.

CSAUSE54	NUM	4		CSA USED*KEY 5*AVERAGE BELOW

average value of CSA used by key 5 below 16 MB.

CSAUSE55	NUM	4		CSA USED*KEY 5*MIN ABOVE

minimum value of CSA used by key 5 above 16 MB.

CSAUSE56	NUM	4	DATETIME19.2	CSA USED*KEY 5*MIN ABOVE TIME

time when minimum value of CSA used by key 5 above 16 MB occurred.

CSAUSE57	NUM	4		CSA USED*KEY 5*MAX ABOVE

maximum value of CSA used by key 5 above 16 MB.

CSAUSE58	NUM	4	DATETIME19.2	CSA USED*KEY 5*MAX ABOVE TIME

time when maximum value of CSA used by key 5 above 16 MB occurred.

CSAUSE59	NUM	4		CSA USED*KEY 5*AVERAGE ABOVE

average value of CSA used by key 5 above 16 MB.

CSAUSE60	NUM	4		CSA USED*KEY 6*MIN BELOW

minimum value of CSA used by key 6 below 16 MB.

CSAUSE61	NUM	4	DATETIME19.2	CSA USED*KEY 6*MIN BELOW TIME

time when minimum value of CSA used by key 6 below 16 MB occurred.

Variable	Type	Length	Format	Label
CSAUSE62	NUM	4		CSA USED*KEY 6*MAX BELOW

maximum value of CSA used by key 6 below 16 MB.

CSAUSE63	NUM	4	DATETIME19.2	CSA USED*KEY 6*MAX BELOW TIME

time when maximum value of CSA used by key 6 below 16 MB occurred.

CSAUSE64	NUM	4		CSA USED*KEY 6*AVERAGE BELOW

average value of CSA used by key 6 below 16 MB.

CSAUSE65	NUM	4		CSA USED*KEY 6*MIN ABOVE

minimum value of CSA used by key 6 above 16 MB.

CSAUSE66	NUM	4	DATETIME19.2	CSA USED*KEY 6* MIN ABOVE TIME

time when minimum value of CSA used by key 6 above 16 MB occurred.

CSAUSE67	NUM	4		CSA USED*KEY 6*MAX ABOVE

maximum value of CSA used by key 6 above 16 MB.

CSAUSE68	NUM	4	DATETIME19.2	CSA USED*KEY 6*MAX ABOVE TIME

time when maximum value of CSA used by key 6 above 16 MB occurred.

CSAUSE69	NUM	4		CSA USED*KEY 6*AVERAGE ABOVE

average value of CSA used by key 6 above 16 MB.

CSAUSE70	NUM	4		CSA USED*KEY 7*MIN BELOW

minimum value of CSA used by key 7 below 16 MB.

CSAUSE71	NUM	4	DATETIME19.2	CSA USED*KEY 7*MIN BELOW TIME

time when minimum value of CSA used by key 7 below 16 MB occurred.

CSAUSE72	NUM	4		CSA USED*KEY 7*MAX BELOW

maximum value of CSA used by key 7 below 16 MB.

CSAUSE73	NUM	4	DATETIME19.2	CSA USED*KEY 7*MAX BELOW TIME

time when maximum value of CSA used by key 7 below 16 MB occurred.

CSAUSE74	NUM	4		CSA USED*KEY 7*AVERAGE BELOW

average value of CSA used by key 7 below 16 MB.

CSAUSE75	NUM	4		CSA USED*KEY 7*MIN ABOVE

minimum value of CSA used by key 7 above 16 MB.

Variable	Type	Length	Format	Label
CSAUSE76	NUM	4	DATETIME19.2	CSA USED*KEY 7*MIN ABOVE TIME

time when minimum value of CSA used by key 7 above 16 MB occurred.

CSAUSE77	NUM	4		CSA USED*KEY 7*MAX ABOVE

maximum value of CSA used by key 7 above 16 MB.

CSAUSE78	NUM	4	DATETIME19.2	CSA USED*KEY 7*MAX ABOVE TIME

time when maximum value of CSA used by key 7 above 16 MB occurred.

CSAUSE79	NUM	4		CSA USED*KEY 7*AVERAGE ABOVE

average value of CSA used by key 7 above 16 MB.

CSAUSE80	NUM	4		CSA USED*KEY 8-F*MIN BELOW

minimum value of CSA used by key 8-F below 16 MB.

CSAUSE81	NUM	4	DATETIME19.2	CSA USED*KEY 8-F*MIN BELOW TIME

time when minimum value of CSA used by key 8-F below 16 MB occurred.

CSAUSE82	NUM	4		CSA USED*KEY 8-F*MAX BELOW

maximum value of CSA used by key 8-F below 16 MB.

CSAUSE83	NUM	4	DATETIME19.2	CSA USED*KEY 8-F*MAX BELOW TIME

time when maximum value of CSA used by key 8-F below 16 MB occurred.

CSAUSE84	NUM	4		CSA USED*KEY 8-F*AVERAGE BELOW

average value of CSA used by key 8-F below 16 MB.

CSAUSE85	NUM	4		CSA USED*KEY 8-F*MIN ABOVE

minimum value of CSA used by key 8-F above 16 MB.

CSAUSE86	NUM	4	DATETIME19.2	CSA USED*KEY 8-F*MIN ABOVE TIME

time when minimum value of CSA used by key 8-F above 16 MB occurred.

CSAUSE87	NUM	4		CSA USED*KEY 8-F*MAX ABOVE

maximum value of CSA used by key 8-F above 16 MB.

CSAUSE88	NUM	4	DATETIME19.2	CSA USED*KEY 8-F*MAX ABOVE TIME

time when maximum value of CSA used by key 8-F above 16 MB occurred.

CSAUSE89	NUM	4		CSA USED*KEY 8-F*AVERAGE ABOVE

average value of CSA used by key 8-F above 16 MB.

Variable	Type	Length	Format	Label
CSA227A0	NUM	4		CSA SUBPOOL 227*KEY ALL*MIN BELOW

minimum value of CSA subpool 227 (below 16 MB) allocated by all protect keys.

CSA227A1	NUM	4	DATETIME19.2	CSA SUBPOOL 227*KEY ALL*MIN BELOW TIME

time when minimum value of CSA subpool 227 (below 16 MB) by all protect keys occurred.

CSA227A2	NUM	4		CSA SUBPOOL 227*KEY ALL*MAX BELOW

maximum value of CSA subpool 227 (below 16 MB) allocated by all protect keys.

CSA227A3	NUM	4	DATETIME19.2	CSA SUBPOOL 227*KEY ALL*MAX BELOW TIME

time when maximum value of CSA subpool 227 (below 16 MB) by all protect keys occurred.

CSA227A4	NUM	4		CSA SUBPOOL 227*KEY ALL*AVERAGE BELOW

average value of CSA subpool 227 (below 16 MB) allocated by all protect keys.

CSA22700	NUM	4		CSA SUBPOOL 227*KEY 0*MIN BELOW

minimum value of CSA subpool 227 (below 16 MB) allocated by protect key 0.

CSA22701	NUM	4	DATETIME19.2	CSA SUBPOOL 227*KEY 0*MIN BELOW TIME

time when minimum value of CSA subpool 227 (below 16 MB) by protect key 0 occurred.

CSA22702	NUM	4		CSA SUBPOOL 227*KEY 0*MAX BELOW

maximum value of CSA subpool 227 (below 16 MB) allocated by protect key 0.

CSA22703	NUM	4	DATETIME19.2	CSA SUBPOOL 227*KEY 0*MAX BELOW TIME

time when maximum value of CSA subpool 227 (below 16 MB) by protect key 0 occurred.

CSA22704	NUM	4		CSA SUBPOOL 227*KEY 0*AVERAGE BELOW

average value of CSA subpool 227 (below 16 MB) allocated by protect key 0.

CSA22710	NUM	4		CSA SUBPOOL 227*KEY 1*MIN BELOW

minimum value of CSA subpool 227 (below 16 MB) allocated by protect key 1.

CSA22711	NUM	4	DATETIME19.2	CSA SUBPOOL 227*KEY 1*MIN BELOW TIME

time when minimum value of CSA subpool 227 (below 16 MB) by protect key 1 occurred.

Variable	Type	Length	Format	Label
CSA22712	NUM	4		CSA SUBPOOL 227*KEY 1*MAX BELOW

maximum value of CSA subpool 227 (below 16 MB) allocated by protect key 1.

CSA22713	NUM	4	DATETIME19.2	CSA SUBPOOL 227*KEY 1*MAX BELOW TIME

time when maximum value of CSA subpool 227 (below 16 MB) by protect key 1 occurred.

CSA22714	NUM	4		CSA SUBPOOL 227*KEY 1*AVERAGE BELOW

average value of CSA subpool 227 (below 16 MB) allocated by protect key 1.

CSA22720	NUM	4		CSA SUBPOOL 227*KEY 2*MIN BELOW

minimum value of CSA subpool 227 (below 16 MB) allocated by protect key 2.

CSA22721	NUM	4	DATETIME19.2	CSA SUBPOOL 227*KEY 2*MIN BELOW TIME

time when minimum value of CSA subpool 227 (below 16 MB) by protect key 2 occurred.

CSA22722	NUM	4		CSA SUBPOOL 227*KEY 2*MAX BELOW

maximum value of CSA subpool 227 (below 16 MB) allocated by protect key 2.

CSA22723	NUM	4	DATETIME19.2	CSA SUBPOOL 227*KEY 2*MAX BELOW TIME

time when maximum value of CSA subpool 227 (below 16 MB) by protect key 2 occurred.

CSA22724	NUM	4		CSA SUBPOOL 227*KEY 2*AVERAGE BELOW

average value of CSA subpool 227 (below 16 MB) allocated by protect key 2.

CSA22730	NUM	4		CSA SUBPOOL 227*KEY 3*MIN BELOW

minimum value of CSA subpool 227 (below 16 MB) allocated by protect key 3.

CSA22731	NUM	4	DATETIME19.2	CSA SUBPOOL 227*KEY 3*MIN BELOW TIME

time when minimum value of CSA subpool 227 (below 16 MB) by protect key 3 occurred.

CSA22732	NUM	4		CSA SUBPOOL 227*KEY 3*MAX BELOW

maximum value of CSA subpool 227 (below 16 MB) allocated by protect key 3.

CSA22733	NUM	4	DATETIME19.2	CSA SUBPOOL 227*KEY 3*MAX BELOW TIME

time when maximum value of CSA subpool 227 (below 16 MB) by protect key 3 occurred.

Variable	Type	Length	Format	Label
CSA22734	NUM	4		CSA SUBPOOL 227*KEY 3*AVERAGE BELOW

average value of CSA subpool 227 (below 16 MB) allocated by protect key 3.

| CSA22740 | NUM | 4 | | CSA SUBPOOL 227*KEY 4*MIN BELOW |

minimum value of CSA subpool 227 (below 16 MB) allocated by protect key 4.

| CSA22741 | NUM | 4 | DATETIME19.2 | CSA SUBPOOL 227*KEY 4*MIN BELOW TIME |

time when minimum value of CSA subpool 227 (below 16 MB) by protect key 4 occurred.

| CSA22742 | NUM | 4 | | CSA SUBPOOL 227*KEY 4*MAX BELOW |

maximum value of CSA subpool 227 (below 16 MB) allocated by protect key 4.

| CSA22743 | NUM | 4 | DATETIME19.2 | CSA SUBPOOL 227*KEY 4*MAX BELOW TIME |

time when maximum value of CSA subpool 227 (below 16 MB) by protect key 4 occurred.

| CSA22744 | NUM | 4 | | CSA SUBPOOL 227*KEY 4*AVERAGE BELOW |

average value of CSA subpool 227 (below 16 MB) allocated by protect key 4.

| CSA22750 | NUM | 4 | | CSA SUBPOOL 227*KEY 5*MIN BELOW |

minimum value of CSA subpool 227 (below 16 MB) allocated by protect key 5.

| CSA22751 | NUM | 4 | DATETIME19.2 | CSA SUBPOOL 227*KEY 5*MIN BELOW TIME |

time when minimum value of CSA subpool 227 (below 16 MB) by protect key 5 occurred.

| CSA22752 | NUM | 4 | | CSA SUBPOOL 227*KEY 5*MAX BELOW |

maximum value of CSA subpool 227 (below 16 MB) allocated by protect key 5.

| CSA22753 | NUM | 4 | DATETIME19.2 | CSA SUBPOOL 227*KEY 5*MAX BELOW TIME |

time when maximum value of CSA subpool 227 (below 16 MB) by protect key 5 occurred.

| CSA22754 | NUM | 4 | | CSA SUBPOOL 227*KEY 5*AVERAGE BELOW |

average value of CSA subpool 227 (below 16 MB) allocated by protect key 5.

| CSA22760 | NUM | 4 | | CSA SUBPOOL 227*KEY 6*MIN BELOW |

minimum value of CSA subpool 227 (below 16 MB) allocated by protect key 6.

Variable	Type	Length	Format	Label
CSA22761	NUM	4	DATETIME19.2	CSA SUBPOOL 227*KEY 6*MIN BELOW TIME

time when minimum value of CSA subpool 227 (below 16 MB) by protect key 6 occurred.

| CSA22762 | NUM | 4 | | CSA SUBPOOL 227*KEY 6*MAX BELOW |

maximum value of CSA subpool 227 (below 16 MB) allocated by protect key 6.

| CSA22763 | NUM | 4 | DATETIME19.2 | CSA SUBPOOL 227*KEY 6*MAX BELOW TIME |

time when maximum value of CSA subpool 227 (below 16 MB) by protect key 6 occurred.

| CSA22764 | NUM | 4 | | CSA SUBPOOL 227*KEY 6*AVERAGE BELOW |

average value of CSA subpool 227 (below 16 MB) allocated by protect key 6.

| CSA22770 | NUM | 4 | | CSA SUBPOOL 227*KEY 7*MIN BELOW |

minimum value of CSA subpool 227 (below 16 MB) allocated by protect key 7.

| CSA22771 | NUM | 4 | DATETIME19.2 | CSA SUBPOOL 227*KEY 7*MIN BELOW TIME |

time when minimum value of CSA subpool 227 (below 16 MB) by protect key 7 occurred.

| CSA22772 | NUM | 4 | | CSA SUBPOOL 227*KEY 7*MAX BELOW |

maximum value of CSA subpool 227 (below 16 MB) allocated by protect key 7.

| CSA22773 | NUM | 4 | DATETIME19.2 | CSA SUBPOOL 227*KEY 7*MAX BELOW TIME |

time when maximum value of CSA subpool 227 (below 16 MB) by protect key 7 occurred.

| CSA22774 | NUM | 4 | | CSA SUBPOOL 227*KEY 7*AVERAGE BELOW |

average value of CSA subpool 227 (below 16 MB) allocated by protect key 7.

| CSA22780 | NUM | 4 | | CSA SUBPOOL 227*KEY 8-F*MIN BELOW |

minimum value of CSA subpool 227 (below 16 MB) allocated by protect keys 8-F.

| CSA22781 | NUM | 4 | DATETIME19.2 | CSA SUBPOOL 227*KEY 8-F*MIN BELOW TIME |

time when minimum value of CSA subpool 227 (below 16 MB) by protect keys 8-F occurred.

| CSA22782 | NUM | 4 | | CSA SUBPOOL 227*KEY 8-F*MAX BELOW |

maximum value of CSA subpool 227 (below 16 MB) allocated by protect keys 8-F.

Variable	Type	Length	Format	Label
CSA22783	NUM	4	DATETIME19.2	CSA SUBPOOL 227*KEY 8-F*MAX BELOW TIME

time when maximum value of CSA subpool 227 (below 16 MB) by protect keys 8-F occurred.

CSA22784	NUM	4		CSA SUBPOOL 227*KEY 8-F*AVERAGE BELOW

average value of CSA subpool 227 (below 16 MB) allocated by protect keys 8-F.

CSA228A0	NUM	4		CSA SUBPOOL 228*KEY ALL*MIN BELOW

minimum value of CSA subpool 228 (below 16 MB) allocated by all protect keys.

CSA228A1	NUM	4	DATETIME19.2	CSA SUBPOOL 228*KEY ALL*MIN BELOW TIME

time when minimum value of CSA subpool 228 (below 16 MB) by all protect keys occurred.

CSA228A2	NUM	4		CSA SUBPOOL 228*KEY ALL*MAX BELOW

maximum value of CSA subpool 228 (below 16 MB) allocated by all protect keys.

CSA228A3	NUM	4	DATETIME19.2	CSA SUBPOOL 228*KEY ALL*MAX BELOW TIME

time when maximum value of CSA subpool 228 (below 16 MB) by all protect keys occurred.

CSA228A4	NUM	4		CSA SUBPOOL 228*KEY ALL*AVERAGE BELOW

average value of CSA subpool 228 (below 16 MB) allocated by all protect keys.

CSA22800	NUM	4		CSA SUBPOOL 228*KEY 0*MIN BELOW

minimum value of CSA subpool 228 (below 16 MB) allocated by protect key 0.

CSA22801	NUM	4	DATETIME19.2	CSA SUBPOOL 228*KEY 0*MIN BELOW TIME

time when minimum value of CSA subpool 228 (below 16 MB) by protect key 0 occurred.

CSA22802	NUM	4		CSA SUBPOOL 228*KEY 0*MAX BELOW

maximum value of CSA subpool 228 (below 16 MB) allocated by protect key 0.

CSA22803	NUM	4	DATETIME19.2	CSA SUBPOOL 228*KEY 0*MAX BELOW TIME

time when maximum value of CSA subpool 228 (below 16 MB) by protect key 0 occurred.

Variable	Type	Length	Format	Label
CSA22804	NUM	4		CSA SUBPOOL 228*KEY 0*AVERAGE BELOW

average value of CSA subpool 228 (below 16 MB) allocated by protect key 0.

Variable	Type	Length	Format	Label
CSA22810	NUM	4		CSA SUBPOOL 228*KEY 1*MIN BELOW

minimum value of CSA subpool 228 (below 16 MB) allocated by protect key 1.

Variable	Type	Length	Format	Label
CSA22811	NUM	4	DATETIME19.2	CSA SUBPOOL 228*KEY 1*MIN BELOW TIME

time when minimum value of CSA subpool 228 (below 16 MB) by protect key 1 occurred.

Variable	Type	Length	Format	Label
CSA22812	NUM	4		CSA SUBPOOL 228*KEY 1*MAX BELOW

maximum value of CSA subpool 228 (below 16 MB) allocated by protect key 1.

Variable	Type	Length	Format	Label
CSA22813	NUM	4	DATETIME19.2	CSA SUBPOOL 228*KEY 1*MAX BELOW TIME

time when maximum value of CSA subpool 228 (below 16 MB) by protect key 1 occurred.

Variable	Type	Length	Format	Label
CSA22814	NUM	4		CSA SUBPOOL 228*KEY 1*AVERAGE BELOW

average value of CSA subpool 228 (below 16 MB) allocated by protect key 1.

Variable	Type	Length	Format	Label
CSA22820	NUM	4		CSA SUBPOOL 228*KEY 2*MIN BELOW

minimum value of CSA subpool 228 (below 16 MB) allocated by protect key 2.

Variable	Type	Length	Format	Label
CSA22821	NUM	4	DATETIME19.2	CSA SUBPOOL 228*KEY 2*MIN BELOW TIME

time when minimum value of CSA subpool 228 (below 16 MB) by protect key 2 occurred.

Variable	Type	Length	Format	Label
CSA22822	NUM	4		CSA SUBPOOL 228*KEY 2*MAX BELOW

maximum value of CSA subpool 228 (below 16 MB) allocated by protect key 2.

Variable	Type	Length	Format	Label
CSA22823	NUM	4	DATETIME19.2	CSA SUBPOOL 228*KEY 2*MAX BELOW TIME

time when maximum value of CSA subpool 228 (below 16 MB) by protect key 2 occurred.

Variable	Type	Length	Format	Label
CSA22824	NUM	4		CSA SUBPOOL 228*KEY 2*AVERAGE BELOW

average value of CSA subpool 228 (below 16 MB) allocated by protect key 2.

Variable	Type	Length	Format	Label
CSA22830	NUM	4		CSA SUBPOOL 228*KEY 3*MIN BELOW

minimum value of CSA subpool 228 (below 16 MB) allocated by protect key 3.

Variable	Type	Length	Format	Label
CSA22831	NUM	4	DATETIME19.2	CSA SUBPOOL 228*KEY 3*MIN BELOW TIME

time when minimum value of CSA subpool 228 (below 16 MB) by protect key 3 occurred.

| CSA22832 | NUM | 4 | | CSA SUBPOOL 228*KEY 3*MAX BELOW |

maximum value of CSA subpool 228 (below 16 MB) allocated by protect key 3.

| CSA22833 | NUM | 4 | DATETIME19.2 | CSA SUBPOOL 228*KEY 3*MAX BELOW TIME |

time when maximum value of CSA subpool 228 (below 16 MB) by protect key 3 occurred

| CSA22834 | NUM | 4 | | CSA SUBPOOL 228*KEY 3*AVERAGE BELOW |

average value of CSA subpool 228 (below 16 MB) allocated by protect key 3.

| CSA22840 | NUM | 4 | | CSA SUBPOOL 228*KEY 4*MIN BELOW |

minimum value of CSA subpool 228 (below 16 MB) allocated by protect key 4.

| CSA22841 | NUM | 4 | DATETIME19.2 | CSA SUBPOOL 228*KEY 4*MIN BELOW TIME |

time when minimum value of CSA subpool 228 (below 16 MB) by protect key 4 occurred.

| CSA22842 | NUM | 4 | | CSA SUBPOOL 228*KEY 4*MAX BELOW |

maximum value of CSA subpool 228 (below 16 MB) allocated by protect key 4.

| CSA22843 | NUM | 4 | DATETIME19.2 | CSA SUBPOOL 228*KEY 4*MAX BELOW TIME |

time when maximum value of CSA subpool 228 (below 16 MB) by protect key 4 occurred.

| CSA22844 | NUM | 4 | | CSA SUBPOOL 228*KEY 4*AVERAGE BELOW |

average value of CSA subpool 228 (below 16 MB) allocated by protect key 4.

| CSA22850 | NUM | 4 | | CSA SUBPOOL 228*KEY 5*MIN BELOW |

minimum value of CSA subpool 228 (below 16 MB) allocated by protect key 5.

| CSA22851 | NUM | 4 | DATETIME19.2 | CSA SUBPOOL 228*KEY 5*MIN BELOW TIME |

time when minimum value of CSA subpool 228 (below 16 MB) by protect key 5 occurred.

| CSA22852 | NUM | 4 | | CSA SUBPOOL 228*KEY 5*MAX BELOW |

maximum value of CSA subpool 228 (below 16 MB) allocated by protect key 5.

Variable	Type	Length	Format	Label
CSA22853	NUM	4	DATETIME19.2	CSA SUBPOOL 228*KEY 5*MAX BELOW TIME

time when maximum value of CSA subpool 228 (below 16 MB) by protect key 5 occurred.

Variable	Type	Length	Format	Label
CSA22854	NUM	4		CSA SUBPOOL 228*KEY 5*AVERAGE BELOW

average value of CSA subpool 228 (below 16 MB) allocated by protect key 5.

Variable	Type	Length	Format	Label
CSA22860	NUM	4		CSA SUBPOOL 228*KEY 6*MIN BELOW

minimum value of CSA subpool 228 (below 16 MB) allocated by protect key 6.

Variable	Type	Length	Format	Label
CSA22861	NUM	4	DATETIME19.2	CSA SUBPOOL 228*KEY 6*MIN BELOW TIME

time when minimum value of CSA subpool 228 (below 16 MB) by protect key 6 occurred.

Variable	Type	Length	Format	Label
CSA22862	NUM	4		CSA SUBPOOL 228*KEY 6*MAX BELOW

maximum value of CSA subpool 228 (below 16 MB) allocated by protect key 6.

Variable	Type	Length	Format	Label
CSA22863	NUM	4	DATETIME19.2	CSA SUBPOOL 228*KEY 6*MAX BELOW TIME

time when maximum value of CSA subpool 228 (below 16 MB) by protect key 6 occurred.

Variable	Type	Length	Format	Label
CSA22864	NUM	4		CSA SUBPOOL 228*KEY 6*AVERAGE BELOW

average value of CSA subpool 228 (below 16 MB) allocated by protect key 6.

Variable	Type	Length	Format	Label
CSA22870	NUM	4		CSA SUBPOOL 228*KEY 7*MIN BELOW

minimum value of CSA subpool 228 (below 16 MB) allocated by protect key 7.

Variable	Type	Length	Format	Label
CSA22871	NUM	4	DATETIME19.2	CSA SUBPOOL 228*KEY 7*MIN BELOW TIME

time when minimum value of CSA subpool 228 (below 16 MB) by protect key 7 occurred.

Variable	Type	Length	Format	Label
CSA22872	NUM	4		CSA SUBPOOL 228*KEY 7*MAX BELOW

maximum value of CSA subpool 228 (below 16 MB) allocated by protect key 7.

Variable	Type	Length	Format	Label
CSA22873	NUM	4	DATETIME19.2	CSA SUBPOOL 228*KEY 7*MAX BELOW TIME

time when maximum value of CSA subpool 228 (below 16 MB) by protect key 7 occurred.

Variable	Type	Length	Format	Label
CSA22874	NUM	4		CSA SUBPOOL 228*KEY 7*AVERAGE BELOW

average value of CSA subpool 228 (below 16 MB) allocated by protect key 7.

Variable	Type	Length	Format	Label
CSA22880	NUM	4		CSA SUBPOOL 228*KEY 8-F*MIN BELOW

minimum value of CSA subpool 228 (below 16 MB) allocated by protect keys 8-F.

| CSA22881 | NUM | 4 | DATETIME19.2 | CSA SUBPOOL 228*KEY 8-F*MIN BELOW TIME |

time when minimum value of CSA subpool 228 (below 16 MB) by protect keys 8-F occurred.

| CSA22882 | NUM | 4 | | CSA SUBPOOL 228*KEY 8-F*MAX BELOW |

maximum value of CSA subpool 228 (below 16 MB) allocated by protect keys 8-F.

| CSA22883 | NUM | 4 | DATETIME19.2 | CSA SUBPOOL 228*KEY 8-F*MAX BELOW TIME |

time when maximum value of CSA subpool 228 (below 16 MB) by protect keys 8-F occurred.

| CSA22884 | NUM | 4 | | CSA SUBPOOL 228*KEY 8-F*AVERAGE BELOW |

average value of CSA subpool 228 (below 16 MB) allocated by protect keys 8-F.

| CSA231A0 | NUM | 4 | | CSA SUBPOOL 231*KEY ALL*MIN BELOW |

minimum value of CSA subpool 231 (below 16 MB) allocated by all protect keys.

| CSA231A1 | NUM | 4 | DATETIME19.2 | CSA SUBPOOL 231*KEY ALL*MIN BELOW TIME |

time when minimum value of CSA subpool 231 (below 16 MB) by all protect keys occurred.

| CSA231A2 | NUM | 4 | | CSA SUBPOOL 231*KEY ALL*MAX BELOW |

maximum value of CSA subpool 231 (below 16 MB) allocated by all protect keys.

| CSA231A3 | NUM | 4 | DATETIME19.2 | CSA SUBPOOL 231*KEY ALL*MAX BELOW TIME |

time when maximum value of CSA subpool 231 (below 16 MB) by all protect keys occurred.

| CSA231A4 | NUM | 4 | | CSA SUBPOOL 231*KEY ALL*AVERAGE BELOW |

average value of CSA subpool 231 (below 16 MB) allocated by all protect keys.

| CSA23100 | NUM | 4 | | CSA SUBPOOL 231*KEY 0*MIN BELOW |

minimum value of CSA subpool 231 (below 16 MB) allocated by protect key 0.

Variable	Type	Length	Format	Label
CSA23101	NUM	4	DATETIME19.2	CSA SUBPOOL 231*KEY 0*MIN BELOW TIME

time when minimum value of CSA subpool 231 (below 16 MB) by protect key 0 occurred.

CSA23102	NUM	4		CSA SUBPOOL 231*KEY 0*MAX BELOW

maximum value of CSA subpool 231 (below 16 MB) allocated by protect key 0.

CSA23103	NUM	4	DATETIME19.2	CSA SUBPOOL 231*KEY 0*MAX BELOW TIME

time when maximum value of CSA subpool 231 (below 16 MB) by protect key 0 occurred.

CSA23104	NUM	4		CSA SUBPOOL 231*KEY 0*AVERAGE BELOW

average value of CSA subpool 231 (below 16 MB) allocated by protect key 0.

CSA23110	NUM	4		CSA SUBPOOL 231*KEY 1*MIN BELOW

minimum value of CSA subpool 231 (below 16 MB) allocated by protect key 1.

CSA23111	NUM	4	DATETIME19.2	CSA SUBPOOL 231*KEY 1*MIN BELOW TIME

time when minimum value of CSA subpool 231 (below 16 MB) by protect key 1 occurred.

CSA23112	NUM	4		CSA SUBPOOL 231*KEY 1*MAX BELOW

maximum value of CSA subpool 231 (below 16 MB) allocated by protect key 1.

CSA23113	NUM	4	DATETIME19.2	CSA SUBPOOL 231*KEY 1*MAX BELOW TIME

time when maximum value of CSA subpool 231 (below 16 MB) by protect key 1 occurred.

CSA23114	NUM	4		CSA SUBPOOL 231*KEY 1*AVERAGE BELOW

average value of CSA subpool 231 (below 16 MB) allocated by protect key 1.

CSA23120	NUM	4		CSA SUBPOOL 231*KEY 2*MIN BELOW

minimum value of CSA subpool 231 (below 16 MB) allocated by protect key 2.

CSA23121	NUM	4	DATETIME19.2	CSA SUBPOOL 231*KEY 2*MIN BELOW TIME

time when minimum value of CSA subpool 231 (below 16 MB) by protect key 2 occurred.

CSA23122	NUM	4		CSA SUBPOOL 231*KEY 2*MAX BELOW

maximum value of CSA subpool 231 (below 16 MB) allocated by protect key 2.

Variable	Type	Length	Format	Label
CSA23123	NUM	4	DATETIME19.2	CSA SUBPOOL 231*KEY 2*MAX BELOW TIME

time when maximum value of CSA subpool 231 (below 16 MB) by protect key 2 occurred.

CSA23124	NUM	4		CSA SUBPOOL 231*KEY 2*AVERAGE BELOW

average value of CSA subpool 231 (below 16 MB) allocated by protect key 2.

CSA23130	NUM	4		CSA SUBPOOL 231*KEY 3*MIN BELOW

minimum value of CSA subpool 231 (below 16 MB) allocated by protect key 3.

CSA23131	NUM	4	DATETIME19.2	CSA SUBPOOL 231*KEY 3*MIN BELOW TIME

time when minimum value of CSA subpool 231 (below 16 MB) by protect key 3 occurred.

CSA23132	NUM	4		CSA SUBPOOL 231*KEY 3*MAX BELOW

maximum value of CSA subpool 231 (below 16 MB) allocated by protect key 3.

CSA23133	NUM	4	DATETIME19.2	CSA SUBPOOL 231*KEY 3*MAX BELOW TIME

time when maximum value of CSA subpool 231 (below 16 MB) by protect key 3 occurred.

CSA23134	NUM	4		CSA SUBPOOL 231*KEY 3*AVERAGE BELOW

average value of CSA subpool 231 (below 16 MB) allocated by protect key 3.

CSA23140	NUM	4		CSA SUBPOOL 231*KEY 4*MIN BELOW

minimum value of CSA subpool 231 (below 16 MB) allocated by protect key 4.

CSA23141	NUM	4	DATETIME19.2	CSA SUBPOOL 231*KEY 4*MIN BELOW TIME

time when minimum value of CSA subpool 231 (below 16 MB) by protect key 4 occurred.

CSA23142	NUM	4		CSA SUBPOOL 231*KEY 4*MAX BELOW

maximum value of CSA subpool 231 (below 16 MB) allocated by protect key 4.

CSA23143	NUM	4	DATETIME19.2	CSA SUBPOOL 231*KEY 4*MAX BELOW TIME

time when maximum value of CSA subpool 231 (below 16 MB) by protect key 4 occurred.

CSA23144	NUM	4		CSA SUBPOOL 231*KEY 4*AVERAGE BELOW

average value of CSA subpool 231 (below 16 MB) allocated by protect key 4.

Variable	Type	Length	Format	Label
CSA23150	NUM	4		CSA SUBPOOL 231*KEY 5*MIN BELOW

minimum value of CSA subpool 231 (below 16 MB) allocated by protect key 5.

Variable	Type	Length	Format	Label
CSA23151	NUM	4	DATETIME19.2	CSA SUBPOOL 231*KEY 5*MIN BELOW TIME

time when minimum value of CSA subpool 231 (below 16 MB) by protect key 5 occurred.

Variable	Type	Length	Format	Label
CSA23152	NUM	4		CSA SUBPOOL 231*KEY 5*MAX BELOW

maximum value of CSA subpool 231 (below 16 MB) allocated by protect key 5.

Variable	Type	Length	Format	Label
CSA23153	NUM	4	DATETIME19.2	CSA SUBPOOL 231*KEY 5*MAX BELOW TIME

time when maximum value of CSA subpool 231 (below 16 MB) by protect key 5 occurred.

Variable	Type	Length	Format	Label
CSA23154	NUM	4		CSA SUBPOOL 231*KEY 5*AVERAGE BELOW

average value of CSA subpool 231 (below 16 MB) allocated by protect key 5.

Variable	Type	Length	Format	Label
CSA23160	NUM	4		CSA SUBPOOL 231*KEY 6*MIN BELOW

minimum value of CSA subpool 231 (below 16 MB) allocated by protect key 6.

Variable	Type	Length	Format	Label
CSA23161	NUM	4	DATETIME19.2	CSA SUBPOOL 231*KEY 6*MIN BELOW TIME

time when minimum value of CSA subpool 231 (below 16 MB) by protect key 6 occurred.

Variable	Type	Length	Format	Label
CSA23162	NUM	4		CSA SUBPOOL 231*KEY 6*MAX BELOW

maximum value of CSA subpool 231 (below 16 MB) allocated by protect key 6.

Variable	Type	Length	Format	Label
CSA23163	NUM	4	DATETIME19.2	CSA SUBPOOL 231*KEY 6*MAX BELOW TIME

time when maximum value of CSA subpool 231 (below 16 MB) by protect key 6 occurred.

Variable	Type	Length	Format	Label
CSA23164	NUM	4		CSA SUBPOOL 231*KEY 6*AVERAGE BELOW

average value of CSA subpool 231 (below 16 MB) allocated by protect key 6.

Variable	Type	Length	Format	Label
CSA23170	NUM	4		CSA SUBPOOL 231*KEY 7*MIN BELOW

minimum value of CSA subpool 231 (below 16 MB) allocated by protect key 7.

Variable	Type	Length	Format	Label
CSA23171	NUM	4	DATETIME19.2	CSA SUBPOOL 231*KEY 7*MIN BELOW TIME

time when minimum value of CSA subpool 231 (below 16 MB) by protect key 7 occurred.

Variable	Type	Length	Format	Label
CSA23172	NUM	4		CSA SUBPOOL 231*KEY 7*MAX BELOW

maximum value of CSA subpool 231 (below 16 MB) allocated by protect key 7.

CSA23173	NUM	4	DATETIME19.2	CSA SUBPOOL 231*KEY 7*MAX BELOW TIME

time when maximum value of CSA subpool 231 (below 16 MB) by protect key 7 occurred.

CSA23174	NUM	4		CSA SUBPOOL 231*KEY 7*AVERAGE BELOW

average value of CSA subpool 231 (below 16 MB) allocated by protect key 7.

CSA23180	NUM	4		CSA SUBPOOL 231*KEY 8-F*MIN BELOW

minimum value of CSA subpool 231 (below 16 MB) allocated by protect keys 8-F.

CSA23181	NUM	4	DATETIME19.2	CSA SUBPOOL 231*KEY 8-F*MIN BELOW TIME

time when minimum value of CSA subpool 231 (below 16 MB) by protect keys 8-F occurred.

CSA23182	NUM	4		CSA SUBPOOL 231*KEY 8-F*MAX BELOW

maximum value of CSA subpool 231 (below 16 MB) allocated by protect keys 8-F.

CSA23183	NUM	4	DATETIME19.2	CSA SUBPOOL 231*KEY 8-F*MAX BELOW TIME

time when maximum value of CSA subpool 231 (below 16 MB) by protect keys 8-F occurred.

CSA23184	NUM	4		CSA SUBPOOL 231*KEY 8-F*AVERAGE BELOW

average value of CSA subpool 231 (below 16 MB) allocated by protect keys 8-F.

CSA241A0	NUM	4		CSA SUBPOOL 241*KEY ALL*MIN BELOW

minimum value of CSA subpool 241 (below 16 MB) allocated by all protect keys.

CSA241A1	NUM	4	DATETIME19.2	CSA SUBPOOL 241*KEY ALL*MIN BELOW TIME

time when minimum value of CSA subpool 241 (below 16 MB) by all protect keys occurred.

CSA241A2	NUM	4		CSA SUBPOOL 241*KEY ALL*MAX BELOW

maximum value of CSA subpool 241 (below 16 MB) allocated by all protect keys.

Variable	Type	Length	Format	Label
CSA241A3	NUM	4	DATETIME19.2	CSA SUBPOOL 241*KEY ALL*MAX BELOW TIME

time when maximum value of CSA subpool 241 (below 16 MB) by all protect keys occurred.

CSA241A4	NUM	4		CSA SUBPOOL 241*KEY ALL*AVERAGE BELOW

average value of CSA subpool 241 (below 16 MB) allocated by all protect keys.

CSA24100	NUM	4		CSA SUBPOOL 241*KEY 0*MIN BELOW

minimum value of CSA subpool 241 (below 16 MB) allocated by protect key 0.

CSA24101	NUM	4	DATETIME19.2	CSA SUBPOOL 241*KEY 0*MIN BELOW TIME

time when minimum value of CSA subpool 241 (below 16 MB) by protect key 0 occurred.

CSA24102	NUM	4		CSA SUBPOOL 241*KEY 0*MAX BELOW

maximum value of CSA subpool 241 (below 16 MB) allocated by protect key 0.

CSA24103	NUM	4	DATETIME19.2	CSA SUBPOOL 241*KEY 0*MAX BELOW TIME

time when maximum value of CSA subpool 241 (below 16 MB) by protect key 0 occurred.

CSA24104	NUM	4		CSA SUBPOOL 241*KEY 0*AVERAGE BELOW

average value of CSA subpool 241 (below 16 MB) allocated by protect key 0.

CSA24110	NUM	4		CSA SUBPOOL 241*KEY 1*MIN BELOW

minimum value of CSA subpool 241 (below 16 MB) allocated by protect key 1.

CSA24111	NUM	4	DATETIME19.2	CSA SUBPOOL 241*KEY 1*MIN BELOW TIME

time when minimum value of CSA subpool 241 (below 16 MB) by protect key 1 occurred.

CSA24112	NUM	4		CSA SUBPOOL 241*KEY 1*MAX BELOW

maximum value of CSA subpool 241 (below 16 MB) allocated by protect key 1.

CSA24113	NUM	4	DATETIME19.2	CSA SUBPOOL 241*KEY 1*MAX BELOW TIME

time when maximum value of CSA subpool 241 (below 16 MB) by protect key 1 occurred.

CSA24114	NUM	4		CSA SUBPOOL 241*KEY 1*AVERAGE BELOW

average value of CSA subpool 241 (below 16 MB) allocated by protect key 1.

Variable	Type	Length	Format	Label
CSA24120	NUM	4		CSA SUBPOOL 241*KEY 2*MIN BELOW

minimum value of CSA subpool 241 (below 16 MB) allocated by protect key 2.

| CSA24121 | NUM | 4 | DATETIME19.2 | CSA SUBPOOL 241*KEY 2*MIN BELOW TIME |

time when minimum value of CSA subpool 241 (below 16 MB) by protect key 2 occurred.

| CSA24122 | NUM | 4 | | CSA SUBPOOL 241*KEY 2*MAX BELOW |

maximum value of CSA subpool 241 (below 16 MB) allocated by protect key 2.

| CSA24123 | NUM | 4 | DATETIME19.2 | CSA SUBPOOL 241*KEY 2*MAX BELOW TIME |

time when maximum value of CSA subpool 241 (below 16 MB) by protect key 2 occurred.

| CSA24124 | NUM | 4 | | CSA SUBPOOL 241*KEY 2*AVERAGE BELOW |

average value of CSA subpool 241 (below 16 MB) allocated by protect key 2.

| CSA24130 | NUM | 4 | | CSA SUBPOOL 241*KEY 3*MIN BELOW |

minimum value of CSA subpool 241 (below 16 MB) allocated by protect key 3.

| CSA24131 | NUM | 4 | DATETIME19.2 | CSA SUBPOOL 241*KEY 3*MIN BELOW TIME |

time when minimum value of CSA subpool 241 (below 16 MB) by protect key 3 occurred.

| CSA24132 | NUM | 4 | | CSA SUBPOOL 241*KEY 3*MAX BELOW |

maximum value of CSA subpool 241 (below 16 MB) allocated by protect key 3.

| CSA24133 | NUM | 4 | DATETIME19.2 | CSA SUBPOOL 241*KEY 3*MAX BELOW TIME |

time when maximum value of CSA subpool 241 (below 16 MB) by protect key 3 occurred.

| CSA24134 | NUM | 4 | | CSA SUBPOOL 241*KEY 3*AVERAGE BELOW |

average value of CSA subpool 241 (below 16 MB) allocated by protect key 3.

| CSA24140 | NUM | 4 | | CSA SUBPOOL 241*KEY 4*MIN BELOW |

minimum value of CSA subpool 241 (below 16 MB) allocated by protect key 4.

| CSA24141 | NUM | 4 | DATETIME19.2 | CSA SUBPOOL 241*KEY 4*MIN BELOW TIME |

time when minimum value of CSA subpool 241 (below 16 MB) by protect key 4 occurred.

Variable	Type	Length	Format	Label
CSA24142	NUM	4		CSA SUBPOOL 241*KEY 4*MAX BELOW

maximum value of CSA subpool 241 (below 16 MB) allocated by protect key 4.

| CSA24143 | NUM | 4 | DATETIME19.2 | CSA SUBPOOL 241*KEY 4*MAX BELOW TIME |

time when maximum value of CSA subpool 241 (below 16 MB) by protect key 4 occurred.

| CSA24144 | NUM | 4 | | CSA SUBPOOL 241*KEY 4*AVERAGE BELOW |

average value of CSA subpool 241 (below 16 MB) allocated by protect key 4.

| CSA24150 | NUM | 4 | | CSA SUBPOOL 241*KEY 5*MIN BELOW |

minimum value of CSA subpool 241 (below 16 MB) allocated by protect key 5.

| CSA24151 | NUM | 4 | DATETIME19.2 | CSA SUBPOOL 241*KEY 5*MIN BELOW TIME |

time when minimum value of CSA subpool 241 (below 16 MB) by protect key 5 occurred.

| CSA24152 | NUM | 4 | | CSA SUBPOOL 241*KEY 5*MAX BELOW |

maximum value of CSA subpool 241 (below 16 MB) allocated by protect key 5.

| CSA24153 | NUM | 4 | DATETIME19.2 | CSA SUBPOOL 241*KEY 5*MAX BELOW TIME |

time when maximum value of CSA subpool 241 (below 16 MB) by protect key 5 occurred.

| CSA24154 | NUM | 4 | | CSA SUBPOOL 241*KEY 5*AVERAGE BELOW |

average value of CSA subpool 241 (below 16 MB) allocated by protect key 5.

| CSA24160 | NUM | 4 | | CSA SUBPOOL 241*KEY 6*MIN BELOW |

minimum value of CSA subpool 241 (below 16 MB) allocated by protect key 6.

| CSA24161 | NUM | 4 | DATETIME19.2 | CSA SUBPOOL 241*KEY 6*MIN BELOW TIME |

time when minimum value of CSA subpool 241 (below 16 MB) by protect key 6 occurred.

| CSA24162 | NUM | 4 | | CSA SUBPOOL 241*KEY 6*MAX BELOW |

maximum value of CSA subpool 241 (below 16 MB) allocated by protect key 6.

| CSA24163 | NUM | 4 | DATETIME19.2 | CSA SUBPOOL 241*KEY 6*MAX BELOW TIME |

time when maximum value of CSA subpool 241 (below 16 MB) by protect key 6 occurred.

Variable	Type	Length	Format	Label
CSA24164	NUM	4		CSA SUBPOOL 241*KEY 6*AVERAGE BELOW

average value of CSA subpool 241 (below 16 MB) allocated by protect key 6.

CSA24170	NUM	4		CSA SUBPOOL 241*KEY 7*MIN BELOW

minimum value of CSA subpool 241 (below 16 MB) allocated by protect key 7.

CSA24171	NUM	4	DATETIME19.2	CSA SUBPOOL 241*KEY 7*MIN BELOW TIME

time when minimum value of CSA subpool 241 (below 16 MB) by protect key 7 occurred.

CSA24172	NUM	4		CSA SUBPOOL 241*KEY 7*MAX BELOW

maximum value of CSA subpool 241 (below 16 MB) allocated by protect key 7.

CSA24173	NUM	4	DATETIME19.2	CSA SUBPOOL 241*KEY 7*MAX BELOW TIME

time when maximum value of CSA subpool 241 (below 16 MB) by protect key 7 occurred.

CSA24174	NUM	4		CSA SUBPOOL 241*KEY 7*AVERAGE BELOW

average value of CSA subpool 241 (below 16 MB) allocated by protect key 7.

CSA24180	NUM	4		CSA SUBPOOL 241*KEY 8-F*MIN BELOW

minimum value of CSA subpool 241 (below 16 MB) allocated by protect keys 8-F.

CSA24181	NUM	4	DATETIME19.2	CSA SUBPOOL 241*KEY 8-F*MIN BELOW TIME

time when minimum value of CSA subpool 241 (below 16 MB) by protect keys 8-F occurred.

CSA24182	NUM	4		CSA SUBPOOL 241*KEY 8-F*MAX BELOW

maximum value of CSA subpool 241 (below 16 MB) allocated by protect keys 8-F.

CSA24183	NUM	4	DATETIME19.2	CSA SUBPOOL 241*KEY 8-F*MAX BELOW TIME

time when maximum value of CSA subpool 241 (below 16 MB) by protect keys 8-F occurred.

CSA24184	NUM	4		CSA SUBPOOL 241*KEY 8-F*AVERAGE BELOW

average value of CSA subpool 241 (below 16 MB) allocated by protect keys 8-F.

Variable	Type	Length	Format	Label
CYCLE	NUM	4		SAMPLE*CYCLE*TIME(MS)

sample cycle time (milliseconds).

| DURATM | NUM | 4 | TIME12.2 | DURATION*OF*INTERVAL |

duration of RMF interval.

| FLPAADHI | NUM | 4 | | FLPA*ADDRESS*ABOVE |

FLPA address above 16 MB.

| FLPAADLO | NUM | 4 | | FLPA*ADDRESS*BELOW |

FLPA address below 16 MB.

| FLPASZHI | NUM | 4 | | FLPA*SIZE*ABOVE |

FLPA size above 16 MB.

| FLPASZLO | NUM | 4 | | FLPA*SIZE*BELOW |

FLPA size below 16 MB.

| IMPLSPHI | NUM | 4 | | PLPA*INTERMODULE*ABOVE |

inter-module space in the PLPA above 16 MB.

| IMPLSPLO | NUM | 4 | | PLPA*INTERMODULE*BELOW |

inter-module space in the PLPA below 16 MB.

| MLPAADHI | NUM | 4 | | MLPA*ADDRESS*ABOVE |

MLPA address above 16 MB.

| MLPAADLO | NUM | 4 | | MLPA*ADDRESS*BELOW |

MLPA address below 16 MB.

| MLPASZHI | NUM | 4 | | MLPA*SIZE*ABOVE |

MLPA size above 16 MB.

| MLPASZLO | NUM | 4 | | MLPA*SIZE*BELOW |

MLPA size below 16 MB.

| MVSLEVEL | CHAR | 8 | | MVS*LEVEL*NUMBER |

MVS software level (which consists of an acronym, and the version, release, and modification level numbers).

| NRSAMPLE | NUM | 4 | | NUMBER*OF*SAMPLES |

number of samples in this RMF interval. (Samples are taken at CYCLE intervals.)

Variable	Type	Length	Format	Label
NUCLADHI	NUM	4		NUCLEUS*ADDRESS*ABOVE

nucleus address above 16 MB.

Variable	Type	Length	Format	Label
NUCLADLO	NUM	4		NUCLEUS*ADDRESS*BELOW

nucleus address below 16 MB.

NUCLSZHI	NUM	4		NUCLEUS*SIZE*ABOVE

nucleus size above 16 MB.

NUCLSZLO	NUM	4		NUCLEUS*SIZE*BELOW

nucleus size below 16 MB.

PLPAADHI	NUM	4		PLPA*ADDRESS*ABOVE

PLPA address above 16 MB.

PLPAADLO	NUM	4		PLPA*ADDRESS*BELOW

PLPA address below 16 MB.

PLPASZHI	NUM	4		PLPA*SIZE*ABOVE

PLPA size above 16 MB.

PLPASZLO	NUM	4		PLPA*SIZE*BELOW

PLPA size below 16 MB.

PRVTADHI	NUM	4		PRIVATE*ADDRESS*ABOVE

private area address above 16 MB.

PRVTADLO	NUM	4		PRIVATE*ADDRESS*BELOW

private area address below 16 MB.

PRVTSZHI	NUM	4		PRIVATE*SIZE*ABOVE

private area size above 16 MB.

PRVTSZLO	NUM	4		PRIVATE*SIZE*BELOW

private area size below 16 MB.

PSRMSPHI	NUM	4		PLPA REDUND*MLPA/FLPA*ABOVE

PLPA space that is redundant with MLPA or FLPA above 16 MB.

PSRMSPLO	NUM	4		PLPA REDUND*MLPA/FLPA*BELOW

PLPA space that is redundant with MLPA or FLPA below 16 MB.

Variable	Type	Length	Format	Label
RELEASE	CHAR	4		OPERATING*SYSTEM*RELEASE
operating system release.				
SMFTIME	NUM	8	DATETIME19.2	SMF*RECORD*TIME STAMP
time when this RMF record was written.				
SQAADHI	NUM	4		SQA*ADDRESS*ABOVE
SQA address above 16 MB.				
SQAADLO	NUM	4		SQA*ADDRESS*BELOW
SQA address below 16 MB.				
SQAALOC0	NUM	4		SQA*ALLOC*MIN BELOW
minimum value of SQA allocated area size below 16 MB.				
SQAALOC1	NUM	4	DATETIME19.2	SQA*ALLOC*MIN BELOW TIME
time when minimum value of SQA allocated area size below 16 MB occurred.				
SQAALOC2	NUM	4		SQA*ALLOC*MAX BELOW
maximum value of SQA allocated area size below 16 MB.				
SQAALOC3	NUM	4	DATETIME19.2	SQA*ALLOC*MAX BELOW TIME
time when maximum value of SQA allocated area size below 16 MB occurred.				
SQAALOC4	NUM	4		SQA*ALLOC*AVERAGE BELOW
average value of SQA allocated area size below 16 MB.				
SQAALOC5	NUM	4		SQA*ALLOC*MIN ABOVE
minimum value of SQA allocated area size above 16 MB.				
SQAALOC6	NUM	4	DATETIME19.2	SQA*ALLOC*MIN ABOVE TIME
time when minimum value of SQA allocated area size above 16 MB occurred.				
SQAALOC7	NUM	4		SQA*ALLOC*MAX ABOVE
maximum value of SQA allocated area size above 16 MB.				
SQAALOC8	NUM	4	DATETIME19.2	SQA*ALLOC*MAX ABOVE TIME
time when maximum value of SQA allocated area size above 16 MB occurred.				
SQAALOC9	NUM	4		SQA*ALLOC*AVERAGE ABOVE
average value of SQA allocated area size above 16 MB.				

Variable	Type	Length	Format	Label
SQAEXPN0	NUM	4		SQA*EXPAND*MIN BELOW

minimum value of SQA expansion into CSA below 16 MB.

SQAEXPN1	NUM	4	DATETIME19.2	SQA*EXPAND*MIN BELOW TIME

time when minimum value of SQA expansion into CSA below 16 MB occurred.

SQAEXPN2	NUM	4		SQA*EXPAND*MAX BELOW

maximum value of SQA expansion into CSA below 16 MB.

SQAEXPN3	NUM	4	DATETIME19.2	SQA*EXPAND*MAX BELOW TIME

time when maximum value of SQA expansion into CSA below 16 MB occurred.

SQAEXPN4	NUM	4		SQA*EXPAND*AVERAGE BELOW

average value of SQA expansion into CSA below 16 MB.

SQAEXPN5	NUM	4		SQA*EXPAND*MIN ABOVE

minimum value of SQA expansion into CSA above 16 MB.

SQAEXPN6	NUM	4	DATETIME19.2	SQA*EXPAND*MIN ABOVE TIME

time when minimum value of SQA expansion into CSA above 16 MB occurred.

SQAEXPN7	NUM	4		SQA*EXPAND*MAX ABOVE

maximum value of SQA expansion into CSA above 16 MB.

SQAEXPN8	NUM	4	DATETIME19.2	SQA*EXPAND*MAX ABOVE TIME

time when maximum value of SQA expansion into CSA above 16 MB occurred.

SQAEXPN9	NUM	4		SQA*EXPAND*AVERAGE ABOVE

average value of SQA expansion into CSA above 16 MB.

SQAFREE0	NUM	4		SQA*FREE*MIN BELOW

minimum value of free SQA below 16 MB.

SQAFREE1	NUM	4	DATETIME19.2	SQA*FREE*MIN BELOW TIME

time when minimum value of free SQA below 16 MB occurred.

SQAFREE2	NUM	4		SQA*FREE*MAX BELOW

maximum value of free SQA below 16 MB.

SQAFREE3	NUM	4	DATETIME19.2	SQA*FREE*MAX BELOW TIME

time when maximum value of free SQA below 16 MB occurred.

Variable	Type	Length	Format	Label
SQAFREE4	NUM	4		SQA*FREE*AVERAGE BELOW
average value of free SQA below 16 MB.				
SQAFREE5	NUM	4		SQA*FREE*MIN ABOVE
minimum value of free SQA above 16 MB.				
SQAFREE6	NUM	4	DATETIME19.2	SQA*FREE*MIN ABOVE TIME
time when minimum value of free SQA above 16 MB occurred.				
SQAFREE7	NUM	4		SQA*FREE*MAX ABOVE
maximum value of free SQA above 16 MB.				
SQAFREE8	NUM	4	DATETIME19.2	SQA*FREE*MAX ABOVE TIME
time when maximum value of free SQA above 16 MB occurred.				
SQAFREE9	NUM	4		SQA*FREE*AVERAGE ABOVE
average value of free SQA above 16 MB.				
SQALARG0	NUM	4		SQA*LARGEST*MIN BELOW
minimum value of largest free block of SQA below 16 MB.				
SQALARG1	NUM	4	DATETIME19.2	SQA*LARGEST*MIN BELOW TIME
time when minimum value of largest free block of SQA below 16 MB occurred.				
SQALARG2	NUM	4		SQA*LARGEST*MAX BELOW
maximum value of largest free block of SQA below 16 MB.				
SQALARG3	NUM	4	DATETIME19.2	SQA*LARGEST*MAX BELOW TIME
time when maximum value of largest free block of SQA below 16 MB occurred.				
SQALARG4	NUM	4		SQA*LARGEST*AVERAGE BELOW
average value of largest free block of SQA below 16 MB.				
SQALARG5	NUM	4		SQA*LARGEST*MIN ABOVE
minimum value of largest free block of SQA above 16 MB.				
SQALARG6	NUM	4	DATETIME19.2	SQA*LARGEST*MIN ABOVE TIME
time when minimum value of largest free block of SQA above 16 MB occurred.				
SQALARG7	NUM	4		SQA*LARGEST*MAX ABOVE
maximum value of largest free block of SQA above 16 MB.				

Variable	Type	Length	Format	Label
SQALARG8	NUM	4	DATETIME19.2	SQA*LARGEST*MAX ABOVE TIME

time when maximum value of largest free block of SQA above 16 MB occurred.

| SQALARG9 | NUM | 4 | | SQA*LARGEST*AVERAGE ABOVE |

average value of largest free block of SQA above 16 MB.

| SQASZHI | NUM | 4 | | SQA*SIZE*ABOVE |

SQA size above 16 MB.

| SQASZLO | NUM | 4 | | SQA*SIZE*BELOW |

SQA size below 16 MB.

| SQAUSED0 | NUM | 4 | | SQA*USED*MIN BELOW |

minimum value of SQA usage below 16 MB.

| SQAUSED1 | NUM | 4 | DATETIME19.2 | SQA*USED*MIN BELOW TIME |

time when minimum value of SQA usage below 16 MB occurred.

| SQAUSED2 | NUM | 4 | | SQA*USED*MAX BELOW |

maximum value of SQA usage below 16 MB.

| SQAUSED3 | NUM | 4 | DATETIME19.2 | SQA*USED*MAX BELOW TIME |

time when maximum value of SQA usage below 16 MB occurred.

| SQAUSED4 | NUM | 4 | | SQA*USED*AVERAGE BELOW |

average value of SQA usage below 16 MB.

| SQAUSED5 | NUM | 4 | | SQA*USED*MIN ABOVE |

minimum value of SQA usage above 16 MB.

| SQAUSED6 | NUM | 4 | DATETIME19.2 | SQA*USED*MIN ABOVE TIME |

time when minimum value of SQA usage above 16 MB occurred.

| SQAUSED7 | NUM | 4 | | SQA*USED*MAX ABOVE |

maximum value of SQA usage above 16 MB.

| SQAUSED8 | NUM | 4 | DATETIME19.2 | SQA*USED*MAX ABOVE TIME |

time when maximum value of SQA usage above 16 MB occurred.

| SQAUSED9 | NUM | 4 | | SQA*USED*AVERAGE ABOVE |

average value of SQA usage above 16 MB.

Variable	Type	Length	Format	Label
SQA226X0	NUM	4		SQA*SUBPOOL 226*MIN BELOW
minimum value of subpool 226 below 16 MB.				
SQA226X1	NUM	4	DATETIME19.2	SQA*SUBPOOL 226*MIN BELOW TIME
time when minimum value of subpool 226 below 16 MB occurred.				
SQA226X2	NUM	4		SQA*SUBPOOL 226*MAX BELOW
maximum value of subpool 226 below 16 MB.				
SQA226X3	NUM	4	DATETIME19.2	SQA*SUBPOOL 226*MAX BELOW TIME
time when maximum value of subpool 226 below 16 MB occurred.				
SQA226X4	NUM	4		SQA*SUBPOOL 226*AVERAGE BELOW
average value of subpool 226 below 16 MB.				
SQA239X0	NUM	4		SQA*SUBPOOL 239*MIN BELOW
minimum value of subpool 239 below 16 MB.				
SQA239X1	NUM	4	DATETIME19.2	SQA*SUBPOOL 239*MIN BELOW TIME
time when minimum value of subpool 239 below 16 MB occurred.				
SQA239X2	NUM	4		SQA*SUBPOOL 239*MAX BELOW
maximum value of subpool 239 below 16 MB.				
SQA239X3	NUM	4	DATETIME19.2	SQA*SUBPOOL 239*MAX BELOW TIME
time when maximum value of subpool 239 below 16 MB occurred.				
SQA239X4	NUM	4		SQA*SUBPOOL 239*AVERAGE BELOW
average value of subpool 239 below 16 MB.				
SQA245X0	NUM	4		SQA*SUBPOOL 245*MIN BELOW
minimum value of subpool 245 below 16 MB.				
SQA245X1	NUM	4	DATETIME19.2	SQA*SUBPOOL 245*MIN BELOW TIME
time when minimum value of subpool 245 below 16 MB occurred.				
SQA245X2	NUM	4		SQA*SUBPOOL 245*MAX BELOW
maximum value of subpool 245 below 16 MB.				
SQA245X3	NUM	4	DATETIME19.2	SQA*SUBPOOL 245*MAX BELOW TIME
time when maximum value of subpool 245 below 16 MB occurred.				

Variable	Type	Length	Format	Label
SQA245X4	NUM	4		SQA*SUBPOOL 245*AVERAGE BELOW
average value of subpool 245 below 16 MB.				
STARTIME	NUM	8	DATETIME19.2	START OF*INTERVAL
start time of RMF interval.				
SYSTEM	CHAR	4	4.	SYSTEM*ID
identification of this system.				
TYPEIOML	CHAR	4		PROCESSOR*COMPLEX*TYPE
processor complex type. Value is 4381 or 308X.				
USERSPHI	NUM	4		MAXIMUM*USER REGION*ABOVE
maximum possible user region above 16 MB.				
USERSPLO	NUM	4		MAXIMUM*USER REGION*BELOW
maximum possible user region below 16 MB.				
VERSNRMF	NUM	4		RMF*VERSION*NUMBER
RMF version number.				

TYPE79
Monitor II Session

The TYPE79 data set contains one observation for every type 79 SMF record written when requested by a Monitor II session. Currently, this data set contains very
little useful information since the type 79 record has not yet been decoded.

Variable	Type	Length	Format	Label
SMFTIME	NUM	8	DATETIME19.2	SMF*RECORD*TIME STAMP

approximate ending time stamp of RMF interval. (Actually, the time the record is moved to
SMF.)

SYSTEM	CHAR	4	4.	SYSTEM*ID

identification of this system.

TYPE80
RACF Processing

The TYPE80 data set contains one observation for every type 80 SMF record written by RACF. This data set currently contains little useful information since the type 80 record has not yet been decoded.

Variable	Type	Length	Format	Label
SMFTIME	NUM	8	DATETIME19.2	SMF*RECORD*TIME STAMP

approximate ending time stamp of RMF interval. (Actually, the time the record is moved to SMF.)

SYSTEM	CHAR	4	4.	SYSTEM*ID

identification of this system.

TYPE81
RACF Initialization

The TYPE81 data set contains one observation for every type 81 SMF record writ-ten by RACF. Currently, this data set contains very little useful information since the type 81 record has not yet been decoded.

Variable	Type	Length	Format	Label
SMFTIME	NUM	8	DATETIME19.2	SMF*RECORD*TIME STAMP

approximate ending time stamp of RMF interval. (Actually, the time the record is moved to SMF.)

Variable	Type	Length	Format	Label
SYSTEM	CHAR	4	4.	SYSTEM*ID

identification of this system.

TYPE82
CRYPTO Security

The TYPE82 data set contains one observation for every type 82 SMF record written by RACF. Currently, this data set contains very little useful information since the type 82 record has not yet been decoded.

Variable	Type	Length	Format	Label
SMFTIME	NUM	8	DATETIME19.2	SMF*RECORD*TIME STAMP

approximate ending time stamp of RMF interval. (Actually, the time the record is moved to SMF.)

| SYSTEM | CHAR | 4 | 4. | SYSTEM*ID |

identification of this system.

TYPE90
Operator Changes

The TYPE90 data set contains multiple observations for every type 90 SMF record written when any one of the following commands is issued by an operator:

SET TIME	SETDMN	SET SMF	SET MPF
SET DATE	SET IPS	SETSMF	SET DAE
IPL PROMPT	SET ICS	SWITCH SMF	IPL SRM
IPL SMF	SET OPT	HALT EOD	

Variable	Type	Length	Format	Label
ACTIVE	CHAR	10		ACTIVE*MAN*DATA SET

name of current active SMF data set.

Variable	Type	Length	Format	Label
BITS	CHAR	32		SMF*RECORD*BITMAP

bit map (hex) that describes which SMF records (0-255) are to be written for each subsystem.

Variable	Type	Length	Format	Label
CHANGE	CHAR	6		DOMAIN*VALUES*CHANGED

domain values changed by the SET DMN command (see appropriate NEW*xxx* variable): MIN, MAX, WEIGHT, AOBJ, DOPJ, FWKLD.

Variable	Type	Length	Format	Label
CMD	NUM	4	MG090CM13.	COMMAND*ISSUED*(FORMATTED)

name of command issued by operator. This is a formatted value. The coding of internal to formatted value is accomplished by the MG090CM format in member FORMATS of SOURCLIB. Note that the formatted value contains the actual internal value:

value	formatted value
1	1:SET TIME
2	2:SET DATE
3	3:SET DOMAIN
4	4:SET IPS
5	5:SET SMF
6	6:IPL SMF
7	7:HALT EOD
8	8:IPL PROMPT
9	9:IPL SMF
10	10:IPL SRM

Variable	Type	Length	Format	Label
		11	11:SET OPT	
		12	12:SET ICS	
		13	13:SETSMF	
		14	14:SET MPF	
		15	15:SET SMF (RESTART SMF)	
		16	16:SET DAE.	
DETAIL	CHAR	1		DETAIL*RECORDING*ON?

detail recording on. The values are either Y or blank. Subtype 5, 9, 13, and 15.

DOMAIN	NUM	4		DOMAIN*NUMBER

domain that was changed.

DOWNTIME	NUM	8	DATETIME19.2	CRASH TIME*OPERATOR*ENTERED

value of time of system crash (IPL PROMPT that is entered by operator).

EVENTIME	NUM	8	DATETIME19.2	EVENT TIME

time of this command.

EXIT01	CHAR	8		NAME*OF*EXIT 1

name of first exit to be taken for each subsystem.

EXIT02	CHAR	8		NAME*OF*EXIT 2

name of second exit to be taken for each subsystem.

EXIT03	CHAR	8		NAME*OF*EXIT 3

name of third exit to be taken for each subsystem.

EXIT04	CHAR	8		NAME*OF*EXIT 4

name of fourth exit to be taken for each subsystem.

EXIT05	CHAR	8		NAME*OF*EXIT 5

name of fifth exit to be taken for each subsystem.

EXIT06	CHAR	8		NAME*OF*EXIT 6

name of sixth exit to be taken for each subsystem.

EXIT07	CHAR	8		NAME*OF*EXIT 7

name of seventh exit to be taken for each subsystem.

EXIT08	CHAR	8		NAME*OF*EXIT 8

name of eighth exit to be taken for each subsystem.

Variable	Type	Length	Format	Label
EXIT09	CHAR	8		NAME*OF*EXIT 9

name of ninth exit to be taken for each subsystem.

EXIT10	CHAR	8		NAME*OF*EXIT 10

name of tenth exit to be taken for each subsystem.

EXIT11	CHAR	8		NAME*OF*EXIT 11

name of eleventh exit to be taken for each subsystem.

EXIT12	CHAR	8		NAME*OF*EXIT 12

name of twelfth exit to be taken for each subsystem.

EXIT13	CHAR	8		NAME*OF*EXIT 13

name of thirteenth exit to be taken for each subsystem.

EXIT14	CHAR	8		NAME*OF*EXIT 14

name of fourteenth exit to be taken for each subsystem.

EXIT15	CHAR	8		NAME*OF*EXIT 15

name of fifteenth exit to be taken for each subsystem.

ICSNAME	CHAR	8		IEAICSXX*MEMBER*NAME

name of (new) Installation Control Specification (ICS).

INTERVAL	NUM	4	TIME12.2	SMF*INTERVAL*DURATION

interval duration.

IPLREASN	CHAR	65		IPL*REASON*ENTERED

reason for this IPL (entered by operator).

IPSNAME	CHAR	8		IEAIPSXX*MEMBER*NAME

name of (new) Installation Performance Specification (IPS).

JWT	CHAR	4		JOB*WAIT*TIME

job wait time parameter.

LISTDSN	CHAR	1		LISTDSN*OPTION

LISTDSN option. The values are either Y or N.

MAXBUFF	NUM	4		MAXIMUM*SMF BUFFERS*FILLED

maximum SMF buffers permitted.

Variable	Type	Length	Format	Label
MAXDORM	CHAR	4		CURRENT*MAXDORM*VALUE

maximum time before which SMF record is to be written.

Variable	Type	Length	Format	Label
MINBUFF	NUM	4		BUFFERS*ON THE*FREE QUEUE

minimum SMF buffers permitted.

Variable	Type	Length	Format	Label
MPCNAME	CHAR	8		OLD MPC*COLOR*NAME

old MPC color parmlib name.

Variable	Type	Length	Format	Label
MPFNAME	CHAR	8		CURRENT*MPF*NAME

new MPF parmlib name.

Variable	Type	Length	Format	Label
NEWAOBJ	NUM	4		NEW*AOBJ*VALUE

new AOBJ value.

Variable	Type	Length	Format	Label
NEWDOBJ	NUM	4		NEW*DOBJ*VALUE

new DOBJ value.

Variable	Type	Length	Format	Label
NEWDSN	CHAR	10		NEW*SMF*DSN

name of new SMF data set to which SMF will now record.

Variable	Type	Length	Format	Label
NEWEIGHT	NUM	4		NEW*WEIGHT*VALUE

new weight value.

Variable	Type	Length	Format	Label
NEWFWKLD	NUM	4		NEW*FWKLD*VALUE

new FWKLD value.

Variable	Type	Length	Format	Label
NEWMAX	NUM	4		NEW*MAX*VALUE

new max value.

Variable	Type	Length	Format	Label
NEWMIN	NUM	4		NEW*MIN*VALUE

new min value.

Variable	Type	Length	Format	Label
NEWTIME	NUM	8	DATETIME19.2	NEW TIME*AFTER*SET

time after set time or set date issued.

Variable	Type	Length	Format	Label
NOWNAME	CHAR	8		NAME*AFTER*COMMAND

new name after change.

Variable	Type	Length	Format	Label
OLDDSN	CHAR	10		OLD*SMF*DSN

old SMF data set name.

Variable	Type	Length	Format	Label
OLDNAME	CHAR	8		OLD*MEMBER*NAME

old name before change.

| OLDTIME | NUM | 8 | DATETIME19.2 | OLD TIME*BEFORE*SET |

time before set time or set date issued.

| OPERNAME | CHAR | 20 | | OPERATOR*NAME*ENTERED |

operator's name (IPL PROMPT).

| OPTNAME | CHAR | 8 | | IEAOPTXX*MEMBER*NAME |

name of OPT member.

| PRODUCT | CHAR | 8 | | PRODUCT*NAME |

product name (SMF, SRM, SUP, and so forth).

| PROMPT | CHAR | 4 | | IPL*PROMPT*DESIRED |

IPL PROMPT desired: IPLR, NONE, LIST.

| REC | CHAR | 4 | | SCRATCH*RECORDS*WRITTEN |

temporary data set records: PERM or ALL. (See discussion in TYPE17 for recommendation of PERM.)

| RELEASE | CHAR | 4 | | OPERATING*SYSTEM*RELEASE |

release number.

| SMFTIME | NUM | 8 | DATETIME19.2 | SMF*RECORD*TIME STAMP |

time this record was written to SMF.

| STATUS | CHAR | 6 | | IO*STATUS |

status in HHMMSS.

| SUBSYS | CHAR | 4 | | SUB*SYSTEM |

detail flag: X '80'.

| SYSTEM | CHAR | 4 | 4. | SYSTEM*ID |

identification of this system.

| VERSN90 | NUM | 4 | | VERSION*NUMBER |

version number.

chapter forty-one

Utilities and Miscellaneous Programs Provided with MXG

This chapter describes the members of the MXG SOURCLIB partitioned data set that do not directly process SMF, RMF, and other data, which were described in the preceding chapter. These remaining programs on the SOURCLIB provide reporting or analysis of specific interest, and they usually use one or more SAS data sets built from TYPE.... members as their input. These programs are documented in the SAS code itself; an examination of the member identifies the input and output of the program. The naming conventions followed in SOURCLIB members are:

SOURCLIB Member Naming Conventions

Member starts with	Purpose
ANAL....	is an analysis or report program
BUILDPDB	builds the PDB, described in chapter thirty-four
CHANGES	documents current change (FIX) level of MXG
CLST....	is a TSO command list to execute a SAS program under TSO
FORMATS	is SAS Source from which formats are created
IMAC....	is installation MACROS, described in chapter thirty-two
JCL.....	is job control language to execute a SAS program in batch
PRINTING	is part of JCLTEST execution to print all data sets
RMFINTRV	is part of BUILDPDB execution to build RMFINTRV data set
TYPE*nnnn*	is a SAS program to build TYPE*nnnn* data sets from SMF/RMF

UTIL....	is a SAS Utilities, written in the SAS language, that is useful for CPE
VMAC....	is SAS macro definitions used in TYPE*nnnn* members
X.......	is eXtra programs that are documented, unsupported, but free.

The specific purpose of each of these programs is described in alphabetical order below.

Program	Purpose
ANALAVAL	Availability analysis. Relates to chapter twenty-five.
ANALBNCH	Benchmark analysis. Relates to chapter thirty.
ANALCICS	CICS report examples from type 110 SMF (CICS CMF records). Relates to chapter twenty-one.
ANALDALY	Daily PDB Report analysis examples. Relates to chapters thirty-four through thirty-six.
ANALDOS	DOS/POWER report examples, including partition usage. Relates to chapter five.
ANALDSET	Data Set analysis. Processes type 14 and 15 (non-VSAM) I/O records with the step records (either TYPE30_4 direct from SMF or PDB.STEPS from the MXG PDB) to build (ultimately) data set DATABASE. Relates to chapter thirteen.
ANALESV	Tape error analysis from type 21 SMF records. Relates to chapter fourteen.
ANALMPL	Multiprogramming level analysis. Relates to chapter sixteen.
ANALNPA	Network Performance Analyzer analysis from type 38 SMF record. Relates to chapter eighteen.
ANALPRNT	Printer usage and queue analysis. Relates to chapter fifteen.
ANALPROG	Program resource usage analysis. Tabulates ranking of all programs by program name. Relates most to chapter nineteen.

ANALRMFI	RMFINTRV (RMF Interval) analysis from combined RMFINTRV data set.
ANALTAPE	Tape drive delays and usage analysis from step records. Relates to chapter fourteen.
ANALTSOR	Average TSO response analysis from RMF type 72 transaction data.
ANALTURN	Batch turnaround analysis. Relates to chapter nineteen.
ANALVM	VM accounting card analysis. Relates to chapter six.
BUILDPDB	Builds the Performance Data Base. Described in detail in chapter thirty-four.
CHANGES	Maintenance status of MXG. This member contains the change level of the MXG software you have. Please look at this member and note the highest change you have installed before reporting a problem to Merrill Consultants.
CLSTIMER	Measure actual TSO response as it happens with this CLIST. A very good measurement tool, described in chapter twenty.
CLSTXREF	TSO CLIST for MXG utility to cross-reference all variables in any number of SAS data sets in any number of SAS data libraries, identifying variables with dissimilar attributes (type, length, format, and so forth). Used originally to prevent such conflicts in MXG variables. Note also JCLUXREF, which is generally superior.
~~JCLDBANL~~	~~JCL to execute ANALDSET program.~~
JCLFIRST	JCL to read the MXG distribution tape. Chapter thirty-two.
JCLPDB	JCL to build the MXG Performance Data Base. Chapter thirty-four.
JCLTEST	JCL to exercise the MXG system. Chapter thirty-three.
JCLUXREF	JCL to execute MXG cross-reference utility. See CLSTXREF.
JCLZERO	JCL that created the MXG distribution tape.
PRINTING	Print all MXG data sets (used with JCLTEST).
TYPETEST	Build all MXG data sets (used with JCLTEST).

UTILDBLK	Deblock VBS records with the SAS System.
UTILDUMP	Produce hex dump of SMF records.
UTILGETM	Select 10 SMF records of each type (used with JCLTEST).
UTILPRAL	Execute PRINT procedure against all data sets in a SAS data library. Actually, can execute any SAS procedure against all SAS data sets in a data library.
UTILXREF	Cross-reference utility for SAS data libraries. See CLSTXREF and JCLUXREF.
XCACHLST	Analyze 3880-11 cache controller buffer hit ratio.
XGEFANAL	Read GTF tape and decode into multiple data sets. Last tested under MVS/370 SP1.1.
XPAII	Read CICS performance analyzer records and decode all fields.
XREADTMC	Read Tape Management System (TMS) Catalog (TMC) to analyze size of tape data sets. Relates to chapter fourteen.
XTAPECER	Complete scratch tape management system, based on TMS and type 21 tape error records. Takes as input today's scratch tape list (from TMS) and today's PDB type 21 records. Updates permanent file of errors on all current tapes, and then compares scratch tapes to errors to produce three tape lists: those scratched, those to be cleaned (because they had temporary errors), and those to be certified (had permanent errors). Relates to chapter fourteen.
XTEACH	Simple interactive example to teach arithmetic, showing how to use the SAS System to interact with a TSO user.
XTSOBATC	JCL to execute TSO session in batch, printing output of a TSO command. Also used to stimulate benchmarks and to act like many TSO users by executing many copies of this job at the same time. Relates to chapter twenty.
XTYPEMVT	Build original *Merrill's Guide* PDB from OS/MVT SMF records.
XTYPEVS1	Build original *Merrill's Guide* PDB from OS/VS1 SMF records.

chapter forty-two
The Last Chapter of the Book

This chapter contains two research papers by the author. The first paper was accepted for presentation at The First International Conference on Computers and Applications, Beijing, China, June 20-22, 1984, sponsored jointly by the Institute of Electrical and Electronic Engineers (IEEE) Computer Society and the Chinese Institute of Electronics (CIE) Computer Society.

The second paper presented in this chapter was delivered at SHARE, March 1984, in Anaheim, California. Although this topic is not a new one, this analysis shows that poor programmer choices of blocksize and buffers account for a significant waste of CPU time.

I. COMPUTER METRICS: MEASURING AND MANAGING THE PERFORMANCE, RESOURCES, AND COSTS OF LARGE COMPUTER SYSTEMS

H. W. Barry Merrill
Network Services
Sun Company

Abstract

Managing and measuring the performance, resources, and costs of a large complex of central and distributed computers with distributed interactive users requires the establishment of repeatable, meaningful, and measurable service objectives (such as interactive response time, batch turnaround, and availability). It requires accurate measures of resource consumption (processor time, I/O device activity, real memory utilization) by which the capacity to meet those service objectives can be acquired in the most timely fashion and at the most cost-effective rate. A case study describes a cost-effective measurement system that captures and analyzes data and answers typical management questions with interactive graphical reporting. The configuration and workload of the computer system are also described.

Introduction

Computer metrics, often called computer performance evaluation, capacity planning, or system tuning, is an emerging technology in large, multi-user computer systems. Motivated by the conflicting goals of increased user productivity and reduced costs, the data center management of these large systems requires hard data to justify requests for resource acquisition. Most of the research to date has been ad hoc and unique to each specific computer installation. Reference (1) has been reviewed as the landmark reference in the field; references (2) and (3) contain 164 of the best current papers ranging from tutorial to technical; and reference (4) describes SAS software.

This paper describes a case study of an approach to computer metrics used in over 1400 installations worldwide. The paper, which is also a brief tutorial on the subject, first describes goals and methods of the technology and then quantifies the environment of the case study. The capabilities and costs of the measurement systems are described, and examples of graphical management reporting are discussed. The cost of the measurement system is shown to be effective, and the conclusions are presented.

Goals and Methods

The basic problem in large installations is the management of shared resources, balanced by the service requirements of users of this network. The most important facet of the solution is the establishment of service objectives. Only when the supplier of computing has quantified the service to be delivered in a measurable fashion can the users of computing evaluate services received relative to the cost of computing.

To be successful, service objectives must:

- be measurable
- be repeatable
- be understandable by the typical user
- correlate directly with the user's perception of service
- allow reflection of true exception conditions
- be directly controllable by the resources applied by the computer installation.

Successful service objectives for the four most important subsystems are described in Table 42.1.

A key additional ingredient in these objectives is the manner in which they are expressed. The use of average (mean) values has been found to be quite misleading. In general, the mean is an unsatisfactory expression of a service objective. Since the primary purpose of the service objective is to allow the supplier to communicate service to the user, the metric used must be human oriented. Mean values, in spite of their strong mathematical heritage, do not relate to human perceptions. A human wants to know what happens most of the time. The average value, which is the sum of all observations divided by the number of observations, is never actually observed by the user. By recognizing this need in computer service objectives and by expressing objectives as frequency of occurrence ("94% of the time this will happen"), we have found not only a metric that relates to the user, but also one that meets the other criteria for effective service objectives. Specific techniques for establishing service objectives are addressed in (1). The actual measure of service used (internal response, turnaround, queue time, and so forth) is dependent on the hardware and software architecture that provides the computing and is a function of the nature and purpose of the specific computing installation. The method of exposition (percentage of occurrences meeting a stated goal), however, appears almost invariant in well-managed computing facilities.

Table 42.1
Service Objectives

Subsystem	Measure	Goal
batch	Percentage of jobs meeting requested IWT, (Initiation Wait Time). Users submit jobs requesting initiation wait times of 15 min., 30 min., 1 hour, 2 hours, or 4 hours. Time to initiate is measured by SMF.	94%
TSO	Trivial transactions meeting 4-second internal response. TSO/MON name table defines trivial. Internal response measured by TSO/MON.	92%
IMS	IMS queue met expected response.	95%
	Service Time met expected response. CONTROL/IMS measures input queue time and service time separately. Expected queue time is calculated based on transaction class or priority. Expected service time is calculated based on resources measured by CONTROL/IMS.	98%
CICS	FAST transactions met 4-second response. Internal response measured by PAII. Transactions classified as FAST if AMCT (I/O count) is less than five and transaction name is not in a table of "bad guys."	92%

Therefore, capturing the service and resource data becomes a crucial element in managing the facility. Without measurable service objectives, when users complain, perhaps the wrong resources are expanded. By correlating service delivered with resources consumed, however, the limiting resource can be identified and options evaluated for cost-effectiveness. Additional resources can be acquired, the application can be rescheduled to a time when that particular resource is plentiful, or the application can be redesigned in light of the limited resource.

Measuring and managing service objectives is necessary for system tuning to identify and eliminate bottlenecks to performance. Management is not interested in the raw power of the configuration to process data but, rather, in knowing the capacity in terms of how much work can be delivered while meeting service objectives. This is called goal level capacity. The specific techniques described in (1) are summarized below.

Analysis of capacity by workload measurement requires these preconditions:

- The system must be tuned. Known bottlenecks to performance have been eliminated and the I/O configuration has been implemented to minimize contention. An untuned system displays erratic response, causing inaccurate capacity measurement.
- Work must execute when needed by the user. The shape of the workload represents real demand required by the business and not an artificial shape created by the supplier's arbitrary resource or scheduling constraints. A batch scheduling system that relates directly to users' requests based on timeliness guarantees this condition. Batch scheduling systems based only on resource requirements generally fail this test since they place arbitrary constraints on when various classes of work are actually executed.

With these preconditions met, hourly resource data are analyzed. Since not all resource utilization is accurately attributed to the workload, linear regression is used to distribute the unattributed (but measured) overhead to the workloads that generated that overhead. The service objectives achieved during each hour are then plotted against workload to measure the knee of the response curve and to quantify the relationship between work and service. The initial result is the hourly capacity in work units per hour of the system (hardware, software, memory, and I/O configuration-dependent) to deliver work and concurrently meet service objectives.

The extension from hourly capacity to daily prime shift capacity is accomplished by first plotting the actual hourly workload profile, hour by hour of prime shift. The shape of the profile is preserved, and that curve with the same shape is raised until the peak value of the profile for any hour equals the hourly capacity value. Integrating under the raised curve then provides the real daily capacity. This technique simply redefines real capacity in terms of the present configuration and the present demand by users. It is a stable measure unless the configuration is changed (by adding resources or by changing system or application software) or the demand profile changes. The shape is usually constant unless personnels' working hours are changed.

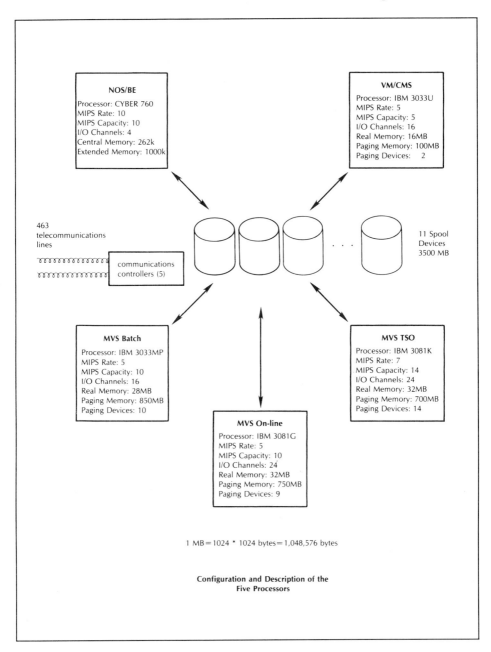

NOS/BE

Processor: CYBER 760
MIPS Rate: 10
MIPS Capacity: 10
I/O Channels: 4
Central Memory: 262k
Extended Memory: 1000k

VM/CMS

Processor: IBM 3033U
MIPS Rate: 5
MIPS Capacity: 5
I/O Channels: 16
Real Memory: 16MB
Paging Memory: 100MB
Paging Devices: 2

463
telecommunications
lines

communications
controllers (5)

11 Spool
Devices
3500 MB

MVS Batch

Processor: IBM 3033MP
MIPS Rate: 5
MIPS Capacity: 10
I/O Channels: 16
Real Memory: 28MB
Paging Memory: 850MB
Paging Devices: 10

MVS TSO

Processor: IBM 3081K
MIPS Rate: 7
MIPS Capacity: 14
I/O Channels: 24
Real Memory: 32MB
Paging Memory: 700MB
Paging Devices: 14

MVS On-line

Processor: IBM 3081G
MIPS Rate: 5
MIPS Capacity: 10
I/O Channels: 24
Real Memory: 32MB
Paging Memory: 750MB
Paging Devices: 9

1 MB = 1024 * 1024 bytes = 1,048,576 bytes

**Configuration and Description of the
Five Processors**

Figure 42.2

Description of the Configuration and Workload

The Sun Company Information Systems Division manages a computer systems network with an annual budget of $36,000,000 for hardware, systems software, communications equipment, and personnel.

Figure 42.2 describes the 5 central processors that support this network and the associated paging subsystems for the virtual memory systems. The 5 processors share 11 direct-access storage devices of SPOOL that are used for staging and exchanging jobs' input and output between systems. Once selected for execution by the job entry system (JES), the job executes completely on 1 of the 5 processors, placing its printed output on the SPOOL. When the job is completed, output is transmitted to the remote locations for printing or display. Users communicate interactively through the telecommunications network to the processor that hosts their particular application.

Table 42.3
I/O Configuration - MVS Systems

TAPE DRIVES

Quantity	Type	Transfer Rate (kilobytes per second)
23	3420-Model 8	1250
40	3420-Model 4	470

ON-LINE DISK VOLUMES

Quantity	Type	Transfer Rate (kilobytes per second)	Storage Capacity per volume (megabytes)
60	3330-1	806	100
400	3350	1198	317
12	3380	3000	630

Total On-Line Disk Storage Megabytes: 140,360

Table 42.3 describes the I/O configuration shared by the three processors using the multiple virtual storage operating system, which accounts for 90% of the workload. Tape drives are fully shareable among processors, with software allocating each drive to a single task when needed. Disk drives are fully shareable among processors so that the failure of a processor does not prevent access to data on a particular disk. However, to minimize contention delays, data on a single disk are application specific; that is, the disk contains data only for a specific application, such as TSO. The path (the control unit and channel) is logically isolated to the processor in which that application normally executes. (Although there always exist some data, such as catalogs, that must be shared, logical isolation is the design objective in the placement of data and is maintained to the highest degree possible.)

Table 42.4 quantifies the telecommunications environment that supports the 4099 terminals that connect to the processor complex. Although host processors are located in two sites in Dallas, Texas, users of the network are located all across the United States and Canada, with heavy concentrations in Dallas, Philadelphia, California, and Illinois.

Table 42.4
Telecommunications Environment

COMMUNICATIONS CONTROLLERS

Quantity	Type	Memory kilobytes	Protocol	Number of lines per controller
4	3705	512	SDLC	60
1	Comten	512	Bisync, Async	240

TELECOMMUNICATIONS LINES

Quantity	Line speed (bits per second)
8	56000
150	9600
203	4800
102	300/1200

Table 42.5 describes the workloads and systems that execute on the three MVS processors. The acronyms may be unfamiliar, so a brief description follows:

Initiators	one batch job owns an initiator during its execution.
IMS	on-line system used for data base inquiry and update, especially with complex data.
CICS	on-line system used for update and inquiry that is simpler but faster than IMS.
TSO	interactive system used heavily for program development and execution of management (end-user oriented) decision-support systems.
WYLBUR	edit and submit interactive system.
ADABAS	data base manager accessed by TSO and batch users.
VTAM	the primary terminal access manager.
JES	job entry subsystem, controls batch and all printing.

Table 42.5
MVS Workloads

3033-MP Batch	3081-D TSO	3081-G On-line
40 Initiators	250 TSO Users	Production IMS Control
Test IMS Control	3 WYLBURS	8 IMS Message Regions
2 Test IMS Regions	4 ADABAS Nucleus	3 Production CICS
2 Test CICS	Backup IMS	VTAM Applications:
	Order Entry TCAM	VTAMPRNT

Table 42.6 quantifies daily workload executed on the three systems. These counts of tasks and concurrent users clearly describe a very large system; there are about fifty installations of similar size in the United States alone.

Table 42.6
Daily Workload Volumes

MVS

Batch Steps	22365
CICS Transactions	223510
IMS Transactions	98436
TSO Prime Transactions	147719
Concurrent TSO Users	213
Concurrent IMS Users	500
Concurrent CICS Users	476
Concurrent WYLBUR Users	10
Concurrent JES2 Remotes	147

CMS

Session Intervals	2123
Concurrent Users	28

CYBER

Batch Jobs	592
Time-Sharing Sessions	80

Table 42.7 quantifies distribution of the budget at a high level. Only the staff that actually operates and manages the hardware and software described before (approximately 150 people) is included in the personnel cost. Application programmers and end users of these systems are excluded from this figure.

Table 42.7
Cost Distribution

Salaries	23%
Local taxes	2%
Electric power	2%
Software rental	2%
Maintenance of facilities	7%
IBM CPUs and channels	12%
CYBER CPU, disk	10%
Voice network	9%
Disk drives and controllers	8%
Dedicated lines	6%
Dial-in lines	4%
Tape drives and controllers	3%
3705 communications controllers	2%
Modems and so forth	1%
Miscellaneous	8%

Annual Budget $36,000,000

Capabilities and cost of the measurement system   To manage an installation of this size, we have found that it is not only mandatory to measure service and resources, but it can be done in an extremely economical fashion, provided some intelligent choices are made. Table 42.8 quantifies volumetrics of the performance data produced that are thought to be required for effective management and measurement in this facility. (A volumetric is a generic term for data elements that describe service or resources.)

Table 42.8
Daily Record Volumes

Source	Average record count	Record length	K bytes of data
MVS			
SMF	780564	248	194214
PAII	223510	88	19668
CYBER	10131	80	810
Dayfile			
CMS Account Cards	13391	80	1071

More specifically, detailed event records written on the MVS systems (Table 42.9) show both the quantity and quality of the data that are automatically created by the operating system's accounting, resource measurement, and service measurement routines. In spite of the breadth of vendor-created event records, we have found it necessary to use the operating system exit facilities to create the additional event records listed in Table 42.10.

Table 42.9
Systems Management Facility (SMF)
Vendor-Created Records Written Daily

		Logical records	K bytes	SAS observations
Type 0	(Sys startup)	1	-	1
Type 2, 3	Dump SMF	12	-	12
Type 4, 34	Step term	22365	7092	25302
Type 5, 35	Job term	8200	1286	8200
Type 6	File print	8035	824	7474
Type 7	Lost SMF data	0	-	0
Type 14	Input file	129115	38310	138
Type 15	Output file	89968	25981	-
Type 17	Scratch	11885	1140	-
Type 18	Rename	104	14	-
Type 20	Initiation	8759	930	2338
Type 21	Tape mount	8172	360	8172
Type 26	Job purge	9316	3205	8257
Type 30	Workload	45031	34057	-
Type 40	Allocation	115736	8711	44252
Type 47-48	RJE Ses	970	69	1116
Type 50	VTAM buffers	314	18	-
Type 52-53	RJE Ses	574	42	-
Type 62-69	VSAM open	31338	8656	-
Type 70	RMF CPU	75	47	150
Type 71	RMF paging	75	31	75
Type 72	RMF workload	8475	1686	2045
Type 73	RMF channels	75	154	2751
Type 74	RMF DASD I/O	150	3442	14548
Type 75	RMF Page I/O	788	123	788
Type 90	Operator acts	8	1	-
Type 110	CICS trans	49	1128	6648
	Record Totals	499584	137370	-

Table 42.10
Systems Management Facility (SMF)
Installation-Created SMF Records Written Daily

		SMF record count	Total SMF K bytes	SAS observations
Type 129	Job initiation	8205	1148	8205
Type 130	Interval	199	105	-
Type 175	VTAM terminal	45334	1587	31794
Type 201	Security	1749	182	-
Type 210	WYLBUR session	195	21	195
Type 214	Archival	14199	1349	-
Type 217	TSO/MON system	653	1730	9713
Type 218	TSO/MON call	2777	690	1560
Type 225	JES operator	4569	258	2353
Type 229	Tape mount	7529	482	7529
Type 230	Audit tape	166	18	166
Type 231	Application	20	1	20
Type 249	IMS program	68367	12852	68367
Type 250	IMS transaction	98436	34156	98436
Type 254	ADABAS trans	876	140	876
	Installation Totals	253953	54723	-

These event records are written to the System Management Facility (SMF) file as their events occur. However, to measure response or resources requires that these event records be processed and synthesized into humanly-perceived events, such as command response time, program memory usage, processor active time for a computer, and so forth. Conversion from raw SMF data to information is a complex software problem because of the complexity of the possible event records that might occur and because of the variety of data formats in the records written by the operating system. The solution was made feasible by a high-level language system, the SAS System, (4) that is powerful enough to handle this variety of data forms and is so efficient in processing this large volume of data records that it is the de facto standard language for processing SMF data. The algorithms (1) that map the raw data to information are written in SAS software. The data are in use at some 1400 installations worldwide, and they are referred to as the

PDB (performance data base, after their end product, a SAS data library of information and reports). The execution resources to process the 200,000 kilobytes of daily event records into the PDB are quantified in Table 42.11. Clearly, this processing of over 1 million records (typically 200 bytes long) daily in 60 CPU minutes per day demonstrates the remarkable power of the SAS System and the PDB algorithms.

Table 42.11
Monthly Resource Costs to Build the
Performance Data Base

Job description	Total monthly 3081-D CPU minutes
CYBER system - total	46
VM system - total	16
MVS systems - total	1760

Major subsystems within MVS:	CPU Min
Dumping accounting data to tape	476
Build daily PDB from accounting data	992
Daily reports and backups	154
Weekly reports	73
Monthly reports	37
Build customer-splitout data base	28
Grand total of all systems	1,822

These 1,822 CPU minutes per month are equivalent to only 60 minutes per day.

Goal level capacity analysis described earlier was performed on these three MVS machines. That study found the prime-time (11-hour shift) goal level capacity to be 2,271 CPU minutes deliverable to batch each day, with batch service goals being met, or a total monthly (prime and nonprime) capacity of 148,653 CPU minutes. If we compare the total cost of 1,822 minutes monthly to build the PDB and to execute all the performance and capacity analysis reports with the configuration's monthly capacity, the cost of executing the total PDB measurement and reporting system represents only 1.2% of the total capacity! Not only does this demonstrate cost-effectiveness of the measurement system, but since the daily running can be scheduled in the least busy time of day, true cost is essentially zero because capacity cost is set by peak time requirements.

Examples of management reporting   The presentation of tables of numbers is often useful during analysis and is appropriate for presentations to technical audiences. However, communication of computer capacity and performance measures to the senior, nontechnical management requires graphical presentation. ("A picture is worth a thousand words.") The graphical capabilities of the SAS System make it simple to create a graphical display of the performance data base data.

The graphs are used to show management the quality of service delivered to the computing users. The use of capacity is also mapped to the internal business organizations that consumed resources. Management can then determine if the business purpose served by a part of the company justifies that part's consumption of computer capacity.

The performance data base contains trend data for each week for the past several years. This permits simple graphical display versus time so that not only is the current service and resource consumption measured and managed (tactical performance management), but also the long-range trends (strategic capacity planning) are tracked.

Management of many businesses is based on monthly data, but we have found the week a far more stable measure. Not only does weekly reporting provide more timely precursors of trouble, but also the trends are significantly more accurate and robust since each week has the same number of days. Monthly resource data points suffer from too much variability because there are as few as 18 and as many as 23 working days in a month. Even weekly data must be cleaned of outliers before mathematical analysis is applied; the 6 weeks during which major holidays occur in the U.S. must be deleted from analysis if typical trends are to be observed.

Using this weekly trend data, management is kept informed of the productivity and efficiency of the computing facility. The following graphs are a subset of the graphs used in presentations to senior management and are available on-line to all levels of management. The manager simply logs on to the TSO application with his CRT terminal, enters a single command, and is presented with a menu from which graphs are selected. Graphs are created on-line in response to the menu selection. Each graph requires approximately 10 seconds elapsed time for creation and transmission on a 9600 BPS line.

Management first asks two questions of the computer facility: how good was the service, and how much work did we deliver? Figures 42.12 through 42.15 answer these quality-of-service questions:

Figure 42.12   CICS (Prime Time) Performance. Percentage of fast CICS transactions in prime time (7 a.m. to 6 p.m.) that received internal response time of less than 4 seconds is tracked. The step decrease in August 1981 was the result of a change in response measurement due to software maintenance. The step increase in October 1982 was the result of additional resources (a new CPU).

Figure 42.13   TSO (Prime Time) Performance. Percentage of fast TSO transactions in prime time that received internal response time of less than 4 seconds

is tracked. In spite of a substantial growth in number of users, tactical management of resources has kept TSO response very stable. Without measures of actual response, tactical movement of work to other processors and the incremental addition of resources (especially memory to meet growth) would not have been possible.

Figure 42.14   Batch (Prime Time) Performance. Percentage of batch jobs that met user-requested initiation wait time (IWT) of 15 minutes is seen to be very consistent except for 5 weeks. The failed weeks correspond to over-capacity weeks because outages usually reduced available capacity. Even bad weeks show 95% satisfaction for this critical 15-minute IWT category, which accounts for over half of prime time batch work.

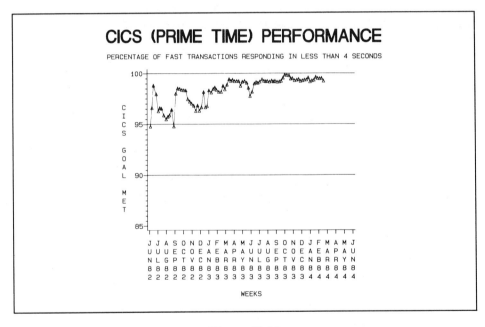

Figure 42.12

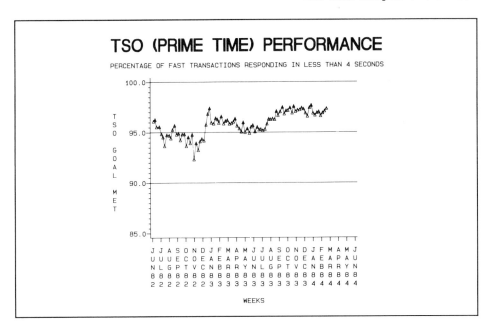

Figure 42.13

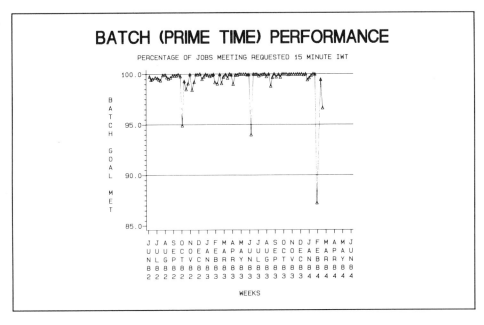

Figure 42.14

Figure 42.15   IMS (Prime Time) Performance. The IMS transaction service time goal shows the service degrade until September 1982 when tactical management applied more resources to support IMS, with the resultant step increase in service. Service remained stable for 4 months until a new application again overloaded IMS, and resources were acquired to restore service levels.

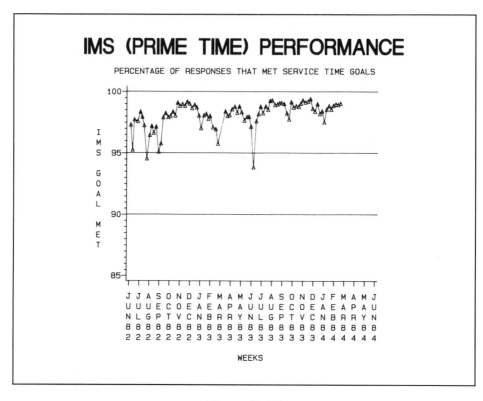

Figure 42.15

Management concern with operating system overhead (which is not usually directly billed but is distributed through the pricing mechanism of the computer facility) is addressed in Figures 42.16 and 42.17, shown in the color section.

Figure 42.16   Prime Time Hardware CRU Totals. The unit of work, the computer resource unit (CRU), is a composite of CPU time and I/O counts, weighing the processor time more heavily. The three lines show the total growth of work (top), work directly measurable and attributable to a task (middle), and the difference in total and identifiable work (bottom). Thus, the bottom line measures the operating system overhead that is not directly attributable to individual tasks.

Downward spikes in the three graphs are the decrease in workload during weeks with a major holiday.

Figure 42.17   Plot of Overhead and Identified Hardware CRU. Data of Figure 42.17 are expressed as percentages of total work. The middle reflects identified work and the bottom reflects operating system overhead. Excluding a brief spike in 1981, which was due to improper installation of software maintenance, the system overhead has remained a consistent percentage of total work, as a well-designed operating system should.

Management is concerned with overall capacity while meeting these goals.

Figure 42.18   Hardware CRU Growth Toward Capacity. Total work delivered is plotted against the installed capacity in absolute computer resource units.

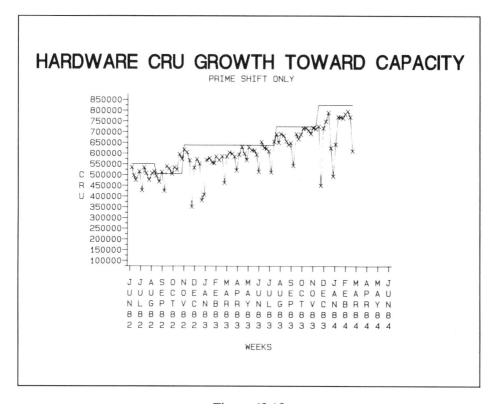

Figure 42.18

Figure 42.19   Weekly Percentage of Current Prime Capacity. Work delivered is expressed as a percentage of installed capacity.

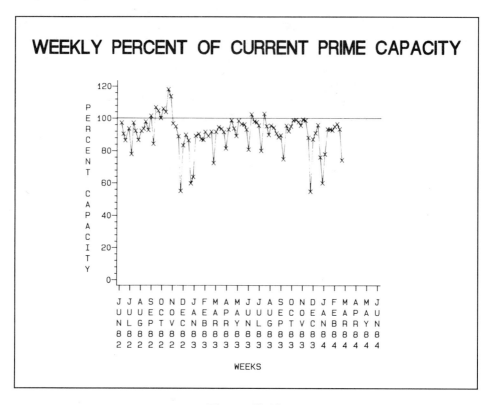

Figure 42.19

Figures 42.18 and 42.19 show that capacity was exceeded for a 7-week period in 1982. This was known in advance, and management chose to ride out the capacity shortage until the new processor was installed because of financial pressure at that time. Because they received advance notice of the decision to ride out, users cooperated, and complaints were minimal.

Management wanted to know the relative usage of prime and nonprime shifts.

Figure 42.20   Distribution of Sun Company Batch by Shift. Percentage of total CRU (nonprime slightly higher than prime) is plotted showing a consistent distribution. Unfortunately, management had hoped to persuade customers to migrate from prime to nonprime time during this period. This plot shows that the particular incentive pricing strategy chosen was ineffective since there was no significant change in the percentage of work in nonprime time. A new incentive pricing was then chosen, which did work.

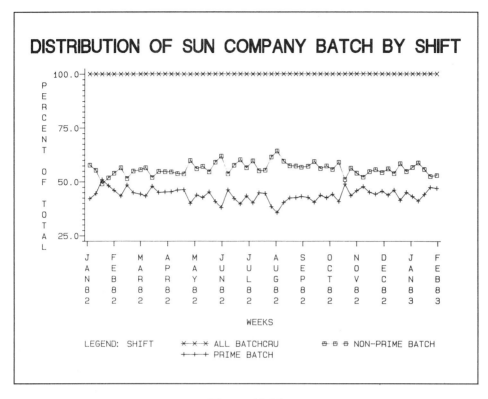

Figure 42.20

Management needs to know how capacity is being used. What categories of work use what portion of the capacity? What business elements (regions or companies) are driving the growth in usage? How are individual companies within the organization using the computing facility? These types of questions are answered in the following graphs, shown in the color section.

Figure 42.21   Overall Category Breakouts. Percentage of work is distributed by the six major workload categories of batch, TSO, CICS, ADABAS, IMS, and non-IWT scheduled batch), in relative order from top to bottom, showing a slight decrease in batch and a slight increase in TSO work.

Figure 42.22   Overall Regional Breakouts. Total CRU distributed by the seven major business elements of the Sun Company (Corporate Financial Division, Exploration and Production, Human Resources, Information Systems Division Staff, Network Services, Refining and Marketing and Sun Information Commercial Services).

Figure 42.23   Regional Breakout by Work Type and Shift. Total CRU of a particular region, SIS, is further plotted as CRU to expose the type of work and relative growth within this business element. This level of detail is necessary in order to project future requirements from past history. It allows planning for the capacity change that will occur when SIS leaves the network in 1985.

Figure 42.24   Category Breakout by Region and Shift. This is the inverse of the prior graph. A work category, CICS, is decomposed into business elements that consume CRU in the CICS subsystems, and highly dissimilar patterns are seen for different divisions.

Figure 42.25   Regional Percentage Breakout by Work type and Shift. This graph shows the usage of one business element, E&P Company, by work type. The upper lines separate batch and TSO. The double-humped bottom line is most interesting because it demonstrates a failed application project. A large application was designed and tested (the first and smaller peak). The commitment was made to implement based on this test, but the actual execution costs were not evaluated during the testing phase. As the system entered production, its resource consumption grew (the second and larger peak), and the design was recognized as too expensive to execute and was terminated. This graph was effective in instituting a new policy to require that execution costs be considered an inherent part of new applications during their testing phase. No table of data was as effective as this graph.

Summary

This paper has shown that a wide range of management questions can be easily answered with data in the performance data base, which is produced from operating system created accounting and performance records. As a brief introduction to computer metrics, it was not the goal to present specific results as much as it was to demonstrate management's need for these analyses and to show that analysis can be done with minimal expense. The use of a common data source for daily performance evaluation and management, system tuning, billing, and capacity planning has significantly reduced conflicts between different operating groups that heretofore reported their own data in their own fashion. By managing the system based on measured service objectives, user and supplier have both agreed on what constitutes acceptable service, and the supplier can manage resource acquisition to ensure that acceptable service is delivered.

Perhaps the best demonstration of the value of computer metrics comes from the continued use of the PDB at Sun Company since 1976 as the single source of data for managing service, capacity planning, and cost recovery of resources while that data center grew from two 2.5 MIP processors to the present 8 CPUs, totaling over 37 MIPs, without any increase in the 5-person staff of the computer metrics group.

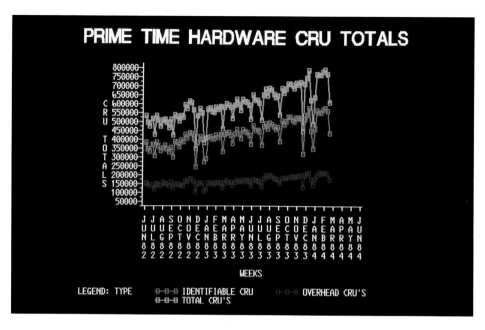

Figure 42.16

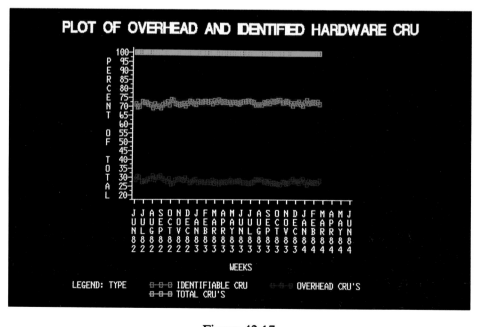

Figure 42.17

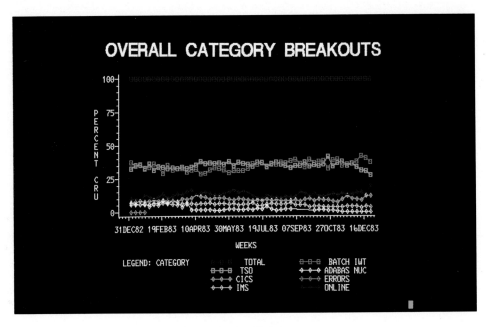

Figure 42.21

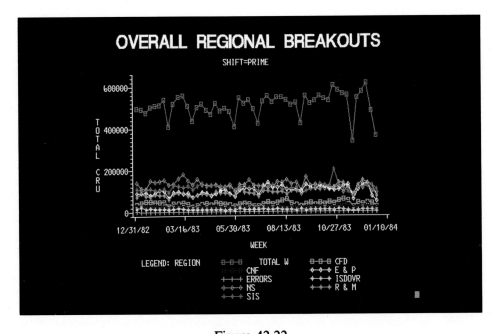

Figure 42.22

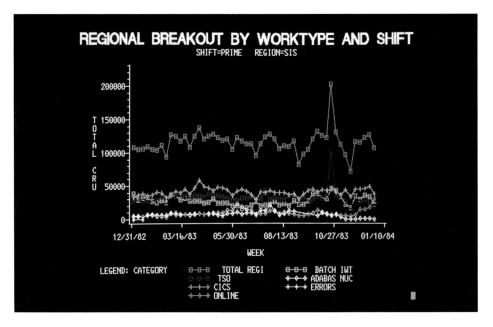

Figure 42.23

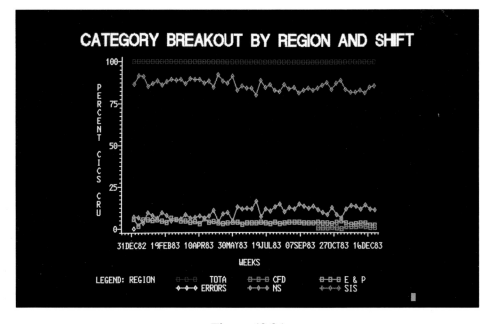

Figure 42.24

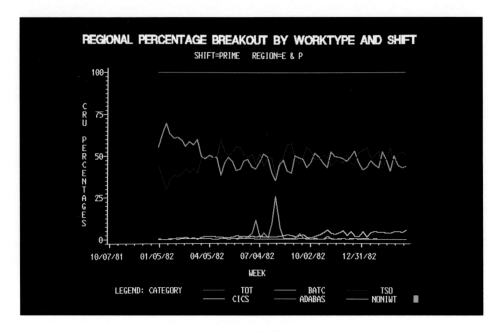

Figure 42.25

References

Because research in computer metrics has been primarily ad hoc, pragmatic, and specific to an installation's needs, references are primarily in the annual proceedings of the Computer Measurement Group, or in the proceedings of Users' Groups of specific vendors' hardware (such as IBM's, SHARE and GUIDE, DEC's DECUS and CDC's VIM).

1. Merrill, H. W. "Barry" (1980), *Merrill's Guide to Computer Performance Evaluation*, Cary, NC: SAS Institute Inc., 336 pp.
2. Dodson, George W., et al. (1983), *Proceedings of the 1983 Computer Measurement Group International Conference*, Phoenix, AZ: The Computer Measurement Group, P. O. Box 26063, 481 pp.
3. Heidel, Ruth (April 1980-July 1982), *Computer Management and Evaluation: Selected Papers from the SHARE Project*, Chicago, IL: SHARE Inc., Volume VI, 662 pp.
4. SAS Institute Inc. (1982), *SAS User's Guide: Basics, 1982 Edition*, Cary, NC: SAS Institute Inc., 923 pp.

II. REDUCING CPU CONSUMPTION WITH PROPER I/O BLOCKSIZE AND BUFFERING

H. W. Barry Merrill, Ph.D.
Sun Company
Box 47803
Dallas, TX 75247
Installation Code: SUN
Jointly Sponsored by
MVS Performance Project and
Computer Management & Evaluation Project
Session Numbers B504/M521

Abstract

This paper postulates that CPU cost, real memory cost, and DASD storage cost are jointly optimized when the blocksize and buffer number are chosen in such a way as to minimize BUFNO while moving one track of data at a time. Furthermore, through exits in DF/DS at open, it appears possible to override poor blocksize choices to reduce the CPU real memory and elapsed time without reblocking the data. Finally, since the true optimum requires maximization of blocksize (and, hence, a potential recompile), another exit is discussed that can allow identification of programs that will need recompiling. These exits allow an installation to migrate user data safely, increase its blocksize, and specify the optimal buffer number, with total user and application transparency.

Introduction

The real resources that a task consumes when performing sequential input or output operations are processor execution time (CPU seconds), real memory pages (average working set size), real memory occupancy time (page-seconds), the number of blocks of data transferred (EXCPs), the number of physical operations necessary to transfer the data (SIOs), and the resultant elapsed run time. These real resources can be reduced when the physical characteristics of the data transfer operations are matched to the hardware and operating system design.

The present sequential I/O design has not changed in principle since OS/360. The user's program requests records that the operating system combines into blocks. A block, when stored on a media, exists as a contiguous physical entity, and the length of a block is its BLKSIZE value. Blocksizes can be as small as 16 bytes or as large as 32,768 (actually, 32,760 is a software limit in MVS), if the media can support that much data.

When I/O is transferred between media and memory, the smallest unit of transfer is a block. However, sequential access methods provide for movement of more than one block in a single operation by allowing you to specify (in JCL or by system default) some number of buffers using the BUFNO parameter.

Although the user requests records that are decoded from a block by the access method, BUFNO of these blocks is transferred by one physical operation called a start I/O, or SIO. Thus, the blocksize is an attribute of the file, and the buffer number is set when the file is opened.

For many years, performance analysts have shown appreciable savings in real resources by increasing the blocksize and buffer number, but few installations have taken aggressive action to correct poor choices.

There are several reasons for their inaction:

- The real cost, in management-understandable terms, had not been shown.
- A systems programmer claimed that more real memory would be needed, and no immediate contradictory evidence was demonstrated.
- The installation was willing to change the blocksize, but it could not guarantee that the change would be transparent. The installation's programs can have internally-specified blocksizes, which would require identification and recompilation.
- The perceived personnel costs of making the changes outweighed the perceived cost savings.
- The application personnel have insufficient knowledge of JCL to be sure of themselves and will not change something that is working now.

This paper shows the real cost of poor choices of the blocksize and buffer attributes, proves that the system programmer's claim is false, and discusses the use of open exits that permit resolution of the final three objections.

The Experiment

Twelve pairs of sequential files containing the same 69,000 80-byte (nonrepeating character) logical records were built with blocksizes of 800, 1680, 2480, 3360, 4800, 5440, 6320, 7440, 9040, 11440, 15440 and 23440 bytes on 3380 disks.

A QSAM assembly program (written by Carol Toll and shown in Appendix I), which did nothing but OPEN, GET, and PUT between each pair of files, was executed repeatedly, iterating the number of buffers from 1 to as many as were necessary for BLKSIZE times BUFNO to exceed the track size. Note that BUFNO is limited to a maximum of 30 by MVS and, thus, only if blocksize is greater than 1076 can full-track I/O be performed on 3380s.

The SMF step termination records were collected and analyzed with the SAS System to determine the impact on real resource costs. Linear regression was used to determine the CPU cost (using total CPU TCB plus SRB) of each block and each SIO. The regression results are provided in Table 42.12. All runs were executed on a 3033-MP under MVS/370 SP1.3.1 in the fall of 1983.

Table 42.26
Regression Results 3033 MP

PROC SYSREG DATA=STEPS;
MODEL CPUTM=SIO EXCP;

	SSE	3.767	F ratio	3823.4
	DFE	273	Prob F	.0001
	MSE	.0138	R-square	.9655

Variable	Parameter estimate	Standard error	T ratio
Intercept	1.1944	0.133	89.88
SIO	0.001389	.000020	68.11
EXCP	.0001516	.0000046	32.73

The equation of the total CPU time (TCB + SRB) in seconds as a function of SIOs and EXCPs for QSAM I/O on an MP3033 with MVS/370 is:

CPU seconds $= 1.1944 + 0.001389 * \text{SIOs} + .0001516 * \text{EXCPs}$

Interpretation of Regression Results

The INTERCEPT is the asymptotic CPU time as the data length transferred per SIO (BLKSIZE times BUFNO) grows infinitely large. The total data in the file were (69000 times 80) 5.52 million bytes. Thus, the CPU cost to process 1 byte of data (excluding the CPU cost of the actual I/O operations, which is described by the SIO and EXCP coefficients) is:

CPU seconds
per byte $= 1.1944/(5.52 * 10^6) = 216$ (nanosecond/byte)

Note: if the processor is rated at 5 MIPS, 1 instruction requires 200 nanoseconds. Thus, it appears that 1 machine instruction on the average is required to process 1 byte.

The SIO coefficient of 0.001389 seconds, or 1.389 milliseconds, is the CPU cost of each physical I/O operation and is independent of how many blocks were transferred. This is the cost of physical transfer.

The I/O UNITS coefficient of 0.0001516, or 151.6 microseconds, is the CPU cost of each block transferred within a QSAM SIO. This is the cost of managing each buffer's data.

Using the Equation

With this equation for CPU cost to perform QSAM I/O, it is easy to calculate the impact of changing the blocksize. For example, a 1000-byte blocksize using the default QSAM BUFNO of 5 can be compared to half-track blocking of 23000 and BUFNO of 2.

BLKSIZE = 1000   BUFNO = 5   EXCPS = 10000 (assumed)
Now SIO   = EXCPS/BUFNO = 10000/5 = 2000
  and CPU = 0.001389 * 2000 + .0001516 * 10000 = 4.294 seconds.
Now if BLKSIZE = 23000 and   BUFNO = 2
then EXCPS = 10000/23 = 435 and SIO = 435/2 = 218
  and CPU = 0.001389 * 218 + 0.0001516 * 435 = 0.3687 seconds.

PERCENT CPU WASTED = (4.294 - 0.3687)/4.294= 91.4%

The CPU cost equation was then applied to all QSAM activity for a day from two 3081Ks and a 3033 MP. Then two possible blocksize choices were compared: IBM's 6K recommendation or the optimum 23K half-track I/O (Table 42.27).

Table 42.27
Daily Cost Savings with Increased Blocksize
DISK

Resource	Present count	6144 blocksize	Half-track blocksize
EXCP (x 1000)	8190	2885	1004
SIO (x 1000)	1711	507	502
CPU Seconds	3618	1141	785

(6K saved = 2447)   half track saved = 2833 seconds

TAPE

Resource	Present count	32760 blocksize
EXCP (x 1000)	10860	3254
SIO (x 1000)	2181	3254*
CPU seconds	4675	2724

saved = 1951 seconds
daily CPU saved (- QSAM) = 4784 seconds

*Increased because buffer was limited to one, whereas there is currently no limit on BUFNO.

Cost extension beyond QSAM   If the true cost of an SIO from the QSAM analysis can be applied to all non-VSAM SIOs, the total processor seconds spent in I/O can be estimated. The daily SIO counts by access method were estimated from the measured EXCP count, and the QSAM SIO cost was applied to the estimate (Table 42.28).

Table 42.28
Estimated CPU Costs Attributed to I/O Operations

Access method	EXCP count	Estimated SIO count	Estimated CPU consumed
QSAM	19,050,000	3,892,000	8,293
BSAM	6,564,000	6,564,000	9,117
BISAM	2,050,000	2,050,000	2,847
EXCP	6,186,000	6,186,000	8,592
QISAM	1,635,000	1,635,000	2,271
BPAM	1,735,000	1,735,000	2,409
BDAM	3,684,000	3,684,000	5,117
SPOOL	25,484,000	509,000	707
I/O Total		25,746,000	39,455

Total daily 3330 seconds recorded	340,000
Total daily MVS seconds recorded	92,349
Total daily TCB seconds	215,793
Total daily SRB seconds	31,858
Total daily TCB + SRB seconds	247,651

Non-VSAM I/O cost is $39,455/247,651 = 16\%$

Optimum Performance

The QSAM DASD experiments were graphically analyzed. Knowing the cost per I/O did not motivate users or management, nor did it answer the system programmer's concern for memory. Each of the nine resources was plotted against the blocksize for all runs. The number of buffers used for that run is printed at the observed intersection, allowing three-dimensional analysis on two dimensions. These nine plots show the range of resource from maximum to minimum, as well as the shape of the trend.

Figure	Title		Ratio of maximum to minimum value
42.29	Elapsed Run Time	ELAPSTM	32:1
42.30	Step CPU TCB Time	CPUTCBTM	4:1
42.31	Step CPU SRB Time	CPUSRBTM	23:1
44.32	Step Total CPU Time	CPUTM	5:1
42.33	Physical I/O Operations	SIO	70:1
42.34	Blocks of Data Transferred	EXCPS	14:1
42.35	Real Memory Page Occupancy	PAGESECS	10:1
42.36	Average Real Memory Working Set Size (K)	AVGWKSET	4:1
42.37	Private Area Virtual Size (K)	MAXADRSP	1.5:1

Figures 42.29 through 42.37 clearly show monotonic, dramatic reductions of resources as blocksize is increased.

The second set of figures shows three of the preceding resources versus data length per SIO (BUFNO times BLKSIZE). Here the effect of full-track I/O per SIO is clear.

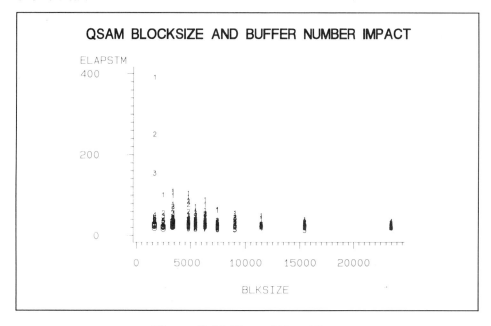

Figure 42.29 Elapsed Run Time

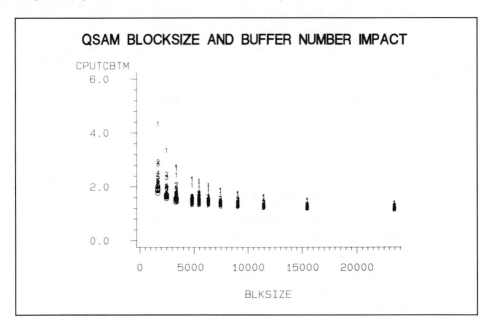

Figure 42.30 Step CPU TCB Time

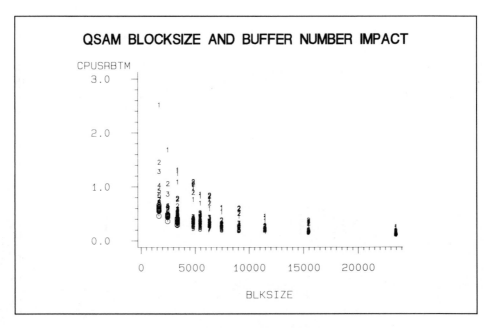

Figure 42.31 Step CPU SRB Time

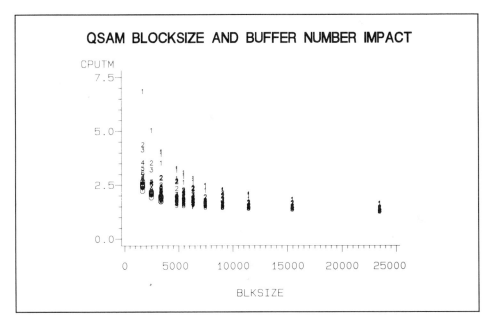

Figure 42.32 Step Total CPU Time

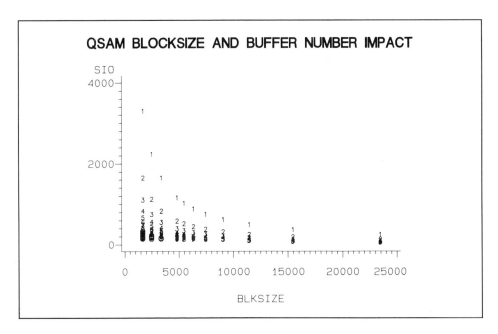

Figure 42.33 Physical I/O Operations

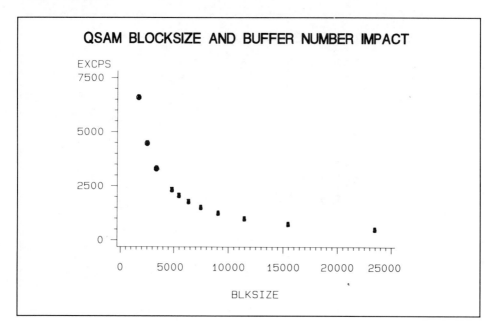

Figure 42.34 Blocks of Data Transferred

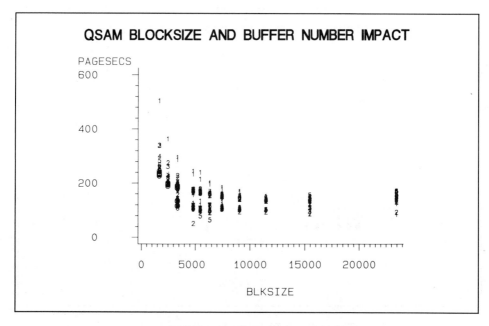

Figure 42.35 Real Memory Page Occupancy

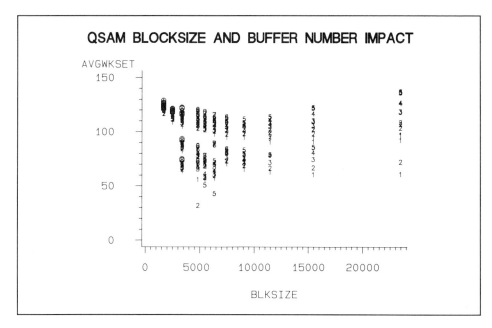

Figure 42.36 Average Real Memory Working Set Size (K)

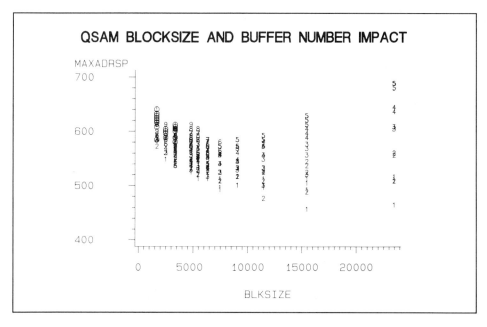

Figure 42.37 Private Area Virtual Size (K)

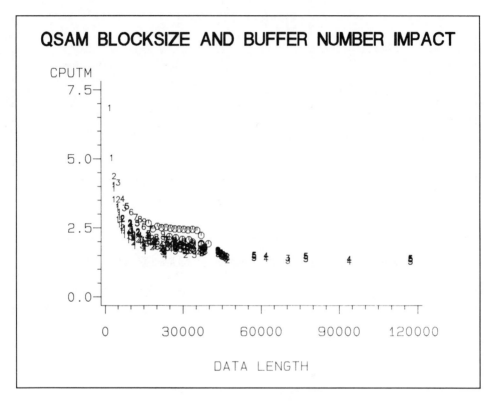

Figure 42.38 Total CPU Time

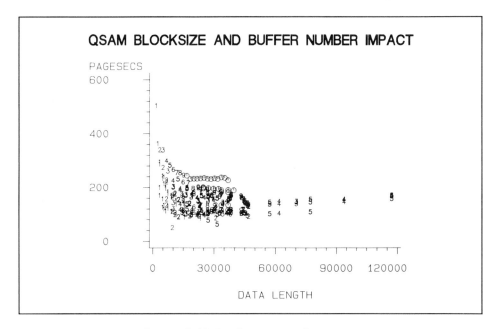

Figure 42.39 Real Memory Occupancy

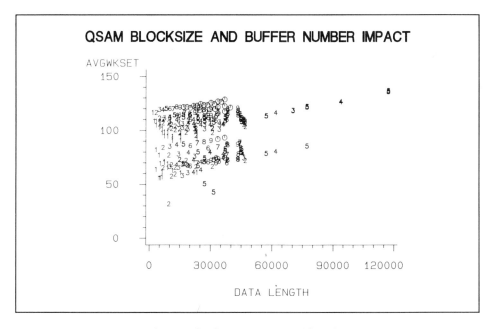

Figure 42.40 Average Working Set

Identifying Programs that Specify DCB Attributes

Implementation of optimal I/O always requires JCL changes. If the installation is wise and demands that all DCB attributes are specified externally to the program, then only JCL changes are required. However, since few installations have such stringent enforcement of standards that can be assumed to be in effect, implementation of optimal blocksize can be accelerated by using the DFDS OPEN EXIT described in the excellent Washington Systems Center Technical Bulletin GG22-9306-00, "Using Data Facility Device Support for DASD Space Management Assistance," by P. J. Henning.

The open exit presents two DCB areas: one is the unmodified user's DCB, and the other is open's DCB area with the JFCB merged into it. You could write your own code that examines the user's DCB area to execute in this exit. If the DCB attributed BLKSIZE is specified in the user's DCB, then an SMF record can be written from the exit, identifying those programs that require recompile before their files can be reblocked. Thus, by use of the DFDS OPEN EXIT, the installation can reblock data sets and guarantee that they will create no ABENDS. A write to programmer (WTO ROUTCDE=11) can also be issued from DFDS OPEN EXIT IFGOEXOB so that (if programmers read their SYSMSG) you can advise them that they are violating standards.

Altering Buffer Number in DFDS Open Exit

Although not yet tested at Sun Company, serious investigation of using the DFDS OPEN EXIT to alter the BUFNO parameter is being studied. Even though the preceding analysis clearly shows that increased blocksize achieves true optimum, there is sufficient return in processor utilization alone to justify the programming and testing time to code this exit. In the exit, the number of buffers can be expanded to the correct number for full-track data transfer, without alteration of either the user's JCL or the user's programs. It is hoped that this work will be presented at a future meeting of SHARE. These additional references are useful for technical examples and discussion of the exit:

Data Facility/Device Support Users' Guide SC26-3952-0
Technical Newsletter to SC26-3952-0 SN26-0888
Search INFO/SYSTEM File A Keywords DFDS EXIT.

Appendix I

Assembler program written by Carol Toll to perform QSAM I/O

```
WITELOOP    ENTER       REGEQUS=YES
            OPEN        (DD1,,DD2,(OUTPUT))
LOOP        GET         DD1,RECORD
            PUT         DD2,RECORD
            B           LOOP
EOF         CLOSE       (DD1,,DD2)
            LEAVE
DD1         DCB         DDNAME=IN,MACRF=GM,DSORG=PS,EODAD=EOF
DD2         DCB         DDNAME=OUT,MACRF=PM,DSORG=PS
RECORD      DS          XL32760
            END
```

Appendix II

Evolvement of Workload Efficiencies Project
at Sun Company

Gary Miley

An opportunity was perceived within Sun Company to improve the efficiency of resource utilization at the business data center. Management support initiated a project team to analyze and study the workload profile and to recommend and implement, where possible, actions to reduce resource consumption of data-processing services.

Initial project activities focused on the preceding analysis of access method I/O usage and performance. Analysis of various blocksizes and numbers of buffers for sequential processing supported the concept of full-track blocking on 3350 storage and half-track blocking on 3380 storage.

Results of the comparison showed a dramatic need to develop installation recommendations for both tape and disk data sets. The resulting blocksize recommendation for DASD sequential data sets was a compromise between the optimum and the actual data center data management environment of mixed device types (3350, 3380). The compromise for DASD was 9080, with no compromise on tapes at 32,760 blocksize. Recognize that even the 9080 DASD blocksize yields a near-optimum data transfer to 3380, with the QSAM BUFNO default of 5 buffers.

Further analysis of the SMF data revealed some surprises that would dictate a data set approach for Sun's workload: tape data sets should be the primary target for improving blocksize performance. The second category of data sets to review was temporary disk files—an analysis of proclibs would be in order here; and finally, permanent disk data sets should be moved with larger blocksize.

The efficiencies project then confronted these issues: how to communicate recommendations to the user community and how to identify the best candidates for reblocking.

The issue of user communication was addressed by the following strategy. An on-line information base was created and referenced by an article in the corporate information systems periodic newsletter announcing the existence of the efficiencies project. After a pilot effort internal to the information systems function, personal visits and presentations would follow in the user organizations.

The issue of identifying reblocking candidates was addressed by the use of UCC's TMS product and Software Module Marketing's DMS/OS product to identify the number of accesses (opens) since data set creation. This strategy allows the information systems function to approach the user community with intelligent information that quantifies the benefit to the user in the form of reduced resource cost. The project acknowledged that not all owners of sequential data sets would increase blocksize to the project recommendation; to improve the system performance for those data sets, a DFDS open exit module will be implemented to increase the number of buffers for sequential access. This exit would calculate the number of buffers required to transfer data at full track data transfer, subject to the SAM-E restriction of 30 buffers per SIO.

To summarize Sun's approach: quantify and communicate to user organizations the benefits to both the users' productivity and resource cost reduction by improving the performance of accessing sequential data, and implement the DFDS OPEN exit to gain system improvements even when users fail to reblock their data sets. In either case, system performance gains will be realized.

Index

D

J

L

M

U

V

About the Author

Barry Merrill first programmed on an IBM 650 while a sophomore at the University of Notre Dame. After a tour of duty in the Navy as a radioman on a diesel submarine, he used FORTRAN II and IV for the PEREC and LARS projects on 7094 and 360/44 processors at Purdue University. He received concurrent BSEE and MSEE degrees there in 1967. He completed Nuclear Power training and served on GATO, a nuclear-powered submarine, and then served at Guantanamo Bay, Cuba.

In 1972, he joined State Farm Mutual Automobile Insurance Company in Bloomington, Illinois, which had just formed a Measurement Unit, and discovered the SAS System for SMF data that November! There he analyzed AUTOCODER emulation on 360/30s through 360/65s and MVT through SVS on 360/15x and 360/16x processors.

In 1976, he moved to Dallas and joined Sun Company (also Sun Information Services and SUNTECH) and migrated from SVS to MVS 2.2 at Release 3.0 that October. In 1979, he completed his dissertation, which is the basis of this book, and was awarded a Ph.D. in Electrical Engineering from the University of Illinois. In 1980, his first book and bundled software were published by SAS Institute Inc. Now he teaches the CPE class that is offered worldwide by the Institute. In 1984, he left Sun and is now fully occupied as president of Merrill Consultants, supporting the MXG Software Product for CPE.

In 1982, the Computer Measurement Group gave him its highest award, the A.A. Michelson Award, for being a pioneer in the areas of processing, using, and archiving accounting and performance data.

His wife Judy is vice president of Merrill Consultants and manages business affairs. Barry, Judy, and their two children, Rachel and Nathaniel, reside merrily in Dallas, Texas.